National Park Style

PATTERNS FROM THE GOLDEN AGE OF RUSTIC DESIGN

ALBERT H. GOOD

LYONS PRESS

Essex, Connecticut

An imprint of The Globe Pequot Publishing Group, Inc.
64 South Main Street
Essex, CT 06426
www.globepequot.com

Copyright © 1990 by Graybooks
First Roberts Rinehart Publishers paperback edition published in 2003.
First Lyons Press paperback edition published in 2026.

All rights reserved. No part of this book may be reproduced in any form or by any electronic or mechanical means, including information storage and retrieval systems, without written permission from the publisher, except by a reviewer who may quote passages in a review.

British Library Cataloguing in Publication Information available

Library of Congress Cataloging-in-Publication Data available
ISBN 9781493094622 (paperback) | ISBN 9781493094653 (epub)

Part I

ADMINISTRATION AND BASIC SERVICE FACILITIES

FOREWORD

IN ANY AREA in which the preservation of the beauty of Nature is a primary purpose, every proposed modification of the natural landscape, whether it be by construction of a road or erection of a shelter, deserves to be most thoughtfully considered. A basic objective of those who are entrusted with development of such areas for the human uses for which they are established is, it seems to me, to hold these modifications to a minimum and so to design them that, besides being attractive to look upon, they appear to belong to and be a part of their settings.

For some years the National Park Service, State park authorities, and other agencies which administer natural park areas have been attaining a constantly improved technique of design and execution for the structures that are required for safe, convenient, and beneficial public use of these parks. Progress in this field has been especially marked since the inception of the Emergency Conservation Work program, with its steadily increasing and sound emphasis on development of recreational facilities, particularly in State parks. Stimulated by the problems this work has presented, competent architects have produced designs—and seen them converted into reality—that denote a real advance in this somewhat specialized field.

Herein are presented some of the successful natural park structures, a group by no means limited to those produced during the past four years or to those designed and erected under National Park Service supervision. Since tastes differ and since varying experience produces varying conclusions, it is hardly to be expected that there will be unanimous agreement as to the wisdom of including certain of the selected designs, or that no one will take issue with any of the points raised in the discussions that form an important part of the work. Selection and discussion alike, however, are the result of most careful and conscientious study.

This book is certain, I believe, to prove of exceptional value to all those who are concerned with the design of park and recreation structures. It should be immensely helpful in stimulating still further improvement in this special field of design. The interest manifested in it in advance of publication indicates a widespread conviction that there is a real place and a real need for such a compilation.

ARNO B. CAMMERER, *Director, National Park Service.*

CONTENTS

	PAGE
FOREWORD	VII
ACKNOWLEDGMENT	IX
APOLOGIA	1
ADMINISTRATION AND BASIC SERVICE FACILITIES	5
ENTRANCEWAYS AND CHECKING STATIONS	9
Plates I A-1 *to* I A-20	
BARRIERS, WALLS, AND FENCES	31
Plates I B-1 *to* I B-6	
SIGNS	39
Plates I C-1 *to* I C-16	
ADMINISTRATION BUILDINGS	57
Plates I D-1 *to* I D-15	
SUPERINTENDENTS' AND STAFFS' QUARTERS	73
Plates I E-1 *to* I E-15	
EQUIPMENT AND MAINTENANCE BUILDINGS	89
Plates I F-1 *to* I F-12	
DRINKING FOUNTAINS AND WATER SUPPLY	103
Plates I G-1 *to* I G-24	
COMFORT STATIONS AND PRIVIES	129
Plates I H-1 *to* I H-20	
INCINERATORS	151
Plates I I-1 *to* I I-3	
FIRE LOOKOUT STRUCTURES	155
Plates I J-1 *to* I J-4	
TRAIL STEPS	161
Plates I K-1 *to* I K-6	
CROSSINGS AND CULVERTS	169
Plates I L-1 *to* I L-5	
BRIDGES	175
Plates I M-1 *to* I M-24	

ACKNOWLEDGMENT

→›› WITH THE APPEARANCE of the National Park Service's publication "Park Structures and Facilities" in November 1935, demand for it soon indicated that another issue must follow. The earlier printing may be said to have been a doubly limited edition—limited in number to such an extent that requests for copies far outran the supply, and limited in scope because of its speedy production, made necessary by a pressing need in connection with the Emergency Conservation Work under way in national parks and monuments, State parks, and other natural park areas throughout the country. Moreover, the two years that have elapsed since the compilation of the original material have witnessed the completion of many park structures and facilities of enlarging variety and unusual merit. It is felt that these, in fact more of them than space permits, definitely deserve recording along with selections from the earlier book. With the intent of bringing the record up to date on a more comprehensive scale and under conditions imposing the least restrictions on its general availability, this revised and enlarged compilation is undertaken.

Civilian Conservation Corps funds sufficient to defray the cost of publication were allotted by Robert Fechner, Director of that popular and successful undertaking. Director Fechner's sympathetic understanding of the major problems of park and recreation development continues to be immensely helpful and encouraging to those whose privilege it is to be associated with him in the work.

In connection with much of the material submitted, there was regrettable lack of information to make possible rendering due credit to the many able planning groups and individuals, earnest artisans and mechanics, responsible for the structures herein illustrated. For this reason, it has seemed fairest to all concerned to credit the material, with few exceptions, to locations rather than to individuals or groups. A kind of equalization of injustice to all has seemed preferable to a discriminatory injustice to some. The practice has been pursued without intent to traffic in the anonymity of others in order to infer credit to the National Park Service. Such an interpretation would be unfortunate and unfair. Regardless of their source, it has been sought to include structures suitable to natural parks. Many, including some of the most notable accomplishments herein shown, were created entirely independent of Service participation. For the distinction these bring to this publication, and for the privilege of including them, the Service is most grateful.

The wonderful success of the first edition of this book two years ago may be attributed to the personal and untiring efforts of Albert H. Good, and, therefore, he was naturally selected as the author for this edition. Those who will have occasion to use these books will appreciate and realize the great amount of study and thought that he has put into his work. We are deeply indebted to him, and we acknowledge his high professional attainments.

Although the final selection of material and the writing of the general discussions and comments have devolved upon one individual, no publication could have been possible without the generous assistance of innumerable associates in the Service who submitted needed material with a tireless helpfulness which is the essential spirit of the National Park Service organization. To these, and to friends of the Service whose interest in park and recreation development has led them to hearty cooperation in this undertaking, we extend appreciative thanks.

CONRAD L. WIRTH, *Assistant Director, National Park Service.*

APOLOGIA

A CHERISHED DICTUM of the many friends of the natural park concept through its formative years has been that structures must be regarded as intrusions in areas set aside to be conserved in their natural state. This unequivocal pronouncement indeed nourished the budding park idea, and has been a favorable and protective influence in its flowering. General acceptance of the principle has so held in check structural desecration of parks that few persons have been moved to brand the statement a half truth, standing very much in need of qualifying amendment to suit today's many-sided park concept. To do so will doubtless be received as a minority report, if not as shameless heresy; nevertheless, the case will be here argued.

Time was when only areas of superb scenery, outstanding scientific interest, or major historical importance held interest for the sponsors of natural parks. There was proper concentration on saving the outstanding natural wonders first, and it was probably along with the acquisition of the first superlative areas that structures in parks came to be frowned on as alien and intrusive. Recall that among the sites early dedicated to the idea were the Valley of Yosemite and the Canyons of the Yellowstone and the Colorado! Quick resentment of invasion of such scenic splendor is altogether understandable. Here man must first have felt that his best-intentioned structural efforts had reached an all-time high for incongruity, that structures, however well designed, do not contribute to the beauty, but only to the use, of a park of conspicuous natural distinction. When he concluded that only the most persistent demands for a facility should trap him into playing the jester, he established a principle that remains paramount today for such areas—to build only structures which are undeniably essential, and to know he is not equipped to embellish, but only to mar, Nature's better canvases. Now and forever, the degree of his success within such areas will be measurable by the yardstick of his self-restraint.

Outstanding, inspiring, breath-taking superlatives in Nature exist by reason of the fact that some comparatively few acres stand out in sharp contrast with hundreds of thousands of relatively unexciting others. Park areas of transcendent quality are often too remote from population centers to be within reach of any great number of citizens. Broad sections of the land, densely populated, are without scenically superb endowment by Nature.

Sensing these facts, the natural park movement could not long remain preoccupied with top-flight Nature alone. The natural park idea was destined for a truly liberal evolution, influenced by such weighing factors as distribution of population, development of the automobile, increase of leisure time, and tardy realization that important among conservational responsibilities of parks was the human crop.

The fact that superlative Nature was beyond gunshot of concentrations of five or ten million people happily did not result in these populations being denied the recreational and inspirational benefits that subsuperlative Nature can provide. It was wisely reasoned that there is more nourishment in half a loaf in the larder than a full loaf beyond the horizon—or no loaf at all. Many park preserves have come into being which cannot boast the highest peak or deepest canyon, bluest lake or tallest tree, but do succeed in delivering, f. o. b. metropolitan centers, hills and valleys to pass for superlative in contrast with tenement walls, and swimming, sun, and shade to seem heaven-sent to youth whose wading pools have been rain-flooded gutters of drab city streets.

Tracts, admittedly limited or even lacking in natural interest, but highly desirable by virtue of location, need, and every other influencing factor, bloom attractively on every side to the benefit of millions. It is inexact to term these, in the accepted denotation of the word, parks—they are reserves for recreation. More often than not their natural background is only that contrast-affording Nature which makes other areas superlative. Does such a background warrant the "no dogs allowed" attitude toward structures so fully justified where Nature plays the principal role? Does it not rather invite structures to trespass to a fulfilment of recreational potentialities and needs, and to bolster up a commonplace or ravaged Nature? It seems reasonable to assert that in just the degree natural beauty is lacking structures may legitimately seek to bring beauty to purpose.

Those who have been called on to plan the areas where structural trespass is not a justifiable taboo have sought to do so with a certain grace. We realize that the undertaking is legitimatized or not by harmony or the lack of it. We are learning that harmony is more likely to result from a use of native materials. We show signs of doubting the propriety of introducing boulders into settings where Nature failed to provide them, or of incorporating heavy alien timbers into structures in treeless areas. We sometimes even experience a faltering of faith in the precision materials produced by our machines, and so evidence an understanding of relative fitness.

As we have vaguely sensed these things, we incline to a humble respect for the past. We become aware of the unvoiced claims of those long-gone races and earlier generations that tracked the wilderness, plains, or desert before us. In fitting tribute we seek to grace our park structures by adaptation of their traditions and practices as we come to understand them.

Thus we are influenced by the early settlers, English and Dutch, along the Atlantic seaboard; something of Old France lingers along the trail of Pere Marquette and the fur traders. Reaching up from New Orleans, Florida, and Old Mexico, Spanish traditions and customs rightfully flourish. Over the covered wagon routes the ring of the pioneer's axe is echoed in the efforts of today. The habits and primitive ingenuity of the American Indian persist and find varied expression over wide areas. Interpreted with intelligence, these influences promise an eventual park and recreation architecture, which, outside certain sacrosanct areas, need not cringe before a blanket indictment for "unlawful entry."

CONFRONTED WITH THE PRIVILEGE of presenting representative structures and facilities that have found place in parks, from the truly natural park to the recreational reserve, many decisions have been necessary in determining a proper approach. Should such a compilation attribute to the reader no fundamental knowledge of the subject, and become a park primer treating the subject "from the ground up" literally and figuratively? Should it seek to embrace in all detail every subject of possible interest to the park-minded, assuming in the reader a consuming appetite for knowledge—in bulk? Need it concern itself with formulae, diagrams, rules of thumb and rules of fact? Should it become a repository of material, technical and aesthetic, elementary and advanced, and already available from scattered sources?

It is the conclusion that the call is for none of these but only for a comprehensive presentation of park structures and facilities in which principles held in esteem by park planners, landscape designers, engineers, and architects have been happily joined in adequate provision for man's needs with a minimum sacrifice of the natural values present. By avoiding any tendency to be a primer, an encyclopedia, or a handbook of the subject, it is hoped to focus more directly on the current trend in park buildings. It is believed that by making the subjects herein widely available for comparative study, the influence engendered by each will merge into a forceful composite to the advancement of park technique.

The examples shown are considered appropriate to natural parks, as distinguished from naturalistic or formalized city parks. These latter are considered to be a field in themselves, very different in premise, and better treated independently of the natural park areas as exemplified by our national, many of our State, and some of our county and metropolitan parks. It has been elected to present examples of structures, regardless of location, if in their expression they promise to be quite at home in little-modified environment.

For more convenient reference it has seemed advisable to arrange items of closely related purpose

→»> APOLOGIA

into three groups representative of certain broad functions. Hence, Part I is titled Administration and Basic Service Facilities, and embraces structures identified with boundary, access and circulation, supervision and maintenance, and those basic services in park areas which can be termed the counterparts of public utilities in urban communities.

The scope of Part II—Recreational and Cultural Facilities—requires no detailed exposition. The structures treated therein are those in facilitation of picnicking, active recreation, and cultural pursuits representative of the day use of a park area.

The title of Part III—Overnight and Organized Camp Facilities—is self-explanatory. Discussed and illustrated therein is the range of individual overnight accommodations and dependencies, from tent campsite to hotel, together with the full complement of structures that make up an organized camp. The latter will, of course, repeat some of the previously explored classifications but will focus on examples adapted physically to the specific requirements of group camping, and scaled economically to the social aspect of this field of public recreation.

THE SCOPE OF MATERIAL has suggested three varieties of presentation. There are minor facilities, developed to a pleasing expression within certain utilitarian or technical limitations, which might with propriety be duplicated in many localities. In such instances, it has been the endeavor to provide information in such detail that adaptation approaching duplication is possible. This is by no means so much an invitation to indiscriminate copying as a suggestion that little objects once well done are often a more satisfactory solution to a recurring problem than a new creation claiming the sole and debatable distinction of being different.

Another group embraces subjects eminently suited to particular locations, but promising little success with outright transplanting into another environment. Such subjects are shown in limited detail. They are included simply in the hope that the charm and fitness of the subjects in their specific settings and expressions may offer inspiration while flying a warning against too literal translation. It is intended to offer the spirit but not the letter of such examples. Only reliance on the best professional advice can reasonably insure against structures appropriate in one locality becoming caricatures elsewhere. Only consummate skill and rare good judgment in adaptation can avoid a half-caste development, the very counterfeit exactness of which is pathetic testimony of the bar sinister.

The third presentation is of successful accomplishments of highly individual problems, the factors fixing which are unlikely ever to be approximated in another problem. These are included in recognition of worthy attainment, to inspire in those to whom the more complex park design problems may fall in the future a high purpose to approach them with equally refreshing individuality, ingenuity, and forthrightness. Plagiarism, subtle or obvious, in structures within this category is a crowning stupidity.

It is felt that inclusion of examples of extraordinarily complex structures would bring little to the practical usefulness of this collection. The more involved and extensive the structure, the more evident that it is the result of an altogether unique interplay of needs, topography, traditions, materials, and many other factors. Beyond the borders of utter simplicity lie innumerable possible patterns, complex in varying degree. Duplication of any one such pattern is without rhyme; approximation of it, without reason. Readers will note the absence of many well-known and admired large-scale buildings of incontestable park character. These are held to be sanctified in a sense by their very success, and are omitted to avoid possible inference that they are imitable material.

The placing of some of the combination structures herein presented, within the chapter classifications established, may stand in need of explanation and defense. Such combination buildings are so numerous that to create a separate classification for them would result in a loosely related group, bulking to an unreasonable relationship with other classifications. For this reason a so-called combination structure is allocated to the heading which seems best to define the apparently dominant use of the building.

IN THE SELECTION OF MATERIAL one issue, long an inviting subject for debate, arose again and again. This involves the use of materials in that wide-ranging style in park structures which we loosely identify, and as loosely term, "rustic" or "pioneer."

APOLOGIA

One opinion holds that park buildings should not appropriate the semblance of primitive structures without appropriating as well all the primitive elements and structural methods of the prototypes. It insists, for instance, that there is no allowable compromise with true log construction; such must be rigidly adhered to in every detail if employed at all. Contrary opinion argues that there are not at hand today the timber resources of pioneer days, that to insist on the use of logs in today's park structures in the spendthrift fashion of our forefathers may be logic in the aesthetic abstract, but in practice wastes those resources the conservation of which largely motivates park expansion.

Taking into account the demands of present day economy and conservation principles, how far may departure from the forthright but prodigal construction of the pioneers properly be urged? What substitutes may be recommended as an acceptable wall surface material for park buildings? Is a proper direction pointed by the fact that the amount of timber stock required for one true log structure will provide material for several more or less adequate and pleasing structures to bloom or blight (the partisan reader may choose his own verb) in its place?

The author carries water on both shoulders. Where wood is the material indicated for use, some of the more important structures may well reproduce faithfully pioneer log construction to create, and so preserve for study, the fast disappearing construction methods of the frontier. On the other hand, minor and oft-repeated units, such as cabins, do well to utilize more economical, even if less picturesque and durable, materials and methods.

The purpose of this publication will be misconstrued if it is interpreted by readers as providing source material for park structures, denying need for competent professional assistance in the creation of park buildings that may follow. The intent is the very opposite. The most completely satisfying subjects included herein are so, not as a result of chance, but because training, imagination, effort, and skill are conjoined to create and fashion a pleasing structure or facility appropriate to a particular setting. Who then but those of professional training and experience are equipped to decide that a perfect structural interpretation for one setting will sanction adaptation to another, and in what detail or degree modification will make the most of the conditions presented by another environment? If an existing structure is so admired that it persuades duplication, careful analysis will inevitably demonstrate that admiration springs from a nice perfection of the subject within one circumstantial pattern. As that pattern changes so must the structure change. To venture in translation without benefit of technical idiom foredooms to mediocrity, if not to failure.

THE STRUCTURAL ACCOMPLISHMENTS presented herein mirror the skills and devotions of many men who have striven to translate into gratifying actuality the creative abilities of many others. It is ventured to hope that the discussions and comments also do not inaccurately mirror the thoughts and philosophies of friends and associates endowed with capacity for viewing clearly and pointing the way. From the following, among unnamed others, the author exposes himself to the jibes "parrot" or "pirate" and if deserving of neither, he is shamed into a realization that he has proved inept.

Bows to Herbert Maier, when the park museum concept and many principles basic to a fitting park architecture enunciated by him are appropriated herein—to Julian H. Salomon, when a theory and standards for organized camping are outlined—to Edward B. Ballard, when winter sports activities and structures are discussed. Acknowledgments to John D. Coffman and his associates for material in exposition of fire lookout structures, to Thos. C. Vint and his associates for collaboration in pioneering trailer campsite lay-outs. Tribute to Colonel Richard Lieber, Conrad L. Wirth, and Herbert Evison—when there is digression into phases of park and recreation philosophy which they have expounded or sponsored

Readers will underwrite the author's deep indebtedness to Mr. Evison, Mentor Extraordinary, for a generous counsel that ranged from the grim business of reading much of this material in manuscript to a helpful and frequent checking and recharting of wavering course. The drawings so ornamental to these pages reflect the talents of a little band of master draftsmen, to whom individually the author acknowledges a very great debt.

A. H. G.

ADMINISTRATION AND BASIC SERVICE FACILITIES

As HAS ALREADY BEEN STATED, administration and basic service facilities are considered to embrace park structural developments necessary for the control, supervision, and maintenance of an area together with those basic services which might be termed the park equivalents of the city's public utilities. Included are entrance and boundary structures, administration buildings as the seat of order and authority, signs as an instrument of control, equipment and maintenance buildings functioning to give continuity to desirable physical conditions attained, and structures for housing those persons charged with administering and maintaining the park preserve. Here also are those "first things" needed for safe use of an outdoor area by the public, namely, drinking water supply, toilets, rubbish disposal, and fire lookout structures, paralleling respectively the city's water, sanitation, rubbish disposal, and fire alarm systems. These are topped off with trail steps, crossings, culverts, and bridges—all of which seem somehow analogous to the accomplishments of the public roads agency of any governmental unit.

All the foregoing have highly practical functions to fulfil, to express and to aid which we do well to provide practical structures. Some are most properly located beyond the horizon of public view and such need carry no economic overburden of park-consciousness. No one of the several kinds of facilities here classified can be termed other than completely requisite in a park area of size, developed for a proper public use. Because so patently essential in a park, the most fitting conception of most of these will be without frills, which are better indulged in, if at all, in the less essential, but more importantly placed, public use structures that should follow only when the fundamental things have been provided.

What follows in this chapter has been said and written many times by the park-minded. It is something of a creed for construction environed by Nature and a pardonable repetition as preamble to any consideration of the many major and minor structures given place in natural parks. Because of their truly basic character, the points here recited may not be omitted, for all it is fully appreciated they will reach the ears of many readers as all too familiar echoes. They are the deep roots of a sound park construction, from which any new growth must stem.

The present discussion by no means applies solely to structures concerned with administration and basic facilities. In point of fact the fullest application of the principles will probably involve those structural items less committed to a stern practicability and more concerned with aesthetics by reason of greater contact by the public.

THE STYLE OF ARCHITECTURE which has been most widely used in our forested national parks, and in other wilderness parks, is generally referred to as "rustic." It is, or should be, something more than the worn and misused term implies. It is earnestly hoped that a more apt and expressive designation for the style may evolve, but until it appears, "rustic", in spite of its inaccuracy and inadequacy, must be resorted to in this discussion. Successfully handled, it is a style which, through the use of native materials in proper scale, and through the avoidance of severely straight lines and over-sophistication, gives the feeling of having been executed by pioneer craftsmen with limited hand tools. It thus achieves sympathy with natural surroundings and with the past.

In high, mountainous and forested regions the various structural elements of rustic construction—logs, timbers, rocks—must be reasonably overscaled to the structure itself to avoid being unreasonably underscaled to surrounding large trees and rough terrain. In less rugged natural areas, the style may be employed with less emphasis on oversizing. For

ADMINISTRATION AND BASIC SERVICE FACILITIES

pleasing harmony, the scale of the structural elements must be reduced proportionately as the ruggedness and scale of the surroundings diminish. When this recession in scale reaches a point at which there is any hint of "twig" architecture masquerading under the term "rustic", the understanding designer will sense immediately its limitations and take refuge in some widely different style.

That the so-called rustic style offers, if anything, more pitfalls to failure than do the more sophisticated expressions, is not widely enough understood. And while generally speaking it lends itself to many semiwilderness regions perhaps better than the others, its use is by no means appropriate to all park areas. This is instantly demonstrated by recalling the wide range of dominant characteristics of our parks. Spectacular snow-covered mountain parks, dramatic primeval forests, open expanses of arid desert or limitless prairie, shifting sand dunes, gently rolling woodland and meadow, semitropical hammock are not to be served appropriately by a single structural expression. A range of architectural styles as varied as these backgrounds must be employed before our park architecture will have come of age.

Nothing is more indicative of lack of a proper sense of values in park technique than the frequently expressed determination to "make a feature" of a shelter or other park structure. The features to be emphasized and stressed for appreciation in parks with which we are here concerned are the natural features, not the man-made. After all, every structural undertaking in a natural park is only a part of a whole. The individual building or facility must bow deferentially before the broad park plan, which is the major objective, never to be lost sight of. The park plan determines the size, character, location, and use of each and every structure. Collectively, these should be properly interrelated; at the same time they must be closely and logically related to the park plan to insure its workability and harmony. Otherwise, there will result, as someone has expressed it, a costly but ineffectual collection of "spare parts."

Although a park structure exists solely for the use of the public, it is not required that it be seen from some distance. In its most satisfying expression, the park structure is designed with a view to subordinating it to its environment, and it is located so that it may profit from any natural screening that may exist. Suitable signs marking the way to a particular park building which has been appropriately retired are to be preferred to the shock of finding a building intruding at a focal point or visible for great distance.

THE SUBORDINATION OF A STRUCTURE to environment may be aided in several ways. One of these is to screen the building by locating it behind existing plant material or in some secluded spot in the terrain partly screened by some other natural feature. In the absence of such screening at a site otherwise well-suited for the function of the building, an adequate screen can be planted by repeating the same plant materials that exist nearby. Preferably, structures will be so located with reference to the natural features of the landscape that it is unnecessary to plant them out.

The color of the exteriors, particularly the wooden portions of park structures, is another most important factor in assimilation. Naturally such colors as occur in, and are commonest to, the immediate surroundings serve best. In general, warm browns will go far toward retiring a wooden building in a wooded or partly wooded setting. A light driftwood gray is another safe color. Where contrast is desired to give architectural accent to minor items, such as window muntins, a light buff or stone color may be sparingly used. Strangely enough, green is perhaps the hardest of all colors to handle, because it is so difficult to get just the correct shade in a given setting and because it almost invariably fades to some very different hue. A green roof might be expected to blend with the green of the surrounding trees, yet because a mass of foliage is an uneven surface, intermingling other colors, and broken up by patches of deep shadow and bright openings, and because a roof is a flat plane which reflects a solid continuous color, anything but harmony results. Brown or weathered gray roofs, on the other hand, blend with the colors of earth and tree trunks to much happier results.

While structures should be so designed and so located that it will not be necessary to plant them out, the proper introduction of vegetation along the foundations will gracefully obliterate the other-

ADMINISTRATION AND BASIC SERVICE FACILITIES

wise unhappy line of demarcation between building and ground. Rough rock footings artfully contrived to give the impression of natural rock outcroppings are a means of blending the structure to the site. A batter to a stone wall, with skillful buttressing of the corners, if done with true finesse, will often bring to the building that agreeable look of having sprung from the soil. Park structures giving that impression are of the elect.

Some park structures give hint of their designers' long dalliance in cities, where architectural design has become a matter of one façade. It should be remembered that park buildings will be viewed from all sides, and that design cannot be lavished on one elevation only. All four elevations will be virtually front elevations, and as such merit careful study. Admittedly, one side of major park buildings will always provide for service, and while enclosures on park areas are to be deplored and only installed where necessary, a palisade or some other suitable enclosure on this side of the building should completely screen all service operations.

As a rule, park structures are less conspicuous and more readily subordinated to their settings when horizontal lines predominate and the silhouette is low. Where snow conditions will permit, any feeling of verticality will be avoided by adopting a roof low in pitch, perhaps not more than one-third. Too frequently roofs needlessly dominate both structure and setting.

THE DEGREE OF PRIMITIVE CHARACTER in park structures that native materials can contribute depends entirely on intelligent use. Not alone the fact, but the quality of "nativeness" of materials is to be sought. Local stone, worked to the regularity in size and surface of cut stone or concrete block, and native logs, fashioned to the rigid counterpart of telephone poles or commercial timber, have sacrificed all the virtue of being native.

Rock work needs first of all to be in proper scale. The average size of the rocks employed must be sufficiently large to justify the use of masonry. Rocks should be placed on their natural beds, the stratification or bedding planes horizontal, never vertical. Variety of size lends interest and results in a pattern far more pleasing than that produced by units of common or nearly common size. Informality vanishes from rock work if the rocks are laid in courses like brick work, or if the horizontal joints are not broken. In walls the larger rocks should be used near the base, but by no means should smaller ones be used exclusively in the upper portions. Rather should a variety of sizes be common to the whole surface, the larger predominating at the base. Rock should be selected for its color and hardness.

Logs should never be selected because they are good poles. There is nothing aesthetically beautiful in a pole. Logs desirable in the park technician's viewpoint are pleasingly knotted. The knots are not completely sawed off. The textural surface of the log after removal of the bark is duly appreciated and preserved. Strong as may be the immediate appeal of structures built of logs on which the bark is left, we do well to renounce at once this transitory charm. If the bark is not intentionally stripped, not only will this process naturally and immediately set in, but the wood is subjected to aggravated deterioration through the ravages of insects and rot. It is in the best interests of the life of park structures, as well as in avoidance of a long period of litter from loosening bark, and of unsightliness during the process, that there has come about general agreement that the bark should be entirely sacrificed at the outset.

When the timber resources of the American frontier seemed limitless, it was usual to lay the sills of a log cabin directly on the ground, without supporting stone foundations. When after a time the logs in contact with the earth had rotted to a point where the cabin commenced to list and sag, another cabin was built, and the earlier one abandoned. This, it seems, in the economy of the frontier, was more reasonable than to have provided a foundation under the earlier cabin. Regardless of the pious respect a log cabin builder of the present must have for the traditions of the past, the changed economy of our day demands that his cabin be preserved against deterioration by the use of masonry or concrete supporting walls or posts that extend well above grade.

THIS OUTLINE OF THE FACTORS which make for the desirable and appropriately rugged, handcrafted character of park structures would be woefully incomplete if the matter of roof texture were left unconsidered. The heavy walls of rock and timber which are urged as fitting to a natural environment are assuredly created in vain unless crowned with roofs having related character. Surmounted with roofs trivial in aspect and thin in fact, the heavy walls appear robbed of justification. Verge members in gables should tend to be oversized, eave lines to be thick, and the roofing material to appear correspondingly heavy and durable. Where wood shingles or shakes are used on a roof, these should be fully an inch in thickness if possible, and the doubling of every fifth course or so, unless the building is quite small, will bring the roof texture into more appropriate scale with the structure itself and with the other materials that compose it. The primitive character we seek to create is furthered tremendously if we shun straight rigid eave and course lines in favor of properly irregular, wavering "freehand" lines. The straight edge as a precision tool has little or no place in the park artisan's equipment.

Since structures exist in parks through sufferance, it follows that it is highly desirable in every area to keep down the number of them. A small area can be ruined by a clutter of minor buildings which, however necessary their purpose, seem to have been forced into every vista to inflict a consciousness of the hand of man. Two functions, or even more, where closely related at a given location, should be combined under one roof. This is not in defense of excessively large buildings. It is sound practice only within reasonable limits. It is based on a belief that a localizing of infection is preferable to an irritating rash of trivial structures all over an area. The grouping of two or more facilities under one roof tends to bring welcome variety to park structures generally. The limited range of expression of any simple, one-purpose building is vastly widened as other purposes are combined in it.

The structures necessary in a park are naturally less obtrusive if they are reasonably unified by a use of one style of architecture, limited construction methods, and not too great variety in materials. When a truly inappropriate style of architecture already exists in a park in which new work is contemplated, it is urged that the new buildings do not stubbornly carry on the old tradition. The best judgment available should be consulted to determine the style most appropriate to the area, and this then frankly and courageously launched. If the new style is the more appropriate one, it will prevail. Time will eliminate the earlier, inappropriately styled buildings for the disturbing contrasts they produce.

Bridge, Dutchess County, New York

ENTRANCEWAYS AND CHECKING STATIONS

IN ITS SIMPLEST and, theoretically, its most desirable expression, the park entranceway is merely a trail or a roadway taking off from a highway and leading into an area dedicated to public use and enjoyment. But it is not long permitted to retain so simple a form. Immediately demands for traffic safety, through elimination of the hazards of steep grades, sharp turns, and obstructions to vision, assert themselves, and the simple unobtrusive entranceway is doomed.

To increase the safety factor for automobiles leaving or entering the main traffic flow at the entrance take-off, the highway is first widened, then the entrance road, and the intersection is transformed by sweeping curves. Tree and plant growth, and perhaps a hillside, which interfere with 60-mile-speed vision, are eliminated. There must be a striving to overcome the traveling public's quick conclusion that here is a new speedway, or the gateway to some optimistic suburban subdivision. All, doubtless, necessary and inevitable "improvement", but the unself-conscious park entranceway, bleeding from the many wounds, expires.

It will be gloriously reborn, having sacrificed only its naive innocence for a myriad of more worldly values. Prompt to admit that the entranceway is more sinned against than sinning, we can but hope that, when forced to take measures in its own defense, it will not too brazenly flaunt artificiality and sophistication.

A mere sign generally proves insufficient. Pylons are resorted to in the hope of standing off the onrush of trucks and speeders. Gates are proposed, but more often than not these succeed rather in bespeaking the modern "burial park" than the kind of park it is hoped to typify. There results confusion worse confounded; solution seems beyond reach. Is it then any wonder that flanking walls, gate lodges, towers, lights, and arches are introduced as appendages where they seem to give promise of proclaiming beyond doubt just what the entrance does or, failing this, does not serve? The temptation is hardly resistible, and the complex, almost institutional, rendering evolves.

Once fully aware of the factors that deny to the park planner a simplicity of entranceway, while concurrently hampering the success of the complicated alternative, it is well to take stock of just what, in spite of all unfavorable limitations, a park entrance can be and convey.

It should at once invite and deter, encouraging use while discouraging abuse of the park by the public. It should be all things to all men, tempting the devotees of Nature and of the past, while warding off and detouring that bloc of the public primarily bent on a greater gasoline consumption—a kind of semaphore simultaneously reading "stop" and "go", yet somehow avoiding all accidents to traffic and to temperament. Surely no easy accomplishment, perhaps unattainable!

The simple appeal and mystery of the rural lane denied us, we can seek to beckon by means of an approach road of inviting width. But the speeder bent on getting nowhere in particular with all possible haste must somehow be urged diplomatically in another direction. An island dividing the in-and-out traffic will promote safety and restrain recklessness without suggestion of inhospitality. If an entrance fee is to be collected, an island kiosk is a very practical station point for collecting admissions and for the attendant duties of checking and providing information. From a kiosk so located, a guard can conveniently give information to departing patrons without undue interruption to the business of admissions. By recalling the familiar tollbridge entrance, it serves to suggest to the entrant that a fee is to be collected, and saves time that with any other arrangement might be consumed in query and explanation. The checking station, lodge, or sentry box to one side of the roadway is sometimes preferred, especially when the traffic flow is not heavy.

ENTRANCEWAYS AND CHECKING STATIONS

When a ranger or other employe is required to be on duty at an entrance during the hours a park is open to the public, suitable shelter must be provided for him. Often it is necessary to provide heat and toilet facilities in the attendant's room of the checking station or gate lodge. Some of the national parks and the State parks of Indiana have checking stations notable for their attractive character and practical completeness. When any portion of the using public is transported to the park by common carrier, a sheltered waiting space, as an adjunct of the entranceway, has a real function. There are shown on the pages which follow some successful examples of the several possible arrangements mentioned herein.

For convenience of administration and limiting roadways the ideal park plan would have but one entrance. It follows that where affecting conditions of terrain, population centers, and other factors dictate more than one entrance, the fewer of these, the better. Particularly where an entrance fee is an accepted principle is the limiting of entrance points desirable and highly so for the economy it effects. The accessories necessary to any entranceway staffed with an attendant call for greater initial investment than the simple untended entrance, and the employe himself is a continuing operating charge.

For a proper control, entranceways to many parks must serve as barriers during certain hours. Gates become a practical necessity, but any pretentiousness of these is apt to suggest an institution. Probably the low gate, related in appearance to the familiar log barrier of the parking area and pivoting at one end for operation, is the happiest solution. It serves adequately as barrier and does not obscure, complicate, or presume to compete with the landscape beyond. Among examples of this type, the gate of the checking station at Turner Falls, Oklahoma, is of exceptional merit. A chain barrier is an even simpler solution, but should always be equipped with a conspicuous sign or be made otherwise readily visible under automobile headlights.

Overhead construction, utilizing arch or lintel, perhaps overdone in an earlier era, seems not to find wide current favor. Doubtless the changed attitude of mind results from a worthy desire to avoid any feeling of confinement, or any subconscious recall of the triumphal arch and staff creations long associated with street parades and carnivals.

In rare instances, as in the case of a small park not heavily used and requiring a very limited staff, a custodian's dwelling or lodge must necessarily be located so that it is almost a part of the entranceway. The connotation of gate lodge guarding a country estate is then to be avoided. Generally speaking, however, this location for the caretaker's residence is unfortunate for it unfairly places that official and his family in a situation of being on call for 24 hours a day.

The speed and conditions of present day traffic, in which the car is quicker than the eye, dictate that the public be given timely warning and vision of its approach to the park entranceway. In order that brakes may be applied effectively at prevalent, popular speeds, a considerable stretch of highway border is affected. While conservation of all possible forest cover may be the primary and praiseworthy objective of the natural park enthusiast, it is urged that it yield precedence outside the entrance gate to the demands for safety. The practical advantages to be derived from the placement of any entrance features well back from the main highway and from the maintenance of suitably cleared sight lines must be acknowledged by all as paramount.

The park entranceway may meet all the requirements of function and many of the standards of beauty and yet fall far short of its potentialities. As the outpost of a reserved area offering certain distinctive recreational opportunities to the public, it can with subtlety and grace project the promise and lure of the region and its offered recreation to the very public highway. The truly successful entranceway will be contrived to be the simple essence of the characteristics of the park to no resultant interference with the basic and material functions of ingress, egress, and barrier.

Plate I A–1 →»» ENTRANCEWAYS AND CHECKING STATIONS

Boyle Metropolitan Park, Little Rock, Arkansas

Twanoh State Park, Washington

ENTRANCE GATES

Hardly major entranceways but sometimes a necessary part thereof, as when a cattle guard is required across the main roadway, yet provision must be made for admitting animals to the park area on occasion. To such purpose function the gates shown directly above, below, and to the right. The gate at upper right is typical of the Pacific Northwest. The decorative gate at lower right is very definitely regional with the full flavor of the Southwest. Its almost solid pattern suggests that its purpose is to close off a view of what is beyond —a major characteristic of a service gate.

Pueblo Mountain Metropolitan Park, Colorado

Tucson Mountain Park, Arizona

University Ruins, Saguaro Forest State Park, Arizona

ENTRANCEWAYS AND CHECKING STATIONS

Cape San Sebastian State Park, Oregon

Echo Lake, Westchester County, New York

STONE ENTRANCE PYLONS

The outer columns feature stone pylons vertical in feeling. A more squat form is common to those intervening. Between the limits represented by the casual piling of rock that buttresses the pylon at Lincoln Park and the meticulous masonry of the Zion National Park pylon, varying degrees of sophistication of masonry are in evidence. The obligation to employ boulders where these are the only indigenous rock of an area is a heavy handicap to start with. Within the limitations that boulders impose the sign-pylon at Steckel Park,

Pinnacles National Monument

Lincoln Park, Oklahoma City, Oklahoma

Plate I A–3 →→→ ENTRANCEWAYS AND CHECKING STATIONS

Deception Pass State Park, Washington

Zion National Park

California, amounts to an excellent performance.

In the Lincoln Park pylon the transition from convincingly natural rock outcrop at base to the climax of finished masonry with cut stone cap is skillfully handled—here is the evolution of masonry in tabloid.

A sign is usually the necessary accompaniment of the pylon. This may be suspended from an arm, inset as a panel, or otherwise incorporated in the scheme. The squared timber with incised legend set vertically into the corner of the stone pier at Deception Pass State Park has novelty.

Steckel County Park, California

Lassen Volcanic National Park

13

ENTRANCEWAYS AND CHECKING STATIONS   Plate I A-4

Bonham State Park, Texas

Goose Island State Park, Texas

Garner State Park, Texas

STONE PYLONS IN TEXAS

In park development in the Lone Star State, entrance pylons are impressive. Surrounding illustrations exhibit the variety of texture and pattern and the considerable originality of silhouette to be found in that area. Infrequent in park construction, and for that reason, refreshing, is the regularity of the masonry units that form the Goose Island pylon. The Bonham example has dignity and restful proportion; that at Hereford, vigorous personality. The tall pylon at Lake Worth proves that skill in execution can at once assemble in a pylon the fixity of finished masonry, sans its usual

Lake Worth Metropolitan Park, Fort Worth, Texas

Longhorn Cavern State Park, Texas

Plate I A–5   ⇢⇢⇢ ENTRANCEWAYS AND CHECKING STATIONS

Hereford State Park, Texas

Caddo Lake State Park, Texas

harshness, and the informality of piled rock without resulting appearance of instability.

At Longhorn Cavern State Park the entrance road is flanked by the two rock piers shown directly below. The one carries the designative sign, the other symbolizes the cavern that is the outstanding feature of this park area. At Garner State Park the pattern of the masonry and the mass of the pylon command attention. The pylon at lower right has a bulk that permits it to serve as kiosk without sacrifice of pylon silhouette. It is regrettable that a close grouping of subjects as here presented is apt to be misleading as to the size of each.

Lake Brownwood State Park, Texas

Longhorn Cavern State Park, Texas

Bastrop State Park, Texas

15

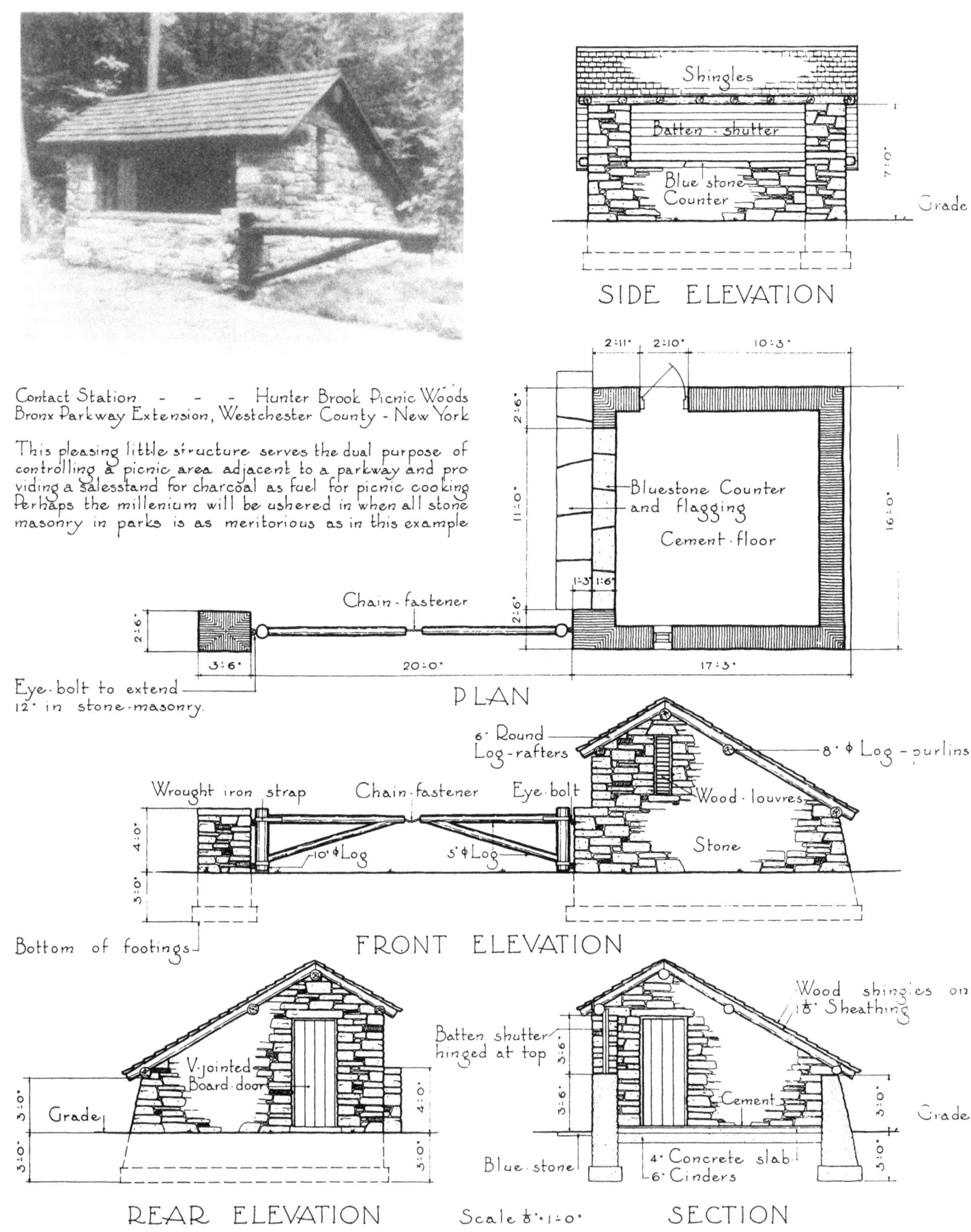

Plate I A-7 — ENTRANCEWAYS AND CHECKING STATIONS

Entrance Way — Mt Penn Park — Reading, Pa.

Not to be judged as a park entrance, but like the example on the facing page, a facility for the control of a park's grounds. From such a station point fees may be collected, charcoal sold, picnic tables allotted, and closing hours and other prevailing regulations enforced.

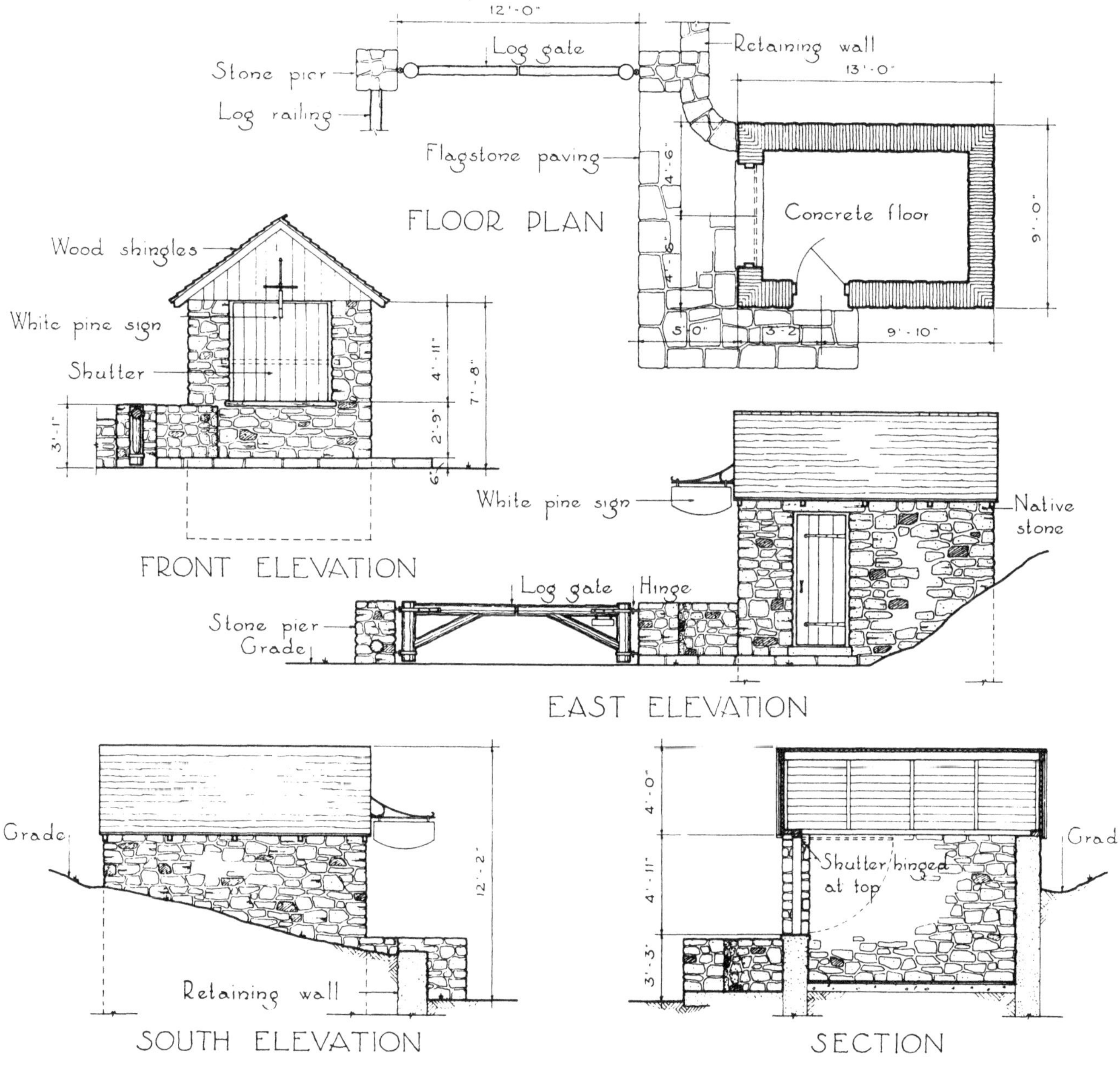

FLOOR PLAN

FRONT ELEVATION

EAST ELEVATION

SOUTH ELEVATION

SECTION

Scale ⅜" = 1'-0"

17

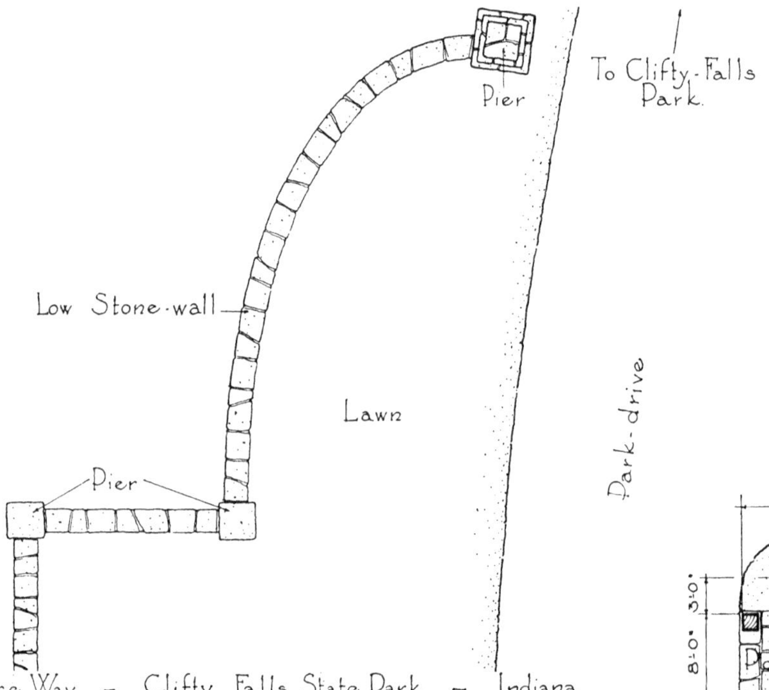

ENTRANCEWAYS AND CHECKING STATIONS

Plate I A-8

Entrance Way – Clifty Falls State Park – Indiana

The stage is here well-set for the softening influence of time and that process of assimilation of structure that only planting will accomplish. The need for a large window in the vestibule has resulted in a slenderness of stone pier that is in unfortunate contrast with the heavy wood post of the porch. The massive chimney, the shake roof with interesting ridge termination are pleasing details.

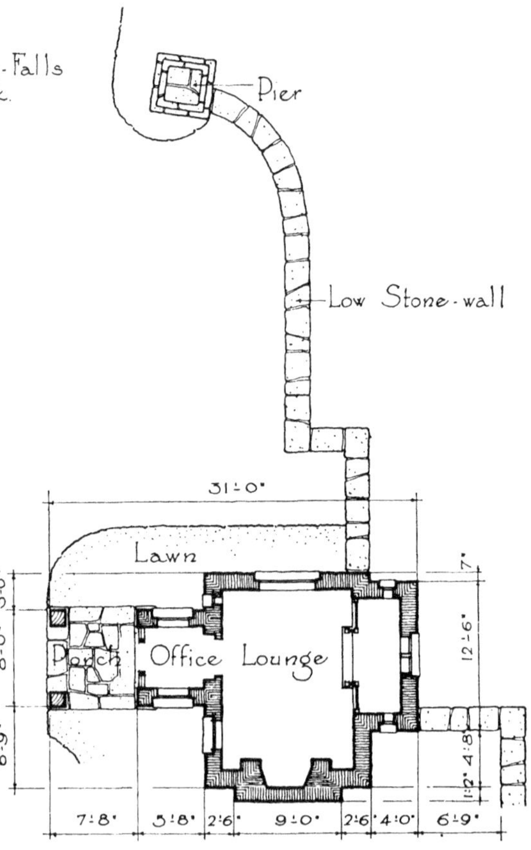

FLOOR PLAN
Scale $\frac{1}{8}" = 1'-0"$

Plate I A–9   ⇶ ENTRANCEWAYS AND CHECKING STATIONS

Brown County State Park, Indiana

Spring Mill State Park, Indiana

INDIANA ENTRANCEWAYS

A page from a family album—counterfeit presentments of five brothers of the Clifty Falls entranceway shown on the facing page. As with members of any family group these gate lodges or checking stations have their points of similarity and surprising points of difference. The Brown County and Spring Mill brothers are Hoosier to the core. Their paternity goes unquestioned. As to the others, although not all the old Hoosier traits persist, there is no question of their general attractiveness however it has been come by.

Turkey Run State Park, Indiana

Pokagon State Park, Indiana

McCormick's Creek State Park, Indiana

ENTRANCEWAYS AND CHECKING STATIONS   *Plate* I A-1

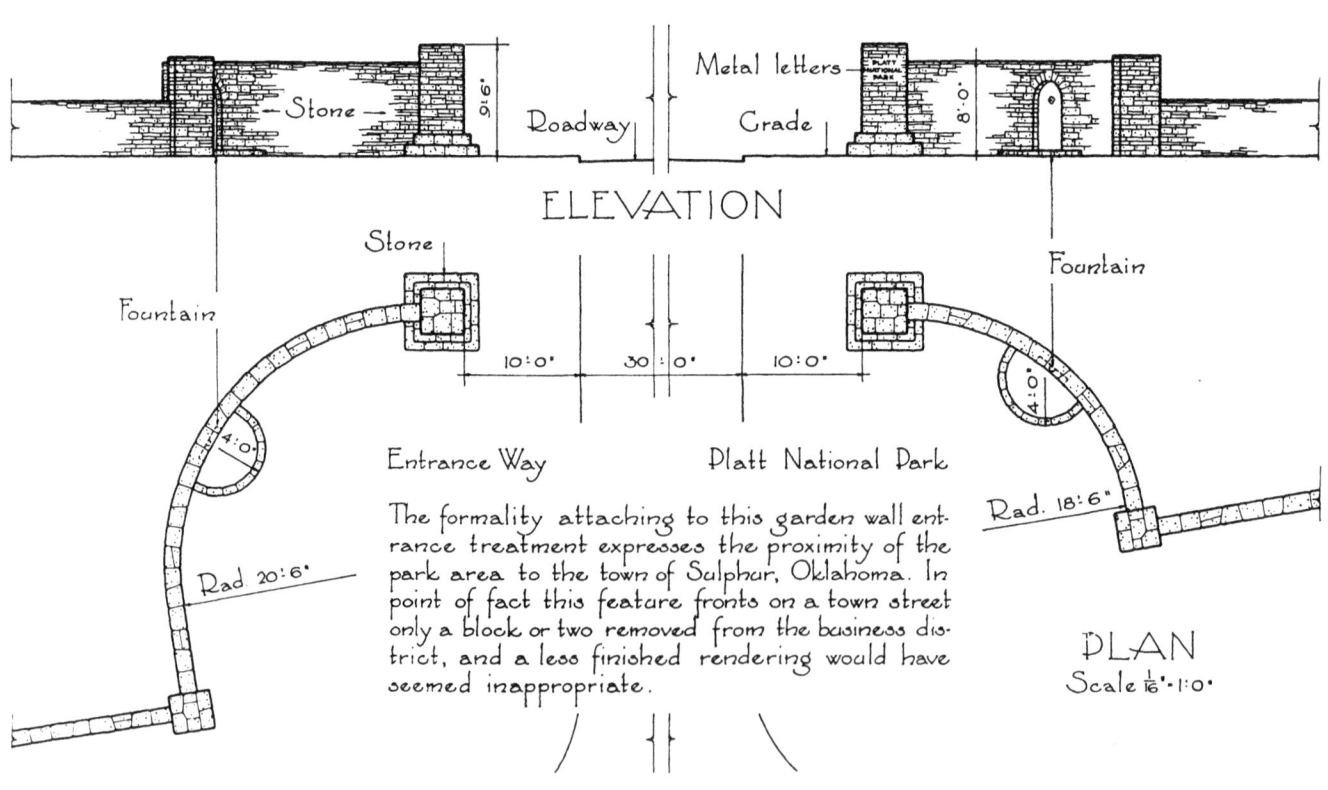

Entrance Way — Platt National Park

The formality attaching to this garden wall entrance treatment expresses the proximity of the park area to the town of Sulphur, Oklahoma. In point of fact this feature fronts on a town street only a block or two removed from the business district, and a less finished rendering would have seemed inappropriate.

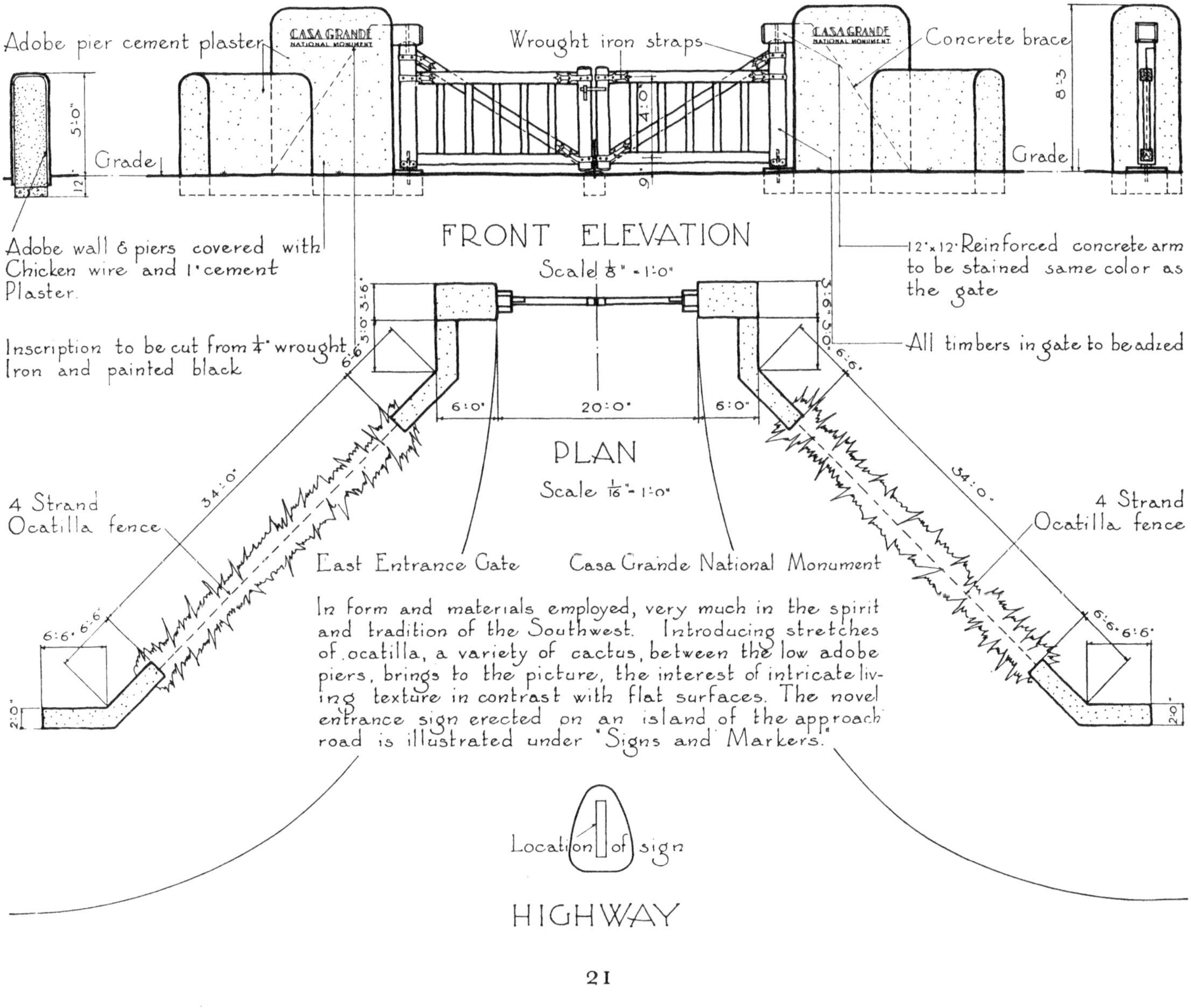

Plate I A-11 → ENTRANCEWAYS AND CHECKING STATIONS

East Entrance Gate — Casa Grande National Monument

In form and materials employed, very much in the spirit and tradition of the Southwest. Introducing stretches of ocatilla, a variety of cactus, between the low adobe piers, brings to the picture, the interest of intricate living texture in contrast with flat surfaces. The novel entrance sign erected on an island of the approach road is illustrated under "Signs and Markers."

ENTRANCEWAYS AND CHECKING STATIONS   Plate I A-12

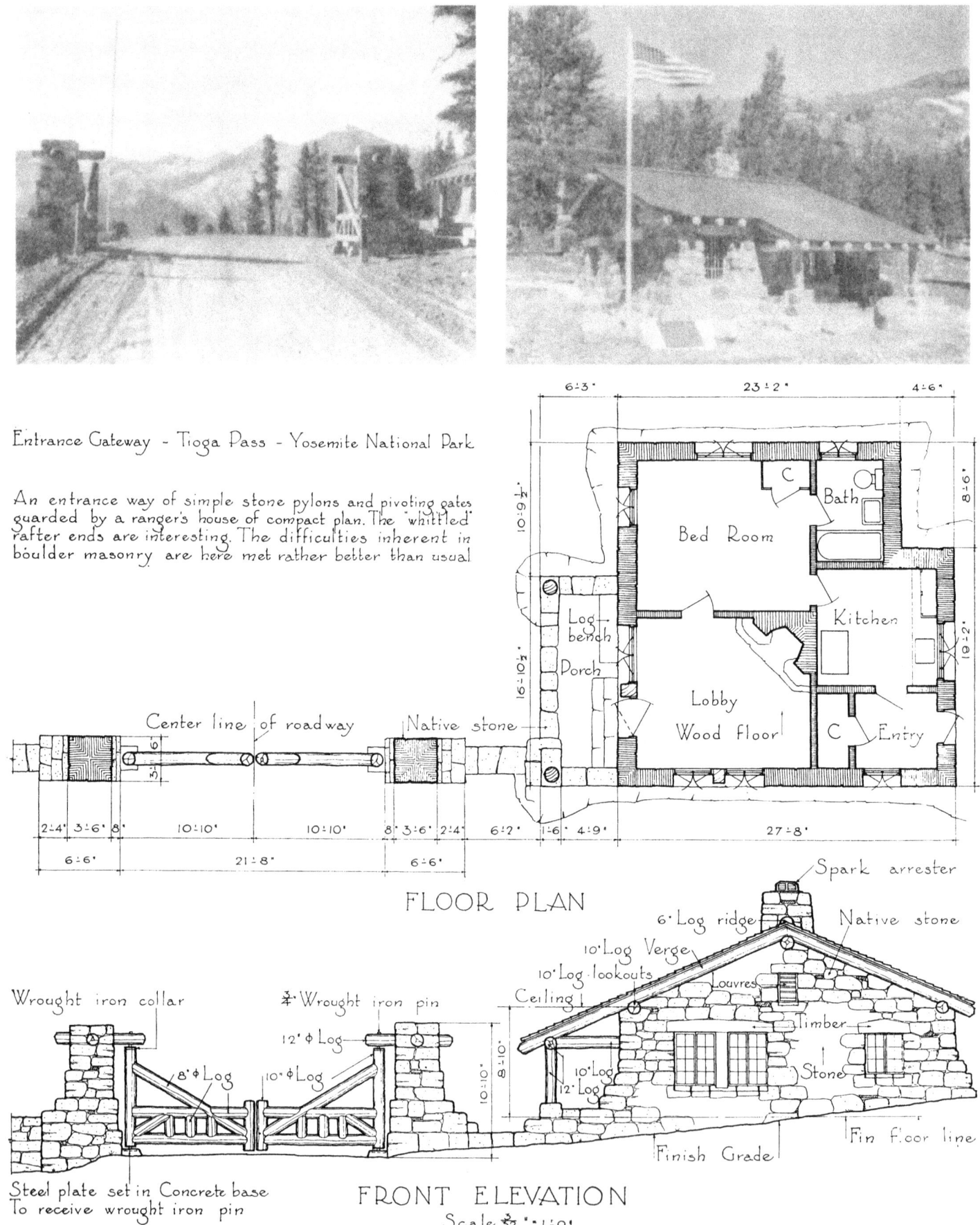

Entrance Gateway - Tioga Pass - Yosemite National Park

An entrance way of simple stone pylons and pivoting gates guarded by a ranger's house of compact plan. The "whittled" rafter ends are interesting. The difficulties inherent in boulder masonry are here met rather better than usual.

Plate I A-13   ENTRANCEWAYS AND CHECKING STATIONS

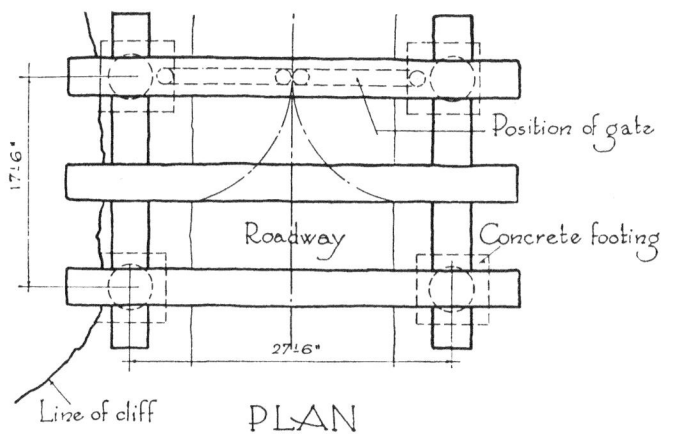

Entrance Way — — Mt. Rainier National Park

Entrance gates with overhead construction do not have their one-time popularity in our natural parks. This example has vigorous proportions and the huge cedar logs used are doubtless representative of the size of the timber that features the region. A ball bearing pivot is highly desirable when gates are of this great size and weight.

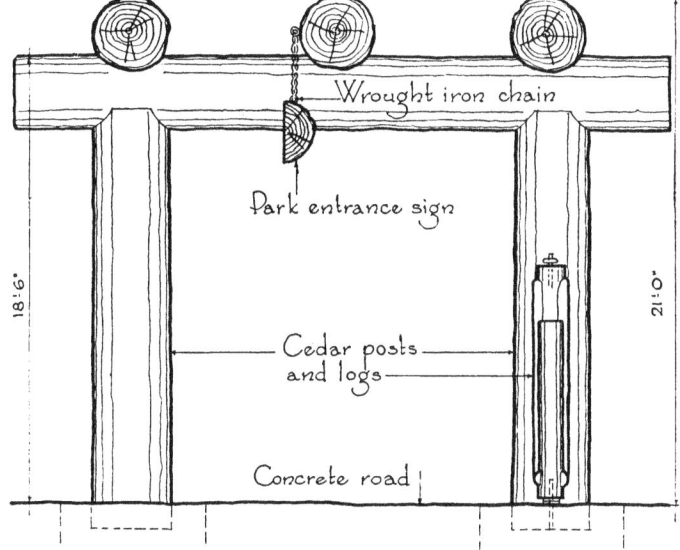
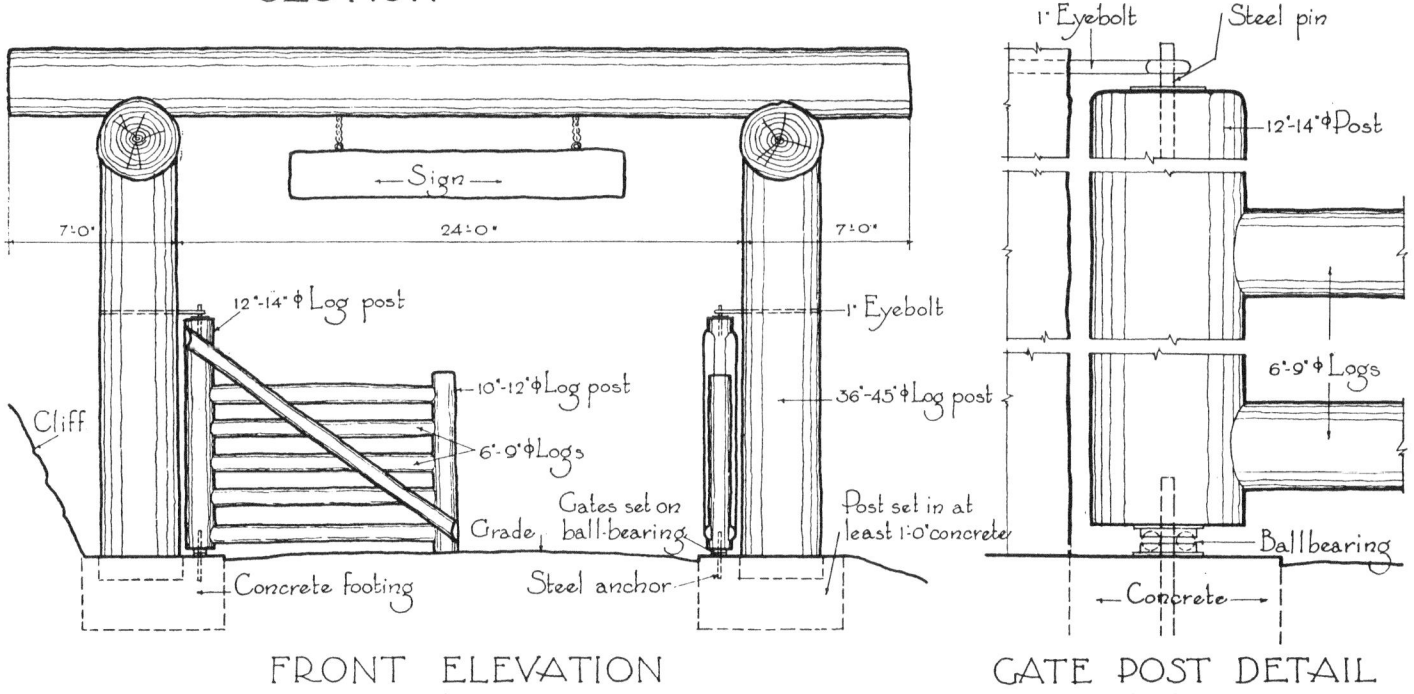

ENTRANCEWAYS AND CHECKING STATIONS

Plate I A–14

Entrance Gateway and Lodge — Perry Lake — Oklahoma

The diminutive lodge adjoining the stone pylons of this entrance-way serves to exaggerate the scale. The transition from rock work laid dry to masonry laid with mortar requires skill and eternal vigilance in the process for satisfying effect. The plan of the little gatehouse is a model for compact utilization of space.

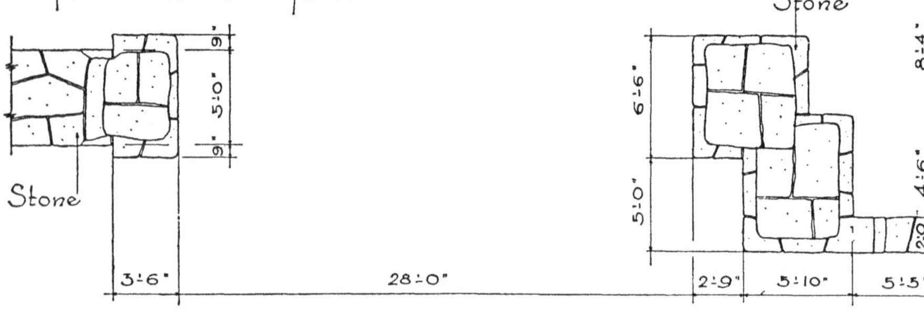

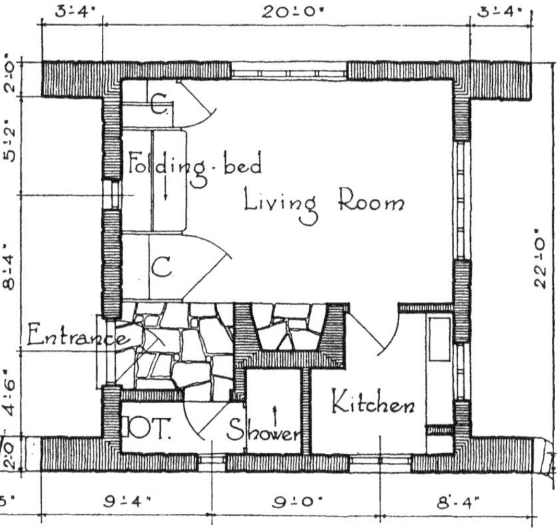

PLAN

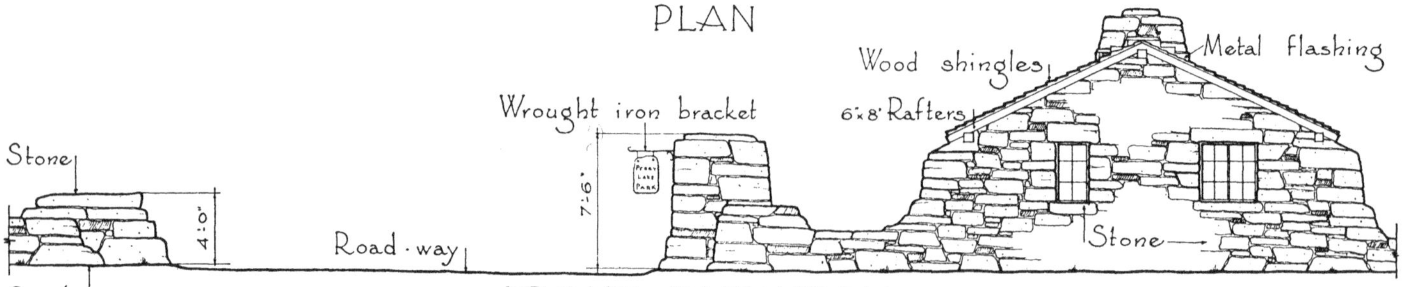

FRONT ELEVATION
Scale 3/32" = 1'0"

24

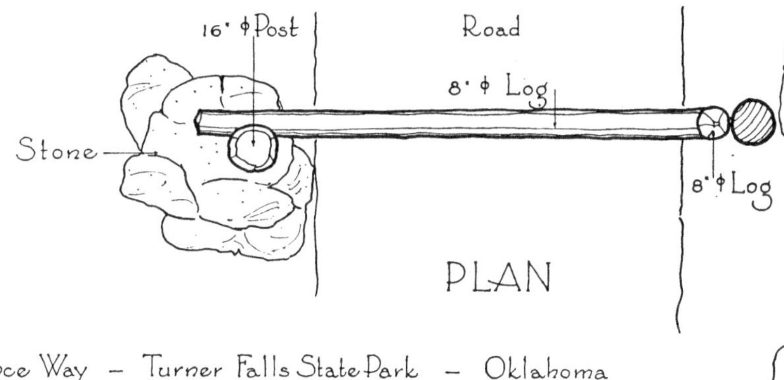

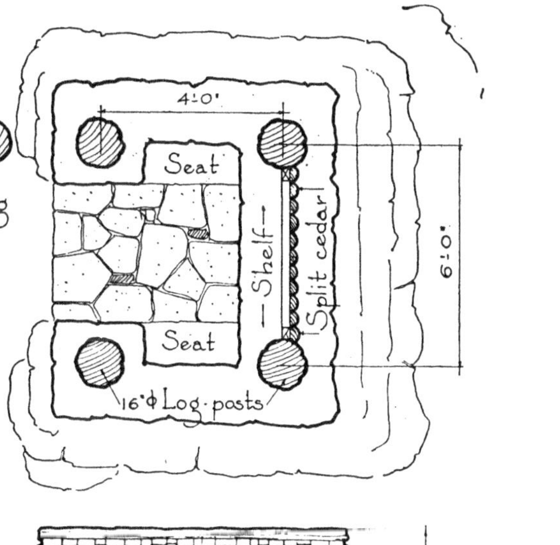

Plate I A–15 ⇒⇒⇒ ENTRANCEWAYS AND CHECKING STATIONS

PLAN

Entrance Way — Turner Falls State Park — Oklahoma

If this be "hill-billy" architecture, let us have more of it; if it be "rustic", it should restore meaning to that abused word. Here is much to admire, little to wish different. Current opinion and cold reason would probably decree the cropping of the shaggy bark whiskers, but aesthetics would as surely plead a special dispensation in this case.

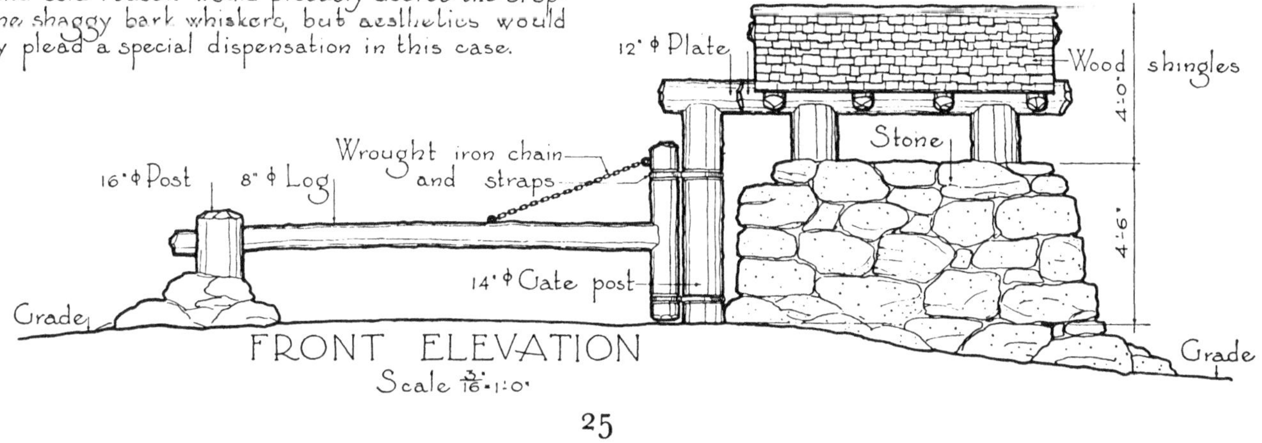

FRONT ELEVATION
Scale 3/16"=1'-0"

25

ENTRANCEWAYS AND CHECKING STATIONS

Plate I A-16

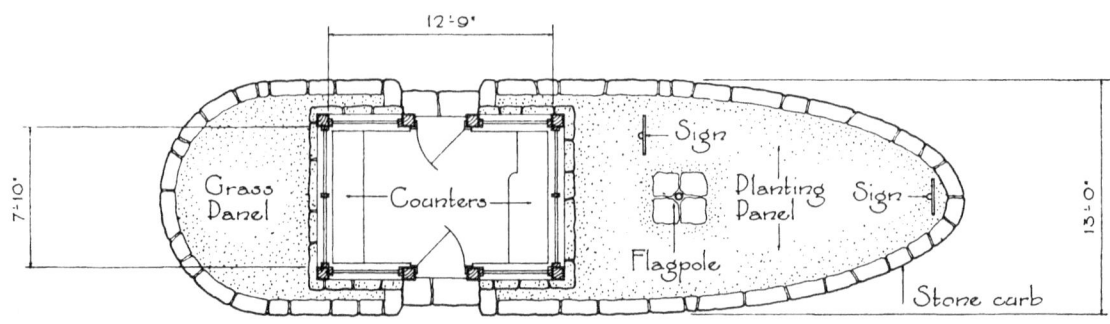

Sequoia National Park

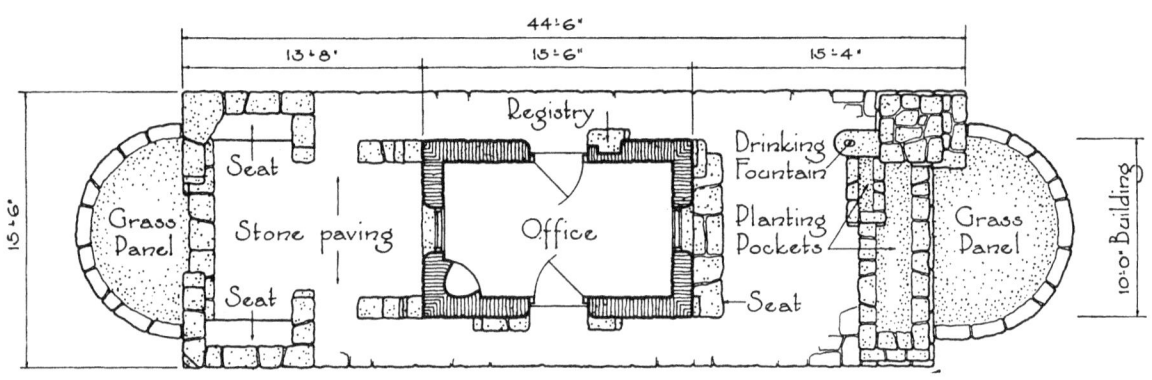

Mesa Verde National Park

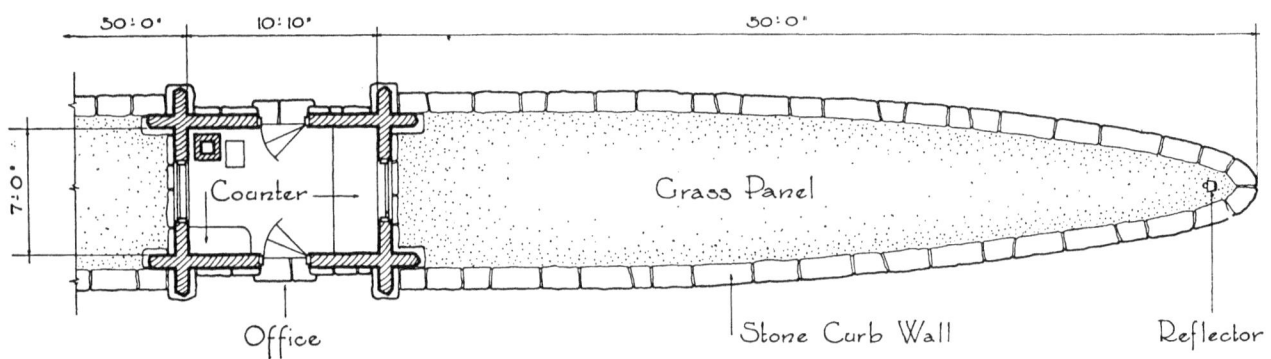

Bryce Canyon National Park

Scale 3/32"=1'-0"

Plate I A–17   ⇶ ENTRANCEWAYS AND CHECKING STATIONS

An island location for the checking station permits effective spotting of the flagpole and the traffic and regulatory signs that are the usual complement of the entranceway. This structure offers clear vision in every direction. Rusticity has tactfully and tactically given way before a well-reasoned practicability to results that invest the facility with a sure air of businesslike control and authority.

Entrance Checking Station, Sequoia National Park

The architectural kinship existing between this appealing little building and the other Mesa Verde structures illustrated under other sections evidences thoughtful design. Interesting features of the island development are the low walls, drinking fountain, outdoor seats, planting pockets and panels, and the registry ledge on the outside wall of the building proper.

Entrance Checking Station, Mesa Verde National Park

This small log building echoes the character present in the administration building of this park, shown elsewhere. The benefits of the island entrance checking station are, of course, well understood. The reflector warning at the point of the island is a practical provision. The position of the chimney well free of all contact with the log walls is sound fire-preventive planning.

Entrance Checking Station, Bryce Canyon National Park

ENTRANCEWAYS AND CHECKING STATIONS   *Plate* I A–18

Entrance Station, Mount Rainier National Park

A splendid log structure deserving of the impressive background it enjoys. Only the trivial chimneys fail to register to the high standards all other details maintain. The log work and the scale of the rafters, purlins, and shake roof with pole-capped ridge are excellently handled. The low log barrier in addition to practical purpose serves to link the log construction with the surroundings. There is a well-tended neatness about this structure and setting untypical of wilderness areas generally, yet somehow not discordant here.

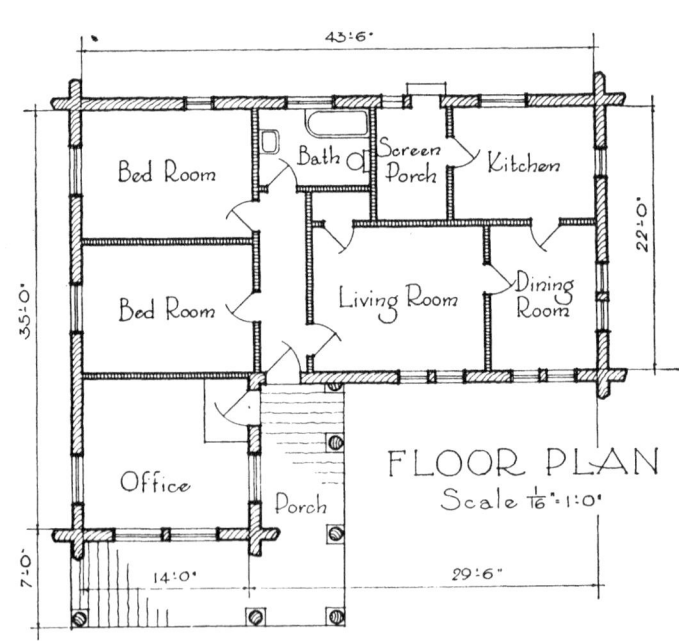

Plate I A-19   ⋙ ENTRANCEWAYS AND CHECKING STATIONS

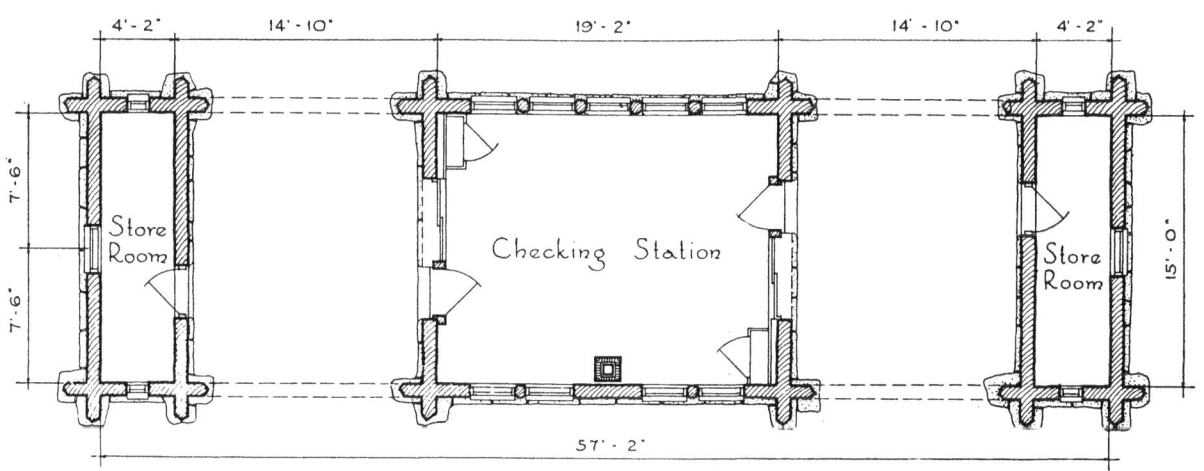

Entrance Station, Yellowstone National Park

FLOOR PLAN
Scale 3/32"=1'-0"

The uncommon and ambitious extent of this entrance feature gives shelter for the ranger as he checks the cars entering or leaving the park—by no means a superfluous provision in many locations. The masonry foundation by its height protects somewhat the log construction in a region of heavy snowfall and by its projection curbs the damage potential in automobiles passing through the covered ways. The practical purposes of the foundation would not be jeopardized, and the total effect of the building would be improved, by some judicious low growth to break the harsh and barren foundation line.

29

ENTRANCEWAYS AND CHECKING STATIONS ««   Plate I A–20

Ticket Stand
Mohawk Metropolitan Park   Tulsa, Oklahoma

The specific purpose of this altogether sightly little facility is unknown, but it can be recommended as entirely reasonable at the entrance to a heavily patronized picnic area where on occasion picnic tables and fireplaces are assigned rather than fought for. It might also serve advantageously as a registration booth when a large group picnic or family reunion was the order of the day.

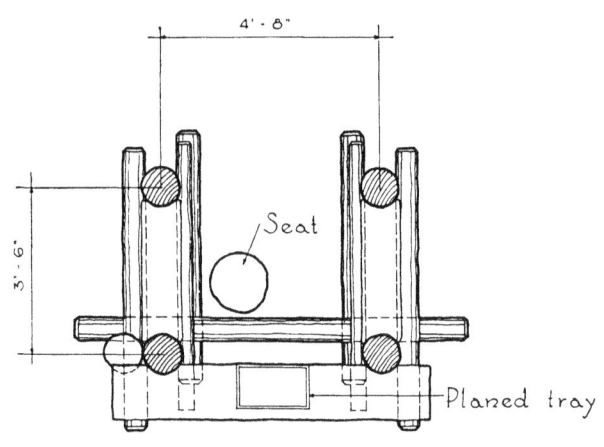

PLAN

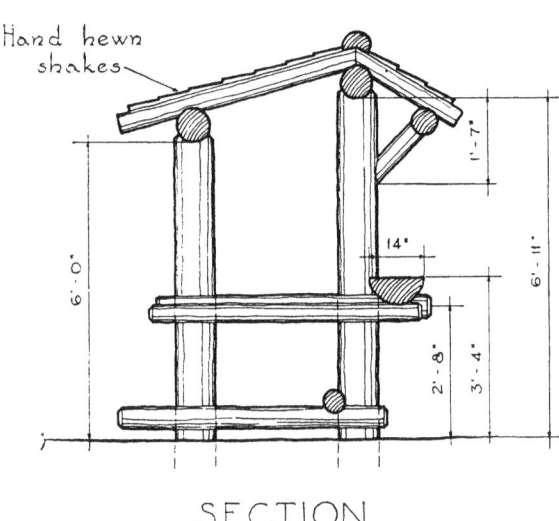

SECTION

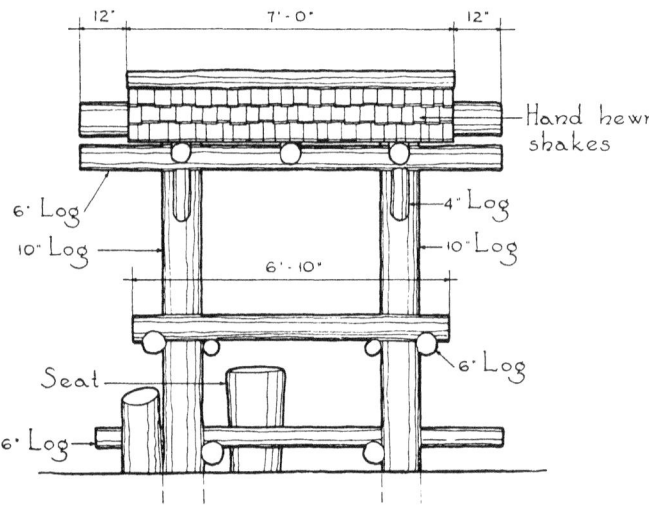

FRONT ELEVATION

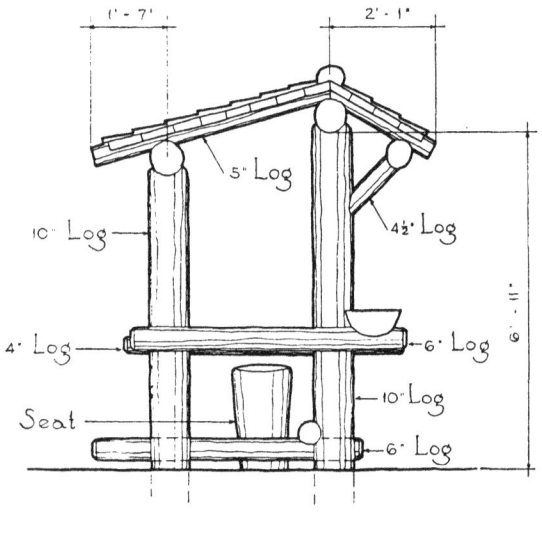

SIDE ELEVATION

Scale ¼" = 1'-0"

30

BARRIERS, WALLS, AND FENCES

IF MAN COULD BRING to his creations in natural parks the protective coloration that Nature bestows on wildlife, with how much more harmony he would endow his trespasses! One particularly longs for this quality in barriers, herein considered to embrace obstacles and obstructions to automobile travel—stone walls and wood fences, guard rails and retaining walls. These are unavoidable necessities in parks, generally so extensively required that any treatment short of the most skillful is a source of quick contamination to natural beauty into the farthermost reaches of the area.

For this reason they deserve to be planned thoughtfully and to be constructed with ever alert willingness to adjust the predetermined treatment to conditions actually encountered in the field. The contrary approach, the attempt to warp conditions of site to some blueprint treatment of barrier or retaining wall, usually leads to disaster. Natural quality is so ready to vanish; artificial quality, so prone to persist.

Barriers of stone have one basic advantage over barriers of wood. Stone is the more permanent, a fact which often predisposes its selection as the material for use. The claim of permanence, however, should not alone determine the choice of stone over wood; each must be further considered for its native suitability. Stone imported into areas to which no stone is native seems always inappropriate. There are parks where native stone suitable for building is not present, yet the landscape is of definitely stony character. Here barriers of imported stone can be made effective if skill and artistry are brought to their contriving. But more often than not, unless barriers can be produced from native stone, it is more reasonable to waive the advantage of greater permanence and make use of wood. Timber for barriers in some localities will offset comparative lack of permanence through native abundance and consequent greater suitability and economy. For wooded areas, regardless of stone supply, there are those who cast their votes in favor of wood, usually log, barriers, which can be made sturdy and unobtrusive and are far from short-lived.

When neither wood nor stone can stake a valid claim to being, or appearing to be, native to a region, the attributes of the area for park purposes may be logically challenged. This premise allowed, we are assured that either wood or stone will appropriately serve as material for the barriers we may require in any tract of true park potentialities. The problem then becomes one of intelligent use of whichever material Nature's bounty indicates.

One cannot visit many parks without becoming conscious of shortcomings of barrier and guard rail treatments in general. Where there is extensive need for guard rail, the use of one type of construction can become very monotonous. This is especially true if the construction is not utterly simple, or is too mathematically precise. Miles of stone barrier with crenelles and merlons of fixed length and height ticking off on the consciousness with pendulumlike routine seem almost to infect Nature itself with dull monotony. Better far to borrow something of Nature's variety. If it is desired to avoid the tiresome regularity of an unbroken coping line, it is merely choosing a different monotony to introduce a system of regular and repetitious breaks into the silhouette. Changes in coping levels to present varying lengths and varying heights are much more in the rhythm of Nature.

There are parks wherein the very extent of necessary guard rail seems to cry out for the variety of more than one type of construction. This is not to suggest merit in a hodge-podge of barrier treatments in one area, or in close coupling two widely different types. But where stretches demanding guard rail construction are separated by distances requiring none, occasionally to introduce variety for an isolated stretch would seem to be well reasoned.

BARRIERS, WALLS, AND FENCES

A long stretch of elaborate guard rail, not only offends and distracts the viewer, but detracts from the view in direct proportion to its complexity of character. Probably the guard rail most generally satisfying to the eye, and as practical and economical as any, is the log barrier hub cap high supported on log posts at the joints. Logs and supports must be first of all of ample diameter, for flimsiness here, as in a bridge, registers adversely on the consciousness. Wood supports below grade should be treated with a preservative to prolong their life. They should extend deep into the ground so as to be truly effectual under impact.

Unpleasant indeed is the barrier of bowed, contorted logs that twists and writhes in its course like an attenuated corkscrew. Just as disturbing is the log barrier that bumps along at the roadside haphazardly rising high above the grade, then dipping almost to meet it. The log barrier should flow along parallel with the grade of the roadway if it is to be harmonious in the picture.

It is possible to detail the log guard rail so that when one section is broken the adjoining sections are unaffected either by reason of the accident itself or the ensuing operation of replacement. These will be favored wherever the limiting of maintenance costs must be considered. Barriers designed with wood rails that build into stone piers usually require an excessive amount of labor when replacement of a broken rail becomes necessary.

The ideal barrier treatment along certain roadways would be guard rocks, bedded deep in the ground in naturalized groupings spaced at irregular but effective intervals. This has been attempted but never, in the examples noted to date, with the measure of success held to be possible if executed with more skill and feeling for natural values.

In his well-presented Camp Planning and Camp Reconstruction, issued by the United States Forest Service, Dr. E. P. Meinecke discusses the choice and use of obstacles, obstructions, and barriers in relation to the principles of camp planning. So much on the subject of barriers therein contained is applicable to their proper use in parks, beyond the confines of campsites, that careful study of Dr. Meinecke's work is recommended.

One of the difficult park problems is the blending of a masonry barrier or retaining wall to a rock outcrop which it surmounts or abuts. The results in general seem to indicate failure to sense that skillful blending of the man-made to the natural was of the essence of the problem, or else that skill was lacking. When the transition is so handled that the precise limits of Nature's handiwork and man's blur to the eye's satisfaction, the accomplishment is praiseworthy.

Of particular import is the wall or fence that adjoins the entranceway. Unless it is to be completely planted out, something of the flavor of the entrance structures should be given it. The stone wall so typical of New England, New York, and other localities, and the snake fence once so widely distributed through the Middle West have the advantage of long familiarity and deep significance to us. Because these bring subconsciously to mind the very values that parks seek to recapture—open spaces, unspoiled Nature, release from cramped and artificial existence—they might well serve as a far more useful instrument than they have to date in our hands.

Unquestionably there are sometimes required in natural areas barriers that must forego protective coloration to warn forcefully of danger ahead, particularly to the motorist. Barriers and obstructions, purposed to prevent traffic accidents, are not to be laughed off. They are an acknowledged, if unwelcome, necessity even in parks, and our public highways provide many precedents more or less effectual in purpose and construction. Probably reflector studs judiciously placed crowd a maximum of warning into a small space, and so interfere least with natural values. To create barriers that shout a warning is no trick at all, but to determine at exactly what locations along park roads barriers having this function are requisite and tolerable needs thoughtful judgment. To provide within a given park area neither one too many nor one too few such barriers is both the problem and the solution. It should be studied in the light of the accepted tenet that park roads exist for leisurely automobile travel only, and with an understanding that traffic speed and barrier need relate to each other. Resultantly we should find in parks fewer blatant barriers than the public highways require, and a prevalence of unobtrusive treatments.

Plate I B–1   ⋙ BARRIERS, WALLS, AND FENCES

Ponca State Park, Nebraska

Denver Mountain Parks, Colorado

WOOD BARRIERS

Common characteristic of the log barriers here illustrated is a recognition of the advantage, from a maintenance viewpoint, of unjoined units in serving to limit, and so to minimize, the spread of damage to result from sharp impact. The simplest expression of the log barrier is a row of posts, so spaced that an automobile cannot pass between them. One here shown is scaled to a modified area, the other, to a more rugged setting. The next step is a series of fabricated units, each a horizontal log with terminal supports and independent of the actuarial risks of the flanking units. Three such are illustrated.

Bastrop State Park, Texas

Devil's Den State Park, Arkansas

Woahink Lake State Park, Oregon

BARRIERS, WALLS, AND FENCES

Plate I B–2

South Mountain County Reservation, New Jersey

Custer State Park, South Dakota

Mohawk Metropolitan Park, Tulsa, Oklahoma

WOOD GUARD RAIL AND FENCES

Here is pictured low guard rail into fence in slow motion—guard rails to the left, fences to the right, and the binding margin the line of cleavage. Above are typical examples of the continuous log barrier riding atop supports, next, in counterclockwise progression, the barrier log bolted to the side of the supporting posts, then a doubling of the horizontal member, and finally a doubling of the supports.

The take-off into fences begins at upper left of the right hand page with an increase in normal

Cumberland Falls State Park, Kentucky

DuPage County Forest Preserve, Illinois

Plate I B–3   ⇶ BARRIERS, WALLS, AND FENCES

South Mountain County Reservation, New Jersey

Cook County Forest Preserve, Illinois

guard rail height and the addition of a buffer rail at hub cap height, a very practical provision in limitation of maintenance. Next, now reading clockwise, is a variation of this idea, followed by three fences that have lost all trace and, probably due to location, all need of functioning as barriers to vehicle traffic. The fence that combines stone piers with wood construction is more pleasing than practical. The wood members will eventually decay, and replacement of them, because of the connection with masonry, will be a troublesome matter.

Devil's Punch Bowl State Park, Oregon

Mount Penn Metropolitan Reservation, Reading, Pennsylvania

Caddo Lake State Park, Texas

35

BARRIERS, WALLS, AND FENCES

Plate I B–4

Quartz Mountain State Park, Oklahoma

Devil's Den State Park, Arkansas

Tucson Mountain Park, Arizona

ROCK BARRIERS, CURBS, AND WALLS

Three illustrations at upper left picture employment of rocks as a roadside barrier in semi-naturalistic distribution—always seemingly very difficult to execute and here better done than usual, especially so at Quartz Mountain State Park. At lower left is a related barrier, rather more of a wall but still quite informal and disclosing the use of but little mortar. This and the barrier to the right of it feature a buffer curb that permits pedestrians to pass between parked automobiles and the barrier proper.

Other examples on these facing pages are gen-

Petit Jean State Park, Arkansas

Rocky Mountain National Park

Plate I B–5   ⇢⇢⇢ BARRIERS, WALLS, AND FENCES

Crater Lake National Park

Yellowstone National Park

erally typical of protective masonry barriers laid with mortar. For the most part these are crenellated. In masonry technique there is considerable range of character.

On the next following page stone curbs and walls are paraded in variety. The low formal curb reflects fittingly its location in a groomed metropolitan area; the other curbs typify surroundings less intensively used, settings more primitive. All the walls pictured in the right hand tier suggest modified and mild country in great contrast with most of the landscape to be seen on this present page.

Great Smoky Mountains National Park

Grand Canyon National Park

Turner Falls State Park, Oklahoma

BARRIERS, WALLS, AND FENCES　　　　　　　　　　　　　　　　　　　　　　　　　　Plate I B-6

Cook County Forest Preserve, Illinois

Greenwich, Connecticut, Eric Gugler, Architect

Voorhees State Park, New Jersey

Butler Memorial State Park, Kentucky

Boyle Metropolitan Park, Little Rock, Arkansas

Cook County Forest Preserve, Illinois

SIGNS

⇛As DEVELOPMENT of any preserve for recreational use proceeds there is bound to be coincident multiplication in the number and kinds of required signs and related objects. If their purpose is directional, designative, regulatory, or cautionary, they are classified as "Signs" in this compilation. If their intent is to be informative of matters of historical or natural interest pertinent to the park area, they are herein termed "Markers" and, being thus incident to cultural recreation, they are discussed along with structures which facilitate that phase of recreational pursuit.

Nothing in parks, unless it be the entranceway, offers wider legitimate scope for individuality in conveying the characteristics or background of the particular area than the signs and markers. These can be the embodiment of those rare and distinguishing features that have dictated the establishment of the park—park motifs-in-miniature.

Well-keyed to an historical period are the signs at Morristown National Historical Park. Here of course the theme is the Revolutionary era.

A visitor on pilgrimage to the reconstructed village of Lincoln's young manhood in New Salem State Park, Illinois, is subtly put in receptive and reverent mood for the illusion of a midwestern backwoods village of the 1830's by the very character of the stylized signs and markers. The black, uncertain lettering on white background, in its hand-made irregularity and wavering course lines, recalls the crude typography of the newspapers and handbills of the period and place. Instantly imagination is in pitch, and understanding in tune, with the melody about to be resung for us.

The number of signs actually purposeful in any area and the strategic placing of them should be thoughtfully determined. Signs too generously provided quickly bring protests from those who crave their Nature uncluttered. A shortage of directional information will annoy those who have neither time nor liking for groping their way along roads and trails without benefit of adequate sign service.

A proper scale in the structural members of a sign is especially to be desired. In such a minor item as a sign it is obligatory wherever possible to evidence the employment of native materials. When the trees on an area are stunted or a second growth, it is unfitting to import massive materials for signs that will sharply accent the deficiency of the natural surroundings. It is equally inappropriate to underscale the structural members of a sign placed in an area of large trees.

The scale and legibility of the lettering employed on signs also merit careful consideration. The legends of cautionary and directional signs, more than those of other purpose, call for terseness and instant legibility at a proper distance. Hence the scale of letters reading "Sharp Curve", "Stop", "Low Water Crossing", and the like is subject to standards entirely different from a lengthy recital of rules for campers or picnickers. However appealing and appropriate in respect to an area may be the qualities of quaintness and individuality in stylized lettering, legibility has the call over other considerations for all signs of cautionary intent.

Where there is need for signs in great numbers as in parks and park systems of vast extent, cost and durability are matters of budgetary importance. The well-considered sign will be sturdy. It will "read" well and continue to do so with the least maintenance expense. The metal sign with baked-on enamel lettering may win the pennant in the Minimum Maintenance League, but in the Park Character League it surely rates what the sports scribes refer to as the "cellar position." Lettering painted on wood must be frequently renewed. This adds to maintenance charges. The renewal of lettering painted on a flat surface is painstaking work. If the lettering be initially incised, or embossed by the blow torch and template technique of burning away the background, the

39

renewal of the paint on the letters is more quickly done because there is a definite guide for the painter's brush.

Lettering by burning, avoiding all use of paint, has been done in many parks, but probably nowhere on the scale or with more successful results than in the metropolitan mountain parks of Colorado. So many signs were required in those areas that it was found practical to make heavy sheet iron stencils of a selected alphabet in several sizes and burning irons fashioned to fit them. The desired lettering is marked out on the wood panel only to insure proper spacing. From this point the making of the sign is a mechanical operation. The stencils are placed in their proper position and the letters burned into the wood with the hot irons to a depth of about three-quarters of an inch. This produces signs legible and durable. Barring an act of God, like a cyclone, or assault by that instrument of Satan, the initial carver, signs like these promise long life.

The jackknife vandalism to which all park construction is subject can be somewhat checked in the case of signs by the practice of placing them either well below or well above the convenient working range of the jackknifer. This most vulnerable stratum is between three and six feet off the ground. In spite of all the evidence in our parks to the contrary, this type of predator is a physical, as well as mental, sluggard and is likely to think twice (we flatter him) before he will stand on his head or shinny up a post to accomplish his scandalous, vandalous ends.

Twin to the jackknife pest is the souvenir hunter. Signs too appealingly picturesque and easy to get at and carry away fall prey to his pack rat instincts. His depredations put very definite limits on what it is within reason to attempt in the way of signs.

The day when the quintessence of naturalism for park signs was to paint them on boulders and cliffs is within the memory of many of us. Happily our developing sense of fitness has had a swing away from this sort of thing. The utter inappropriateness of nailing signs to trees is also better understood in the light of today's park-mindedness. Perhaps a warning should be sounded against a noted recent tendency to bring to the park sign something of modern, commercial, eye-arresting technique. By no means need the park entrance sign seek to compete with the 24-sheet cigarette poster farther down the road nor is there merit in three or four messages conveyed by as many different signs wherever all might logically be accumulated to one sign. Several sign groupings that successfully exemplify this point are included among the illustrations on the following pages.

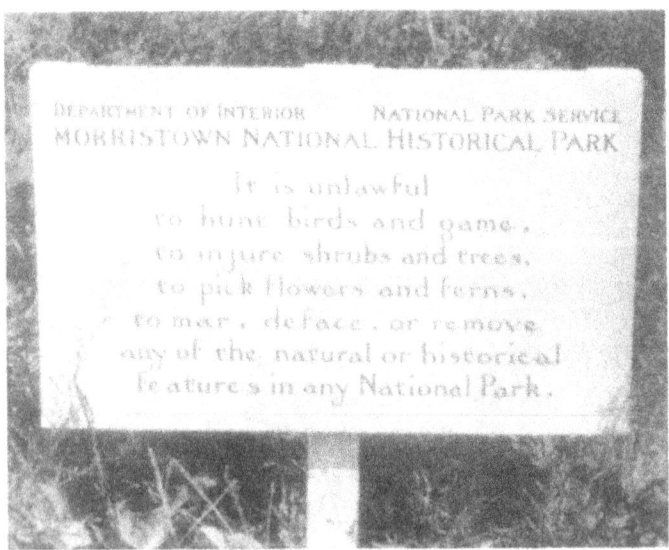

Morristown National Historical Park

New Salem State Park, Illinois

Plate I C–1 　　→›› SIGNS

Fort Dupont, Washington, D. C.

Fort Dupont, Washington, D. C.

LOW HORIZONTAL SIGNS

This page and the two pages next following demonstrate structural simplicity in sign devices—single log in horizontal or vertical position. The recumbent log is satisfyingly unobtrusive but unless vigilantly tended can be quickly lost to view where vegetation grows rapidly. The "To the Lodge" sign lacks painfully a ground cover to obliterate its miserable rock garden foreground. Bark left on structural logs is never to be countenanced—well, hardly ever. The very character of the Lincoln Log Cabin State Park sign would vanish along with the bark. The alternative—probable replacement of this sign every few years—seems here justified.

Gull Point, Okoboji State Park, Iowa

Saratoga Hot Springs State Park, Wyoming

Lincoln Log Cabin State Park, Illinois

41

Garden of the Gods Park, Colorado

Garden of the Gods Park, Colorado

Boyle Metropolitan Park, Little Rock, Arkansas

POST SIGNS

Sturdy durability is the keynote of signs of this type. A genuine "sign" language, understandable and brief, is the ingenious feature of some here shown, and fittingly simple carving brings interest to others. Burned lettering is almost the rule and the effectiveness of deep burning is well demonstrated. It seems to be proved by this group that the singular appeal of an unperfected alphabet is

Rib Mountain State Park, Wisconsin

Garden of the Gods Park, Colorado

Garden of the Gods Park, Colorado

more appropriate to the open spaces than the stodgy professional touch.

The cluster of posts at Boyle Metropolitan Park is at once sign and entrance pylon and has interesting mass and considerable individuality. The "Her–Him" sign at this same park is also more than a sign—it is light-hearted mutiny against the drearily stereotyped.

Boyle Metropolitan Park, Little Rock, Arkansas

Boyle Metropolitan Park, Little Rock, Arkansas

Zilker Metropolitan Park, Austin, Texas

Longhorn Cavern State Park, Texas

Saguaro Forest State Park, Arizona

SINGLE POST AND CROSS ARM SIGNS

"Sign" language persists in the example at upper left, as a footprint instead of the hackneyed index finger points the way. Next right is a sign in character only in the Southwest, for the upright is of cactus. Failure to remove bark from the supporting posts of the two signs to the left is hardly subject to censure. A tousled picturesqueness is added for so long as the bark shall remain, and any resultant acceleration of decay would be inconsequential.

Lake Worth Metropolitan Park, Fort Worth, Texas

Plate I C-5 ⇢ SIGNS

Turner Falls State Park, Oklahoma

Denver Mountain Parks, Colorado

Where there is no vegetation threatening to obscure them, signs are best kept low, as exemplified by the "Trail" and "Trail to Falls" signs. The "Fillius Park" sign rates a very high score; it seems to have everything, including an interesting spiral twist of upright that is a unique talent among signs of our acquaintance.

The sign at lower right has sturdy mass, and displays a competence for directing traffic in all directions at once to make the most accomplished traffic officer envious.

Dolliver Memorial State Park, Iowa

Lake Worth Metropolitan Park, Fort Worth, Texas

45

SIGNS

Plate I C-6

Sequoia National Park

Petit Jean State Park, Arkansas

Santa Rosa County Park, California

SINGLE POST AND BRACKET SIGNS

Here are signs fabricated of post and directional arm, the top row in the singular, shall we say, and the bottom row in the plural. As a group these display a wide range of scale and considerable variety of pattern.

There would be gain of legibility if the incised or burned lettering of several examples were deeper, or painted in a sharply contrasting tone. Because of their hand-hewn weathered character the two signs in Moran State Park might almost be survivals of pioneer days. The wraithlike support of

Deception Pass State Park, Washington

46

Plate I C–7 ⇢ SIGNS

Moran State Park, Washington

Pickett State Forest, Tennessee

the sign illustrated at lower right calls to mind the tree forms of an Arthur Rackham drawing. It is here shown because it is an interesting "sport", fantastic within bounds. If it were often repeated it would probably annoy.

It is a matter for regret that it is not possible to show all subjects of a given group in a proper scale relationship to each other. The reader is warned of the tendency throughout this publication to a certain unavoidable distortion of the true scale of many of the grouped examples illustrated.

Moran State Park, Washington

Crowley's Ridge State Park, Arkansas

SIGNS ⋘ Plate I C-8

Mount Nebo State Park, Arkansas

Wildcat Hills Game Reserve, Nebraska

Boyle Metropolitan Park, Little Rock, Arkansas

SINGLE POST AND SUSPENDED SIGN

This sign group parades the simple hanging sign, reared on a single supporting post. The urge to capture naïveté and rusticity in a park sign should not trap us into using letter forms not readily legible. These qualities are best sought for in and confined to the form of the sign panel itself and the upright supporting member. The alphabets employed in the signs of the enframing illustrations follow generally familiar forms without prejudice to wilderness character.

Humbug Mountain State Park, Oregon

48

Plate I C–9 ⇢⇢⇢ SIGNS

Crowley's Ridge State Park, Arkansas

Crater Lake National Park

Comments disparaging to the subjects here shown would be difficult to frame. The fine entrance sign at Crater Lake National Park merits a better photograph than we are able to show. The head-on approach to the multi-directional sign at Devil's Den State Park is by way of a bridge. The recessed setting in a retaining wall is unusual and interesting, and reduces the vulnerability of the sign to the hazards of traffic.

Humbug Mountain State Park, Oregon

Devil's Den State Park, Arkansas

49

SIGNS Plate I C-10

Humboldt-Redwoods State Park, California

Robbers Cave State Park, Oklahoma

Steckel County Park, California

TWO-POST SIGNS

In general the character of the signs shown on the left hand page seems predicated on locations subjected to more or less modification of Nature. Those signs to the right characterize regions of rugged topography and heavy timber growth. Though all the signs have two supporting posts as a common factor, beyond that are wide differences.

The incised lettering at upper left and upper right of these pages appears to be excellently de-

Bronx River Parkway, New York

Virginia Kendall State Park, Ohio

Plate I C–11   →» SIGNS

Lake Guernsey State Park, Wyoming

Wildcat Hills Game Reserve, Nebraska

signed and skillfully wrought. The greater legibility of incised letters that are additionally painted a contrasting color is demonstrated by the three signs at upper left. The painted legend of the Lake Guernsey Park sign has a nice simplicity. The staggering of the letters in the second line of the "Kitchawan Tavern" sign will have its critics. Signs like this are produced by sheet metal or asbestos templates, a blow torch, and, "for the lower line, just the right degree of intemperance", as has been said before.

Humbug Mountain State Park, Oregon

Black Hawk State Park, Illinois

Crowley's Ridge State Park, Arkansas

51

White Pine Forest State Park, Illinois

Papago State Park, Arizona

Caddo Lake State Park, Texas

TWO-POST SUSPENDED SIGNS

Sign panel hanging from lintel carried by two posts is the theme of the subjects here pictured. From upper left to lower right is a crescendo of scale and mass embracing suitability to almost every character our park terrain presents, not omitting desert country as represented by the Papago State Park example with its uprights of cactaceous growth. Several illustrations strikingly disclose how the best designed of signs are depreciated by immediate

Gull Point, Okoboji State Park, Iowa

Jewel Cave National Monument

Plate I C–13 ⇒⇒ SIGNS

Lake Worth Metropolitan Park, Fort Worth, Texas

Spavinaw Hills State Park, Oklahoma

surroundings lacking natural ground cover and low planting.

Two signs shown at lower right suggest special site considerations, presumably in the case of one, a fork in a road, which would be served well by the angled plan, or in the other, a junction of roads creating an island, which would be served by the sign of triangular plan. The vigorous scale of these is astonishing—an ingratiating fault, if fault it is.

Beavers Bend State Park, Oklahoma

Mount Nebo State Park, Arkansas

Petit Jean State Park, Arkansas

Loveland Mountain Metropolitan Park, Colorado

Mount Nebo State Park, Arkansas

Custer State Park, South Dakota

HOODED SIGNS

The addition of a hood above a sign panel lends prominence and importance to a sign, probably on occasion justified. The hood serves practicably and measurably to protect the lettering and other matter displayed by the sign panel from deteriorating exposure to weather.

From the form of the hooded sign it is no far cry to the typical expression of trailside nature shrine or marker. The sign directly to the left, incorporating as it does the map of a campground, is close indeed to what in this compilation has been classed as marker rather than sign.

Boyle Metropolitan Park, Little Rock, Arkansas

Mount Nebo State Park, Arkansas

Bastrop State Park, Texas

Bastrop State Park, Texas

MISCELLANY

Too novel rather than too late to classify are the "sports" of this aggregation. The metal silhouettes tell their story with a well-rendered cleverness that should silence objections from latter day Puritans. Although "charming" and "delightful" have been shunned as the plague in commenting herein on park construction, both are bestowed on the Mohawk Metropolitan Park example and are far from being a reproach. Note that the sign at Crowley's Ridge State Park is one of a trinity standing guard at the corners of a traffic island.

Mohawk Metropolitan Park, Tulsa, Oklahoma

Crowley's Ridge State Park, Arkansas

Millersylvania State Park, Washington

Humboldt-Redwoods State Park, California

The use of cross-grained slabs for tops of picnic tables is to be discouraged if only because these are impractical. Their use for signs is not universally looked on with favor, yet when cut from trees of impressive girth these become educational exhibits as well as signs and so gain in justification. The annular structure of a giant tree, in this case a redwood, is ever a matter of interest to the inquiring.

Turner Falls State Park, Oklahoma

Strikingly characteristic of the country around Turner Falls are outcropping, folded, limestone strata marching over the hills like tombstones row on row. These break up in layers of comparatively equal thickness. This block of laminae was moved in sections from another location where it was found very much as here reerected. It is a tour de force suitable only in this particular area. The lettering is cut out of boiler plate, pegged and cemented into the limestone.

Casa Grande National Monument

This unusual sign, hammered out of sheet copper and filled with concrete, is a clever conception. In addition to functioning to designate the park entrance, this sign by virtue of location serves as a traffic guide in separation of the in-and-out flow of traffic. The lettering of modern character is of interest. The entranceway in its entirety is shown under that section of this book.

ADMINISTRATION BUILDINGS

>>> IF IN THE ARRANGING OF MATERIAL of this collection, a certain latitude, not to say license, could not be assumed to be granted the compiler by the readers, this heading would have little reason for being. For while if asked to name a half dozen structures justified by need within parks, a reader will probably name an administration building as one of them, he might be somewhat in a fog if asked to describe just what, specifically, constitutes one. The embarrassing question will not be pressed upon the reader. Rather will the difficult duty of seeking the answer be here assumed and herein attempted without, however, any certain expectancy of pulling a rabbit from an empty hat.

In theory the administration building is headquarters for directing effort and business management of the park area. Actually it may be a vest pocket, a desk, a room supplemented with typewriter, adding machine, safe, or some multiplication of these accessories. Frequently we find gate lodges, custodians' dwellings, community buildings, recreation pavilions, dining concessions, and numerous combinations of several functions, all termed administration buildings.

Few examples of administration buildings are known to exist as entities separate from other functions, except in national parks of vast extent. In these the need for space for the superintendent and a considerable staff engaged in the varied operations of dealing with the public and the park operator or concessionaire, keeping accounts, directing maintenance, planning the further development of the area, etc., is very considerable, and it results in a building of some size and of single purpose. In smaller national parks and monuments the combining of administration point and museum is often advantageous for the concentration of required supervisory effort that results.

It is probably usual in State parks to conduct on-the-area administration with less formality from an office attached to the custodian's or caretaker's dwelling. Sometimes this control point is in connection with a lodge or other dominant structure in the nature of a community building; again, under conditions requiring limited contact with the public and almost constant supervision of development and maintenance, the administration headquarters may be more conveniently placed with the service group. An analysis of most combined use buildings and of the space devoted to this sometimes intangible business of administration will often demonstrate that the designation of the building as the administration building is something of a courtesy title, if not actually a misnomer.

This widespread paradox exists very naturally and with some logic. It is probably proper that the point of control, the symbol of supervisory authority, should have importance, even dominance, among park buildings. It is quite pardonable that the limited space demand of administrative function should augment itself by the borrowed bulk of less significant space requirements and give name to the resulting combination structure. The tail is allowed to wag the dog with more than usual justification.

Structures dignified by the designation "administration building" sometimes tend to a prominence of location and an ostentatious treatment that arrogantly imply special prerogative to compete with Nature as the "feature" of the natural park. Such boorish behavior can no more be condoned in Park Building No. 1 than in lesser park structures.

Illustrated hereinafter are numerous buildings, one function of which is administration. Some include closely related functions, others combine facilities unrelated or only slightly related to the business of administration. Insofar as these avoid the blight of several scattered structures to result in a single structure free of pompous pretensions, the multi-purpose building masquerading as administration building is not unreasonable. Rather does it seem to be a solution worthy of encouragement.

| ADMINISTRATION BUILDINGS | *Plate* I D-1 |

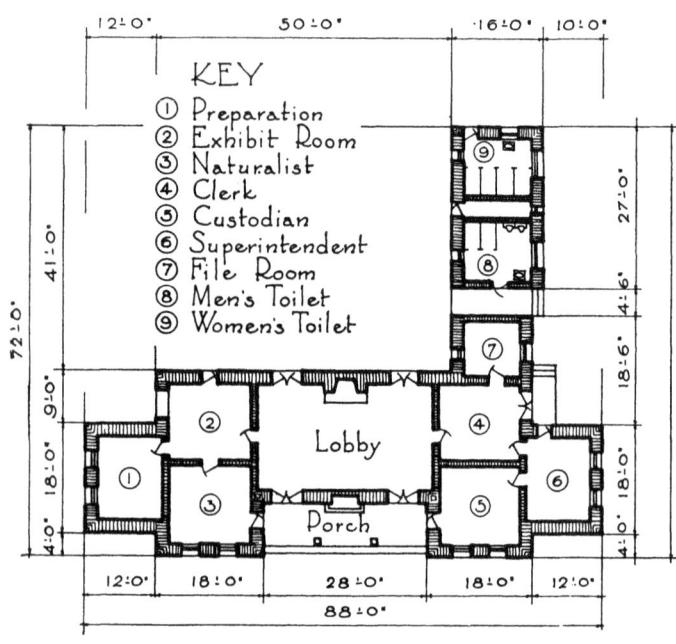

Administration Building, Casa Grande National Monument

Adobe, in gesture to tradition, and low, in keeping with the surrounding expanse of level terrain, this building is definitely and excellently custom-tailored to the Southwest. It houses various facilities that have legitimate function as phases of park administration and conveys impressively a feeling of organized administrative authority. The architectural style is related to that of the entrance-way and entrance sign of this same park. These subjects are shown elsewhere in this collection.

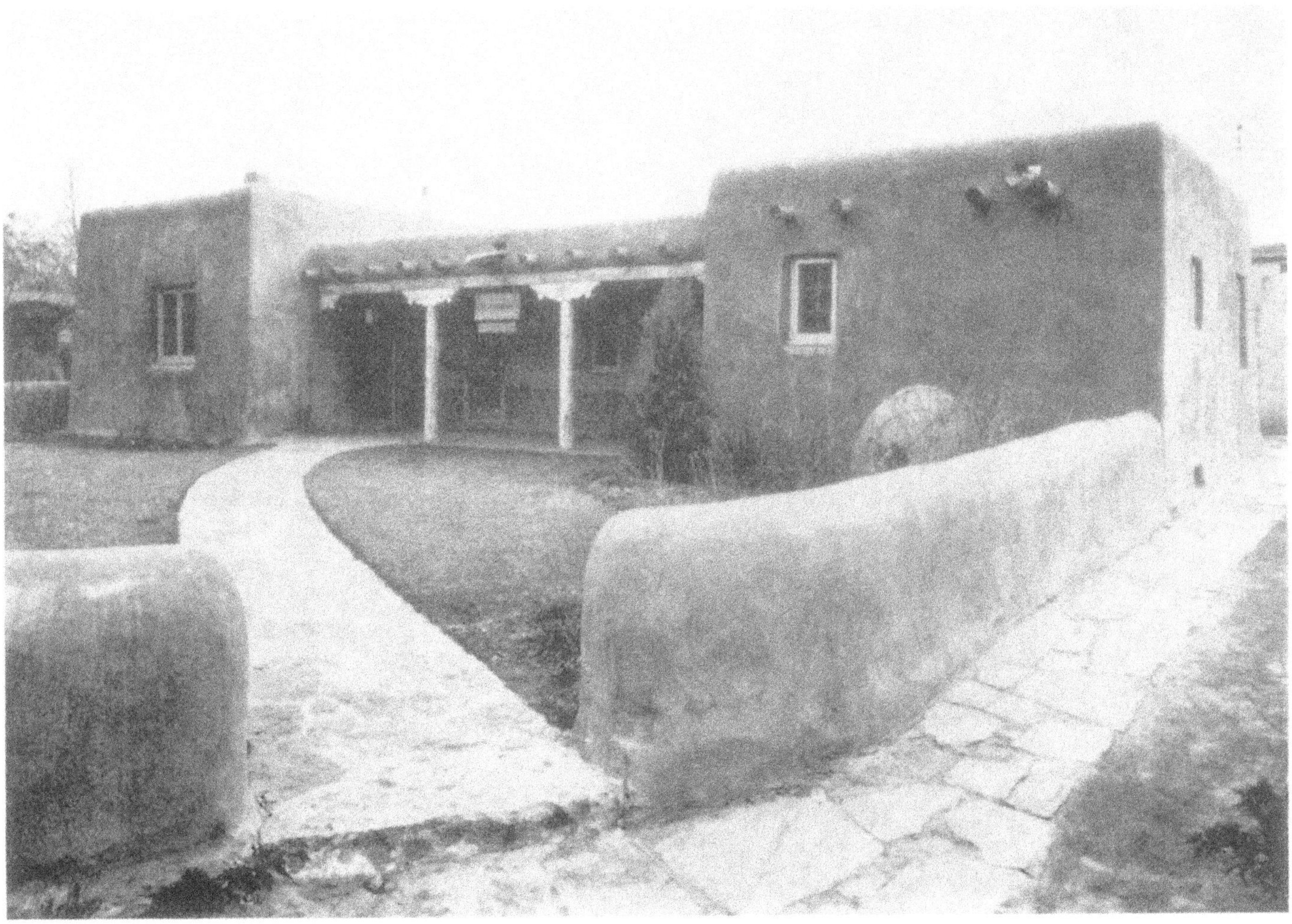

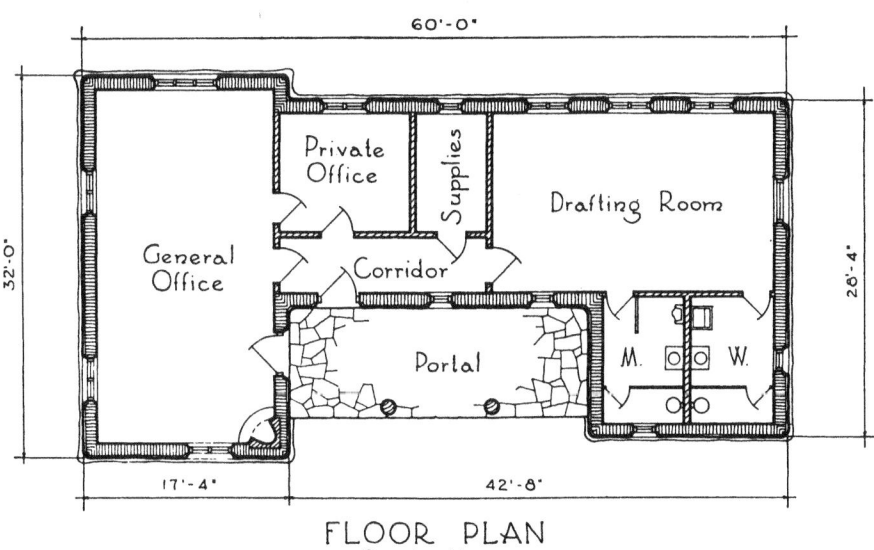

State Park Administration Building, Santa Fe, New Mexico

FLOOR PLAN
Scale 1/16" = 1'-0"

Here are headquarters from which presumably a system of State parks is administered. It carries on the traditions of the adobe architecture of the Southwest in its few and small window openings, the projecting pole rafters, the rounding of all corners, and the shaped brackets surmounting the log posts of the recessed porch. Its location in a town explains the unfortunately cramped setting.

ADMINISTRATION BUILDINGS

Plate I D-3

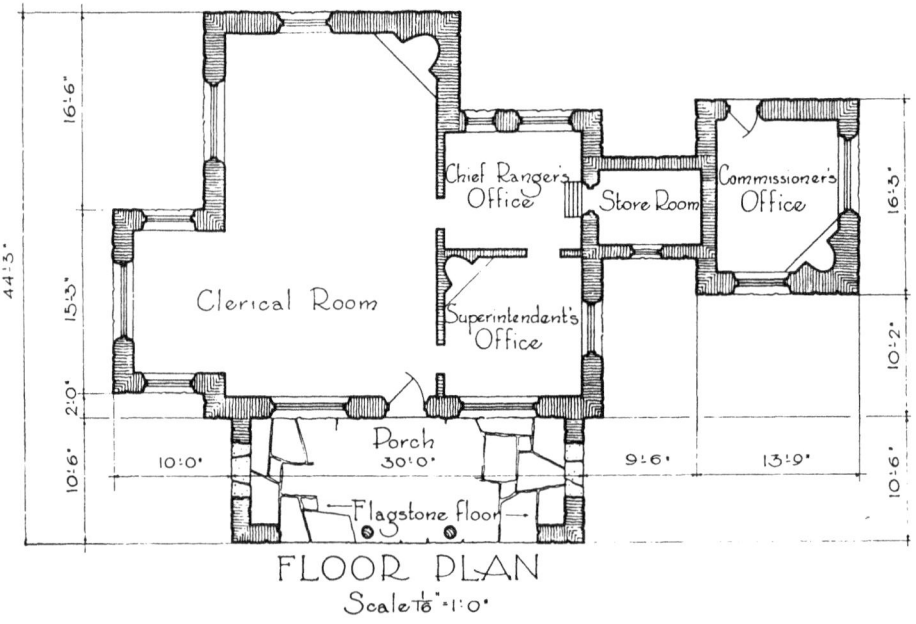

Administration Building, Mesa Verde National Park

Here is exemplified that unusual park structure, an administration building that does not accumulate other functions to gain impressive bulk. Informal in plan and exterior, it relates well to the other buildings in this national park, several of which are included under other classifications.

Plate I D-4   ⇛ ADMINISTRATION BUILDINGS

Administration Building, Bandelier National Monument

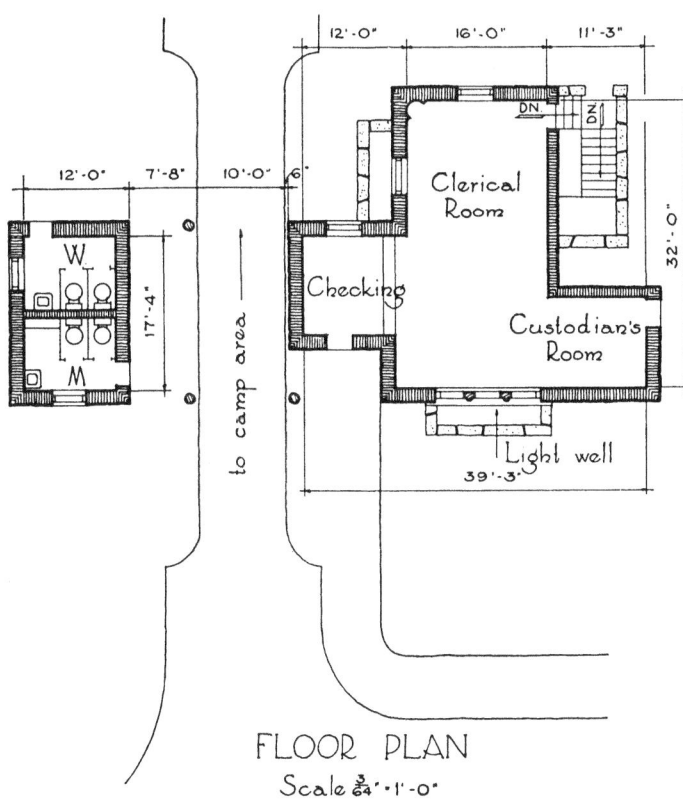

Some buildings win admiration for their very simplicity and modest size, if reinforced with good proportions and textures harmonious with surroundings. Here is one such. It is repesentative of structure housing administration in minimum terms. For an illustration of the meaning and desirability of singleness of architectural expression or theme in one area, the service group at Bandelier National Monument shown elsewhere should be compared with this plate.

FLOOR PLAN
Scale ¾" = 1'-0"

61

ADMINISTRATION BUILDINGS Plate I D-5

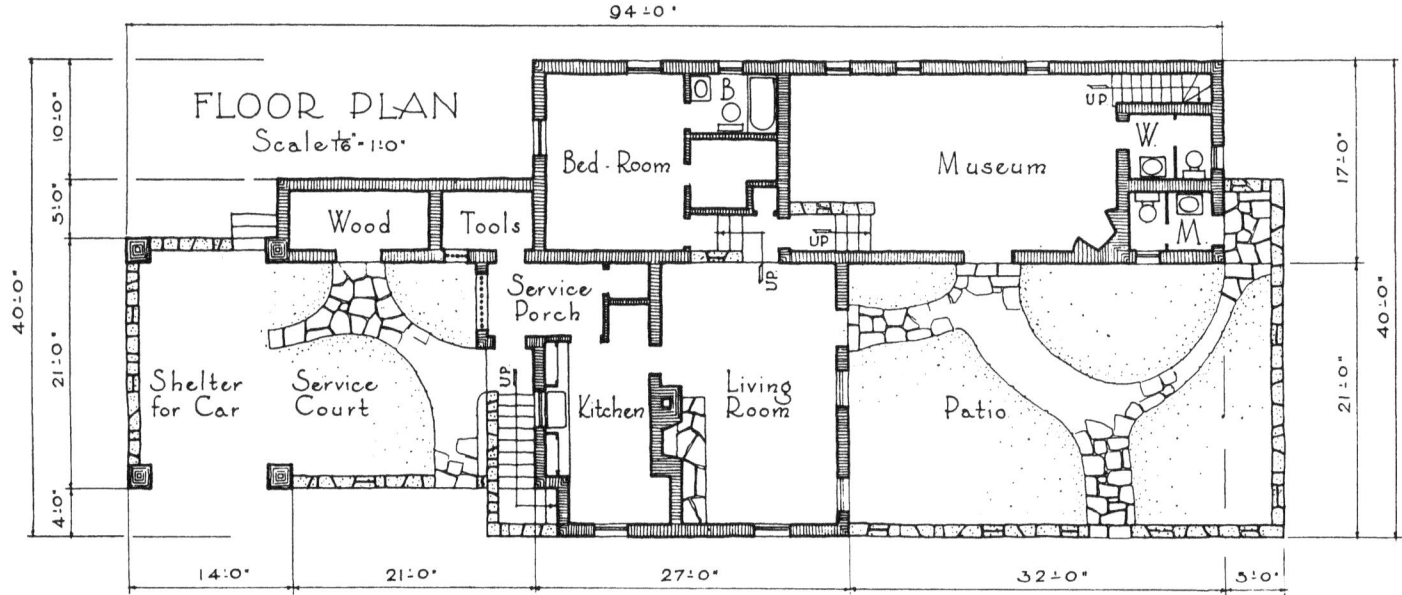

Administration Building, Phoenix South Mountain Metropolitan Park, Arizona

In continuing prehistoric Pueblo structural tradition this building extends the vocabulary of park architecture to include a pleasing and welcome regional expression eminently suited to the Southwest. Interest is caught by the unusual character of the masonry, the several levels of the roof, the haphazard lift and drop of the parapets, and the rhythmic shadows cast by the projecting pole vigas. As is so frequently the case with administration buildings, the plan shown above does not particularly evidence administrative function. The combination of caretaker's quarters, service courtyard, and museum forms more accurately administration "point" than administration building.

Plate I D-6 → ADMINISTRATION BUILDINGS

Administration Building, Zion National Park

The routine functions of administration and contact with the public are here combined in a small building of straightforward plan and the appearance of fitting very well its site at the base of the towering walls of Zion Canyon. Impression is gained that in any future need for expanding administrative facilities the present building will lend itself to alterations and additions with a minimum of disturbance to existing construction.

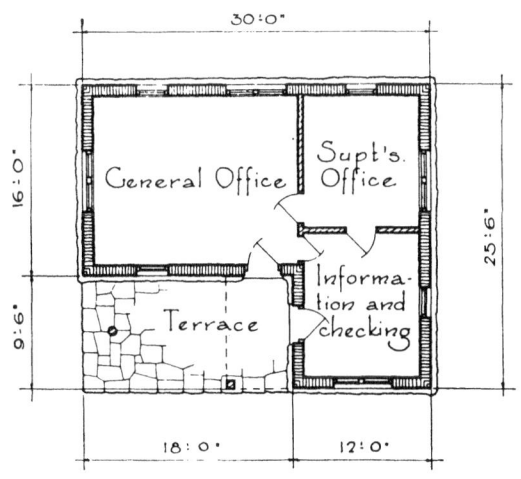

FLOOR PLAN
Scale ⅙" = 1'0"

63

ADMINISTRATION BUILDINGS

Plate I D-7

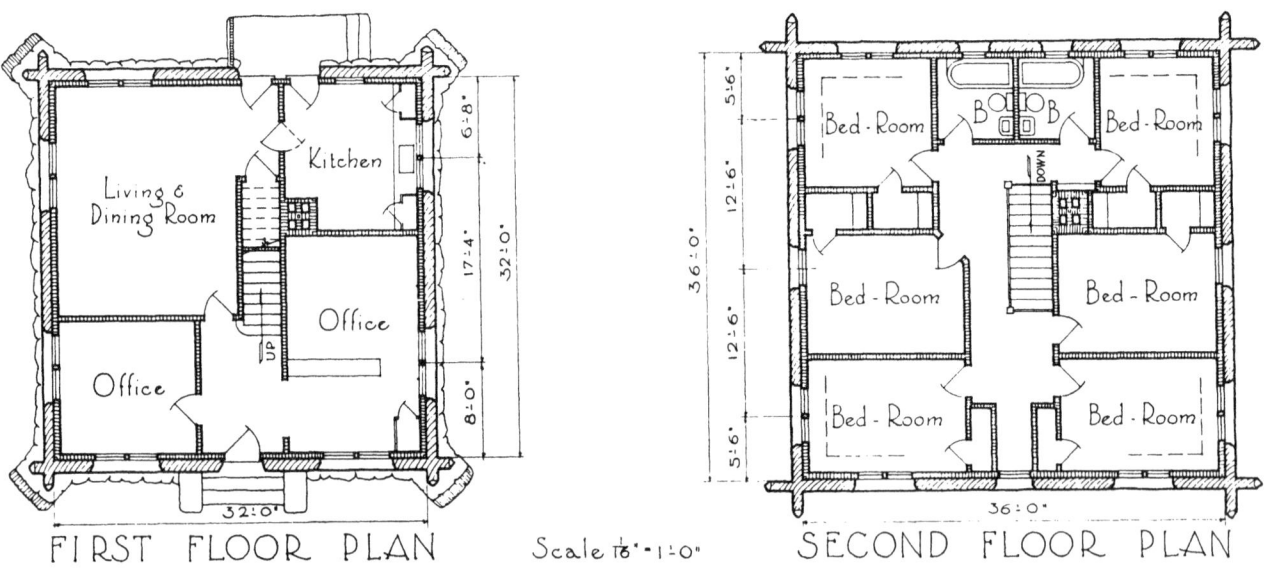

Administration Building, Yakima, Mount Rainier National Park

FIRST FLOOR PLAN   Scale ⅛"=1'-0"   SECOND FLOOR PLAN

Even without benefit of the magnificent background afforded by Mount Rainier this log building would be an outstanding contribution to park architecture. Obviously, but not too self-consciously, inspired by the early blockhouse, here is a building representative of logical and legitimate adaptation of a traditional form. The log work is neither too precise nor too laboriously rustic.

64

Plate I D-8 →»› ADMINISTRATION BUILDINGS

Administration Building, Bryce Canyon National Park

In parks not accessible to great hordes of visitors, uncomplicated administration functions and a modest museum display can often be housed in one building to practical advantage. Such is the case here. It permits a limited personnel to do double duty and accumulates into one building of suitable size space that as two buildings could hardly avoid seeming trivial and inappropriate in a park of the magnificent distances offered by Bryce Canyon.

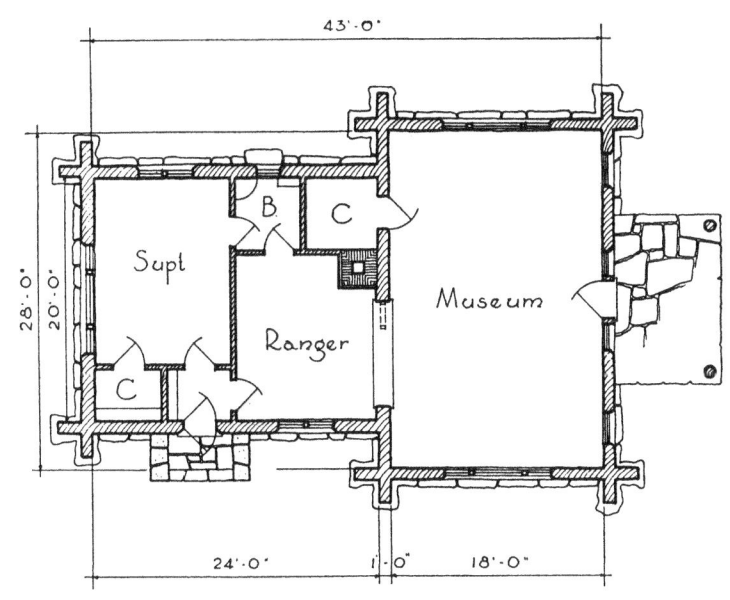

FLOOR PLAN
Scale 1/8" = 1'-0"

65

ADMINISTRATION BUILDINGS

Plate I D-9

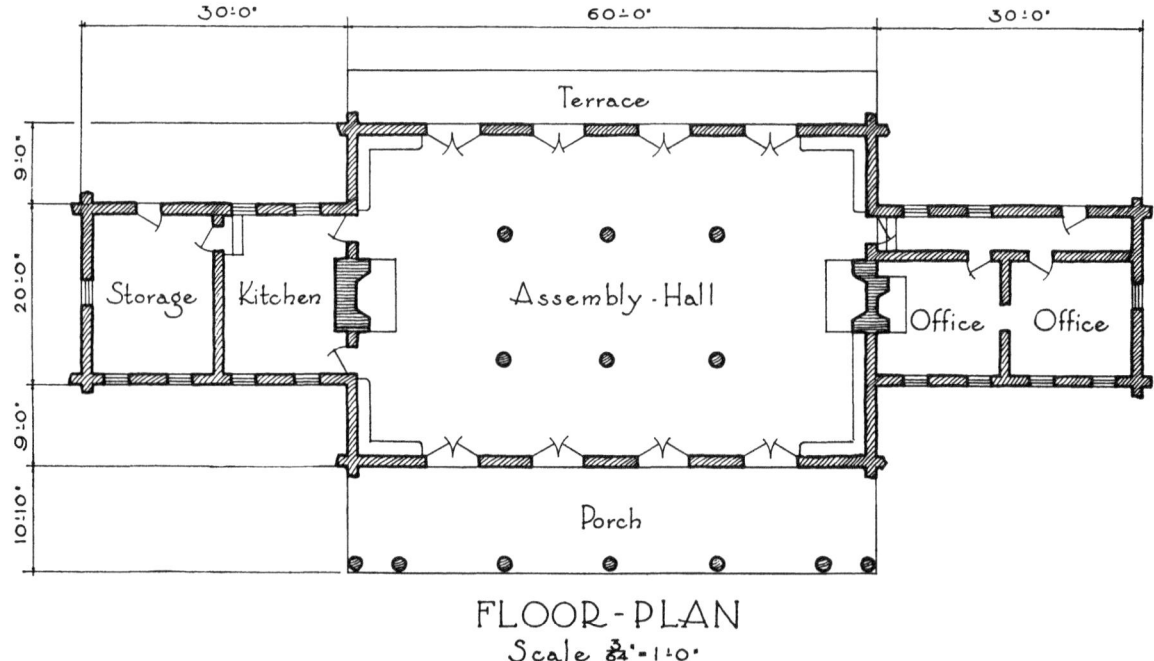

Administration Building, Selkirk Shores State Park, New York

FLOOR-PLAN
Scale ¾'=1'-0"

Impressive in extent for a log building and notable for the workmanship of the log construction and the broad sweep of the roof. The severity of the concrete base, the trivial boulder masonry of the chimneys, and the thinness of the covering material of the roof are disturbing details.

Plate I D–10   ⇢⇢⇢ ADMINISTRATION BUILDINGS

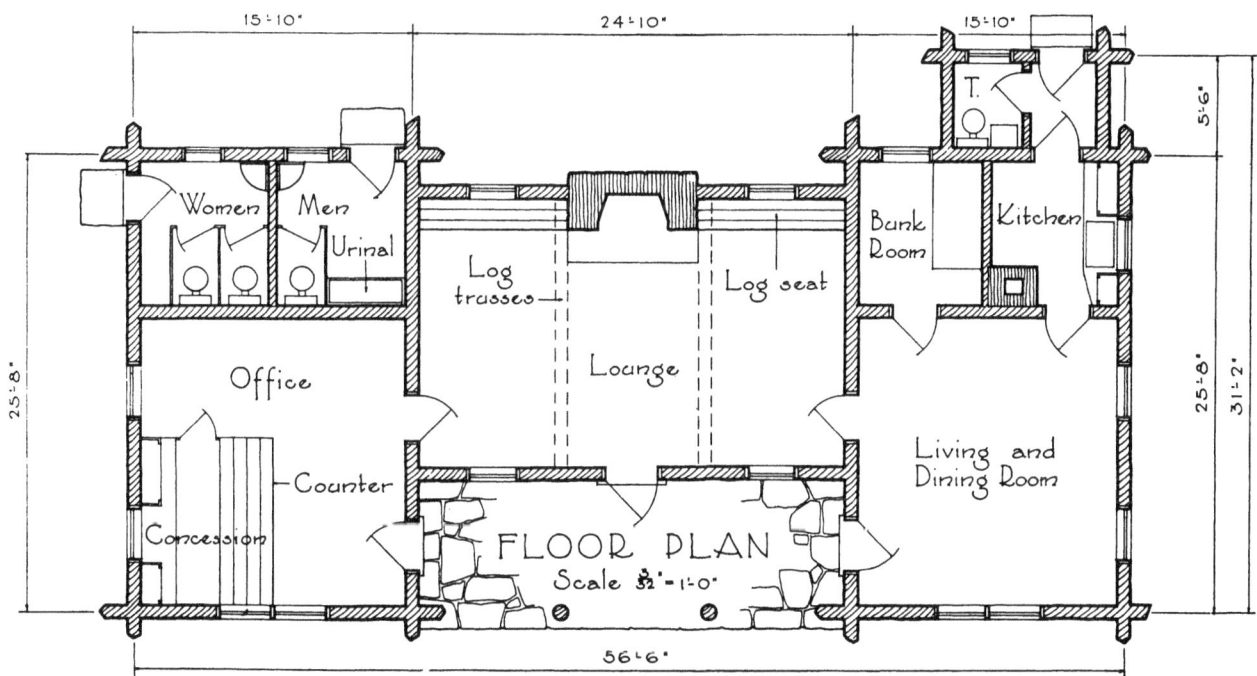

Administration Building, Mohawk Trail State Forest Park, Massachusetts

This altogether amiable building is rated a ten-strike in an area where the availability of long, straight logs is far from what it once was. The proportions and details of design and workmanship seem quite beyond reproach. Along with an ambitious log bridge at this same park, illustrated under "Bridges", this structure offers convincing testimony that all skilled craftsmanship in log construction did not march westward with the course of empire.

ADMINISTRATION BUILDINGS

Plate I D–11

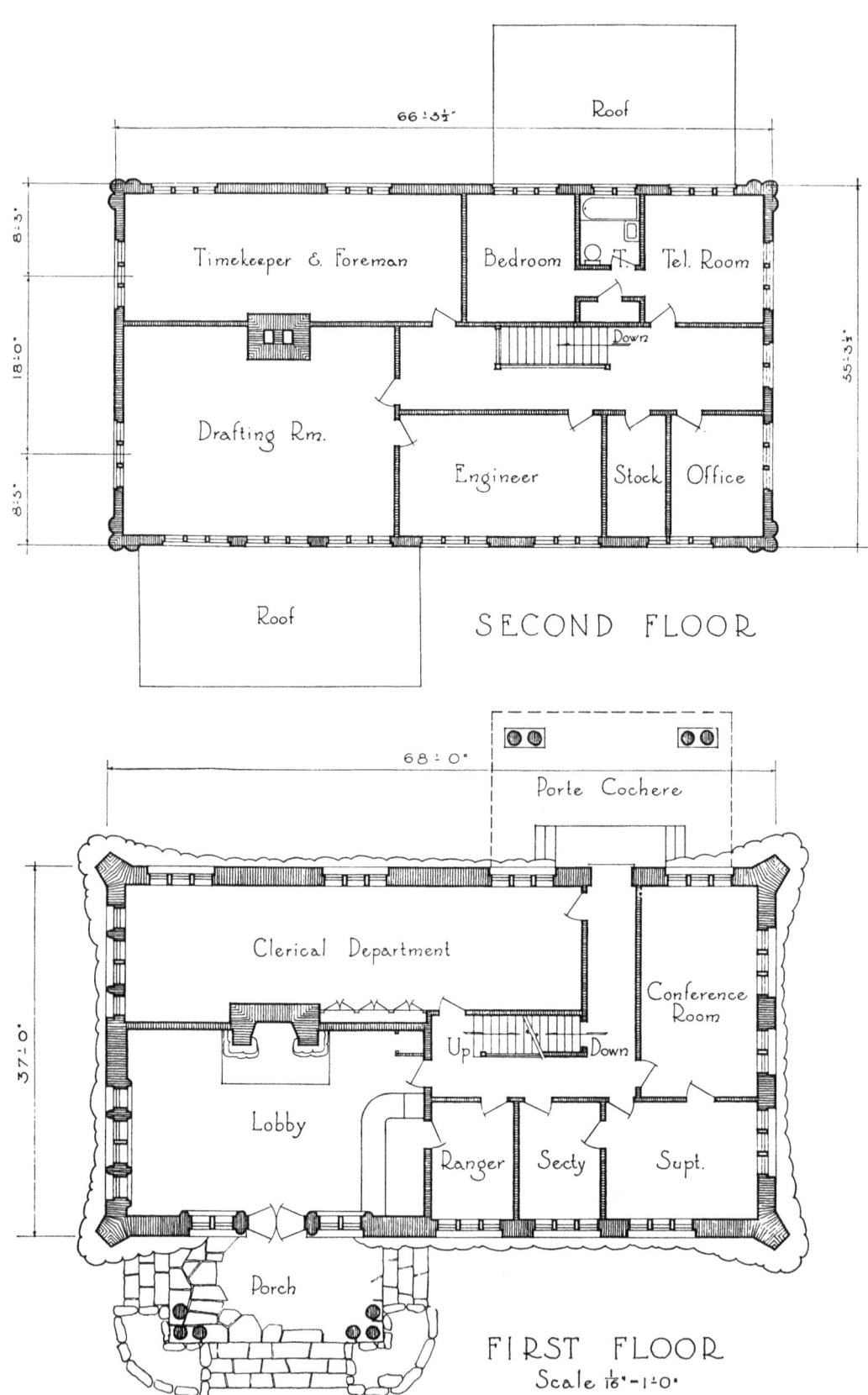

Plate I D–12 ⇶ ADMINISTRATION BUILDINGS

Administration Building, Longmire, Mount Rainier National Park

The plans on the opposite page exhibit the several functions that may accrue to an administration building in a major park. The employment of boulder masonry as here illustrated is usually dictated and only justified by the absence of more workable rock material within reasonable distance. However well handled, it seems impossible to attain a satisfying appearance of stability. The rafters are appropriately vigorous in scale, and the blunted terminations of them are most agreeable. There is abundant provision of windows to insure a well-lighted interior without sacrifice of wall surfaces to the point where the exterior suffers in appearance.

ADMINISTRATION BUILDINGS

Plate I D–13

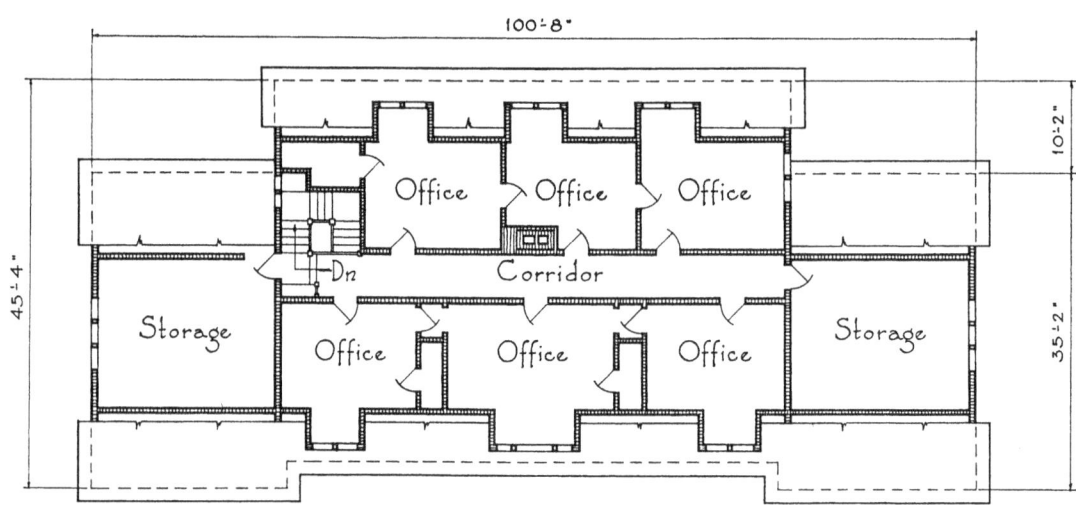

SECOND FLOOR PLAN

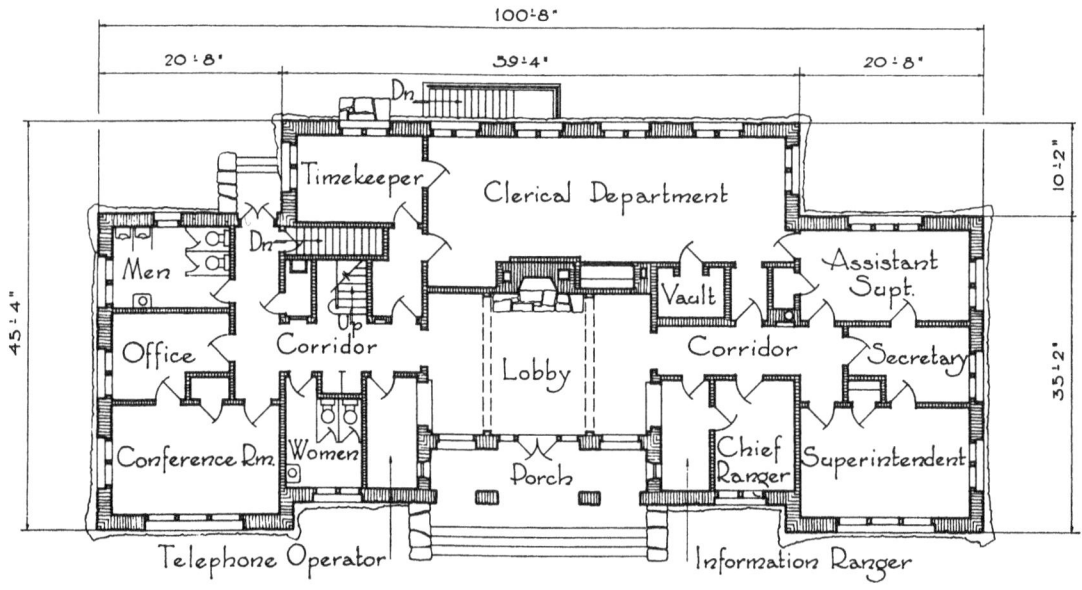

FIRST FLOOR PLAN
Scale 3/64" = 1'-0"

Plate I D–14 →›› ADMINISTRATION BUILDINGS

Administration Building, Crater Lake National Park

This large administration building and the example at Longmire, Mount Rainier, presented on a previous page, represent typical structural accommodations for the administrative activities and needs of a large park of national importance. First and second floor plans are delineated on the opposite page. The steep roof is dictated by the heavy snows of this area, which often accumulate and drift to levels above the first story windows. Attention is called to the several structures for housing personnel at Crater Lake, illustrated under "Superintendents' and Staffs' Quarters", for the study of a pervading unity of structural treatment, the usual recommendation for all buildings of a particular area. Massive boulder masonry, stained timbers, steep roofs, and dormer windows are common to all.

| ADMINISTRATION BUILDINGS | *Plate* I D–15 |

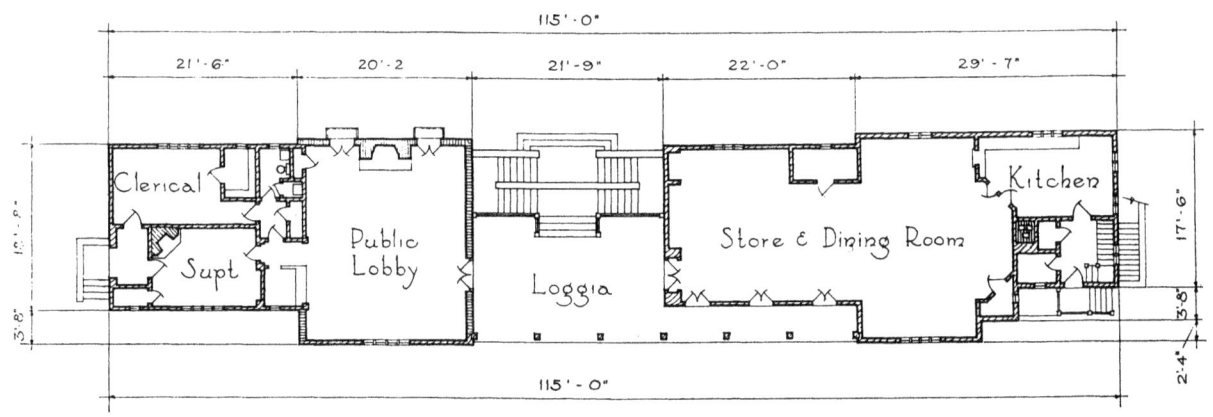

Administration Building, Wind Cave National Monument

FLOOR PLAN
Scale ¾" = 1'-0"

The architectural expression found here departs in materials and manner of use from what one almost comes to expect in park construction. The widening of vocabulary is welcome, and this particular treatment is well undertaken in surroundings which are comparatively unwooded. The long-drawn-out, narrow plan produces an exterior which gives the illusion of a building low in height. This also seems a proper effort in the setting pictured. The plan indicates the many related functions that accrue to the administration of a park domain of considerable extent.

SUPERINTENDENTS' AND STAFFS' QUARTERS

⇛ OFTEN family living quarters for the park superintendent, custodian, or caretaker and other staff members can with propriety reflect in externals the pioneer homesteads of a locality. And being somewhat similar to the pioneer dwellings in most essentials, the modern housing can recall traditional lines without too evident struggle, not always true of adaptations in which the old forms and the modern needs are less closely related. Subject to the dictates of regional influence, we may appropriately house park personnel in structures which derive from the log and stone cabins of the pioneer, from the Spanish, Pueblo, and several manifestations of the Colonial, and from many other traditional structural expressions born of history, local materials, and climate.

The typical problem is simply an efficiently planned five- or six-room rural dwelling that stresses the importance of fitness to environment. Climate, comfort, traditions, and above all the budgets of the park and of the occupant, whether superintendent or naturalist, warden or workman, should be duly weighed.

Where the park personnel group is comparatively large, it is sometimes deemed expedient to resort to small apartment buildings. Although such concentration sacrifices something of park character by bringing an urban solution into a park, it is in accord with the tenet that a single building is better than many minor ones.

In large, isolated, yet heavily attended parks the problem of housing groups of unmarried employes, especially those only seasonally employed, is solved by a barracks or dormitory building. A rangers' club providing comfortable and wholesome living conditions contributes much to the esprit de corps of this group of employes. In Yosemite National Park is a notable example of this institution, made possible by the generosity of Mr. Stephen T. Mather, the first Director of the National Park Service.

Comfortable, well-maintained living quarters in which the occupants can take personal pride will undoubtedly find reflection in the attitude of each employe toward maintenance of the public area. Patched-up, ramshackle living quarters can influence the standards of general park operation adversely.

Inasmuch as quarters in a final analysis supplement the employe's salary, it seems only fitting that quarters and salary be reasonably scaled to each other. Neither commodious residence in lieu of a fair salary, nor more generous stipend in lieu of decent living quarters is a satisfactory substitute for living quarters and salary in appropriate relationship. A more general understanding of this would remove a frequent cause of dissatisfaction.

Sometimes, for purposes of control, economy, or other reason, living quarters are combined with other park needs in structures, such as administration and concession buildings, entranceways and checking stations. In a small park this is logical, avoiding as it does small independent buildings ruinously crowding the area.

Worthy of most careful study is the locating of buildings that house park personnel. To aid effectively in supervision, such structures must be distributed with respect to the areas of concentrated use; employes' quarters should be convenient to, without obtrusively invading, the intensively used areas. Perhaps the Far East custom of a compound which isolates the foreign colony is adaptable to personnel housing in our larger parks. To say that this would serve to protect the park from the personnel and the personnel from the park is not a flippant observation. Too widespread scattering of quarters to achieve maximum supervision can result in unwarrantable modification of the far reaches of the park. It tends, moreover, to place the isolated staff members at the command of the public 24 hours a day, a situation unfair to them and to the best interests of the park.

SUPERINTENDENTS' AND STAFFS' QUARTERS

Plate I E–1

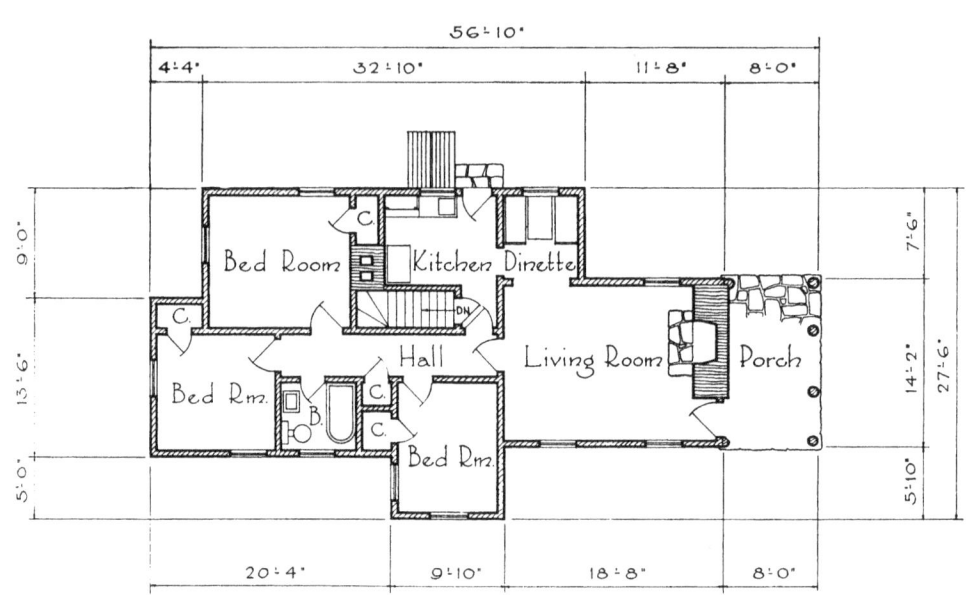

Cumberland Falls State Park – Kentucky

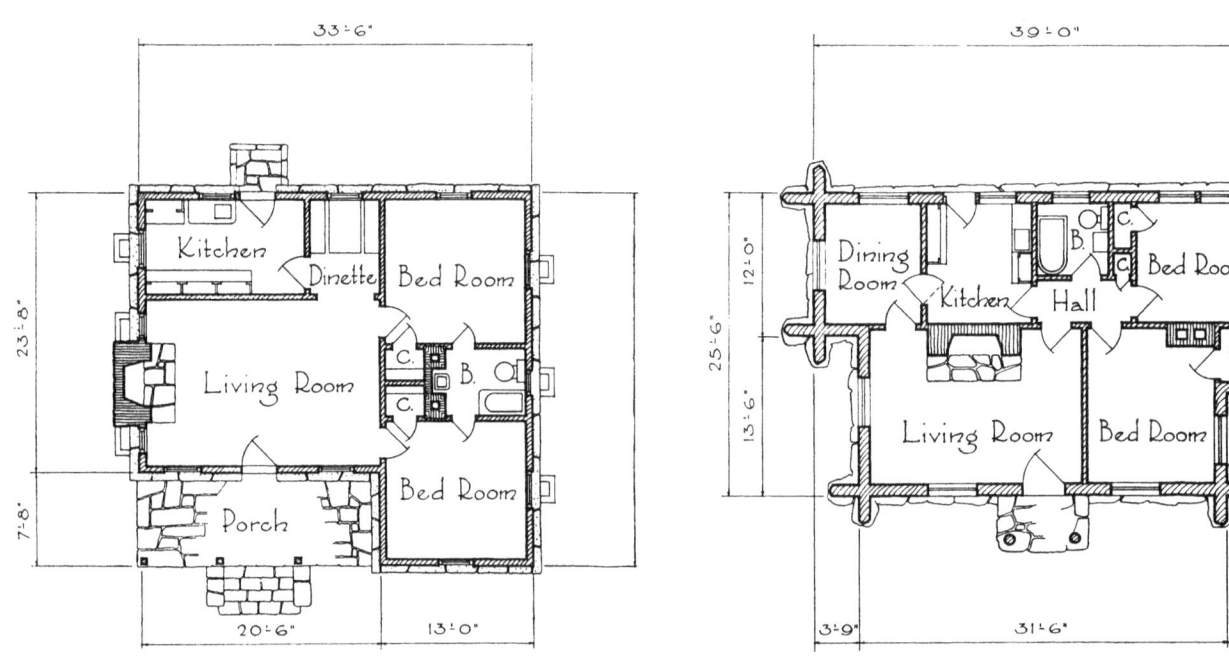

Weogufka State Park – Alabama

Crowley's Ridge State Park – Arkansas

Scale ⅛"–1'-0"

Plate I E–2 ⇶ SUPERINTENDENTS' AND STAFFS' QUARTERS

Simple in design, well-arranged, and employing inexpensive materials, here is illustrated an adequate caretaker's house. Siding of wide boards and battens, placed vertically, succeeds rather better than other economical wood constructions in appearing harmonious with a wooded setting. With the providing of an outside door to any one of the bedrooms, an acceptably accessible office would be created.

Custodian's Dwelling, Cumberland Falls State Park, Kentucky

Contrasting methods of wood construction are displayed by the three housing units shown on this page. This example employs half logs in a manner traditional to this part of the South. The smooth side forms the inside face of the walls; the rounded side, slabbed off, is exposed on the exterior. The economy of this construction over that of a full log construction is obvious.

Custodian's Dwelling, Weogufka State Park, Alabama

This custodian's house and one shown on another page have a family resemblance to demonstrate that the parks of Arkansas enjoy an architectural style that is definite and yet varied. Readers who more than casually scan these pages will come to expect, and will usually find, a vigorous scale and a sympathetic handling of rustic materials in this State's park buildings to rate high commendation and invite study.

Custodian's House, Crowley's Ridge State Park, Arkansas

75

SUPERINTENDENTS' AND STAFFS' QUARTERS   Plate I E–3

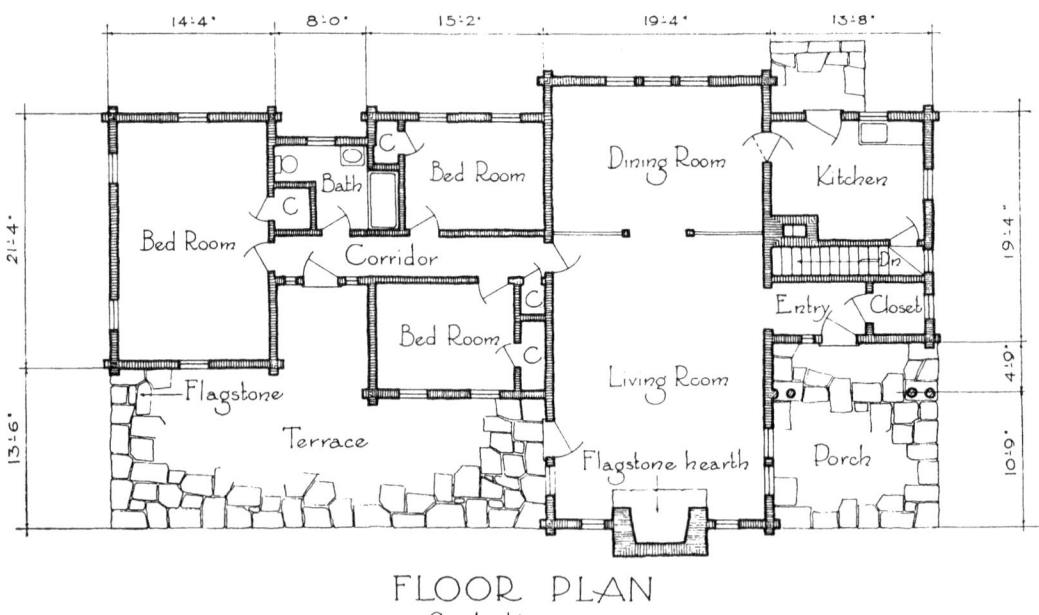

Custodian's Cabin, Douthat State Park, Virginia

FLOOR PLAN

Here is proof that a log structure can be varied and exciting without breaking with tradition. A stickler for perfection might wish for a shaggier roof, closer joints between logs, and a less pronounced terrace line, but he would be a stickler indeed in the face of such high merit in other essentials.

76

Plate I E–4   ⇛ SUPERINTENDENTS' AND STAFFS' QUARTERS

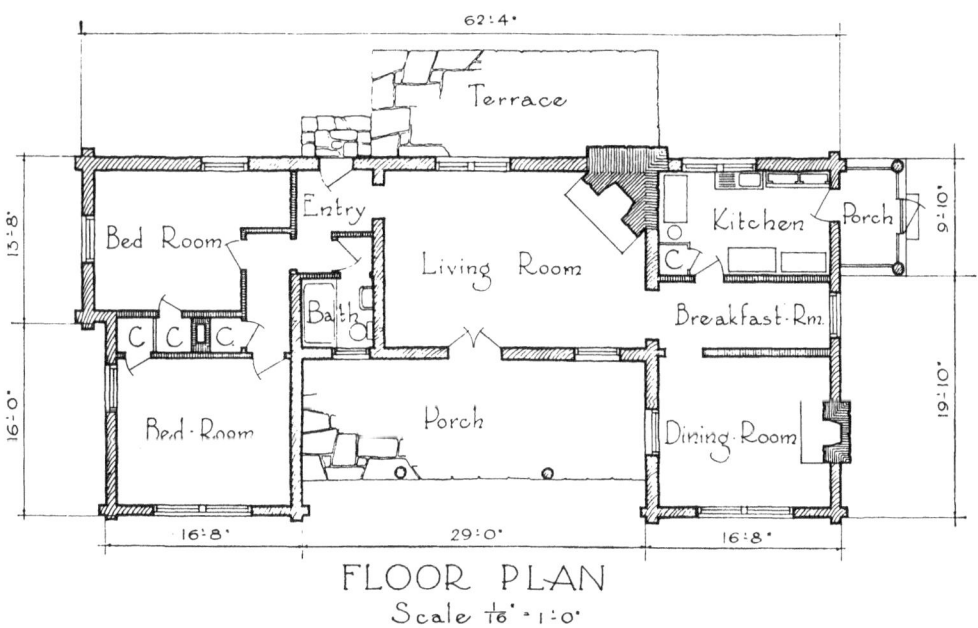

Custodian's House, Boyle Metropolitan Park, Little Rock, Arkansas

FLOOR PLAN
Scale 1/16" = 1'-0"

Although not specifically warned in the moral code against coveting a custodian's house among those worldly holdings that might incite envy, it was surely because such an example as this did not exist at the time. We may forego coveting, but are not to be denied admiring, this excellent plan and the fine use of the materials that so satisfactorily clothe it.

SUPERINTENDENTS' AND STAFFS' QUARTERS

Plate I E-5

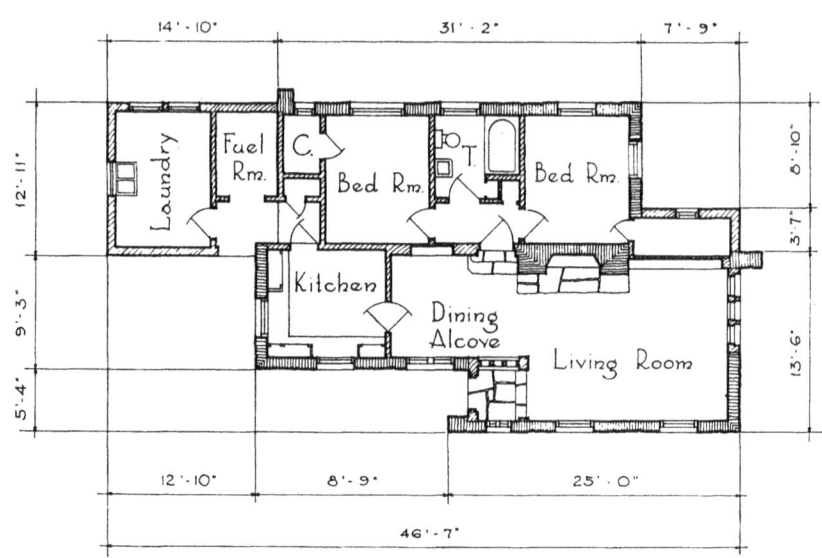

Heyburn State Park, Idaho.

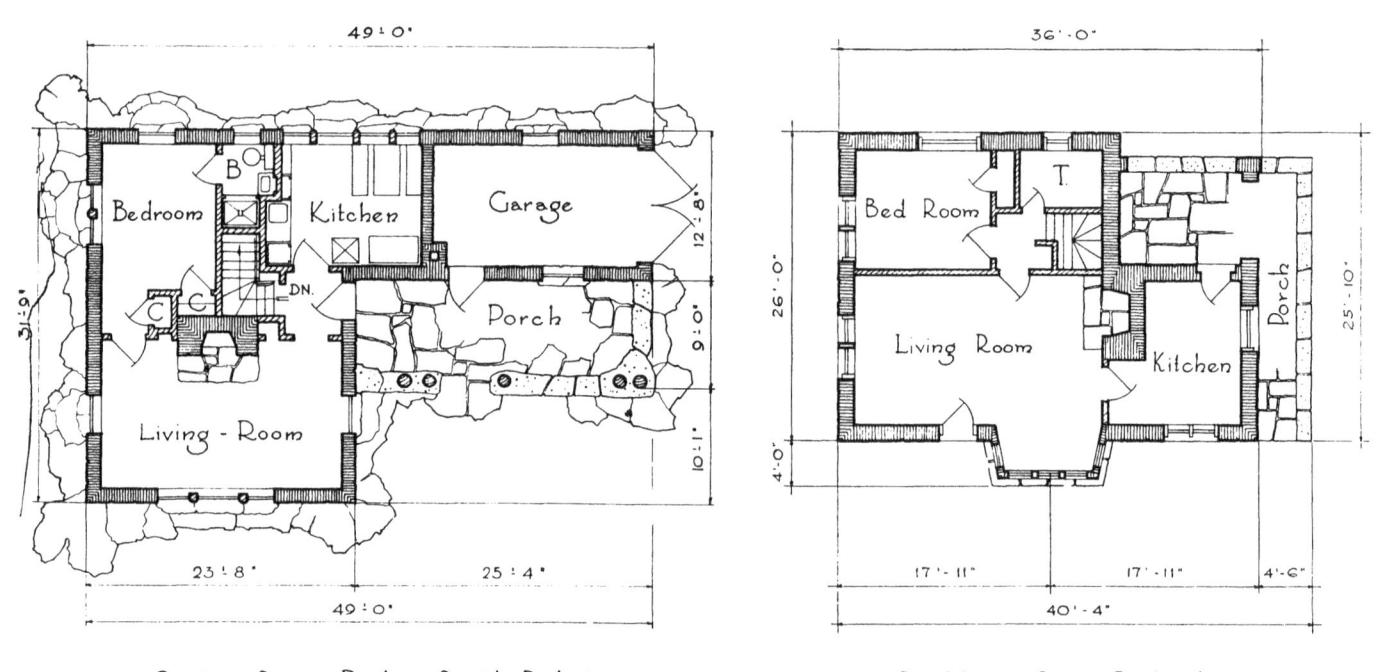

Custer State Park, South Dakota.

Backbone State Park, Iowa.

Scale 1/8" = 1'-0"

Plate I E–6 ⇛ SUPERINTENDENTS' AND STAFFS' QUARTERS

An admirably arranged caretaker's cottage, hardly completed, and so standing greatly in need of, and greatly to benefit from, future foundation planting. The stone work, shake roof, and low lines generally are factors in the eventually satisfying picture the building seems to promise.

Custodian's Dwelling, Heyburn State Park, Idaho

This compact, attractive little dwelling houses the keeper of the game farm of this large park. The materials employed recall the museum and several shelters of this area, shown elsewhere. The enclosing fence is elaborate and in a degree inconsistent with the almost barren immediate surroundings.

Custodian's Dwelling, Custer State Park, South Dakota

A space-conserving plan arrangement rendered in finished architectural terms which suggest an outpost of the East where the West has begun. There is a meticulousness in the laying of the masonry less and less frequently encountered in park architecture beyond the Mississippi. Such is in very proper deference to the claims of cumulative ruggedness of terrain and enlarging distances.

Custodian's Dwelling, Backbone State Park, Iowa

SUPERINTENDENTS' AND STAFFS' QUARTERS

Plate I E-7

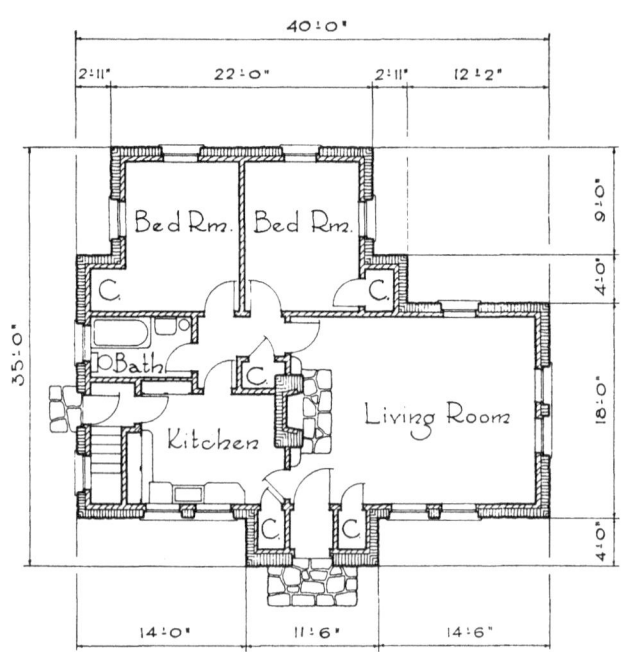

Riverside State Park - Washington

Silver Creek Falls State Park - Oregon

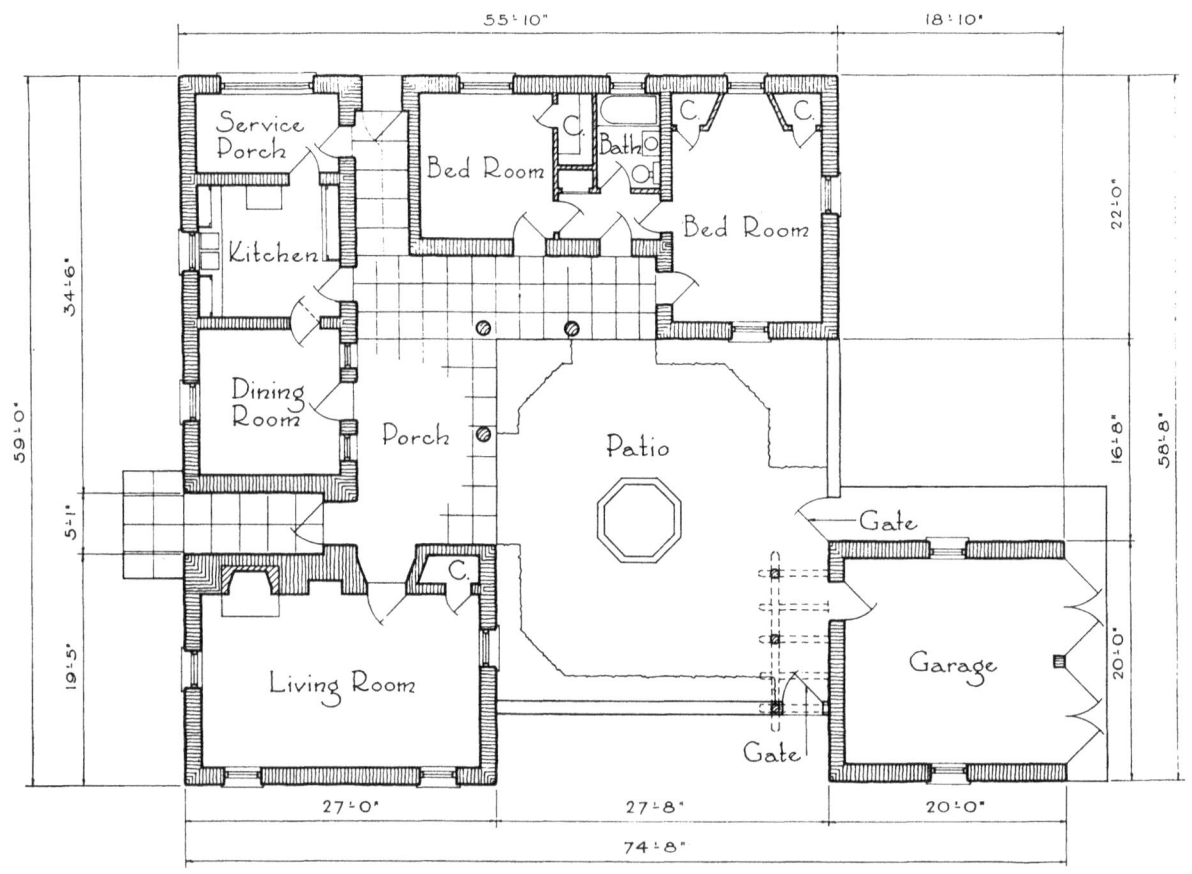

Zoological State Park - California

Scale 1/16" = 1'-0"

Plate I E–8 ⇛ SUPERINTENDENTS' AND STAFFS' QUARTERS

An attractive and convenient coordination of the elements that can be said to be typical of custodian's quarters in a park of average size. The ensemble rates far above average. Only improvement wished for—a horizontal bedding of the masonry. When viewed in the flesh, so to say, the lichens on the stone and the moss in the joints serve to stifle even that deprecative comment on the masonry technique.

Custodian's Dwelling, Riverside State Park, Washington

The excellencies of plan cannot make us blind to the unfortunate masonry of the chimneys and the mechanical overperfection of log construction that here robs this material of the very quality that has made it preeminent for park construction. Some more equitable distribution of skill between carpenter and mason would have produced more satisfying results.

Custodian's Dwelling, Silver Creek Falls State Park, Oregon

The arrangement of living quarters for custodian to create a patio is particularly desirable in the Southwest and doubly so where the distances are great and the country unwooded. The oasislike result is productive of a degree of intimacy and sense of security not otherwise achieved. A patio of size is hardly possible in connection with the very small dwelling unless service buildings and walls are joined with it, as here.

Custodian's Dwelling, Zoological State Park, California

81

SUPERINTENDENTS' AND STAFFS' QUARTERS «« Plate I E–9

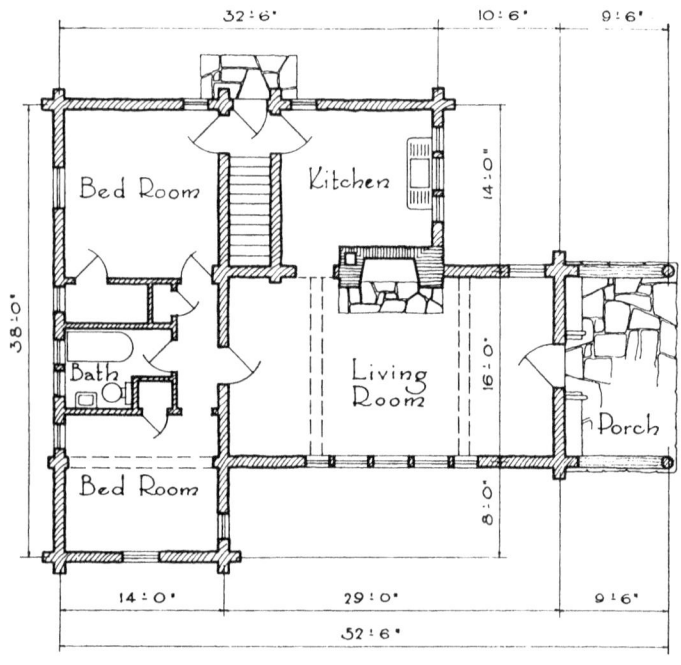

Custodian's House, Lewis and Clark State Park, Washington

FLOOR PLAN
Scale ⅛"=1'-0"

Here is well exemplified the charm of simple unbroken surfaces strongly horizontal in feeling. Perhaps to describe this quality as poise is expressive. Whatever the word for it, it is here present in large measure, along with minor details of interest, among which are the wide muntins of the windows and the excellent scale of log work and roof covering. This building is typical of custodians' dwellings generally in the parks of the State of Washington. An approximate standardization of this particular facility for all parks within a park system forestalls any possible charge of discrimination in favor of an employe or a locality.

82

Plate I E-10 →→→ SUPERINTENDENTS' AND STAFFS' QUARTERS

Superintendent's Residence, Mesa Verde National Park

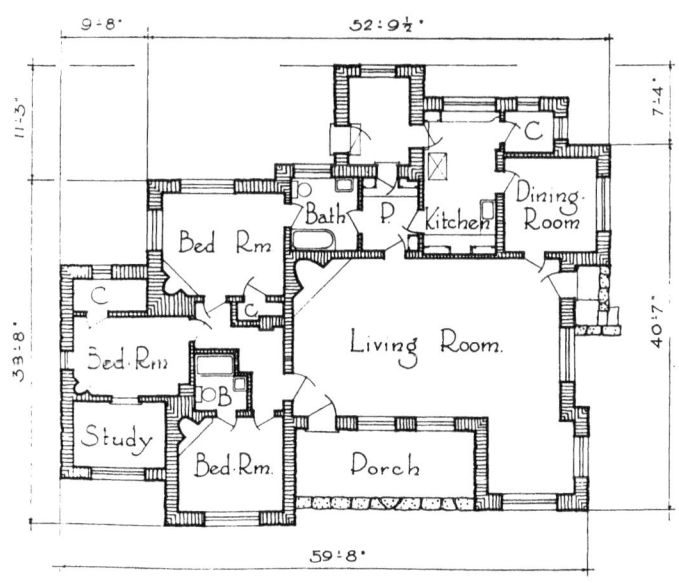

FLOOR PLAN
Scale $\frac{3}{64}" = 1'-0"$

Definitely regional by reason of the technique of its masonry, the projecting vigas, and the shifting parapet levels surmounting flat roofs, this example is rather larger than most of the dwellings shown herein for the accommodation of the family of park custodian or superintendent. The building seems particularly well suited to site and to region. The several corner fireplaces are in the spirit of the architectural prototypes of the American Southwest.

SUPERINTENDENTS' AND STAFFS' QUARTERS

Plate I E-11

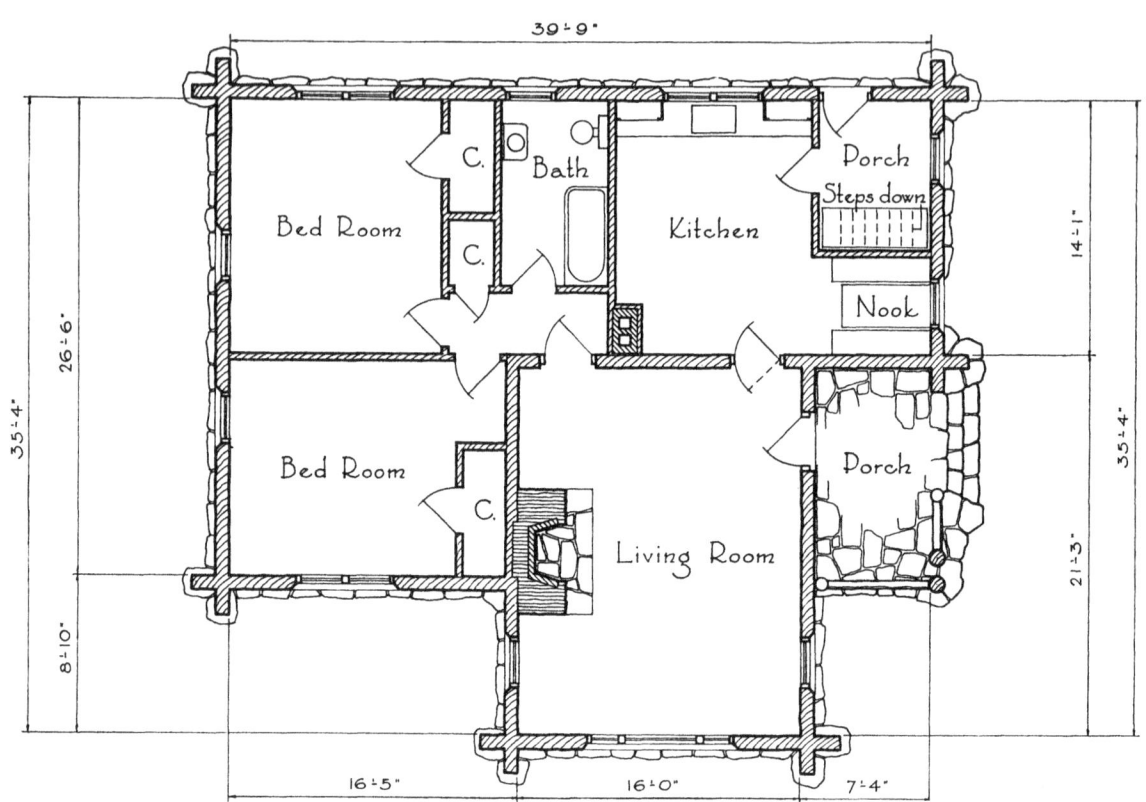

Rocky Mountain National Park

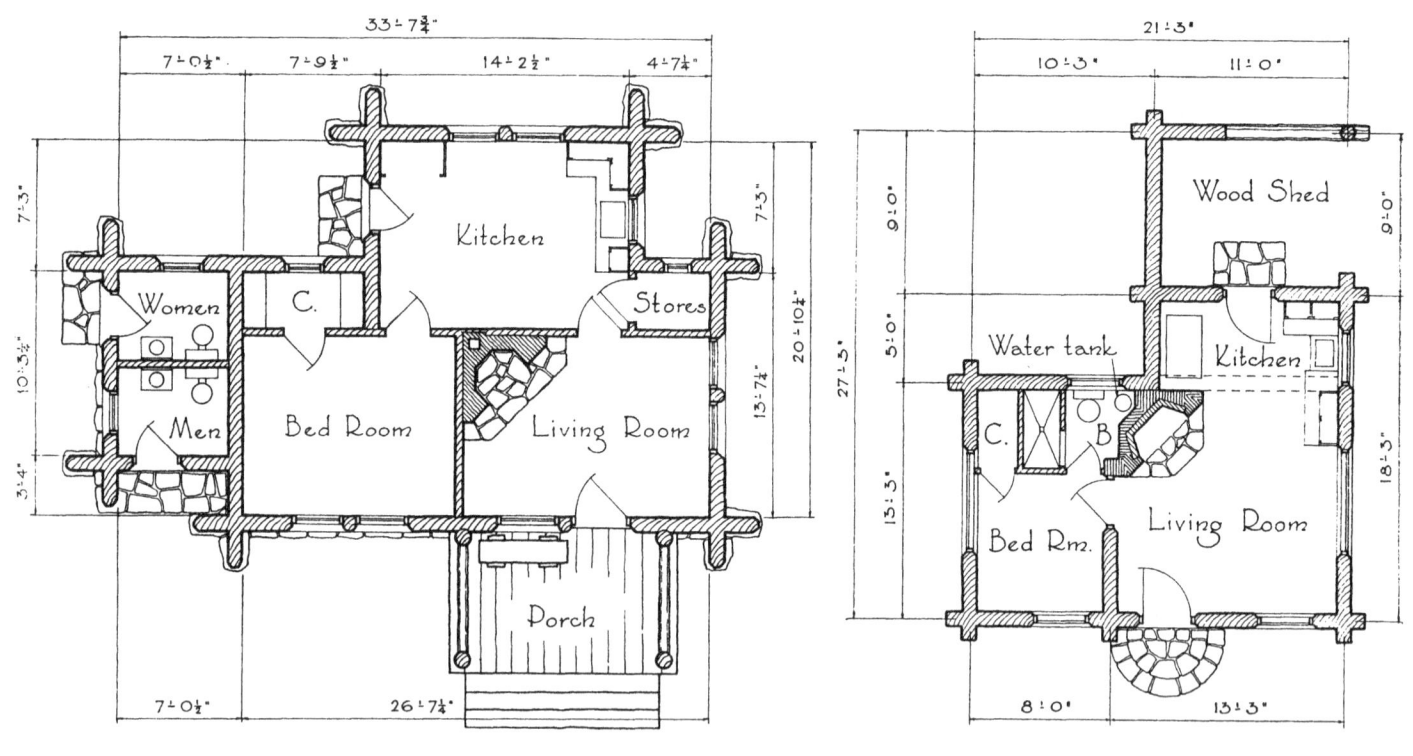

Jewel Cave National Monument

Moran State Park - Washington

Scale 3/32" = 1'-0"

Plate I E–12   ⇶ SUPERINTENDENTS' AND STAFFS' QUARTERS

On the evidence of this page logs are apparently the favored construction material for rangers' stations. Subtle differences of technique, as well as of space needs, may here be compared. In all cases the recommended practice of raising the logs off the ground on a masonry foundation, thus eliminating the Achilles' heel of log construction, has been followed.

Ranger's Station, Rocky Mountain National Park

Being almost a miniature in scale, this cabin is something of a concentrated essence of log cabin structural technique. Logs are employed for the puncheon floor and steps of the porch, both details which, in modern log cabins, usually compromise with more modern and less sturdy building methods.

Ranger's Station, Jewel Cave National Monument

Multum in parvo is the phrase for this little dwelling which marries the split millimeter proportions of a Pullman section and the spendthrift technique of the pioneer builder. Its compactness is a masterly accomplishment, probably most appreciated by the person who must carry the firewood in a climate where the woodshed can claim so large a share of the floor area.

Ranger's Cabin, Moran State Park, Washington

SUPERINTENDENTS' AND STAFFS' QUARTERS

Plate I E–13

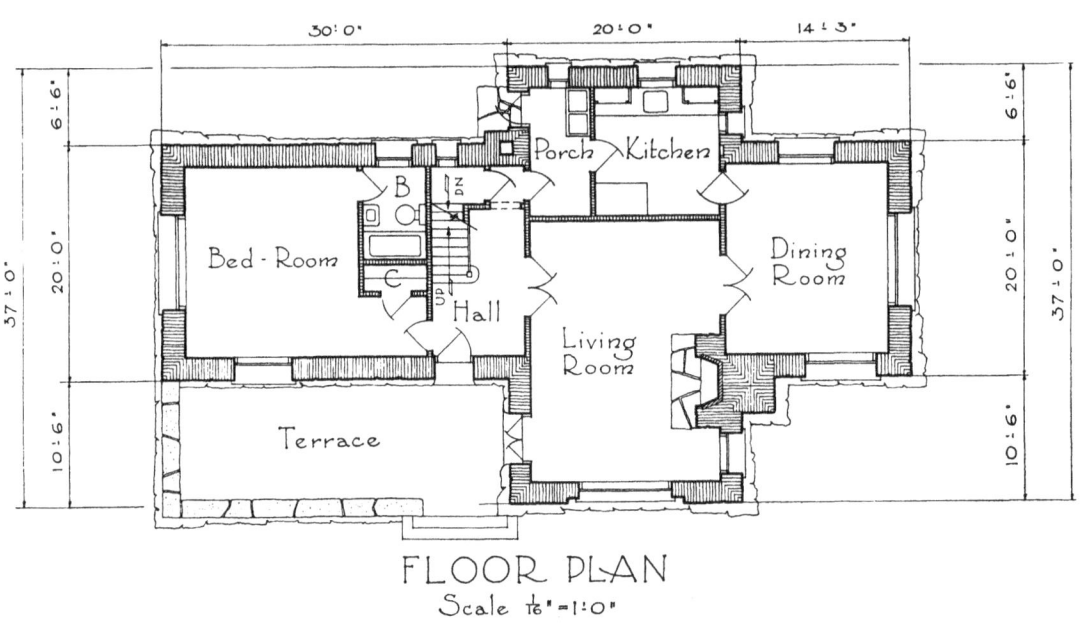

FLOOR PLAN
Scale 1/16" = 1'-0"

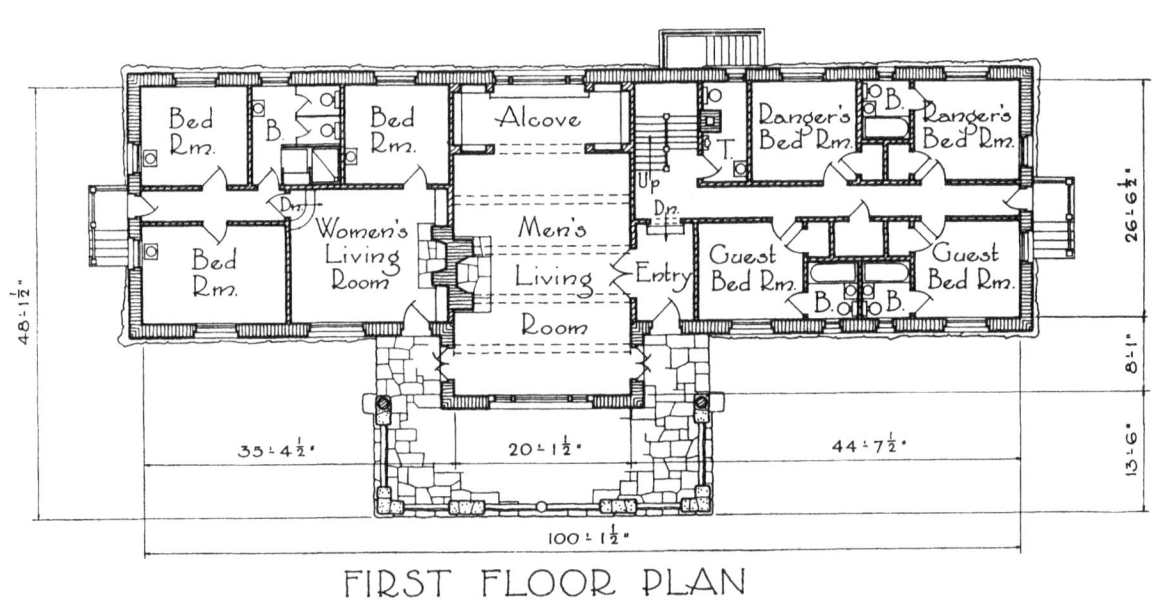

FIRST FLOOR PLAN
Scale 3/64" = 1'-0"

Plate I E–14   ⇢⇢⇢ SUPERINTENDENTS' AND STAFFS' QUARTERS

Superintendent's House

Naturalist's Cottage

STAFF HOUSING, CRATER LAKE NATIONAL PARK

In all buildings for housing superintendent, staff, and employes at this park, unifying, well-defined structural traits persist. Steep roof pitch, dictated by the heavy snowfall in the high altitude here, and masonry employing boulders of impressive size, combined with rough-sawn siding or vertical boards and battens, are chief among the factors common to all. The quarters illustrated typify the ideal provision of living accommodations to meet the needs of a large national park. Ground floor plans of the superintendent's house and the rangers' dormitory are shown opposite.

Employe's Cottage

Rangers' Dormitory

Dormitory and Mess Hall

SUPERINTENDENTS' AND STAFFS' QUARTERS   Plate I E-15

Entrance Side

Garden Side

Service Gateway

CUSTODIAN'S DWELLING,
LOCKHART STATE PARK, TEXAS

Here is a masterful molding of a park building in the traditional forms of early Texas architecture. It should inspire more frequent ventures in adaptation of the colloquial to park structural needs, with consequently less far-flung use of the less regional so-called rustic style. Such a development will mark a significant advance for park architecture. It seems highly probable that tradition has not here been slavishly followed, and equally probable that the very liberties taken are responsible for the satisfying results.

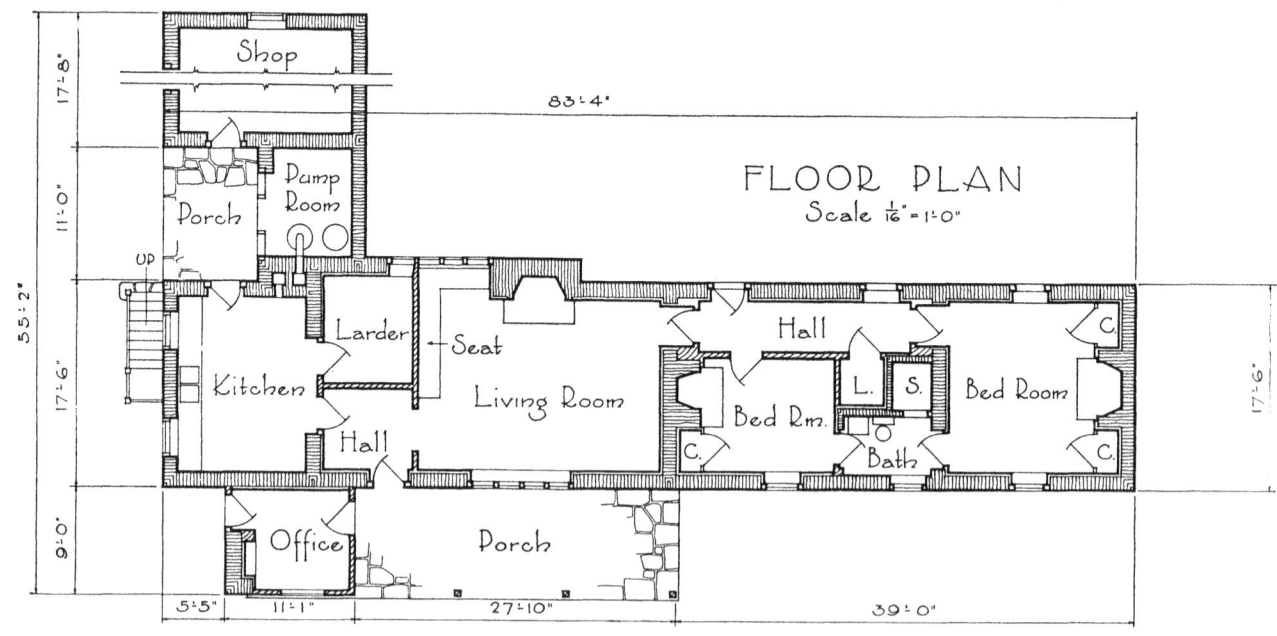

EQUIPMENT AND MAINTENANCE BUILDINGS

→›› THE FACILITATING BUILDINGS least contacted by the using public, those identified with equipment and maintenance of the park area, if properly located need make little effort in gesture to environment. Generally speaking, their best location is off the track beaten by park patrons, and if isolated and well-obscured these stepchildren among park structures need not suffer comparison with necessarily more self-conscious and better groomed members of the family.

This is not to say that these buildings should not be conveniently located. Inconspicuous convenience is the qualification. If such sites are not available, then these buildings must go in for protective coloration, and perhaps in greater degree than other buildings, for they are so completely nonrecreational and without the saving grace of very apparent direct benefit to the public itself. Their reason for being is so inadequately sensed by the unanalytical public mind that their presence is more than likely to be subconsciously resented.

Typical facilitating buildings within parks provide in the main for the housing of trucks, road-conditioning and other equipment, tools and implements of many kinds, and for the storage of supplies, such as firewood, ice, maintenance materials, feed, explosives, gas and oil, and other items, the variety and quantity of which are dictated by the size, character, and geographic location of the park. The generic term is variously equipment, utility, maintenance, or service buildings; but it is clear that the species embraced include garages, woodsheds, storehouses, barns, shops, and numerous other structures.

Often provision must be made for the stabling of work horses, or of one or more saddle horses used by custodian, ranger, or others of the park personnel in the discharge of their duties. This leads to need for space in which to store wagons and feed.

Shops equipped for the work of the motor mechanic, blacksmith, carpenter, and painter are essential to all large parks and extended park systems, and even in minor park areas the need for some space in which part-time work of these trades may be carried on should not be disregarded. There must be space available wherein picnic tables, signs, screens, and other items can be reconditioned, and a truck can be overhauled even though this be the only piece of automotive equipment in the park.

Mobile picnic tables and benches can require much storage space, if conditions affecting park policy dictate that these must be kept under roof during the winter months. An icehouse in which natural ice cut during the winter can be stored against summer demands is sometimes an economic requirement. Regardless of the apparent convenience to result from locating such a building on the shore of the lake from which the ice will be cut, the more valid claim of a shoreline spared such drastic infringement opposes this. It will be found that storage in reasonable proximity to the points where the ice will be used is equally convenient.

Probably in most remote parks wood is used to the exclusion of all other fuels and, where the winter season is long, cold, and rainy, a great quantity of cordwood must be on hand and much of it kept dry. This means a woodshed or shelter, usually semienclosed to give protection against rains driven by the prevailing winds and perhaps also to bring a certain orderly form and appearance to a wood pile which otherwise would tend to be ragged and unsightly. Particularly in the parks of the Pacific Northwest are sizable woodsheds an accepted facility.

These and many other service space needs crop up so progressively during park development that the equipment and maintenance building or group seems always to be in process of change or in crying need of it. Indeed it is foolhardy to look upon the most carefully considered and planned initial

EQUIPMENT AND MAINTENANCE BUILDINGS

structure as the fixed ultimate. It may serve perfectly the need of the moment. But there is nothing more legitimately subject to change than service and facilitating needs during the development of a park, and few parks are recorded as having finally passed that stage. The very choice of site for the service center should be predicated upon expansion possibilities beyond all reasonable limits to be foreseen at the start, and the wise technician will clearly visualize and cannily plan the initial structure as an extensible building, or as one unit with which others can be joined or grouped.

Probably the happiest and most forehanded visualization of the ultimate maintenance group is a square service courtyard surrounded by all the facilitating structures. If at the starting gong the required buildings utilize but one, or at most two, sides of the eventual courtyard, the planner need not feel regretful concern for its incompleteness. Time will correct that, and speedily. His concern might more profitably be for how the threat of future additions will be met after structures have raced their way to enclose all sides of the courtyard. He may almost find that to maintain any opening for access to the service court is his real problem.

The chief advantage of the "hollow square" plan is the confinement of maintenance activities and paraphernalia to an area that becomes ultimately screened from public view as the expanding structures proceed to enclose it. Cavernous openings for entrance of trucks and equipment, factorylike windows so necessary for proper lighting of work spaces—all the inharmonious and unparklike—can be made to open on the court, while the walls exposed to public view need not shout stridently the storage and maintenance activities within. This results in an opportunity to limit "eye appeal" construction, where this must be adopted, to the exposed outer walls, and to resort to strictly practicable and serviceable construction within the court. The "hollow square" serves also to accommodate and screen from view any equipment which need not be kept under roof. It masks the loading and unloading of supplies, the arrival and departure of work crews, and the other necessary activities which can be destructive of the visitor's primary desire for the illusion of Nature unaffected by man's contacts.

Indeed should the building of permanent buildings to hem in an "equipment corral" seem a distant prospect, it is often advantageous to complete the enclosure by means of a temporary (though it should be a substantial) stockade or other type of fence.

The park patron thus is fended from wandering into the activities of the maintenance base with which his recreational use is not properly involved; and limits are created to prevent a loose overflow of maintenance facilities into areas which the public should be privileged to claim for its own. Confined to their own fixed precinct, surrounded and obscured by their own requirements of structure, the activities and facilities which have to do with the mechanics of development and maintenance need not constitute a disfigurement of a preserve of Nature.

Plate I F–1 ⇶ EQUIPMENT AND MAINTENANCE BUILDINGS

Palmetto State Park, Texas

Garner State Park, Texas

SERVICE GATES

Functioning as entrances to service or utility enclosures, the gates here pictured are not without decorative value, particularly the two at the top of the page. The gates directly at right permit the entrance of a vehicle through a fence of good park character which surrounds an incinerator. The example at lower right is likewise of vehicle width and gives entrance to a typical service group enclosure. The gate which continues the palisade fence leads to the service yard of a lodge building and affords a maximum of obstruction to view.

Bonham State Park, Texas

Petit Jean State Park, Arkansas

Lake Brownwood State Park, Texas

91

EQUIPMENT AND MAINTENANCE BUILDINGS

Plate I F–2

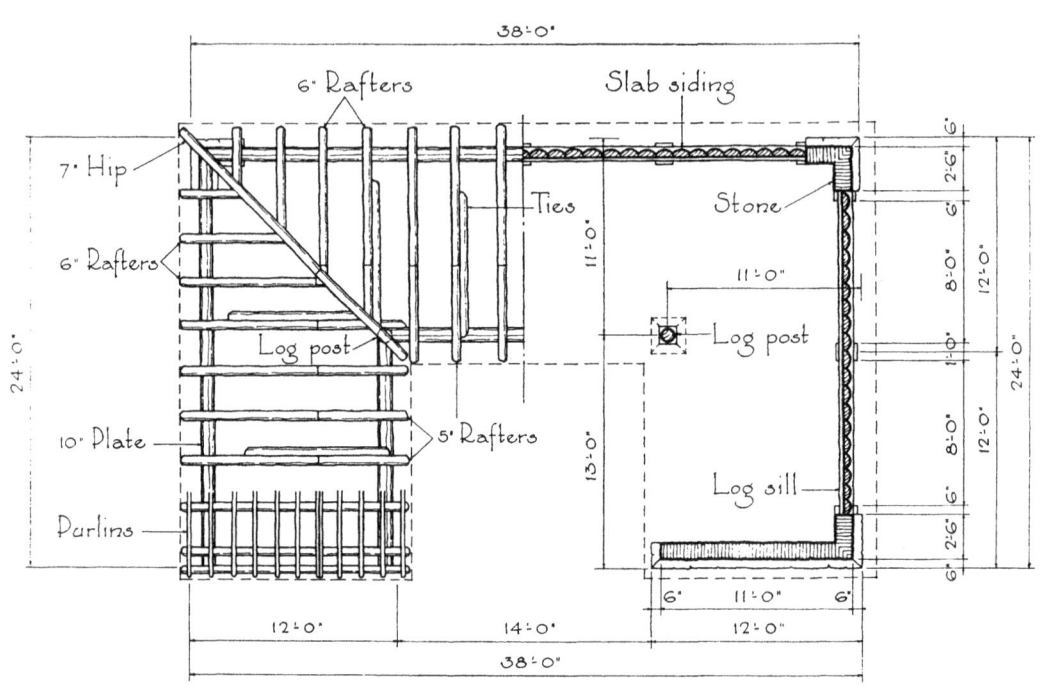

Wood Storage Building

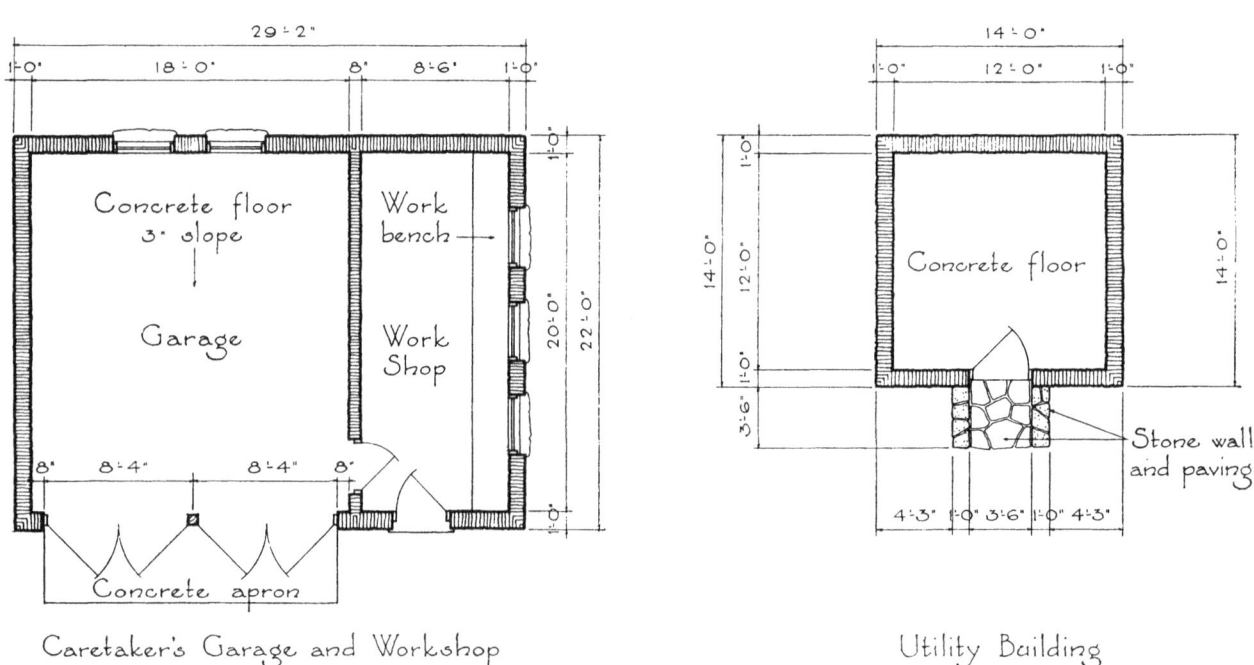

Caretaker's Garage and Workshop

Utility Building

Riverside State Park - Washington

Scale 3/32"=1'-0"

Plate I F–3 →»› EQUIPMENT AND MAINTENANCE BUILDINGS

Here illustrated are three structures of maintenance purpose which, with a custodian's dwelling elsewhere shown in this compilation, indicate a pleasant and consistent unity of structural theme. Together these make up a group as closely related by location and function as by architectural style. The not entirely satisfying masonry may result from characteristics of the local stone which make more structural shape for the units difficult, if not impossible.

Wood Storage Building, Riverside State Park, Washington

In extent this garage with shop space is typical of the facility that complements the caretaker's dwelling in the park of average size. The shop is well lighted. The outcropping rocks in the foreground are indicative of the character of the area and probably explanatory of the imposed limitations of masonry technique here. The lichens on the stone surfaces exposed in the walls and the moss-filled joints go far to compensate for the unstructural pattern of the masonry.

Caretaker's Garage and Workshop, Riverside State Park, Washington

This little building has been allowed to stray from its logical location in this book with geographical justification. Though it is a pumphouse, it is shown here with its near neighbors of an equipment and maintenance group to illustrate at full length the harmony which derives from the employment of similar materials and one architectural expression for a group of related structures.

Utility Building, Riverside State Park, Washington

EQUIPMENT AND MAINTENANCE BUILDINGS

Plate I F-4

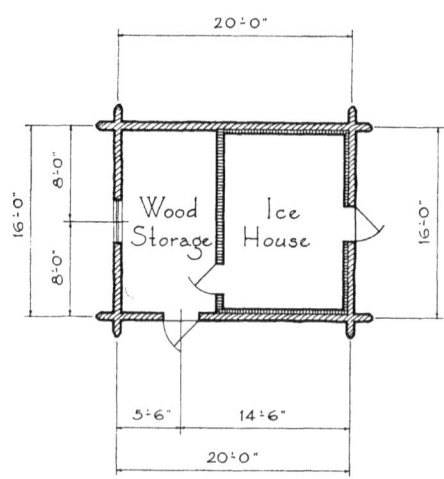

Scenic State Park - Minnesota

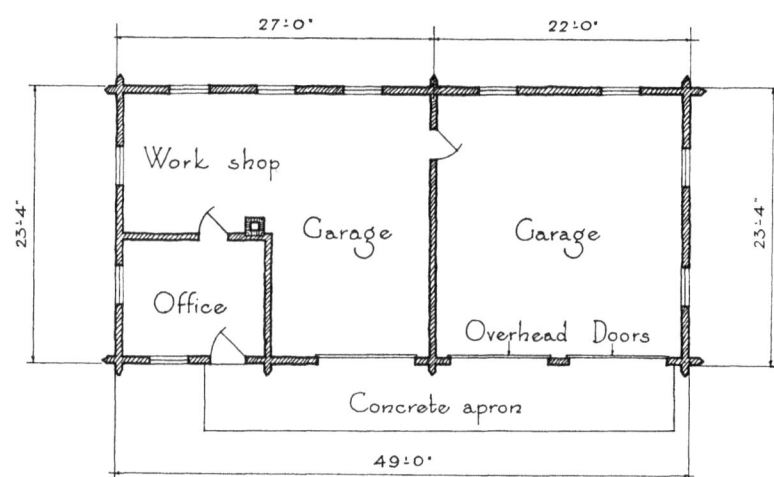

Scenic State Park - Minnesota

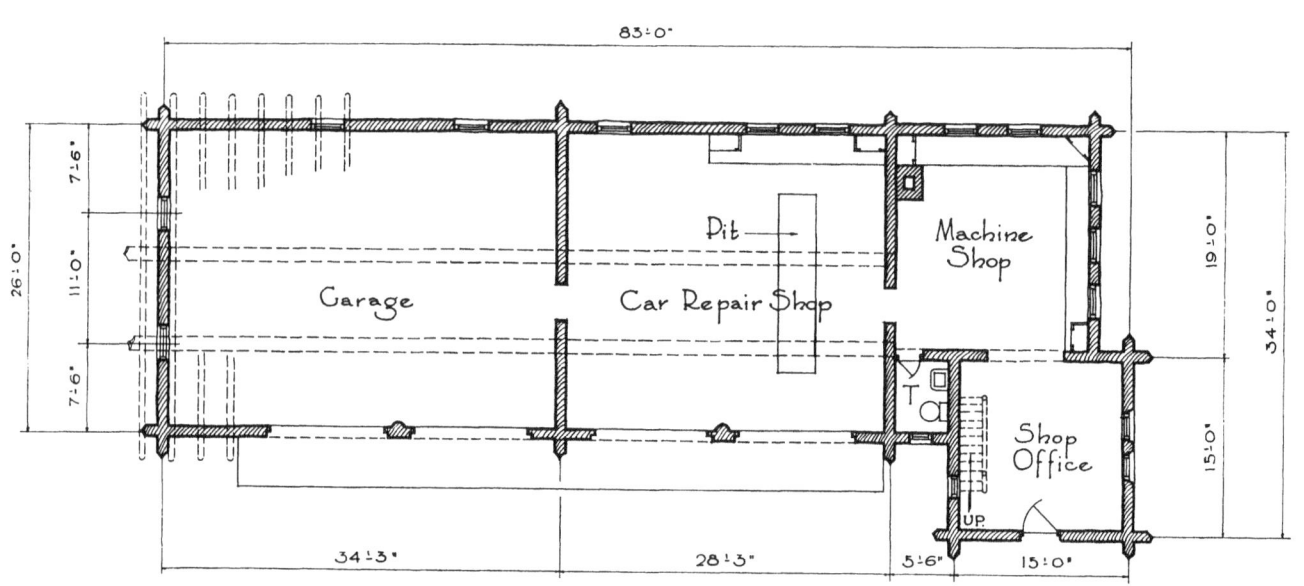

Itasca State Park - Minnesota

Scale 1/16" = 1'-0"

Plate I F–5 →›› EQUIPMENT AND MAINTENANCE BUILDINGS

A little building of humble purpose, glorified by the excellent log work that is almost the invariable accomplishment in Minnesota parks. The projecting logs at the corners keep within allowable limits of rakishness and enliven the general effect. The ridge, capped with pole, and other details should be noted. Ice, wood, and tools are stored in the building. The walls and roof of the section allotted for ice storage are lined with insulating material.

Wood and Ice House, Scenic State Park, Minnesota

An equipment and maintenance building which is obviously close kin to the wood and ice storage building of this same park. The family traits of selected, straight logs and high craftsmanship in joinery are unmistakable. When all park structures built for public view exemplify the sturdy forthrightness of these mere facilitating buildings, much existing construction will have been replaced.

Garage, Scenic State Park, Minnesota

Where construction is so skillfully executed as here, one regrets that its functions and its construction materials combine to produce fire hazards far above the average. The two-story portion contrives to suggest a blockhouse form, but it will be seen that the overhang is instead an optical illusion. The building is too sightly a structure to be allowed to remain long without the added benefit of some foundation planting where this is possible.

Equipment Building, Itasca State Park, Minnesota

EQUIPMENT AND MAINTENANCE BUILDINGS

Plate I F-6

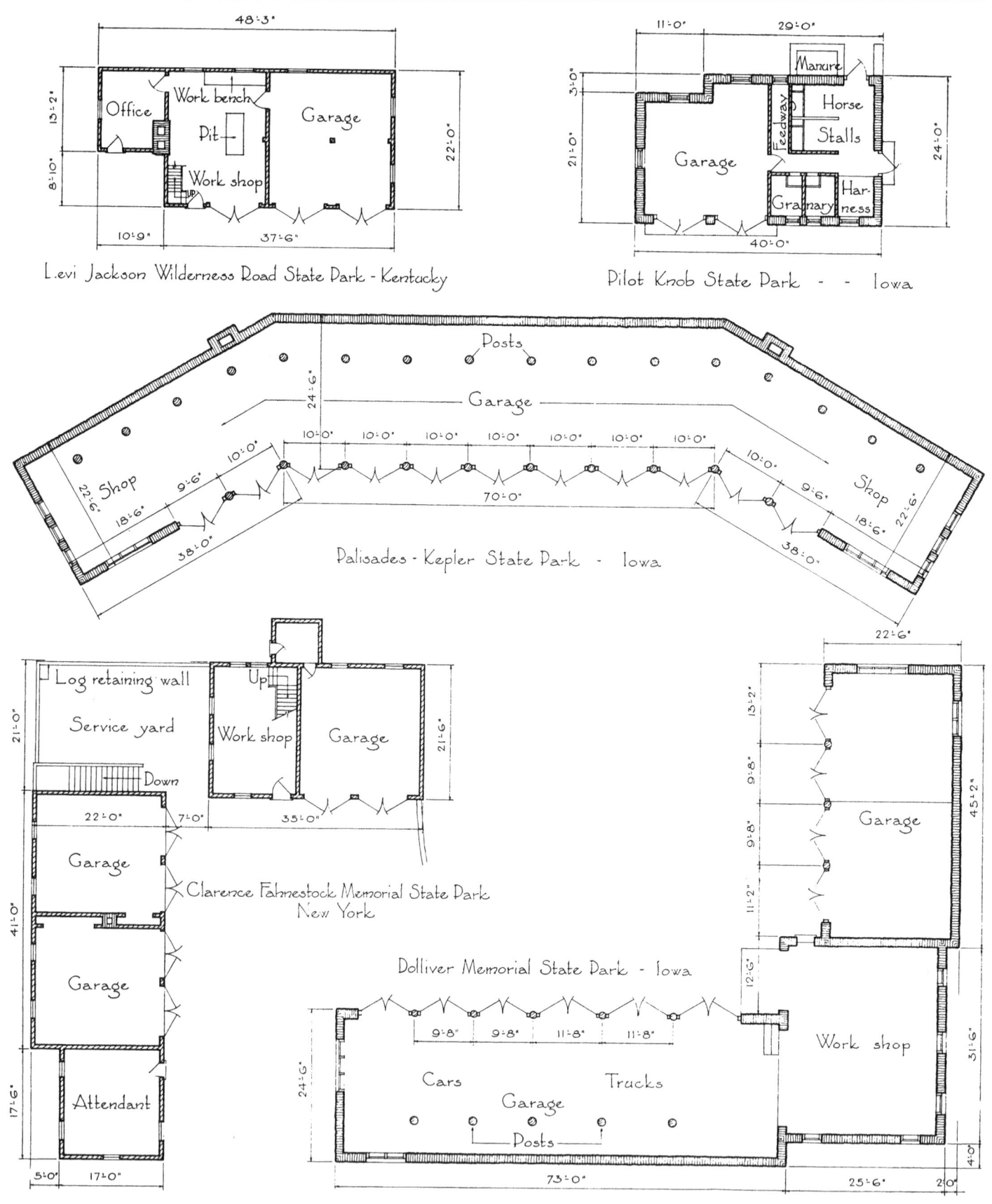

Plate I F–7 →›› EQUIPMENT AND MAINTENANCE BUILDINGS

Levi Jackson-Wilderness Road State Park, Kentucky

Pilot Knob State Park, Iowa

THE SERVICE QUADRANGLE IN DEVELOPMENT

The small Iowa and Kentucky examples illustrated above are typical of the modest beginnings of storage facilities for maintenance materials and equipment in connection with a caretaker's group in a small park. The other three here shown well illustrate the tendency to expand, inherent in service buildings. Happily, the two at the bottom of the page suggest expansion along recommended lines—to an eventual equipment and maintenance courtyard or enclosure.

Palisades-Kepler State Park, Iowa

Clarence Fahnestock Memorial State Park, New York

Dolliver Memorial State Park, Iowa

EQUIPMENT AND MAINTENANCE BUILDINGS

Plate I F-8

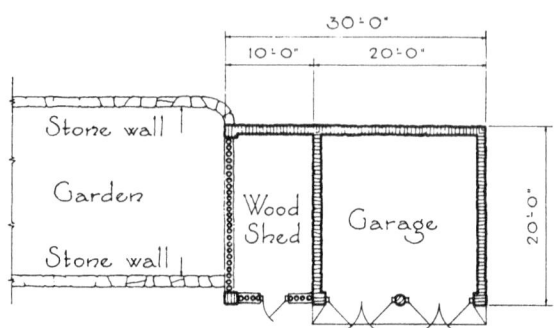

Palomar Mt. State Park - California

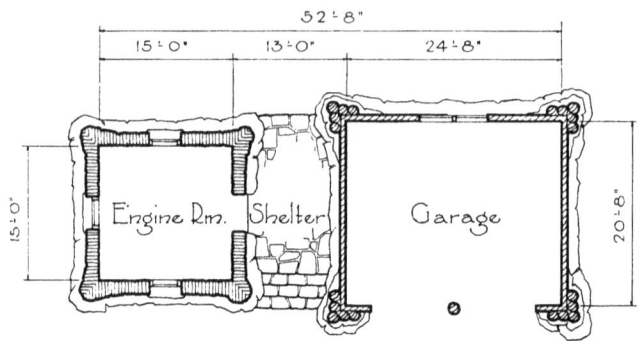

Boyle Metropolitan Park - Arkansas

Scale 3/4" = 1'-0"

Garner State Park - - - Texas

Scale 3/4" = 1'-0"

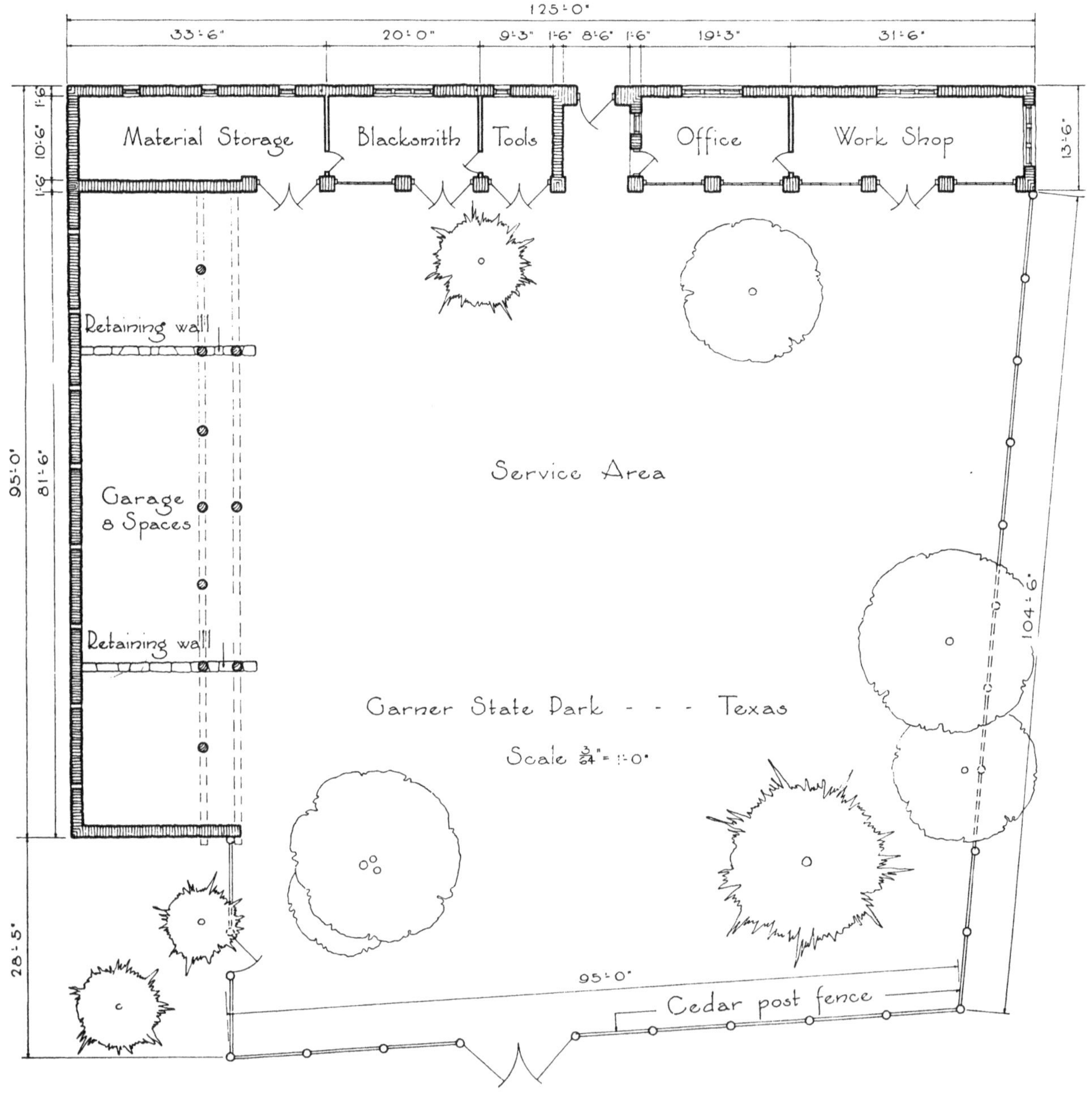

Plate I F–9 — EQUIPMENT AND MAINTENANCE BUILDINGS

Again is presented a garage building with storage space meeting in general a custodian's needs in a park. There is novelty in the combination of stone masonry and vertically placed slender poles serving as curtain wall. Depreciative of the total effect of the building is the flat, thin roofing, too meticulously laid to be completely harmonious with the setting.

Custodian's Garage, Palomar Mountain State Park, California

This spirited rendering of a custodian's garage departs from the typical in its link with a pumphouse and water storage tank. There is a surprising variety of materials in this design. The texture of the shake roof and the batter of the rude rock base, suggesting a sparing use of mortar, are details of great interest.

Custodian's Garage, Boyle Metropolitan Park, Little Rock, Arkansas

The case for the equipment and maintenance courtyard or enclosure rests on this exhibit and two which follow. In this instance equipment sheds supply one side of the quadrangle, shops, another. Palisade fence completes this "introvert" lay-out, which safeguards the public's right to a park area unblemished by long-range views of gaping garage doors, mechanical equipment, and other such disillusioning paraphernalia.

Service Group, Garner State Park, Texas

99

EQUIPMENT AND MAINTENANCE BUILDINGS ⋘   *Plate* I F-10

Service Group, Goliad State Park, Texas

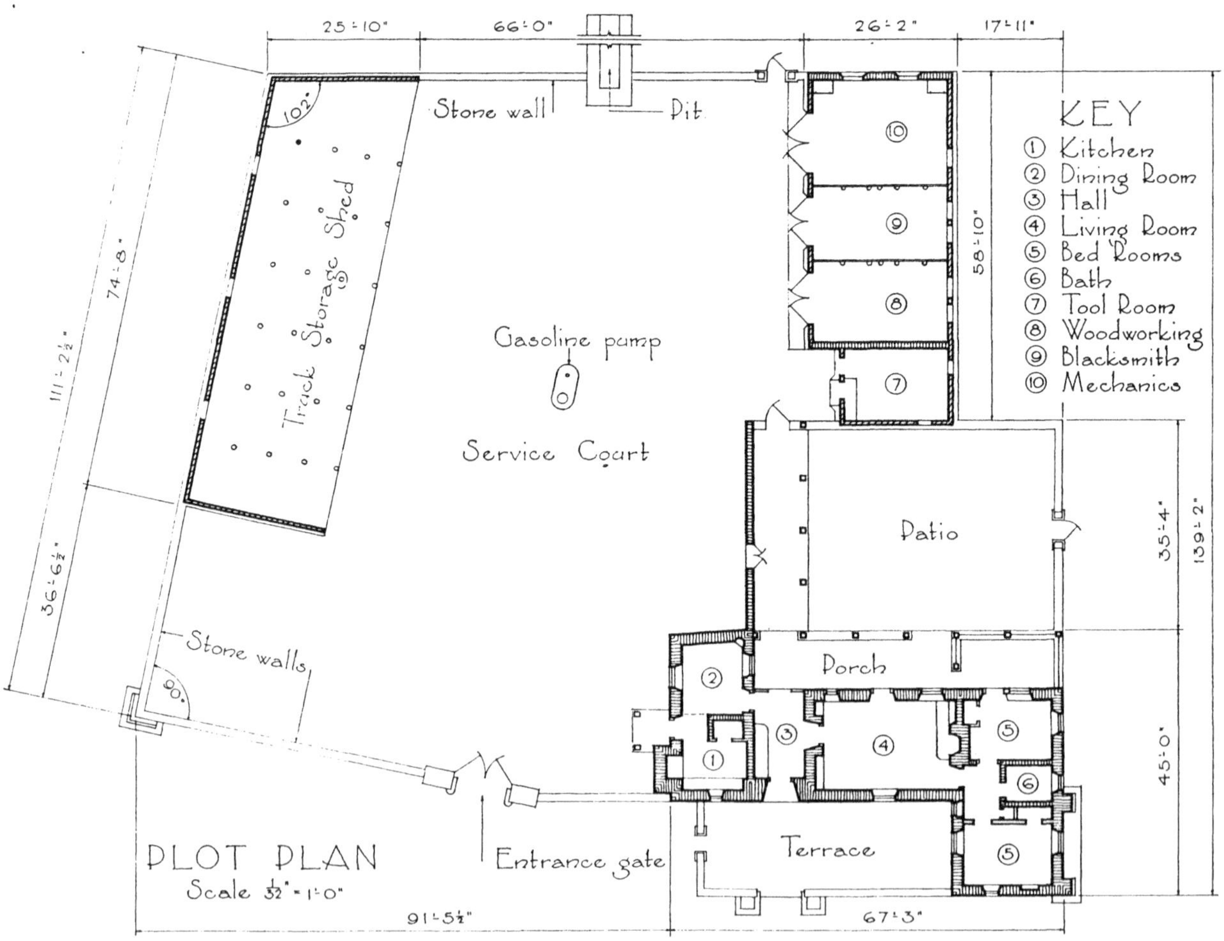

KEY
1. Kitchen
2. Dining Room
3. Hall
4. Living Room
5. Bed Rooms
6. Bath
7. Tool Room
8. Woodworking
9. Blacksmith
10. Mechanics

PLOT PLAN
Scale 32" = 1'-0"

Plate I F-11 →»> EQUIPMENT AND MAINTENANCE BUILDINGS

SERVICE GROUP IN EXTENSO, GOLIAD STATE PARK, TEXAS

Not content with supplying a full complement of structural units for equipment and maintenance needs, and connecting with the caretaker's house in a logical plan arrangement, this service group arrays itself with exquisite care in the traditional south Texas architecture that characterizes the dwelling. In a general prevalence of a certain "down-at-heelness" among buildings meeting these needs in parks, the nice attention here lavished on detail is as welcome as it is startling.

101

EQUIPMENT AND MAINTENANCE BUILDINGS　　　　　　　　　　　　　　　　Plate I F–12

Service Group, Bandelier National Monument

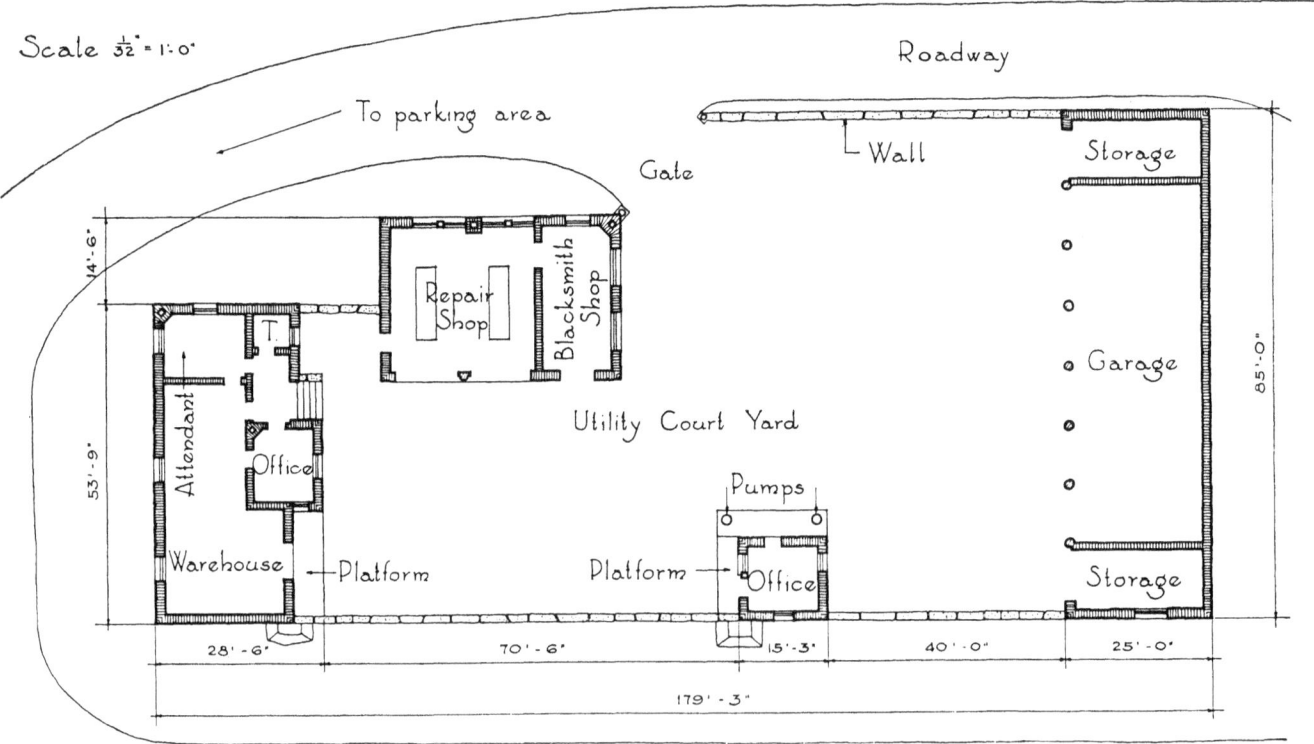

The sufficient-unto-itself service yard enclosure as it has found expression on a national area. Necessary buildings and connecting walls close in a work yard promising comparative freedom from interruptions by a curious public, as well as from pilfering. Certain minor elements of the plan wait upon future construction although the plan fails to disclose this fact. The simple character of the stuccoed buildings and walls seems very suitable to the location in the Southwest.

DRINKING FOUNTAINS AND WATER SUPPLY

IT IS ASSUMED to be unnecessary to dwell more than momentarily on the two absolute essentials in provision of drinking water in park areas. Primary of these most important considerations is the unalterable requirement that the water supply shall be completely safeguarded against contamination. Hardly second to this is the need for dispensing it at so many points over the park area that it is always easier for the park patron to avail himself of the protected water supply than to seek out brooks and other possible sources of drinking water not policed against pollution. Treatment of the bubbler, well, or spring as an architectural or landscape feature can hardly claim consideration until these two major demands have been met. Only a firm conviction that a safeguarded and widely distributed water supply may be taken for granted universally in the park planning thought of today encourages a venture in consideration of the form and character, in an architectural and landscape sense, of the dispensing media.

The cleaning out of a spring and the erection of some suitable enclosure to minimize the danger of pollution are in the direction of a safe water supply. However, if the public is to have free access to the spring at the source, the human equation enters and renders problematical continuing cleanliness. Poetic in fancy is the cool, clear pool from which to drink on bended knee, but subject in fact to the careless habits of that considerable section of the public which can be perfectly unaware that others both precede and follow.

The ungarnished rendering of a facility for the dispensing of drinking water is a vertical pipe terminating with a tap, the tap perhaps inverted to serve as a simple, but far from sanitary, "bubbler." Such a contrivance set out in the open will satisfy thirst, but certainly not the eye. If it is decided to mask its gaunt utilitarianism by locating it amongst low growth of planting, it is not readily discoverable, and a sign must point out its location. If provision is not made for disposing of drip and overflow, the tap is soon the center of a muddy wallow, and only accessible if planks or stepping stones are provided. All of which soon demonstrates that the utterly simple facility suffers from very real disadvantages, and leads logically and necessarily to its being accepted as something of a feature, its functionalism neither so starkly naked as to offend the eye nor so elaborately draped as to fail to declare itself. With the imperative need for suitable disposal of waste water and for bubbler of truly sanitary type, and such desirable refinements as steps to accommodate children, tap for the filling of pails, and in some climates or locations even roof protection against the heat of the sun, the feature becomes multi-functional, and demands careful study in any pursuit of satisfying results.

Important in connection with a piped water supply out-of-doors is a suitable arrangement for shutting off and draining the pipes in winter weather. This provision should not be overlooked wherever climate would indicate need for it.

Because the treatment of the drinking fountain or bubbler as an isolated unit is so difficult, every opportunity should be embraced to incorporate this facility within any suitable building situated near the spot where drinking water is a requirement. It is possible and desirable to include bubblers as features of structures erected primarily for other purposes, and thus to eliminate some of the separate installations. Many bubblers have been installed separately that need not have been.

Sometimes the source of drinking water at a park location is a shallow well equipped with a hand-operated pump. This piece of mechanism, as currently quantity-produced, has strayed far from the picturesqueness of its forerunner, the town pump, though very definitely not into the arms of any industrial designer. It displays nothing of good old-fashioned primitive substance and has strangely escaped the face-lifting manipulations of the streamliners. It is not to be wondered at then that the plight of this neglected ugly duckling so challenges the chivalry of designers of park facilities that they ride forth in shining armor to see justice done.

Rescue may take the form of a round or squared log hollowed out to sheathe or encase as much as possible of the unprepossessing mechanism. Often the handle that is standard equipment with the pump is replaced by one shaped out of wood, and the spout on occasion is hooded by a fortuitously occurring forking branch. This is not to be tolerated of course if it must be interpreted as a reprehensible device for making a new-fangled metal pump look as though it were a primitive wooden one. Justification lies rather in the fact that something unsightly may be masked by the use of a material more natural to a park setting, just as the hood, covering and concealing the automobile engine, is accepted without any very general eyebrow-lifting.

Of course there are those who are for open plumbing openly arrived at and who will decry the foregoing solution as being utterly unprincipled. It is our great good fortune that for them there remains an alternative method for bringing a measure of charm to the creaking, clanging pump without resorting to the immoral trickery of the aforementioned handcrafted figleaf. This is to cloister the unadorned pump in the dark shadows of a small shelter.

The well or pump shelter can be so happily executed that we are made blind to the ugliness of the pump in our admiration for the shelter. The effective disposal of the waste water from a pump located in a shelter is an important detail. This is sometimes provided for by a sump at the base of the pump, but the more positive method for preventing damp and unpleasant conditions within the shelter is to lead the waste outside the building by means of a trough where it can leach into a dry well. Seats of one form or another are usually incorporated with the pump shelter.

Another structural item often required in a park as a part of the water supply system, though probably seldom for drinking purposes, is an elevated storage tank. The "theory of approach" to design of this structure presents much the same quandary as that of observation and fire towers. There is at once an urge to give it skeletonized directness revealing of purpose and an inclination to enclose it in a degree concealing of its function. When the former approach can be followed to the high accomplishment of the example at Mount Nebo State Park, Arkansas, we are convinced that this is the one admissible "theory" of design. When some of the examples that enclose and conceal the tank are studied, we waver to the point of admitting that the second approach has its points.

Accessory to an elevated storage tank is a minor building housing the electric or gasoline operated mechanism that lifts the water from the well, spring, or other source to the elevated tank. While it is possible to imagine unusual conditions under which the pump machinery might be in the base of the tower enclosing the elevated tank, it is customarily a small separate building, determined by the source of the water supply and hence more or less remote from the location logical for the storage tank. If the water is to be pumped from a well, a hatch should be provided in the roof of the pumphouse directly above the well to anticipate the pulling of the casing or making of other repairs without affecting fixed construction.

The problem becomes one of knowing how far to go and where to stop in glorification of the drinking fountain, the pump shelter, and other water supply structures. The examples shown herein illustrate various stages of the process. Personal preference alone will dictate at what point and in what particular the bounds of reason and good taste have been overreached.

Plate I G–1   →» DRINKING FOUNTAINS AND WATER SUPPLY

Crowley's Ridge State Park, Arkansas

Parvin State Park, New Jersey

PUMPS SYLVANESQUE

Here are pumps which strive valiantly to be Roman in Rome by wrapping a wooden toga around their barbaric functionalism. The ethics of it all will doubtless be cried down by many. Suffice it to be recommended here that 'twere done when 'tis done with the measure of ingenuity and skill evidenced in the surrounding illustrations.

Saratoga Hot Springs State Park, Wyoming

Boulder Mountain Park, Colorado

105

DRINKING FOUNTAINS AND WATER SUPPLY

Plate I G–2

Drinking Fountain
Lewis and Clark State Park — — — Washington

Recommended to the consideration of those who are repelled by the impropriety of an unprocessed log, serving (masquerading, they will say) as a drinking fountain, or a drinking fountain borrowing the protective coloring of (pretending to be, they will say) a natural log. This duly processed wood pedestal may be the ethically sound and acceptable compromise that can effect a truce between the warring partisans in this very vital issue involving legitimacy of use.

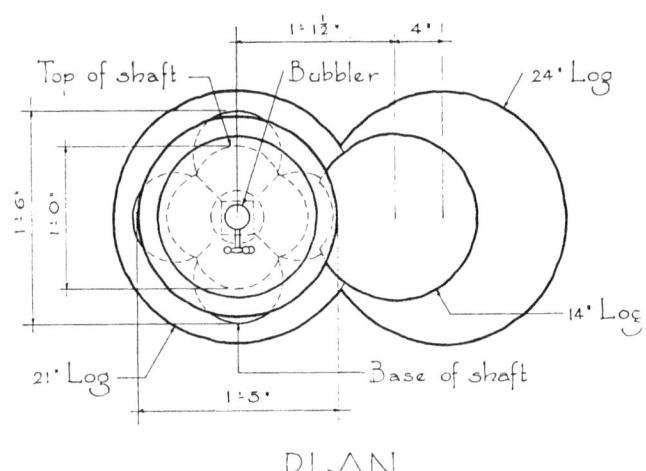

PLAN

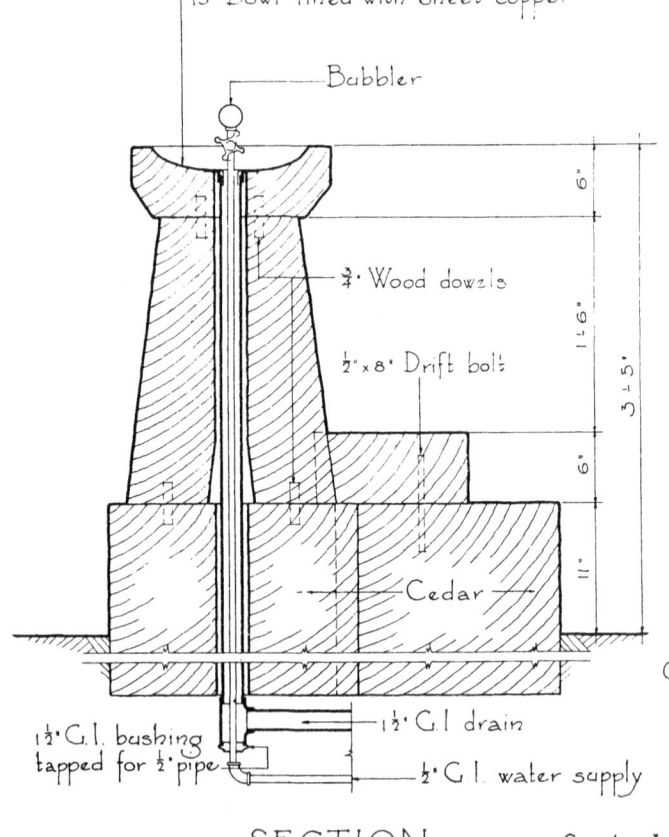

SECTION Scale ¾"=1'-0"   FRONT ELEVATION

106

Plate I G–3   ⋙ DRINKING FOUNTAINS AND WATER SUPPLY

Mohawk Metropolitan Park, Tulsa, Oklahoma

Stackhouse Metropolitan Park, Johnstown, Pennsylvania

LOG PEDESTAL DRINKING FOUNTAINS

In the above example the additions of log posts and designative sign evidence substance, protection, and dignity brought to an exposed pipe terminating in a tap. Other illustrations demonstrate wood-encased drinking fountains to embrace one from which it was neglected to remove bark and another which can boast many steps in assorted heights. Fair appraisal of the suitability of wood to this use must base from whether it was premised to make a drinking fountain look like a tree trunk or to lend substance to the facility by the use of a material abundantly at hand.

Mount Penn Metropolitan Reservation, Reading, Pennsylvania

Crowley's Ridge State Park, Arkansas

Humbug Mountain State Park, Oregon

107

DRINKING FOUNTAINS AND WATER SUPPLY

Plate I G-4

Drinking Fountain
Lake Guernsey State Park — — — Wyoming

Here certainly is the peak accomplishment in naturalistic masking of a provision for bubbler and tap. It is a temptation hardly resistible to state that the rock was smitten with a rod and that the water gushed forth in the best biblical tradition. However, the section drawing below evidences too plainly to the contrary — a laborious business of drilling and pipe fitting. Smiting with a rod would have been easier.

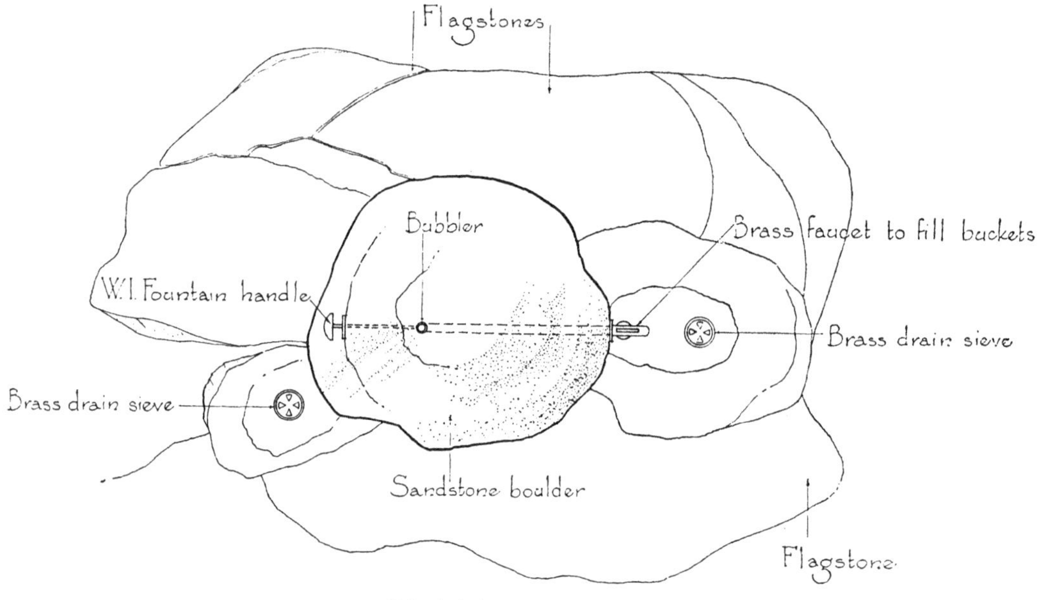

PLAN

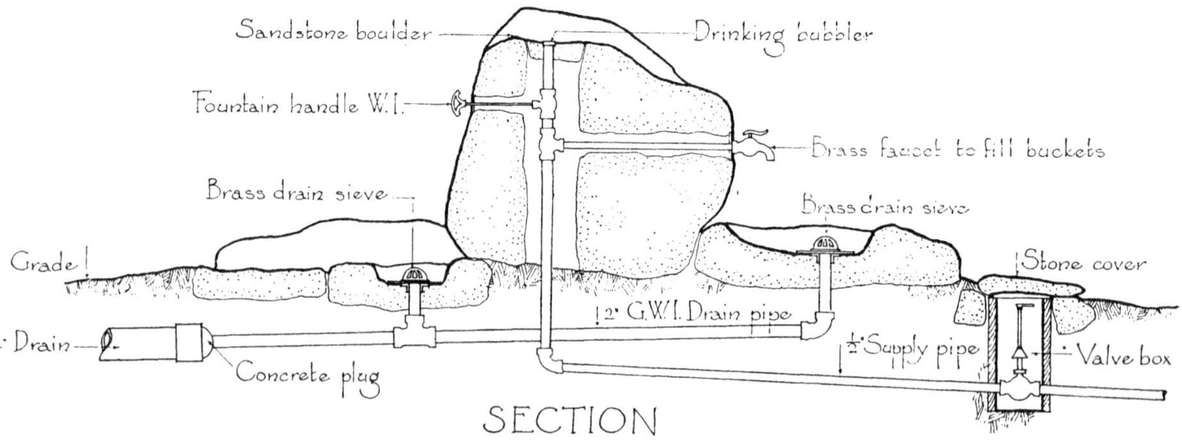

SECTION
Scale ¾" = 1'-0"

108

Plate I G–5 ⋙ DRINKING FOUNTAINS AND WATER SUPPLY

Palmer Park, Colorado Springs, Colorado

Mount Tamalpais, California

STONE DRINKING FOUNTAIN IN DEVELOPMENT

The two fountains above-pictured continue to exploit attractively the naturalism characteristic of the rock fountain shown on the facing page. The subject at Crater Lake National Park is a single native stone with top hollowed out. The examples below begin to take on familiar bubbler form. One is still single stone but roughly squared; the other is polylithic but involves fewer stones than occur in the more sophisticated bubbler pedestals that follow. At this stage the step for the accommodation of little people becomes almost standard equipment for the drinking fountain.

Crater Lake National Park

Steckel County Park, California

Millersylvania State Park, Washington

109

DRINKING FOUNTAINS AND WATER SUPPLY

Plate I G-6

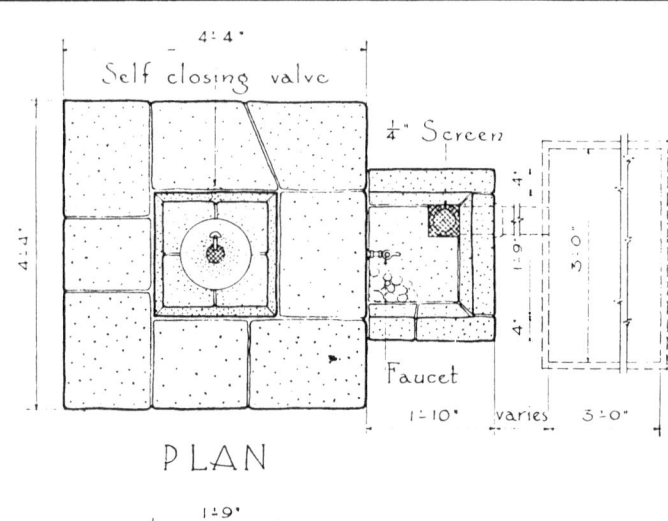

PLAN

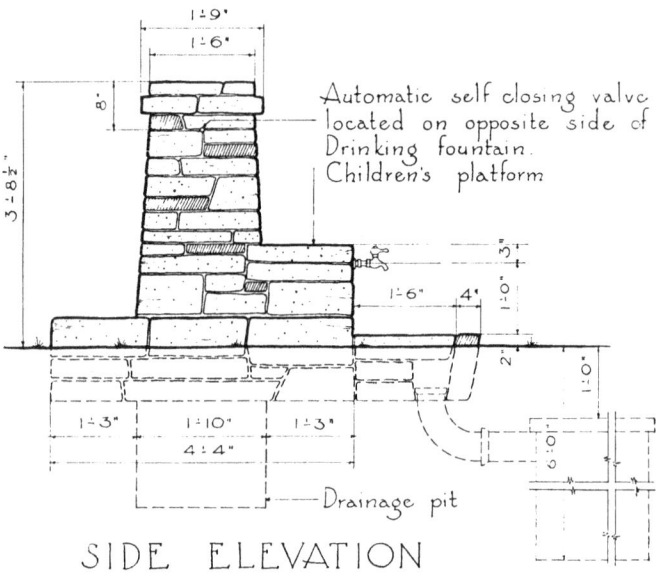

SIDE ELEVATION

Bubbler   Letchworth State Park   New York

This stone drinking fountain is generally typical of this facility as built in many parks through New York State. Designed with sanitary bubbler and step to make it accessible to small children, and with low tap for the filling of buckets above the gravel-filled sump receiving the waste, all essential factors are met without over-elaboration.

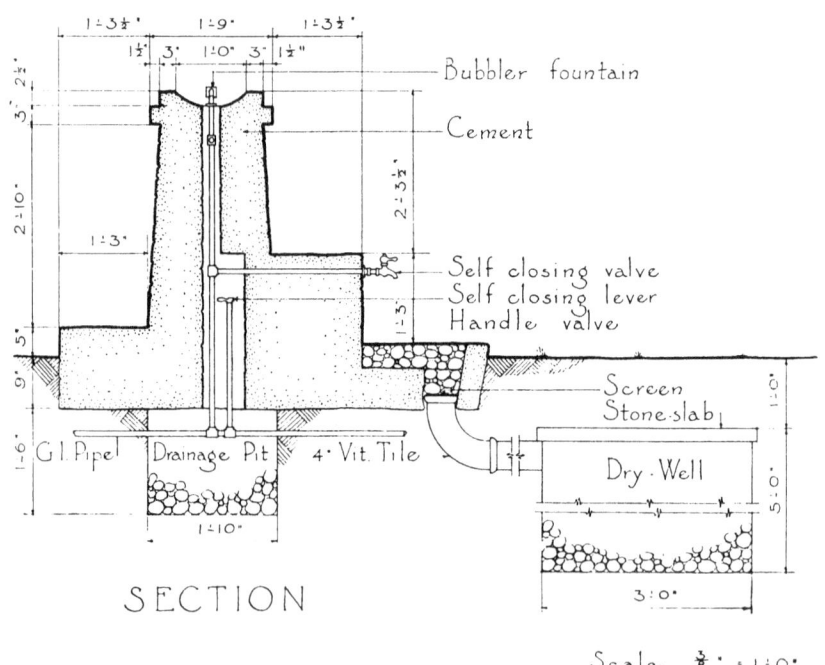

SECTION

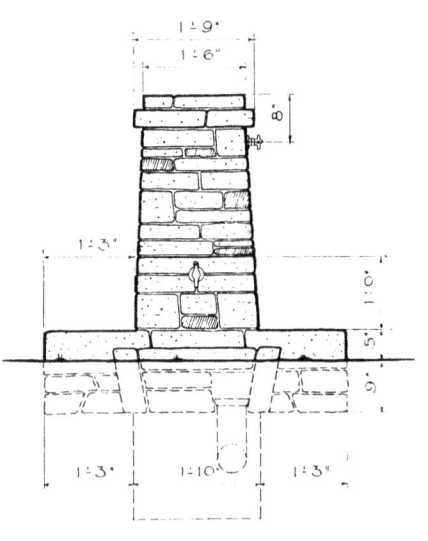

FRONT ELEVATION

Scale ⅜" = 1'-0"

110

Plate I G-7 — DRINKING FOUNTAINS AND WATER SUPPLY

Bonham State Park, Texas

Cook County Forest Preserve, Illinois

MASONRY PEDESTAL DRINKING FOUNTAINS

Surrounding this panel are colloquial renderings of the basic masonry pedestal detailed on the facing page. It is interesting to study this array of subjects for differences in characteristics of stone and workmanship, scale of masonry units, and the surprising variety that can prevail within narrowly fixed limits. Thus there are three varieties rather rigid in outline and character, mounted on platforms at or near grade level. Features of the two other subjects are recess to receive pail, buried natural boulder to serve as stepping stone, and pedestal of markedly horizontal coursing suggesting ledge rock.

Sibley State Park, Minnesota

New Salem State Park, Illinois

Foster County Park, California

DRINKING FOUNTAINS AND WATER SUPPLY

Plate I G-8

Lake Worth Metropolitan Park, Fort Worth, Texas

Pere Marquette State Park, Illinois

Spring Mill State Park, Indiana

MISCELLANY OF DRINKING FOUNTAINS

Above is a bubbler with circular pedestal, set in the recess of a retaining wall—uncommon features. The column at the left ranges fountains equipped with two or more bubbler fittings, culminating at lower left in a development that begins with the pious idea of recalling an ancient well curb, only to fall from grace when it breaks the commandments for good masonry. Directly below is a well curb, roofed, and somewhat in the stride of the unusual specimen detailed on the facing page.

I & M Canal State Park, Illinois

Bastrop State Park, Texas

112

Plate I G–9   ⇶ DRINKING FOUNTAINS AND WATER SUPPLY

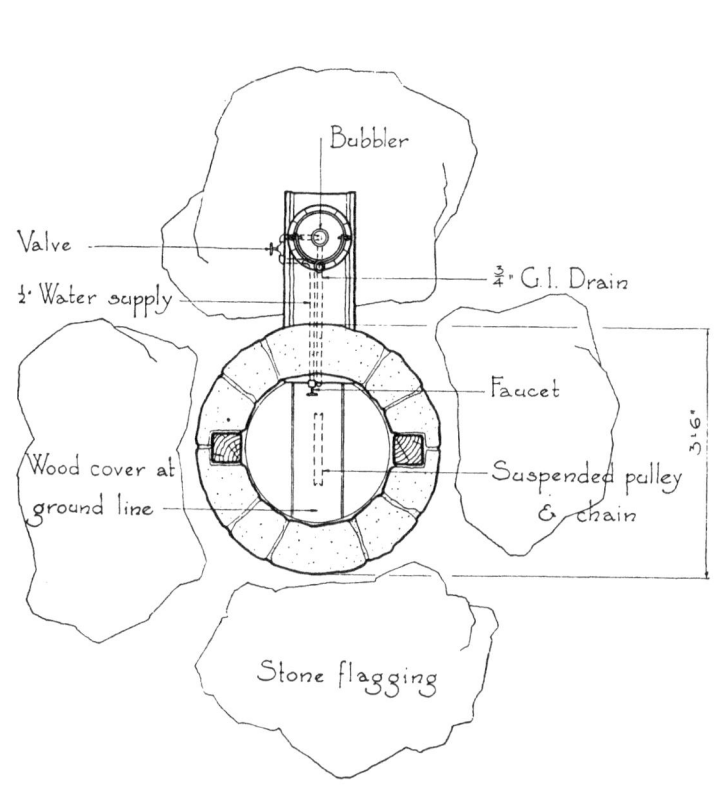

Drinking Fountain - Ledges State Park - Iowa

Mannered and perhaps forced, if you will, but capable of inspiring in many of us a recall of things long gone -- not the least among the more subtle benefits a park can offer.

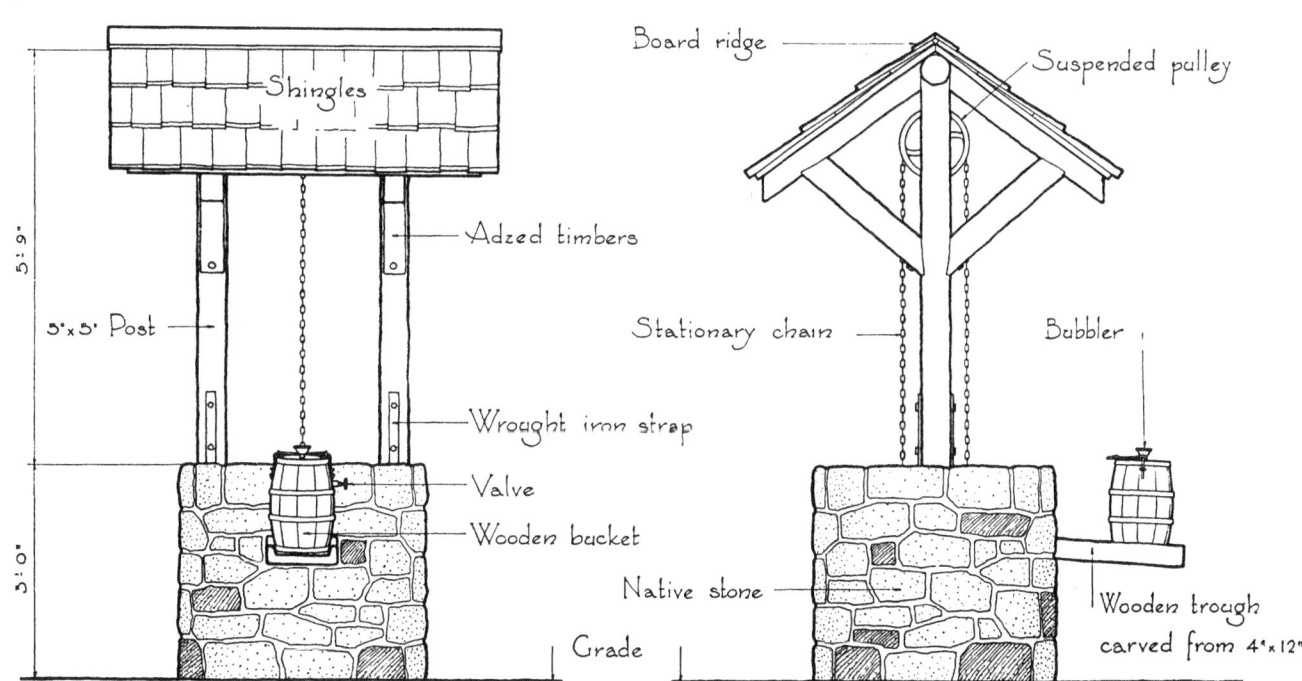

Scale 3/8" = 1'-0"

DRINKING FOUNTAINS AND WATER SUPPLY

Plate I G-10

Pump Shelter
Crowley's Ridge State Park — — — Arkansas

There is a rakish spontaneity in this shelter-for-pump that is very winning. It is unspoiled by the over-professional touch, which is likely to wither the essential personality of primitive construction in its too conscious effort. The iron-banded log-encased pump is a detail of interest.

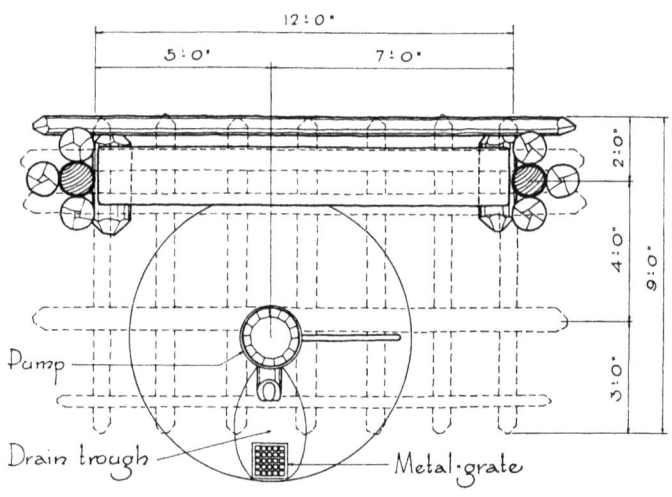

PLAN

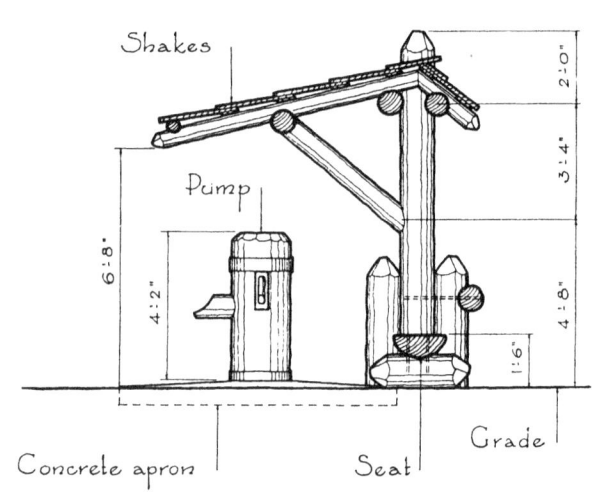

SECTION

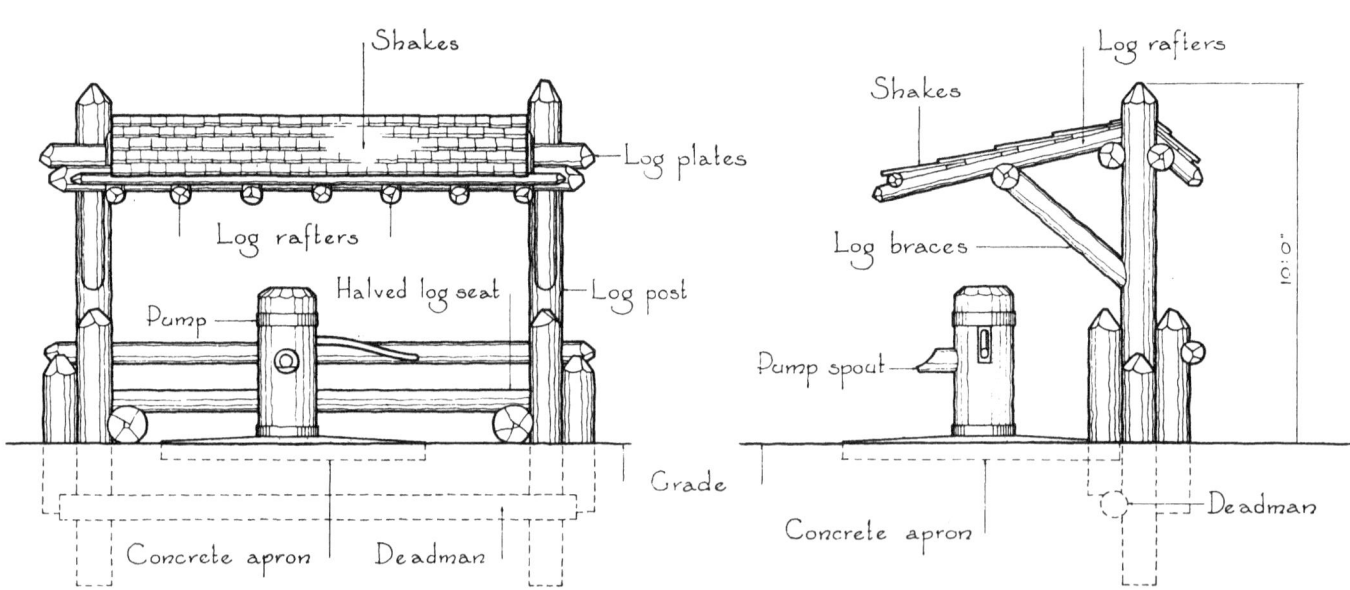

FRONT ELEVATION   Scale 3/16" = 1'-0"   SIDE ELEVATION

114

Plate I G-11 — DRINKING FOUNTAINS AND WATER SUPPLY

Well Shelter — Itasca State Park — Minnesota

Certainly exempt from any accusation of "twiginess" this little structure perhaps exemplifies ideal proportions for a truly rustic construction. The idea of hollowed-out log as a receptacle for the piped spring water is novel. The ragged shake roof is particularly well-done. There is neither economy of materials nor of originality to detract from this example.

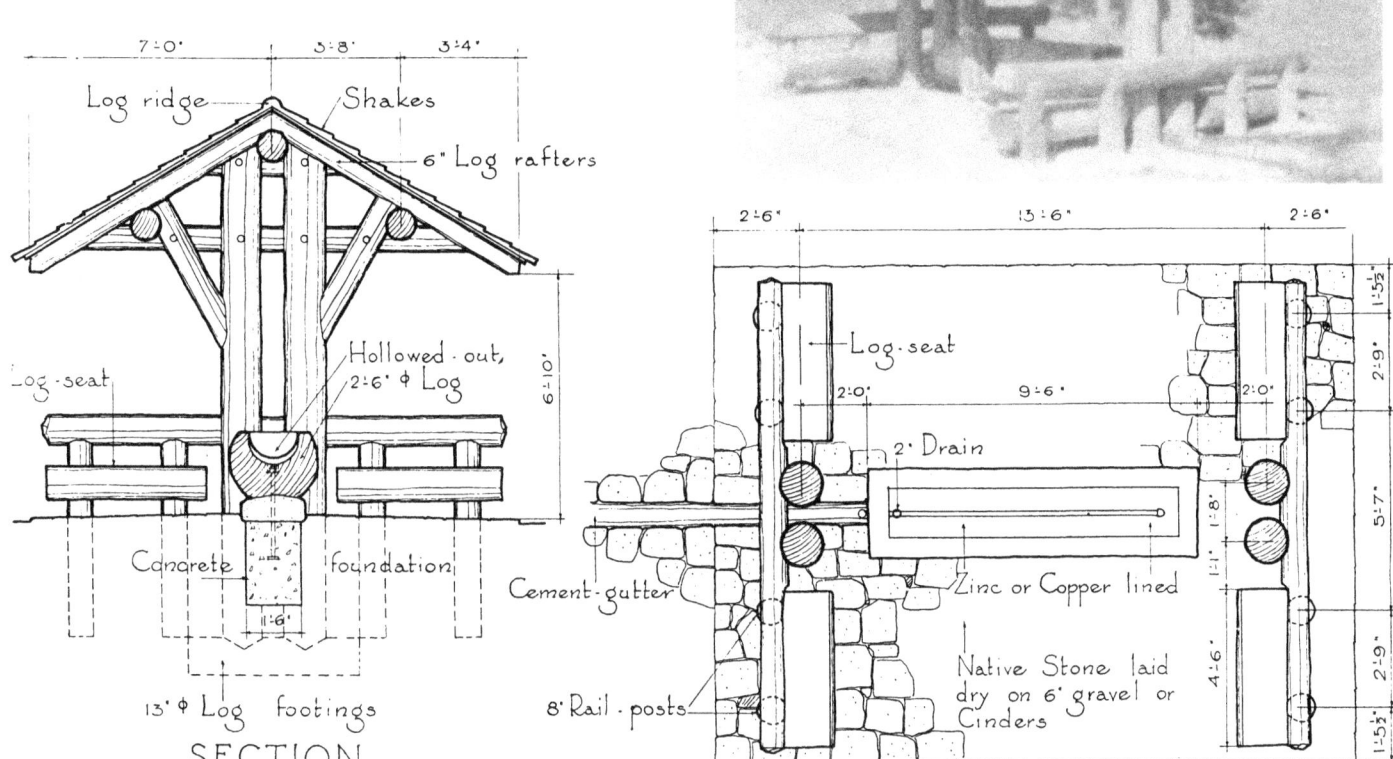

115

DRINKING FOUNTAINS AND WATER SUPPLY

White Pine Forest State Park, Illinois

Willow Springs State Park, Illinois

Starved Rock State Park, Illinois

PUMP AND WELL SHELTERS

The town pump in the open spaces can be variously and agreeably sheltered. Illinois is here represented by three examples which speak with a considerable range of vocabulary. These evidence thoughtful design, the one at upper left having especially pleasing, sturdy proportions. The shelter directly above is roofed with slabs, never a very positive weatherproofing. Below are illustrated a pump shelter in the West and a spring shelter in the East. These may not be strictly representative of standards of scale and proportion generally prevalent in these broad regions and so an odious comparison which might be drawn is not indulged in.

Custer State Park, South Dakota

Lost River State Park, West Virginia

Plate I G–13 — DRINKING FOUNTAINS AND WATER SUPPLY

Pump Shelter – Custer State Park – South Dakota

A shelter altogether amiable except that its rugged timbers put to shame the surrounding tree growth. In this it sets a proper goal for the trees to strive for and attain in due course, and evidences a degree of durability to last out their present embarrassment. Its pleasing proportions and appropriate weather vane merit attention.

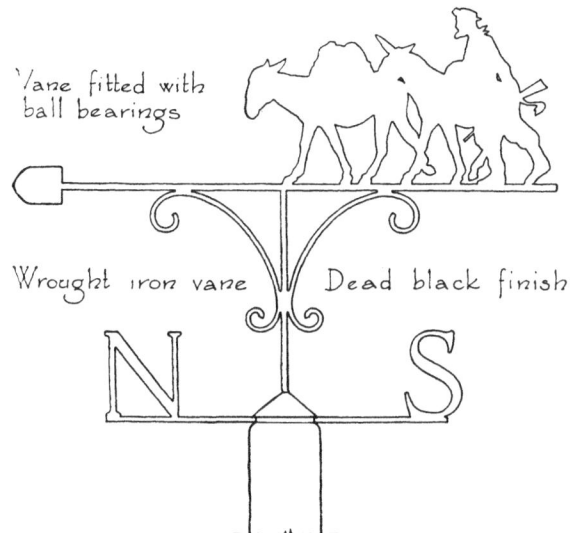

DETAIL OF WEATHER VANE
Scale ¾" = 1'-0"

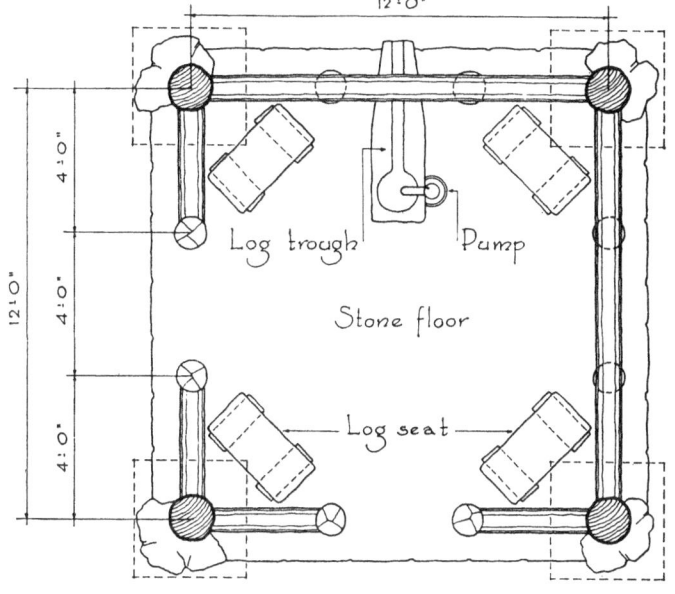

FLOOR PLAN

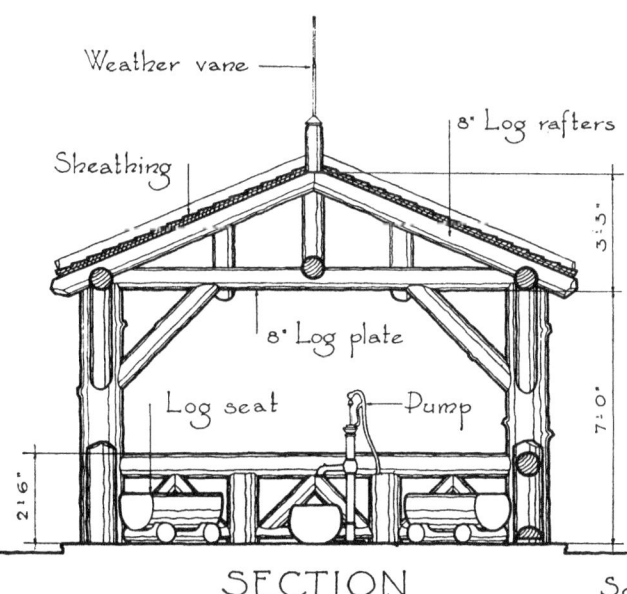

SECTION   Scale ³⁄₁₆" = 1'-0"   ELEVATION

DRINKING FOUNTAINS AND WATER SUPPLY

Plate I G-14

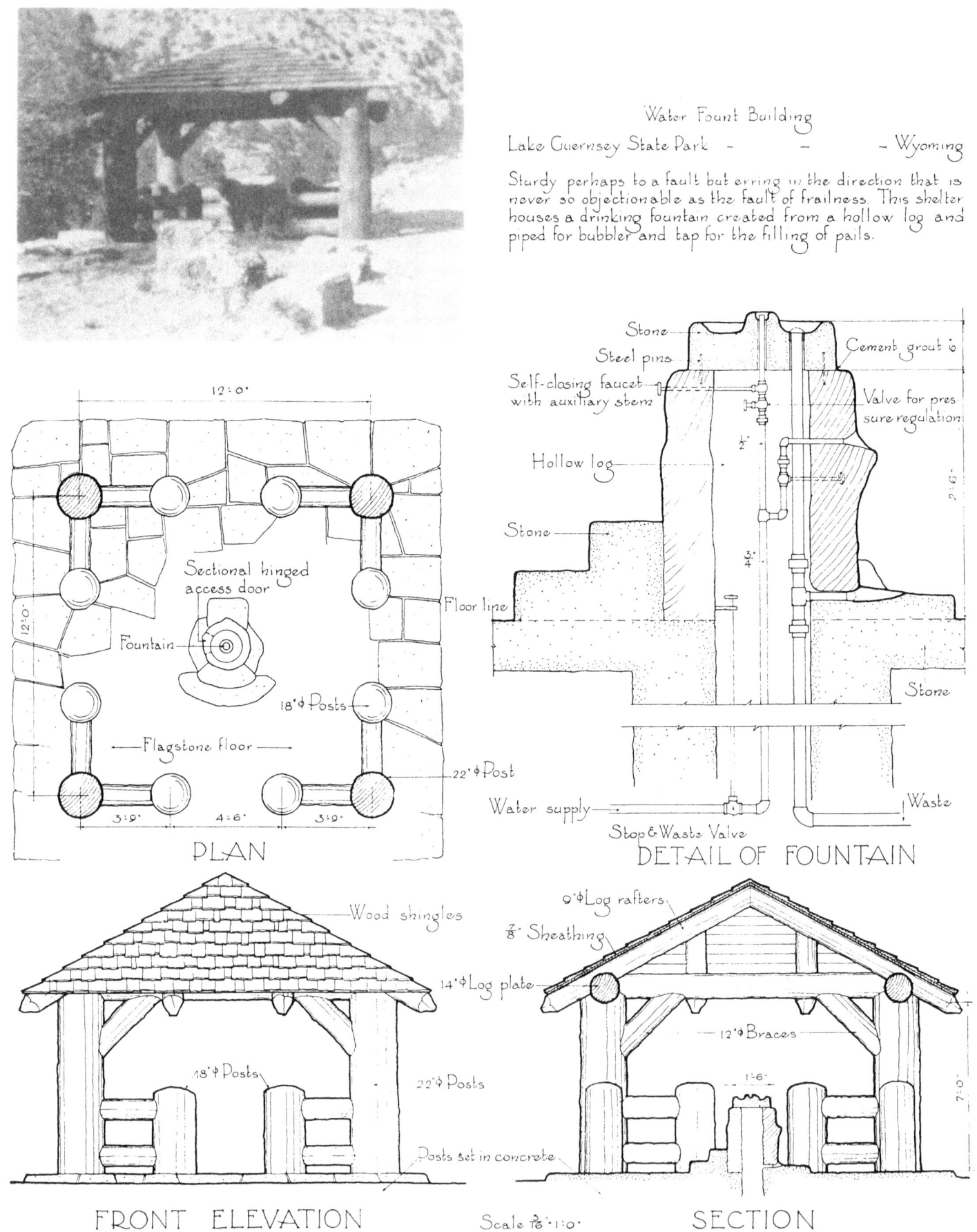

Water Fount Building
Lake Guernsey State Park – – – Wyoming

Sturdy perhaps to a fault but erring in the direction that is never so objectionable as the fault of frailness. This shelter houses a drinking fountain created from a hollow log and piped for bubbler and tap for the filling of pails.

Plate I G–15 ⇢⇢⇢ **DRINKING FOUNTAINS AND WATER SUPPLY**

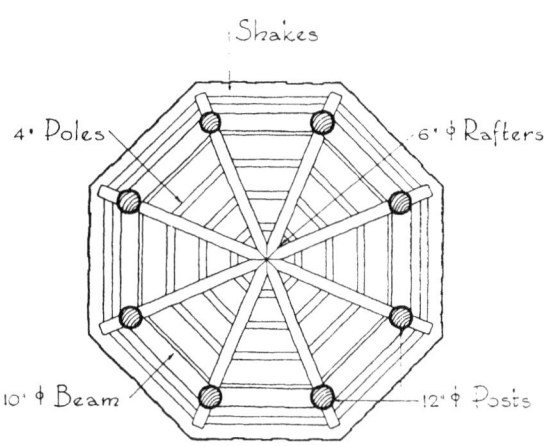

ROOF PLAN

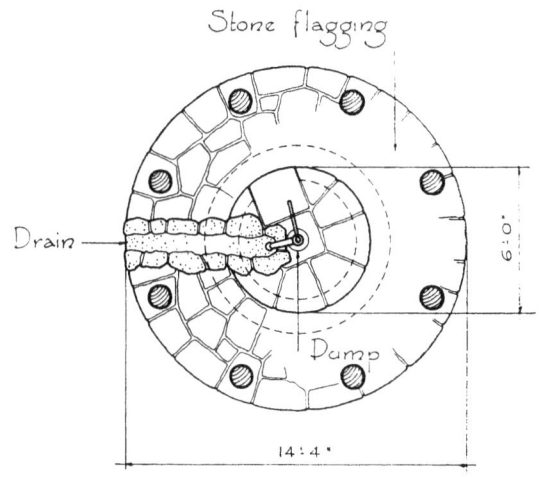

FLOOR PLAN

Pump Shelter — Moran State Park — Washington

To provide shelter at a pump, buildings of octagonal or hexagonal plan have been seldom used, yet seem well adapted to the purpose. The "close-up" of this one is unflattering, cropping as it does its surroundings, which in the actual, seem very much a part of it.

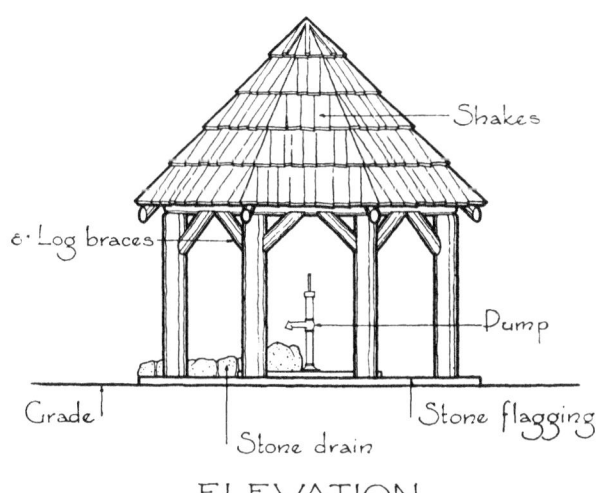

ELEVATION

Scale ⅛"=1'-0"

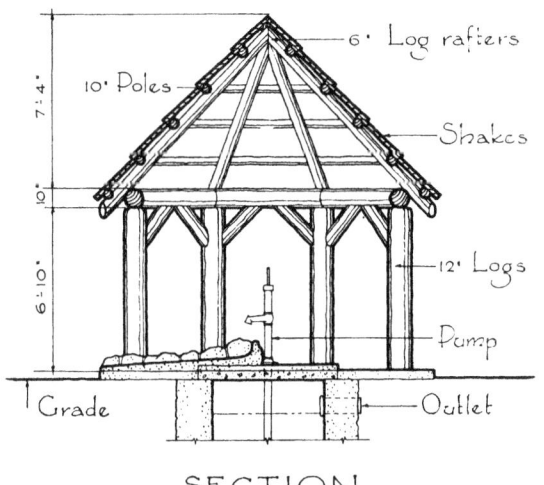

SECTION

119

| DRINKING FOUNTAINS AND WATER SUPPLY | Plate I G–16 |

Spring House, Boyle Metropolitan Park, Little Rock, Arkansas

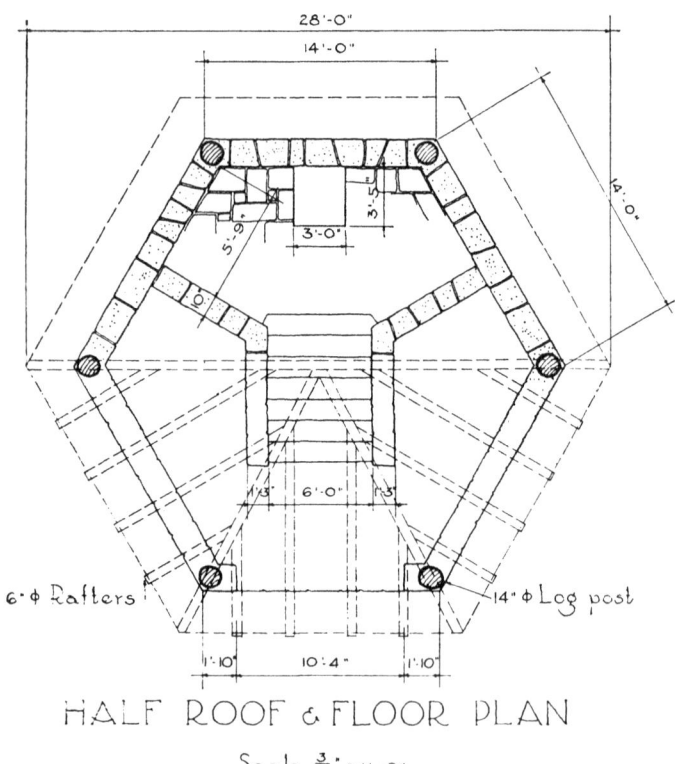

HALF ROOF & FLOOR PLAN
Scale 3/32"=1'-0"

If a rustic structure may ever properly be termed a temple, here is one. A veritable shrine for a woodland spring, this shelter seems in every detail beyond legitimate criticism. Roof texture, "whittled" rafter ends, character of stone work—all combine to render a structural symphony. Even the almost invariably unpleasant perching of a log post upon a built-up rock base does not here seem an offense. There is invitation in the width of the approach and in the well-shaded interior with its short flight of steps down to the level of the spring.

Plate I G–17   ⇢⇢⇢ DRINKING FOUNTAINS AND WATER SUPPLY

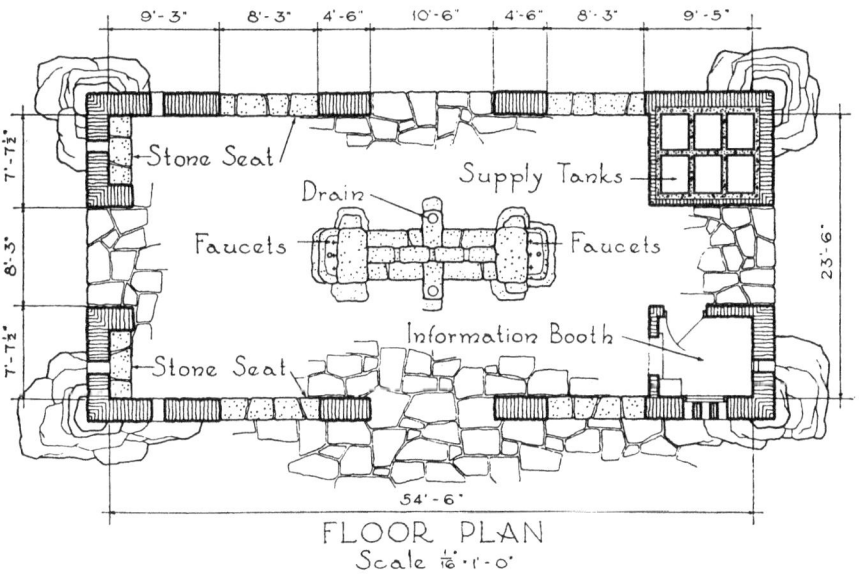

Bromide Pavilion, Platt National Park

Distinctive features of this park are the many springs having mineral properties. This structure shelters a bromide spring. It is something of an outdoor equivalent of the "Pump Room" which at Bath and other watering places in the England of Beau Brummel was a foregathering place of great social importance. This pavilion gives onto a terrace which looks out over a sunken area centered by a formal pool and surrounded by the benches, seen in the illustration.

DRINKING FOUNTAINS AND WATER SUPPLY   Plate I G–18

Pump House — Lake Murray State Park — Oklahoma

A characterful little building that makes a strong case for the proposition that the most minor facilities in parks are deserving of great pains in designing and executing. If the pump house of utterly prosaic purpose can suggest with a decent restraint the habitation of the Three Bears, or the Big Bad Wolf, why not? The pleasant gesture does not hamper its practicability, as witness the hatch for the pulling of the well casing.

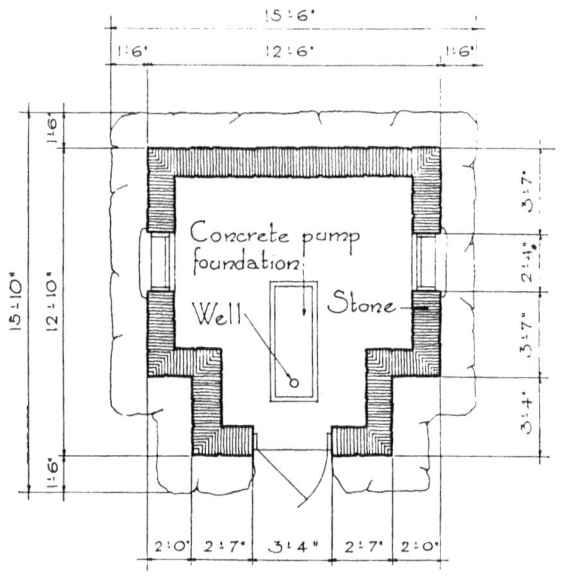

FLOOR PLAN

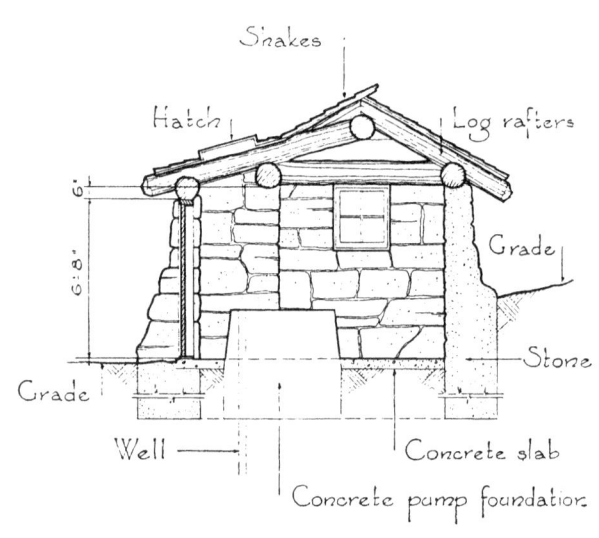

SECTION

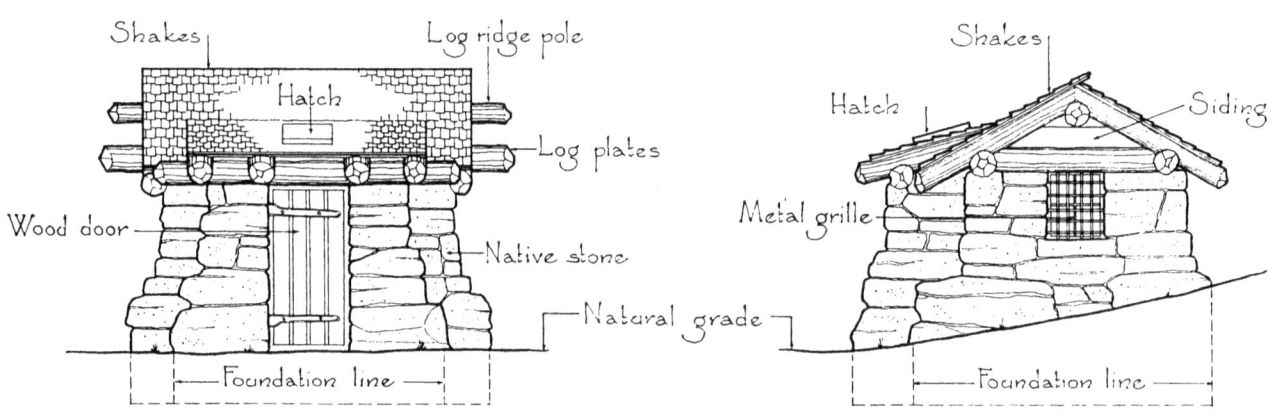

FRONT ELEVATION   Scale ⅛"=1'-0"   SIDE ELEVATION

122

Plate I G–19   ⇛ DRINKING FOUNTAINS AND WATER SUPPLY

This little structure will benefit greatly in appearance by the rising waters of a created lake from which the water supply will be drawn. The lake level will climb halfway up its spread foundation and much improve its proportions. Readers are asked to visualize this change in appraising the building with a critical eye. This pumphouse and the one shown directly below relate definitely, in an architectural sense, to the Lake Murray pumphouse detailed on the facing page.

Pumphouse, Devil's Den State Park, Arkansas

The bulk and picturesqueness of this pumphouse result from the provision of settling basins, roofed over by the wing to the right. The vigorous scale of the masonry and roof timbers and the thick and raggedly coursed shakes of the roof effect a harmony in which no false note is to be detected. The main portion of the building, as the hatch visible in the roof suggests, houses the pumping machinery.

Pumphouse, Robbers Cave State Park, Oklahoma

In character this structure stands at some point between the heavy rusticity of the pumphouses we have just seen and the more finished building of similar purpose delineated on the following page. Here there is unmistakable suggestion of ancient minor farm buildings in Italy, probably not consciously sought, and if unwarranted as precedent for a structure in our parks, nevertheless far from unpleasant.

Pumphouse, Pere Marquette State Park, Illinois

123

DRINKING FOUNTAINS AND WATER SUPPLY

Plate I G—20

Pump House — — Wilderness State Park — — Michigan

This little building succeeds in being at once completely practical and extraordinarily attractive. This, in a few words, defines the objective so consciously pursued in most pretentious park structures, and very often achieved, probably with a certain casualness, in the minor ones. Practicability is evident in the wide doorway and in the lean-to roof detached from the main roof and readily removable whenever the well casing must be pulled for repairs.

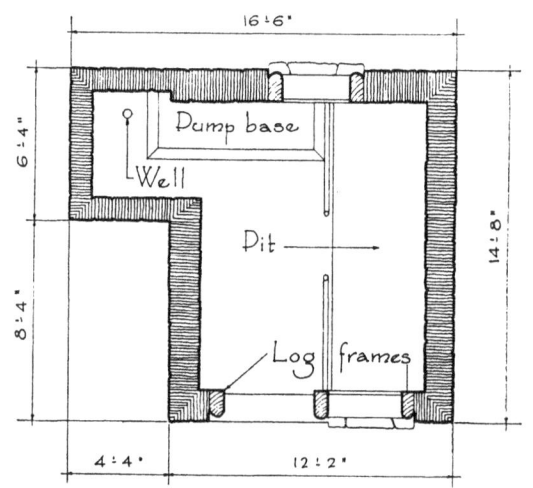

FLOOR PLAN

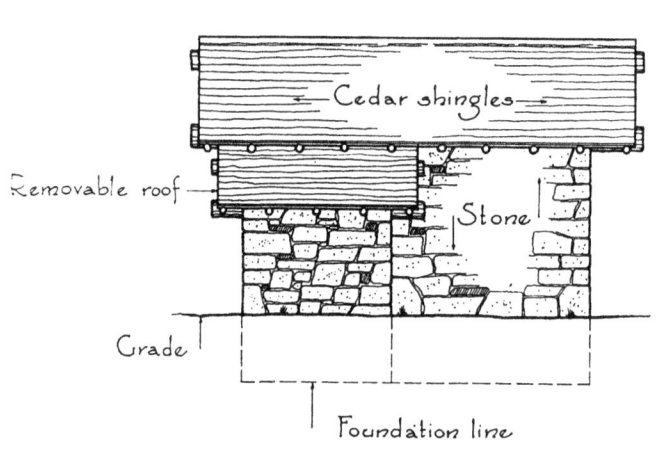

SIDE ELEVATION

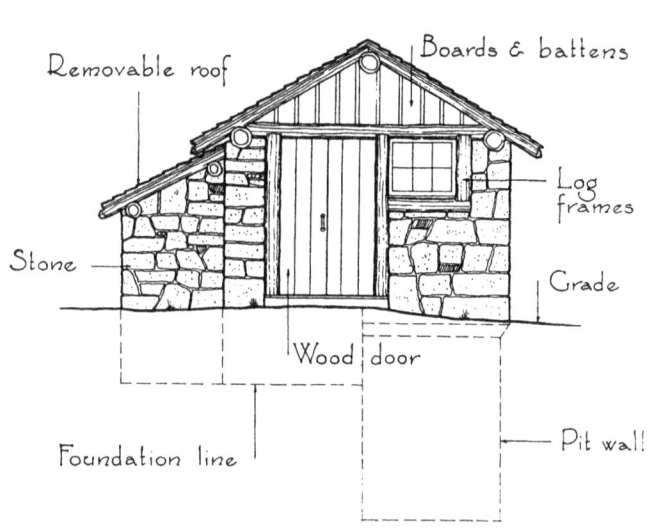

FRONT ELEVATION

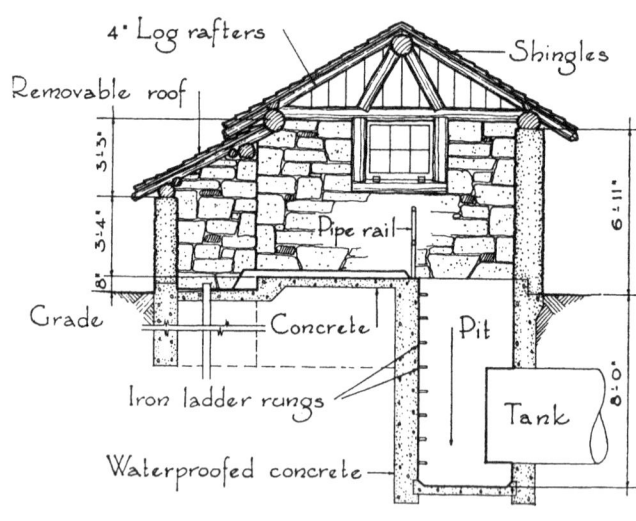

SECTION

Scale ⅛" = 1'-0"

124

Plate I G–21   ⇛ DRINKING FOUNTAINS AND WATER SUPPLY

Water Tank - Mt. Nebo State Park - Arkansas

A structure of practical purpose, which, satisfied to parade its function forthrightly, quite satisfies us. Here is no mistaken urge to appear a ruined watchtower, -- no overweening affectation of being some more aesthetic something which it is not. All honor to the greater glory of beauty so openly and honestly arrived at.

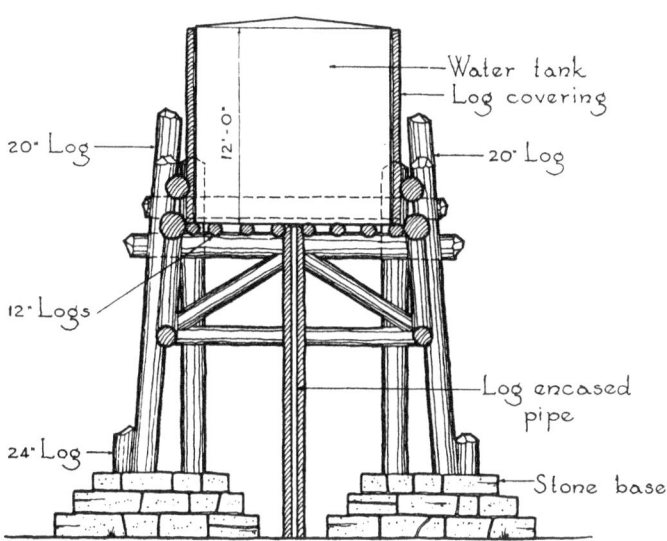

SECTION

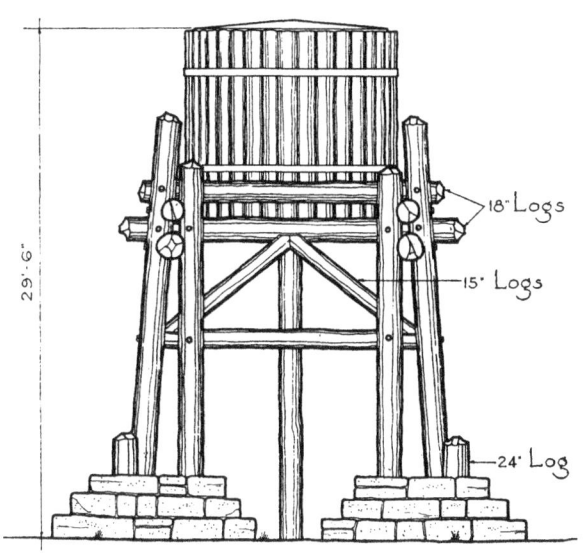

ELEVATION

PLAN

Scale ⅜" = 1'–0"

125

DRINKING FOUNTAINS AND WATER SUPPLY

Plate I G–22

Pump House   Bonham State Park   Texas

Elevated water tank and shelter for a pump are combined in this attractive building. There is definite character to the masonry, with its variety of unit sizes and deeply raked joints, and to the board and batten construction by reason of the heavy battens. This character persists in other structures at Bonham, as witness the boathouse, bathhouse and entrance pylon, elsewhere illustrated.

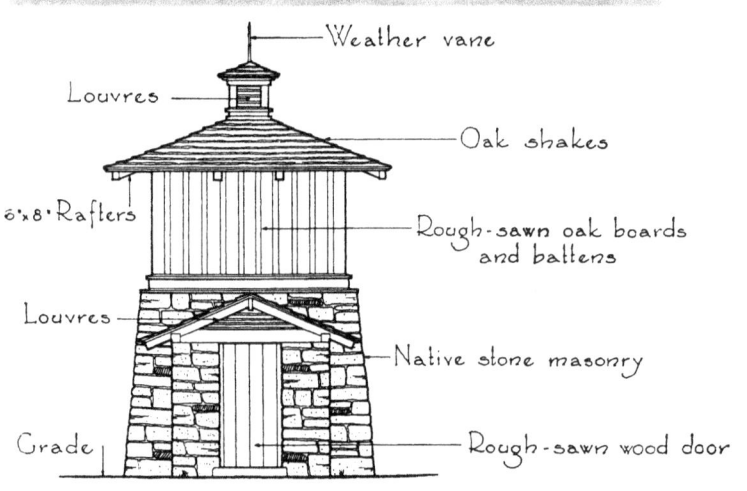

ELEVATION

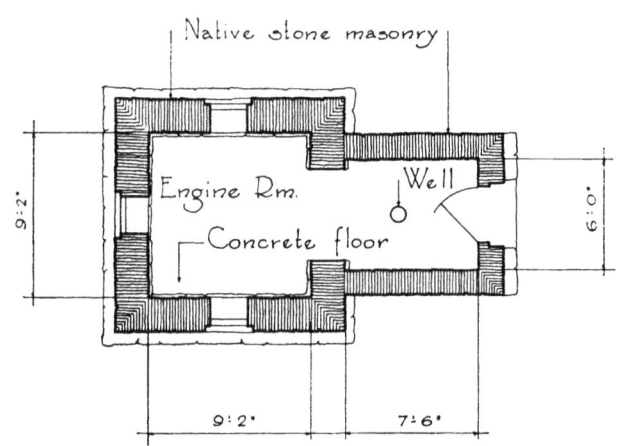

FLOOR PLAN

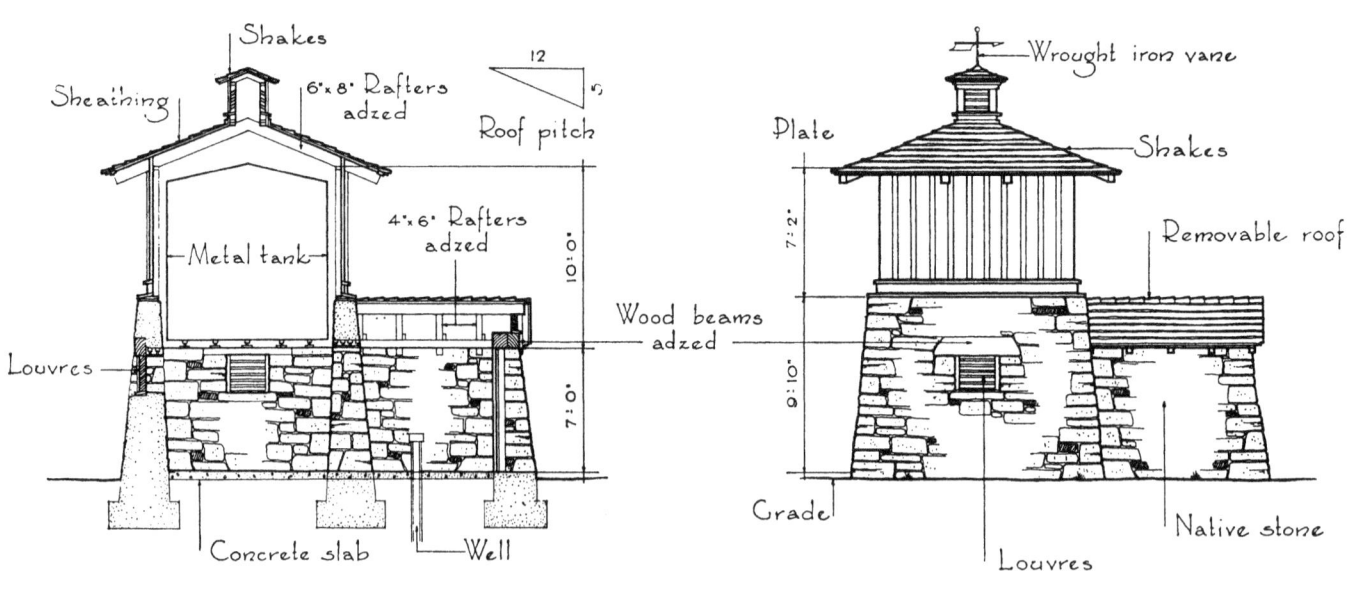

SECTION   Scale 3/32"=1'-0"   ELEVATION

Plate I G–23 — DRINKING FOUNTAINS AND WATER SUPPLY

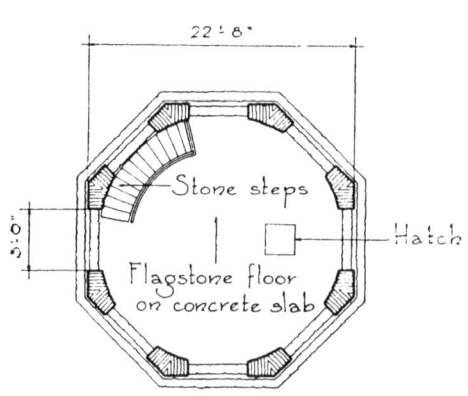

PLAN AT LOOKOUT

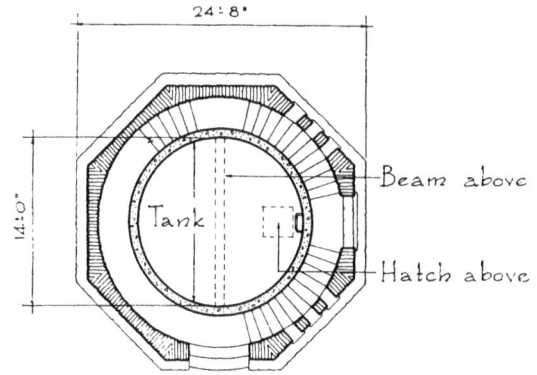

PLAN AT TANK
Scale ⅛" = 1'0"

Observation Tower – Lake Taghkanic State Park – New York

The case for combining in one structure a required elevated storage tank and a desired elevated observation point has been stated. Here is an exhibit in support of it.

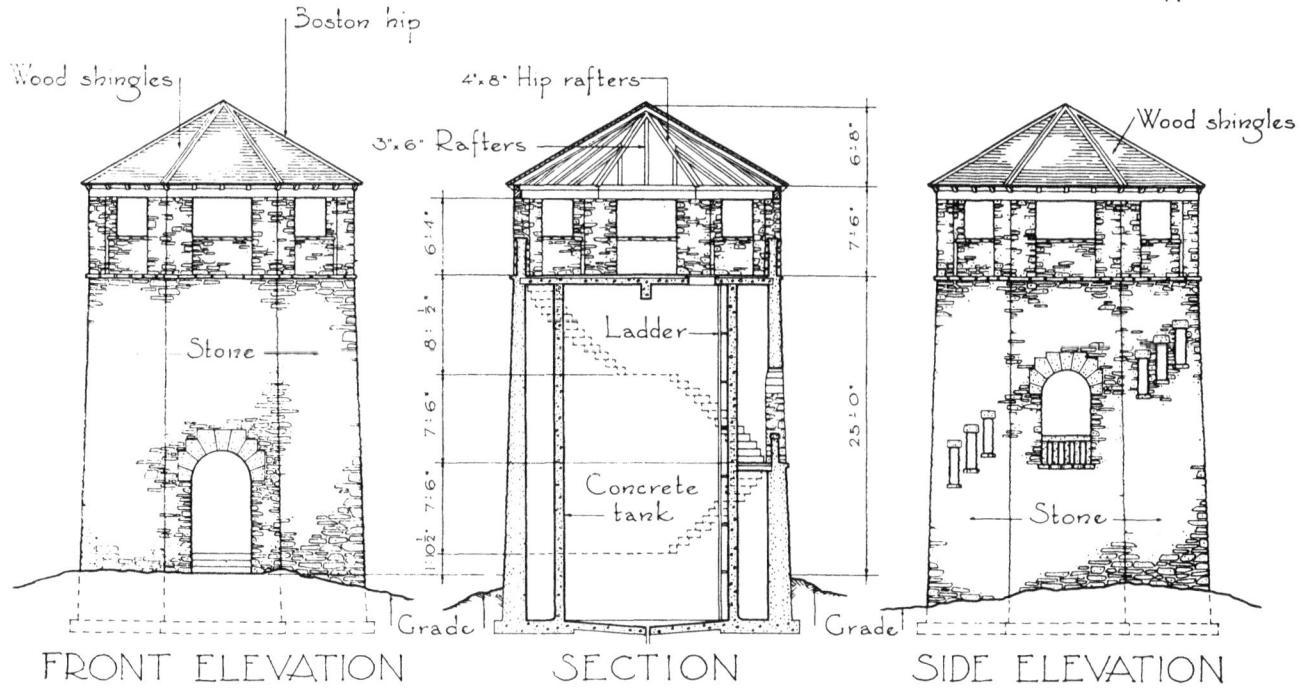

FRONT ELEVATION SECTION SIDE ELEVATION

DRINKING FOUNTAINS AND WATER SUPPLY   Plate I G–24

Crowley's Ridge State Park, Arkansas

Lake Murray State Park, Oklahoma

WATER TOWERS

Above, a water storage tank enclosed by rock wall so well blended to rocky site as to constitute something of a puzzle and suggest a "Find the Water Tower!" caption. Below, a more revealing rendering of masonry enclosure. Both provide lookout platforms, reached by outside stairways. At the left, two wood-framed towers of greater elevation and of contrasting exterior treatments. It should be realized that the vertical slab surfaces of the Palmetto State Park tower do not assume to appear the structural support, but rather the curtain enclosure, of the trussed timber structural frame.

Palmetto State Park, Texas

Mother Neff State Park, Texas

128

COMFORT STATIONS AND PRIVIES

IT IS GENERALLY CONCEDED that toilets are the most necessary among structures built in natural parks, and that if only safe water and proper toilets are provided in these areas, the essentials of development have been accomplished. It has even been said that those who will not lead the field in proper sanitation should get out of it and allow those who are "not ashamed to be proud of their toilet buildings" to take over.

In general usage any distinction between "comfort station" and "privy" may be merely one of gentility of phrase. Within this discussion, and perhaps more generally distinguishing than is assumed, "comfort station" applies to buildings equipped with flush toilet facilities and "privy" to those equipped with nonflush toilet facilities.

It is elected herein to consider the more modern comfort station at greater length than the more primitive privy. The former, for the higher standard of sanitation it provides, is the unqualified recommendation of the National Park Service and the great majority of public health agencies for all park toilets wherever conditions, physical and economic, make its adoption possible. This recommendation embraces a positive sewage disposal by natural processes, and decries, along with the pit toilet, treatment by chemical processes alone. The chemical sterilization of effluent, it should be understood, is quite another matter. Such is often desirable subsequent to a sewage disposal treatment by bacterial action.

For those who may be concerned with the details of sanitation in respect to park toilets, the National Park Service Engineering Manual, Part 700—Sewage Disposal, is cited.

If the comfort station is located in an area subject to freezing temperatures, and if at such times it will not be heated, provision must be made for completely draining all piping and fixtures. Whether or not to make a comfort station suitable for operation during freezing winter weather depends largely on the volume of use, and the economics of each case is an individual problem. Sometimes limited winter use of such areas makes more reasonable the provision of temporary chemical toilets during those periods when a flush toilet must be drained or heated. Under such conditions it will probably be more satisfactory to erect small portable pit privies as discussed in the Manual of Engineering Design previously referred to.

In the park toilet building we have another facility not to be taken seriously as a landscape or architectural feature until every demand for sanitation and practical need has been properly met. Any economy in fulfilment of these primary requirements makes absurd any indulgence of a too impetuous urge to dress up the structure. The comfort station not a part of a building housing other park facilities is very properly so subordinated by location that there is little reason for embellishing it structurally. Preferable and usually more effective alternative is to screen both building and approach to it by planting and careful choice of site. The comfort station is often incorporated in a park building which combines other park needs. Linked up with a shelter or concession building, or as part of a multiple use building designated as administration, it is forced to a certain elaborateness of dress that, as a half-hidden separate entity, it does not require.

When comfort stations are a part of buildings housing several facilities, it is generally desirable that direct outside entrance to them be provided in addition to any inside communication. Some park patrons may feel reluctant to make use of toilets requiring approach through what may not be conspicuously enough a public space. Access to comfort stations through a lodge or concession might imply availability only to guests or patrons of these. If intended for free use by the general public, there should be no confusing of the fact of accessibility.

COMFORT STATIONS AND PRIVIES

The paramount practical need of proper sanitation implies first of all thorough knowledge of, and strict compliance with, all laws, ordinances, and other regulatory provisions of governing and jurisdictional agencies. Beyond these are other practical and aesthetic considerations which may not be disregarded. The importance of smooth and impervious materials for floors, walls, partitions, and other such interior surfaces is not to be minimized. Funds tend to be scant enough for the maintenance of readily cleaned and durable materials, and are certainly hopelessly less than adequate for the upkeep of materials without such merits. Ease of cleaning will determine the degree of cleanliness that will prevail over the long run. In consequence, any conscious effort at rusticity in suiting the exterior of the comfort station to park environment should be just as consciously forsworn on the interior. Equipment and materials conforming to present day standards of sanitation should be adopted for all interior details.

In the case of the comfort station there is obvious saving in cost to result from grouping men's and women's toilet rooms under one roof. When the facilities are of the privy type, separate structures for the sexes can be built at but little greater cost, and this is recommended. Privies are apt to be less soundly constructed than comfort stations; therefore, greater distance between the men's and women's toilets is desirable.

When comfort stations or privies serve both sexes under one roof, the arrangement of the separate entrances so that each section is suitably remote from the other is important. If on opposite sides of the building, the maximum in desirable separation of the approaches of course results. The approaches and entrances should be clearly marked. A substantial soundproof partition should completely separate the two toilet rooms, and in the case of pit privies there should be complete separation of the vaults serving the men's and women's sections. Unless vestibule and properly swinging door break the sight lines into the toilet rooms, an effective exterior sight barrier in the nature of a wall, trellis, or stockade must be provided to screen the entrance opening.

Toilet buildings, whether comfort stations or privies, must be well lighted and ventilated, and properly protected from the weather. Windows should be placed above the eye level for privacy. When not so placed, and obscure window glass is resorted to instead, the windows can often be opened in summer only with sacrifice of privacy, or remain closed at a sacrifice of ventilation. Windows should so operate that it is possible to equip them with insect screens on the outside. A most practical toilet room window is hinged at the bottom to open inward with chain fastening, which gives some measure of protection against rain, wind, and snow, while providing continuous ventilation and opportunity for a screen on the outside. In milder climates, and elsewhere when winter use is not intended, there is a current tendency to make use of louvres rather than windows. These give a desirable maximum of ventilation, and may also be screened as effectively as windows against insects. However, unless louvred openings are very generously provided, the rooms are apt to be insufficiently lighted. Because ample light and ventilation are prerequisite to a clean and well-maintained room and go far to curb abuse by the using public, an abundance of window or louvred area is to be sought.

Doors to toilet rooms should always be self-closing, by the employment of a high-quality door-closer if possible, or failing this, a less costly but positive substitute device. If window or other openings are screened, door openings should, of course, be fitted with screen doors. The ventilation in summer will be greatly helped. All screening in equipment of toilet rooms must be at least 14 wires to the inch, and preferably finer. While galvanized or black-enameled wire-cloth is satisfactory for the more temporary buildings, bronze or copper employed for permanent structures will, by its longer life, more than offset the greater initial cost involved.

Readers scanning the drawings which follow are reminded to view these only through an architectural lens. Bifocal exploration seeking also details of sanitation will by intent prove unrewarding.

Plate I H-1 — COMFORT STATIONS AND PRIVIES

Privy — Mt. Tamalpais State Park — California

An unpretentious housing of toilet facilities that, with the benefit of properly retired location, would not be unsuitable in parks over a wide area. Its simple exterior is free of strictly regional characteristics. It can be built at small cost and is not unsightly. The wide overhang of the roof shelters the ventilation openings but makes for a dark interior where other light admission is as limited as here.

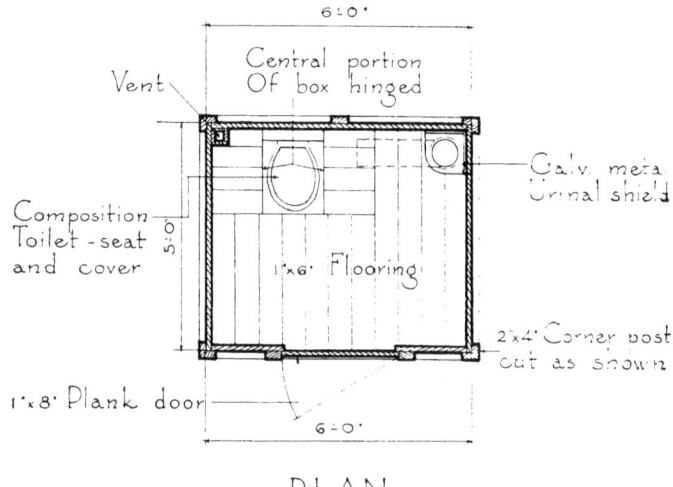

PLAN

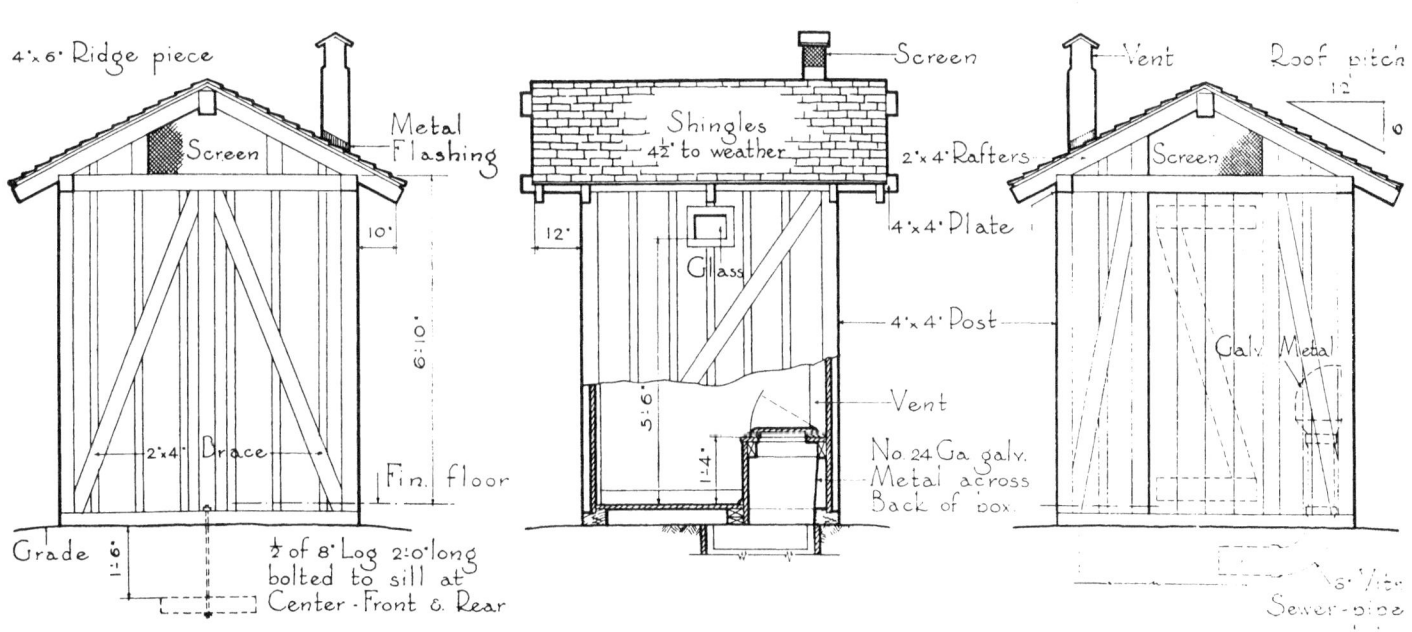

REAR ELEVATION   SIDE ELEVATION   FRONT ELEVATION
Scale ¼" = 1'-0"

131

COMFORT STATIONS AND PRIVIES

Plate I H-2

Privy
Egg Harbor River Parkway – Camden County – New Jersey

This privy is so unassuming and decorous in its externals as hardly to be an offense in any location, retired or not. It is the simplest expression of the type which allows direct outside entrance to each toilet stall, and might be expanded indefinitely to include more than the two stalls here shown. The screening of the doors by lattice is a desirable feature. The trim cornice is especially appropriate to so small a building.

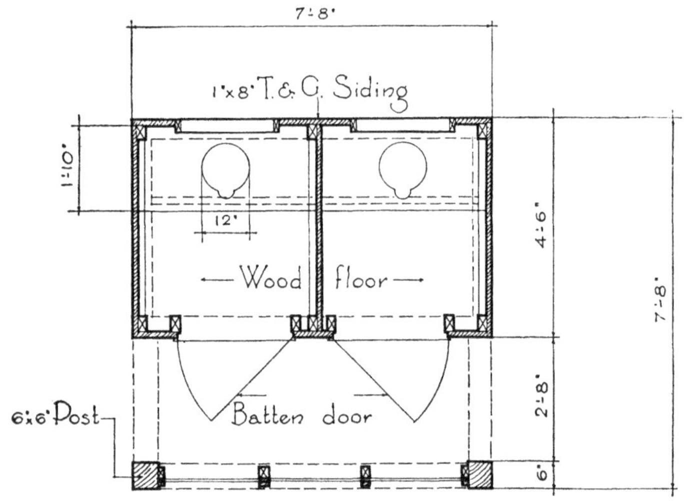

PLAN

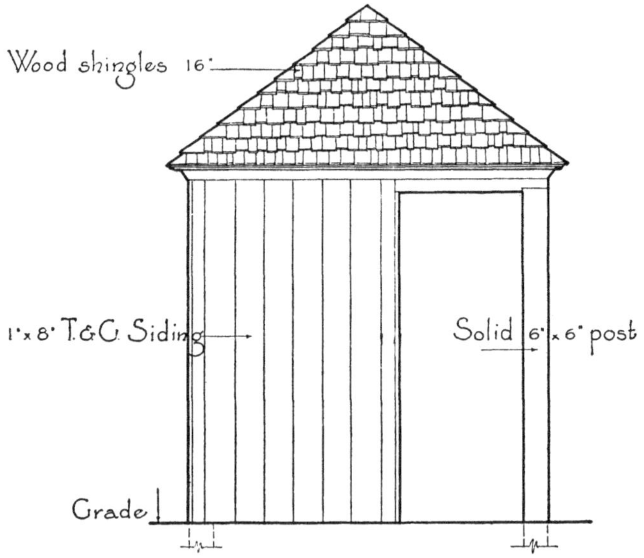

SIDE ELEVATION

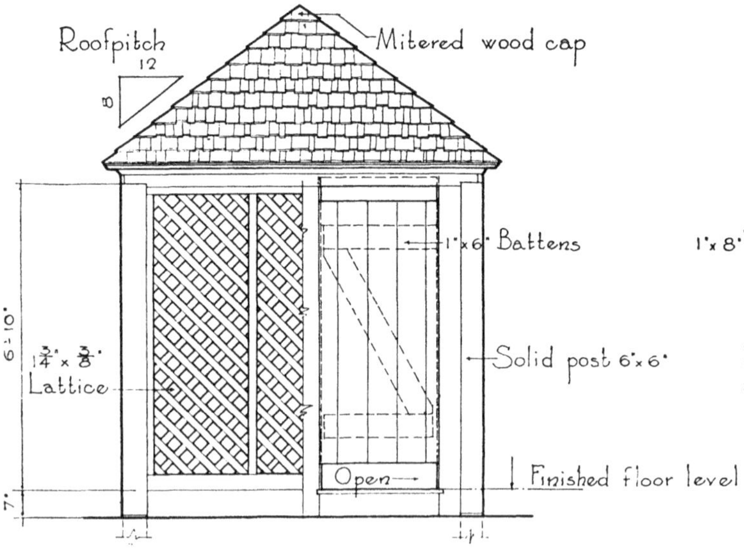

FRONT ELEVATION

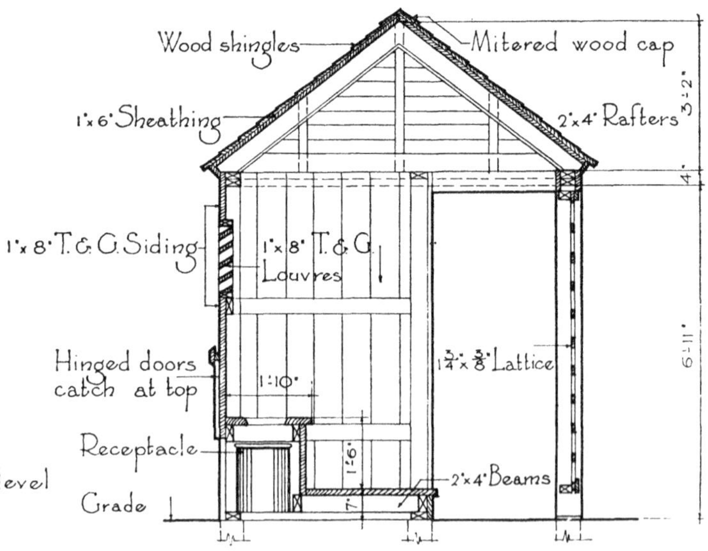

Scale ¼" : 1'0"

SECTION

Plate I H-3 — COMFORT STATIONS AND PRIVIES

Privy — Marseilles State Park — Illinois

In connection with a picnic area which must be shifted periodically for purposes of recuperating a wornout site, a toilet facility on skids capable of being moved readily is of great practical advantage. The construction of slabs applied vertically over sheathing boards is one that gestures in the direction of pioneer woodcraft character at economical cost. The entrance door is well-screened by the stockade barrier.

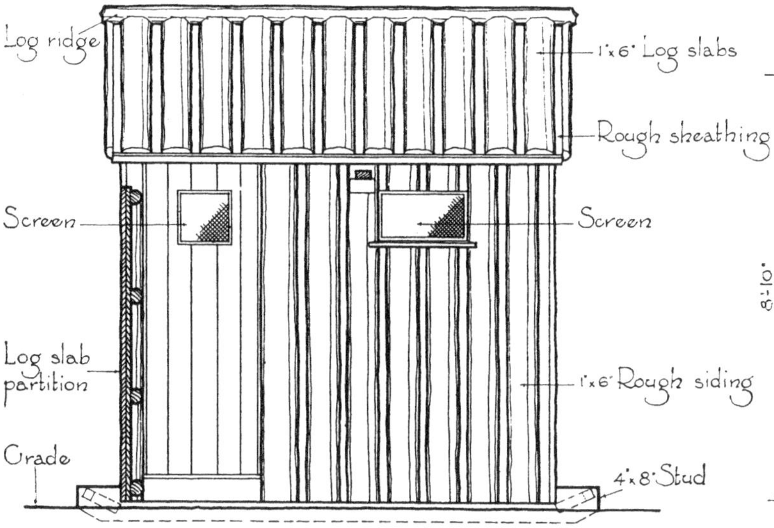

FRONT ELEVATION

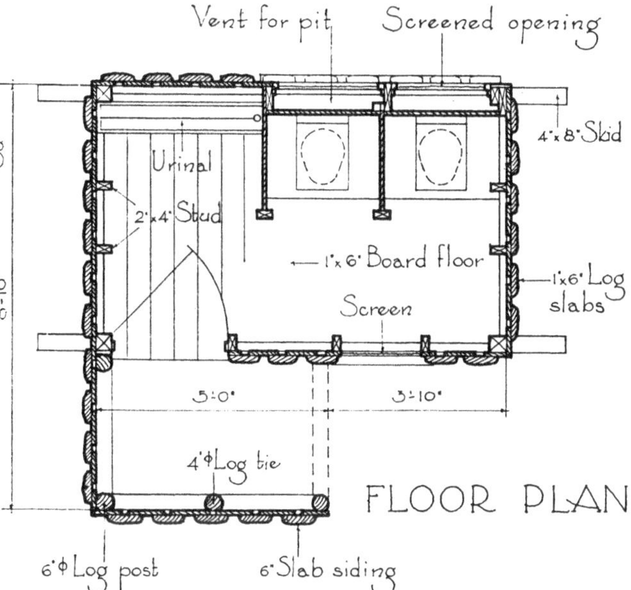

FLOOR PLAN

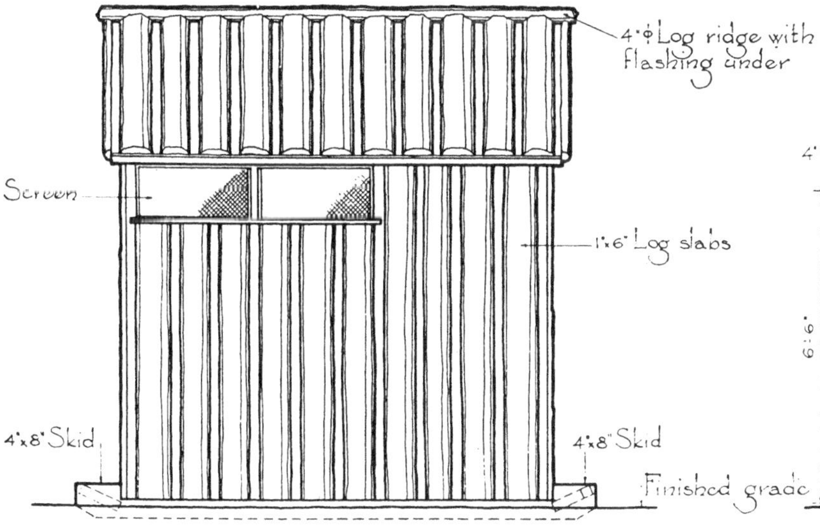

REAR ELEVATION

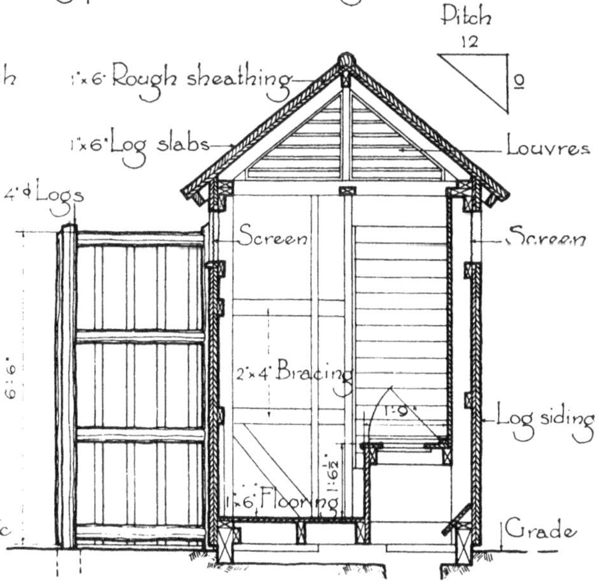

SECTION

Scale ¼" = 1'-0"

133

COMFORT STATIONS AND PRIVIES

Plate I H-4

Privy   Devil's Den State Park   Arkansas

Certain unpretentious park structures, it will be observed, have a definite woods character -- a homespun propriety -- difficult to analyze. Here is one.

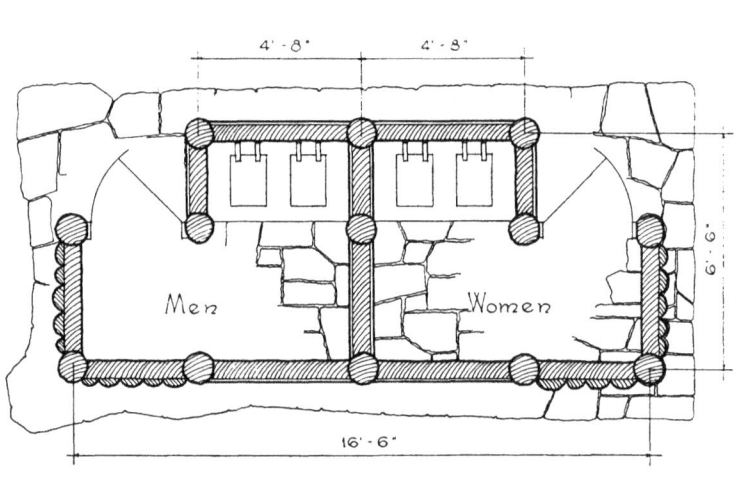

PLAN   SECTION

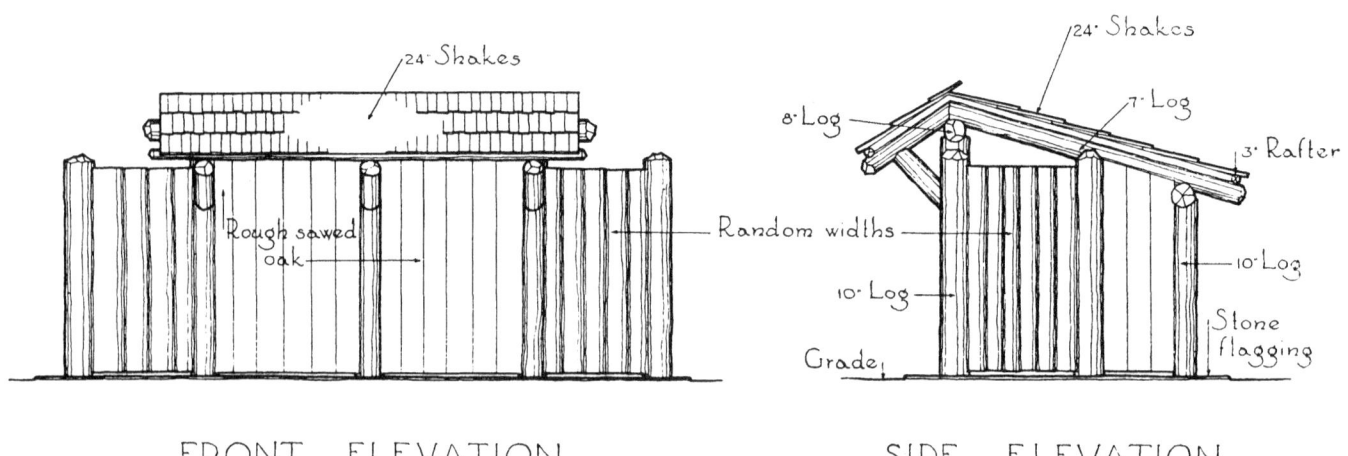

FRONT ELEVATION   SIDE ELEVATION

Scale $\frac{3}{16}$ = 1'-0"

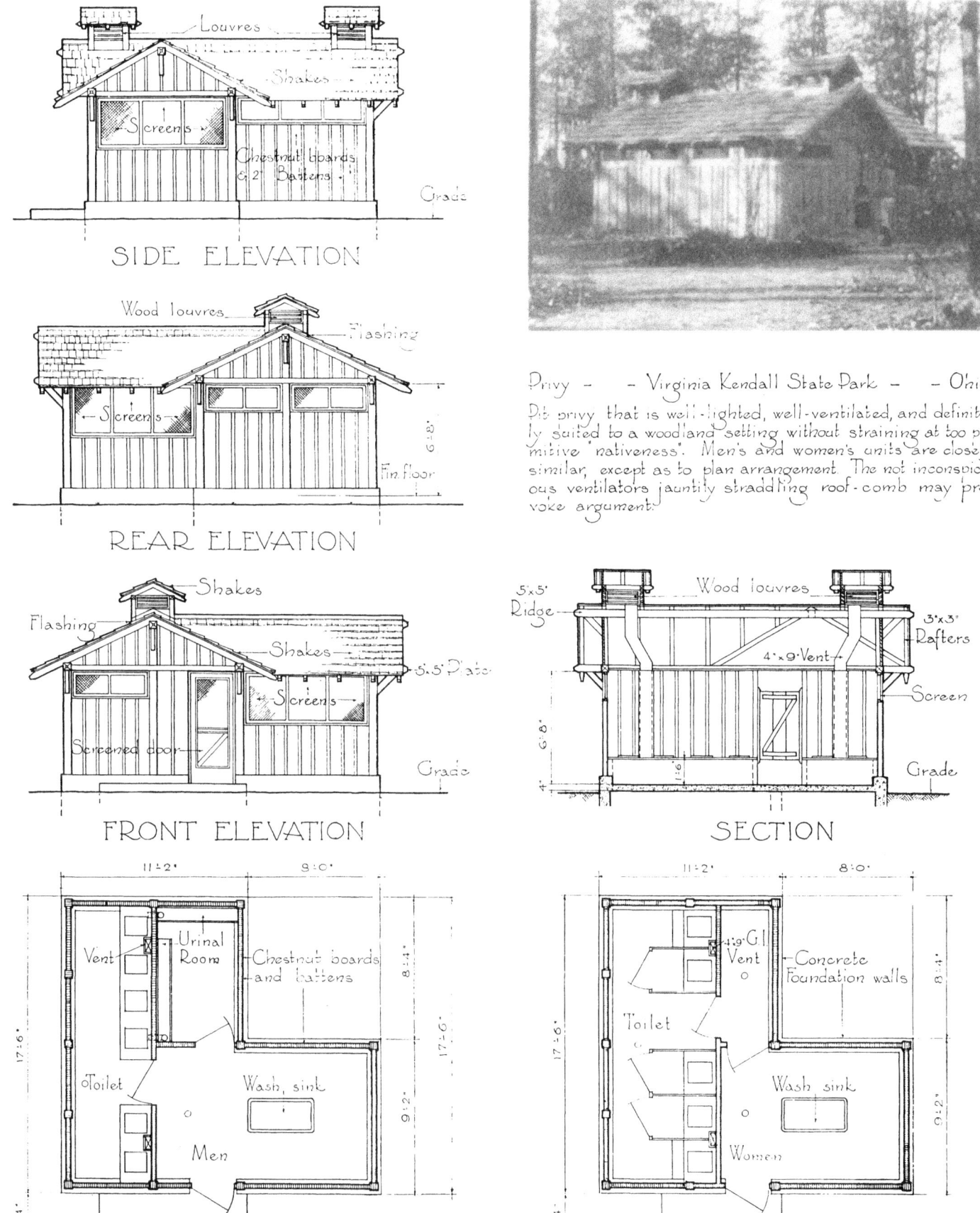

Privy - - Virginia Kendall State Park - - Ohio.
Pit privy that is well-lighted, well-ventilated, and definitely suited to a woodland setting without straining at too primitive "nativeness". Men's and women's units are closely similar, except as to plan arrangement. The not inconspicuous ventilators jauntily straddling roof-comb may provoke argument.

COMFORT STATIONS AND PRIVIES

Plate I H-6

Privy — Mt. Penn Park — Reading, Pennsylvania

An utterly simple and sightly provision of a basic facility, that can be scrapped without great capital loss whenever flush toilets and lavatories in a more permanent structure are possible on the area.

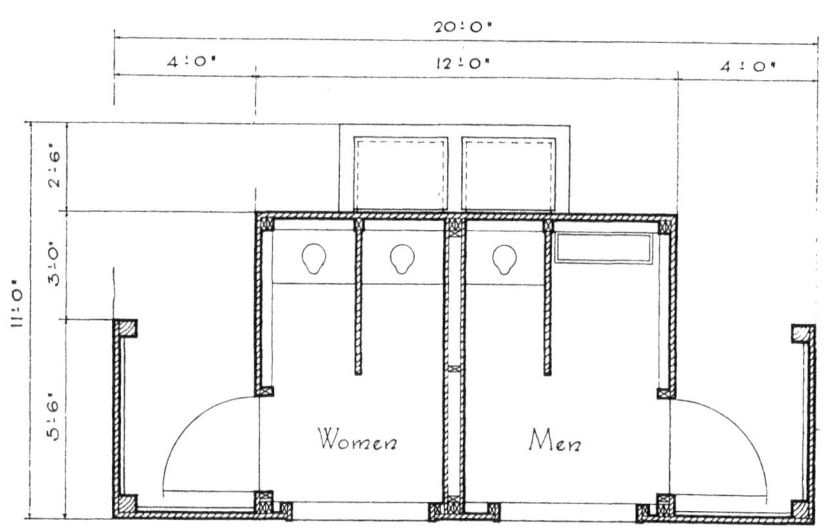

FLOOR PLAN

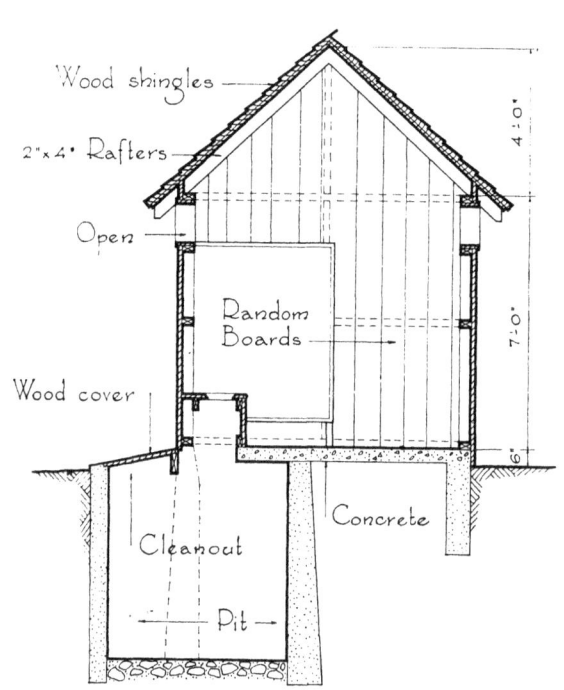

SECTION

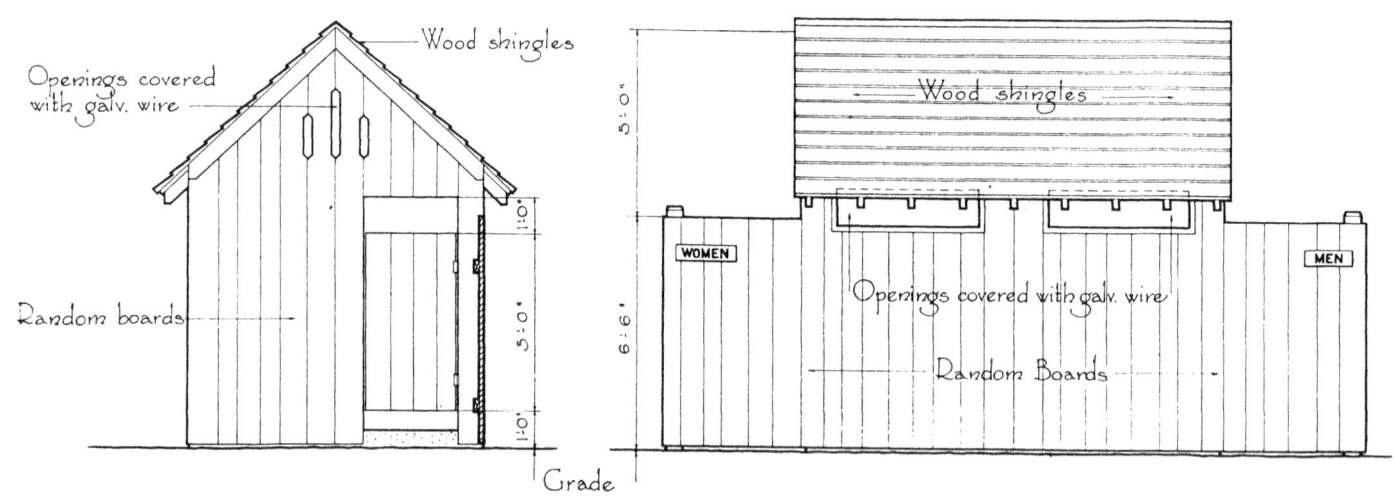

SIDE ELEVATION   Scale 3/16" = 1'0"   FRONT ELEVATION

136

Plate I H-7 >>> COMFORT STATIONS AND PRIVIES

Comfort Station
Humboldt Redwoods State Park - - - California

A one-seat comfort station retaining the simple exterior contrived from minimum materials more usual in the privy. Elaboration has made its appearance where it properly should - - the more positive sanitation offered by a flush toilet fixture. The men's and women's toilets are identical spaced about twenty-five feet apart

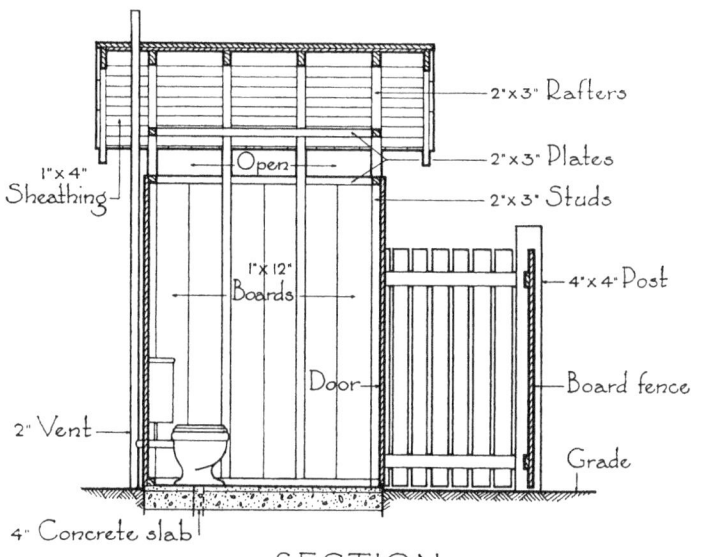

SECTION

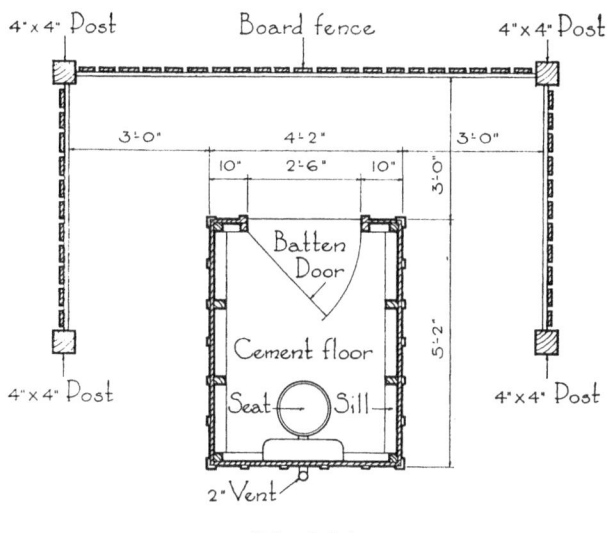

PLAN

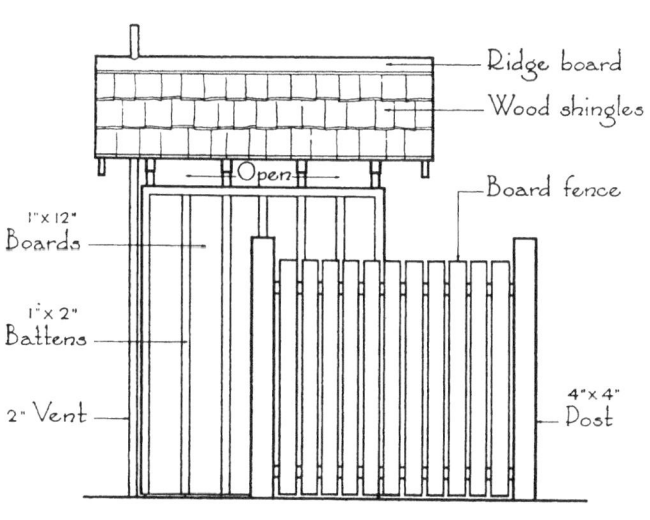

SIDE ELEVATION

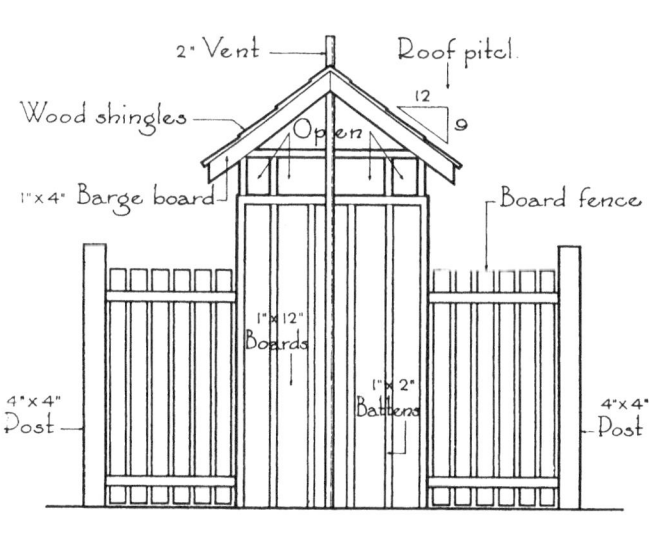

REAR ELEVATION

Scale ¼"=1'-0"

137

COMFORT STATIONS AND PRIVIES

Plate I H-8

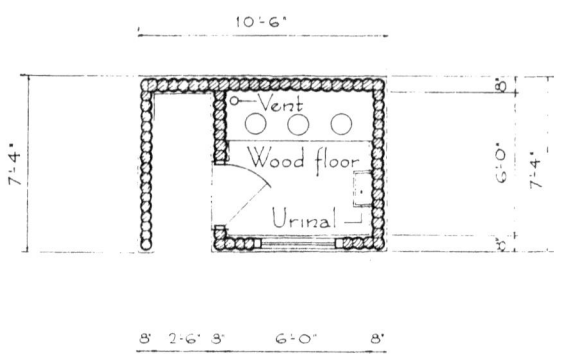

Coos Head Metropolitan Park – Oregon

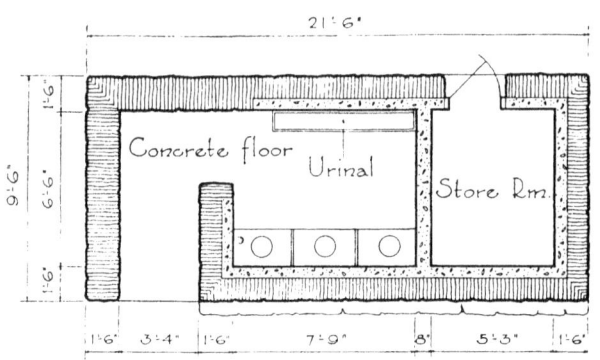

Mohansic Reservation – Westchester County – New York

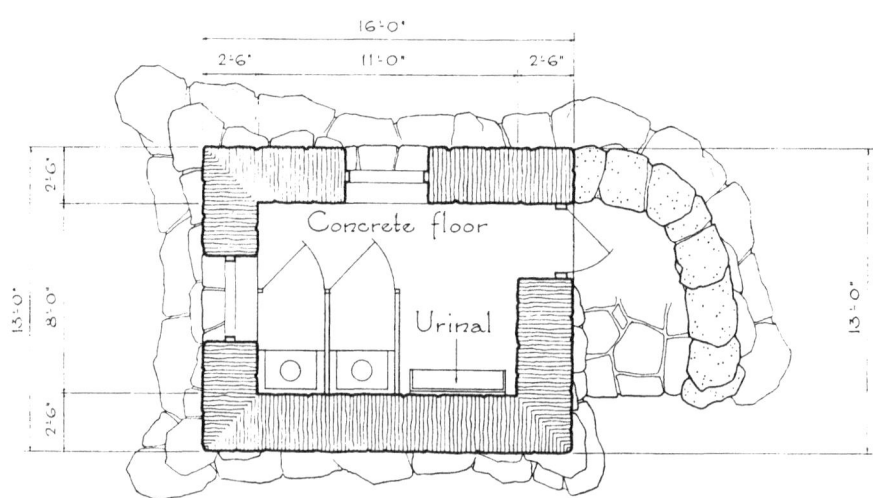

Boyle Metropolitan Park – Arkansas

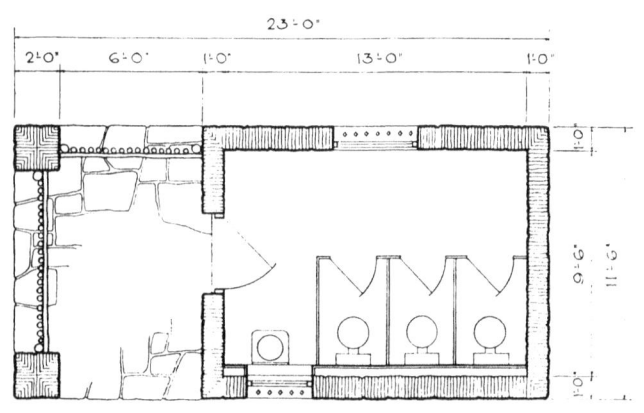

Santa Rosa County Park – California

Woahink Lake State Park – Oregon

Scale ⅛" = 1'-0"

Plate I H-9 ⇒⇒ COMFORT STATIONS AND PRIVIES

Coos Head Metropolitan Park, Oregon

Mohansic County Reservation, New York

TOILET STRUCTURES FOR SINGLE SEX

The plans on the facing page indicate the housing of toilet facilities for the sexes in separate buildings, probably less usual than a single building with two well-separated sections. The latter arrangement in general characterizes the toilet buildings shown on the following pages. Fixtures here range from the primitive to the flush type. There is just as wide variation in the construction materials employed and in the degree of rusticity these produce. Three of the structures have open gable ends to provide abundant light and ventilation.

Boyle Metropolitan Park, Little Rock, Arkansas

Santa Rosa County Park, California

Woahink Lake State Park, Oregon

COMFORT STATIONS AND PRIVIES

Plate I H-10

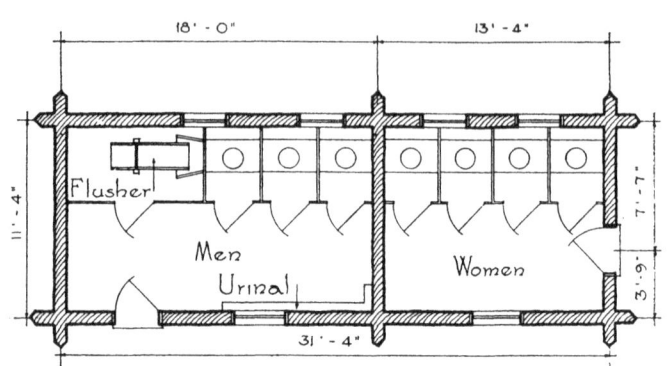

Vogel State Park, Georgia.

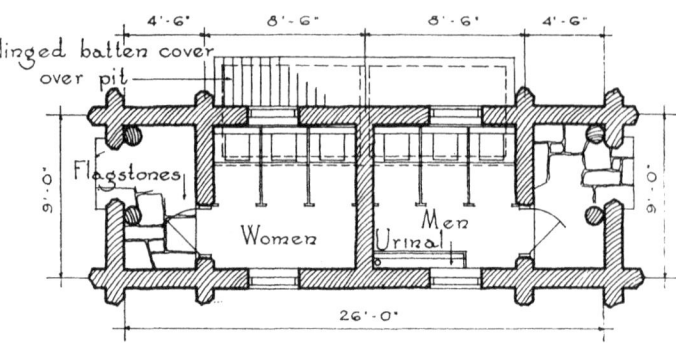

Custer State Park, South Dakota.

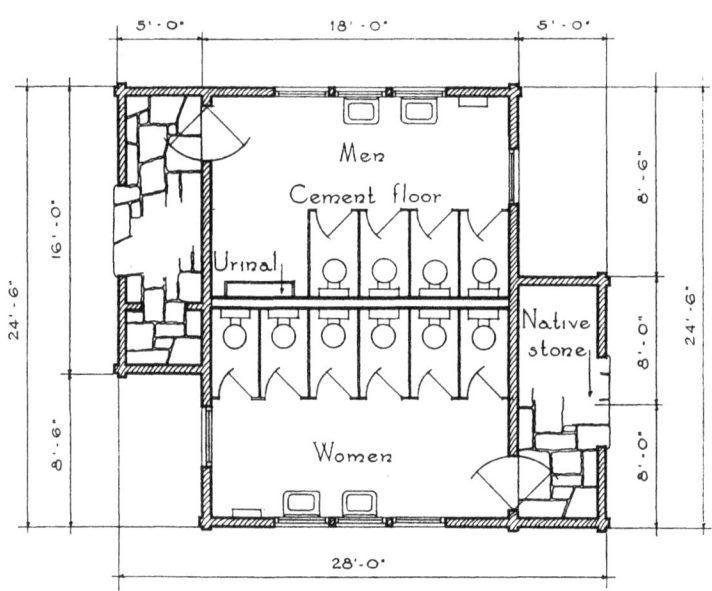

Spring Mill State Park, Indiana.

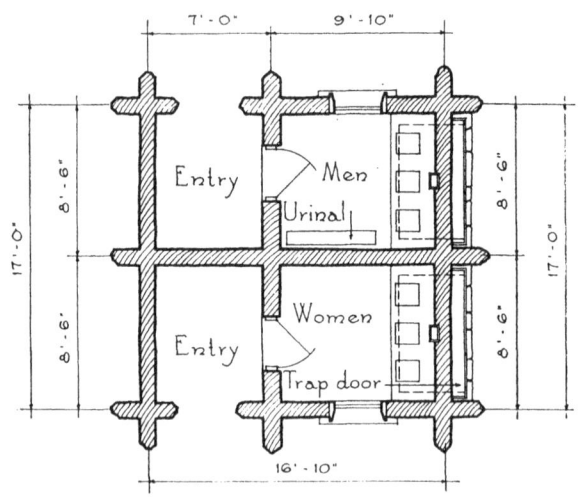

Fargo Metropolitan Park, North Dakota.

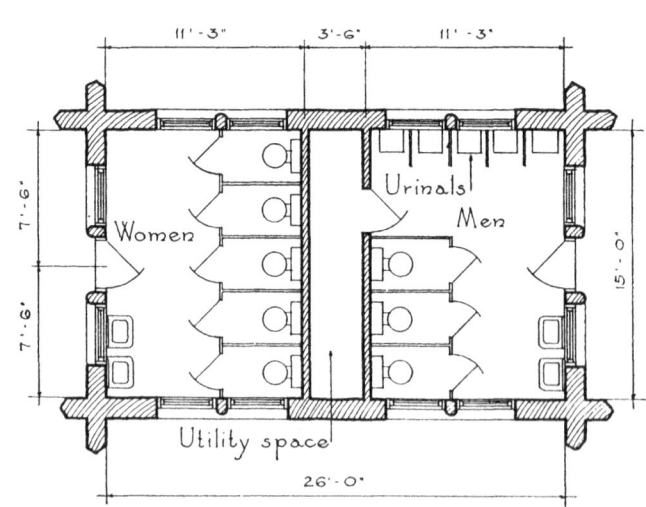

Yosemite National Park.

Scale 3/32" = 1'-0"

Plate I H–11 ⇨ COMFORT STATIONS AND PRIVIES

Vogel State Park, Georgia

Custer State Park, South Dakota

LOG TOILET STRUCTURES FOR BOTH SEXES

Common to these toilet buildings, plans of which are shown opposite, is log construction. In quality and in scale the log work is generally excellent. The single example of squared logs is in "Indiana Primitive" in continuation of the traditions of a reconstructed early village in this park. The low lines of the Custer State Park example are especially pleasing. Two typical "back-to-back" plan arrangements are shown. The other three are less usual in lay-out. A partition wall of logs is likely not to prove as positive a separation between sections as is desirable.

Spring Mill State Park, Indiana

Fargo Metropolitan Park, North Dakota

Yosemite National Park

COMFORT STATIONS AND PRIVIES

Plate I H-12

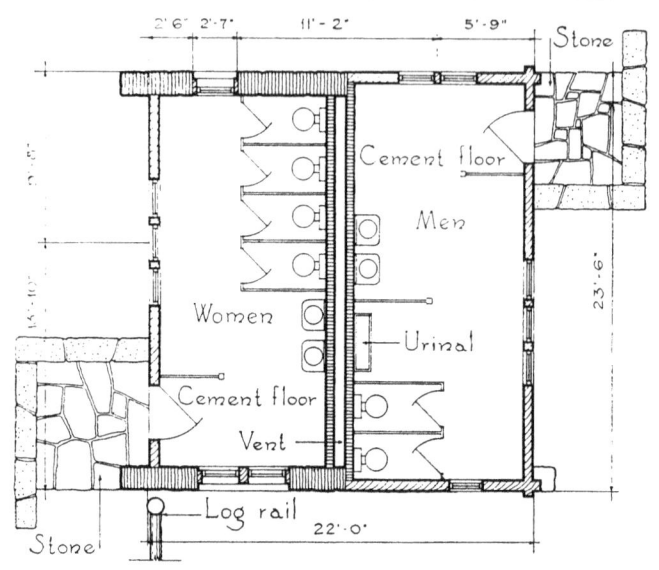
Clifty Falls State Park, Indiana

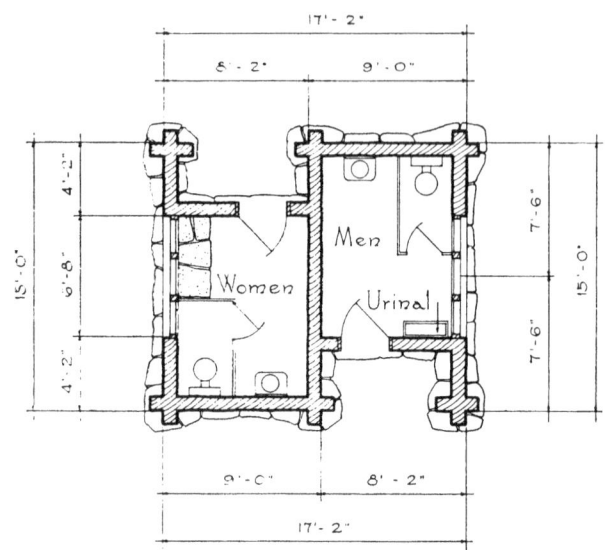
Mohawk Metropolitan Park, Tulsa, Oklahoma

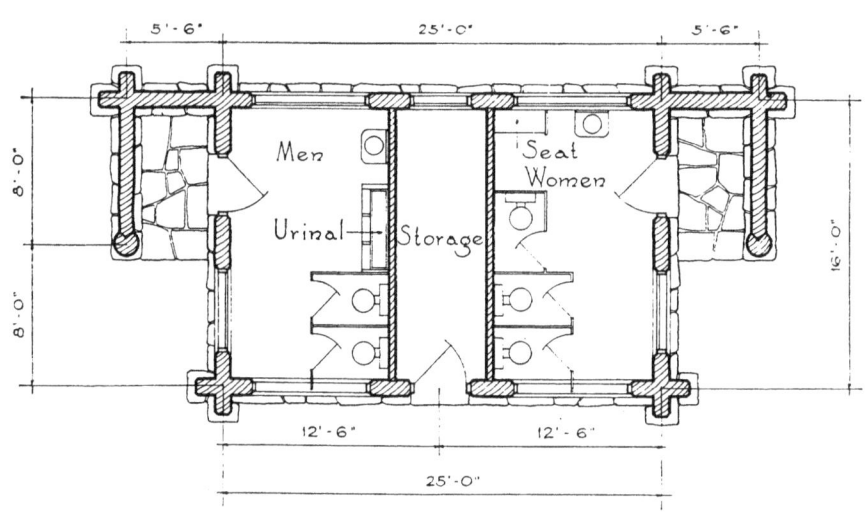
Lewis and Clark State Park, Washington

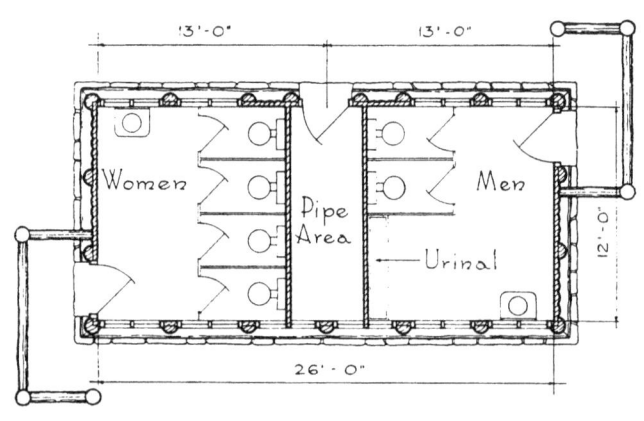
Mt. Rainier National Park

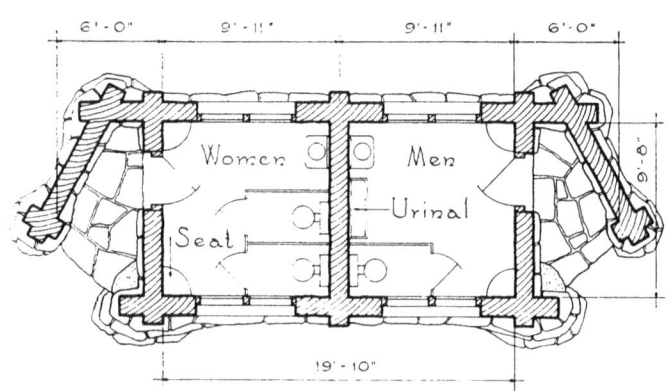
Mohawk Metropolitan Park, Tulsa, Oklahoma

Scale ½"=1'-0"

Plate I H–13   ⇒⇒ COMFORT STATIONS AND PRIVIES

Clifty Falls State Park, Indiana

Mohawk Metropolitan Park, Tulsa, Oklahoma

LOG AND STONE IN COMBINATION

There is great practicability in toilet structures having stone walls below and log walls above. The stone walls provide both secure anchorage for fixtures and suitable base for impervious surfacing. The log walls lend themselves readily to the extensive louvred or other openings necessary for ample light and ventilation. The buildings at Mohawk Metropolitan Park belong in the very front rank for their rustic park character. Picturesque is the pioneer construction of adzed, squared logs and local stone, adapted to a hillside site at Clifty Falls State Park.

Lewis and Clark State Park, Washington

Mount Rainier National Park

Mohawk Metropolitan Park, Tulsa, Oklahoma

COMFORT STATIONS AND PRIVIES

Plate I H-14

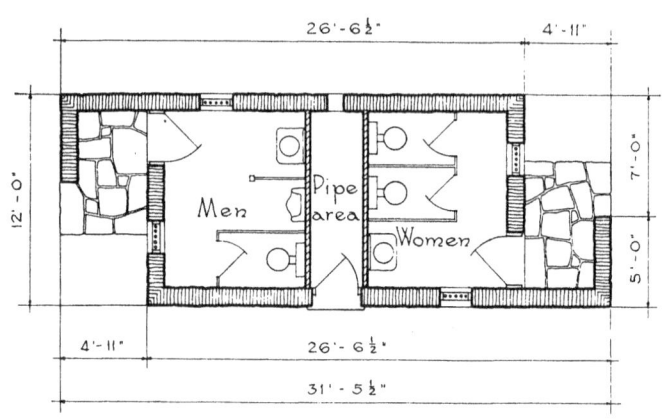

Phoenix South Mountain Metropolitan Park, Arizona

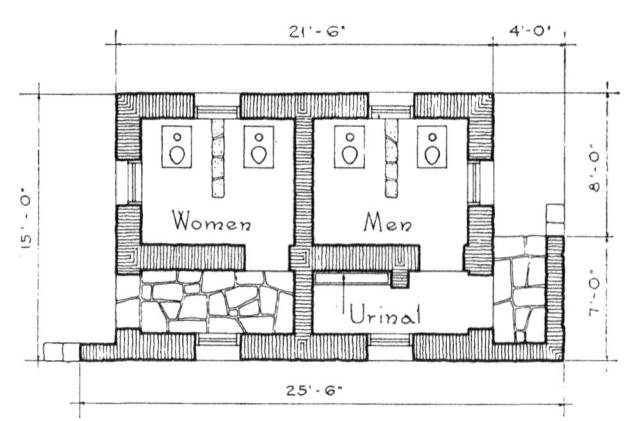

Palo Duro State Park, Texas

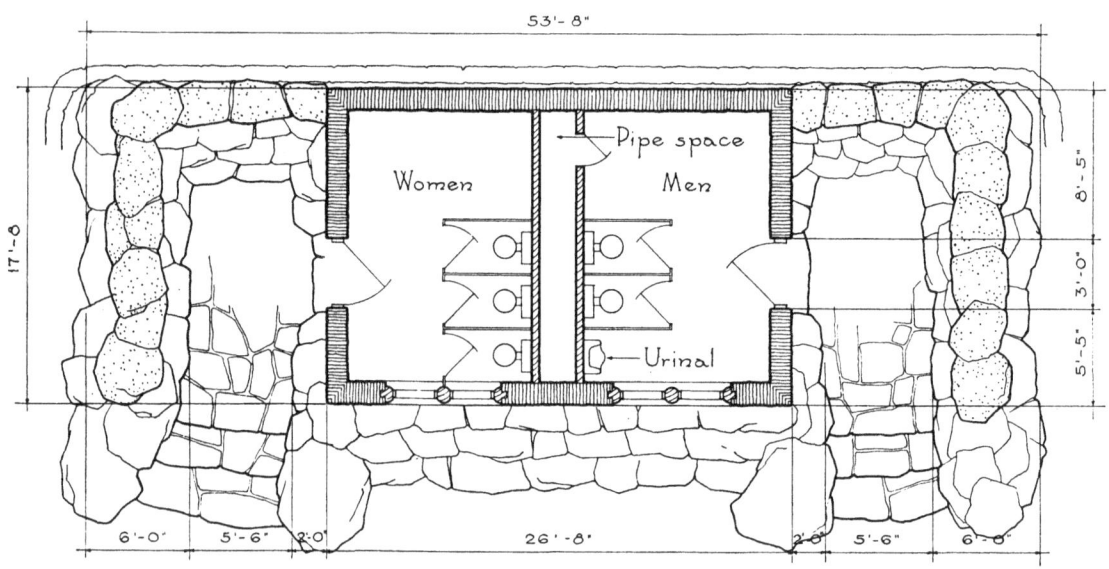

Lake Murray State Park, Oklahoma

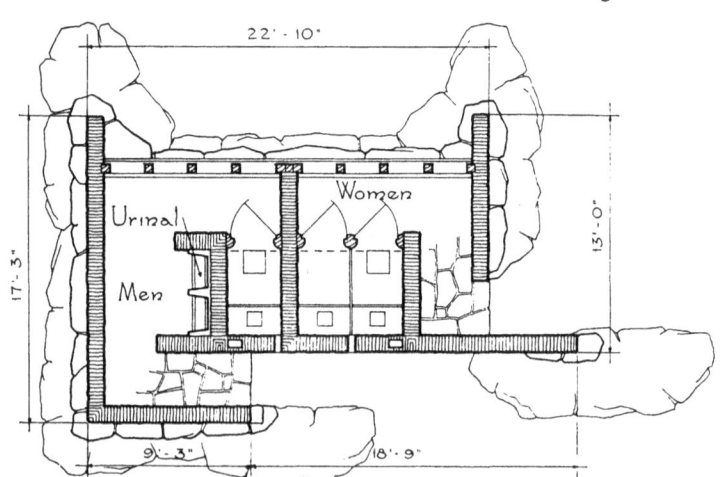

Perry Lake Metropolitan Park, Oklahoma

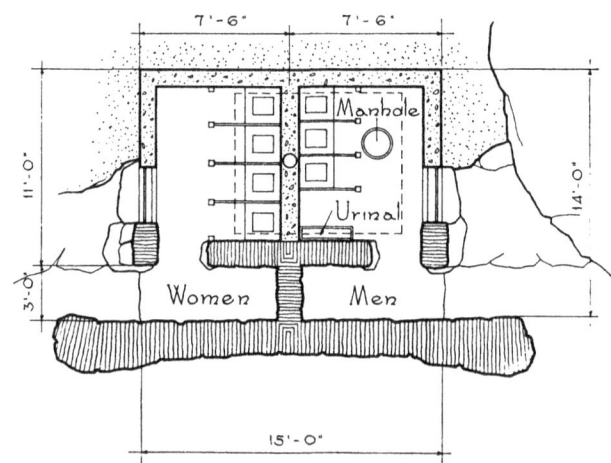

Garden of the Gods, Colorado Springs, Colorado

Scale 3/32"=1'-0"

Plate I H–15   ⇝ COMFORT STATIONS AND PRIVIES

Phoenix South Mountain Metropolitan Park, Arizona

Palo Duro State Park, Texas

TOILET BUILDINGS IN THE SOUTHWEST

The roof which is flat or very low-pitched is a favored means for insinuating structure into surroundings in the Southwest. So, also, is a well-defined horizontal coursing of the masonry. The treatment of the hillside latrine at Lake Murray amounts almost to camouflage. The burrowing structure in the Garden of the Gods is the all-time high for conversion of a natural site to structural purpose.

Lake Murray State Park, Oklahoma

Perry Lake Metropolitan Park, Oklahoma

Garden of the Gods, Colorado Springs, Colorado

COMFORT STATIONS AND PRIVIES   Plate I H-16

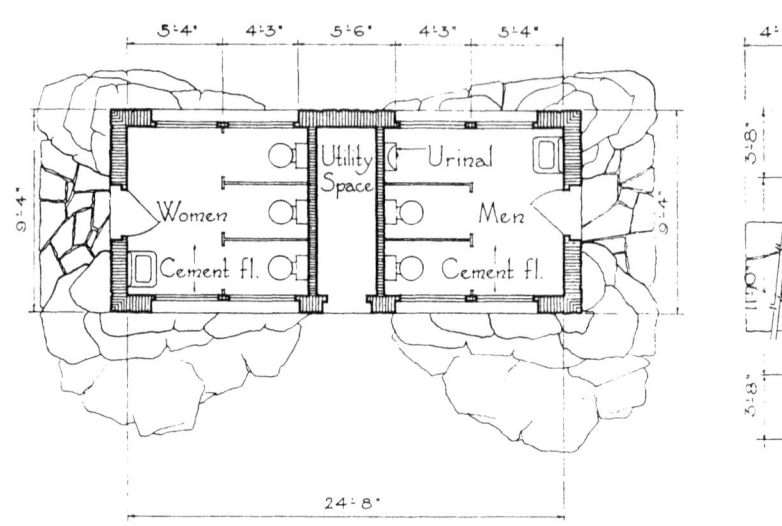

Yosemite National Park

Yosemite National Park

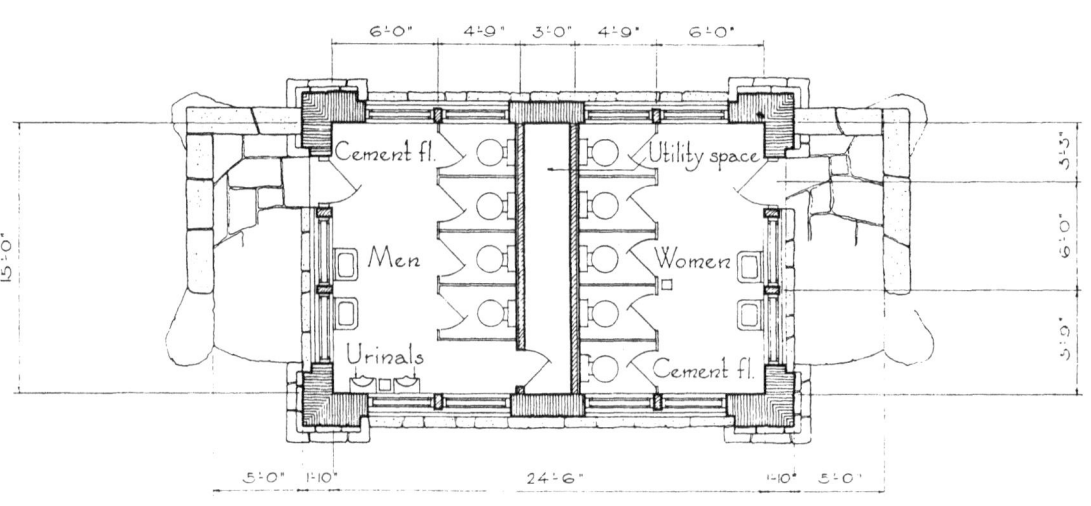

Platt National Park

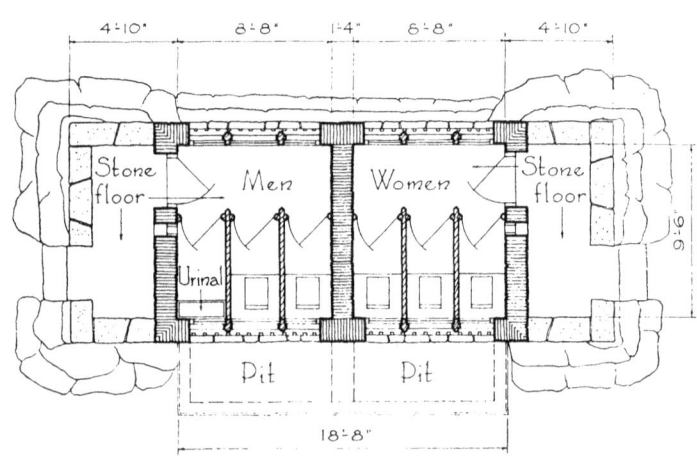

Lake Guernsey State Park, Wyoming

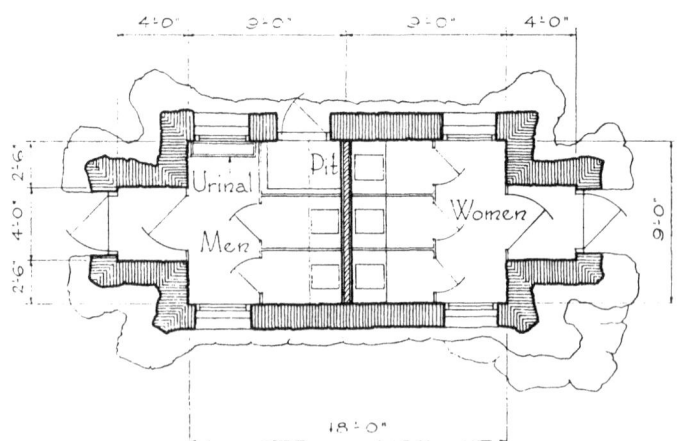

Saratoga Hot Springs State Park, Wyoming

Scale ½" = 1'-0"

Plate I H–17   ⇶ COMFORT STATIONS AND PRIVIES

Yosemite National Park

Yosemite National Park

TOILETS IN FAR WESTERN PARKS

Three structures here shown typify comfort stations in the western national parks. Scale of structure is keyed to a rough terrain. Three illustrated exemplify that treatment of rough rock walls variously described as "battered", "buttressed", and "blended to outcrop." It is not to be denied that there results assimilation into site in a degree not attained by other approaches. A variety of roof surface textures is here presented for comparative study.

Platt National Park

Lake Guernsey State Park, Wyoming

Saratoga Hot Springs State Park, Wyoming

COMFORT STATIONS AND PRIVIES

Plate I H–18

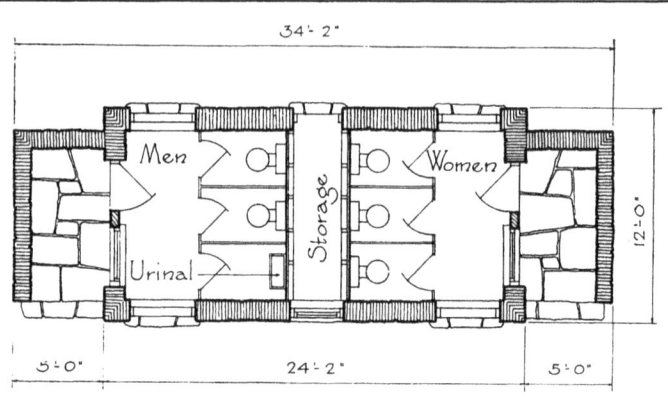

Eldora Pine Creek State Park, Iowa

Lampasas State Park, Texas

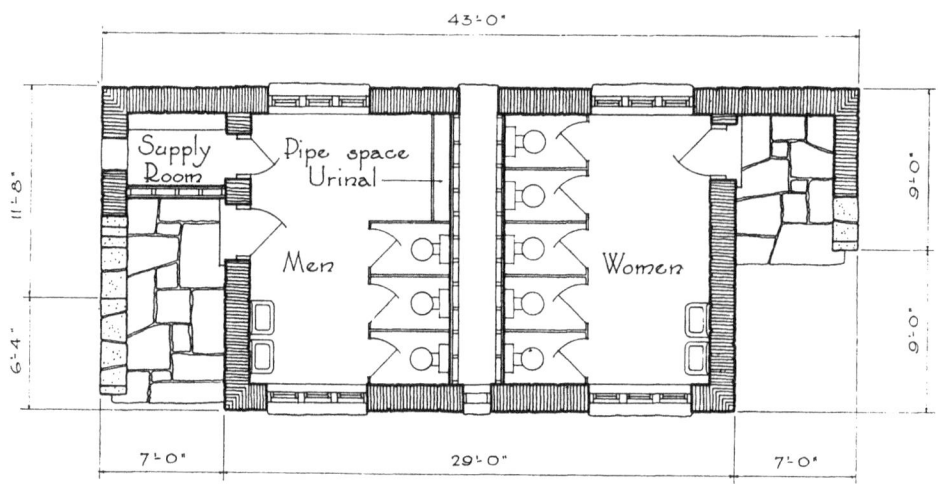

Fort Ridgely State Park, Minnesota

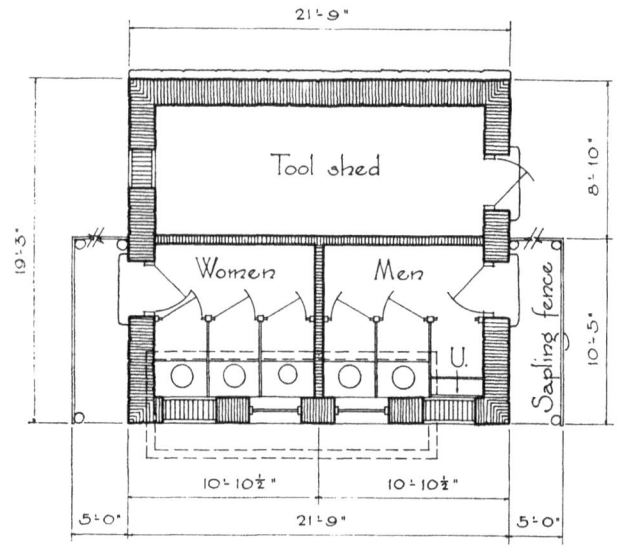

Saxon Woods, Westchester County, New York

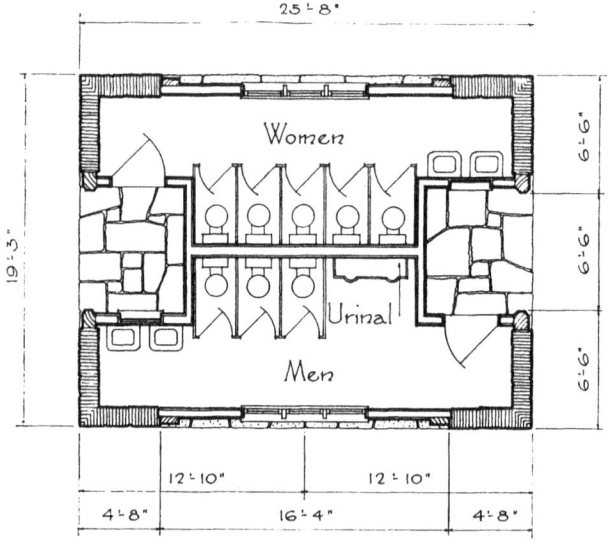

Turkey Run State Park, Indiana

Scale 3/32" = 1'-0"

148

Plate I H–19 ⇛ COMFORT STATIONS AND PRIVIES

Eldora Pine Creek State Park, Iowa

Lampasas State Park, Texas

MISCELLANY

These examples have in common a certain more finished (in the sense of less rustic) treatment than we have just observed in the handling of masonry. It may be inferred that the surroundings are likewise less rugged, even modified, in character. Whereas all examples suggest the many varieties of masonry possible; and Whereas there are details here present, to wit: shapeless units, directionless coursing, suggestion of concrete block, unbroken vertical joints, stones placed on end (all of which might have been avoided to happier results): Therefore be it *Resolved*, That such shortcomings shall not merit repetition.

Fort Ridgely State Park, Minnesota

Saxon Woods, Westchester County, New York

Turkey Run State Park, Indiana

COMFORT STATIONS AND PRIVIES

Plate I H-20

Comfort Station, Logan Pass, Glacier National Park

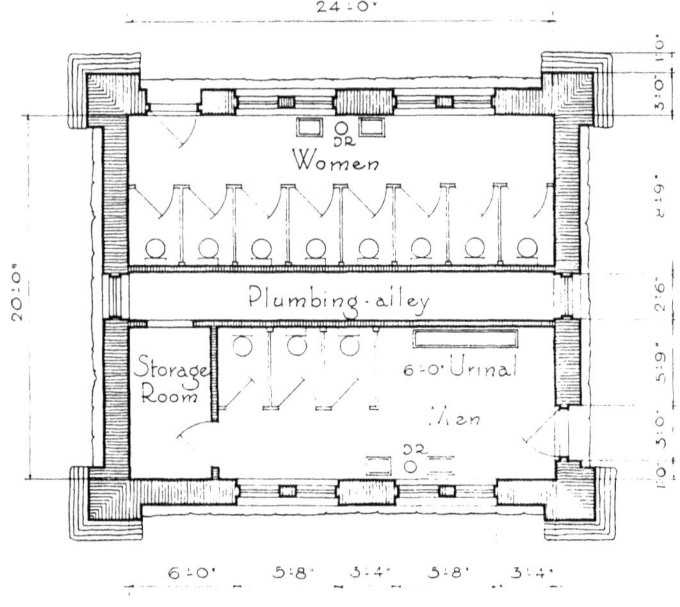

FLOOR PLAN

Here is a comfort station of considerable size, the exterior treatment of which is no less than very highly distinguished in its appropriateness to site. The degree of this accomplishment is hardly exceeded by any other subject herein illustrated. The bold masonry of heroic scale, projecting pole beams and rafters, and the skillful blending with the rugged terrain are important contributions to this completely satisfying structure.

INCINERATORS

SAFE DRINKING WATER and sanitary toilets are often cited as the "first things" to be provided in a park for its safe use by the public. Also in this category and hardly of secondary importance is the need for the positive disposal of garbage and rubbish to insure the maintenance of healthful and inviting conditions. As surely as drinking water must be provided and kept uncontaminated and sewage disposal provided and kept uncontaminating, so must garbage and rubbish collection and disposal be positive and complete. The undertaking may not be haphazard. The incinerator is the structural medium, but it is not automatic and depends entirely on the human equation for its effectiveness.

Incinerators provided in the picnic area for operation by the public itself have not proved efficacious, generally speaking. They are most certainly short of positive in disposal of the variety of waste that is the byproduct of picnicking. Picnickers in the mass seem not to be endowed with the knack of operating an incinerator and even their most sincere attempts are not effective in a degree to leave the incinerator a very salutary object in a use area.

A policy that looks to the public to burn its combustible rubbish in picnic fireplaces, deposit its cans and bottles in pits and its garbage in surface containers, assumes public cooperation in a degree that is probably subrealistic. Experienced park men recognize that the missionary work necessary to promote public cooperation in that degree is a formidable undertaking in itself. They willingly take over as operations functions the collection and disposal of refuse beyond that point. Some find the responsibility must be assumed before that point is reached.

Undertaken as a public service operation, the business of collecting garbage and rubbish and of operating and tending the incinerator must be diligent and routine. The schedule will be determined by the measure of the public's preliminary cooperation, the fluctuating use of the picnic facilities, and the types and capacities of containers, pits, and incinerator.

The incinerator can take one of a number of forms. Important details are the determination of a proper capacity, the employment of heat resisting materials, and, for a maximum combustion, the provision for draining accumulated waste prior to burning. An abundant draft is absolutely essential. Overhead shelter for the attendant operating the incinerator is desirable, because for efficiency in operation more than a casual attendance may be necessary, particularly in heavy, rainy weather.

The method of charging the incinerator is deserving of consideration. When the garbage is delivered in truck load quantities, there is saving of labor in an arrangement that permits it to be dumped or shoveled into the combustion chamber from above.

It is regrettable if the flue must be tall and unsightly, but it is more regrettable if, in attempting to overcome this, the draft is reduced beyond the desirable maximum and unnecessary smoke and stench are the result. Prevailing air currents should be studied before the site is determined. Tree growth and other natural screening from view are advantageous only if in that capacity they do not also become obstructions to draft.

Incinerators should be located conveniently near the intensively used areas, yet must be decently retired so that their nuisance quality is minimized.

It might be said in short that incinerators, like equipment and maintenance buildings, and all such other phases of park operation which by their nature are capable of functioning without direct contact with the public, function best if kept from its sight and from its path.

INCINERATORS
Plate I I-1

Incinerator, Fargo Metropolitan Park, North Dakota

The most elementary form of incinerator is this type. It is merely picnic fireplace of exaggerated size. The examples on this page are more restricted in capacity than those which follow. The open top incinerator is not adapted to regions of heavy rainfall.

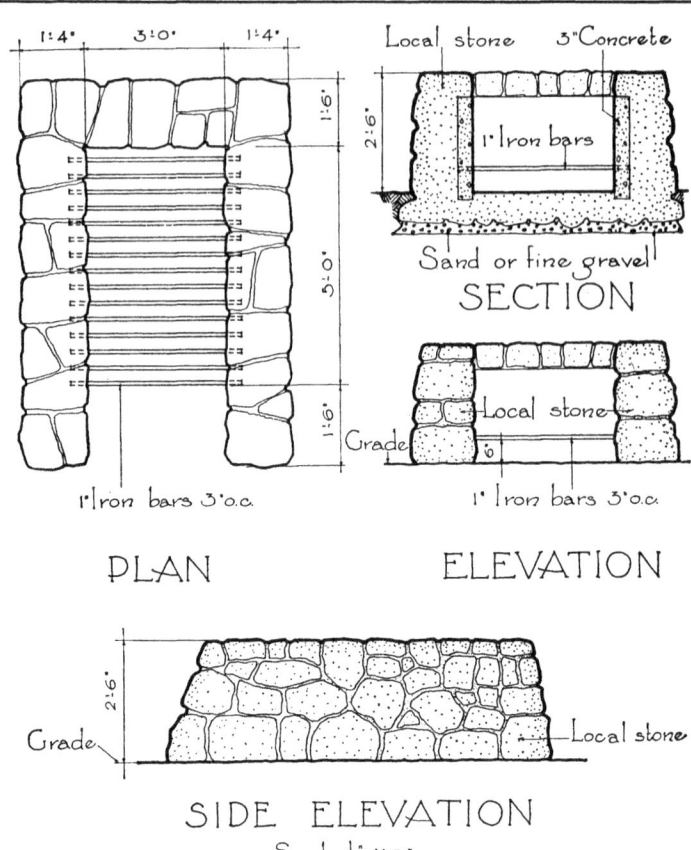

Incinerator, Bonham State Park, Texas

An exceedingly simple design in which the drying out of wet refuse before burning is probably accelerated by the open top. The illustration shows a fence of good park character which hides from public view the disposal of rubbish and unsightly service items—supplies, equipment, and the like.

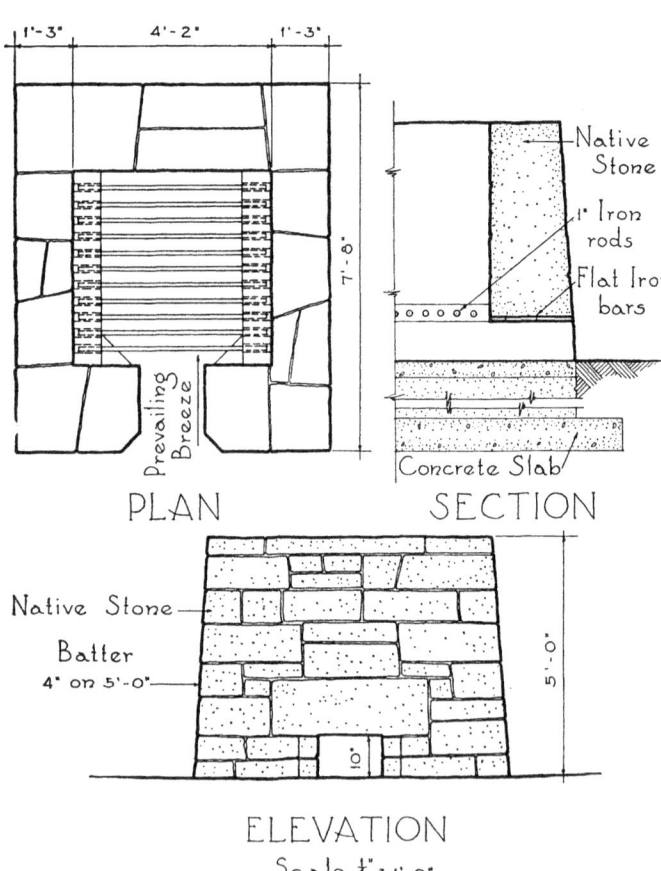

152

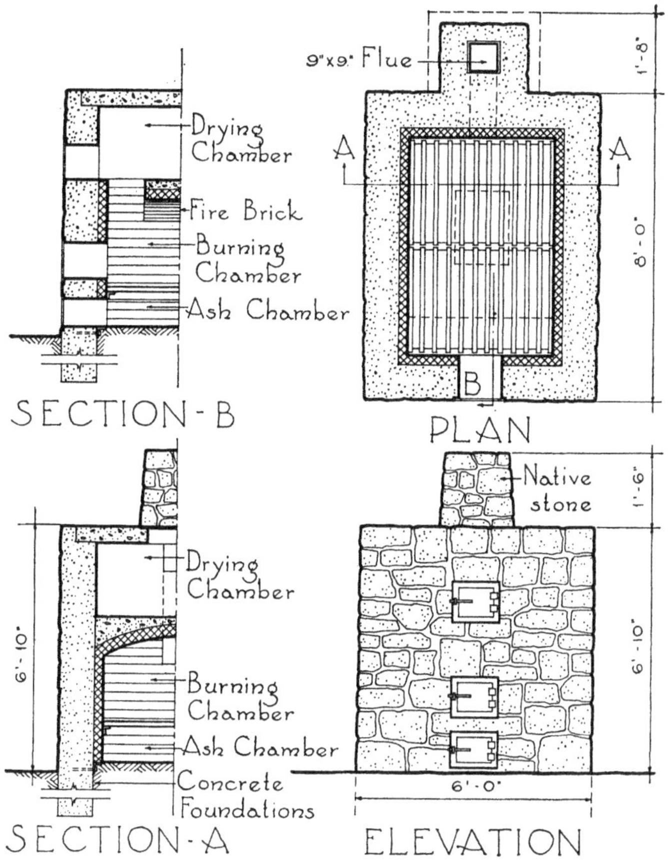

Plate I I-2 　　　　　　　　　　　　　　　　　　　　　　　»» INCINERATORS

Incinerator, Backbone State Park, Iowa

Although of moderate size for a park incinerator, this one buries from sight some of its bulk by reason of its hillside location. Important aid to complete combustion is the draining and drying of the collected refuse prior to firing, here provided for. The surroundings suggest that draft may be hampered by the woods growth.

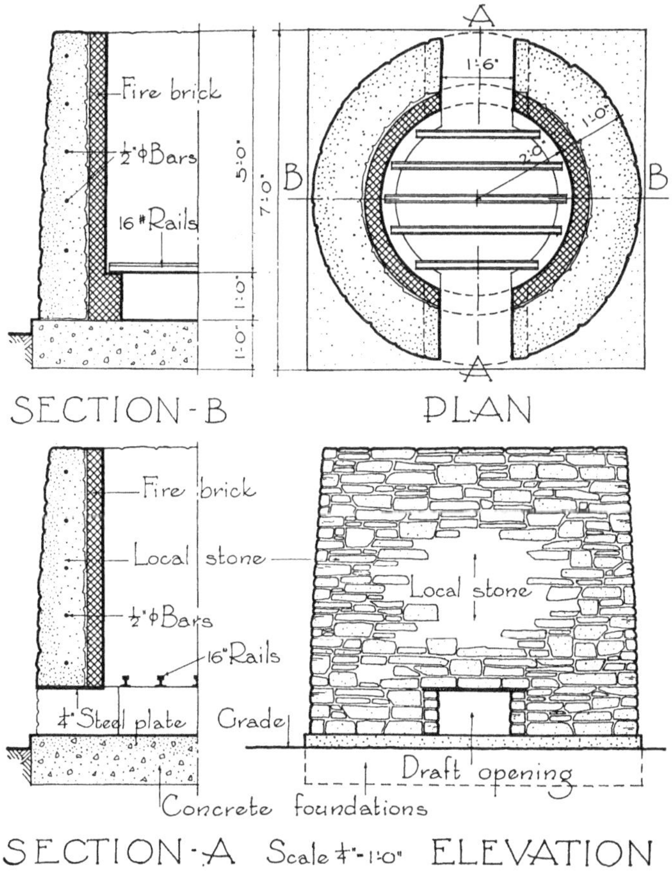

Incinerator, Taughannock Falls State Park, New York

The refuse is lowered into this circular incinerator from the level of truck or wagon, approach for which is supplied by the concrete pavement to the left of the unit. This design is not unsightly in appearance and provides large capacity. A well-cleared site insures an adequate draft for this example.

153

INCINERATORS

Incinerator, Sharon Woods, Cincinnati, Ohio

Monumental in size, and almost so in its character, is this utilitarian incinerator. It is fed directly from refuse collection trucks which reach the charging door by means of the elevated earth ramp. The capacities of this chimneyed facility and the one below greatly exceed those of the previously shown examples.

Incinerator, Audubon Memorial State Park, Kentucky

The soaring chimney is considerably softened by the roofed structure at its base which houses the incinerator itself and provides shelter for attendant operating it. The charging of the unit is from the front wall, not overhead opening as in the example above. The wire-screen spark arresters that equip both units are important safeguards.

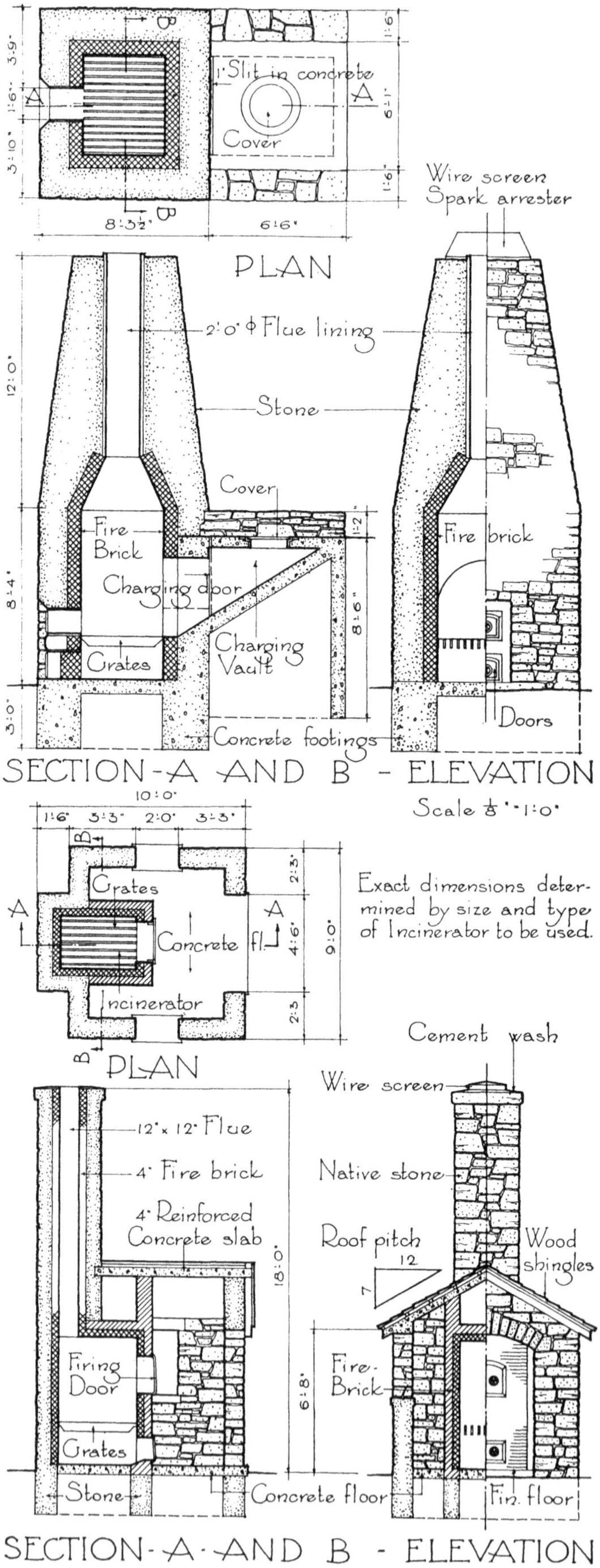

FIRE LOOKOUT STRUCTURES

THE PROMPT DETECTION of any forest fire that may start is a basic necessity for the efficient protection of forested parks. In order to provide for early discovery and immediate report of size, location, and condition of fires before they become large, it is necessary that trained observers be so stationed that they can keep the forest under constant observation. These stations are usually located on heights which overlook the greatest possible expanse of danger area, and particularly on those which cover the most probable points of fire origin.

The need, location, and number of lookouts required for adequate fire detection in a given park are determined after carefully conducted lookout studies, not by arbitrary selection of the highest vantage points. The best single point or combination of points to afford the maximum coverage of fire danger areas is selected. Efficient range of visibility does not exceed 10 to 15 miles, due to haze and other vision-limiting factors; therefore, even though a point may provide views of areas much further removed, this additional coverage cannot be given much weight in determining lookout locations.

In selecting the type of structure best adapted for any particular site several considerations are involved.

Unobstructed visibility in all directions in which a fire may occur is of primary importance. If the site is on flat topography, or a shoulder of ridge or mountain cuts off the view, or trees are nearby, which for aesthetic or other reasons cannot be removed, it is necessary to raise the observatory above the ground. On sites which provide clear visibility of the entire danger area, the structure can be a one- or two-story building.

Adequate, safe, and comfortable living quarters for the observer are another important consideration. For efficient fire detection it is essential that the observer live in his lookout unless precluded by height of structure. Since fires can and do start at all hours of the day and night, he must be constantly on the alert and in a position to observe them promptly. If the observer lives away from his station, the fire may burn a long time before being discovered. Since most lookout structures are on exposed sites, adequate protection from lightning, wind, storm, and sun must be provided. Where high towers (exceeding 16 feet in height) are necessary for detection, the lookout's living quarters should be close to the base of the tower, so located that all possible detection of the area is provided from that point. Provision should be made for storage of food and other supplies and equipment, and also for water, if no source of supply exists on the site. This storage space for supplies is especially necessary in isolated locations where servicing of lookouts is made at infrequent intervals.

Efficient detection of fires requires the use of delicate and costly equipment including the telephone or radio and fire locating and other instruments. It is vitally necessary that these be protected from exposure by adequate housing.

Since lookouts are located on vantage points selected for their broad coverage of forest, they are also the best points from which the public can view the finest scenic panoramas. A well-designed structure and a properly trained lookout observer can contribute to the enjoyment of the park by the public, and the observer is offered a chance to sell fire protection painlessly to the visitors.

SEVERAL TYPES OF STRUCTURES have been designed for efficient fire protection, including a simple single-room building 14 by 14 feet which combines living quarters and observatory, a two-story building with observatory above and storage space below, a low tower with 14 by 14 feet observatory on top, and finally the higher steel towers, some of which are 65 feet high with smaller enclosures. In

FIRE LOOKOUT STRUCTURES

designing the structure it is essential that the observatory provide the maximum of unobstructed visibility, using plate glass and narrow corner posts. Adequate protection against lightning, high winds, and winter storms, and the factor of live load due to a concentration of visitors must be taken into account in designing the lookout.

The safety of the visitors must be considered if it is anticipated that the public will visit the lookout. It is generally desirable to provide a walkway or platform around the observatory to accommodate visitors and to permit the observer to examine the area from outside the observatory. High towers must be provided with railings along the steps, platforms, and landings. Landings are desirable to break a monotonous and strenuous climb to the top of a high tower. Ladders are not satisfactory on towers visited by the public.

Since fire lookouts must be placed on prominent points for efficient fire protection, they are frequently visible for considerable distances. They should, therefore, be designed with thought for their appearance. It is possible by employing native rock or logs in the construction to achieve a certain harmony with the surroundings, especially if, when located on a rocky summit, the structure is blended to it and made to appear to grow out of it. However, where it is not feasible to hide the structure without decreasing the efficiency of the lookout, or there is not opportunity for blending the structure to location, the benefits derived from fire detection and the public's interest in the operation itself as a conservational activity of the park area go far to offset any aesthetic shortcomings of the facility itself.

The fire lookout shown directly below exemplifies the functional fire lookout tower, divested of all the gestures to park environment so conspicuous in the timber-framed tower delineated on the following page.

Fire Lookout Tower, Grand Canyon National Park

Plate I J-1   ⇶ FIRE LOOKOUT STRUCTURES

Lookout Tower - Custer State Park - South Dakota

Here is a timber framed lookout tower that includes highly practicable features without the sacrifice of park character, which is peculiarly and agreeably here present. Favoring practical purpose is the wide overhang of roof, for reducing glare, and the white painted cab and soffit of this overhang, for diffusing and reflecting light. Favoring the claim of its location in a park are the log-cabined parapet of the cab, the vigorous scale of the supporting timbers, and the considerable rake of the corner posts so that the tower seems almost to swagger.

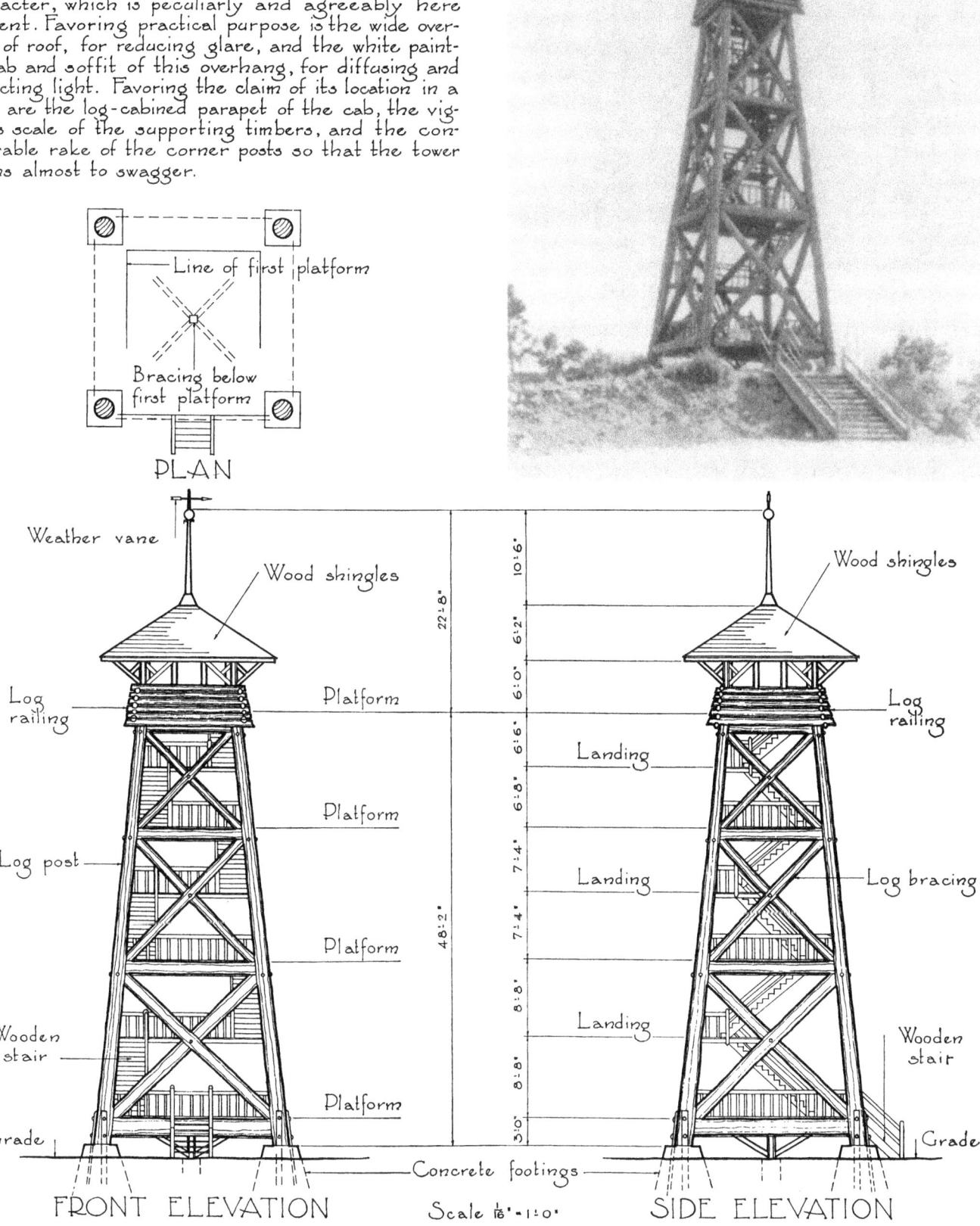

157

FIRE LOOKOUT STRUCTURES

Plate I J-2

Fire Lookout, Crater Lake National Park

There is novelty in the provision of museum and toilet facilities in the ground floor space of this example. It is probably close to some trail and readily accessible to the public. The recommended maximum of glass and minimum of obstructing posts in the lookout cab are here in evidence. The surrounding balcony is put to practical use by both attendant and visiting public.

Fire Lookout, Lassen Volcanic National Park

Two-story structure offering minimum obstruction to vision in the details of fenestration of the lookout level. The vigorous proportions in the railing and its bracing are satisfying. The masonry leaves something to be desired. Ventilators, here just beneath the cornice, are necessary in a room so completely enclosed by glass.

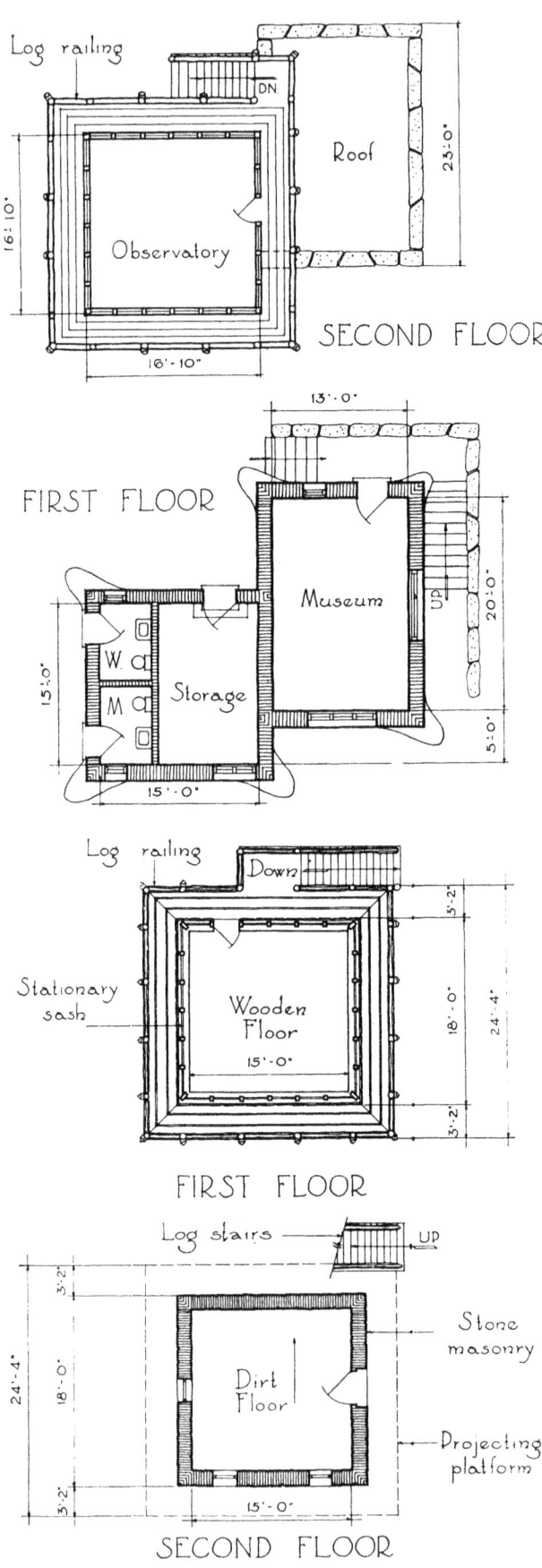

158

Plate I J–3   ⇢⟫ FIRE LOOKOUT STRUCTURES

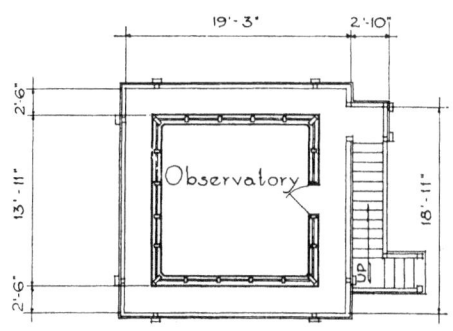

SECOND FLOOR PLAN

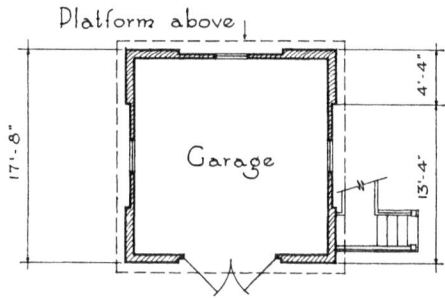

FIRST FLOOR PLAN

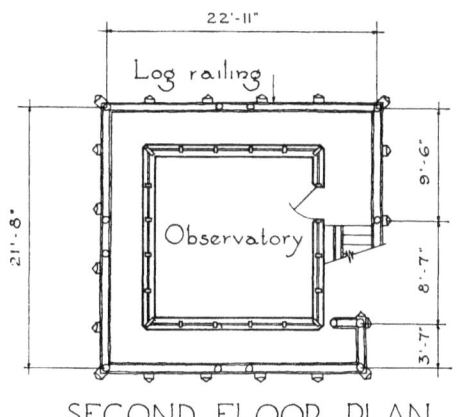

SECOND FLOOR PLAN

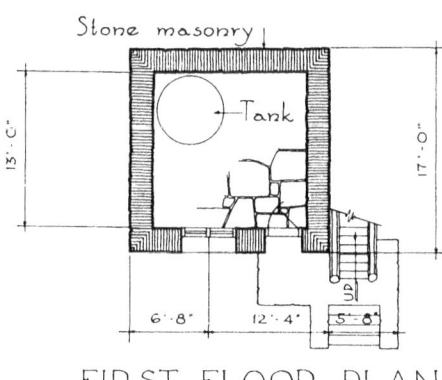

FIRST FLOOR PLAN

Scale 1/8" = 1'-0"

Fire Lookout, Crane Flat, Yosemite National Park

Perhaps unusual in its provision of automobile storage space at the ground level, but typical, in its maximum of glazed wall and in the catwalk and overhanging cornice features, of the primary structural needs of the fire lookout facility. The garage as a part of the building indicates a location more readily accessible than is perhaps usual to fire lookouts.

Fire Lookout, Shadow Mountain, Rocky Mountain National Park

More pleasing in its proportions than the foregoing examples and illustrative of the happy results where a masonry structure can appear to grow out of a natural rock outcrop. The technique of the masonry retains characteristics of the rock on the site. The observatory and surrounding balcony are typical.

159

FIRE LOOKOUT STRUCTURES

Plate I J–4

Fire Lookout, Sugar Loaf, Chiricahua National Monument

Terrain and absence of tall growth here permit the fire lookout observatory to be placed practically at grade level, to results that hardly interrupt the park scene. Topography and other affecting conditions seldom allow this solution to obtain.

Fire Lookout, Paradise, Sequoia National Park

However prominent this lookout may appear, the enormous scale of the rocks on which it is perched must dwarf it to a point where its intrusion is not serious. It rather serves to accent the vastness of scale of the primitive areas into which man has penetrated.

Fire Lookout, Henness Ridge, Yosemite National Park

The fire lookout forced up and up, to three-story structure in this instance, the ultimate, probably, before it must abandon being a building to become a skeleton tower of steel or wood members. The finished character of the details here observable is less appealing in park areas than the more rustic structures already reviewed.

TRAIL STEPS

>>> DESIRABLE AS STEPS ARE at many points in many trails, by no means are they ever to be created for their own sake. It is perhaps not generally sensed that if as much study were given to trail planning as to modern road planning, lesser grades and consequently fewer trail steps would result. In any case, only an unavoidably sharp grade not readily negotiable as such, with no reasonable alternative of an easier grade, will justify resorting to steps at all.

That the first purpose in providing steps along steep trails is to facilitate walking is undeniable. Less obvious perhaps, but not less important, is another consideration. This is the safeguarding of the aspect of naturalness in every detail of the construction of trail steps.

Trail steps, to justify their presence in natural areas, must facilitate walking to just such extent as will not corrupt this natural quality. Conversely, trail steps must strive to emulate Nature only to a degree that will not make them extremely hazardous in use. Either approach should result in approximately the same satisfying compromise. The facilitation of walking along trails in natural areas can hardly lay claim to all the considerations of uniformity of rise and tread, and relationship between these, that may be demanded of steps in almost every other location. It is not unreasonable to assume that the typical park trail is created for the use of hardy hikers entitled to acquaintance with Nature unarrayed with safety treads and handrails.

There are admittedly within most parks limited areas of concentration visited by persons of all ages and of differing capacities for physical activity. Obviously, for steps within such areas, the claim of easy and safe walking should rank in importance above the claim of complete naturalness, and the time-proved principles and practices in satisfaction of the former are applicable at such locations in greater degree. But for the trails into areas of less intensive use, and with these we are here principally concerned, steps will not demand of the natural setting unreasonable and discordant compromise in adaptation to human use.

In park reservations where there are rock outcroppings, and especially where these are of ledge rock, the very background goes far to contribute naturalness to man-made trail steps. Yet even with the most sympathetic collaboration of Nature, the execution of steps requires considerable skill for wholly satisfying results. The characteristics of the stratifications of ledge rock can often be utilized or reproduced in the creation of steps to such results that they are almost without trace of the artificial. Where rock outcroppings do not exist to provide liaison with the landscape, the naturalizing of rock steps requires a sculptor's skill and sense of form if an anomalous creation is to be avoided. Even here the effort should be to give the constructed steps the appearance of natural ledges. To create such aspect it is most important that the width of treads vary. Rocks forming cheeks at either side of the steps should vary in horizontal alignment, as well as in height, and should be tied and blended into the setting by being occasionally and irregularly extended some distance into the vegetation to either side. No mortar should be evident—greater naturalness will result from dry construction. Width of treads and height of risers will be governed in large measure by the natural slope. Treads should be as wide as possible and risers, except under unusual conditions, should not exceed six inches in height. Rock ledges may naturally exist in the trail where the grade is not so steep as actually to require step forms, yet because the rock is present, steps with risers lower and treads deeper than usual become a logical treatment.

For trails where rock is not an indicated characteristic of the environment, and where the attempt to naturalize it will evidence much of struggle, the steep grades of trails can be made more

TRAIL STEPS

negotiable by forming risers of timbers, and providing treads by filling in with gravel or earth. There are various techniques in the fashioning of the timbers, and in methods of anchorage, which achieve different degrees of practical and artistic attainment, as some illustrations suggest. Trail steps of this construction cannot be termed naturalistic with accuracy, but it should be possible to claim them harmonious with environment and not hazardous in use. As with all use of logs in park construction, the timber risers should be stripped of bark, not only because this will in time naturally occur, but because in the certain process of loosening, bark will constantly be a source both of hazard and of litter. Sometimes timber risers are roughly squared or carefully hand-hewn. Such, while not "going native" to the extent of timbers left in the round, probably boast a higher safety rating in the sprain and fracture statistics. Timber risers should be staked in place to insure against loosening and shift in position. Exposed stakes should be driven well below the tread surfaces so there is no projection in which a heel might catch. Better still are methods that admit of anchorage by invisible stakes.

There are numerous examples of unusual methods or solutions in provision of trail steps. Often the abruptness of grade makes necessary a veritable stairway steeper than the easy rise and tread we know to be ideal. On occasion a ladder must be built when the grade is precipitous. In a land of giant trees, one that has fallen across a gorge or ravine will provide a picturesque foot bridge which, when out of level beyond a certain degree, can be notched to form steps and equipped with rustic handrail.

A handrail is often a necessary safeguard in connection with trail steps narrowly confined between a rising cliff on the one hand and a precipitous drop on the other. It is vital that a handrail be thoroughly substantial in character and in fact, inviting as it does the reliance of adventurous recreation seekers. Better no handrail in any location than one that cannot be trusted both in use and abuse. Far too many structurally adequate and safe handrails are an offense by reason of flimsy appearance.

Palmetto State Park, Texas

Plate I K-1   ⇾ TRAIL STEPS

Cascades State Park, Minnesota

Mount Penn Metropolitan Reservation, Reading, Pennsylvania

TRAIL STEPS OF LOGS

Here grouped for comparative study are shown logs in provision of steps in trails. The practical and aesthetic values of logs in the round and of squared timbers, and the several methods employed in contriving them to this purpose, are here on parade. The combination of log risers and stone paved treads at lower right is unusual. The litter that results when bark is not removed from the logs used in building trail steps is noticeable in the illustration at lower left. The construction method in this example is none the less interesting.

Letchworth State Park, New York

Spring Mill State Park, Indiana

Alleghany State Park, New York

TRAIL STEPS ⋘   Plate I K-2

Bronx River Parkway, New York

Bronx River Parkway, New York

Petit Jean State Park, Arkansas

TRAIL STEPS OF STONE

The illustrations surrounding this caption show rocks employed with temperate informality for grade negotiation of foot trails. All suggest that the objective was hardly concealment of their man-made origin but rather uneffusive gesture toward natural surroundings. Present in some examples is appropriate blending to the characteristics of the adjacent terrain. In others, notably toward the upper left, is there hint of the informal garden, rarely and only justified in parks if the immediate surroundings have undergone very considerable modification of original character. In

Mammoth Cave National Park

Perry Lake Metropolitan Park, Oklahoma

Plate I K–3 ⟶ TRAIL STEPS

Mammoth Cave National Park

Cascades State Park, Minnesota

the illustrations shown at upper right and immediately below there is uncompromising and disturbing rigidity of line which breeds a conclusion that here the full potentialities of site were not realized.

Honesty requires the admission that the steps in the illustration at lower right are not actually trail steps, nor is all the surrounding rock work a natural formation. The steps lead to an overlook atop a cairnlike water storage tank, shown elsewhere in this volume. The accomplishment as to the steps is deserving of the "close-up" that is here given them.

Apollinaris Springs, Yellowstone National Park

Wheeler Dam Reservation, Tennessee Valley Authority

Lake Murray State Park, Oklahoma

165

TRAIL STEPS ⋘ Plate I K-4

Pueblo Mountain Metropolitan Park, Colorado

Wintersmith Municipal Park, Oklahoma

Pueblo Mountain Metropolitan Park, Colorado

TRAIL STEPS OF STONE

"Trail step sculpturing" is a phrase that might aptly be applied to most of the examples here illustrated; certainly it describes the two examples in Wintersmith Park. There is commendable blending to the flanking slopes at Pueblo Mountain Park. Some subjects below do not "read" clearly—the trail steps are discovered with difficulty. If due to bad photography, our regrets; if the result of good trail building, kudos for the rock sculptor!

Most surrounding subjects succeed in reflecting Nature in greater degree than the examples shown on the preceding pages, probably indicating

Interstate State Park, Wisconsin

Lake Guernsey State Park, Wyoming

Plate I K–5   →» TRAIL STEPS

Wintersmith Municipal Park, Oklahoma

Dolliver Memorial State Park, Iowa

less heavily trafficked areas as the setting for the steps here shown. The illustration at lower right is noteworthy because the man-contrived steps skillfully imitate the rounded, weathered outcropping rocks that frame them.

Examples on the following page depart from the imitation of Nature in the direction of more frankly man-made steps. Steeper grades and heavier use constitute the problem there encountered. More uniform steps geared to time-proved relationships of rise to tread are the solution very properly adopted, and are certainly neither unpleasantly conventional nor too mathematically exact.

Petit Jean State Park, Arkansas

Mesa Verde National Park

Quartz Mountain State Park, Oklahoma

TRAIL STEPS   Plate I K-6

Crowley's Ridge State Park, Arkansas

Turner Falls State Park, Oklahoma

Wheeler Dam Reservation, Tennessee Valley Authority

Crater Lake National Park

Taughannock Falls State Park, New York

Palo Duro State Park, Texas

CROSSINGS AND CULVERTS

→→→ CLOSE COUPLING of these facilities is premised on a conception that the function of the culvert is to permit a trail or roadway to pass over a drainage obstacle, while the function of the crossing is to permit the drainage to pass over a trail or roadway. Paradoxically, their very difference thus closely relates them.

If in our approach to a park technique the primitive has the right of way, stepping stones for pedestrians and the ford have place as picturesque survivals. For horse trails and secondary motor roads in parks where traffic is leisurely and light, the ford is a legitimate and economical provision for crossing a shallow stream. This is subject to further reservations if tolerance of its quaintness is not to give way to annoyance on the part of the public. The low water crossing will not meet with favor if it is frequently impassable due to flood. Equally intolerable are a soft stream bed, treacherous holes, or other hazards to safe negotiation. The approaches must not incline too sharply, nor may sight lines, as the ford is approached, be obscured by planting. Lack of these requisites to public acceptance of the ford is apt to provoke clamor of disapproval and lead to demand for its replacement with a culvert or bridge, to the eventual voiding of the economy it was sought to effect.

In a sense the crossing is the bridge in embryo, the culvert, the boy that is father to the bridge. We are never unconscious of the presence of a bridge, however well it may be insinuated into environment. In its most minor expression it cannot possibly be truly inconspicuous. A culvert, on the contrary, being in reality merely a retaining wall pierced by a drain, can often be so treated that the casual passerby is unaware of its presence in a natural area. If culvert and fill are extended far enough to either side of the roadway, roadside planting may be extended across the culvert without interruption, and head walls may be omitted above grade. Planting will limit the width of traveled way with more naturalism and finesse than can possibly be achieved by obtrusive head walls. The latter close to the traveled roadway are at once alien and artificial and a traffic hazard.

If this procedure for subordinating culverts to surroundings is impractical or uneconomical by reason of terrain, head wall barriers then become a very necessary safeguard. Worthy of study is the character given the required barrier. Its artificiality can be held to a minimum. Like many another facility in natural parks, it should be first and always informal in treatment and blended to its surroundings. Materials and workmanship should be such that facing and culvert itself, once constructed, make no demands whatever upon maintenance appropriations.

The culvert proper is sometimes of local stone when this is abundant and workable, but if it must be of concrete or of galvanized iron, reasonable concealment of the fact is to be striven for. The head wall, by extending well into the culvert opening, should avoid disclosing that it is a mere veneer. Natural rock is certainly the preferred material for the head wall, laid either dry or in mortar. The former method to be lasting must employ stones of suitably large size. If stone is not available, concrete or wood may be resorted to for the retaining wall. In a park sense, neither is a very satisfactory substitute for the stone wall.

Quite as much care should be given to the design and execution of culvert head walls as other park structures. Usual mistakes are insufficient care in the handling of mortar, resulting in sloppy joints, stone of trivial size, and lack of variety in sizes, leading to monotony and formality of surface pattern. These faults are common to much contemporary stone work, not limited to park construction only.

CROSSINGS AND CULVERTS

Plate I L–1

Platt National Park

Ludington State Park, Michigan

Loveland Mountain Metropolitan Park, Colorado

CROSSINGS AND CULVERT TREATMENTS

The crossings illustrated above give indication of the possibilities for picturesqueness in such a facility. Of particular interest is the crossing of stepping stones meeting the well-executed flight of trail steps on the brook bank in Platt National Park. The marsh crossing provided by wood piling at Ludington State Park is novel.

A casual, natural appearance is rather general in the culvert treatments shown on these facing pages. In several the presence of this not easily attained quality is marked. In fact, these culvert

Bronx River Parkway, New York

Boyle Metropolitan Park, Little Rock, Arkansas

170

Plate I L–2   ⇛ CROSSINGS AND CULVERTS

Hereford State Park, Texas

Lake Murray State Park, Oklahoma

treatments scarcely classify or are recognizable as culvert head walls except in two illustrations at lower right. It should be realized that it has been necessary to include in this collection many culvert head walls almost at the moment of their structural completion, and that these stand to benefit greatly from the toning influence of a return of natural vegetative growth. In presenting some in their new-born nakedness there is at least the compensatory advantage of disclosing their structure in maximum.

Loveland Mountain Metropolitan Park, Colorado

Spavinaw Hills State Park, Oklahoma

Roman Nose State Park, Oklahoma

[171]

CROSSINGS AND CULVERTS

Plate I L-3

Spavinaw Hills State Park, Oklahoma

Robbers Cave State Park, Oklahoma

Arbuckle Trail, Oklahoma

CULVERT HEAD WALL INTO CULVERT-BRIDGE

The masonry head wall of the minor culvert usually employs the lintel to bridge the span. It will be seen that the lintel is sometimes assisted by corbeling, as in the example from the Arbuckle Trail, or by a suggestion of relieving arch, as at Vogel State Park, before the segmental arch in the example from the Blue Ridge Parkway appears. Here revived in miniature are the architectural milestones between the stone age and Imperial Rome. The bottom row of illustrations indicates a

Beavers Bend State Park, Oklahoma

Arbuckle Trail, Oklahoma

Plate I L-4   ⇶ CROSSINGS AND CULVERTS

Lake Corpus Christi State Park, Texas

Wyandotte County Park, Kansas

Vogel State Park, Georgia

solution where heavy flow of surface water will overtax a single culvert.

At upper right is more than culvert, less than bridge—probably culvert-bridge is a fitting term for it. On the following page will be seen more of these, ranging from a finished character to rocky treatments suitable to mountainous terrain. In a majority the arch appears in full development, and the blending of head wall to site is generally very skillfully executed.

Lake Worth Metropolitan Park, Fort Worth, Texas

Blue Ridge Parkway, North Carolina

173

CROSSINGS AND CULVERTS

Plate I L-5

Mount Vernon Memorial Highway

Hillcrest Park, Durango, Colorado

Longhorn Cavern State Park, Texas

Wyandotte County Park, Kansas

Lake Murray State Park, Oklahoma

Lake Murray State Park, Oklahoma

BRIDGES

>>> BRIDGES IN PARKS include foot trail, bridle trail, and vehicle bridges. There should be proved necessity for every bridge before it is undertaken to build it. This refers chiefly to foot trail and bridle trail bridges. Many such trails, certainly those crossing a dry ravine or gully at remote distances from intensive use areas, can make the dip rather than be kept to a constant grade by a bridge. The location of the trail with respect to intensive use areas and the extent of the drainage obstacle are determining factors in the justification of bridges.

This presentation seeks merely to focus on the characteristics that bring to park bridges of varying widths, spans, heights, and types of construction the most promise of compatibility with natural environment. There is elsewhere abundant information, including diagrams, rules, and formulae, for the design of structurally enduring bridges. Much more limited is the presentation of source material concerning itself with bridges which, by reason of appropriateness to natural environment, truly deserve to endure. There are far too many bridges which, after having broken every commandment for beauty and fitness, seem to have sought to wash away all sins through the awful virtue of permanence. Such penitent bridges surely have no place in our parks. The quality of permanence cannot be considered a virtue unless every other virtue, big or little, is present. It is otherwise only a vicious attribute.

In outward appearance, the bridge calls most importantly for visible assurance of strength and stability. To be entirely successful, it is not enough for the bridge to be functionally adequate within the exact knowledge of the engineer; it must proclaim itself so to the inexact instincts of the layman. It is pardonable park practice to venture well beyond sheer engineering perfection in the scaling of materials to stresses and strains, not alone in gesture to the lay concept of structural sufficiency, but to satisfy the claims of comparative scale. Overemphasis of the structural elements of the bridge is usually necessary in order to maintain a good scale relationship with the natural elements of the more or less rugged landscape widely prevailing in park areas.

THE ATTAINMENT of "the little more" that is so desired by those who would have an eye-appeal scale brought to the slide rule is all too rare in park bridges. Rather is there a too prevalent flimsiness, ocular rather than structural. Considerably fewer bridges fail to satisfy by seeming too ponderous for their function.

Of perhaps equal importance is the choice of materials for the bridge. Only those which are native to the area and predominate near the bridge site will constitute a convincingly appropriate and harmonious medium of structural interpretation. While this applies, of course, to all structures in parks, it is particularly important to stone bridges, which in their most happily successful expressions seem almost to spring from the stream or river bank when truly related in color, texture, and scale to adjacent rock outcrops.

After wise choice of a native material, used in a sufficiency pleasing to the eye, the next demand to be made upon bridges would be for variety within reason, avoiding the commonplace at one extreme, and the fantastic at the other. The ranges of use, span, and height, and the broad fields of materials, arch and truss forms, local practices (to name a few variety-making possibilities) promise endless combinations and cross-combinations making for much individuality among bridges.

In general, bridges of stone or timber appear more indigenous to our natural parks than spans of steel or concrete, just as the reverse is probably true for bridges in urban locations or in connection with broad main highways. Probably there are few structures so discordant in a wilderness environment as bridges of exposed steel construction.

Too great "slickness" of masonry or timber technique, however, is certain to depreciate the merits of these materials for park bridges. Rugged and informal simplicity in use is the indisputable specification for their proper employment.

In no park structure more than in bridges is it of such importance to select a type of stone masonry construction that will reflect the natural formations in the immediate area and steer clear of the common errors in masonry. Shapeless stones laid up in the manner of mosaic are abhorrent in the extreme, having no precedent in Nature or in the traditions of sound masonry. In bridges particularly is there merit in pronounced horizontal coursing, breaking of vertical joints, variety in size of stones—all the principles productive of sound construction and pleasing appearance in any use of masonry. Often the creation of an effect that recalls any natural ledge stone formations in the vicinity is the indicated technique for the masonry of the bridge. The curve of the arch, the scale of the arch stones and masonry generally, the size of the pier, the height of the masonry above the crown of the arch are all factors vital to the success of the masonry bridge.

TIMBER BRIDGES may utilize either round or squared members to agreeable results. Squared timbers gain mightily in park character when hand-hewn. Simplicity of constructional pattern is a paramount consideration. It offers lesser contrast with natural elements, and is less distracting where competition between rigid artificial forms and free natural forms is an acknowledged taboo.

For practical as well as aesthetic reasons, bridges of open wood-truss type are in general disfavor. Arguments to their advantage seem to be lacking, whereas many are raised against them. When trusses are not structurally required, they are to be condemned for complicating the design and obstructing the view. In spite of most careful detailing to prevent water entering and lying in the joints, this is hard to overcome entirely. Shrinking of the timbers, rack under impact and strain, and rot developing in the opening joints speed the deterioration of this type of construction. It is short-lived and soon unsafe. It was practical effort to overcome this inherent weakness of the open wood-truss bridge by sheltering the trusses from exposure to the weather that brought about the development of the old-time covered bridge.

Many an otherwise altogether satisfying bridge fails of complete success through careless disregard in the matter of finishing touches. These, in relation to total effect, are actually far from so trivial as the frequent neglect of them might indicate or the man-days they involve. The parapet, railing, or wing wall should not terminate abruptly as though content with a mere toe-hold on the abutment, but should carry well back from the face of it to a very evidently sufficient bearing. Sometimes there is great merit in splaying the parapet or railing at the point of approach to a bridge, particularly if the bridge is narrow. Often the silhouette is much enhanced by stepping down, "easing" or "merging" parapet or railing into the grade at the terminals. Logical transition, convincing structurally, is desirable to relieve any abrupt change of materials in construction, especially in bridges that combine wood spans and stone piers. A similarly unpleasant and sharp transition sometimes occurs along the grade line of a bridge structure. A disturbing, unfinished, unassimilated appearance, noticeable in a number of the illustrations that follow, might have been dispelled by a mere warping of grade or bank slope, a suitable clean-up, and some cooperation with Nature to encourage the return of natural ground cover for the softening effect that is always its contribution.

Plate I M–1   ⋙ BRIDGES

Petit Jean State Park, Arkansas

Deception Pass State Park, Washington

MINOR FOOT AND HORSE TRAIL BRIDGES

Surrounding are bridges of the most elementary pattern, mere platform bridging an obstacle, a type termed in France a passerelle. Enhanced by a sylvan setting, the casual simplicity of these seems the concordant note for a narrow trail in a wilderness tract, wherein a narrow and shallow brook is hardly an obstacle to call for protective curb or handrail. The example with low curbs shown at lower left is transitional between this group and that shown on following page.

Denver Mountain Parks, Colorado

Sequoia National Park

Parvin State Park, New Jersey

Deception Pass State Park, Washington

Prairie Creek State Park, California

Great Smoky Mountains National Park

MINOR FOOT BRIDGES WITH SINGLE HANDRAIL

Greater hazard in the obstacle to be crossed is met by the foot bridge with a single handrail. Each example here shown has distinct individuality. The Prairie Creek representative is two fallen redwood trees, one dressed on top to provide level walking surface, the other, still sending off living shoots, serving as picturesque guard on the off-handrail side. Equally novel are the bridge that changes handrails in the middle of the stream, the colloquial cantilever example in Great Smoky Mountains, and the stairway bridge in Moran State Park, notched from a fallen tree.

Grand Teton National Park

Moran State Park, Washington

Plate I M-3 →»> BRIDGES

Turner Falls State Park, Oklahoma

Custer State Park, South Dakota

FOOT BRIDGES WITH HANDRAIL AND CURB

On this page will be noted a vigorous scale which is at once the common bond between the five examples shown and the main point of difference between this group and that shown on the facing page. Another common factor is the employment of a handrail on one side and a curb on the other—the latter a mere log in every example save that at lower left where there is evidence of a developing second handrail. This promise becomes a fact in the bridges of the next group.

Loveland Mountain Metropolitan Park, Colorado

Humbug Mountain State Park, Oregon

Devil's Den State Park, Arkansas

BRIDGES

Plate I M-4

Wildcat Hills Game Reserve, Nebraska

FOOT BRIDGES WITH TWO HANDRAILS

We put our best foot bridge forward in this initial bursting into a half-page cut of a bridge and stoutly deny that we are victimized by the artful maneuvering of a clever photographer. After faithful editorial effort to discount the unfair advantage this conscienceless fellow has heaped on it, the bridge still seems to rate as a bull's-eye for those who designed and executed it.

Pleasing overscale, the subtle camber of the handrails, logical interrelation of the sizes of the various timbers, the exaggerated rake of the outrigger braces—all add up to a score that is impressive. The reader is implored to see only the good and to go along with us in being blind to the inferior masonry of the abutment. This feature certainly cannot be recommended to serve as a model.

All the bridges illustrated on these facing pages comprise a related group. There is great variation in scale ranging between the pudgy example at upper left and the rather attenuated construction of the bridge at lower right. The former is so very ample for performing its obviously light task that it may seem ridiculous to plead that the diagonal handrail braces (which might have been omitted altogether with logic) should have taken the other diagonal and made a pretense at functioning.

It should be noted that outrigger construction for bracing the railings, hardly encountered up to this page, here becomes almost the rule.

Plate I M-5 ⋙ BRIDGES

Custer State Park, South Dakota

Saratoga Hot Springs State Park, Wyoming

Lake Guernsey State Park, Wyoming

Alderwood State Park, Oregon

Devil's Den State Park, Arkansas

Savoy State Forest Park, Massachusetts

Great Smoky Mountains National Park

FOOT AND HORSE TRAIL BRIDGES IN VARIETY

In the scale of the bridge shown above there is happily present that visible assurance of adequate strength so strongly urged for park bridges. The suggestion of invitation with which the splayed approach invests the narrow foot bridge is here well exampled.

As a group the bridges on the facing page are not so well integrated as the group just reviewed. Individuality is more the note. Only the bridge at Crater Lake National Park is comparable in sturdiness with the bridge shown above. A bridge of the left hand column of the facing page, an example in Parvin State Park, borrows the graceful and pleasing crown or segmental arch form characteristic of oriental garden bridges. The bridge in Clifty Falls State Park brings on the scene for the first time squared timber members, and this bridge and the Wind Cave National Park subject illustrate the possibilities for extending the masonry abutment of a wood span bridge to the height of the railing. Both also show a sophisticated and careful masonry construction that has not appeared in any of the bridges shown up to this point. Such masonry is more typical of large bridges. The somewhat elaborate rail pattern of the Scenic State Park bridge is more at home in its birch thicket setting than it would be either among larger trees or in the open.

Plate I M-7 ⋙ BRIDGES

Parvin State Park, New Jersey

Crater Lake National Park

Parvin State Park, New Jersey

Scenic State Park, Minnesota

Clifty Falls State Park, Indiana

Wind Cave National Park

BRIDGES ‹‹‹ Plate I M-8

Fort Collins Mountain Metropolitan Park, Colorado

TIMBER FOOT BRIDGES OF MULTIPLE SPAN

In the examples shown on these pages, stone piers in support of the bridge spans appear almost to be the rule, with but one bridge employing wood for the purpose. This exception does not prove the rule, however, for there are possibilities in wood bents and log cribbing to bring greater variety to multiple span foot and horse trail bridges than is manifested here. The multiple span vehicle bridges later shown give proof of this.

The Crowley's Ridge State Park and the Ponca Lake Metropolitan Park bridges illustrate the results that can obtain when the terminations of the handrails are "brought to ground." Such satisfying features as ample bearing, firm anchorage, and exaggerated crown sum up to a total effect that is at once suggestive of strength and of skillful adaptation to site.

The superiority—practical, logical, and aesthetic—of a considerable batter to masonry bridge piers may be readily appreciated by a close study of this series. Noteworthy for this important feature are the examples from Colorado, Oklahoma, and Wyoming here pictured. Likewise does this group afford a suitable opportunity for appraising the merits of outrigger bracing and of the scale of individual wood members in relation to adjoining parts, to length of span, and to length of the bridge itself.

Plate I M–9 ⇛ BRIDGES

Crowley's Ridge State Park, Arkansas

Yosemite National Park

South Mountain Reservation, New Jersey

Saratoga Hot Springs State Park, Wyoming

Ponca Lake Metropolitan Park, Ponca, Oklahoma

Ledges State Park, Iowa

BRIDGES

Plate I M-10

New Salem State Park, Illinois

FOOT AND HORSE TRAIL BRIDGES

A common denominator of this aggregation of bridges is squared timber members. These may be smooth-dressed, rough-sawn, or hewn and dressed with axe or adze. The aesthetic value of an axe- or adze-dressed surface is hardly apparent in a photograph, but the quality such surfaces bring to park construction is quickly sensed when observed in the actual. The two New Jersey bridges benefit greatly from hewn surfaces.

The bridge at New Salem State Park, wherein is a reconstructed pioneer village, seeks and achieves a primitive quality related well to its surroundings by virtue of hand-split rails and hand-hewn posts, smoothed of all sharp edges to a convincing simulation of great age and long weathering.

The crown or camber of the vigorous bridge at Whitewater State Park, Minnesota, seems in very proper amount and contributes, along with the sensibly trussed rail pattern, to the eye-appeal of this bridge.

Common to the bridges of the outer column of the facing page is the slender, segmental arch form. In Illinois this is usually of laminated wood, occasionally of reinforced concrete with the offhand appearance of wood. The Rock Creek Park bridge is frankly concrete. There is a soaring grace about bridges of this profile that is very appealing. Large suspension bridges have made the profile familiar to us in this usage, and a present day streamline-mindedness must on occasion be served.

Plate I M-11 　　　　　　　　　　　　　　　　　　　　　　　　　　　　⇛ BRIDGES

Cooper River Parkway, New Jersey

Gebhards Woods, I. & M. Canal State Park, Illinois

Egg Harbor River Parkway, New Jersey

White Pine Forest State Park, Illinois

Whitewater State Park, Minnesota

Rock Creek Park, Washington, D. C.

BRIDGES

Custer State Park, South Dakota

MINOR VEHICLE BRIDGES

At this point the bridge comes of age and accommodates vehicles. Once again in the choice of the key illustration of this group, a clever photographer is suspect of having played friend-at-court, although it is contended the bridge has real merit on its own. The graceful birch may artfully mask formless masonry abutments but the wood span—its braces, railing members, outriggers—all appear of pleasing proportion in an attractive pattern.

On the facing page is illustrated the development of the vehicle bridge, from vehicular equivalent (at upper right) of the passerelle which ushered in foot bridges, to the full-fledged bridges at the bottom of the page, having abutments that grow into approaches. There is an appealing, humorous quality about the little bridge at Goose Island State Park, Texas—Mother Goose is the name for it. As the illustrations well disclose, the droughts of recent years have made it difficult to obtain photographs of some bridges in any convincing relationship to the obstacles involved. This is especially noticeable in this series and should not be held in disparagement of these bridges in the light of more normal function.

Plate I M-13 ⋙ BRIDGES

Roosevelt Regional State Park, North Dakota

Goose Island State Park, Texas

Letchworth State Park, New York

Lewis and Clark State Park, Washington

Osage Hills State Park, Oklahoma

Mohawk Metropolitan Park, Tulsa, Oklahoma

BRIDGES ««   *Plate* I M–14

Sequoia National Park

WOOD SPAN VEHICLE BRIDGES

There is in the bridge above-illustrated a robustness of scale that qualifies it for preeminence among the examples shown on these facing pages. The positional as well as the scale relationship between the posts of the railings and the log girders, and the great size of the latter members conspire to produce a bridge extraordinarily harmonious with the boulder-strewn creek and the wilderness setting.

Facing are vehicle bridges which in the left column employ round timbers and in the right column squared timbers. The bridge at upper left is very much the bridge above in miniature, and retains its heroic scale. Note in the bridge just below it that the abutment constructed of log cribbing makes its entrance on the scene.

In the trio of bridges of squared timbers we have the grade-high abutment at the top, next it extends half the height of the rail, and finally to the full height of the rail and steps down to grade on the approach side. The refinements of axe- or adze-dressed surfaces and of wood-pegged connections appear in these bridges.

Plate I M–15 ⇶ BRIDGES

Bandelier National Monument

I & M Canal State Park, Illinois

Yellowstone National Park

Cook County Forest Preserve, Illinois

Lassen Volcanic National Park

Spring Mill State Park, Indiana

BRIDGES Plate I M–16

Margaret Lewis Norrie State Park, New York

MINOR VEHICLE BRIDGES OF MASONRY

The masonry arch bridge offers variety by reason of the many arch profiles, stone colors and textures, and masonry techniques it is possible to employ. The proportion between length of arch stones and span of arch is an always important consideration. An arch that appears inadequate to support the bridge is a major aesthetic blunder, even though the roadway is actually carried by a concrete construction for which the stone wall is merely a surfacing.

The arch of the example above has in satisfying degree that look of being competent to perform its job, as have also the arches of the Texas bridges at the bottom of the facing page. In the others it exists in lesser degree. The Missouri bridge waives this consideration aside as unimportant, and brazenly "tells all" about modern bridge construction by choosing to substitute an arch fillet of concrete for any mere vestige of a true stone arch.

There is informality in a stepped silhouette for the parapet wall of park bridges, as at Lockhart and Longhorn Cavern State Parks, which is held to be in better "park character" than any use of a thin, projecting, and more formal cap stone.

The little masonry bridge in Dutchess County, New York, shown as tailpiece illustration on page 8, belongs in the group shown here. If the information regarding this bridge is accurate, it is passed along with embarrassment, for it is said to be an ancient structure—not consciously created for its superlative park character. Achievement will be considerable, when, purposing to build park bridges of distinction, actual accomplishment in equivalent degree is more the rule.

Plate I M–17 ⋙ BRIDGES

October Mountain State Forest Park, Massachusetts

Bennett Springs State Park, Missouri

Canyon Park, Oklahoma City, Oklahoma

Wintersmith Metropolitan Park, Ada, Oklahoma

Lockhart State Park, Texas

Longhorn Cavern State Park, Texas

BRIDGES «« Plate I M–18

Enfield Glen State Park, New York

LARGER STONE VEHICLE BRIDGES

Unfortunate among larger stone arch bridges is a tendency to a thin and structurally weak appearance at the crown of the arch. Even the annointed of this group shown above suffers slightly from this occupational defect. So also does the Arbuckle Trail, Oklahoma, bridge although not actually a long span. It is more conspicuously present in many otherwise pleasing and graceful park bridges that are not here illustrated, and for that reason.

As the length of stone arch increases, it of course follows that it is increasingly difficult to maintain the same arch-stones-to-arch-span proportion we admire in the smaller arch bridge. We do not then bay the moon but adapt our standards of judgment in this regard to the limits of the possible. The arch stones of the bridge in Zion National Park seem happily scaled to the size of the arch.

Among this group are shown a variety of stone patterns and techniques and a varying merit. In an age when the carrying arch is almost invariably of concrete, and the stone sidewalls and their vestigial arches are mere veneer, it is thrilling to observe that the stone arch of the McCormick's Creek bridge is functional, carrying through the width of the bridge. The disillusionment when a veneer-arch barely turns the corner to give way to a characterless concrete surface comes always as something of a shock.

Plate I M–19   ⋙ BRIDGES

Cheaha State Park, Alabama

Arbuckle Trail, Oklahoma

Yellowstone National Park

Zion National Park

McCormick's Creek State Park, Indiana

Watkins Glen State Park, New York

BRIDGES

Plate I M-20

Devil's Den State Park, Arkansas

VEHICLE BRIDGES OF MULTIPLE WOOD SPAN

The conditions indicating a bridge construction as a succession of wood spans are usually a comparatively shallow declivity, a considerable distance between banks, and the absence of any necessity for maintaining a clear span. The highly interesting bridge on this page has greater height than any shown opposite, and the resulting lofty and massive piers are impressive. The observant will note that many otherwise well-executed bridges terminate too abruptly after gaining what often seems a precariously slight bearing on the bank or abutment. The Devil's Den bridge rolls magnificently and hospitably on to join hands with the guard rails of the transverse road construction with such unmistakable grace that it easily wins place as the key example of this group.

The bridges of the left column on the facing page are of log construction (except for the stone abutments of the one) and illustrate that the intermediate supports may be posts with bracing, bents, cribbing, or any of these in combination, as at Mohawk Trail State Forest Park, Massachusetts.

The bridges shown in the outer column opposite employ intermediate piers of masonry. The bridge at the top has floor construction of wood, and the next below, steel and concrete masked by log stringers. At the bottom will be seen a bridge of concrete floor construction undisguised, supported on stone piers and abutments, and utilizing log handrails—a combination of modern and time-honored materials and methods that is both reasonable and forthright.

Plate I M–21 ⇶ BRIDGES

Levi Jackson-Wilderness Road State Park, Kentucky

Giant City State Park, Illinois

Mohawk Trail State Forest Park, Massachusetts

Backbone State Park, Iowa

Yellowstone National Park

Yellowstone National Park

BRIDGES   Plate I M–22

Whitewater State Park, Minnesota

MULTIPLE ARCH AND SUSPENSION BRIDGES

Streamlining has not yet drummed the pleasing rhythm of the repeating arch form out of our consciousness. And when the melody is echoed in still waters as it is above, we are reassured that it will forever continue within the range of our appreciation.

A pitfall in the designing of the multiple arch stone bridge is insufficient mass in the piers. A tendency in this direction is noticeable in the bridge illustrated at the bottom of the left hand column opposite. Pleasing in the top example are the subtle crowning of the parapet silhouette and equally subtle splay of the terminals, so that these suggest rather than actually become wing walls. The arch stones of this double-arched example are very happily scaled and have a face-to-back thickness that is not glaringly disclosing of the concrete inner construction.

The suspension constructions shown in the right hand column embrace two foot bridges, top and bottom, and a vehicle bridge at Mount Rainier National Park. The suspension bridge probably more than any other type will provoke controversy among the park-minded as to its fitness in a wilderness. There are those who will accept the log constructions and ban the type represented by the example at Jay Cooke State Park, and there are some who will approve, and others who will deplore, both types. Space here permits the showing of these bridges, but by great good fortune does not allow for comment or analysis disclosing of other than a neutral position regarding them.

Plate I M–23 ⇒⇒ BRIDGES

Mount Vernon Memorial Highway

Rainbow Falls State Park, Washington

Cook County Forest Preserve, Illinois

Mount Rainier National Park

Bennett Springs State Park, Missouri

Jay Cooke State Park, Minnesota

BRIDGES

Quartz Mountain State Park, Oklahoma

Roman Nose State Park, Oklahoma

Palmetto State Park, Texas

LOW WATER BRIDGES

Where terrain and other affecting conditions are such that the approach roads to the bridge and nearby streamside use areas are unusable during flood periods, it is purposeless to elevate the bridge above flood stage to a resulting awkward relationship with the terrain. In such locations the low water bridge has proper place. Predicated on frequent submersions by flood, this type of bridge calls for a rugged, "weighted" scale that gives unmistakable assurance of permanence.

Boyle Metropolitan Park, Little Rock, Arkansas

Boyle Metropolitan Park, Little Rock, Arkansas

Part II

Recreational and Cultural Facilities

CONTENTS

	PAGE
RECREATIONAL AND CULTURAL FACILITIES	1
PICNIC TABLES	7
Plates II A–1 *to* II A–17	
PICNIC FIREPLACES	27
Plates II B–1 *to* II B–11	
REFUSE RECEPTACLES AND PITS	41
Plates II C–1 *to* II C–3	
PICNIC SHELTERS AND KITCHENS	45
Plates II D–1 *to* II D–26	
CONCESSIONS AND REFECTORIES	73
Plates II E–1 *to* II E–13	
TRAILSIDE SEATS, SHELTERS, AND OVERLOOKS	87
Plates II F–1 *to* II F–29	
DAMS AND POOLS	119
Plates II G–1 *to* II G–6	
BATHHOUSES AND DEPENDENCIES	127
Plates II H–1 *to* II H–15	
BOATHOUSES AND DEPENDENCIES	145
Plates II I–1 *to* II I–9	
MISCELLANEOUS SPORTS STRUCTURES	155
Plates II J–1 *to* II J–10	
MARKERS, SHRINES, AND MUSEUMS	169
Plates II K–1 *to* II K–13	
HISTORICAL PRESERVATIONS AND RECONSTRUCTIONS	185
Plates II L–1 *to* II L–9	
CAMPFIRE CIRCLES AND OUTDOOR THEATERS	197
Plates II M–1 *to* II M–14	

RECREATIONAL AND CULTURAL FACILITIES

WE ARE PRONE to assume that all forms of day use recreation in parks are readily classifiable as "active" or "cultural." In point of fact "Active and Cultural Recreational Facilities" was the tentative title of the discussion here being launched until picnicking, probably the most popular recreational pursuit in parks, was put under the microscope.

Memory, observation, research—all seemed to substantiate a feeling that picnicking, while certainly recreation, is actually a brief life cycle, intemperately active at the start and tapering off rapidly to a state of comparative inaction, not to say torpor, and hardly fittingly classifiable at any stage as cultural in any sense. As between promoting a campaign to overhaul the institution of picnicking as it exists and a tactical retreat to "Recreational and Cultural Facilities" as a more apt title, the positive promise of the latter seemed to "have the edge." So picnicking can remain for the present just recreational, neither active nor inactive by fiat, its state of culture not a matter of public concern. Let us get the discussion of picnic facilities, as a disturbing borderline case, behind us before indulging our taste for dissecting recreational facilities which can be neatly tagged "active" or "cultural."

CHARACTERISTIC OF NATURAL VALUES in park picnic areas generally is a congenital tendency to quick decay, eternally threatening to infect the natural fabric of entire park areas. Careful diagnosis and heroic remedies are very much in order. Notwithstanding constant vigilance, human use "like a worm i' the bud" feeds on the damask cheek of Nature, in which figure our prayers should probably be for a potent insecticide to retard, if it may not altogether exclude, the processes of deterioration.

That the natural values present and potential in a park are best preserved and fostered by confining the wear and tear of human use to well-defined concentration points has become almost axiomatic in sound park planning thought of today. The exact degree of concentration of facilities conducive to a supportable concentration of use is by no means so generally understood. In certain areas the theory has been so reservedly applied that the damaging effect of human activities continues to spread out over a disproportionate share of the park. In others, with equally destructive results, it has been too literally embraced.

It is hardly possible to devise for existing areas a universal formula for determining whether closer concentration of picnic facilities or retreat from overconcentration is in the direction of the double objective sought—improving the immediate environment of the picnickers and preserving in proper maximum the natural aspect of the less modified surrounding area. Although a divining rod be lacking, the remedy for a particular area should be perfectly obvious to anyone who will (1) closely and dispassionately observe it suffering average attendance, (2) coordinate his observations, and then (3) follow through to a rational conclusion, when, it is devoutly to be wished, he will do something about it.

Because the happy mean between an overcrowded picnic area and an overextended one is so very difficult to formulate and because when it is missed the horns of the dilemma offer a repellant scar or a menacing infection, something more promising and positive in the way of a solution invites study.

The most reasoned suggestion yet advanced is for rotating the use of picnic areas. In place of the usual complement of facilities for serving adequately the needs of a given patronage it has been proposed to double the number of facilities in some feasible arrangement of lay-out which will permit roughly half of the area to be withdrawn from intensive use in alternate years. Perennial regener-

RECREATIONAL AND CULTURAL FACILITIES

ation of the values that make a picnic area attractive should result from such a development. The processes of renewal might not be entirely automatic but should hardly require any great burden of management.

A stand-by area with its duplicating facilities may appear at first thought to add to initial development cost. Actually it merely anticipates by a few years, and only in part, the greater outlay forced when year-in and year-out concentrated use has made a shambles of a picnic area. Over the years, recurrent seeking of greener pastures for the continuously used picnic area will lead to deterioration needlessly extended and to the multiplied costs of progressive removals. It can be claimed with reason that the stand-by area in the long run is as economical of cost and space as it is conservational of attractive natural surroundings.

The cost of providing a stand-by picnic area can be greatly reduced by a Siamese plan arrangement which will avoid the need of duplicating some of the picnic facilities, especially the more expensive ones. If toilets, shelters, and kitchens are placed on the boundary between the biennially alternative picnic areas, a great saving in cost is effected without any great sacrifice of convenience in their use, regardless of which picnic ground is active.

Especially recommended for these dual lay-outs are heavy wooden picnic tables movable only by exertion of just that degree of effort which forestalls the public and causes satisfaction among the maintenance crew that table movings—thank heaven!—are a twelvemonth apart. If tables are of a type incapable of being moved by the park crew to an alternate location, it will be difficult to keep the public out of the portion of the area being rested. Stone tables have this defect. Mobility in the degree recommended will not only save the resting area from a bootleg use, so to say, but will limit the first cost of tables to those actually needed for normal use. Where the recommendation for alternating picnic sites as above-outlined can be practically followed to the letter, the overburden of cost can be held to the duplication of drinking fountains, refuse pits, and fireplaces. Even the cost of duplicating fireplaces may be evaded where the use of one or another of the metal or concrete fireplaces of movable type, hereinafter illustrated, is looked on with favor.

Hence it appears that the proposition of the stand-by picnic area may not, after all, be so much a matter of cost as one of whether the acreage and topography of the park—and the scope of the park planner's understanding—are receptive to it.

THERE IS ANOTHER IMPORTANT ADVANTAGE of the stand-by picnic area. Holiday crowds heavily overtax facilities that are quite sufficient for a normal patronage. These overloads tend to influence the park authority to provide picnic tables and fireplaces out of all proportion to normal needs. Such a solution is not ingenious. But by having "up its sleeve", so to speak, a stand-by area in process of regeneration, the park is prepared to absorb the shock of a peak load. So long as peak load is not interpreted to include all week ends but is confined to holidays and similarly infrequent special events, the opening up of the alternative picnic area for such occasions should not unwarrantably retard the recuperative process. If the recommended withdrawal of picnic tables from the resting area has been practiced, there can be a reserve supply of light folding tables temporarily placed in the "out-of-season" area for the holiday crowds.

Another planning procedure in the direction of preventing devastating wear and tear in a picnic area is the substitution of several minor shelters or kitchen shelters for a single large building. The latter, as the hub of all picnicking activity, tends to acquire a threadbareness in its immediate environs that can spread rapidly along the many paths that converge on it. On the other hand, a small concession building, if necessary in the scheme of things, and several minor scattered supplementing picnic shelters or kitchen shelters can often so distribute destructive wear that the recuperative powers inherent in Nature are enabled to keep abreast of the wearing-out process.

Similarly the site destructiveness of the drinking fountain will not so rapidly outstrip natural regenerative processes if, instead of one such facility, heavily taxed by use, several of very simple type are judiciously scattered through the large picnic area.

Some measure of privacy is certainly sought by many picnic parties and should in reasonable degree be vouchsafed to those groups desiring it. If the area dedicated to picnicking is devoid of, or but sparsely provided with, low growth contributory to reasonable suggestion of seclusion, then wider separation of table and fireplace facilities is almost an alternative requirement. Natural environment, in terms of low-growing vegetation and shrubs, thus proves its worth in terms of practical economy. It is something to be carefully preserved for the very check it provides against a sprawling expansion of the acreage given over to picnicking.

Among the facilities needed in picnic areas are two items which, in heavily used areas, provoke divergent theories in justification of approach. These are table and bench combinations and fireplaces. For picnic areas of moderate size in little modified settings, there is probably negligible opinion deprecatory of the appropriateness and appeal of the sturdy handcrafted picnic table. So also of the naturalistic rock fireplace skillfully insinuated into its setting with a sculptor's finesse. Yet in respect to parks to which picnickers swarm like locusts demanding weekly, or even daily, use of hundreds upon hundreds of tables and fireplaces (the many picnic areas of the Cook County Forest Preserve come to mind as examples of this heavy use), one may well wonder if endless repetition of the overconsciously primitive, painstakingly mannered facility could not become more than slightly nauseating.

For quantity consumption is there not perhaps greater logic and appropiateness, and even real art, in an out-and-out product of quantity production? The sheet steel "cheese box" fireplace devised for the picnic groves massed in the Chicago metropolitan district is exactly that. In addition, it is economical in materials, conserving of space and fuel, intensely practical and efficient, and if these attributes are not truly those of a facility in the real meaning of the term, then it has been misapplied.

We find the picnic table, handcrafted from heavily scaled native materials, an ingratiating thing where distributed by the dozen or even by the score through scenic areas, but in settings scenically substandard and commonplace, to the number of hundreds in supply of use-demand, is it not possible that it is malapropos? There are many to hold that it is, and that only tables produced by assembly line methods truly tune in on the wave length of our times.

Among the More Active recreational offerings in parks, most indulged in is hiking, an unsuitable term, but one which, like the word rustic, must serve us until something more appropriate appears. The sport becomes a recreational feature immediately the park is born. It can be enjoyed (never more completely by some) before any development and construction are brought to the refinement of foot trails. These have a way of developing without the benefit of conscious planning, and there are those who will say that the trail which just grows, marking a line of least resistance to some point of vantage or of interest, is not always improved by conscious efforts. The potential weakness of the unplanned trail is the tendency to become needlessly wide with unrequired forks and bypasses. There generally comes a time in the developing use of the trail which has "laid itself out" when conscious and careful planning must rescue it, and there is always danger of the step being too long deferred.

Of course it is obvious that many items necessarily or desirably incidental or auxiliary to a trail by no means just grow. Eventually there must be drains and gutters built at locations vulnerable to erosion. Seats, sometimes roofed, and small shelters are welcome for the rest and protection from sun and storm they afford. Guard rails will make for safety at stretches where steep slope or narrowness of trail is a hazard. A prospect point will suggest the betterment of view to derive from an overlook structure rising above the natural elevation.

Overnight cabins, of which the Adirondack shelter is the prototype, are a needed refuge along cross country routes like the Appalachian Trail, which invite week end or longer hikes, or where the going is difficult. They are especially needed at strategic intervals along trails where winter journeys on skis and snowshoes are offered and high altitudes induce sudden and heavy snowfalls. Under such conditions it is desirable to provide some means for closing the open front of the typical trail shelter.

RECREATIONAL AND CULTURAL FACILITIES

IN MANY NATURAL PARKS, particularly those close to great centers of population, and in most recreational reserves, active recreation beyond picnicking and hiking means largely water recreation. Where rivers have limited recreational value, due to flood tendency, pollution, or other influences, and where natural lakes are few or nonexistent, the urge to create water area for swimming and boating is a natural and understandable one. The appropriateness of an artificial lake depends entirely on whether the chief potential of an area is the preservation of natural beauty, historical values, or scientific interest, or is the development of recreational facilities. Whether it will flood a disproportionate amount of the area at the expense of the claims of land recreational activities, or can be effected only by a dam which produces an ineradicable scar, or will be a muddy torrent for the rainy season and lapse into a stagnant, mosquito-breeding puddle for the remainder of the year—all these are considerations to be solemnly weighed.

"The lusty mania for building artificial lakes in natural surroundings" has been noted as threatening, and warning has been flown against "rash and ill-considered action" in the widespread creation of lakes that are invading misfits.

The artificial lake can add nothing of scenic value where scenic values exist. Rarely has it been imposed without diminishing the natural values originally present. Its benefits are chiefly recreational. It has no place where the preservation of scenic, scientific, or historical values is the theme.

However, with some groups, charged with the development of park and recreation systems, the impounding of a considerable body of water by the construction of a large dam is apparently, and regardless of other considerations, the "be-all and the end-all" of park planning. There is a confused scrambling of preservation principles and recreation objectives.

The current pointing with pride to acres and acres of exotic water surface, which have sacrificed certain values in reaching for others, smacks of the same pathetic provincialism which led the last generation to boast of the tallest bank building in the south-central section of the State, and the generation before that to glory in its red plush Grand Opera House. The latter has long since become a market or a burlesque house. The bank is in the hands of a receiver. May some equally appalling fate lie in store for the ill-conceived artificial lake intruded to a marring of scenic beauty or a modification of a setting of historic or scientific interest!

In point of fact there have been brought into being some publicly owned areas so flooded that it would seem perfectly reasonable to enlarge the nomenclature of parks and recreation to include "public lake" along with "park", "historic site", "recreational reserve", and the other familiarly known designations.

Due to the perversities of topography, the shore line of a made lake will almost never exactly coincide with the boundary lines of the publicly owned tract, and there will always be some elevated stretches here and there which will not submerge. This wastage is a thorn in the side of the advocates of bigger and better lakes, and distresses them greatly. They get what consolation they can from the fact that these remnants are as small as may be, and strive mightily not to be overconscious of them. Eventually this ragged fringe is taken over by old-fashioned folk who are apathetic to any need for a complete rearrangement of the continental and marine surfaces of the planet. These reactionaries get a simple satisfaction from sprawling in the shade of a remaining cottonwood or picnicking among the few sycamores not sacrificed in clearing the lake site.

If the only defect of the artificial lake is having appropriated a disproportionate share of the area for itself, this, fortunately, is often possible of correction. The acreage can perhaps be added to in the future so that there evolves finally a well-rounded plan, giving proper space for land recreation activities.

The ultimate idiocy, of course, is reached in impounding a lake so extensive that lands privately owned beyond the boundaries of the public holding are generously presented with a shore frontage. Uncontrolled frontage on a recreation lake is a constant threat against the high standards we would insure for park and recreation areas. It is a potential for all the subversive manifestations of shoddy, commercial amusement enterprise—dance halls, concessions, and the like—which, even in remote contact, cannot but affect unfavorably the natural

RECREATIONAL AND CULTURAL FACILITIES

park values and the recreation ideals we would preserve.

AFTER BATHING AND BOATING there are other sports and active recreational pursuits which, if not so widely demanded, are yet attracting constantly increasing popular participation.

Winter sports, as a group, are prominent among these and embrace many activities. Few are actually dependent on construction for their existence as recreational offerings in a park, yet all are greatly promoted and more widely enjoyed by reason of the availability of certain accessory structures. Thus, while perhaps only tobogganing and bobsledding may be said really to require construction (in the form of tracks when a suitable hillside is lacking or when maximum safety and satisfaction are sought), outdoor winter pursuits generally will make auxiliary use of heated shelters, concessions, and such other facilities as are basic to a recreational program at other seasons of the year. The range of cross country skiing and snowshoeing is obviously widened by the availability of shelter cabins at strategic locations on an overland trail, but these again usually meet a dual or multiple need not confined to the winter sports program alone.

Horseback riding is currently enjoying an increasing popularity in some localities, hardly second to the great interest in winter sports prevailing in New England and in some areas of the West. It has long been a popular pursuit in the larger national parks, ranging from a form of exercise of a few hours' duration to extended trips of several days into remote and often otherwise inaccessible areas. More recent has been its introduction into parks smaller in area and nearer to population centers. Structures directly facilitating riding embrace stables and corrals, and where horse trails are extensive and the country rugged and little developed, trail shelters and overnight accommodations for riders, and trail shelters and corrals for the riding and pack animals are not unusual.

THE POTENTIALITIES FOR CULTURAL RECREATION in natural parks were only realized long after facilities for active recreation had won place there. In spite of this comparatively short span of recognition and development, the propriety of facilities for cultural pursuits in such publicly owned areas is now almost universally admitted.

During recent years there has been a healthy overhauling of old theories that too long governed museum interpretation of outdoor life, and history as well. Emerges the modern viewpoint that it is more civilized and more illuminating to view Nature and its phenomena in situ, and the automobile has made this possible, sooner or later, for everyone.

There are those who claim that the trend reversal that is sending the interpretation of Nature from city museums to the outdoors results from the constant threat of dust explosions in many metropolitan museums. This is a moot point among authorities, but it deserves passing mention if any inquiry into cause is pressed.

The Great Enlightenment has had its depressing effect on the bid price for museum specimens of geological fragments, dinosaur tracks in concrete, and Cardiff giants. Quite possibly it may have made some contribution to the appalling mortality among examples of that once far-flung and glamorous institution—the small town zoo. But there are gains to balance these tragic losses, and parks of natural and scientific interest are the beneficiaries.

Structures functioning to interpret the natural, scientific, and historic phases of parks are today many and diverse, and have greatly widened the field of usefulness and appeal of the public preserve. Parks which have added the interpretation of cultural interests to the provision of active recreation will be found to attract many visitors who might never be lured by a foot trail, bridle path, or diving board, or even Nature itself—uninterpreted.

Facilitating media for projecting the story of Nature, in terms of the natural sciences dealing with earth, sky, elements, phenomena, flora, and fauna, and the story of man, by the exposition of events, preservation of survivals, and reconstruction of memorabilia, in record of his progress, may be said to fall within two groups.

One group depends upon the eye for reception. It embraces markers, shrines, and museums, a series in ascending scale, each springing from and elaborating the simpler facility next preceding it.

5

RECREATIONAL AND CULTURAL FACILITIES

Historical preservations and reconstructions and so-called exhibits-in-place belong to this group.

The other group functions rather through the ear. It is a shorter series, embracing the campfire circle and outdoor theater, or amphitheater. Here again there are stages of elaboration, as the outdoor theater develops out of the campfire circle. It is altogether possible that the community building, particularly as it functions in many national parks, is the ultimate of this series, for it brings under roof some of the activities of the campfire circle and outdoor theater. Inasmuch as its offerings are usually not limited to lectures and exhibitions, but include a variety of entertainments such as concerts and dancing, its purpose is perhaps more social than cultural. Herein it is chosen to consider it among the complement of facilities identified with the overnight use of a park or recreation area.

Picnic Shelter, Dr. Edmund A. Babler Memorial Park, St. Louis, Missouri

PICNIC TABLES

AN AVERAGE of the dimensional limits of the human frame and uniformity of a sort in the distribution of the hinges thereof have long since determined certain basic dimensions for the picnic table. In general, the seat surface is 16 to 18 inches and the table surface 28 to 30 inches off the ground or floor, and the front edge of the seat is from one to three inches removed from the edge of the table. These dimensions have been held to in practically all successful picnic tables, and probably in the majority of the unsuccessful ones. The measure of success is determined by numerous and varied other factors, not so easily reducible to rule.

Tables in wide variety are illustrated herein. It is appreciated that differing climates, resources, and habits of use prevailing through the length and breadth of the land call for diversity of materials and details in this necessary item of park equipment. Desirable as are the qualities of sturdiness, nativeness, woodcraft, and handcraft in these minor objects in some locations, in others, it must be recognized that a too much forced effort to achieve them is ill-advised.

Picnic tables may be built entirely of wood or stone, or they may be cleverly contrived combinations of both materials. It is quite possible that tables built wholly or in part of rock blend into some landscapes more readily than do those of logs or sized lumber. They may have aesthetic advantages, and they are durable in the extreme, but their immobility offsets these benefits. The picnic ground is usually an area of intensive use, and its equipment is subject to hard wear. It may seem farsighted to create picnic units of stone because these will "stand the gaff" over a long period. They do meet abundantly this requirement, but their potential life is hardly begun before the site, especially the average picnic site, has lost most of its value as a natural area due to concentrated use, and must be evacuated and left to the healing processes of Nature. The most cumbersome wood table could be moved under these conditions, but the stone picnic table, through no frailty of its own, becomes nonproductive, so to say, and the capital investment therein omits the dividend for the duration of the recuperative period of the site.

There are other less formidable factors militating against the use of masonry for tables. They are executed with great difficulty because, due to the freehand lines desired, workmen find it hard to construct them from a blueprint with a nice balance of freedom and accuracy. The units must be located in almost permanent shade, else they become thoroughly heated and radiate heat for a long period. Furthermore, only the smoothest stone slabs serve satisfactorily as table tops, and these are not always readily obtainable. Cement slab tops in substitution seldom give a satisfactory appearance. Because only a broad base looks reasonable for supporting a table top of stone, there is danger of leg-room interference. With a growing understanding of the many disadvantages of the stone table, the picnic unit entirely of wood has met with increasing favor.

THE VERY FIRST DECISION to be made by the creator of a wooden picnic table is one around which much controversial argument centers. To him it may be only a matter of whim whether the picnic unit in a rustic setting will be built of commercial lumber or of native-cut material, but he should be warned from the first that, whichever his choice, he will be heartily condemned by approximately 50 percent of the arbiters of such matters.

On whichever side he may innocently and squarely range himself, it seems only fair that he be fortified with, and forewarned against, all invokable arguments.

If he elects to use commercial lumber:

(Pro) He has made commendable and honest use of the production facilities of our times to meet all functional requirements of strength, comfort, and economy in a utility, or

(Con) He has with unpardonable insolence desecrated a natural beauty spot by the introduction of utter incongruities, makeshift, uncompromising in line, ugly.

If he elects to use native-cut timber:

(Pro) He has with artistry graced a natural setting with an harmonious facility, not alone of practical usefulness, but of sturdy, handcrafted beauty, or

(Con) He has ruthlessly felled trees which were the park's very reason for being, despoiling a glory of Nature to produce in an outworn craftsmanship trivial accessories that were better produced by today's machines.

If, fully apprised of the pitfalls all around him, the artisan now dares to make a choice, the picnic table may be undertaken. For his encouragement be it said that after this choice is made the further going is comparatively smooth.

If he is not himself definitely of the left or of the right in this issue, he can take a middle course, daring moderate scorn to win moderate approval from the extremists of both views. He can gesture in one direction by deciding that the machine-made product is in truth rigidly uncompromising in line, and in the other, by avoiding cutting any trees within the confines of the park to obtain material needed for the more rugged and freehand table. If the required native material can be had from some source near at hand without sacrifice of the timber resources of the park itself, the table maker can run for a touchdown with cheering from all sections of the stands. Another compromise approach which produces very sightly picnic tables is a combination of dimension lumber for table and seat tops and rustic timbers for the understructure.

The desirability of preventing the public from moving tables about has already been mentioned. Dragging tables around a picnic area is highly destructive of ground cover. The fixed position—fixed insofar as the public is concerned—if a good one, is desirable. It is achieved by means of weight or by anchoring.

WORTHY OF WIDE ADOPTION in the contriving of the picnic unit are numerous practical refinements. Regardless of the soundness of material and workmanship, the boards forming a wooden top tend to pull apart on exposure to the weather. More or less narrow cracks develop between them in which food particles are apt to lodge and are removable with difficulty. How much better that the table top be constructed with open joints about a quarter of an inch wide between the boards, from which food particles, if they do not drop through, can easily be dislodged.

Rough edges on seats and tables should be guarded against. Unfortunately, the picturesque unit of rustic wood material will take high toll in the tearing of silk stockings and light clothing. The unit built of milled materials should have all edges and roughnesses likely to come in contact with clothing, or to produce splinters, smoothed and rounded. Much can be done even to the handcrafted type to eliminate the worst among such hazards without sacrificing rustic character entirely. There is a measure of defense against the use, and consequent abuse, of table tops for uncapping bottles when a convenient device for this purpose is securely fastened within a recess at an end of the table top.

When the anchoring of tables is accomplished by extending their wood supporting members into the ground, in most instances the portions below grade should be treated with creosote, tar, or other preservative. Where the wood is western red cedar or redwood, the use of tar or creosote is considered unnecessary. In general, exposed wood above ground should also be treated against weather by oiling, shellacking, creosoting, or other tried and proved methods. In the Far West this is not encouraged; the natural wood color is preferred and the preservative treatment of the native woods is held to be unnecessary. Especially are treatments carrying color out of favor. With this we are quick to agree once we have observed the surprising number of shades of green and blue which can be bought in paint cans, and how invariably these clash with the colors of Nature.

There are sectional preferences in tables in our parks which veer away from the usual and prosaic. For example, in California round and octagonal tables seem to meet with favor in camp and picnic grounds. It is alleged that they are more useful for playing cards! They are usually fashioned from cross sections of the large redwood and fir trees available on the West coast. But the cross sections split as they weather, and are far from satisfactory for this reason. Therefore none of this type is shown in the accompanying illustrations. Table tops in which the grain of the wood is *with* the slab can be kept cleaner, are longer lived, and in consequence are recommended.

There are conditions and considerations, such as a great need for extra tables on holidays, to dictate that some tables be readily mobile, and collapsible or knock-down for compact storage. Knock-down units should be designed to be assembled easily, and to be as light in weight as is consistent with the structural requirements. The fewer pieces, the better. When parts can be made interchangeable, time is not wasted in sorting them. Cabin or screen door hook fastenings are to be preferred to loose fastenings wherever practicable. Seat and table tops of knock-down units should be of material heavy enough or sufficiently braced to avoid spring or sag.

Mention has already been made of a developing sense of the incongruity of heavy, primitive wooden tables massed in crowded picnic groves where scenic values, particularly woods growth, are deficient. There has been some recent experimentation purposed to evolve practical, comfortable, and lasting picnic tables of "contemporary" aspect— loosed from the fetters of tradition to acknowledge the claims of new materials and methods. Two interesting efforts in this direction have been undertaken in Texas parks, and these are detailed among the plates which follow. One makes use of stock metal tubing for a frame and slabs of reinforced concrete for a table top. The streamlined result is at once practically indestructible and indestructive. Its materials foil the jackknifer, and its weight discourages that other park pest, the table mover. The other table experiment on contemporary lines is of wood, except for the cast metal shoes which serve to keep the wood from contact with the ground. The unit is low and comfortable. This employment of commercial lumber in a functional design is frankly in the technique of the machine age, and many will applaud it as a firm first step in a logical direction.

It would seem reasonable to accentuate on occasion the informality which is the very spirit of picnicking by varying the standardized table and bench combination. There is novelty in an arrangement of naturalized stone buffet table located in shade near a fireplace and seats ranged informally round about through clever naturalizing of boulders, flat rocks, or down logs, or exposing of natural rock outcroppings.

There are park reservations wherein shade is lacking or rainfall is unusually heavy. In such locations picnic units logically include a sheltering roof. They may even require a windbreak against prevalent high winds. Any complexity or increase in size of objects which are desirably kept inconspicuous is unfortunate, but form must always follow demonstrated need.

PICNIC TABLES 　　　　　　　　　　　　　　　　　　　　　　　　　　　Plate II A-1

Picnic Unit — — Bonham State Park — — Texas

Here is pictured the most appealing of the picnic units contrived from squared lumber of commercial sizes. The well proportioned, splayed legs are the outstanding factor in furthering the superiority of this example to the variants shown on the opposite page. There is in this specimen an admirable appearance of being substantially braced against overturning.

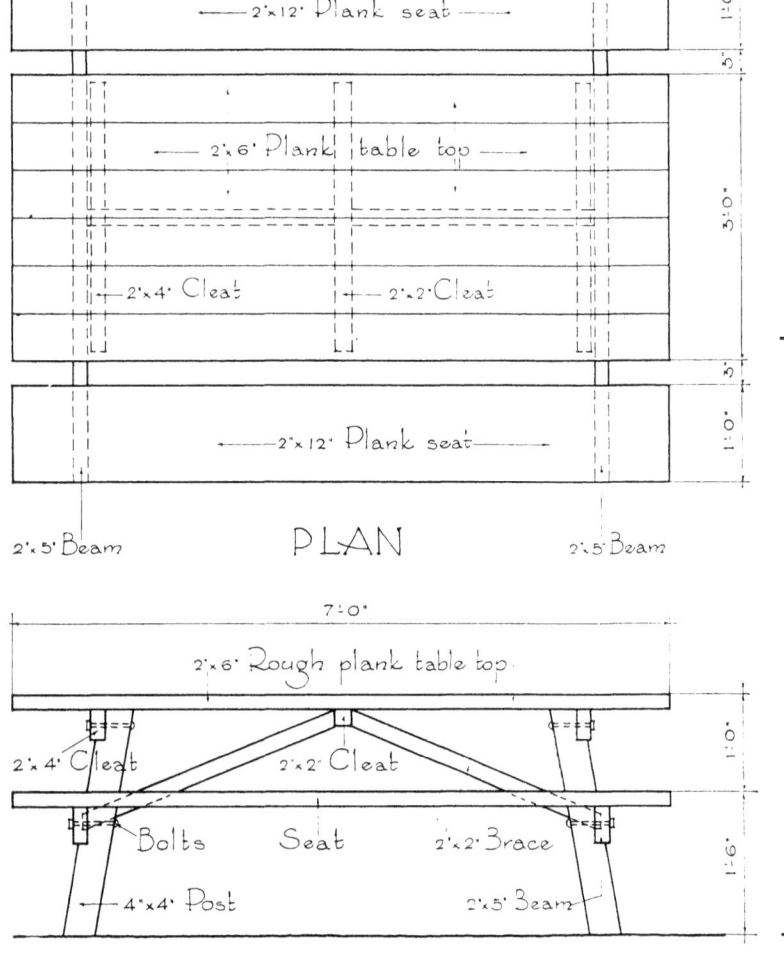

PLAN

SIDE ELEVATION

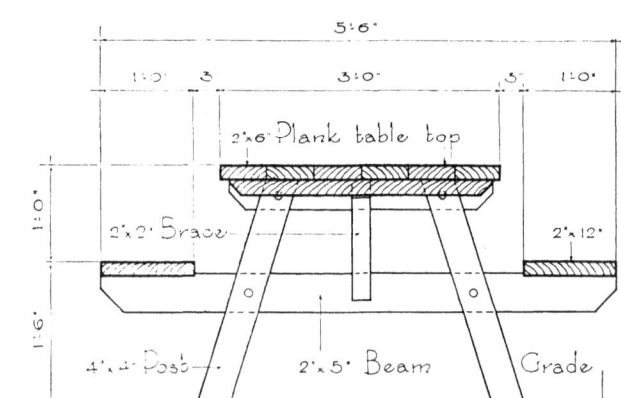

SECTION

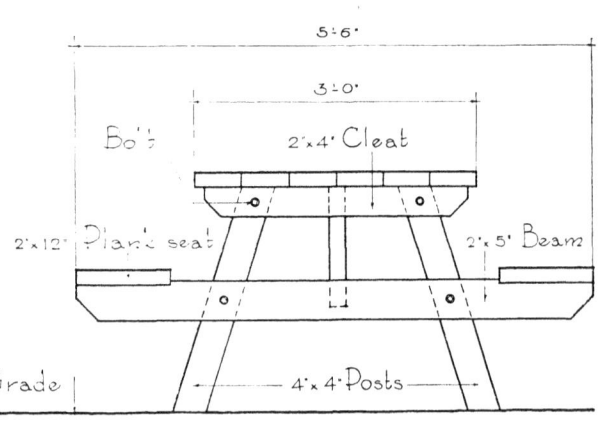

END ELEVATION

Scale ½" = 1'-0"

10

Plate II A–2   →» PICNIC TABLES

American Island Metropolitan Park, Chamberlain, South Dakota

Millersylvania State Park, Washington

PICNIC TABLES OF SQUARE-SAWN MATERIAL

The examples here pictured are more or less closely related to the table detailed on the facing page. Square-sawn lumber of generally commercial sizes is the material used for all, except for the exceedingly thick slabs which are the seat and table tops of the Millersylvania State Park example. The freehand lines of these hewn slabs do much to insinuate this man-made object into a harmony with its surroundings.

Two examples illustrate fabrication of table top with spaces between the component members so that there are no narrow cracks or joints in which food and other accumulations can lodge. The South Dakota table indicates a careful rounding of the edges of seat and table tops so that danger of damage to clothing is minimized. The Pickett Forest table appears particularly sturdy and well-braced. The Platt National Park table is also substantially braced and has a center of gravity so low that it could only be overturned by intent and much effort. All might, and perhaps some do, have a buried length of leg to give fixity of location.

Pickett State Forest, Tennessee

Platt National Park

PICNIC TABLES

Plate II A-3

Picnic Unit
Guernsey Lake State Park — — — Wyoming

A heavy rustic type in which the seats are carried on crossbeams bolted to the legs of the table. There is the possibility of extending the length of the legs to allow for planting in the ground to prevent casual moving of the unit. This basic type of table is widely used in the plains and mountain states. Happily the very nature of the rustic material employed serves to save any one unit from appearing to be the exact duplicate of its next neighbor as the opposite illustrations demonstrate.

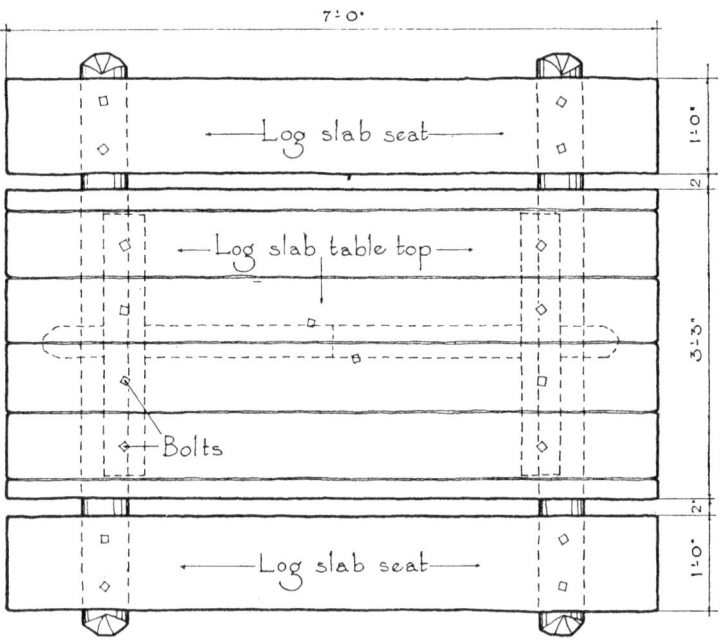

PLAN

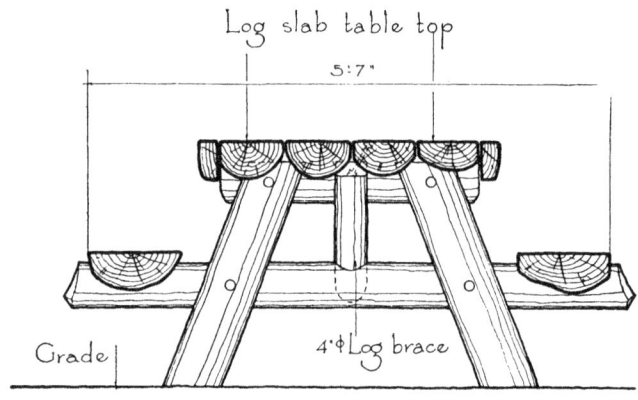

SECTION

All logs and slabs to be peeled

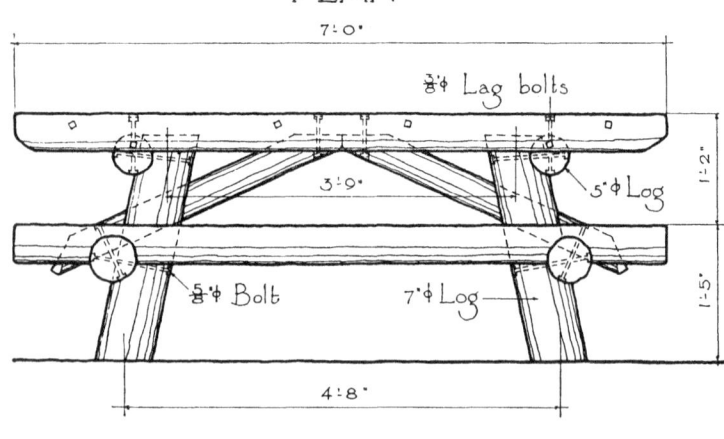

SIDE ELEVATION

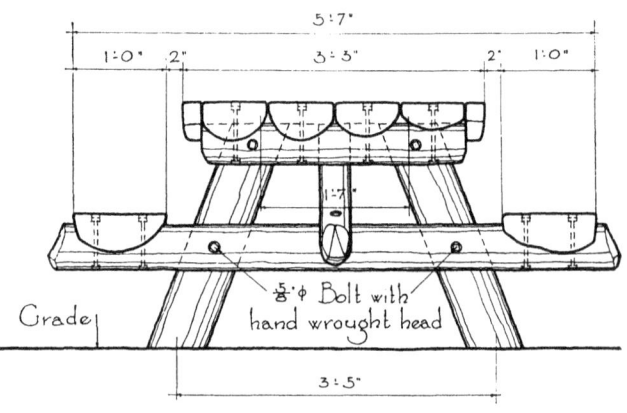

END ELEVATION

Scale ½" = 1'0"

Plate II A-4 →›› PICNIC TABLES

Crowley's Ridge State Park, Arkansas

Dolliver Memorial State Park, Iowa

PICNIC TABLES WITH SUBSTRUCTURE MEMBERS IN THE ROUND

These variants of the table detailed on the opposite page exhibit the quality of handcraftedness in a wide range of scale. The more noticeable differences between them are in seat and table tops. At upper left these are of sawn lumber; at upper right only the top of the table is dressed material—the seat tops are half logs. The examples shown below employ half logs for both seat and table surfaces.

It will be noted that the legs of the Crowley's Ridge table, apparently, and of the Gebhards Woods table, certainly, are buried in the ground. In point of fact the lack of any longitudinal bracing in the latter example makes firm anchoring of the legs a virtual condition of stability under the rack of use. Rigid bracing, both lateral and longitudinal, is very necessary if the picnic unit is to withstand the stresses and strains to which a single season in facilitation of picnicking is certain to subject it. To this the experienced park man charged with maintenance will be quick to testify.

Denver Mountain Metropolitan Parks, Colorado

Gebhards Woods State Park, Illinois

PICNIC TABLES

Plate II A-5

Picnic Unit

South Mountain Reservation — — New Jersey

Squared and round timbers in satisfying combination that is neither too mannered nor too machined in appearance. An excellent compromise favoring equally wilderness setting and the need for great numbers of practical picnic units, appropriate and yet not costly. Present are suitable thickness of seat and table planks, adequacy of cleats to prevent the warping of the table top, and assurance of desirable fixity of location by virtue of the deep-planted supporting members.

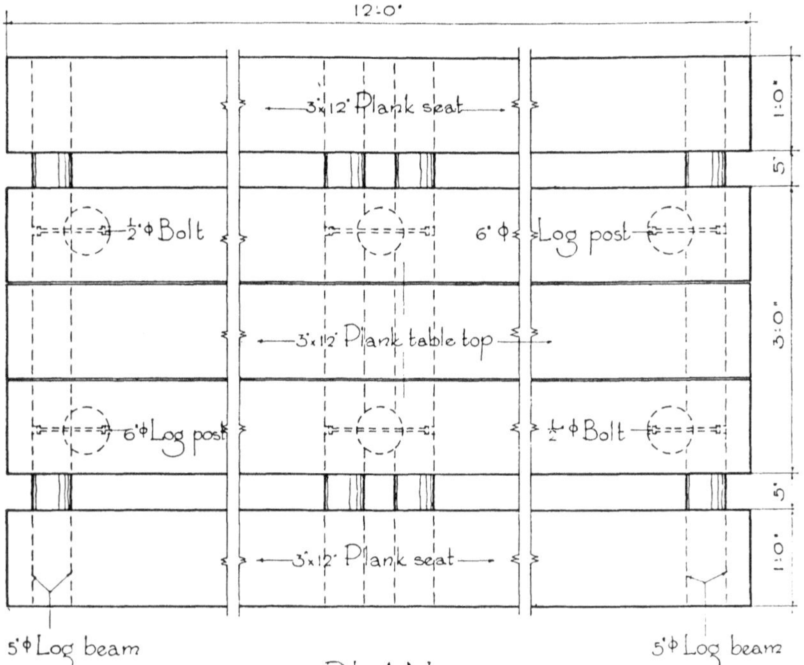

PLAN

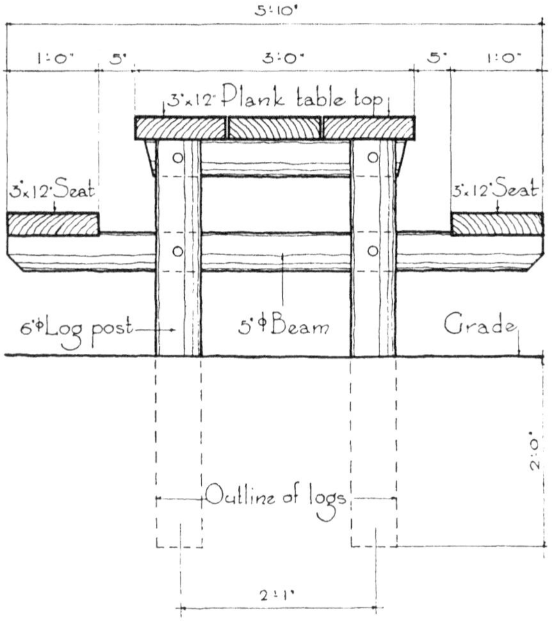

SECTION

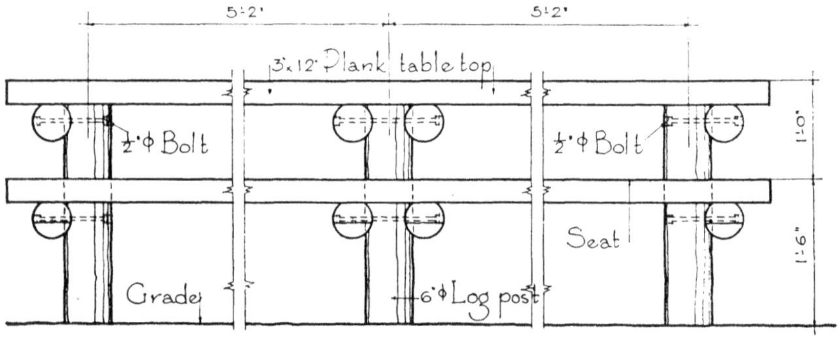

SIDE ELEVATION

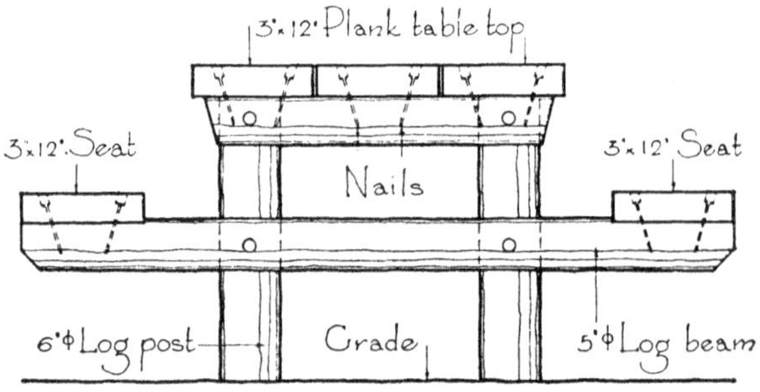

END ELEVATION

Scale ½" = 1'-0"

Rocky Creek State Park, Oregon

Riverside State Park, Washington

PICNIC TABLES OF FIXED LOCATION

Common to these variants of the picnic table detailed on the facing page is that degree of anchorage which effectively discourages the public's inclination to move tables about, and yet does not prevent the maintenance crew from moving them when the picnic ground must be vacated for a period of recuperation.

The subtle differences in these examples hold interest if studied in the light of such potent affecting and related influences as climate, location, and available timber supply. The wide slabs which serve as table tops in three examples are, generally speaking, indigenous only to the Pacific slope. The top of the Oklahoma table is not a single board it is true, but the several pieces that comprise it are of a very satisfying thickness and are spaced sufficiently far apart to do away with unsightly, clogged joints.

The two illustrations above show a substructure of squared material in contrast with one in the round. The fine slabs which serve for table top and seats in the Deception Pass State Park example have astonishing bulk, and show an agreeable disregard for true planes and straight edges.

Deception Pass State Park, Washington

Osage Hills State Park, Oklahoma

PICNIC TABLES

Plate II A-7

Picnic Table

Crater Lake National Park — — — Oregon

A table of substantial proportions that fully acknowledges the impressive scale of the trees native to the Pacific slope and so is appropriate in this and other western National Parks where it has been built. A practical advantage in the type is the absence of underbracing so often inconveniently restrictive of leg room.

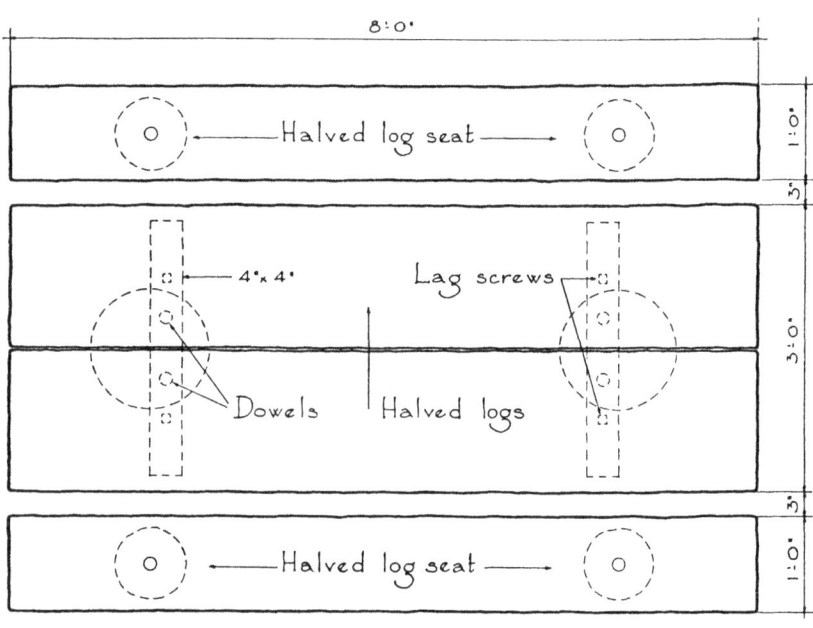

PLAN

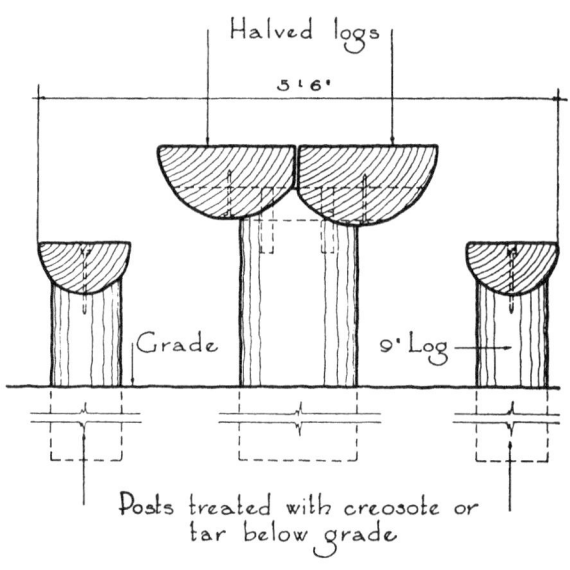

SECTION

All logs to be peeled and stained

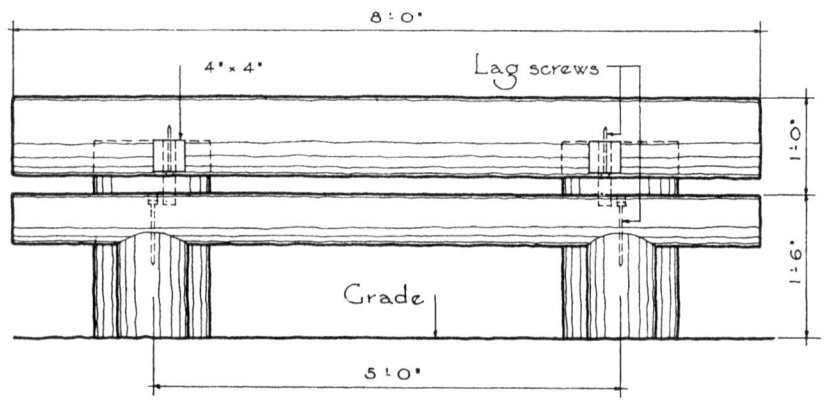

SIDE ELEVATION

END ELEVATION

Scale ½" = 1'-0"

Plate II A-8 →» PICNIC TABLES

Rocky Mountain National Park

Mohawk Metropolitan Park, Tulsa, Oklahoma

PICNIC TABLES WITH BURIED SUPPORTS

The table and bench combination detailed on the facing page and the variations here pictured have in common vertical round supports buried in the ground and benches quite independent of table construction.

At upper left is an example that substitutes three half logs for the two which form the top of the Crater Lake table. At upper right is shown a table with single half log, roughly squared, serving as table top. The Woahink Lake table frankly adopts a sawn slab for this purpose, but half logs still provide the seating. The Deception Pass example goes all the way. Its table and bench top parade the unexcelled timber resources of that region in the form of massive slabs having hewn surfaces and freehand edges.

Shifting of tables of this type is not impossible, yet hardly a light task to be assigned annually to the maintenance crew. There are other types better suited to areas where the wearing-out process is rapid, and frequent relocating of picnic tables is practiced as a maintenance measure.

Woahink Lake State Park, Oregon

Deception Pass State Park, Washington

PICNIC TABLES

Plate II A–9

Picnic Unit

Caddo Lake State Park — — — Texas

Free from accusation of fragility, yet capable of being relocated if occasion demands, this unit and the variations shown on the plate opposite rate well for primitiveness and practicability. Wood construction of this husky character is only truly appropriate if the surrounding standing timber is in scale with the log members of the table and benches.

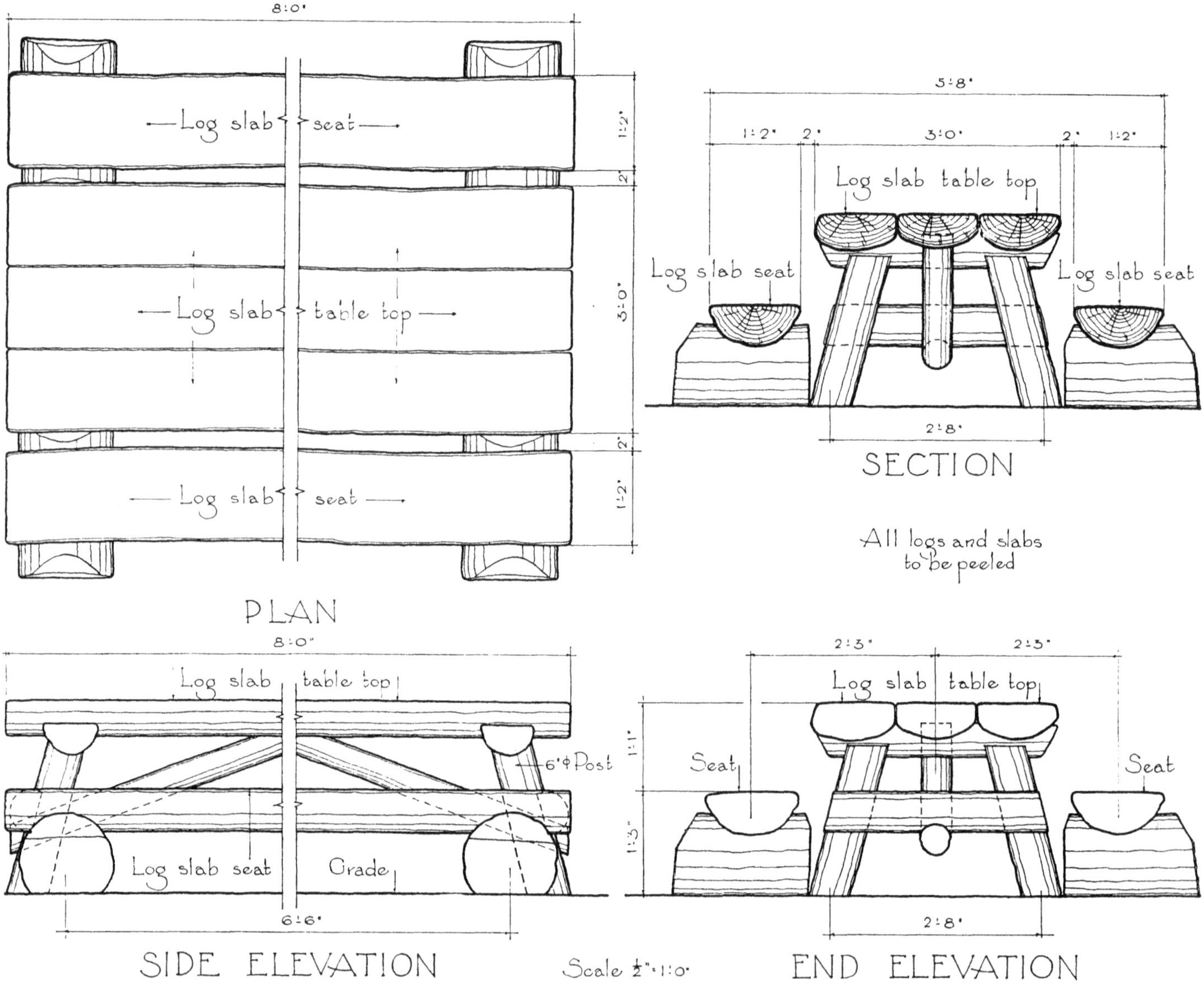

All logs and slabs to be peeled

PLAN

SECTION

SIDE ELEVATION

END ELEVATION

Scale ½"=1'0"

Plate II A-10 →» PICNIC TABLES

Caddo Lake State Park, Texas

Scenic State Park, Minnesota

LOG PICNIC TABLES IN VARIETY

The table at upper left is a virtual duplicate of the one detailed and illustrated on the opposite page. Both are of interest as illustrations of the subtle differences of line which can result between units built from the same blueprint. Though the table tops of these Caddo Lake units are supported by legs, the method of supporting seats on short lengths of log laid on the ground here makes its initial appearance.

In the three other tables pictured, this style of support is variously and interestingly developed to carry the table top as well. The resulting massive appearance should discourage the persistent whim of the public for casually shifting tables about. As with the preceding groups, here are differences in the construction of table and bench tops, and of understructure, which make for considerable individuality in spite of a basic similarity of parti. With tables of this type, probably the major shortcoming, in a strictly practical sense, is the requirement of a perfectly level site. Lacking such, it is surely more desirable to obtain a full bearing by "scooping out" the ground so as partially to bury the supporting logs than to resort to a shim as illustrated at upper right.

Custer State Park, South Dakota

Sibley State Park, Minnesota

PICNIC TABLES — Plate II A-11

Picnic Unit
Mississippi Palisades State Park — — — Illinois

Masonry and split logs combined in a unit of extreme durability that has not the practical advantage of ready mobility when the resting of site becomes desirable. The freehand lines of the split logs are agreeable. The stone masonry has well-related feeling of informality. The disadvantage of the fixed location is perhaps offset by an indicated freedom from maintenance costs. Opposite are shown other picnic units contrived of stone and timber.

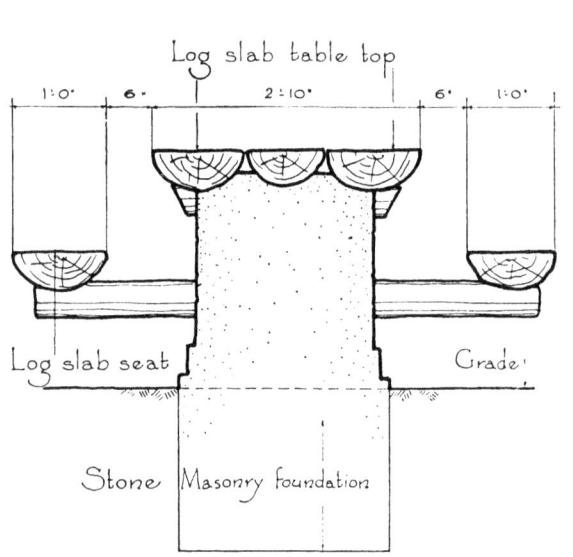

SECTION

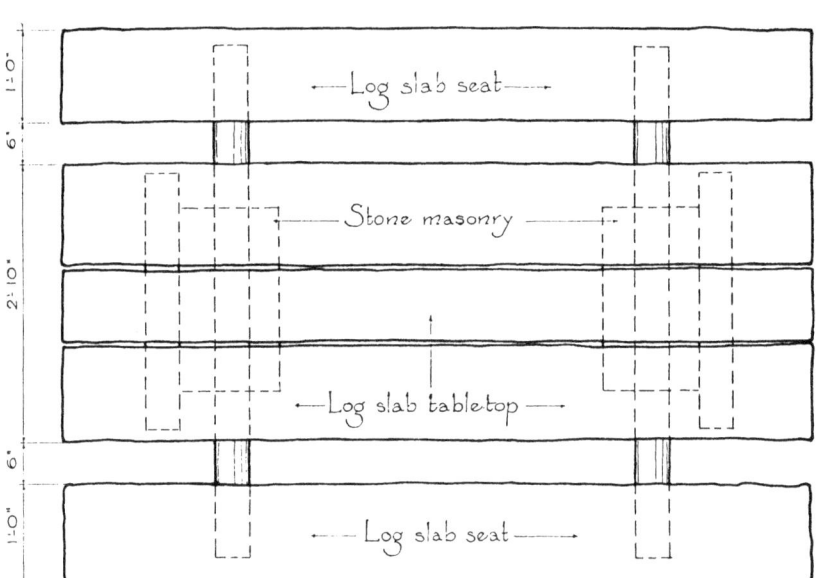

PLAN

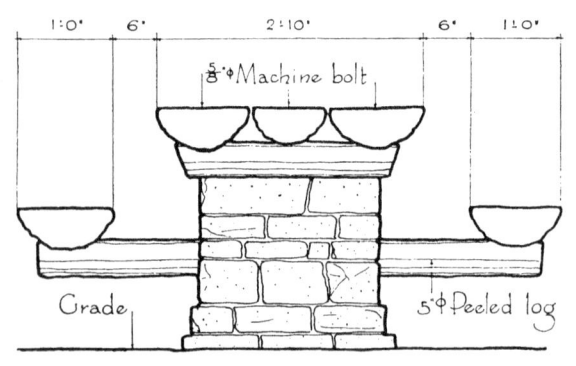

END ELEVATION   SIDE ELEVATION

Scale ½" = 1'-0"

Plate II A-12 →» PICNIC TABLES

Saxon Woods, Westchester County, New York

Foster County Park, California

PICNIC TABLES COMBINING MASONRY AND WOOD

At upper left is an informal combination of masonry table and half log seats for accommodating the short-legged (first aisle to the right) and the gangling (next aisle to the left). Thus is a hillside site utilized to practical and coincidently picturesque advantage. The rock-faced edge relieves the severity of the stone top.

At upper right the starting handicap of an at-hand material difficult to handle has been overcome in large degree by a careful selection and painstaking laying up of the boulders. The weathered, rounded treatment of the wooden parts is a nice gesture toward the "lumpy" character inherent in all boulder masonry, and serves to harmonize the two materials.

The two examples from Minnesota parks illustrate the interesting variety possible in tables developing from the same basic idea. In these two the differences in the seat and table top constructions, and in the character and form of the stone end supports, may be compared with interest. In both there seems to be lack of tone harmony between wooden and masonry parts; in the one case, the apparently untreated wood is glaringly white, in the other, the planks appear to be stained too dark, to an unpleasant contrast with the masonry.

Gooseberry Falls State Park, Minnesota

Whitewater State Park, Minnesota

PICNIC TABLES

Plate II A–13

Picnic Table – – Bastrop State Park – – Texas

Because of general familiarity with porch and lawn furniture having a framework of metal tubing, this experimental picnic table seems novel rather than revolutionary. It evolved from an urge to create a practical, comfortable, durable, inconspicuous unit which would give promise of immunity from vandalism. The copper tubing with "stream line" cast brass fittings, permanently soldered, will take on a natural oxidized weathering. The troweled and pumice stone finished concrete table top may be stained or integrally colored, and the white pine seat tops may be stained, all to a certain harmony with natural surroundings. The principal advantages of the unit are adaptability to mass production methods and a practical indestructibility. It weighs four hundred pounds.

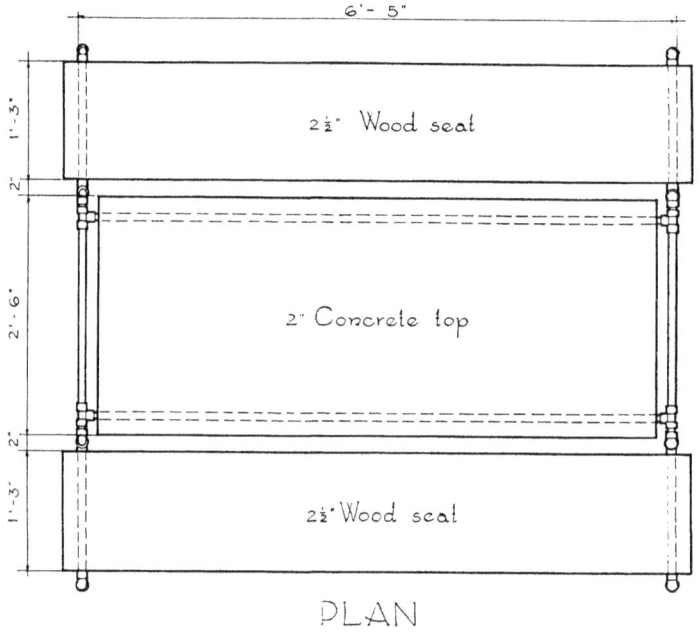

PLAN

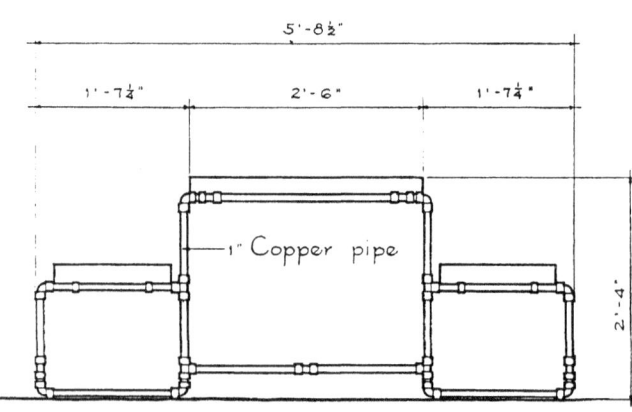

SECTION

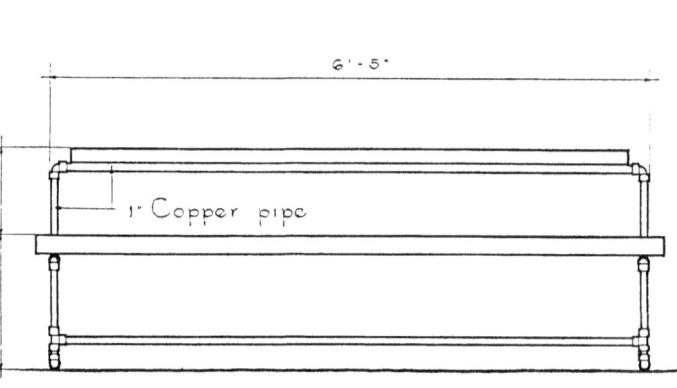

FRONT ELEVATION

SIDE ELEVATION

Scale ½" = 1'-0"

Plate II A-14 — PICNIC TABLES

Picnic Table - - Bastrop State Park - - Texas

Another experimental picnic table purposed to provide a comfortable unit of easily obtainable stock materials, and assemblable without the endless cutting and fitting of joints required for log tables. All surfaces are smooth, the end supports can be easily straddled, no braces interfere with knee-room and the horizontal braces are low and easy to step over. Iron shoes, which might also be cast with extensions to anchor the table to its location, keep all wooden members off the ground and prevent rotting. The unit is lower than average, with wider than usual seats, and has found favor for its inviting comfort and rigid construction. It is furthermore economical of material as to kind and amount, weighing not over one hundred and thirty five pounds.

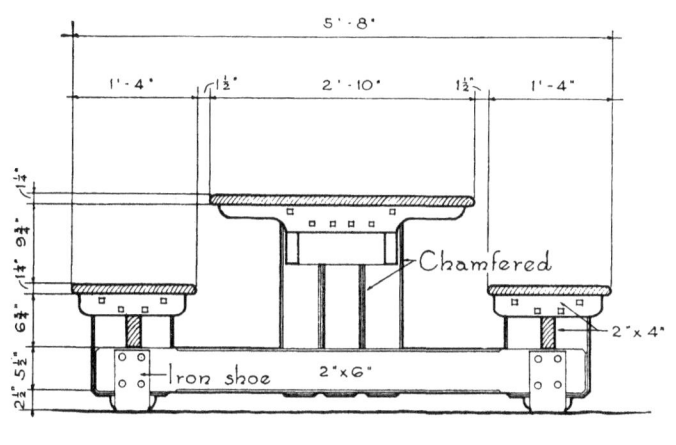

SECTION

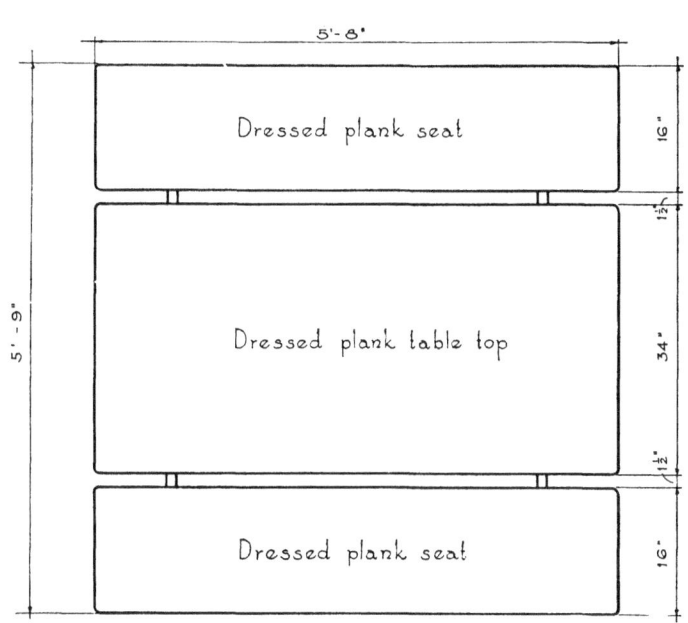

PLAN

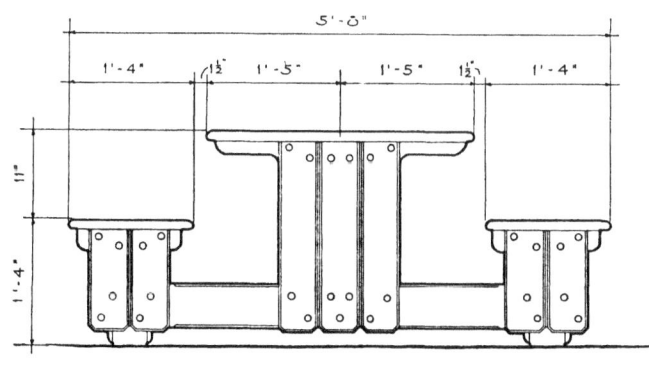

SIDE ELEVATION

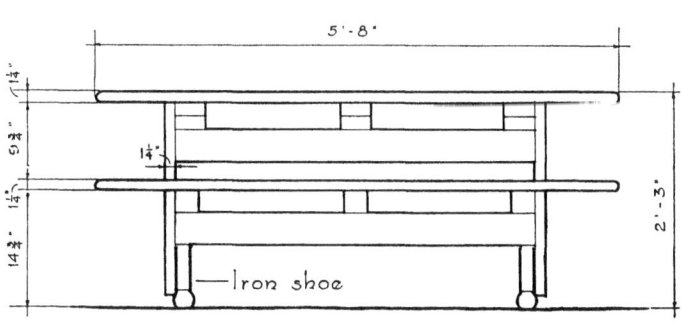

FRONT ELEVATION

Scale ½" = 1'-0"

PICNIC TABLES   Plate II A-15

Moran State Park, Washington

Mount Penn Metropolitan Reservation, Reading, Pennsylvania

VARIFORM PICNIC TABLES

The turnstile or merry-go-round table at upper left passeth understanding and defieth explanation. It deserves some sort of award for originality and doubtless brings a measure of novelty to a jaded picnicker. There is an agreeable freehandedness in the lines of the Pennsylvania table of unusual design at upper right. The California table introduces a ventilated cupboard for stowing away the picnic basket and other picnic gear. The seat and table tops are dressed smooth with edges rounded well for the protection of light clothing against tearing.

The Alabama combination of table and detached benches will wisely be adopted only in areas where destruction of natural values is not likely to attend the casual moving around of picnic facilities by the public, or where nontypical circumstances might make detached and readily movable seats extraordinarily useful equipment. Sturdy and well-braced in a degree that should protect the items themselves from demolition in the process of being moved, they are here shown for their reference. value in special cases.

Palomar Mountain State Park, California

De Soto State Park, Alabama

Springbrook State Park, Iowa

Springbrook State Park, Iowa

RUSTIC WOODEN PICNIC TABLES

At upper left is maximum exemplification of the weather-worn primitive. Rough and raw edges are nonexistent. There is present something of "driftwood" quality that infers great age, unauthentic but ingratiating.

The table at upper right is a rawboned rendering that pleases by its very awkwardness. There is affinity with Nature in man-made things in which it is not sought to eliminate all inherent imperfections of line and surface.

The Deception Pass table evidences opportunism applied in utilization of superlative materials at hand. By converting huge half log to table top and exceedingly heavy planks to seats, a picnic table of massive scale results.

At lower right the typical Caddo Lake picnic unit, detailed on a previous page, is extended to almost indefinite length for the benefit of family reunions and al fresco foregatherings of the gregarious Rotarian or Elk. The most meager picnic fare becomes a banquet when it can be served on a board so vigorously rustic.

Deception Pass State Park, Washington

Caddo Lake State Park, Texas

PICNIC TABLES

Plate II A–17

Mohawk Metropolitan Park, Tulsa, Oklahoma

Round Top Metropolitan Park, Wyoming

MISCELLANY OF PICNIC FACILITIES

Here is a motley assortment, no item of which is any less interesting because unrelated to the others. At upper left is a wood and stone combination, picturesque in the extreme, but very definitely committed to its location, come flood or tornado, or need for recuperation of outworn area, when it becomes a "frozen asset" until the site is renewed.

Judging from its vacant expanse of background, the roofed picnic table at upper right is by way of being the outstanding feature, natural or man-made, of this metropolitan park area. The table pinch-hits for Nature and provides its own shade, certainly a legitimate function in such a setting.

The monumental table at lower left is known in Texas as a barbecue table. Starting in Lampasas State Park, it ends we know not where. The great length is probably a protest against "second table" seating and its usual accompaniment of chicken wings and watered lemonade. At lower right is a first step in the direction of buffet picnicking, touched on in the preliminary discussion. When the hang-over formality exhibited in the bench can be shaken off, the theory of the truly informal picnic unit will have been put into practice.

Lampasas State Park, Texas

Clifton State Park, Texas

PICNIC FIREPLACES

To PROVIDE abundant hospitality for picnicking—unquestionably the most popular recreational offering of natural parks—requisite facilities must be scaled to peak attendances which touch new highs with each succeeding summer holiday. This, in terms of cooking units, means uncounted numbers of them, and in our parks their multiplication has been forced at an alarming pace. Is it then any wonder that critical opinion tends to urge that fireplaces be inconspicuous as well as completely practical? In this little scene Practicality will monopolize the center of the stage, and Aesthetics, if she is to have a speaking part at all, will be heard only from the wings.

But before Aesthetics is summarily driven out into the raging blizzard and biting wind off stage, may we not allow her an exit line? Let her rant that she played no small part when the chimneyed picnic fireplace was an ugly threat and the figurative "inability to see the woods for the trees" could be paraphrased to a literal "inability to see the trees for the chimneys."

In all truth our park vistas until lately were becoming more and more encumbered with chimneyed eruptions of the monumental proportions, and even the appearance, of a dismal mortuary art. It is not gross exaggeration to state that merely topping off with cast iron statues of military aspect the soaring piles of masonry elbowing each other in many antiquated picnic areas would approximate some very typical, and hideously compact, historic battlefields. Happily there is increasing evidence that the chimney blight is currently on the wane, thanks to the clamor raised by Aesthetics. If it is not eventually completely stamped out, then an aggressive campaign for picnic menus without benefit of cooking must be launched to save some of our picnic groves.

The pioneers, the plainsmen, who frequently cooked out-of-doors on the most primitive of contrivances, needed no chimney for their cooking, which on occasion embraced baking as well. Hence the open flueless fire would seem to be adequate for outdoor cooking in any situation and the chimney to be functionally unnecessary to any picnic fireplace.

The essentials of the inconspicuous chimneyless picnic fireplace are few and neither complex nor very rigid. Recently a number of revolutionary departures from principles long held to be inviolable have been taken with apparent success. It was once felt that the firebox, to be truly effective, must be roughly 12 inches wide and 24 inches long. A fireplace developed and now in wide use in parks in Colorado just reverses this and has a firebox width two or three times its shallow front-to-back dimension. Similarly, until lately the grate was very generally set about 12 inches above the hearth, but now there is noted a tendency to reduce this hearth-to-grate dimension. When it is from five to seven inches, economy of fuel consumption results, and the alternative use of charcoal for fuel is possible. The lowered grate means more stooping to use, but this is not a consideration of weight when the preparation of but one or two meals on a day's outing is involved. In such circumstances the importance of subordinating fireplace to surroundings justifies some sacrifice of convenience in use. The alternative of elevating both hearth and grate so that the latter is at a more convenient level is the prerogative of the campstove intended for day-in and day-out use by camping parties over extended periods. With campstoves it is reasonable that convenience have the call over aesthetic considerations. Thus is the line drawn between campstove and picnic fireplace.

Simplification seems to have become the watchword in fireplace design, once the chimney was shaken off. Apparently some observers came to feel that the rear wall was merely a vestigial remnant of the chimney and itself nonessential. In many parks a fireplace having side walls only and a firebox open at front and back evolved. A fireplace with no rear wall to join the side walls together has points of advantage. It will take a wider variety of fuel than more enclosed structures. It will cool more quickly and is less susceptible to breaking as it cools or as the grate expands under heat. In Minnesota and North Dakota the momentum of simplification has resulted in a unit of four low masonry piers to support the grate, with each of the four sides potentially a front and no chance of a draft that is disadvantageous. Whatever the form of the fireplace, some level shelf space as a part of it is useful for setting out cooking utensils and for keeping cooked food hot.

THE DESIGN OF GRATE is affected by several considerations. The interstices should be small enough to prevent, as someone has reasoned, "any but the most emaciated hot dog from dropping through." The Central New York State Parks Commission has developed a cast iron grate which meets well this specification, but has also contrived, at one-tenth the cost of the cast product, a satisfactory substitute, which can be cut to size from diamond mesh culvert reinforcement with a pair of bolt cutters. When the tendency to vanish, seemingly inherent in all unanchored park accessories short of "two-man" size, is borne in on the consciousness, the virtue of cheapness is appreciated. Some type of secure fastening of the grate to the masonry is the only alternative in long-range economy.

Hinged grates or grids make for convenience in the removal of ashes from the firebox. Grates subjected to the weather and intense heat, or in the event of failure to keep ashes removed, deteriorate and must be replaced periodically. When grates are built into the masonry, the disadvantage is obvious. If the side walls are connected by a rear wall or by a foundation, provision should be made to prevent the cracking and breaking of the masonry when the bars or grate expands under heat. Sleeves of pipe or tubing, built into the walls to receive the bars, or a slot for other types of grate, allow for expansion.

Fireplaces should not be placed near enough to trees to injure either branches or roots by heat. Orientation in relation to prevailing air currents is an important consideration.

Of all possible picnic fireplaces, a skillful manipulation of native ledge rock or a few large boulders, to a reasonable compliance with the practical and yet at first glance to suggest a natural arrangement or outcropping, is in the best park character and can take its bow on Nature's stage without blush or apology. This cannot be said for some other solutions which are ever more or less ill at ease in a natural landscape. Of these others, probably the most satisfying is the low stone unit laid up with mortar, and the closer its kinship to a natural formation or a casual piling up of rock, the more pleasing it is.

Because certain kinds of rock crack or explode under intense heat, it is common practice to line rock fireplaces with firebrick. This results in longer life for the unit, and provides a good level bearing for the grate, and is indeed practical, though it may detract from the informality so much favored for the fireplace. Before it is elected to omit the firebrick lining, it should be made certain that the rock is a kind that will not crack or explode in heat.

Because water thrown on rock or masonry heated to high temperatures tends to cause it to fracture, signs should be provided to instruct the public in the proper extinguishing of fires. It is better to put out a fire with earth than water, but recommendations to that effect may result in undesirable prospecting for earth nearby to the detriment of the picnic site.

One blind to the fact that in some regions neither rock nor boulders are indigenous might rule that, even there, fireplaces of any other materials are unthinkable and taboo. This view cannot be sponsored here in the face of a firm conviction that required facilities built of materials of "natural" origin, but "foreign" to an area, are no less than arrant Nature faking. Fireplaces of brick, concrete, or metal are surely to be preferred to this.

Probably such strictly utilitarian solutions are hardly to be considered "landscape units." But they can be not inefficient as to operation, not unskilled as to workmanship, not unsightly as to form, within limitations of their own. They are economical in the current demand for picnic units in greater numbers, and are somehow unmannered and free of false pretense.

THERE HAS BEEN CITED a growing doubt of the complete appropriateness of innumerable self-conscious repetitions of picnic tables of rustic handcraft and fireplaces imitative of rock outcrops on the very fringes of a machine age metropolis. The Cook County Forest Preserve District authorities have long realized that the rock-sculptured fireplace is a quaint anachronism in the perennially convalescent Nature in their charge. Moreover, they know that, in spite of every possible structural precaution to insure long life, this kind of facility remains intact scarcely one season under the hard use to which swarming hordes of picnickers subject it. They have tried experiment after experiment to determine the utmost in practical durability in a use of twentieth-century materials in a contemporary vein. Concrete units have been designed, constructed, tested, with innumerable revisions. Varying mixtures, employing various aggregates, have been subjected to rigid tests. Simultaneously many all-steel designs have been tried by fire and by torture, with resulting changes and constant improvement.

The battle of concrete versus steel for the light middleweight fireplace championship in the Chicago area has been thrilling all the way, and to hear it colorfully and dramatically broadcast round by round by the official observer and referee, Roberts Mann, superintendent of maintenance of the district, is equal to a seat at the ringside. The plates picture the current concrete favorite and what has been described as "the improved one-cylinder 1937 model" of steel. Latest flash from the Chicago front: CONCRETE CHAMPION CRACKING STOP ALL-STEEL CONTENDER WINNING DECISION ON POINTS.

Both concrete and steel fireplace units lend themselves to mass production methods at a central point, and are easily installed. Where the need is for thousands, or only for hundreds, of units, these factors are important. Although in Cook County the concrete fireplace has been perfected to a point where its weaknesses of form seem to have been overcome, no materials mixture has been found which does not show, after a year's time, signs of progressive deterioration under use and abuse, and abuse, unhappily, must ever be reckoned with.

The major drawback of the Cook County all-steel model is that it "requires skilled labor and lots of it." But if this produces a practically indestructible, theftproof, trim, compact, efficient unit which can be rustproofed with a special aluminum heat-resisting paint that weathers to an inconspicuous silver-gray, the high labor cost may prove to be entirely justified over the long run.

There are those who foresee in the expanding demand for picnic facilities the threat of fireplaces more crowded than gopher mounds on a prairie and who propose to meet it by resorting to multiple fireplaces. Obviously, the close coupling of units somewhat reduces smoke annoyance and hazard to tree growth, and can boast a certain economy of construction. The sole opposing argument, however, is formidable because it is based entirely on human nature. The massing of the cooking units brings in too close contact too many cooks, proverbially not conducive to peace and good will. Moreover, the propelling inspiration behind most picnics is a desire to get away from crowds. Confronted with sound reasoning both for and against multiple fireplaces, one shies at making oracular pronouncement sweeping in scope.

The discussion to this point has embraced more or less typical outdoor fireplaces and neglected the very simplest provisions for cooking out-of-doors that for some people are the most fun. A mere rock-bordered hearth will provide for a fire with minimum danger of spreading. This type of open fire is satisfactory only for cooking requiring no utensils. Supplemented by two forked sticks, a cross arm, and wire hooks to hold kettles, this basic facility is not necessarily inconvenient, and its cooking range is widened. In some western areas an iron stake, driven into the ground at the center of the hearth and furnished with revolving cranes and grids, has met with favor.

The one variety of picnic fireplace which dares to be somewhat pretentious is a combination of chimneyed fireplace and campfire ring, exedralike in form and as suitable a structure for a modest memorial to an individual as is to be found in natural parks.

In regions where the barbecue is a religion, the details of the pit are probably too much a part of the ritual itself, and too varied in strictly personal interpretations by the high priests thereof, to risk a controversy by more than mention here.

PICNIC FIREPLACES

Plate II B-1

Picnic Fireplace — — — National Parks

The splayed fire box and style of grate here shown are typical of the picnic fireplaces favored in many of the Western National Parks. When these fireplaces are constructed (or appear to be constructed as in this instance) of but three stones or boulders, they are most happily naturalized in their settings. Salient features of the construction are the dimensions of the fire box, the fire brick lining and base, the stone hearth curb, the paving of the area immediately in front of the fire box (in presuppression of grass fires) and the mounding up of earth against the side and back enframing rocks. The grate is preferably of genuine wrought iron, but may be of open hearth cold-rolled milled steel in stock size bars.

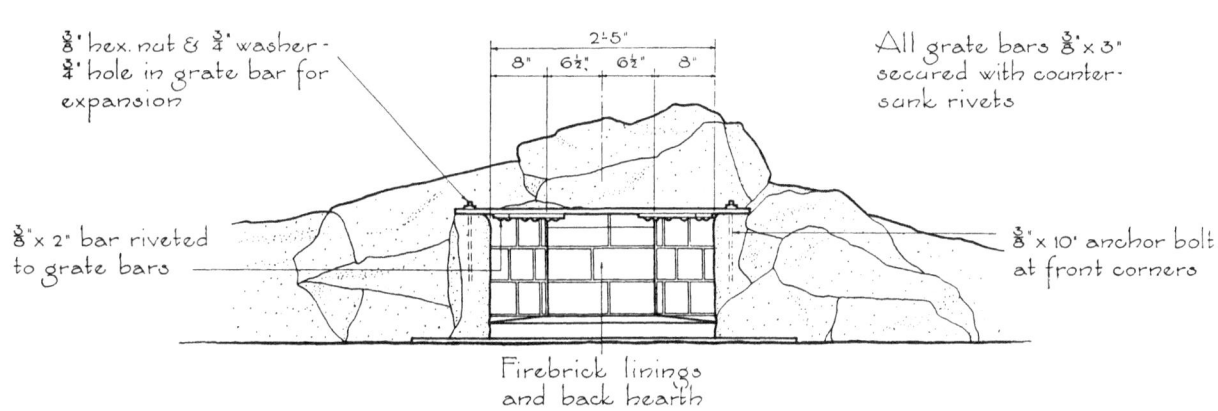

FRONT ELEVATION

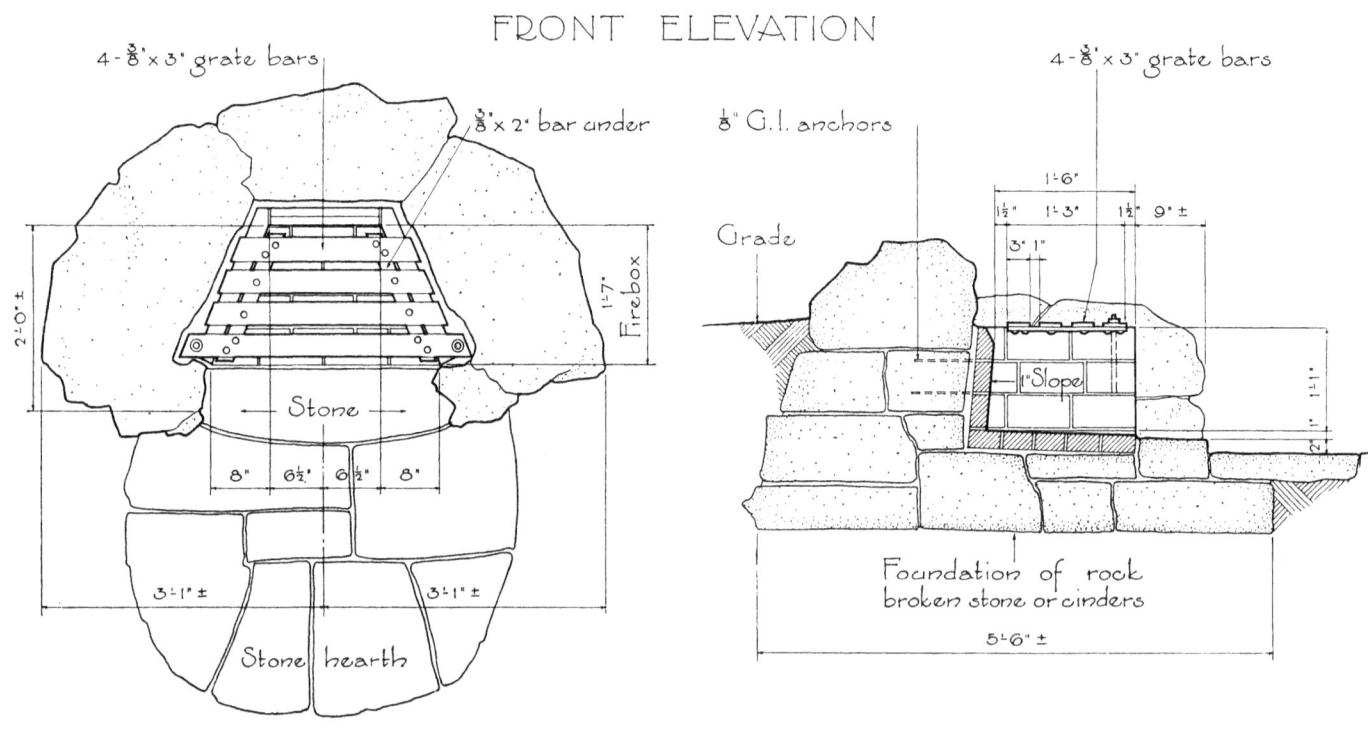

PLAN   SECTION

Scale ½" = 1'-0"

30

Plate II B–2   ❯❯❯ PICNIC FIREPLACES

Myles Standish State Forest Park, Massachusetts

Boyle Metropolitan Park, Little Rock, Arkansas

VARIANTS OF THE WESTERN FIREPLACE

Single trait in common of the fireplaces here pictured is a basic informality. Several appear to employ three stones of large size; others are formed of more and smaller stones. A considerable range of grate construction is represented. Some are lined with firebrick, others are not. Note the hinged grill of the Texas example—an aid to the ready removal of ashes. Note also the raised hearths of the two subjects at the bottom of the page—a feature making for more convenient use.

Bastrop State Park, Texas

Sequoia National Park

Foster County Park, California

31

PICNIC FIREPLACES

Plate II B-3

Picnic Fireplace
Denver Mountain Metropolitan Parks   Colorado

Distinguishing features of the unit, developed in Colorado and here detailed, are the unusual, wide, shallow grate and the fact that mass production methods are brought to picnic fireplace construction. The reinforced concrete hearth, fire brick base, grate bars and back and side plates constitute a unit fabricated and cast at a production point and distributed over wide areas for placement and naturalizing by use of local stone. Few large stone, rather than many small ones are preferable for this function. This type of fireplace is ideally situated on a gentle slope. The very integration and weight of this unit should curb vandalism and theft. Though the grille is set close to the hearth, ashes are easily raked out by reason of the grille being wide and shallow.

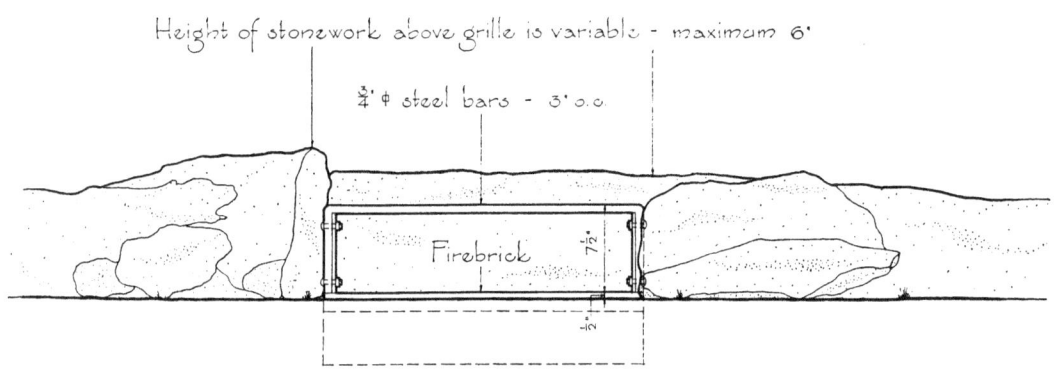

FRONT ELEVATION

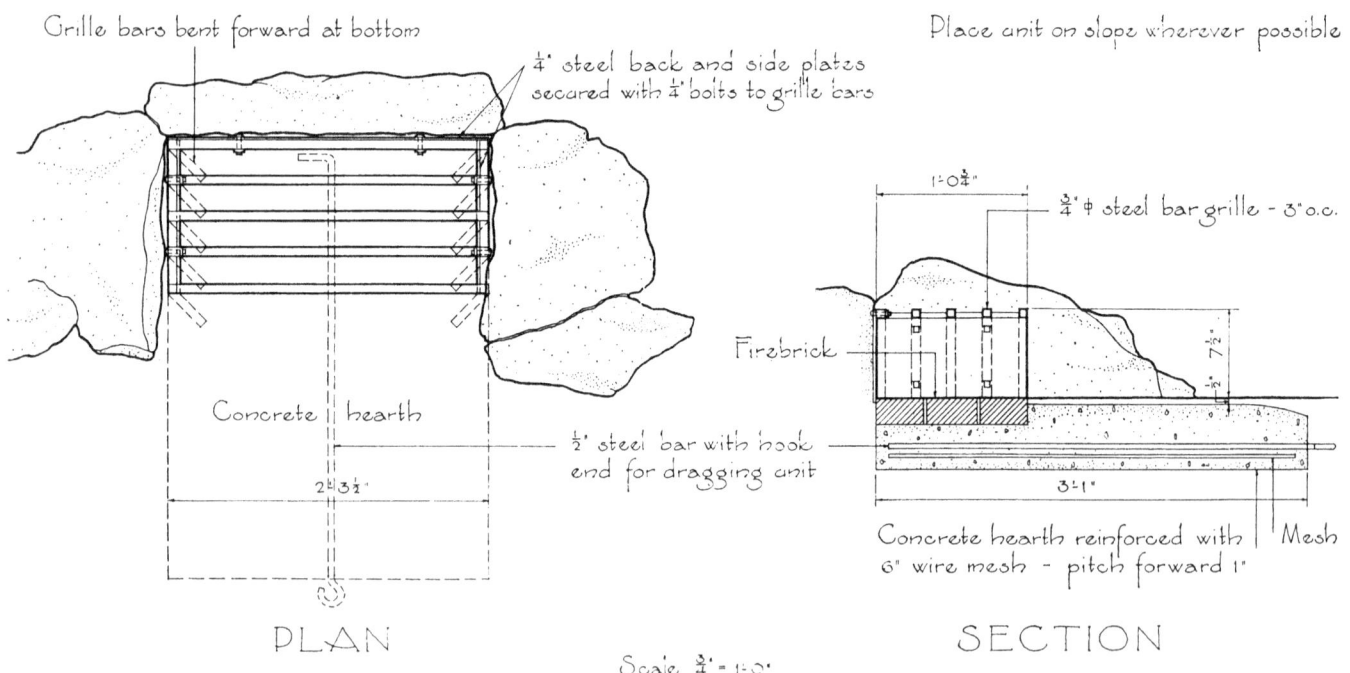

PLAN   SECTION

Scale ¾" = 1'-0"

32

Plate II B–4 →» PICNIC FIREPLACES

Mount Penn Metropolitan Reservation, Reading, Pennsylvania

Ponca Lake Metropolitan Park, Ponca City, Oklahoma

PICNIC FIREPLACES ON SLOPES

None of the subjects pictured on this page reproduces the hearth, prefabricated with related parts, which features the fireplace detailed on the facing page. All, however, are similarly located on slopes. Such placement, because it goes far to make the fireplace less conspicuous in the picnic area, is recommended. The adobe unit in Arizona evidences utilization of a regionally appropriate material where a suitable local stone is probably not available. The different kinds of stone employed in the other examples and the various grill constructions are of interest.

Pickwick Dam Reservation, Tennessee

Randolph Metropolitan Park, Tucson, Arizona

Lake Guernsey State Park, Wyoming

PICNIC FIREPLACES

Plate II B-5

Picnic Fireplace — Parvin State Park — New Jersey

In modified and less rugged areas, the stones surrounding the fire box of the picnic fireplace are rarely the casual placing of half buried rocks we have just observed but tend rather to take on the characteristics of a conscious masonry. The more successful examples of the type evidence an effort to use large stones and hold to a minimum the number of stones in a degree consistent with characteristics of the available local stone. Because the stone is laid in mortar need not mean that the results must be rigidly and unpleasantly mechanical. On the opposite page are pictured in wide range variants of the fireplace here detailed.

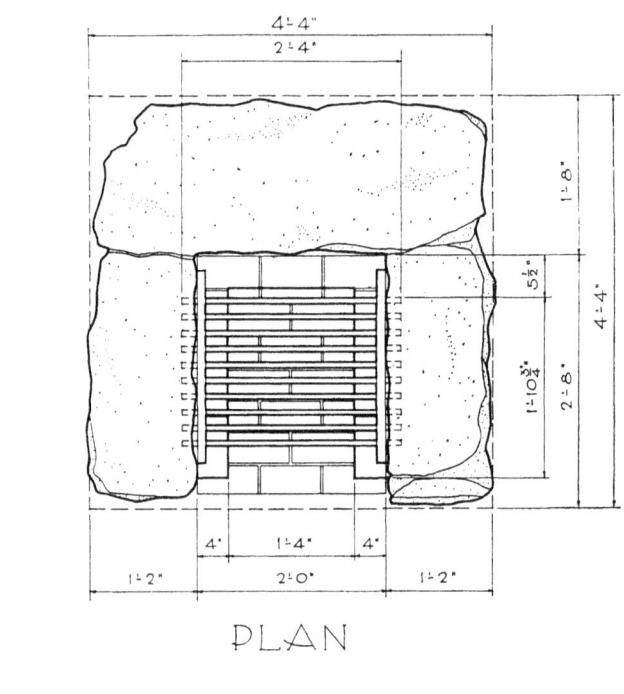

PLAN

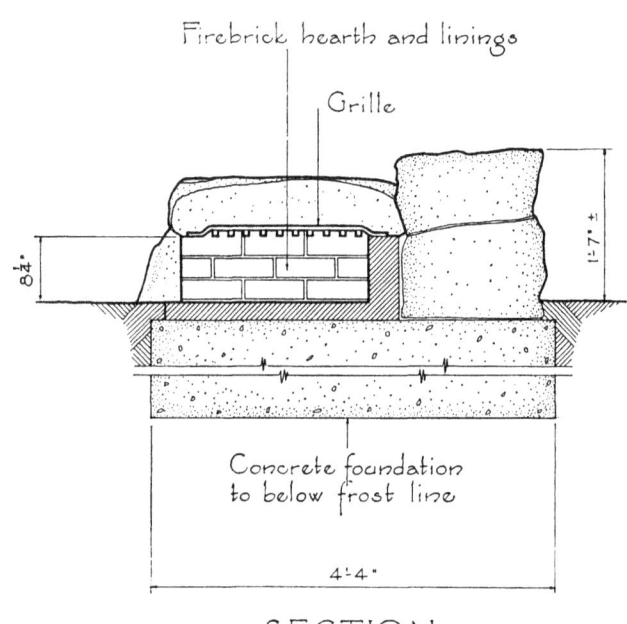

SECTION

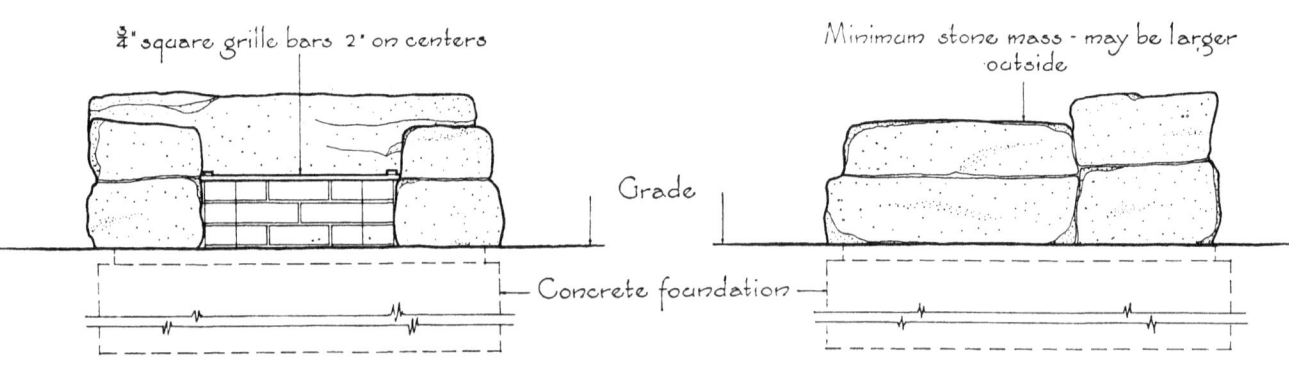

FRONT ELEVATION

SIDE ELEVATION

Scale ½" = 1'-0"

Plate II B–6   →» PICNIC FIREPLACES

Sequoia National Park

Levi Carter Metropolitan Park, Omaha, Nebraska

PICNIC FIREPLACES OF MORTAR-LAID MASONRY

The stone picnic fireplace laid up in mortar is ordinarily U-shaped but by no means always so. Variants include a type open at both ends so that a through draft is possible, and another type, much used in Minnesota and adjacent States, which consists of four stone piers supporting the corners of the grill. Masonry fireplaces have been built in every degree of rusticity. The Sibley State Park subject is very like the all-steel firebox, detailed on a succeeding page, glorified by the addition of masonry side walls.

Sibley State Park, Minnesota

Minnesota State Parks

Fargo Metropolitan Park, North Dakota

35

PICNIC FIREPLACES
Plate II B-7

Picnic Fireplace
Cook County Forest Preserve — — Illinois

A forthright answer to the need for picnic fireplaces in vast numbers in the heavily picnicked parks of the Chicago Metropolitan area. Surely here an endless duplication of "sculptured" rock fireplaces so fitting, for example, in the mountain parks surrounding Denver, would seem reasonable only to those who would limit current traffic on Michigan Avenue to the pioneer's covered wagon and the Indian's travois. Among the advantages of this "cheese box" type are low cost, suitability for quantity production, simplicity of installation, and range of orientation in adaption to prevailing winds. Possibly further development will make possible the unit revolving on its anchorage, which will give it more fixed location without sacrifice of orientation range and further provide it with a smooth hearth.

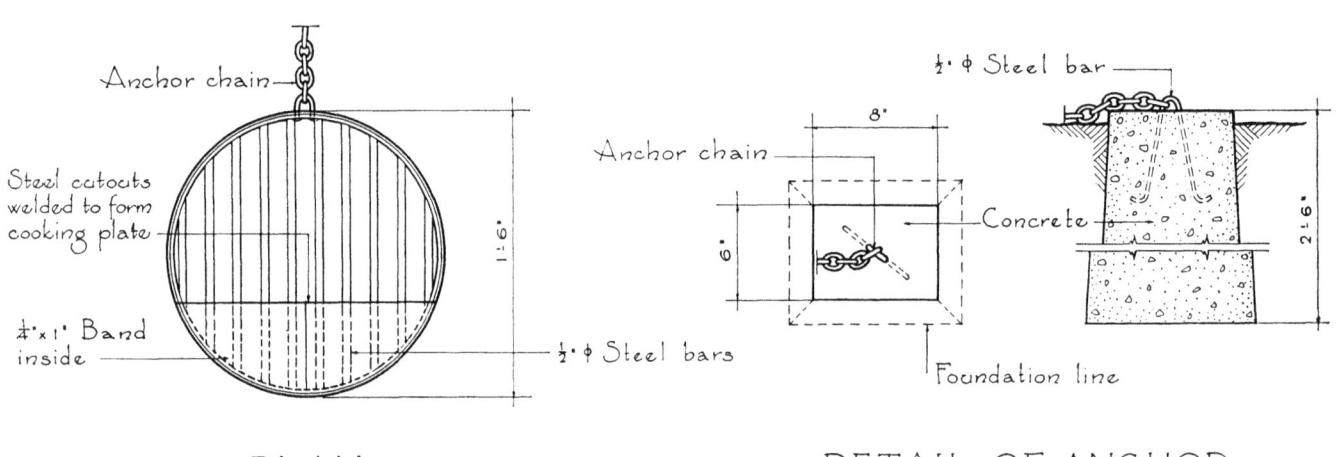

PLAN   DETAIL OF ANCHOR

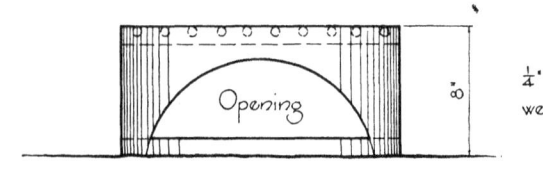
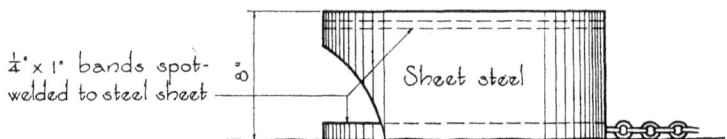

FRONT ELEVATION   SIDE ELEVATION

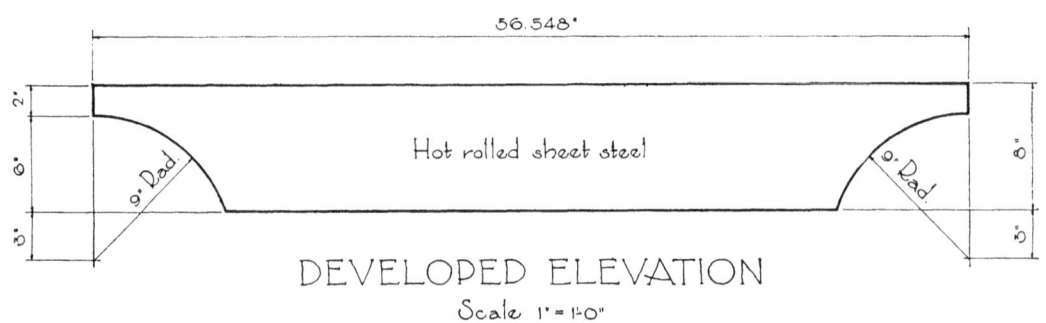

DEVELOPED ELEVATION
Scale 1" = 1'-0"

Plate II B–8 — PICNIC FIREPLACES

Picnic Fireplace — Sibley State Park — Minnesota

Another rendering of an all steel fire box, quantity produced for wide distribution. Although of very different form, its points of advantage closely parallel those of the circular unit developed for the Cook County Forest Preserve. Chief disadvantage of all units of this basic type in heavily wooded areas would seem to be a greater hazard for spread of ground fire than exists in connection with the usual picnic fireplace of stone. Noteworthy are the combination of bar and plate grilles, and the chain and bar anchorage.

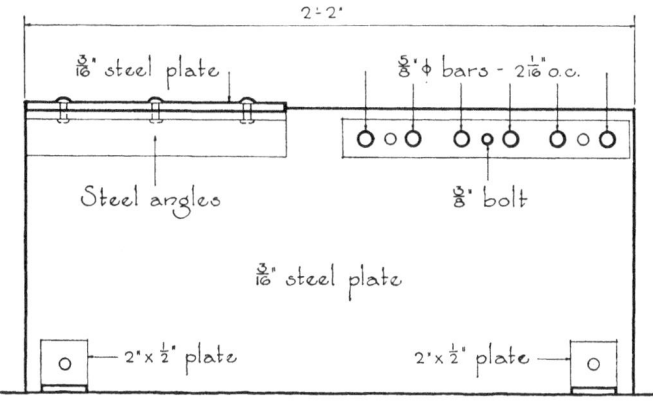

SECTION

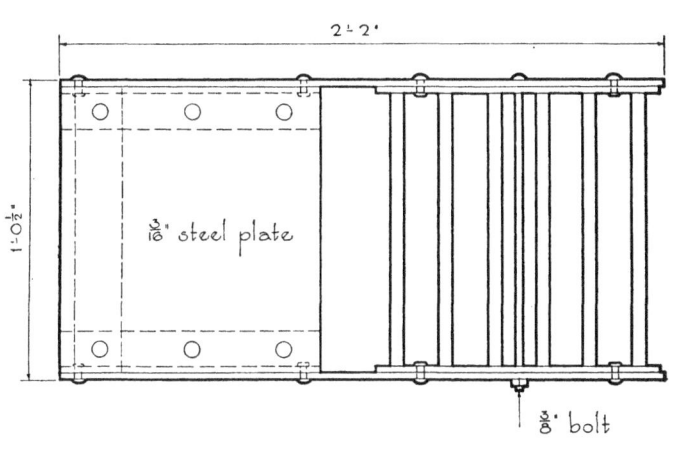

PLAN

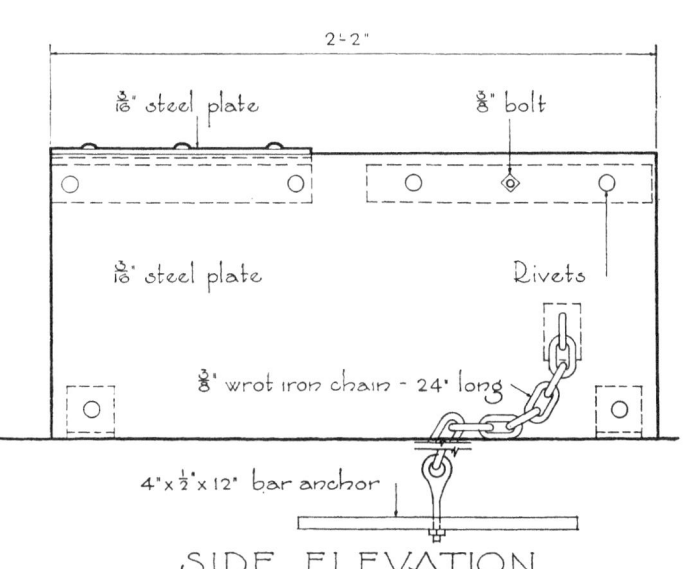

FRONT ELEVATION

SIDE ELEVATION

Scale 1½" = 1'-0"

PICNIC FIREPLACES

Plate II B-9

Picnic Fireplace

Cook County Forest Preserve District — — — Illinois

This latest model of concrete fireplace in this District is known as the "modified Akron type" because it is based upon a fireplace developed in the Akron Metropolitan Park District. Basic features are a monolithic casting using as aggregate a commercial, non-patented material closely resembling ground-up firebrick, and a grate not built into the concrete but held in a slot when the two otherwise unjoined concrete parts are drawn together with bolts through pipe sleeves in the base. Despite extensive experiment and every preventive measure, the type, after a year's use, shows signs of progressive disintegration to indicate that it is good for two or three seasons at the most.

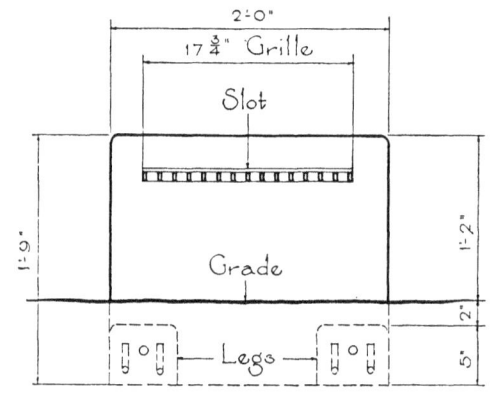

SECTION

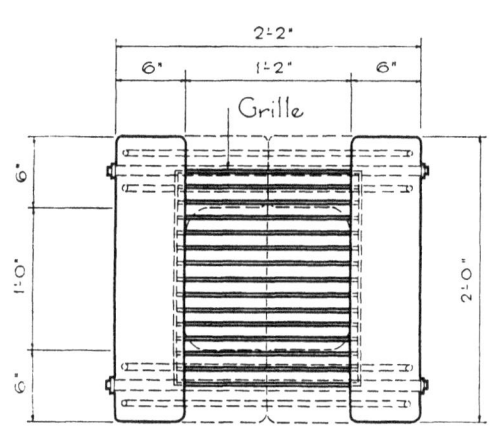

PLAN

Grille is made of 15 bars, $\frac{1}{4}$" x $\frac{3}{4}$" x 15" long, spaced 1" apart, welded to frame, $15\frac{1}{2}$" x $17\frac{3}{4}$", also $\frac{1}{4}$" x $\frac{3}{4}$" bars

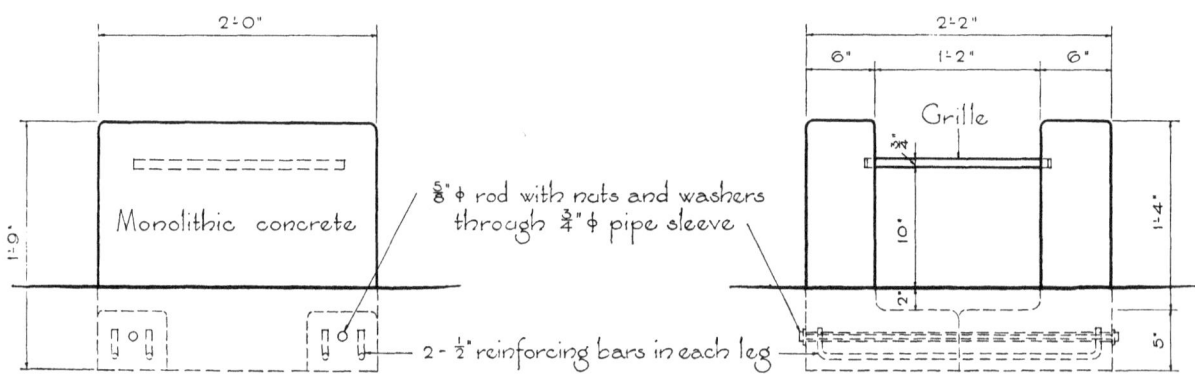

SIDE ELEVATION   FRONT ELEVATION

Scale $\frac{3}{4}$" = 1'-0"

Plate II B–10   ⇢⇢⇢ PICNIC FIREPLACES

Picnic Fireplace - - Pickett Forest - - Tennessee

For intensively used picnic grounds, here is a concrete unit, adaptable to off-the-area mass production and straightforward in its method of approach to present day needs. It is commodious in size and simple in design. The hinged steel flaps have twofold purpose. They function as windbreaks in control of draft and, folded over the grille, provide flat surfaces for cooking. The problem of a materials mix immune to deterioration under use conditions is the point of vulnerability of the unit.

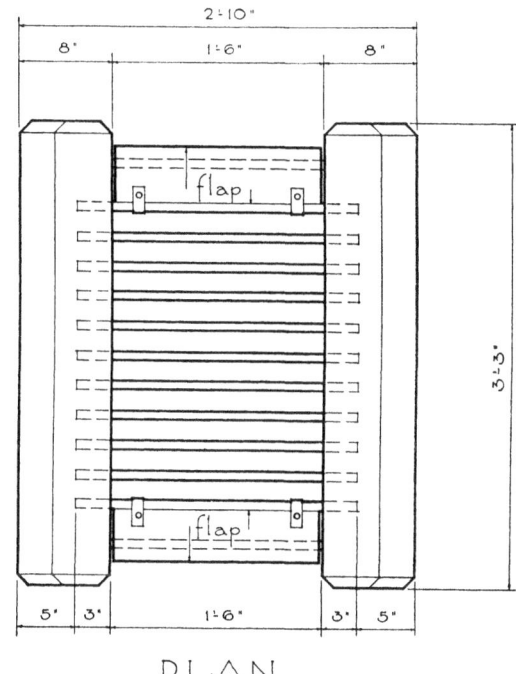

PLAN

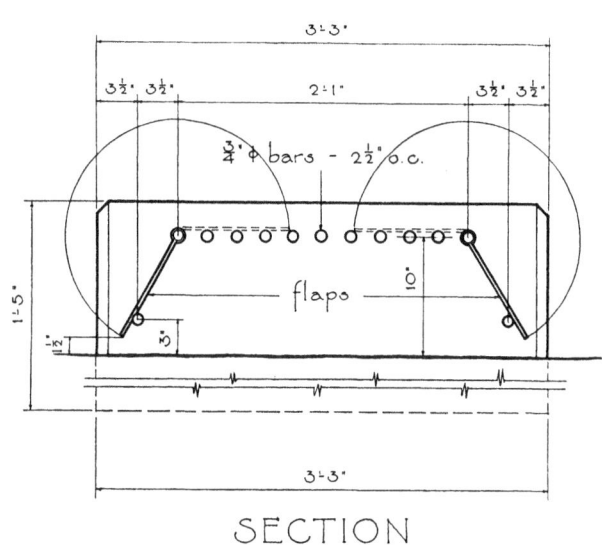

SECTION

Note - steel flaps act as windbreak and also cooking surface over grille

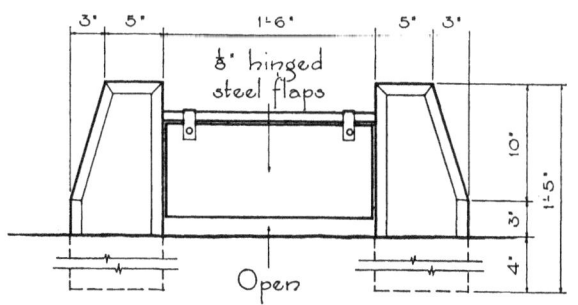

FRONT ELEVATION

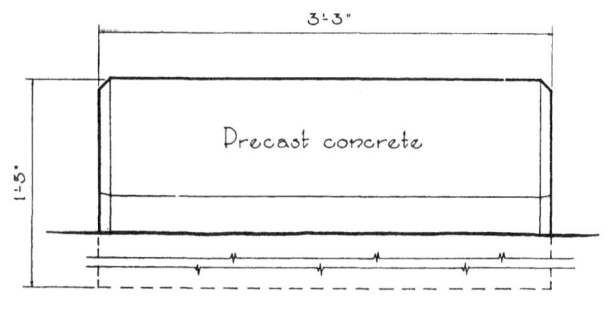

SIDE ELEVATION

Scale ¾" = 1'-0"

PICNIC FIREPLACES   Plate II B-11

Swan Lake State Park, Iowa

Mount Penn Metropolitan Reservation, Reading, Pennsylvania

HEARTH RINGS AND VOTIVE FIREPLACES

The outer column pictures the hearth ring, reborn in its present recreation usage, if not actually originated, in Iowa. A length of axle, reclaimed from a junk yard, with hub and wheel buried for a very positive anchorage, attests the ingenuity and skill of a mechanic at Riverside Park. The Wyoming example affords large cooking capacity, and its high curb supplies a convenient working space for the chef. The illustrations directly above and below show the votive fireplace with flanking seats which, designed and built with a decent restraint, offers an opportunity to create a memorial appropriate in a truly natural park.

Riverside State Park, Washington

Young Mens Literary Society Park, Cheyenne, Wyoming

Spring Mill State Park, Indiana

40

REFUSE RECEPTACLES AND PITS

IF ATTRACTIVE and wholesome conditions are to obtain in a picnic area, receptacles for refuse must be provided. Not only should these facilities be of a highly practical nature, but they should be so abundantly provided that their very convenience induces people to use them.

Refuse receptacles may be of several kinds. It is possible, of course, to distribute through the picnic area garbage cans of commercial type, or oil drums converted to that purpose. However these may be painted, they are unsightly and subject to abuses by picnickers whose ideas of fun have perpetually a Hallowe'en tinge. They attract vermin and animals and are not proof against their depredations. They are tolerable only if regular and frequent collections of their accumulations are made.

If these facilities are placed underground, certain features may be adopted which overcome many of the deficiencies of the surface type. They are hidden from view. They can be more positively flyproof. They are less an invitation to the pranksters and can be made safe from the raids of animals. In permanent locations the walls of the pit are lined with planking or masonry, and the bottom is often undertiled to prevent the accumulation of moisture. The cover of the pit is best designed as a kind of "trap door within a trap door", so fashioned that by opening the inner door garbage may be dropped into the receptacle, and by opening the larger door the receptacle may be removed from the pit for emptying. The feeding door should be of restricted size and so placed that there is no possibility of the dropped refuse missing the receptacle and fouling the pit. Operation of this door by a self-closing foot lever is recommended for greater convenience and cleanliness. If the cover is of wood, it is subject to shrinkage and warp, which soon renders the pit accessible to flies and even small animals. On the other hand, short of malicious abuse, a heavy sheet metal cover will remain flytight indefinitely.

Another subsurface receptacle is a pit without any removable container. Noncombustibles are dropped into the pit itself. Its bottom is sometimes underlaid with broken rock or gravel as a leaching bed for the moisture from any garbage dropped contrary to regulations. If the soil is such that the vertical wall of the excavation will crumble, some form of light bracing or shoring of rough lumber is provided. The pit is floored over at a level about six inches below grade. Over an opening therein is set some form of tight-jointed receiving device. The remainder of the plank top is covered with soil. When the pit has filled almost to grade, the cover is removed intact to another pit in a new location, and the old hole is filled to grade with earth.

The receiving device of a pit of this type may be the aforementioned self-closing trap door, or it may be some raised boxlike or cylindrical form. In any event, it must prevent flies from entering the pit. In order to hold the bulk of the accumulation to a minimum, the public must be schooled to burn waste paper, cartons, and other combustibles in the picnic fireplaces. This will require signs which state regulations and urge compliance with them.

In some picnic areas it is a practice to provide in place of waste containers a small incinerator for public use—usually an oversized picnic fireplace—and to hope that picnickers will conscientiously burn in this their rubbish, wet and dry. This is usually a hope unfulfilled, and between the unregenerate who laugh at regulations, and the uninformed who seem to attribute to the incinerator a kind of human intelligence beyond their own, the gadget and the picnic area itself are rather constantly in an unpleasant state of sanitative deficiency. It is recommended that the alchemy of converting melon rinds and pop bottles into smoke be squarely acknowledged as worthy of the ministrations of a garbage man of talent, on the park pay roll at a prevailing wage scaled to his professional attainments.

REFUSE RECEPTACLES AND PITS

Plate II C–1

Refuse Pit, Mount Nebo State Park, Arkansas

A disposal pit of fixed location, the exposed parts more parklike, though less flytight, than the very utilitarian steel cover used in the Colorado parks and detailed opposite. The feature of small receiving door framed within the large removal door is common to both. The properly low, informative sign is in good character with the pit cover and the wooded surroundings.

Refuse Pit, Crowley's Ridge State Park, Arkansas

Where an excavation does not require shoring, a refuse pit as here detailed is possible. It is important with this type that the decking be covered with tamped clay and made flytight at all joints. When the pit is filled almost to grade, the decking can be removed to a new pit. The old pit is then covered to grade with tamped earth and sodded.

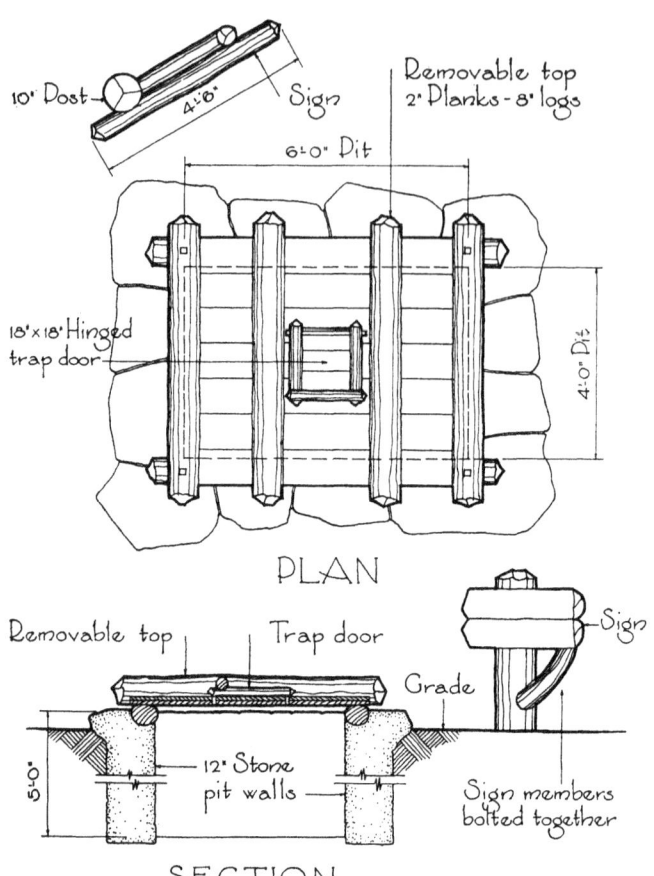

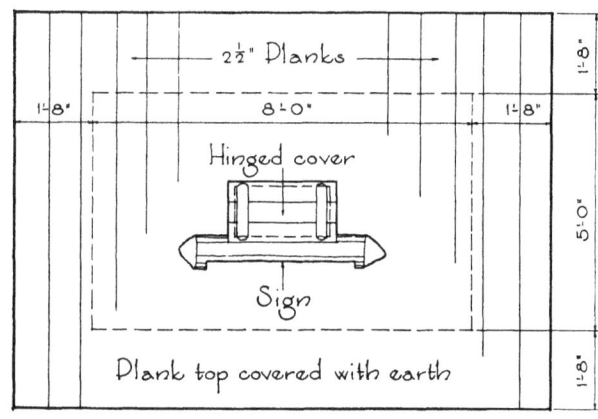

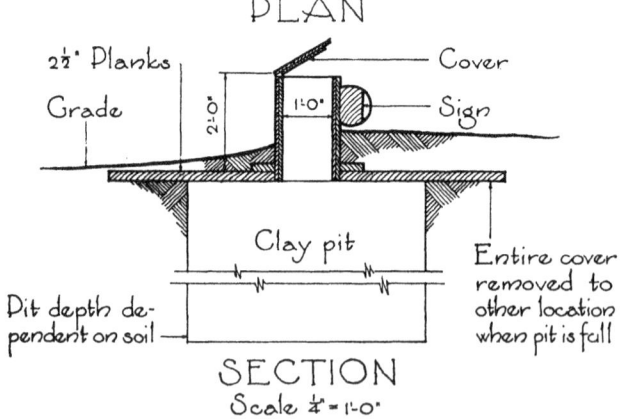

42

Plate II C–2   ⇉ REFUSE RECEPTACLES AND PITS

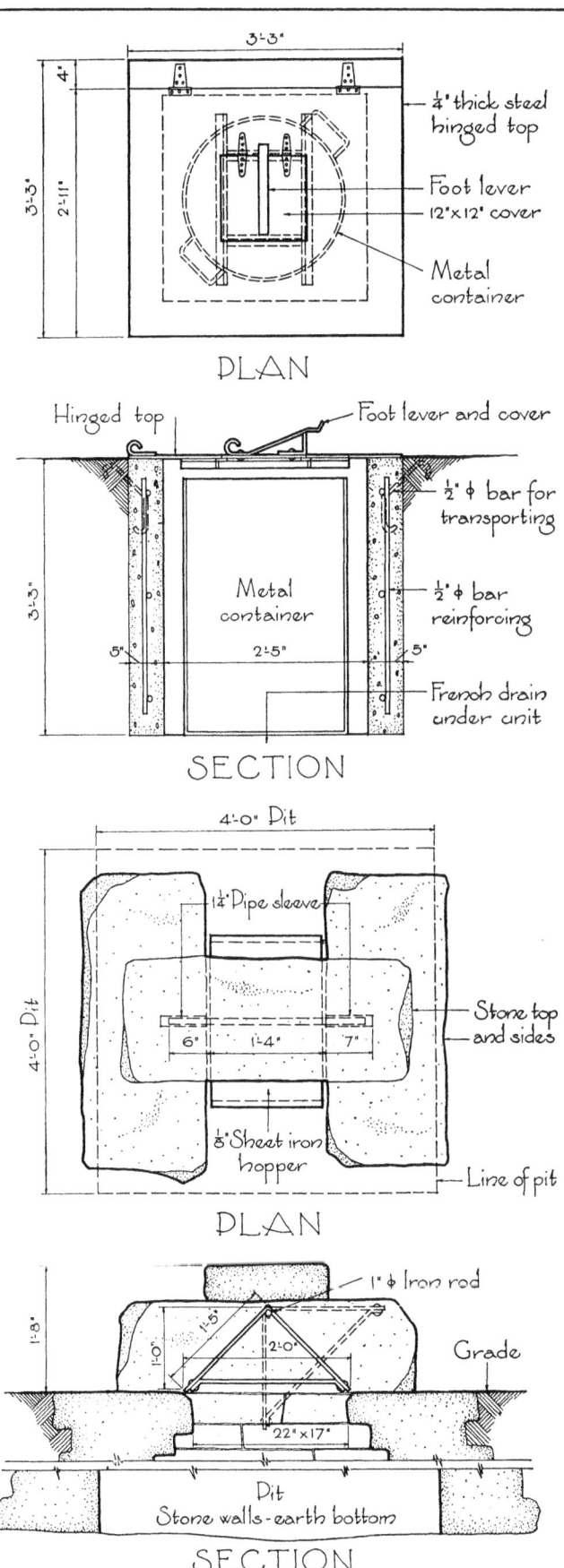

Refuse Pit, Colorado Parks

This contrivance combines a practical grade line steel cover of trap-door-within-trap-door type and a precast concrete underground pit in fixed location. The foot-operated inner door provides for the picnicker's disposal of garbage, and the large outer door permits removal of the receptacle—converted oil drum or some equivalent container—when filled.

Refuse Pit, Devil's Den State Park, Arkansas

The receiving-door device of city trash receptacles borrowed and naturalized in a setting of rocks. Because of the work of providing another rock-walled pit, when one is filled up, and of reerecting the flap door and housing, the type is best suited to parks not heavily used. Unless the opening is kept small, it is a hazard to very small children.

REFUSE RECEPTACLES AND PITS

Plate II C–3

Robbers Cave State Park, Oklahoma

Will Rogers Park, Oklahoma City, Oklahoma

Hualpai Mountain Park, Kingman, Arizona

REFUSE PITS

Above are shown two refuse receptacles of commercial manufacture, in themselves inconspicuous. There is character harmonious with environment in the signs which accompany both and in the rocks massed around the one. Foot operation of the feeding door will be observed in these examples, also in the one to the left.

The doors of both units illustrated below are the less satisfactory hand-operated type, but the designative signs are of interest. Convenient proximity of the example at lower right to the fireplace should be noted.

Boyle Metropolitan Park, Little Rock, Arkansas

Garden of the Gods Park, Colorado Springs, Colorado

PICNIC SHELTERS AND KITCHENS

BEYOND DOUBT the most generally useful building of recreational purpose in any park is a picnic shelter. It is admittedly no trivial task to achieve a desirable and unforced variety in such buildings within the confines of a moderate cost. This is true of other park structures, but it is more apparent of shelters because they are so universally existent in park areas. The almost invariable presence of at least one shelter, and often of several shelters, in every park tends to make us especially and painfully aware of a spiritless monotony of design and execution. Exertion of effort to bring character to a shelter, such as will differentiate it from a thousand and one others, is all too rare; attainment of the objective, without bizarre result, still more rare. The attempt is worth all the creative effort expended; the successful accomplishment is truly worthy of praise.

Because its purpose usually leads to its placement in a very choice location within the park, the shelter finds itself in the very center of a stage with a back drop by the first Old Master. Its role is thus a difficult one, and is ill-played if rendered in the flippant slang or thin syncopated measures of the moment. Slapstick comedy technique is inappropriate; some dignity beyond passing fad or fashion is demanded of the shelter's stellar part.

The chief essential of a picnic shelter is overhead protection from sun and rain. Fixed or mobile benches, table and bench combinations, and fireplaces are the bare needs in the way of accessory equipment for the picnic shelter. In size, it ranges from a structure very small and simple, in a minor rendering, to the large, complex, and ambitious combination building with many extra-functional dependencies, encountered in the heavily used park.

When its development is such that it may be enclosed for winter use, the picnic shelter is confusable with what it has been chosen to term herein community buildings and recreation buildings. If space for a concession is incorporated in the plan, it is difficult to determine at what stage the shelter actually attains the status of concession building or refectory. When there is elaboration of equipment to include sinks and counters, and facilities for cooking more in the nature of stoves than mere open fireplaces, it is customary to designate the shelter a picnic kitchen or kitchen shelter.

This latter well-defined variant of the picnic shelter seems to have originated in the Northwest, where heavy rainfall is presumably an abnormal threat to cooking picnic fare in the open. The type evolved is a kind of picnic shelter in which many of the material benefits of the home kitchen one has fled from are provided. Usually the side walls are widely open except against the prevailing winds. Our countrymen of this region must fairly radiate sweetness and light, for here quite generally the facilities for cooking are double, triple, or quadruple ovens ranged in close proximity about one chimney. The shelters bear no noticeable scars of intergroup ruction and seem almost to refute the widely held conviction that close contact of picnicking groups is provocative of trouble. Perhaps from this peaceable region will spread forth the millennium when the lion and the lamb universally can picnic on the same half-acre and like it.

There are colloquial departures in shelters, their treatment, and their functions which make for other well-defined varieties. Typical of the Southwest is the ramada, functioning in protection of one or more groups of picnickers from the heat and brilliance of the desert sun. Its name is from the Spanish, its style generally derived from the Pueblo. It is built with rock or adobe walls or piers, its practically flat roof carried on round poles, or vigas. Its roof is usually covered with a kind of thatch allowed to hang down over the edges as a fringed protective valance of bewhiskered appearance. The ramada of the desert country is often equipped with an integral open fireplace with chimney. Sometimes there is provided instead a nearby outdoor fireplace for the preparation of food.

There are some oft-repeated plan arrangements of shelters which amount almost to standardization. One such typical arrangement, having a fireplace centered on one end wall, is quite open except that the chimney end wall and adjacent stretches of abutting side walls, for one-fifth to one-third their length, are built solid. Another recognizable type has similar chimney and enclosed treatment at both ends and side walls of open construction between. Both these types have been built far and wide to serve basic practical needs which do not vary greatly for reasons of locale. Almost identical plans may be outwardly clothed to have highly individual regional character.

In their structural elements there is often almost no appreciable difference between some picnic shelters and some trailside shelters, especially the simpler expressions of both. Differentiation between them is largely a matter of location and manner of use.

There are logical combinations of the picnic shelter with other park structural needs which diversify its form and appearance. Custodian's or concessionaire's quarters, concession space, public comfort stations, and storage space have been successfully incorporated with shelters and have produced satisfying variations which avoid the commonplace on the one hand and the fantastic on the other. There are sufficient legitimate combinations and cross-combinations of functions, materials, forms, and other ingredients to make possible an almost infinite number of agreeably different structures, if served up without economy of skill and effort in the contriving and seasoned with a palatable dash of individuality.

Unless it is a pavement of end grain blocks, a wood floor for a shelter has little to recommend it. Better that it be simply a gravel or earth fill, or brick or stone laid on a sand fill. One of several surface materials such as flagstone, brick, slate, and tile laid on a concrete base will give a more durable floor. The variety of soil and frost conditions over the entire country precludes the making of any more definite recommendation of base or surface materials, or depth of enclosing frost wall. Extent of funds and local availability of material also will affect selection of the surface treatment.

Whatever material a thorough consideration of circumstances may designate for use, it is certainly to be urged that intelligent thought be given to the factors of frost wall, base material, and method of laying with respect to durability of the finished product. So many pavements of open shelters have failed to survive the local temperature range and frost action, with such disheartening results, that it is not unfair to assert that there has been too prevalent ignorance or naive disregard of unchangeable facts of Nature. Were it not for the introductory promise to avoid the "primer" approach within these discussions, there would be at this point a yielding to temptation to point out that masonry expands under heat and contracts with cold, and that proper expansion joints are a specific, that foundation walls are unreliable unless carried below the local frost level, and that bounding retaining walls do not long retain if moisture can collect underground above the frost line. A promise being what it is, a recall of these elementary facts must go herein unrecorded and neglected.

Plate II D–1   ⇒⇒⇒ PICNIC SHELTERS AND KITCHENS

Picnic Shelter
Mohawk Metropolitan Park – – Tulsa, Oklahoma

The reader should find some interest in tracing "family traits" through the several structures of this metropolitan park which are illustrated in other sections of this compilation. A boat-house, a refectory and an octagonal shelter have similar characteristics of materials, scale and details to stamp them as of one family, and a rather distinguished one, we should say. Overscale and a certain intimacy in plan are the predominant qualities of the member here shown.

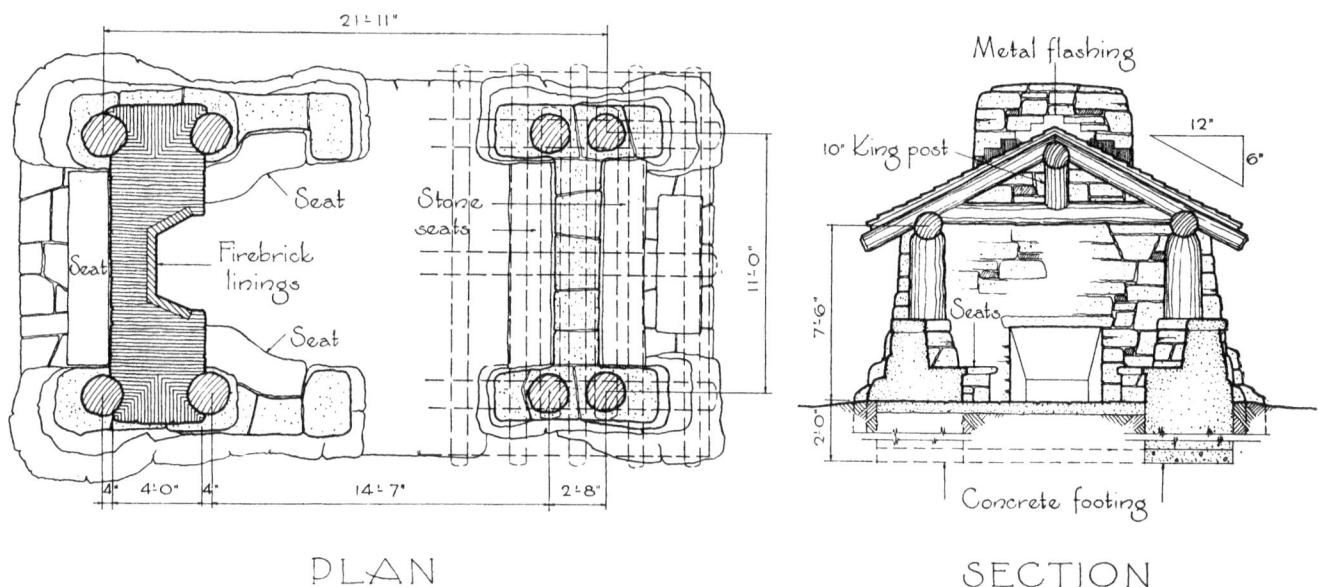

PLAN   SECTION

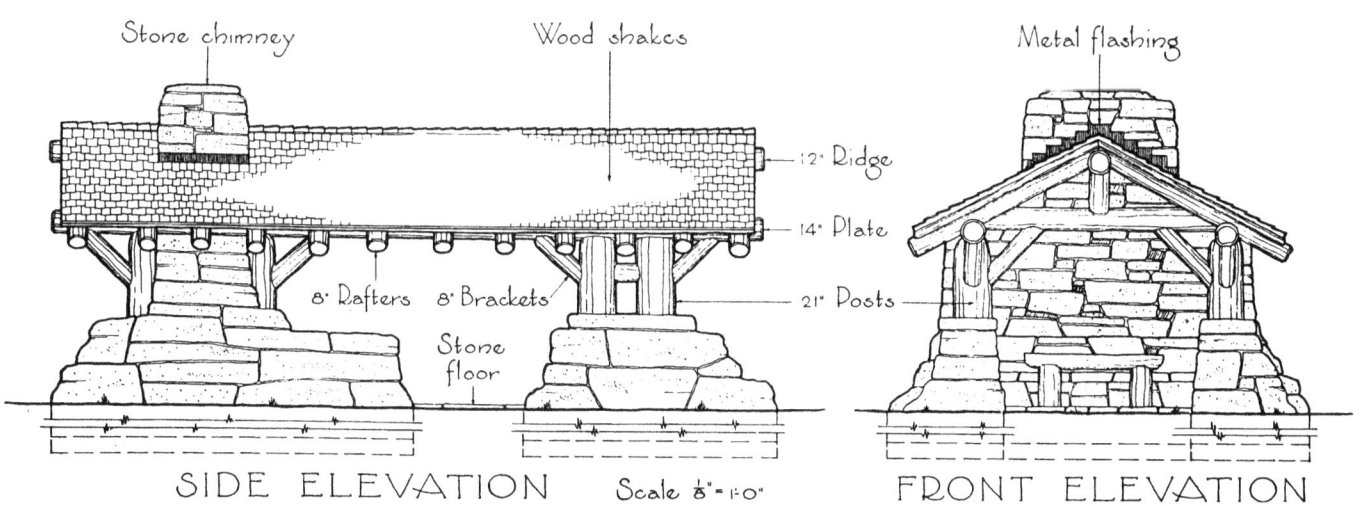

SIDE ELEVATION   Scale 8" = 1'-0"   FRONT ELEVATION

PICNIC SHELTERS AND KITCHENS

Plate II D-2

Picnic Shelter — Parvin State Park — New Jersey

Exampling an appealing simplicity of structure with a nice scale maintained in every detail. Of interest are the half log used as upper rail member serving as back for the seat that carries around the shelter and the trim cornice with close cropped rafter ends.

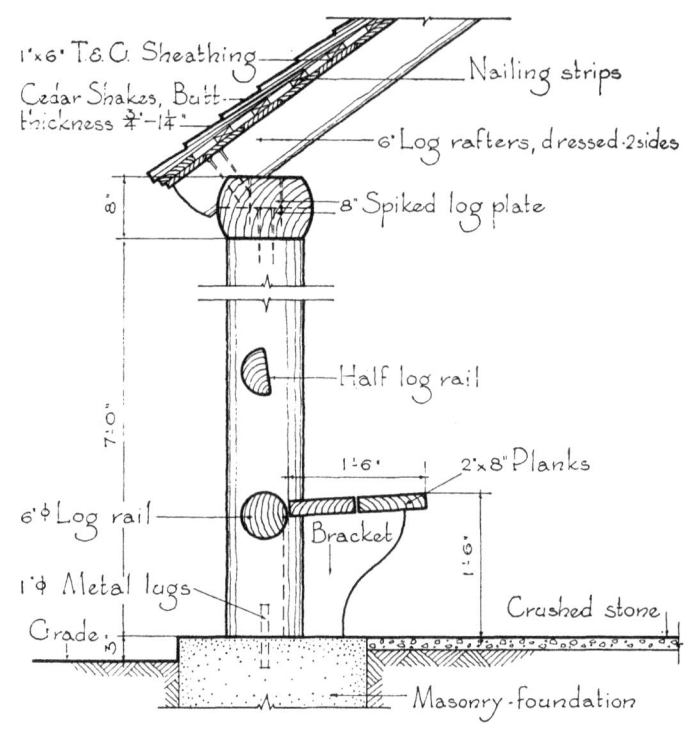

CONSTRUCTION DETAIL

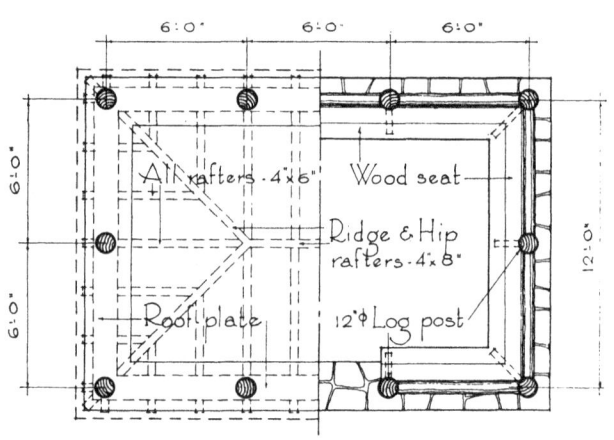

HALF ROOF & FLOOR PLAN

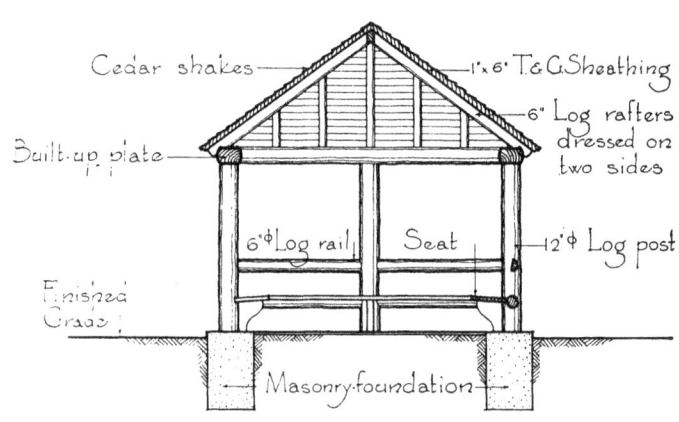

SECTION

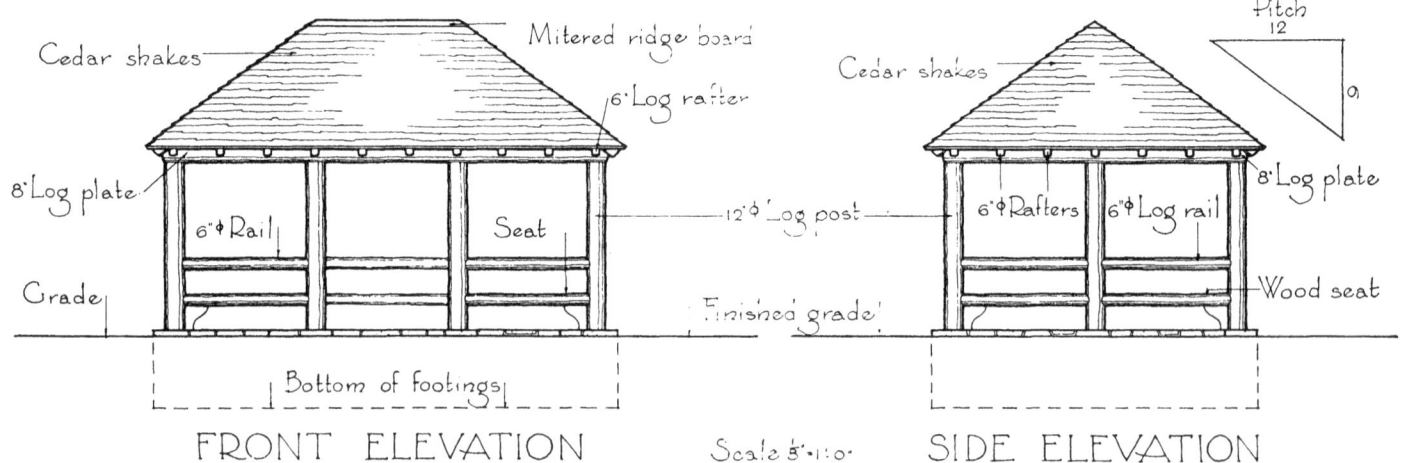

FRONT ELEVATION   Scale ½"=1'-0"   SIDE ELEVATION

Plate II D–3 ⇶ PICNIC SHELTERS AND KITCHENS

Mount Penn Metropolitan Reservation, Reading, Pennsylvania

Mississippi Palisades State Park, Illinois

SMALL SHELTERS EAST OF THE MISSISSIPPI

The two shelters above-pictured reproduce with squared timbers the elements of the shelter detailed opposite, replacing hip roof with ridge roof. The shelter to the right of this caption and the basic shelter detailed are located in the same park, and the former is in every way an expanded version of the latter. Below are two shelters which, in spite of greater size and use of squared timbers, still seem closely related to the shelter detailed.

Parvin State Park, New Jersey

Stackhouse Metropolitan Park, Johnstown, Pennsylvania

Giant City State Park, Illinois

49

PICNIC SHELTERS AND KITCHENS

Plate II D-4

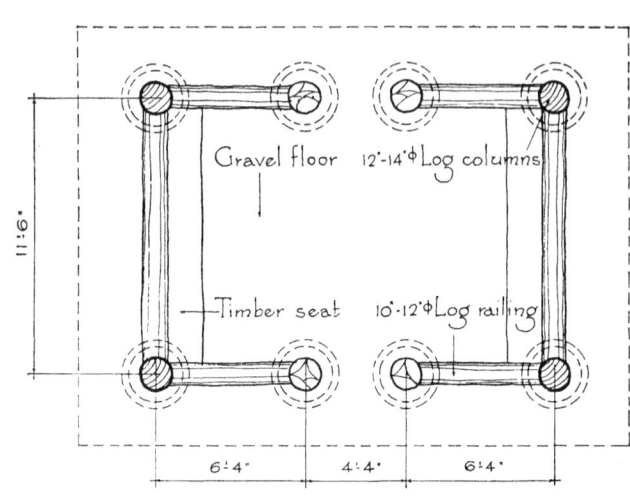

FLOOR PLAN

FRONT ELEVATION

Small Shelter — Fargo Metropolitan Park — North Dakota

The best points of the so-called "rustic" style are here well exampled. The vigorous proportions of the timbers in the round, the free-hand eave and shingle course lines, the blunted rafter ends — all make for a well-proportioned and attractive small shelter in excellent scale, that would be appropriate far beyond the boundaries of the state in which it has been built.

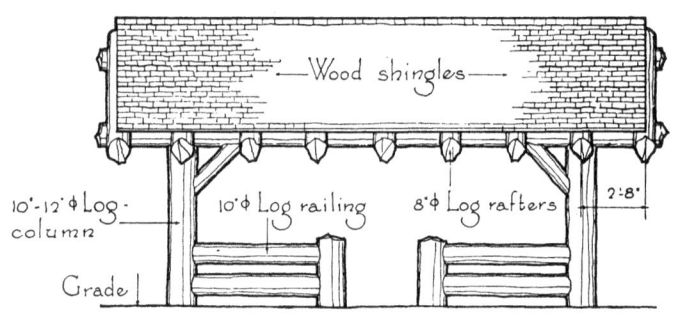

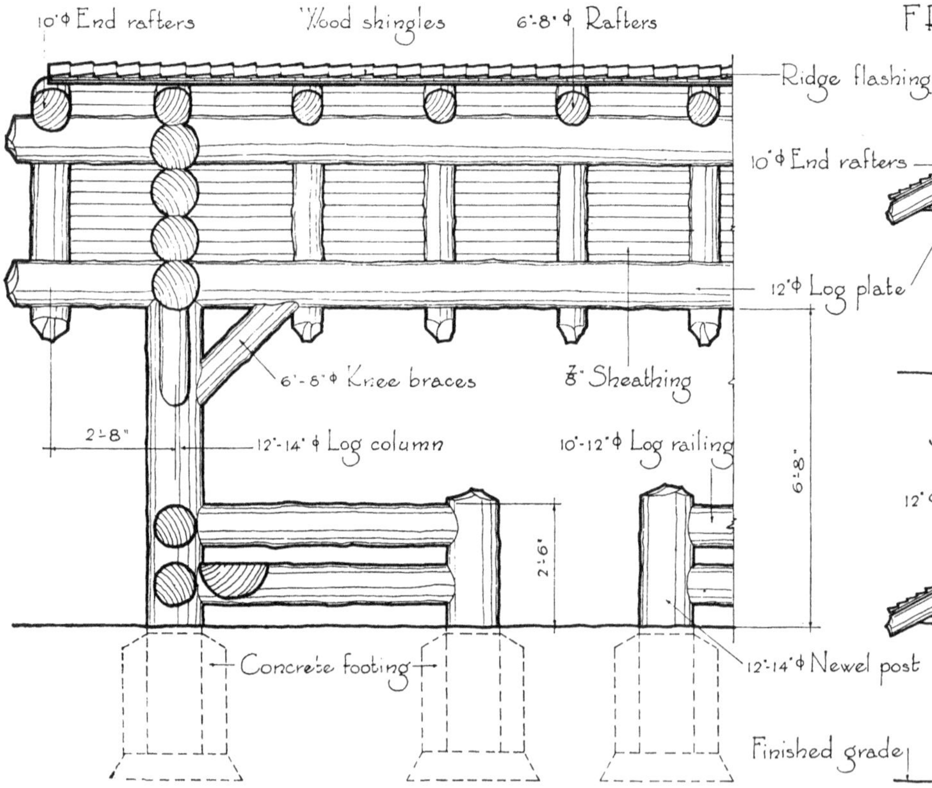

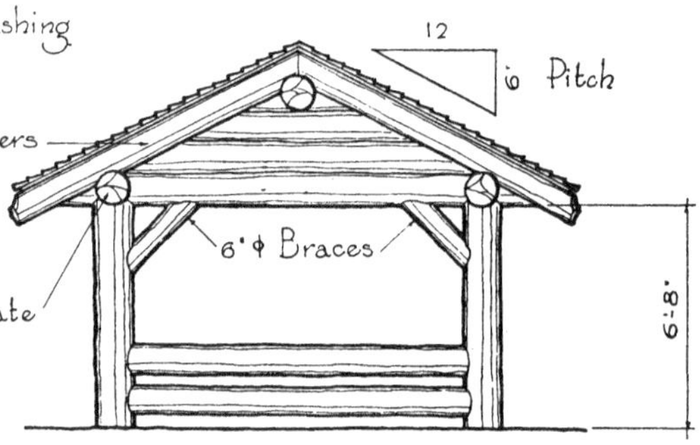

SIDE ELEVATION

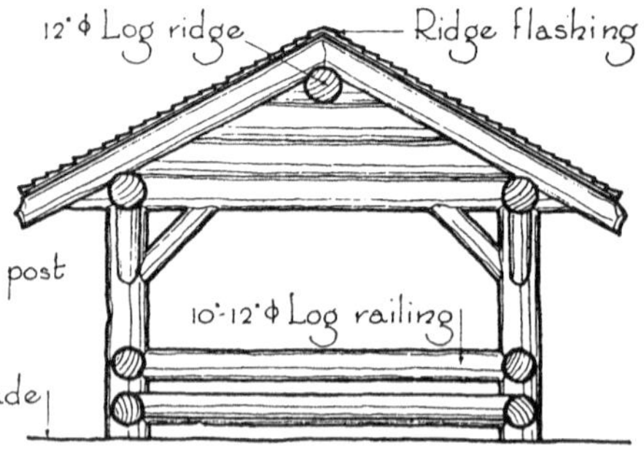

HALF SECTION
Scale ¼" = 1'-0"

SECTION
Scale ⅛" = 1'-0"

50

Plate II D-5   ⇒ PICNIC SHELTERS AND KITCHENS

Itasca State Park, Minnesota

Crowley's Ridge State Park, Arkansas

SMALL SHELTERS WEST OF THE MISSISSIPPI

The general character of the shelter of the facing page is closely held to in the expanded developments pictured above and to the right. Freehand lines, scale of logs, snubbed rafter ends, and other points of regional character are unmistakably western and of the forested parts thereof. The counters of the Itasca building are removable, so that it may function normally as a shelter, and as a concession on "pageant" days. Below are illustrated two shelters in unforested parts of the Southwest. Scanty, twisted wood members and the use of masonry terminal piers in the Nevada example reflect natural environment.

Crowley's Ridge State Park, Arkansas

Colossal Caves County Park, Arizona

Valley of Fire State Park, Nevada

51

PICNIC SHELTERS AND KITCHENS

Plate II D-6

Shelter — Turner Falls State Park — Oklahoma

The carping critic may well skip this subject unless he would merely pause for breath. The free-hand lines of the shingle courses doubled every fourth or fifth course for scale and accent, the well-scaled pole rafter ends, the rugged informality and textural quality of the stone work, the batter of the wall - all combine to the success of this structure.

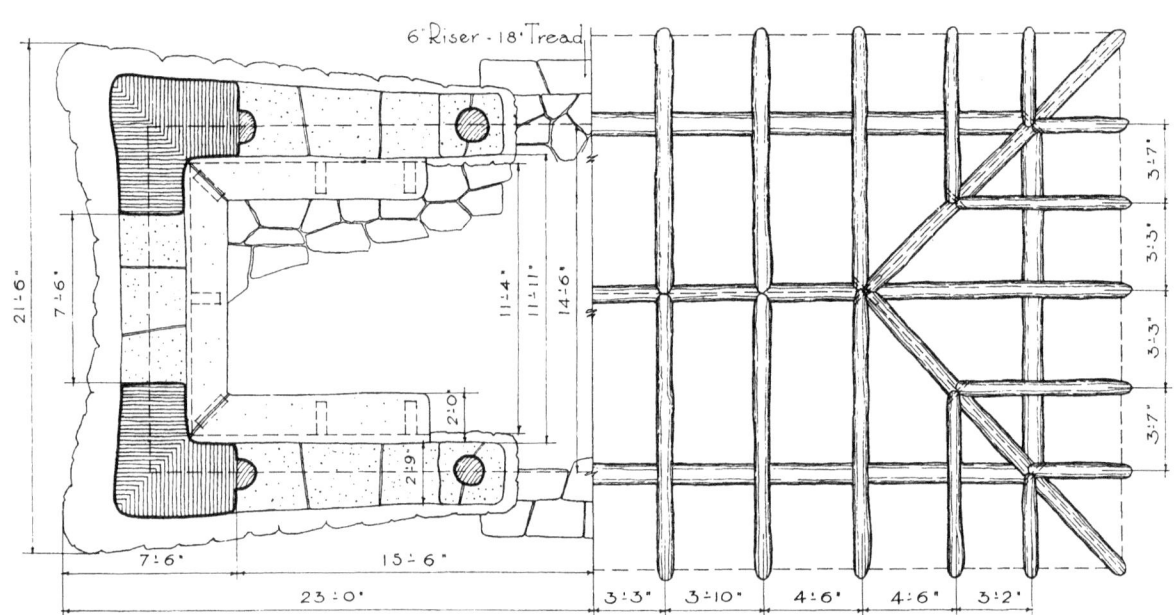

HALF PLAN   HALF ROOF FRAMING

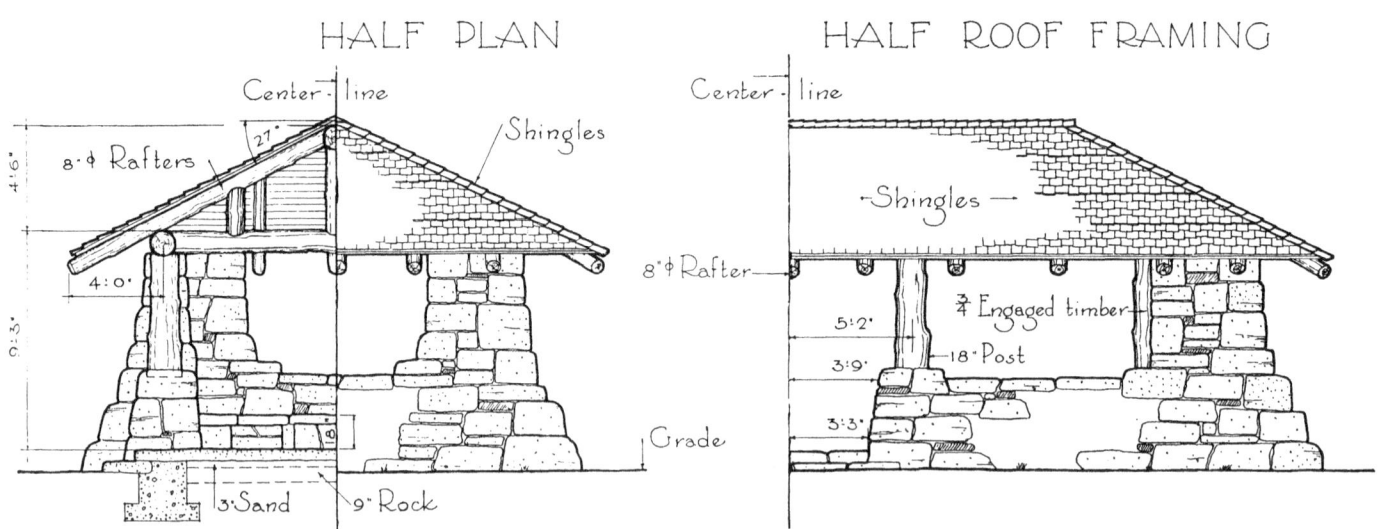

HALF SECTION & SIDE ELEVATION   FRONT ELEVATION

Scale ⅛" = 1'-0"

52

Plate II D-7   ⇶ PICNIC SHELTERS AND KITCHENS

Whitewater State Park, Minnesota

Mount Penn Metropolitan Reservation, Reading, Pennsylvania

SMALL SHELTERS OF STONE AND TIMBER

Here are shown shelters which retain elements of the shelter detailed opposite, varied by regional and personal influences. Two, even without captions, could be quickly tagged as not of the Far West. The Mount Penn example is the earlier illustrated all-wood shelter in this same area, with stone piers introduced. The Fort Worth subject might fittingly be approximated in many environments. Not so the Phoenix South Mountain ramada. Definitely of the desert country are its piers of thin stone slabs, roof of vigas and bearded thatch of old Spanish custom. The scale, mass, and blending to site of the Osage Hills shelter are admirable.

Lake Worth Metropolitan Park, Fort Worth, Texas

Phoenix South Mountain Metropolitan Park, Phoenix, Arizona

Osage Hills State Park, Oklahoma

PICNIC SHELTERS AND KITCHENS *Plate* II D-8

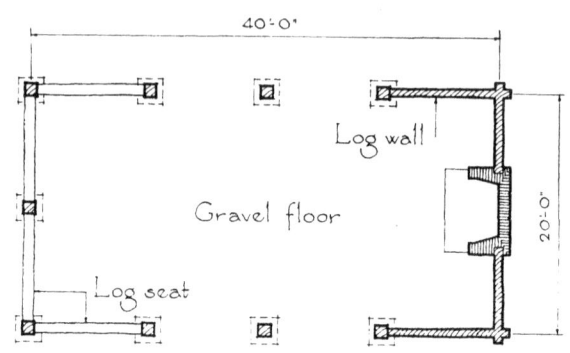

Fort Mountain State Park - Georgia

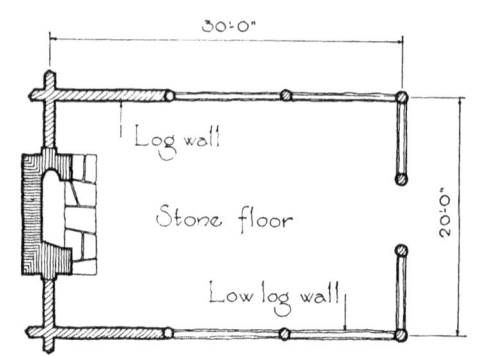

Darling State Forest Park - Vermont

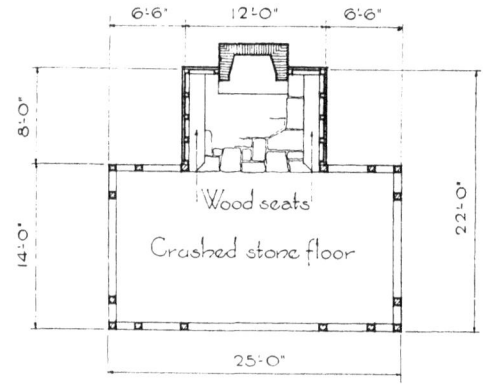

Westmoreland State Park - Virginia

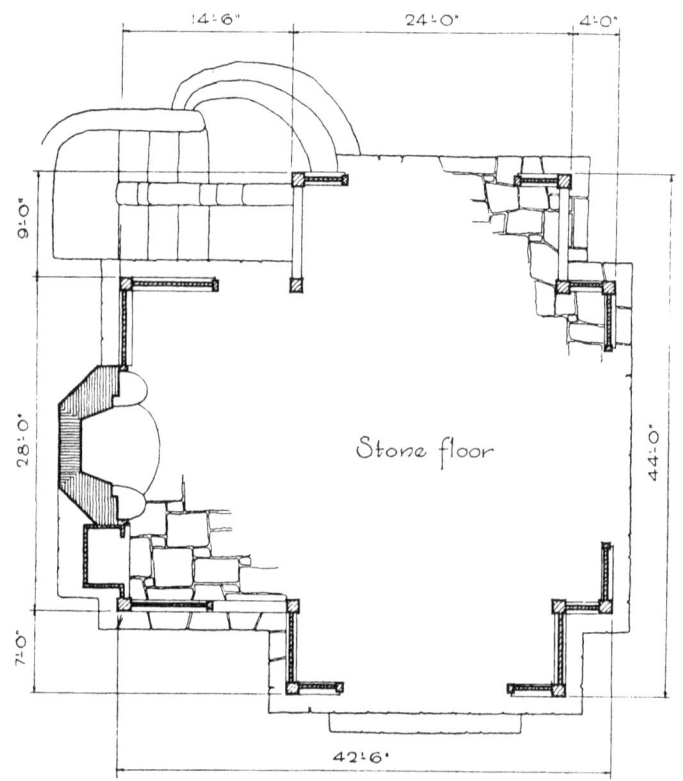

Stony Brook State Park - New York

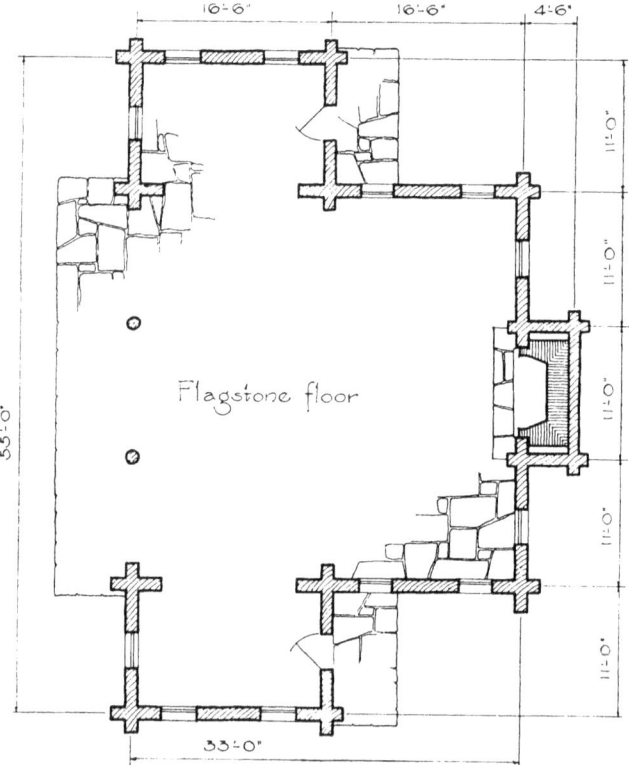

Fillmore Glen State Park - New York

Scale 1/16" = 1'-0"

Plate II D-9   ››› PICNIC SHELTERS AND KITCHENS

Fort Mountain State Park, Georgia

Darling State Forest Park, Vermont

PICNIC SHELTERS WITH SINGLE CHIMNEY

In the development from minor to more complicated picnic shelter, a first step is the addition of a fireplace. A shelter enclosed at one end and open at the other generally follows. Typical are the two examples above. Next step is a T-plan in which the open end expands to both sides with fireplace in an alcove. There is enlarging elaboration in the three shelters of this plan pictured. Wide ranges of material and method are on view, with novel construction details observable in the shelter at lower left.

Westmoreland State Park, Virginia

Stony Brook State Park, New York

Fillmore Glen State Park, New York

PICNIC SHELTERS AND KITCHENS

Plate II D-10

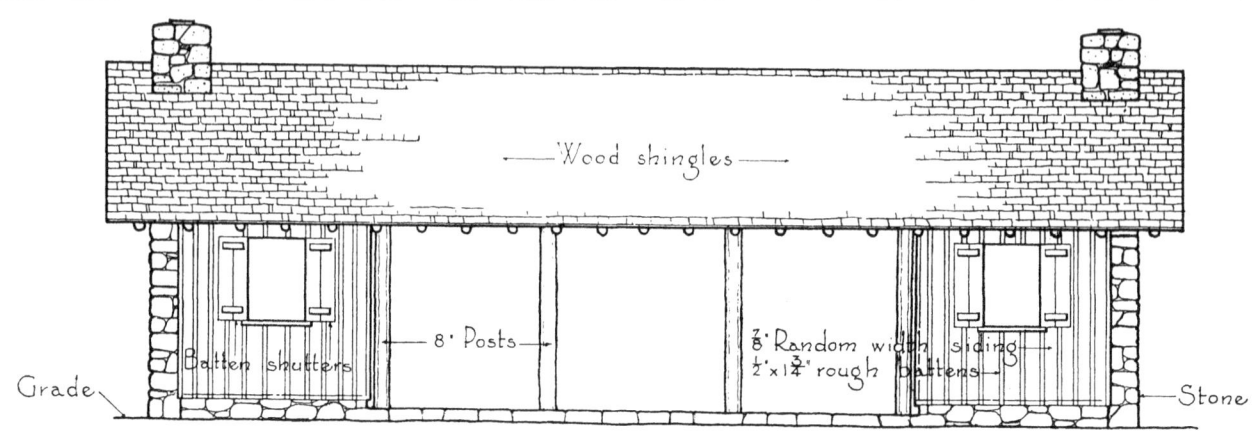

FRONT ELEVATION

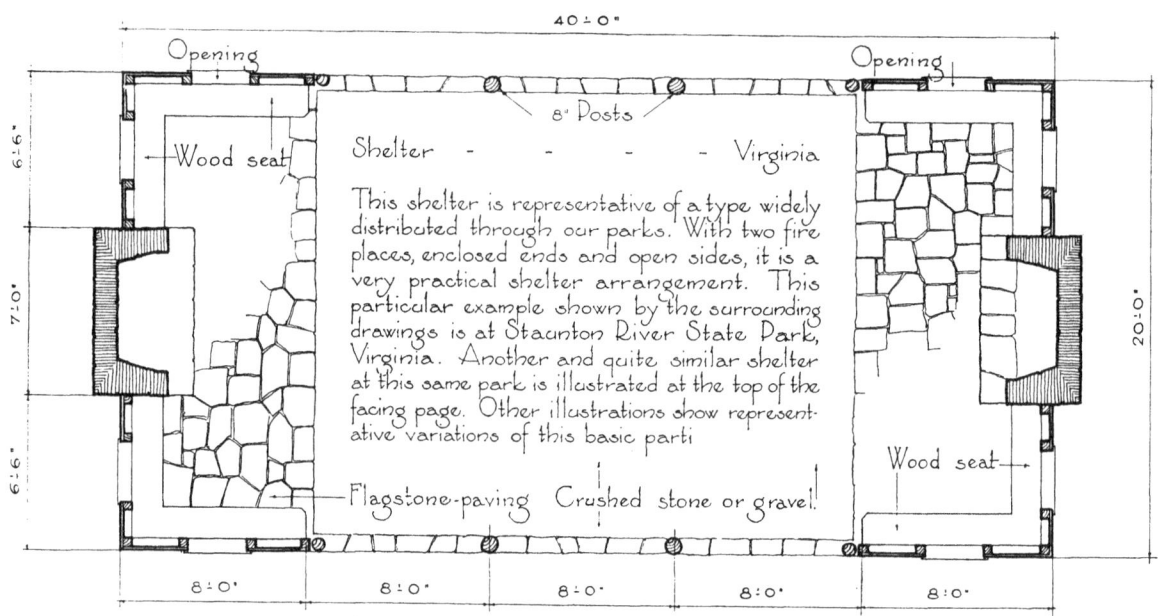

Shelter - - - - Virginia

This shelter is representative of a type widely distributed through our parks. With two fire places, enclosed ends and open sides, it is a very practical shelter arrangement. This particular example shown by the surrounding drawings is at Staunton River State Park, Virginia. Another and quite similar shelter at this same park is illustrated at the top of the facing page. Other illustrations show representative variations of this basic parti.

FLOOR PLAN

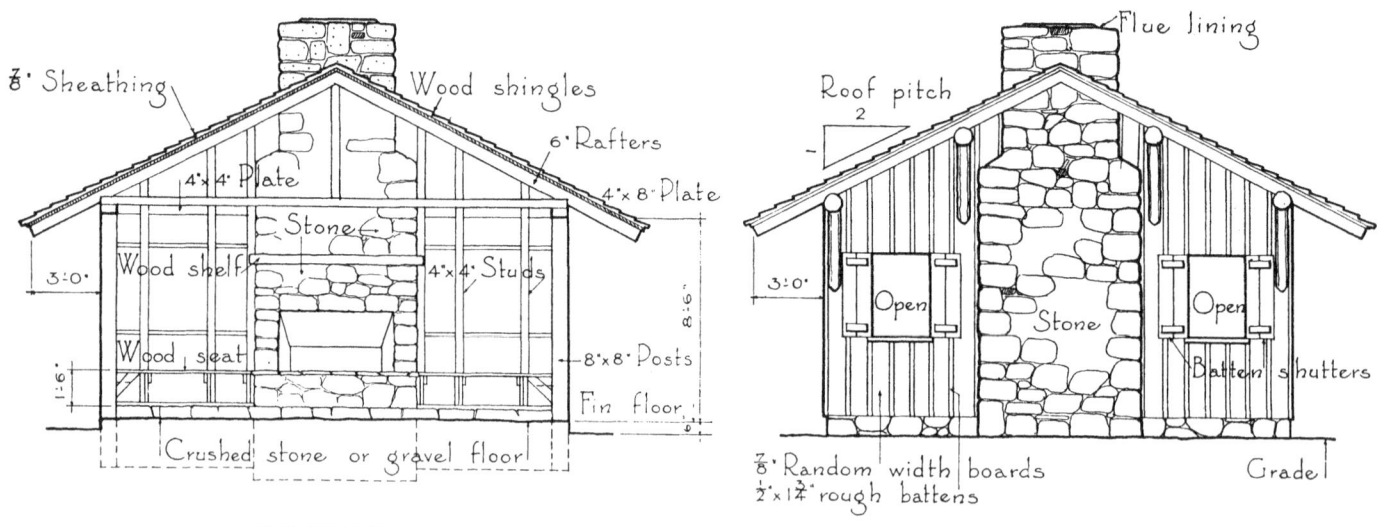

SECTION

SIDE ELEVATION

Scale ⅛" = 1'-0"

56

Plate II D–11 ⇶ PICNIC SHELTERS AND KITCHENS

Staunton River State Park, Virginia

Douthat State Park, Virginia

PICNIC SHELTERS WITH TWO CHIMNEYS

The shelter pictured above and the one detailed on the facing page are not one and the same shelter but illustrate variations within a narrow range on one park area. The other subjects exhibit interpretation of this basic and popular two-chimney type in a variety of materials including vertical logs, rough-sawn siding, and masonry in differing techniques. These serve to demonstrate the wide range of exterior treatments it is possible to obtain from an almost identical floor plan.

Wheeler Dam Reservation, Tennessee Valley Authority

Clarence Fahnestock Memorial State Park, New York

Giant City State Park, Illinois

PICNIC SHELTERS AND KITCHENS Plate II D–12

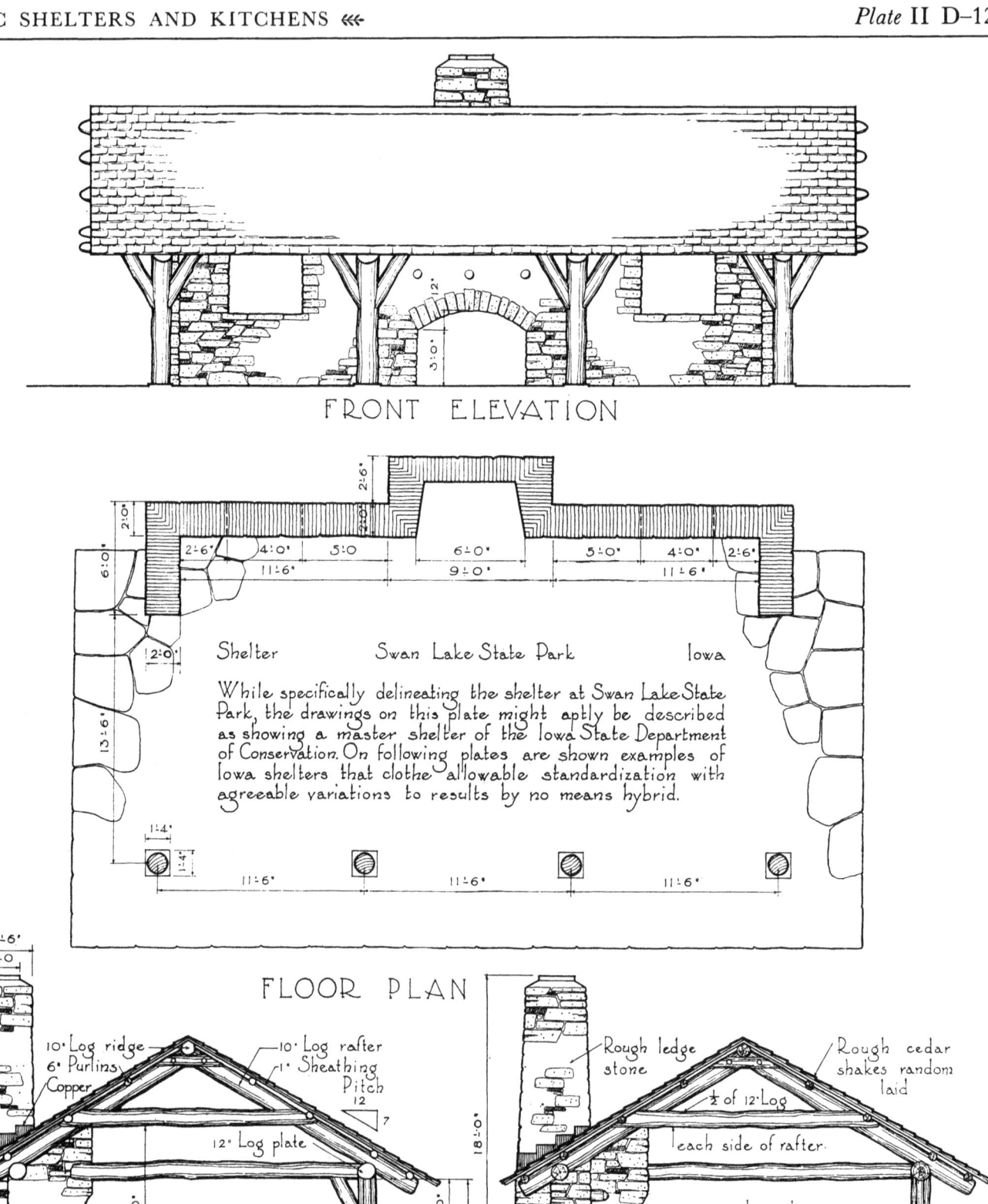

FRONT ELEVATION

FLOOR PLAN

Shelter   Swan Lake State Park   Iowa

While specifically delineating the shelter at Swan Lake State Park, the drawings on this plate might aptly be described as showing a master shelter of the Iowa State Department of Conservation. On following plates are shown examples of Iowa shelters that clothe allowable standardization with agreeable variations to results by no means hybrid.

SIDE ELEVATION   SECTION

Scale ⅛" = 1'-0"

Plate II D-13 ⇶ PICNIC SHELTERS AND KITCHENS

Backbone State Park, Iowa

Forest City State Park, Iowa

IOWA SHELTERS

The surrounding illustrations prove that variations in design within comparatively narrow limits produce a considerable individuality. All bear the stamp of Iowa through kinship with the shelter detailed on the opposing page, yet none evidences slavish duplication. Rather is there indicated a regional structural expression that is agreeable and vigorous. The plan is one appropriate and useful in many settings. The stages from very open shelter to much enclosed one and other points of variation are interesting.

Backbone State Park, Iowa

Gitchie Manitou State Park, Iowa

Springbrook State Park, Iowa

PICNIC SHELTERS AND KITCHENS

Plate II D-14

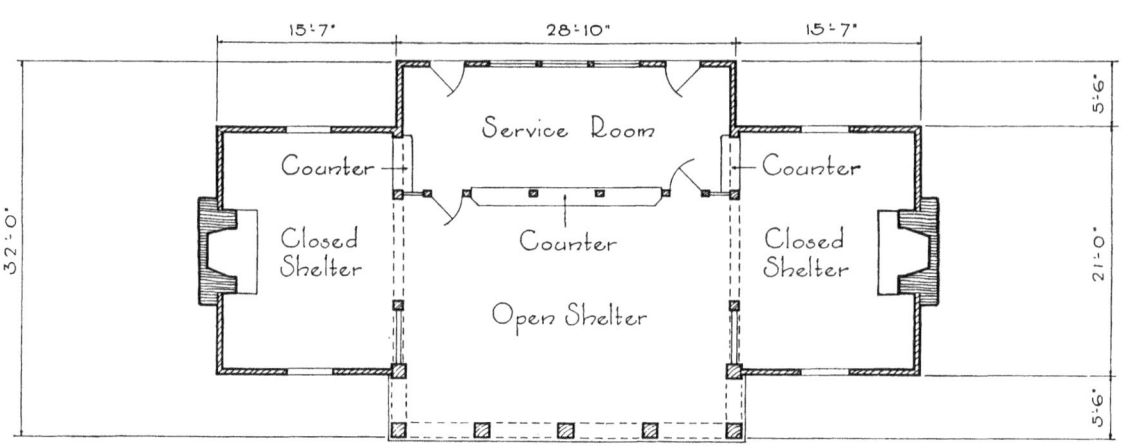

Spring Mill State Park — Indiana

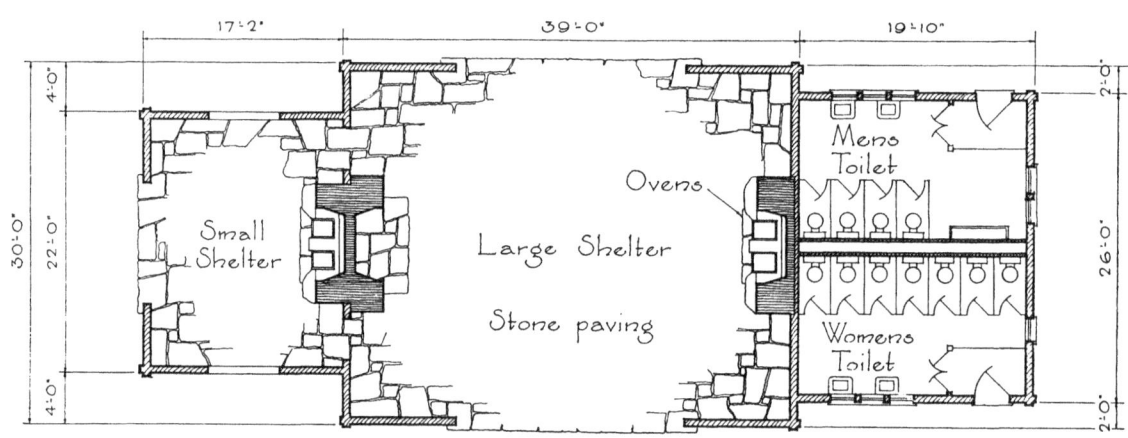

Turkey Run State Park — Indiana

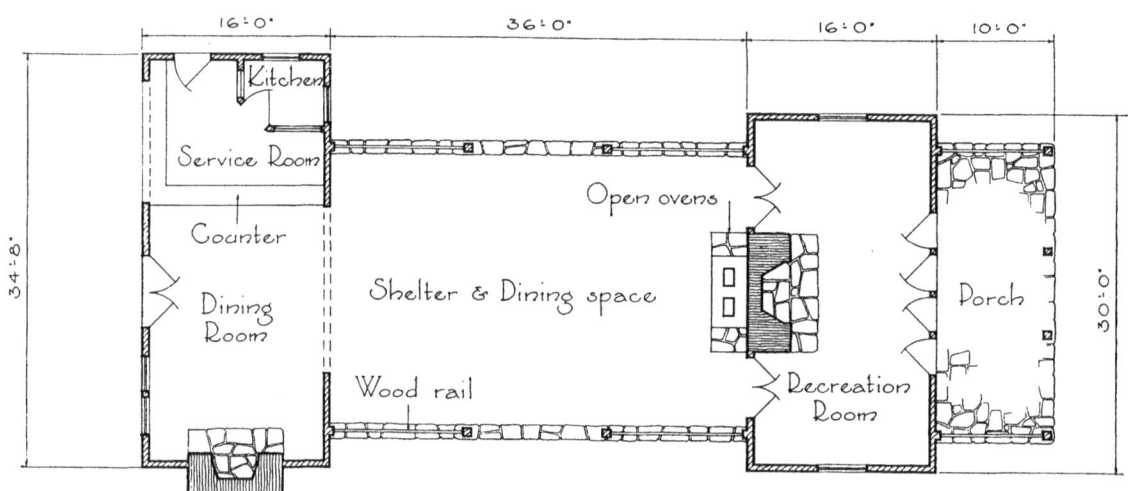

Clifty Falls State Park — Indiana

Scale $\tfrac{1}{16}" = 1'-0"$

Plate II D–15   ⇢⇢⇢ PICNIC SHELTERS AND KITCHENS

Spring Mill State Park, Indiana

Turkey Run State Park, Indiana

LARGE PICNIC SHELTERS IN INDIANA

In their log construction and many minor characteristics, the large shelters or combination buildings shown in plan on the facing page, and here illustrated, are unmistakably of Indiana. The Spring Mill State Park shelter is constructed within a park that centers around an early grist mill, restored to operating condition in a delightful setting. The new shelter gestures deferentially to the venerable mill. The wood posts are chamfered in the manner of the expert joinery of the mill framing.

The Turkey Run subject is in a State park whose chief glory is a last stand of virgin hardwood forest. The squared logs, of astonishing size for the region generally, thus fittingly relate structure to setting and to park "theme."

The low, informal, and picturesque Clifty Falls State Park shelter succeeds in retaining the feeling of the typical primitive log cabin of southern Indiana that must have inspired it. The combination of textures, the denticulation of roof comb by the local practice of alternating the lap of the topping-off shingle courses, the squared logs, and robust chimneys are important details. This is exhibit A in disproof of any contention that a simple structure of character cannot be expanded without sacrifice of its savor.

Clifty Falls State Park, Indiana

Clifty Falls State Park, Indiana

PICNIC SHELTERS AND KITCHENS   *Plate* II D–16

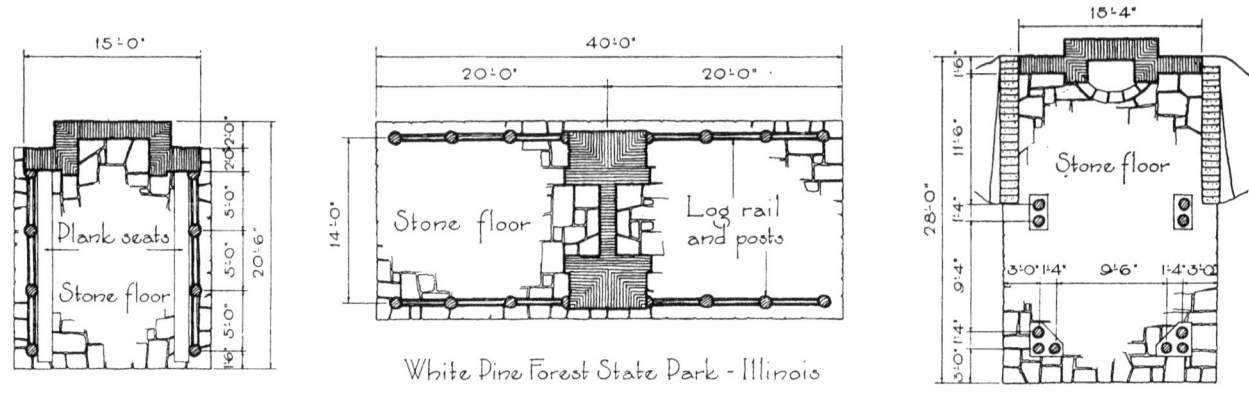

Starved Rock State Park - Illinois

White Pine Forest State Park - Illinois

White Pine Forest State Park - Illinois

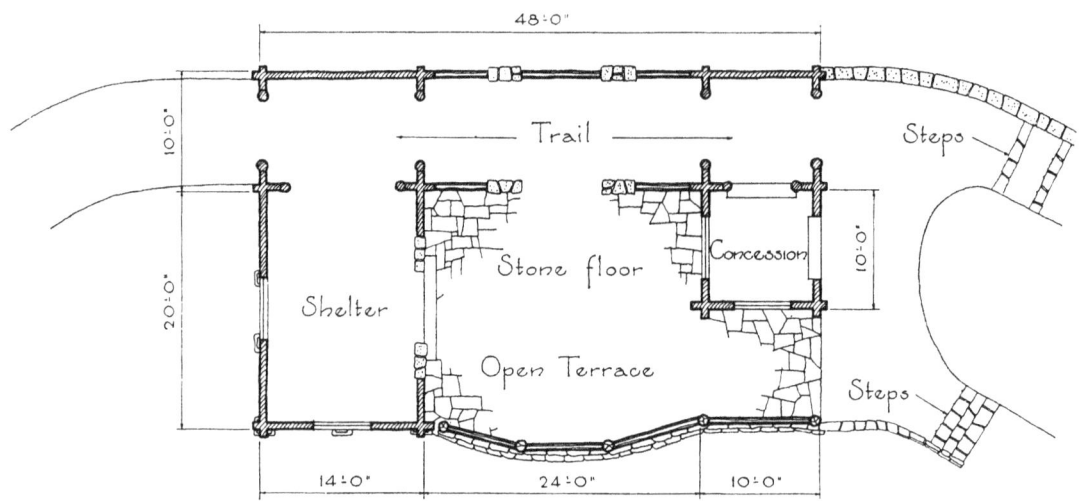

Pere Marquette State Park - - Illinois

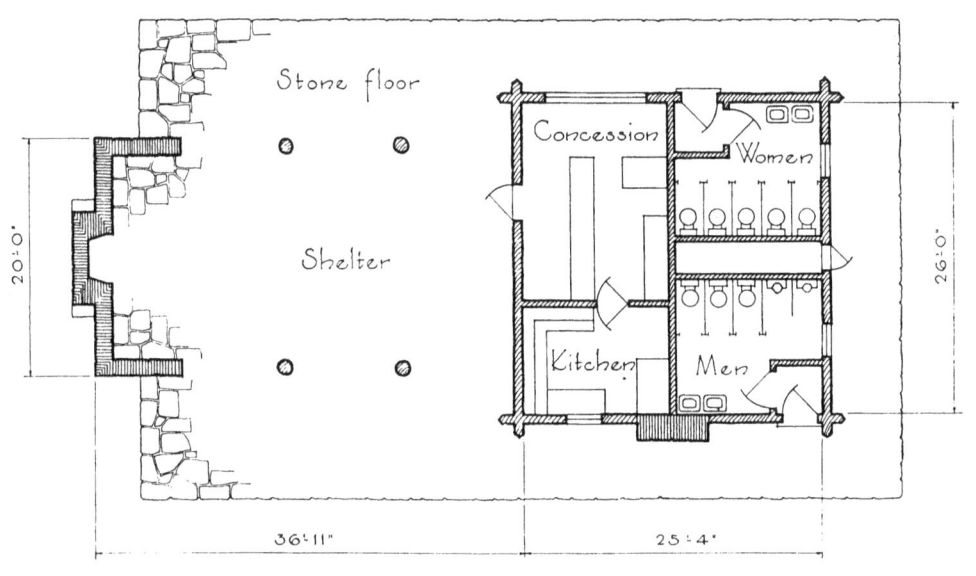

Buffalo Rock State Park - - Illinois
Scale 1/8" = 1'-0"

Plate II D–17   →→→ PICNIC SHELTERS AND KITCHENS

Starved Rock State Park, Illinois

White Pine Forest State Park, Illinois

PICNIC SHELTERS IN ILLINOIS

Here are Illinois picnic shelters in graduated sizes, ranging from one so minor that it would shelter but a single picnic group to an example which includes refreshment concession and comfort stations. In the little shelter at Starved Rock State Park and the Siamese adaptation of it at White Pine Forest there is faint recall of European farm buildings that appears accidental rather than deliberate. The routing of the trail through the Pere Marquette shelter is a unique feature.

White Pine Forest State Park, Illinois

Pere Marquette State Park, Illinois

Buffalo Rock State Park, Illinois

63

PICNIC SHELTERS AND KITCHENS

Plate II D-18

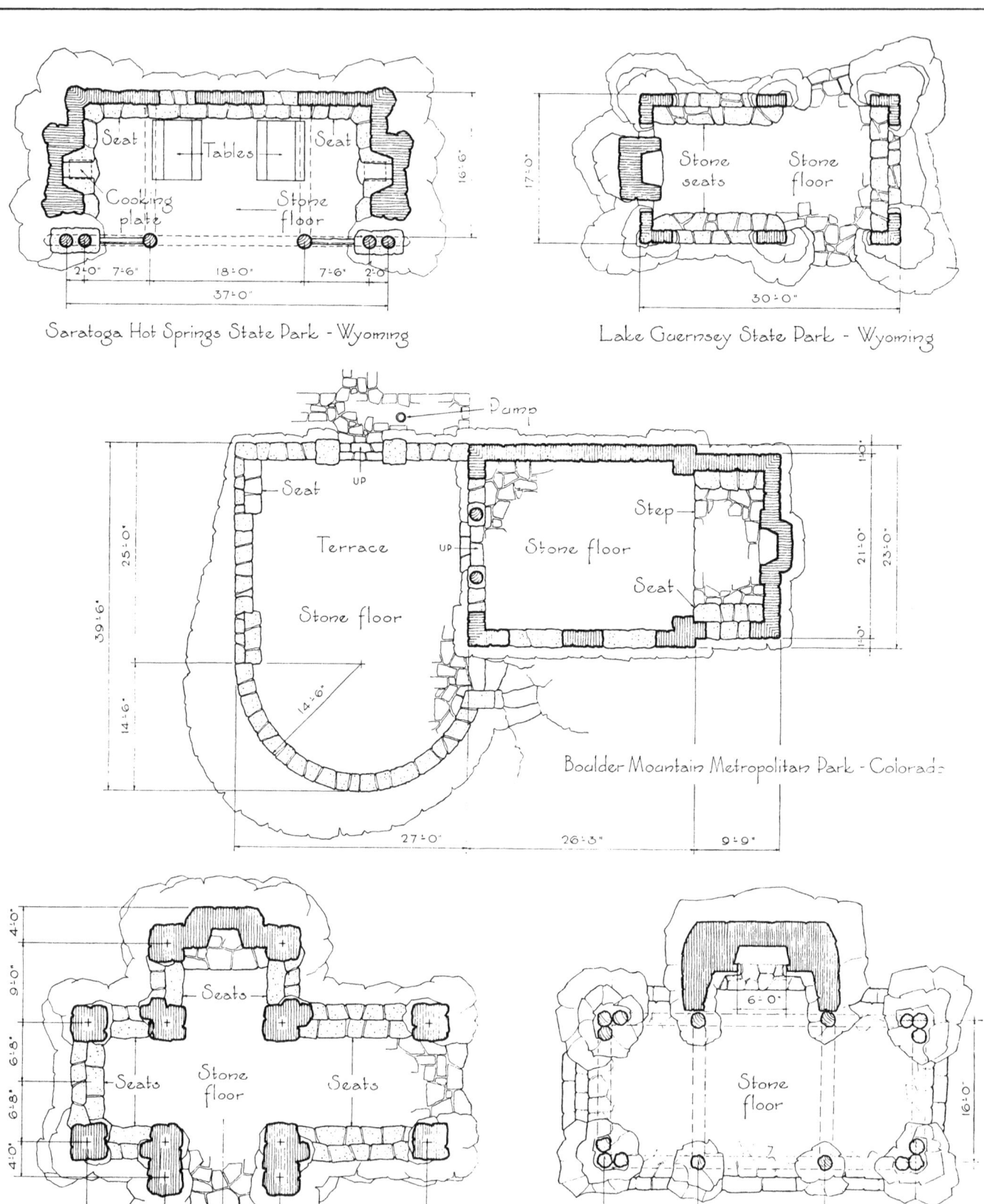

Saratoga Hot Springs State Park – Wyoming

Lake Guernsey State Park – Wyoming

Boulder Mountain Metropolitan Park – Colorado

Lake Okmulgee Metropolitan Park – Oklahoma

Custer State Park – South Dakota

Scale 1/8" = 1'-0"

Plate II D–19   →›› PICNIC SHELTERS AND KITCHENS

Saratoga Hot Springs State Park, Wyoming

Lake Guernsey State Park, Wyoming

PICNIC SHELTERS IN THE WEST

A scale in structural elements suitable to the rugged country of the plains and mountain states was the challenge encountered and well met in the surrounding shelters. Plans of them are shown on the facing page. In the Lake Guernsey example the transition from formless rock outcrop to a topping-off of chimney with well-formed masonry is skillful indeed. There are excellences of detail in all these shelters to merit careful study and to inspire equally vigorous structures wherever harmony with rugged terrain is the goal.

Boulder Mountain Metropolitan Parks, Colorado

Lake Okmulgee Metropolitan Park, Oklahoma

Custer State Park, South Dakota

PICNIC SHELTERS AND KITCHENS

Plate II D–20

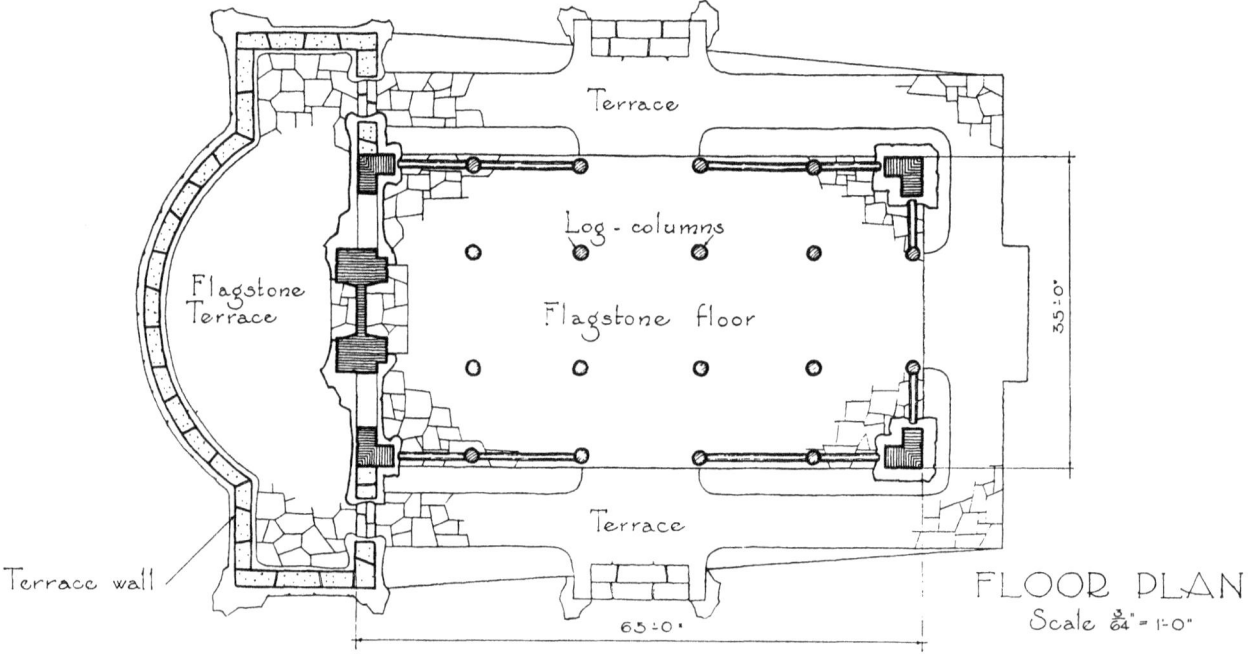

Shelter, Boyle Metropolitan Park, Little Rock, Arkansas

Vigorous in design and sympathetically executed, this shelter ranks near the top by current standards for park architecture. The broad, unbroken roof surface, rough-textured by thick shakes doubled every fourth course, and the informality of masonry and log work are admirable.

66

Plate II D–21   ❯❯❯ PICNIC SHELTERS AND KITCHENS

Picnic Shelter, Voorhees State Park, New Jersey

The supporting posts and brackets of this shelter seem perfectly scaled to the mass, and recall something of the sturdy and workmanlike joinery of the early American barn, a fitting source of precedent and inspiration for a building in our natural parks. The horizontality produced by the three-member railing offsets the considerable pitch of a roof that otherwise might cause the structure to appear too high. The simple gable treatment and the broad approach steps are important contributions to the satisfying effect here created.

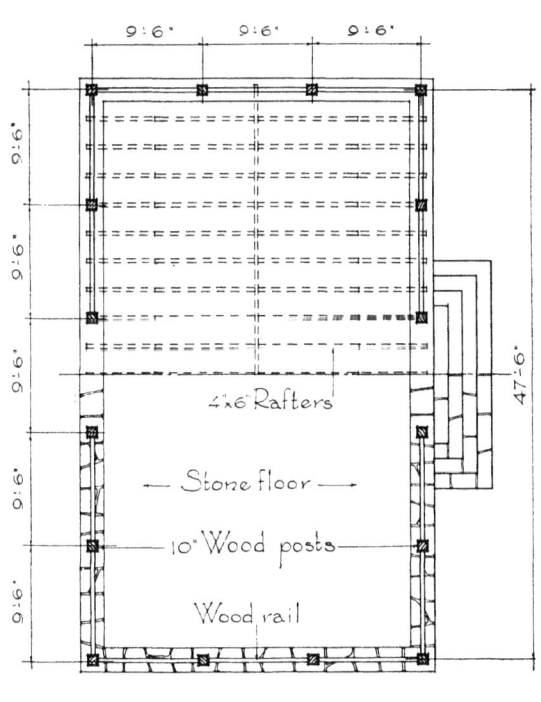

FLOOR PLAN
Scale ⅛" = 1'-0"

PICNIC SHELTERS AND KITCHENS

Plate II D–22

Shelter — Cumberland Falls State Park — Kentucky

A single roof shelters four picnic groups and barricades each against the incursions of the others by means of partition walls that converge on the four-way fireplace. A splendid safeguard against the entire structure being monopolized by one particularly aggressive group.

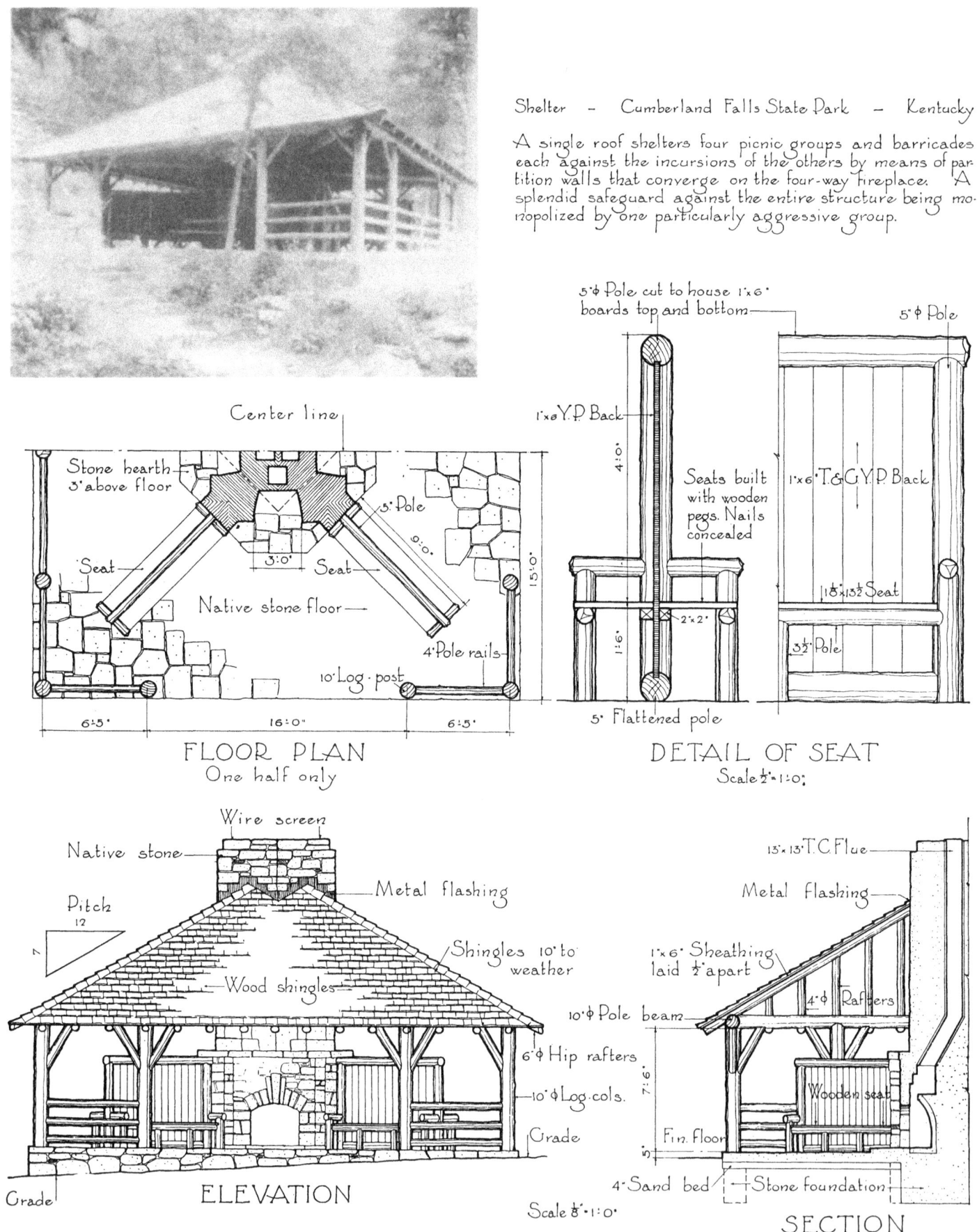

Plate II D–23 ⇶ PICNIC SHELTERS AND KITCHENS

McCormicks Creek State Park, Indiana

Clifty Falls State Park, Indiana

KITCHEN SHELTERS IN INDIANA

Above are illustrated two Indiana versions of the kitchen shelter or community kitchen so generally associated with picnicking in the Northwest. In form these are related to the Kentucky shelter detailed on the facing page. Apparently the Hoosiers do not feel the need for barricades between picnicking groups favored in neighboring Kentucky. They must also regard the enameled sink—standard equipment in the Northwest—as intolerably new-fangled for association with the ancient rites of picnicking.

Below are two views of another Indiana kitchen shelter rendering—this one largely of stone, and in a two-way or back-to-back plan arrangement. There was error in that statement about barricades between picnicking Indiana groups being unnecessary. Here is provided not just a separation, but it is of stone, and of a substantial thickness. The building has a pleasing general informality, and there is great interest attaching to the roof rakes, stone and shake textures, and the dovetailed ridge coursing so typical of Indiana.

Turkey Run State Park, Indiana

Turkey Run State Park, Indiana

PICNIC SHELTERS AND KITCHENS

Plate II D–24

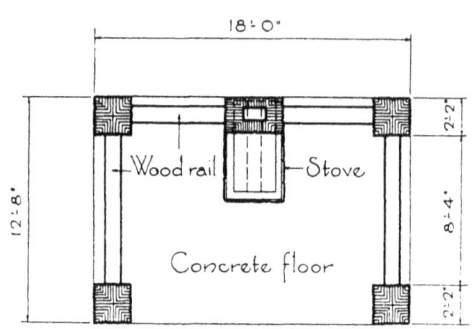

Deception Pass State Park - Washington

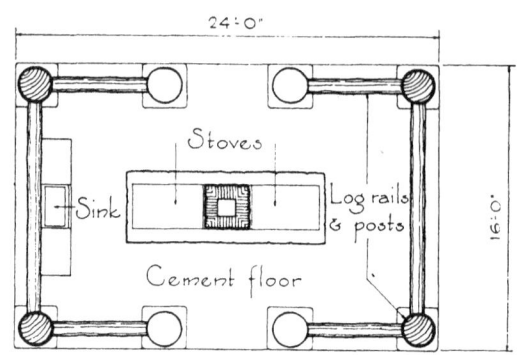

Moran State Park - Washington

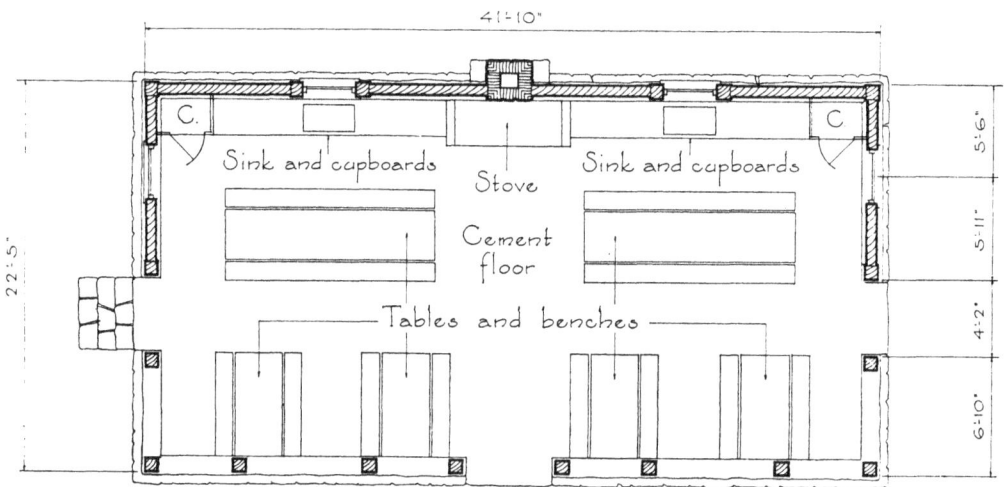

Benson Metropolitan Park - Oregon

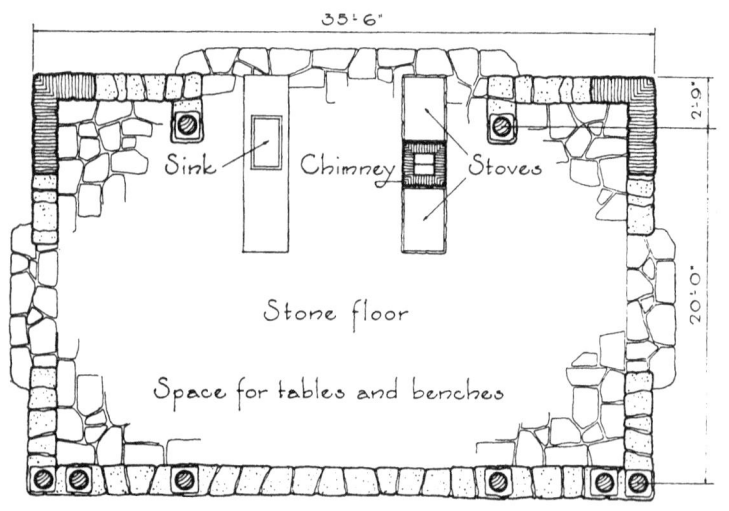

Riverside State Park - Washington

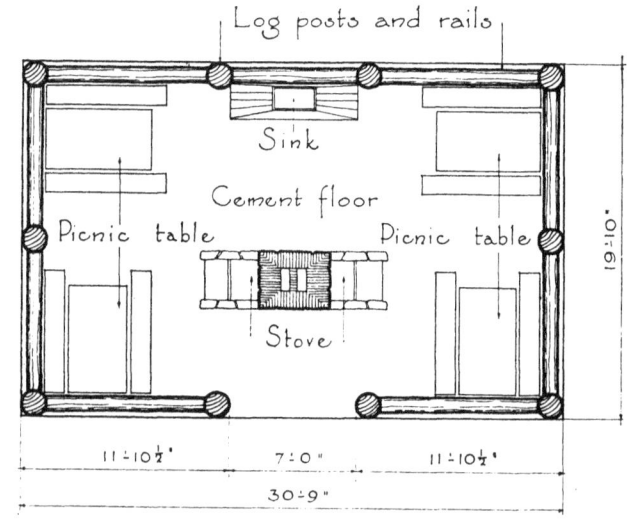

Rainbow Falls State Park - Washington

Scale 3/32" = 1'-0"

Plate II D–25 ⇢ PICNIC SHELTERS AND KITCHENS

Deception Pass State Park, Washington

Moran State Park, Washington

COMMUNITY KITCHENS IN THE NORTHWEST

Here are pictured the various shelter kitchens shown in plan on the facing page. All are in the Pacific Northwest, where the mortality rate of picnics relates directly to the heavy rainfall. Facilitating equipment usually consists of one or more picnic ovens, sinks, and a supply of table and bench combinations, the last sometimes in an intimate proximity that only a torrential downpour would render inviting. Realization that the superlative timber resources of this area have not been conducive to the development of a sound masonry technique tempers somewhat a critical sputtering at the unorthodox masonry here pictured.

Benson Metropolitan Park, Oregon

Riverside State Park, Washington

Rainbow Falls State Park, Washington

71

PICNIC SHELTERS AND KITCHENS ««   Plate II D-26

Shelter Kitchen - Deception Pass State Park - Washington

Typical of a structural facility provided in parks of the Pacific Northwest where heavy rainfall makes sheltered picnic tables and stoves a practical necessity. The hand-rived shakes and their rough-textured collective effect, as here laid, bring to this structure a manifest quality of handcraftedness. There is an agreeable sturdiness about the structure generally

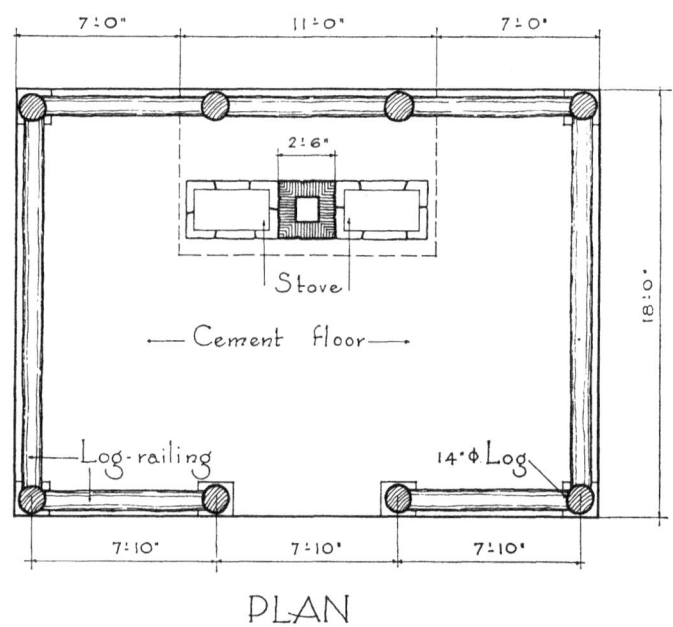

PLAN

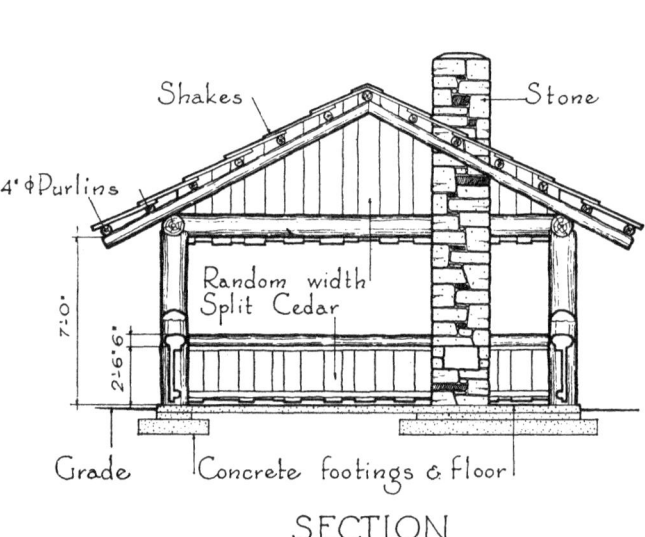

SECTION

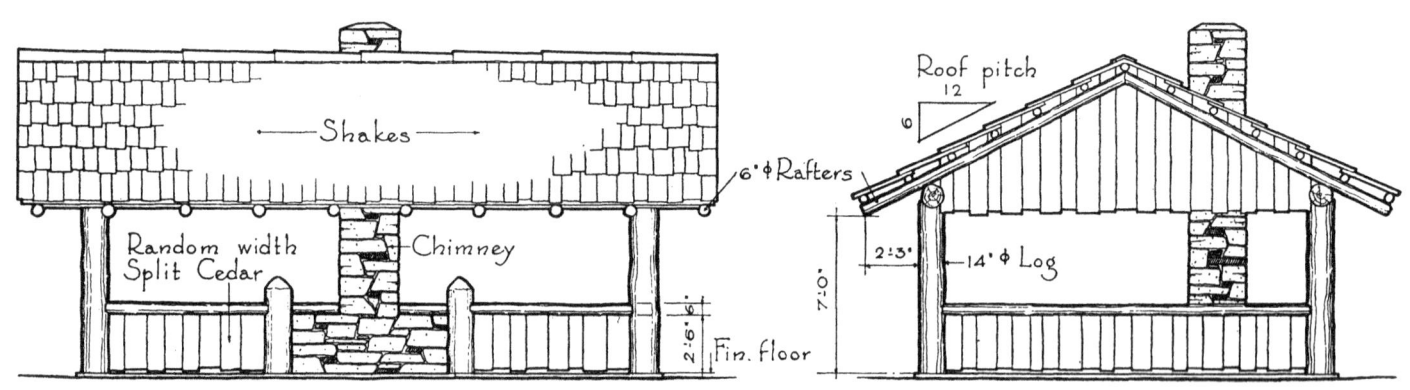

FRONT ELEVATION   SIDE ELEVATION

Scale ½" = 1'-0"

CONCESSIONS AND REFECTORIES

ALTHOUGH MANY of the recreational facilities found in natural parks are with varying frequency let out as concessions, it is elected within this classification to treat only the concession which dispenses by sale rather than by rental, and purveys to the recreationist food supplies, soft drinks, candies, tobacco, toys, novelties, and prepared light lunches. After all, it is this usage that comes first to mind at mention of the word, and the curb on verbosity that this limitation insures, while it comes hard for the pen in hand, will be a source of keen satisfaction to readers. A less restrictive interpretation of the word would mean deadly and duplicating analysis of structural media in promotion of active recreation elsewhere dissected.

Thus, the concession building, as here discussed, is actually the corner store, delicatessen, or restaurant, transplanted into the park area for the convenience of the park visitors. It may be some unpedigreed cross-combination of two or more of these urban facilities, as it settles itself in adjustment to the demands of the recreation crowd and to its new environment. If small in size, the concession is very apt to seek association under the same roof with other facilities, in order that it may borrow their bulk and be where the crowd is. The crowd is as essential to its commercial success in a park as in an urban environment. Other park facilities may exist by virtue of subsidy, but the concession is called upon to pay its way.

Since it must be located at the "cross roads" of the park, and must proclaim itself to the public, it cannot be exactly the shy violet among park buildings. It must announce its commercial traffic unmistakably yet with a certain subtlety. It is the Jekyll and Hyde among park structures. It is asked to walk in the paths of quiet beauty and of commercial solvency at one and the same time, though these may lead in opposite directions. It is scarcely to be wondered at that the concession, successful both as a park structure and as a commercial venture, is not common. Perhaps the greatest fault to be found with concession buildings in some localities is their lag in attaining the standards urged for park structures generally. There is recent evidence to indicate that past tendencies to flimsy and ultracommercial appearance are being overcome.

There is a practical need in connection with concession buildings, large and small, that is too generally underestimated. This is the requirement for working space and storage of supplies. The merchandise dispensed by the park concession involves not only much garbage and rubbish, but the handling and temporary storage of containers for soft drink and milk bottles, and the like, incoming or empty, awaiting collection. All bulk to a space need seldom correctly foreseen, and eventually force the building of an addition or enclosure to screen the unsightly debris from public view. Because funds for second thoughts are grudgingly given, and because the initial shortage of space is apt to lead to an extreme of oversupply on the second try, the addition is often of inferior construction and down-at-heel appearance. Practical need is served, but the quality of the building is depreciated in the process.

It is difficult to fix the stages of development at which the concession building becomes a refectory and the latter in turn becomes a lodge, and it may be pointless to attempt it. However, it seems logical to catalog them as park counterparts of familiar urban institutions—the concession, the store, dispensing food supplies and snacks; the refectory, the restaurant, serving meals; the lodge, the hotel, adding overnight accommodations to the serving of meals. Of these, the lodge is the facility least to be "promoted" in a natural park. It can be a too "civilizing" influence where the true concept of the natural park and the basic interest of the public-at-large in natural areas safeguarded against the artificial constitute first liens.

CONCESSIONS AND REFECTORIES

Plate II E-1

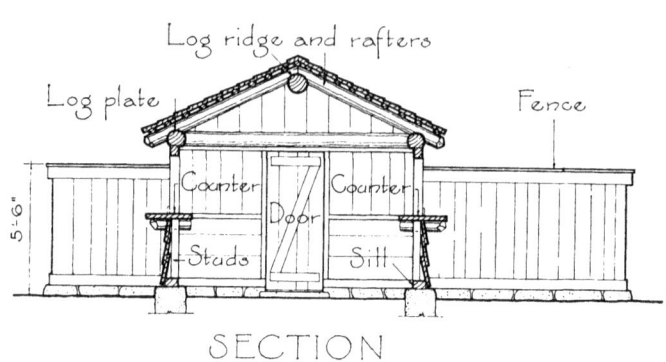

SECTION

Minor Concession
Boyle Metropolitan Park — Little Rock, Arkansas

Here is vibrant personality in structure achieved through economy of kind, but certainly not of scale, in the materials used. The result is convincing of the fact that the measure of a supremely satisfying building is not to be taken in terms of cost. A little building so appealing to the eye by reason of its simple charm might beg indulgence for many a practical shortcoming. It does not stoop to do so however in any detail.

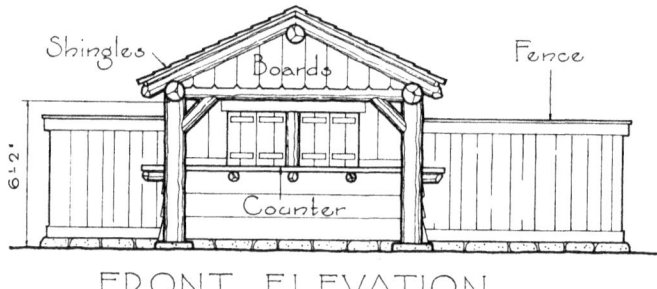

FRONT ELEVATION

SIDE ELEVATION

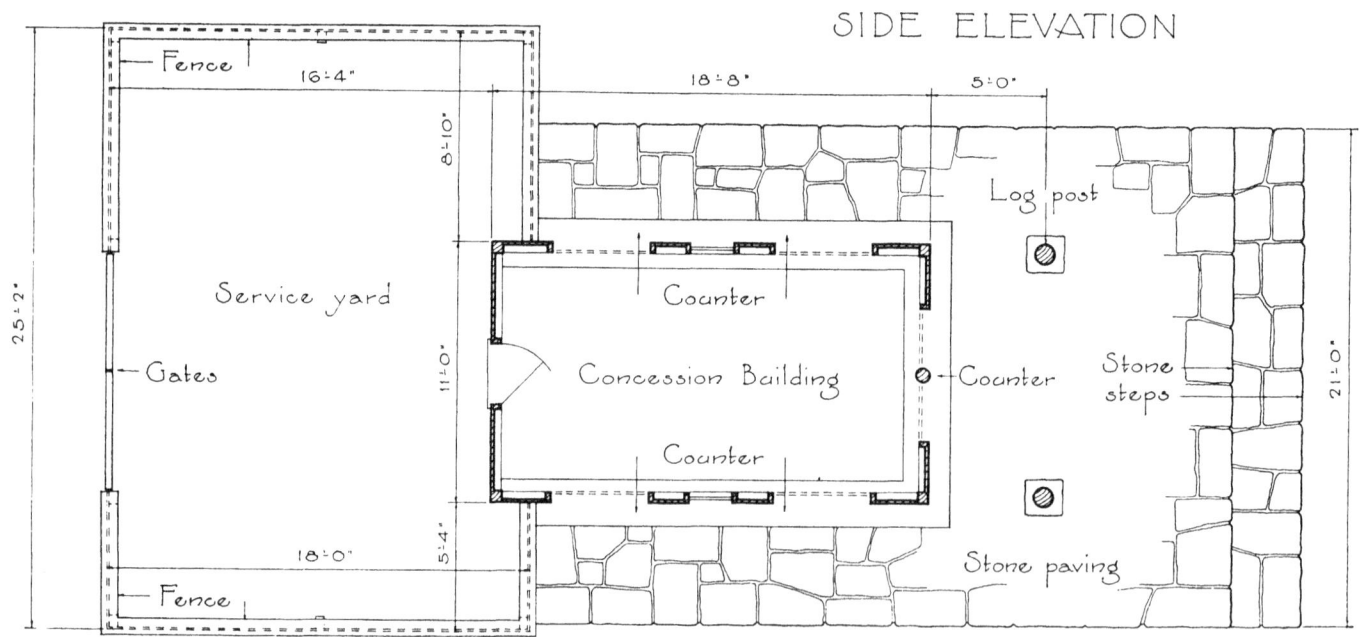

PLAN
Scale ⅛" = 1'-0"

74

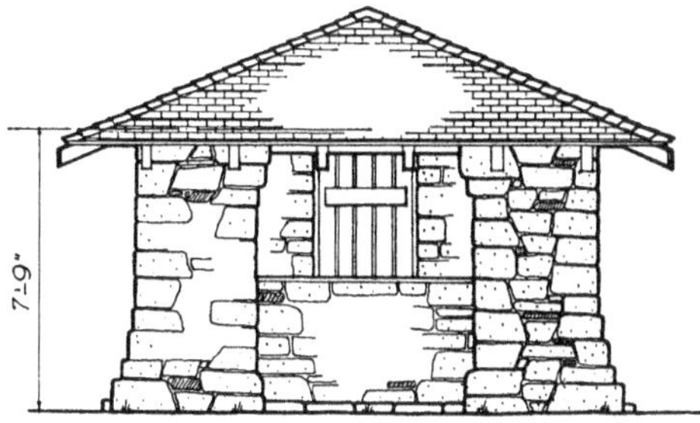

Plate II E-2   ⋙ CONCESSIONS AND REFECTORIES

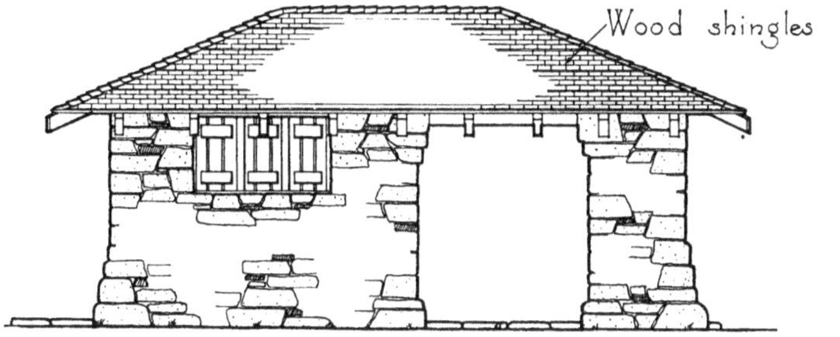

Small Concession Building - Lampasas State Park - Texas

A concession stand that is not so regional in character as to deny inspiration over a wide area. Recommended to the attention of proponents of highway improvement who would kennel the hot dog in greater grandeur. The texture of the stone masonry is worthy of note.

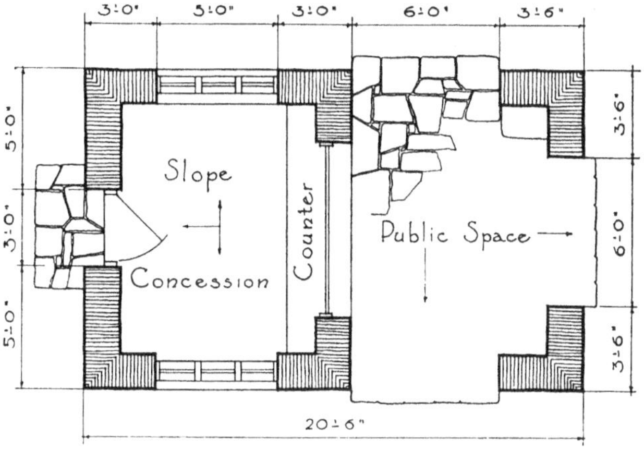

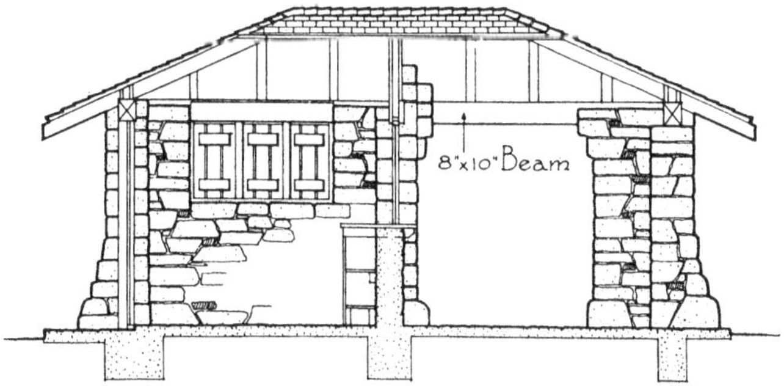

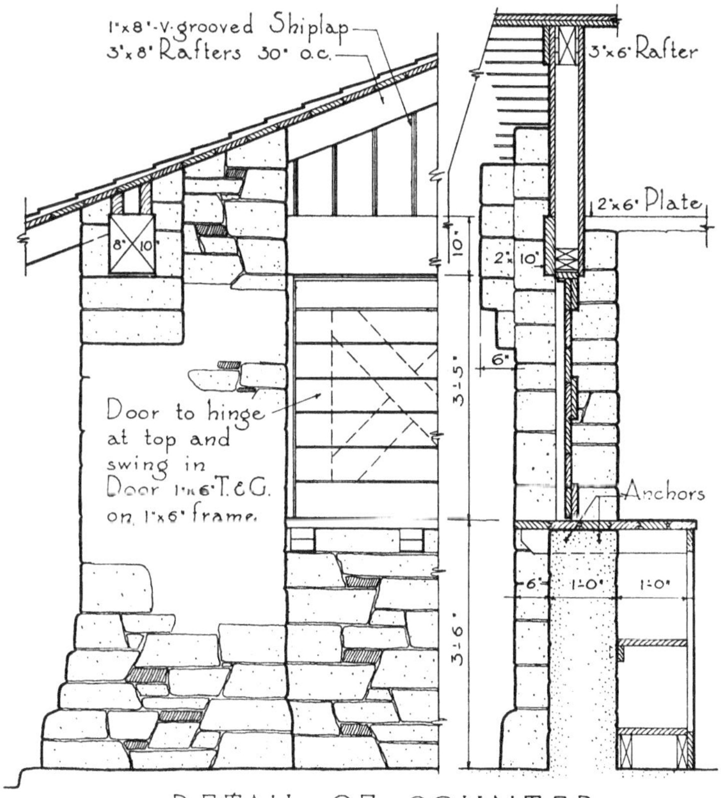

CONCESSIONS AND REFECTORIES ⋘   *Plate* II E-3

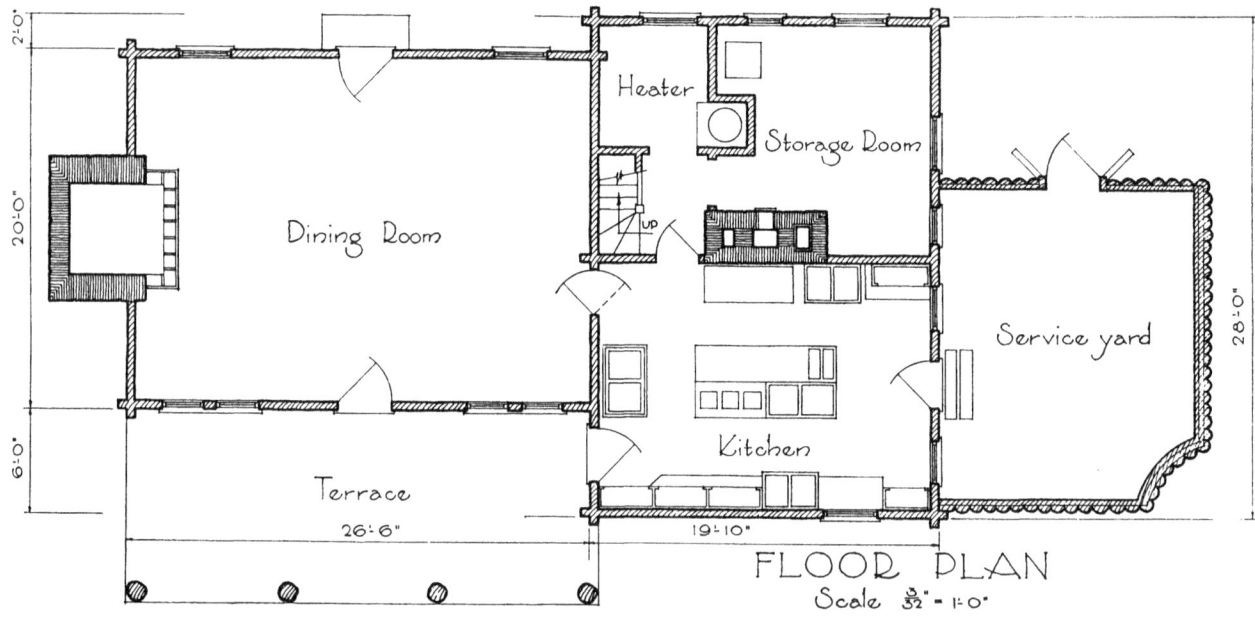

Refectory, New Salem State Park, Illinois

Here is a concession building in which it was sought to re-create a tavern typical of an Illinois backwoods village of the early 1800's. Located on a street lined with log dwellings of the period, and almost directly opposite the little frame building in which Abe Lincoln "kept store", it represents a sincere and successful attempt to clothe appropriately a valid park need. Views of other buildings of the reconstructed village will be found elsewhere herein.

Plate II E–4 ⇉ CONCESSIONS AND REFECTORIES

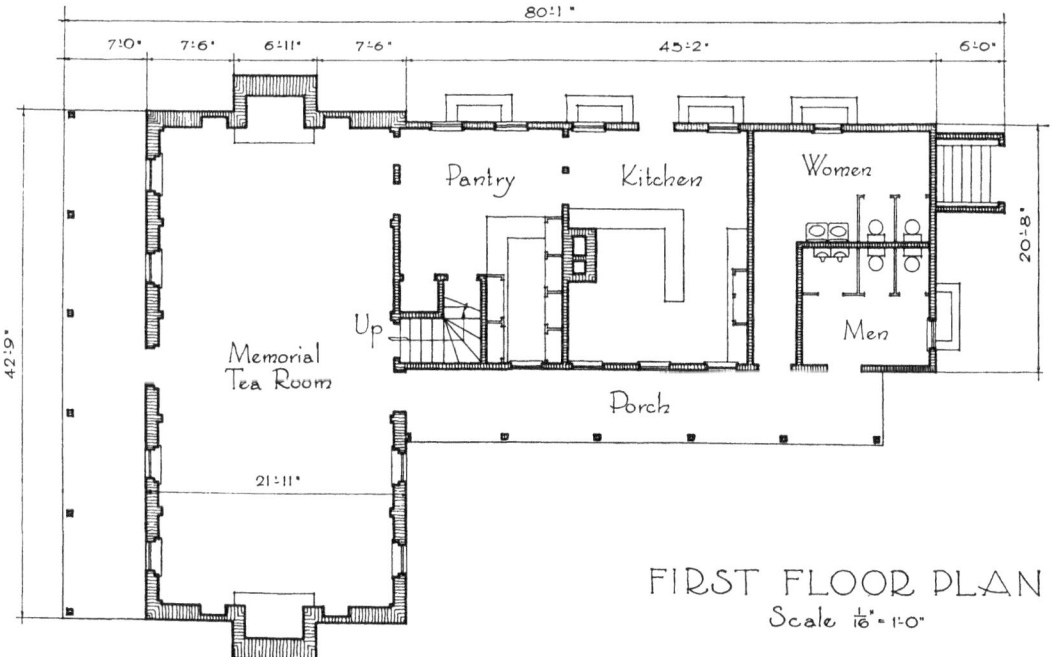

Refectory, "Duck Hall House", George Washington Birthplace National Monument

Designed to harmonize with the architecture of rebuilt Wakefield, this tearoom well exemplifies the stylized and more finished structures that have place in parks. The inspiration of Yorktown and Williamsburg and intelligent adaptation are evident. Edward W. Donn, Jr., architect.

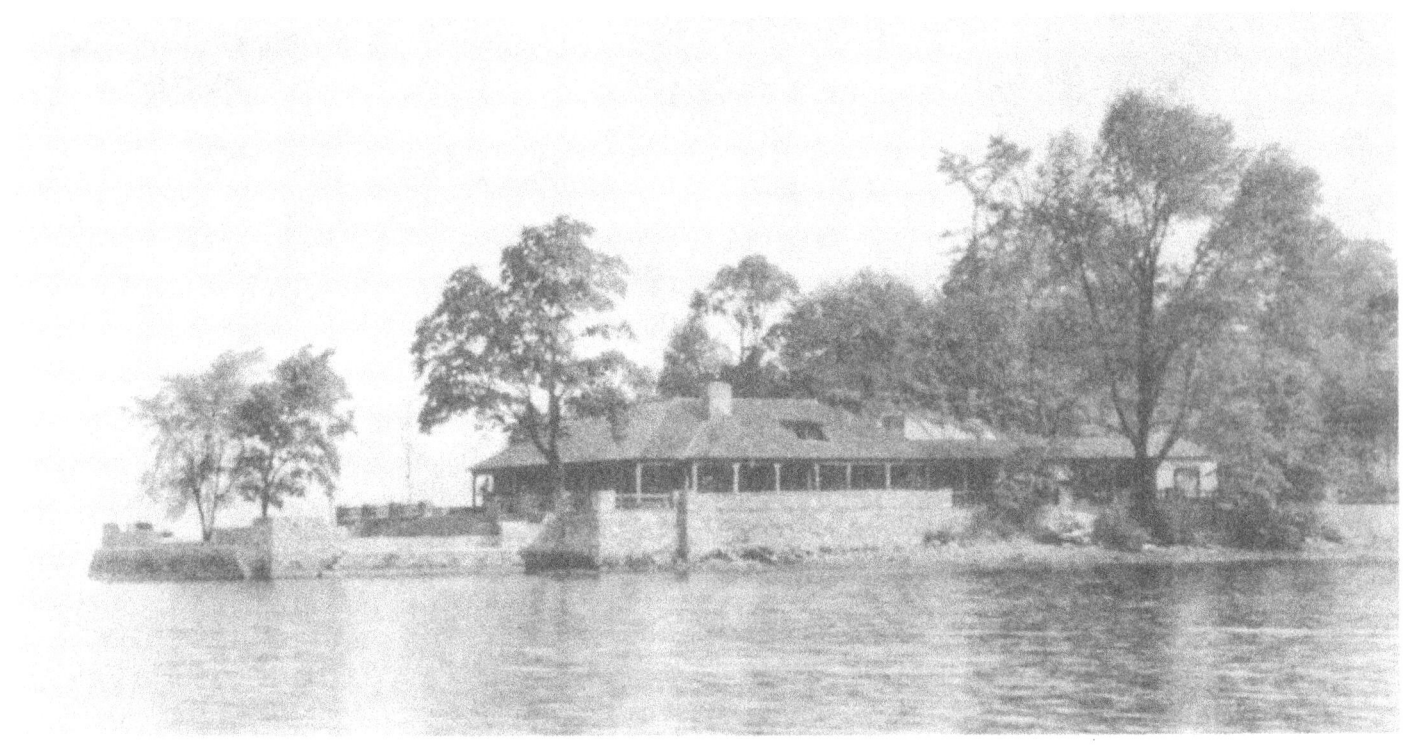

Refectory, Margaret Lewis Norrie State Park, New York

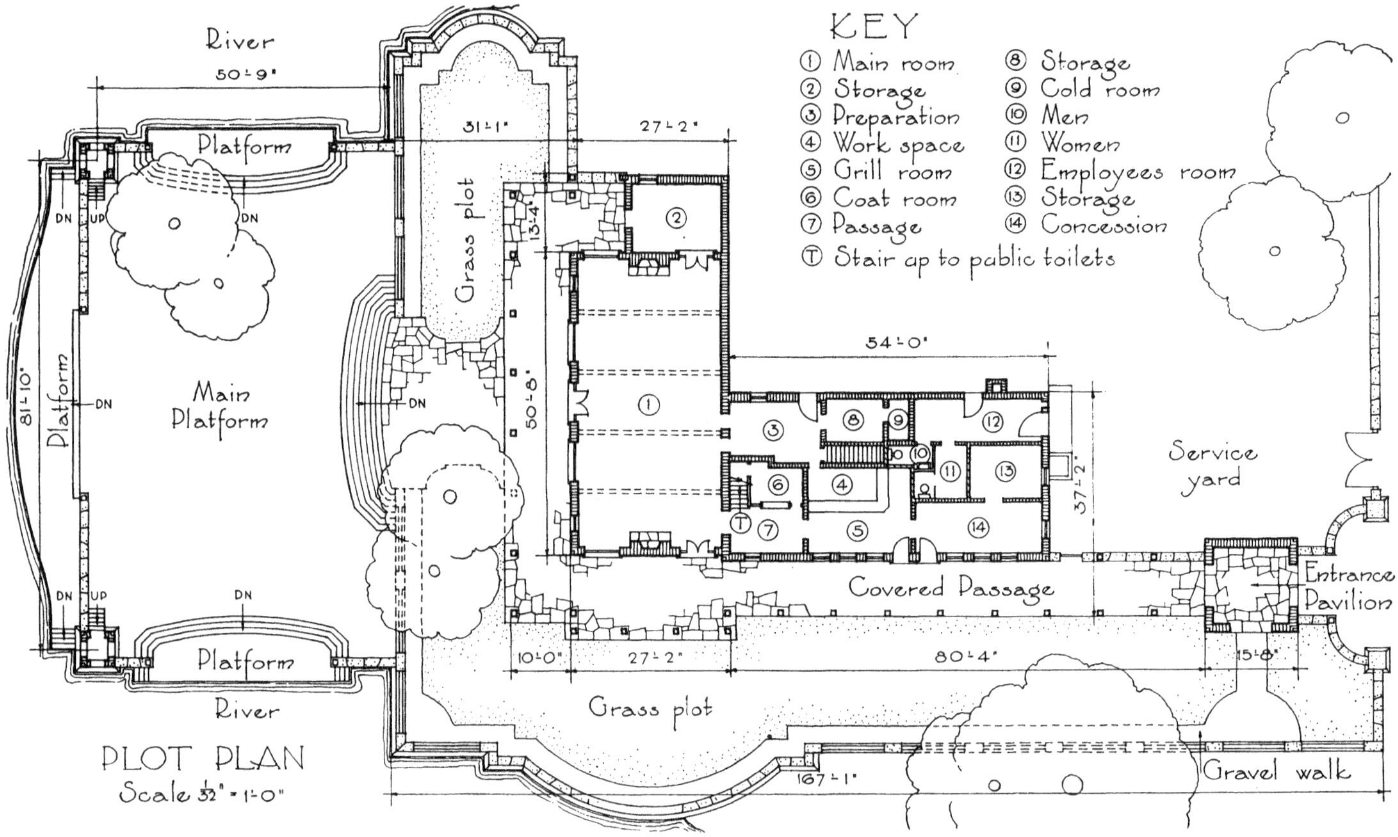
KEY
① Main room
② Storage
③ Preparation
④ Work space
⑤ Grill room
⑥ Coat room
⑦ Passage
⑧ Storage
⑨ Cold room
⑩ Men
⑪ Women
⑫ Employees room
⑬ Storage
⑭ Concession
Ⓣ Stair up to public toilets
River
50'-9"
Platform
Main Platform
Platform
River
81'-10"
31'-1"
27'-2"
Grass plot
13'-4"
50'-8"
54'-0"
37'-2"
Service yard
Covered Passage
Entrance Pavilion
10'-0"
27'-2"
80'-4"
15'-8"
Grass plot
167'-1"
Gravel walk
DN
UP
PLOT PLAN
Scale 1/32" = 1'-0"

This attractive combination building is on the east bank of the lordly Hudson, in a park surrounded by a populous and extensively developed countryside fringing a metropolitan area. Locale thus explains and justifies a more finished character in structure than is general in parks termed natural. The broad water-front terrace actually provides for landing from small river craft.

Plate II E-6   ⇛ CONCESSIONS AND REFECTORIES

Refectory, Santo Domingo State Park, Georgia

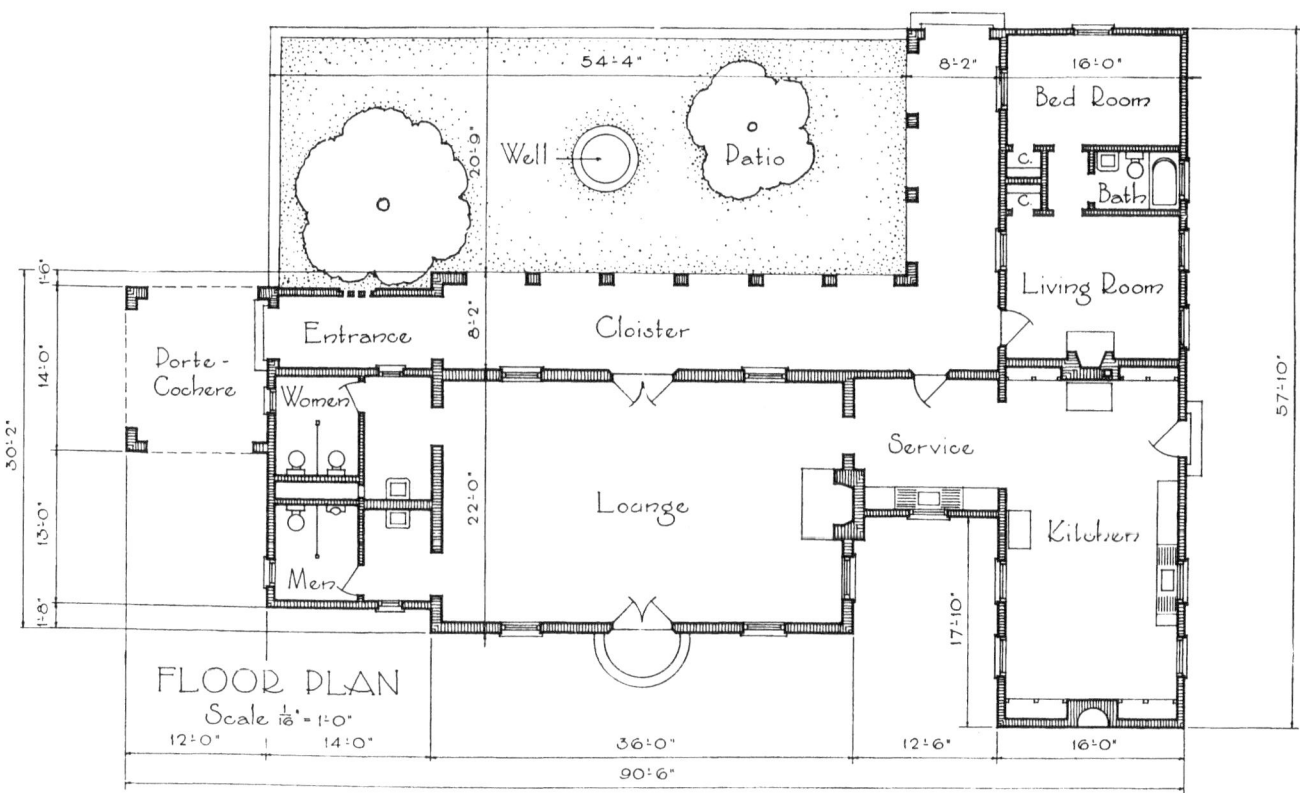

Here is another combination building the architecture of which ranges beyond the usual in natural parks. It gestures toward an interesting and ancient ruin within the park boundaries, and is, of course, keyed to the architectural style become current along the south Atlantic seaboard.

79

CONCESSIONS AND REFECTORIES ≪≪ Plate II E–7

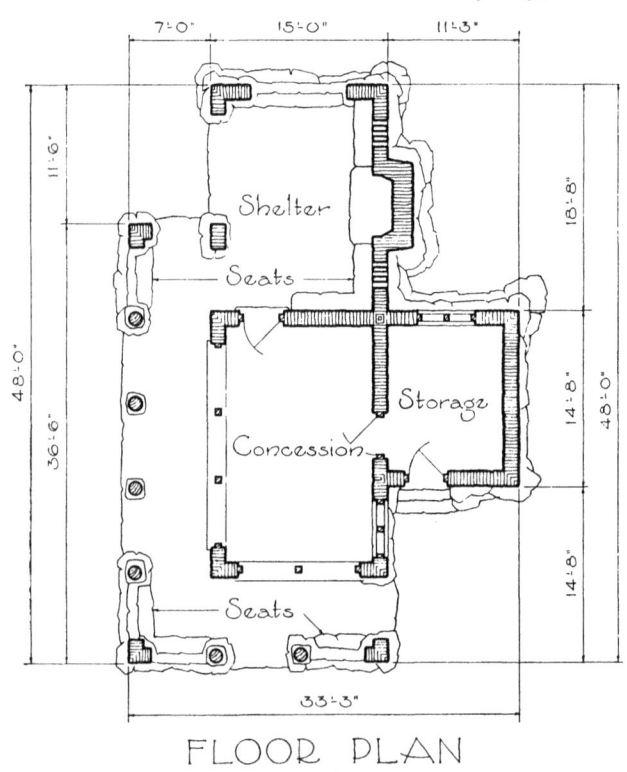

Refectory, Lake Murray State Park, Oklahoma

A concession and shelter combination out of the ordinary in its rambling plan and very practical in the generous storage space it provides. It will be recognized as a formidable contender for the record for size of rocks maneuvered into structure, and not exactly an "also ran" in the matter of freehand quality. The building serves not only picnicking crowds but also the occupants of a group of cabins started nearby. The shelter end overlooks Lake Murray, a large man-made lake.

Plate II E-8   ⇾ CONCESSIONS AND REFECTORIES

Refectory, Mohawk Metropolitan Park, Tulsa, Oklahoma

The combining of concession and concessionaire's quarters with picnic shelter and comfort stations is not unanimously favored. A tendency to inhibit free use of the public facilities by visitors who are not patrons of the concession is argued. But shelters and comfort stations within range of the watchful eye of a concessionaire suffer less from the abuses of the initial carvers and others than do more isolated facilities, because the concessionaire's own best interest leads him to consider the shelter space and toilet facilities as within his sphere of influence to their considerable benefit in clean-up and condition. In this lay-out an altogether reasonable measure of isolation without loss of the benefits of supervision seems to have been accorded the concession, shelter, and comfort stations.

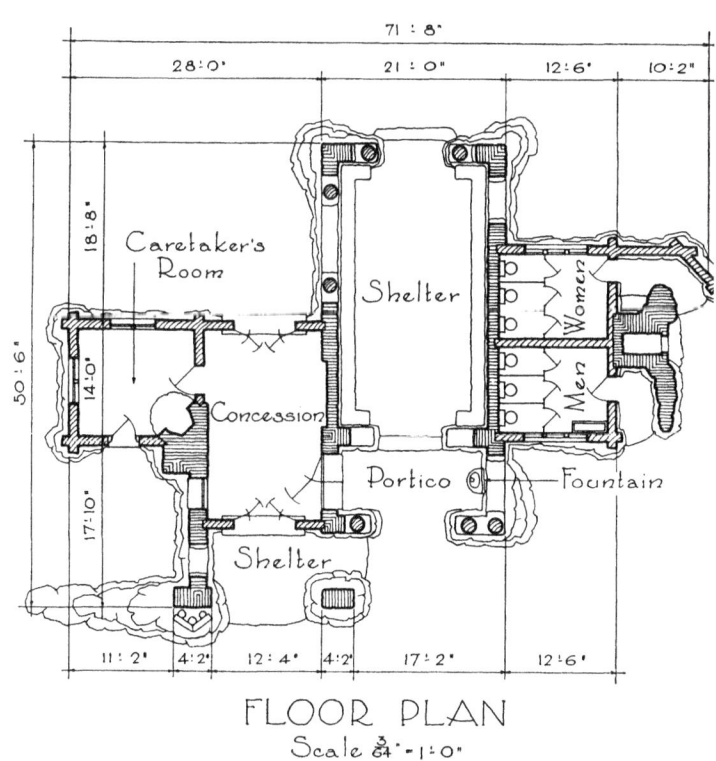

FLOOR PLAN
Scale 3/64" = 1'-0"

81

CONCESSIONS AND REFECTORIES

Plate II E-9

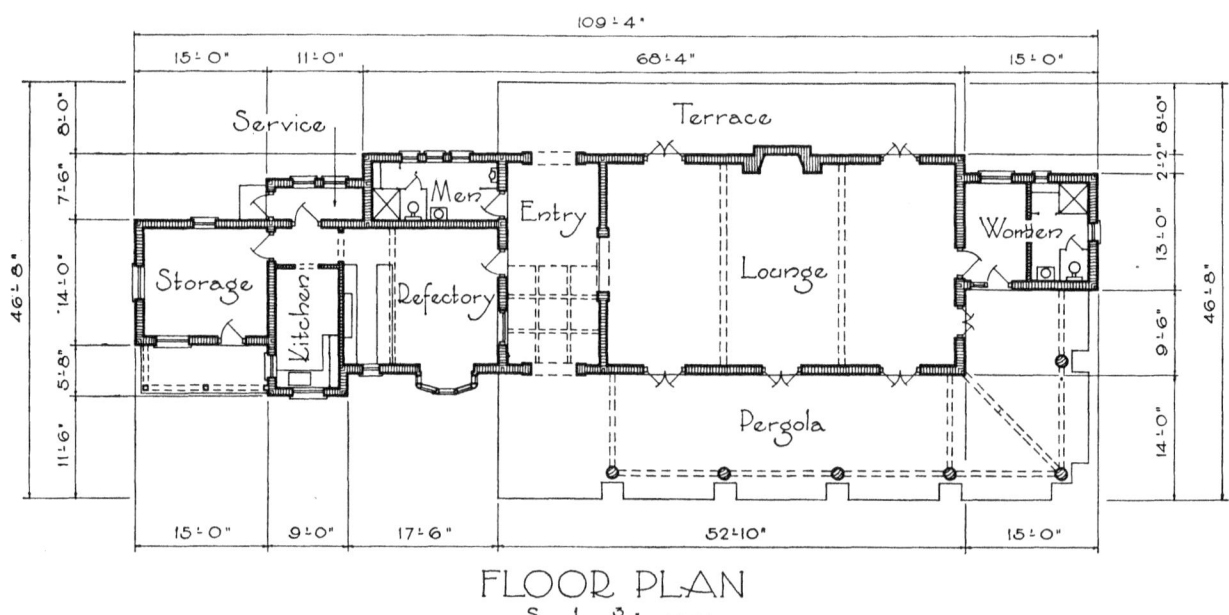

Refectory, Goose Island State Park, Texas

FLOOR PLAN
Scale ¾" = 1'-0"

Where the refreshment concession occupies a space so comparatively small, the refectory building is perhaps more properly classifiable as a recreation or community building. At any rate, here is a most satisfying structure, with strong regional flavor in its use of adobe and in its architectural lines.

82

Plate II E–10   ⇛ CONCESSIONS AND REFECTORIES

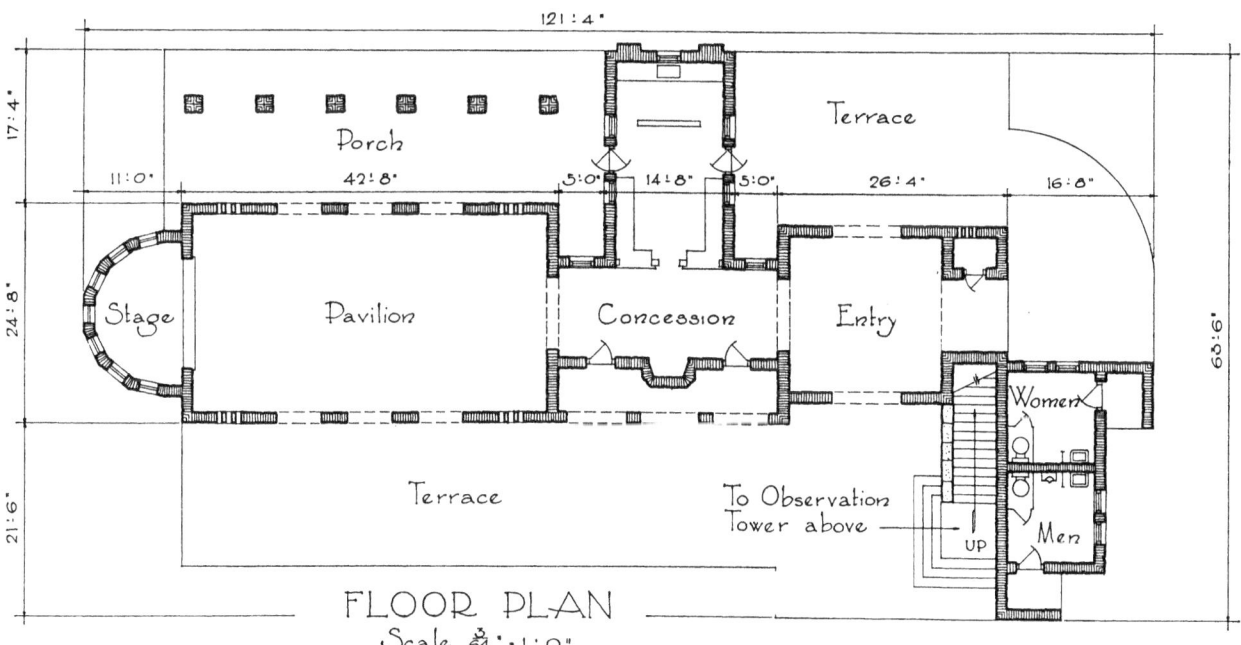

Refectory, Lake Corpus Christi State Park, Texas

Top jewel in the crown of Texas' park structures is the large refectory. In no other part of the country has this multi-purpose facility been so elaborately, variously, and cleverly developed. Usual pattern is shelter space, refreshment concession, and toilet facilities, to which, in this instance, are added small stage and roof deck overlook reached by an exterior stairway. It is of interest to know that no suitable native stone was available here and that a manufactured block is the material employed.

CONCESSIONS AND REFECTORIES ««   *Plate* II E–11

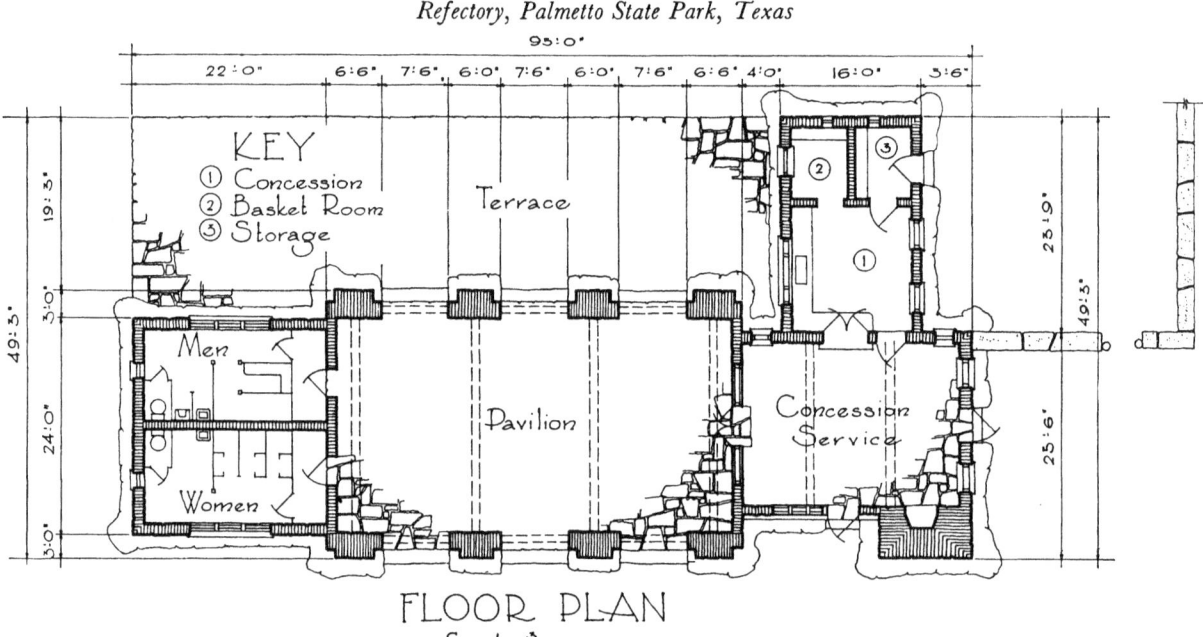

Refectory, Palmetto State Park, Texas

FLOOR PLAN

Although the eye is first attracted by the novel palmetto-thatched roof, it lingers on to observe intently and to admire the masonry with outcrop base, the adzed timbers, and the vigorous treatment generally. No uninspired rehash of a forerunning park building this, but probably commemorative of some circuitous route between the Congo and the Emerald Isle that must once have passed through Texas.

Plate II E–12 ⇶ CONCESSIONS AND REFECTORIES

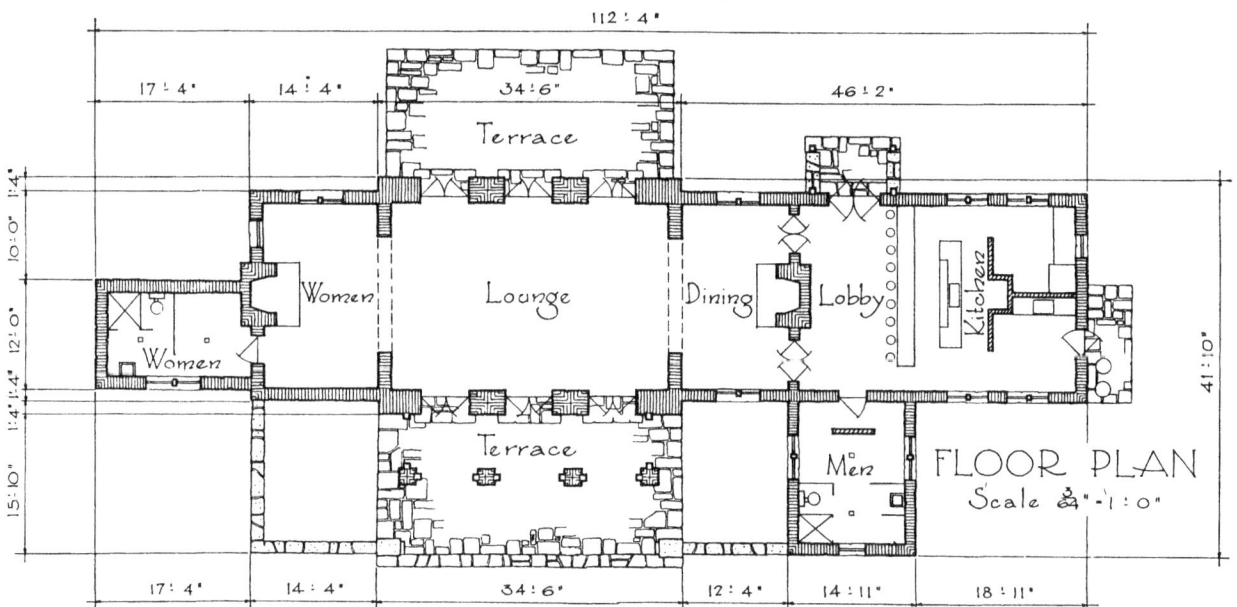

Refectory, Bastrop State Park, Texas

This building combining lunchroom, dining room, lounge space, and toilet facilities is on the sophisticated side in its architectural expression. It is restful in its excellent proportions, long, low lines, and uncomplicated roof surfaces. The arrangement of dining space and women's lounge as alcoves of the main lounge makes possible virtually one large room when occasion demands.

CONCESSIONS AND REFECTORIES ⋘   *Plate* II E–13

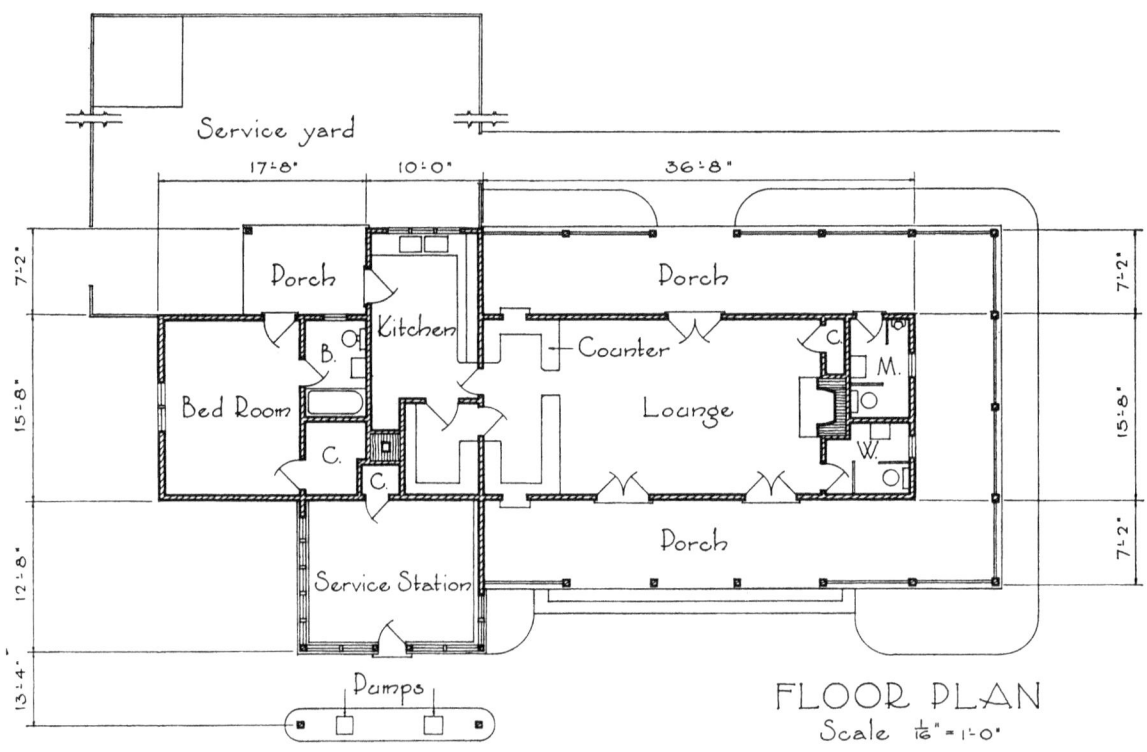

Concession, Chinquapin, Yosemite National Park

In parks of vast size and along extended parkways, concessions to dispense gasoline are necessary. This one dispenses fuel for both man and motor and provides quarters for an attendant in a housing that admirably recaptures the simple character of early California architecture.

86

TRAILSIDE SEATS, SHELTERS, AND OVERLOOKS

SEATS ALONG TRAILS affording hikers a place to rest after a particularly difficult climb or to contemplate a fine view or an object of interest are very properly of much more informal character than the seating provided where use is more concentrated, such as in the picnic or beach area. A trail seat, being often the solitary manmade object within view, makes an extraordinary demand on the park planner for sympathetic treatment in design and execution. The appearance of belonging in its setting is the rightful claim of the trail seat, and to accomplish this is the difficult problem of the designer. If it is to be effectively naturalized, it must appear casual and unforced, free of the appearance of being too cunningly and elaborately devised. There must be no implication of Nature turned upside down, or inside out, into a very parody of itself, in order that the world and his wife may have quaint, if uncomfortable, seats on the aisle. If the term "naturalistic" implies imitation of Nature, then to contrive in the manner of Nature things which Nature itself did not attempt—and trail seats are examples of this—is not only a difficult but a far-fetched undertaking. Completely satisfying naturalistic seats may seem few and far between. Since they are outside the realm of formula, the measure of their success or failure must remain a matter of personal opinion altogether.

Natural objects or formations may be utilized, within the limits of reason, as resting places along the trail. Ledges of stone, boulders, or down logs, with slight adaptations, provide trailside seating without the introduction of foreign elements. Two stumps, or well-buried rocks or boulders, in suitable proximity, provide supports for split logs as a resting place. A huge fallen log is notched to provide seat and back. An ingenious collaboration with Nature almost invariably provokes more genuine acclaim than the more pretentious object of which man can claim sole authorship.

It is possible to incorporate directional signs with trailside seats to picturesque results. Examples at Deception Pass evidence this. A fork in a trail or a crossing of two trails is reason for both seat and sign. The close coupling of two facilities not unsuitably related is always to be recommended over two separate facilities, especially if these are minor items like seat and sign.

In some localities, due perhaps largely to climatic conditions, there is a tendency to expand the simple trailside seat, by the addition of a roof, into something closely approaching a minor shelter. For such elaborations of the trailside seat it is surely reasonable to recommend a quality in both design and execution consistent with the pretentiousness of the object. If this recommendation of a higher quality in pretentious trailside seats results in fewer of them, it is still a sound recommendation.

A TRAILSIDE SHELTER is normally of lesser size than the picnic shelter of the concentrated use area. Its purpose is to offer rest and shelter to those hiking or strolling a trail. Its location, like that of the trailside seat, may be determined by a desire to provide quiet seclusion in an especially beautiful spot or rest along a difficult stretch of trail. It may combine a place to rest with a fine view, which latter feature makes the trailside shelter close kin to the minor overlook and differentiation between them not always possible.

The trail shelter of long tradition is widely known as the Adirondack shelter and was probably first developed by the early hunters and trappers of that region. Originally it was built with three walls of logs and one side open to the weather. It could be heated by a campfire built in front of the open side. For the greatest benefit from the campfire and the utmost in protection from the weather, the true Adirondack shelter was very low in height, barely affording headroom at the open front. The roof overhung this open side somewhat and sloped toward the rear. The scant headroom that resulted was not inconvenient in the original use of this type of shelter—sleeping on evergreen boughs laid on the ground. In adapting the type to present day uses in parks, of which overnight shelter is but one, the roof is generally raised to give greater headroom throughout. The changed proportions often result in a loss of the snug compactness characteristic of the pioneer's Adirondack shelter. If the structure is located so as to "burrow" into a hillside, the illusion of a low building is in a measure maintained, but such a site will necessitate a change from log to stone construction, and this is quite as marked a departure from the typical as is the altered roof line.

As other regions have claimed the Adirondack shelter for their own and adapted it to other materials and climates, and individual needs and tastes, it has undergone great change. Some of the experiments are interesting and successful, some are not. Adaptation, no less than invention, calls for skill. The transplanted Adirondack shelter of logs and of stone is shown in variety in the illustrations that follow.

STRUCTURES FOR PUBLIC OBSERVATION eventuate largely from determination on the part of the hyper-view-conscious for something bigger and better and more distant in views than Nature unaided could provide. Although often erected solely for the use of the public, they occasionally undertake to do double duty by serving also as fire detection towers. Tower structures in which fire detection is the sole or dominant purpose are discussed under the classification "Fire Lookout Structures." The present discussion is concerned with overlooks for public observation in connection with which fire detection is not a part or is merely casual.

Between the grimly functional fire lookout and the utmost in aesthetic structural elevation contrived by the view-for-view's-sakers is greater distance than any park vista will ever provide. When it has been essayed to superimpose the too conscious aspirations of the aesthetic on the structurally sufficient skeleton of the fire detection tower, the literally "crowning" error in park development has been committed. Probably a frank rendering of either extreme, free of gesture toward the other, is better than any hybrid produced by crossing the two irreconcilables.

Examination of existing timber-framed trestle-type observation towers for aesthetic values will prove disheartening. In general, the oil derrick as their inspirational source is painfully undisguised. This conclusion cannot be held in disparagement of the designers if it be honestly admitted that they have valiantly sought to solve the unsolvable. There is such admirable show of there-is-no-such-word-as-can't in every new attempt! It seems heartless to venture a restraining word, but the accumulation in our parks of harrowing skeletons commemorative of past ill-advised best intentions in this direction admits no choice of action.

There are other than purely aesthetic reasons for discouraging the building of high wooden structures. It is very difficult, if not impossible, to fabricate a timber-braced structure with bolted or spiked joints that will hold up under the attack of the elements for any considerable length of time without constant maintenance. Immediately after construction the wood members shrink, and the joints loosen. Decay will proceed rapidly at the joints where water seeps in between the members and finally into the bolt and spike holes. The structure is weakened at its most vulnerable point. With the slightest loosening of the joints the tremendous wind pressures cause movements which increase the stresses in the entire structure. The safety of the public using the towers cannot be assured, since it depends entirely on inspections and maintenance that naturally cannot be assumed and guaranteed into the future.

Because the wood-framed lookout tower is so utterly unappealing, and so potentially a hazard, it is strange that but few stone observation structures have been built. These are not foredoomed to failure, aesthetic and structural, as is the open wooden tower, but on the contrary offer opportunity for picturesqueness, satisfying design, greater permanence, and less maintenance. Particularly does it appear that the possibilities for a stone tower of modest height springing from a rock-crowned summit have not been widely sensed, certainly not widely embraced.

A required elevated water supply tank will often furnish both excuse and means for an observation feature. The utilitarian water tower becomes a less disquieting element in the landscape, when its structural support is masked by an enclosing stone wall surmounted by a lookout platform.

It is held by many that the birth rate for tower-like observation structures in parks is currently too high, and that some measure of control should be instituted. A wise choice of location, duly considered for elevation, vistas, forest cover, and obstructions to view, will sometimes permit a less blatant facility for observation, without aspirations to become a tower of Babel, yet without loss of desired objectives. Wherever in parks of little-modified natural character structural provision for the enjoyment of a view can be limited to something less than a skyline tower of great height, a sane concept of wilderness values is better served.

THE MODEST OVERLOOK STRUCTURE has been designed in many pleasing forms, examples of which are shown in variety by the photographs and drawings that follow. It will be found that the most admired have an ingratiating lack of pretentiousness. It must be admitted that some of these might as logically have been classified as shelters. Perhaps the reader will withhold censure of this straining in classification and wink at the subterfuge as pardonable in the circumstances. The "batting average" of observation structures in general with the overburden of high towers stands very much in need of the beneficial rating that modest overlooks suggestive of simple shelters can contribute.

There is widespread urge to adapt the picturesque blockhouse of the pioneer to useful purpose in parks. This early, usually square building, with second story overhanging for purposes of defense, marched with the frontier from the Atlantic seaboard across the continent to the Pacific slope. There are said to be remains of these outposts of empire in the Puget Sound country. Thus it is a traditional structure over a large part of the United States, and the disposition to recall its interesting silhouette and construction in natural preserves is understandable. When the adaptation is intelligently done, with real feeling for the materials and methods of the original, the reconstruction seems almost to point backward to a once virgin continent and somehow to symbolize and give promise of such regeneration of natural resources as it is hoped park planning can in time effect.

Although the blockhouse form has been the inspiration for administration and other buildings, it is especially adaptable as a vantage point for observation or overlook use, and to such purpose has been re-created in a number of park areas in recent years. Sometimes the lower story is built of stone, but the use of logs throughout, either round or squared, is more typical of the original structures. Some of the adaptations, even those rather freely made, are very appealing. Unfortunately, the defensive purpose of the early blockhouse necessitated very small openings, whereas something much more open is usually felt to be essential in an overlook. Hence, the problem of the designer is to achieve such a balance between tradition and new function that we are not immediately and violently conscious of compromise.

In a sense the emergence of a trail or road at any point well above the surrounding country or at an open prospect point is essentially an overlook. It may be developed only to the extent of widening the trail or roadway, clearing a "window" in the foliage, or constructing a guard rail. In its more elaborate phases it may call for extensive retaining walls, parking area, seats, roofed shelter, sometimes with fireplace. Where the view is distant and spectacular, and supervision permits, fixed telescopic equipment is installed. The observation station on the south rim of the Grand Canyon and the Sinnott Memorial overlooking Crater Lake are so equipped.

There are some who will claim that it is sometimes better to remove the trees that crown a high summit and are the very obstructions to view that make necessary the building of an observation structure of height. The bald crown of the eminence is held to be a lesser, certainly no greater, blemish than the construction rearing itself above trees. There are undoubtedly locations where this solution would be an acceptable alternative to a tower. But it can hardly be urged for universal application. Rather should it be given thoughtful consideration as a possibility, to be weighed in the light of characteristics of hill or mountain top contours, prevalence of forest cover, and interest value of the view.

TRAILSIDE SEATS, SHELTERS, AND OVERLOOKS

Plate II F–1

Giant City State Park, Illinois

Mount Penn Metropolitan Reservation, Reading, Pennsylvania

Camden State Park, Minnesota

TRAILSIDE SEATS IN FIXED LOCATION

Ranging from half log or plank on stone or post supports through benches with several varieties of back, here is run the gamut of simple trail seating. Benches elaborate and sophisticated beyond the limitations of the examples here grouped have less measure of justification in natural parks. The types shown are capable of infinite variation giving scope for wide differences in detail without viola-

Crowley's Ridge State Park, Arkansas

Lake Worth Metropolitan Park, Texas

Plate II F–2   →›› TRAILSIDE SEATS, SHELTERS, AND OVERLOOKS

Saratoga Hot Springs State Park, Wyoming

Lacey-Keosauqua State Park, Iowa

I & M Canal State Park, Marseilles, Illinois

tion of reasonable simplicity. Most of them are rather on the side of park character than the utmost in comfort, which is as it should be. Robustness of scale is almost general. The jaunty Lacey-Keosauqua bench proves that the lines of the gnarled cull are much more in the spirit of a natural setting than the rigid lines of more merchantable timber. It will be observed that a happy choice of location for the trail seat plays no small part in the effect that is created.

Sibley State Park, Minnesota

Mount Penn Metropolitan Reservation, Reading, Pennsylvania

91

TRAILSIDE SEATS, SHELTERS, AND OVERLOOKS

Plate II F–3

Springbrook State Park, Iowa

Dolliver Memorial State Park, Iowa

Springbrook State Park, Iowa

MOBILE TRAILSIDE SEATS

Here are items equally appropriate along trails and in open picnic or trailside shelters. Considerable individuality has been brought to benches in the development of parks in Iowa. There is a note of naive handcraftedness which must command interest even though it may fail to win unqualified approval. From simple half log on splayed legs to complex fabricated bench with back is an expressive vocabulary of seating furniture. Compare the several degrees of freehand quality exhibited. The same primitiveness will be discovered in the Iowa picnic tables. Both in turn relate well to the Iowa shelters illustrated elsewhere.

Dolliver Memorial State Park, Iowa

Springbrook State Park, Iowa

Plate II F–4 → TRAILSIDE SEATS, SHELTERS, AND OVERLOOKS

Deception Pass State Park, Washington

Dolliver Memorial State Park, Iowa

SIGNS AND ROOFS COME TO TRAIL SEATING

Illustrated above and below are picturesque combinations of benches and signs. The outer column shows sheltered trailside or overlook seats. Only when the central support of the umbrella type is vigorous and well-buttressed at the base is this type of shelter to be considered. It is tolerable only if it holds to the canons of sound construction, and beyond the pale when there is economy in its structural members. Compare the finished masonry technique of the McKinley Woods seat and the pronounced batter and freer handling of the Lake Worth example. One tends to appear top-heavy; the other has informal well-rooted stability.

McKinley Woods, Chennahon, Illinois

Deception Pass State Park, Washington

Lake Worth Metropolitan Park, Fort Worth, Texas

TRAILSIDE SEATS, SHELTERS, AND OVERLOOKS

Plate II F-5

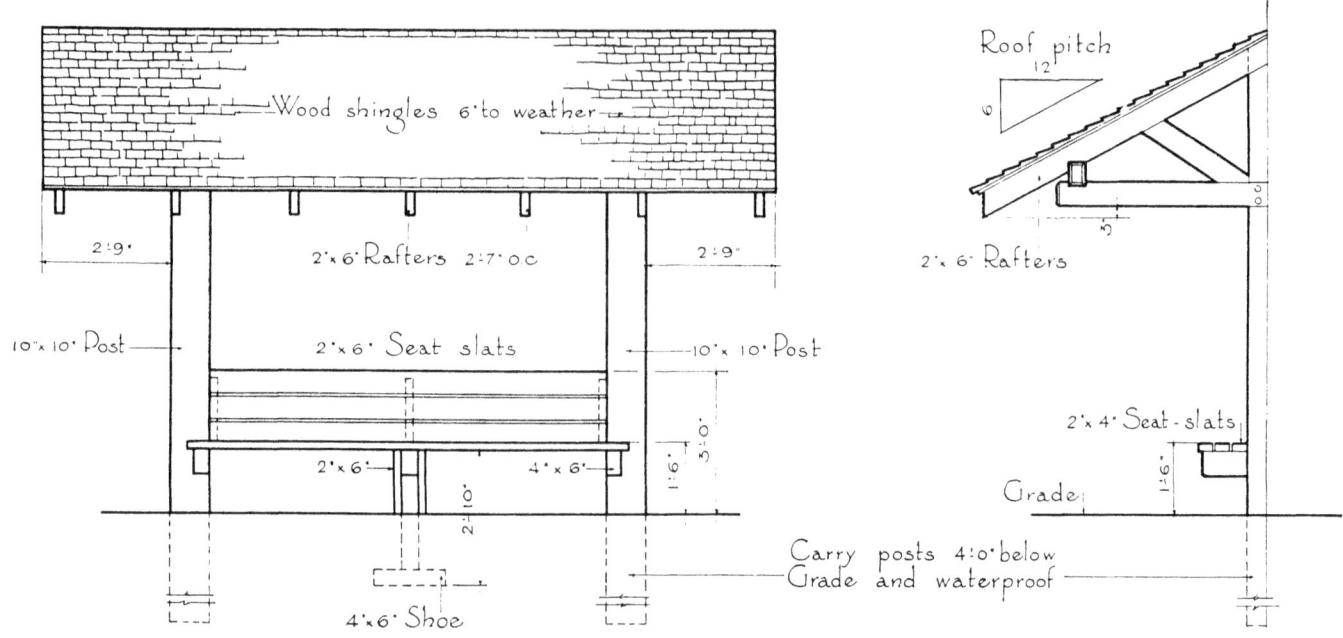

FRONT ELEVATION

HALF SIDE ELEVATION

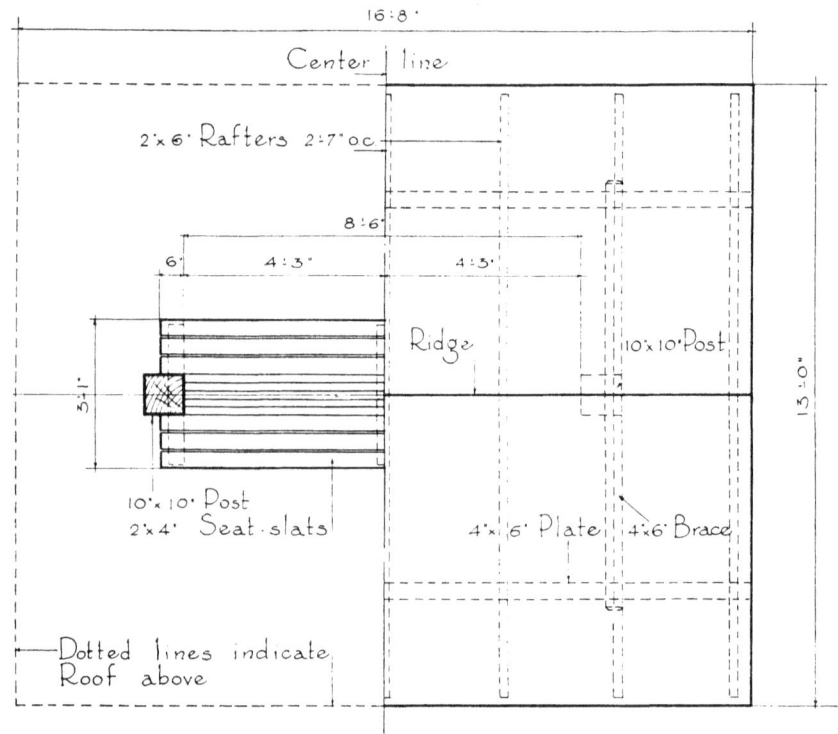

HALF FLOOR & ROOF PLAN
Scale ¼"=1'-0"

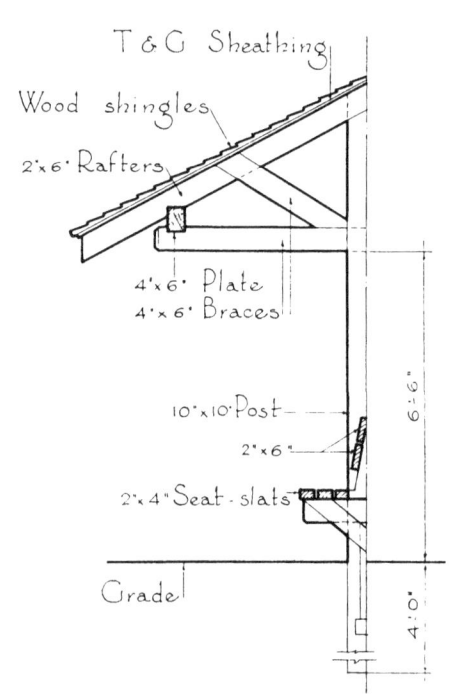

HALF SECTION
Scale ¼"=1'-0"

Plate II F-6   →›› TRAILSIDE SEATS, SHELTERS, AND OVERLOOKS

McKinley Woods, Chennahon, Illinois

Giant City State Park, Illinois

THE ILLINOIS SHELTERED TRAIL SEAT

Above is the basic Illinois seat of sawn commercial lumber detailed on the facing page. The other illustrations are its close kinfolk who have knocked about the State and acquired quite a polish. Reading clockwise we see hand-hewn surfaces applied to the typical, then a portly rendering utilizing timbers in the round, followed by a bench in which arm rests become a prominent feature, and finally, an impressive example which doubles the supporting posts and acquires a center aisle. All in all, a fine old Illinois family of long tradition and notable attainment.

I & M Canal State Park, Marseilles, Illinois

Starved Rock State Park, Illinois

Pere Marquette State Park, Illinois

TRAILSIDE SEATS, SHELTERS, AND OVERLOOKS

Plate II F-7

Adirondack Shelter
Letchworth State Park – – – – New York

In New York State the Adirondack shelter is a tradition, a survival of the primitive shelter of the earliest woodsmen and hunters of this region. The end and rear walls are tightly built of logs, the front is open to the friendly warmth and light of the campfire. The roof slopes gently to the rear and sharply to the open front to give a protective overhang. The following page shows regional variations in the type as it has moved westward; the second following page depicts its translation into stone.

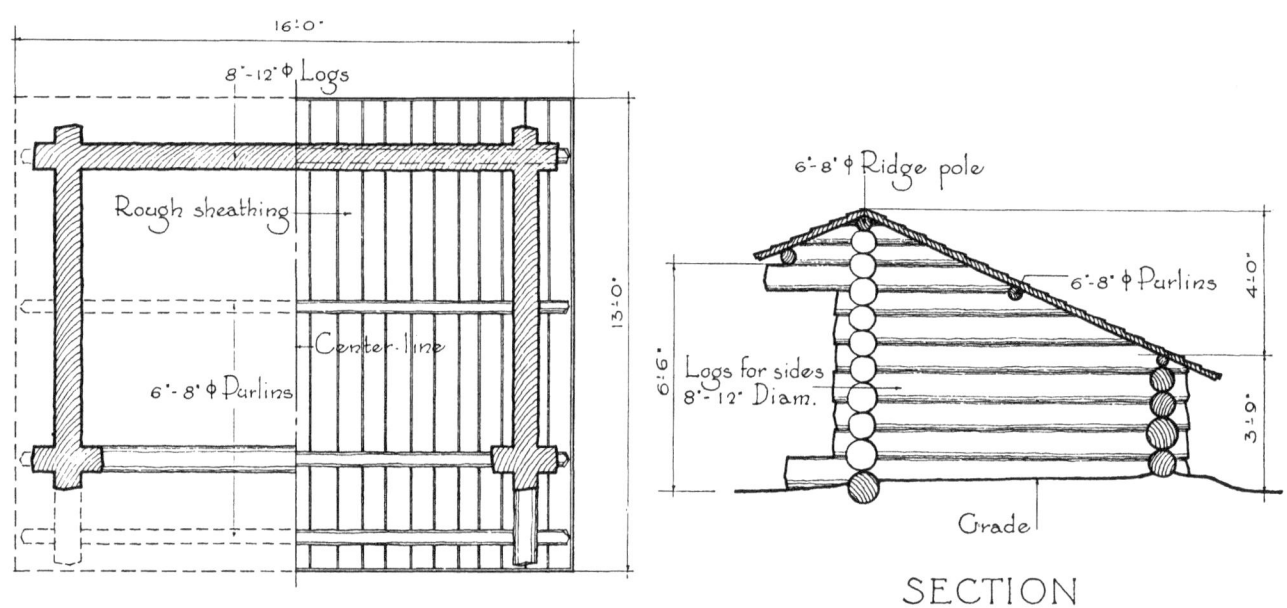

HALF FLOOR- & REFLECTED ROOF PLAN

SECTION

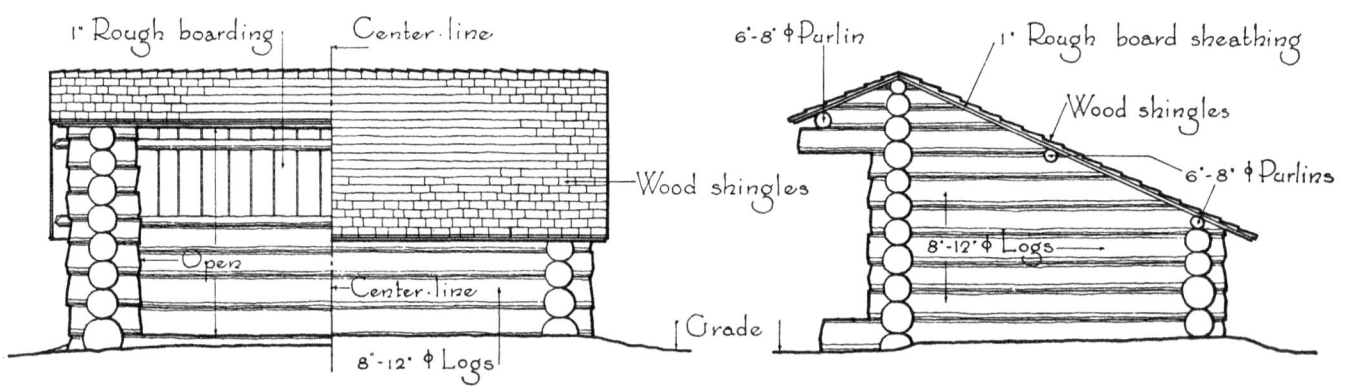

HALF FRONT & REAR ELEVATION

SIDE ELEVATION

Scale 3/16" = 1'0"

96

Plate II F–8   ➢ TRAILSIDE SEATS, SHELTERS, AND OVERLOOKS

Bismarck Metropolitan Park, Bismarck, North Dakota

Scenic State Park, Minnesota

VARIANTS OF THE ADIRONDACK SHELTER

The Adirondack shelter moving westward undergoes changes. Above enter informality of axe-cut log ends and added rakishness of contours. The next example, with forward "log cabin corners" omitted, appears unstable, even though very long spikes doubtless make it structurally safe. Next example indulges in variant details characteristic of location. Below are derivations in the traditional squared log construction of the Indiana pioneer which invoke doubt as to whether they are converted from old cabins, reconstructed from remnants of the old, or are new construction cleverly "antiqued."

Crowley's Ridge State Park, Arkansas

Brown County State Park, Indiana

Clifty Falls State Park, Indiana

TRAILSIDE SEATS, SHELTERS, AND OVERLOOKS

Plate II F-9

Shelter
Clarence Fahnestock Memorial State Park — New York

This simple and pleasing building promises to be a cool retreat during midsummer, and, by virtue of its fireplace and single open side, a well-protected shelter at other seasons. The roof and supporting members have desirable weight, the stonework has informal but structurally satisfying character.

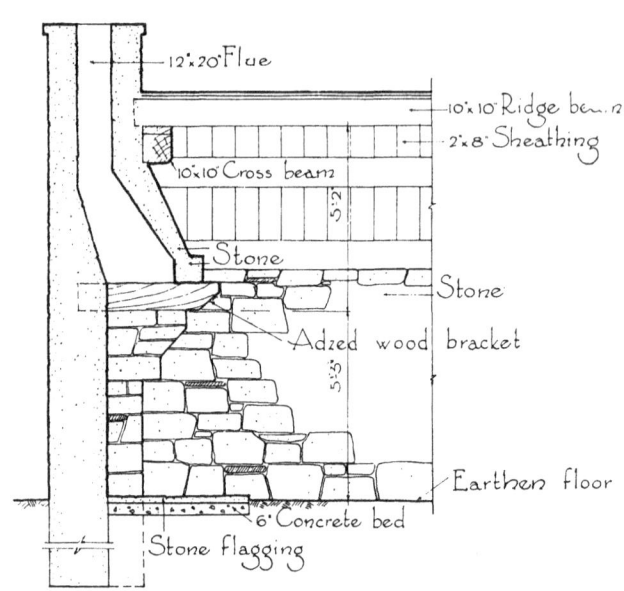

SECTION OF FIREPLACE
Scale 3/8" = 1'-0"

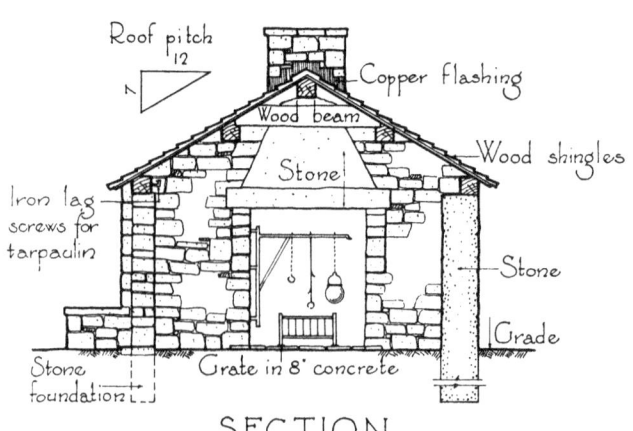

SECTION

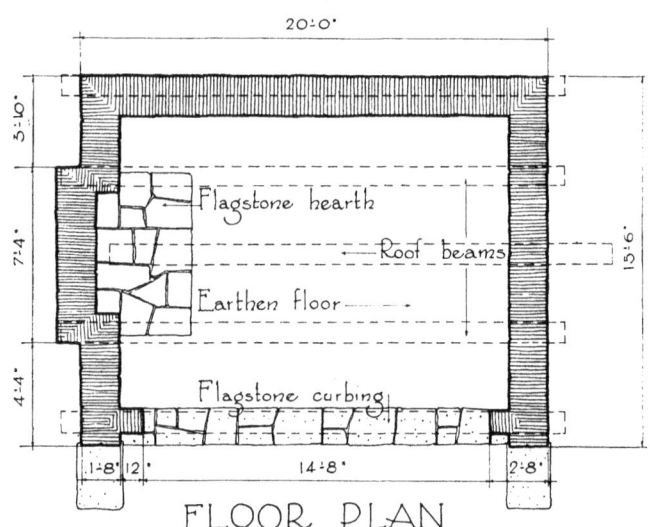

FLOOR PLAN

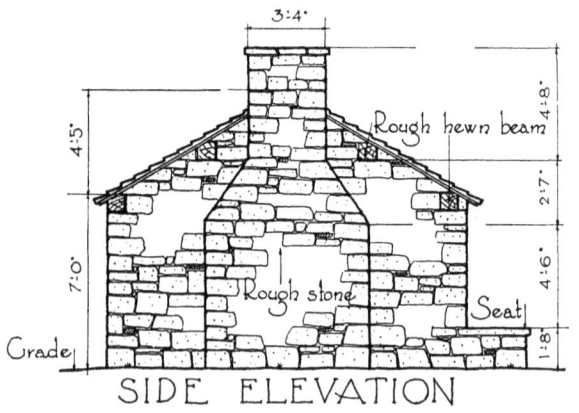

SIDE ELEVATION

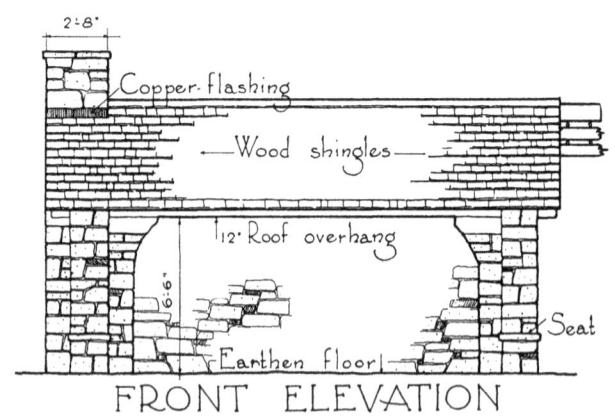

FRONT ELEVATION

Scale 1/8" = 1'-0"

Plate II F-10   →» TRAILSIDE SEATS, SHELTERS, AND OVERLOOKS

High Point State Park, New Jersey

Brown County State Park, Indiana

THE ADIRONDACK SHELTER IN STONE

The trail structure pictured just above interprets so accurately in stone the lines and spirit of the original Adirondack shelter that the inspirational source is never in doubt. Hardly less so, the shelter at upper right. In the example alongside this caption the typical rake of roof lingers, but a certain formality of line and masonry enters the picture. The two shelters below retain a mere trace of the Adirondack prototype, yet are so bountifully supplied with individuality of their own that there can be no regrets for a tradition flouted.

Cook County Forest Preserve District, Illinois

Perry Lake Metropolitan Park, Perry, Oklahoma

Ponca Lake Metropolitan Park, Ponca City, Oklahoma

99

TRAILSIDE SEATS, SHELTERS, AND OVERLOOKS

Plate II F–11

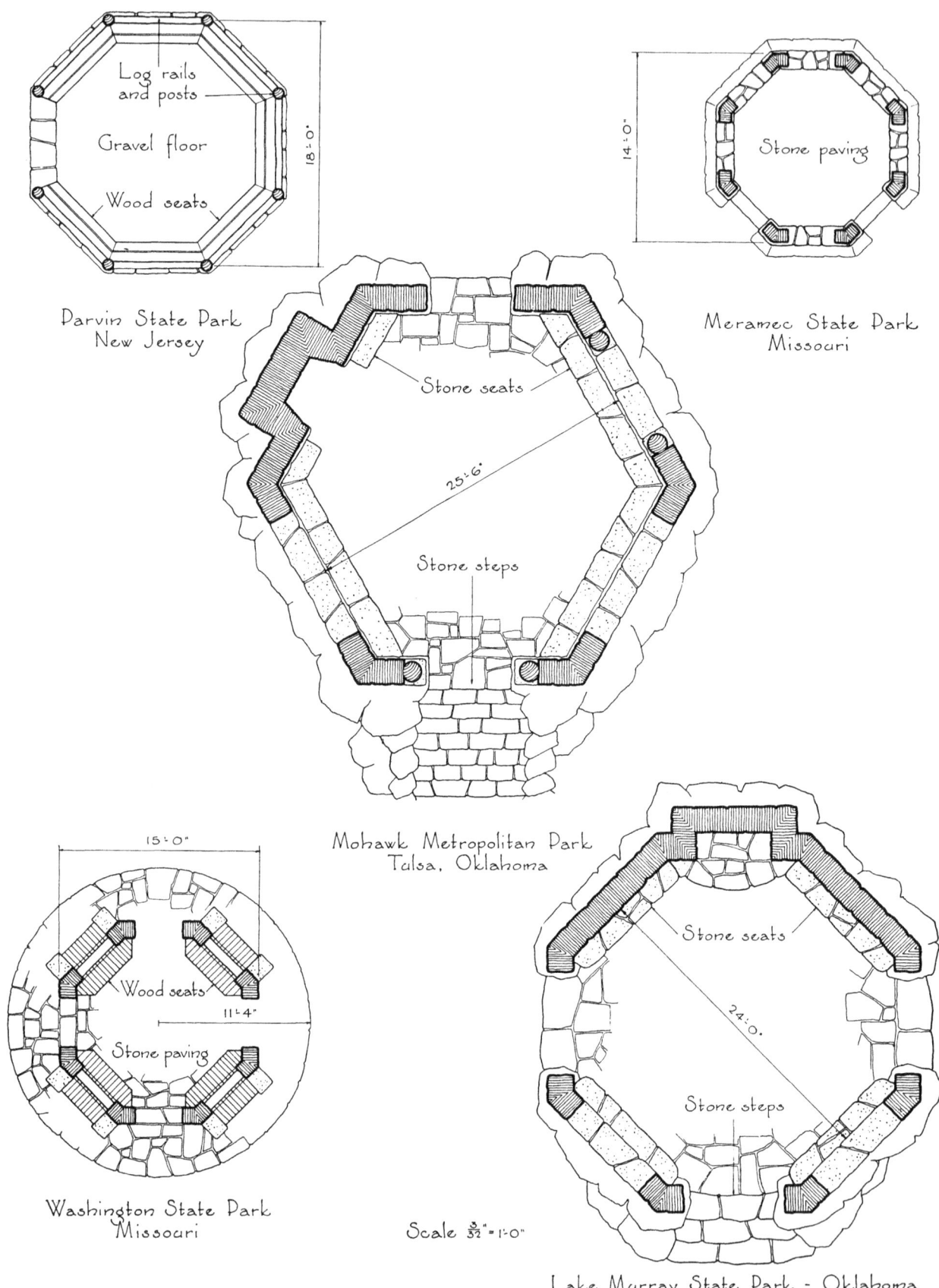

Plate II F–12 →» TRAILSIDE SEATS, SHELTERS, AND OVERLOOKS

Parvin State Park, New Jersey

Meramec State Park, Missouri

OVERLOOK SHELTERS OF POLYGONAL PLAN

Park structures, based on the hexagonal and the octagonal plan, occur rather infrequently, although the forms are particularly well-suited to overlooks having views in several directions. Various stages of sophistication of architectural treatment are here in evidence. There is great excellence in the proportions of the New Jersey log-built example here shown. The two Oklahoma subjects illustrate skillful blending of structure to site and afford opportunity to compare the merits of the two plan forms similarly clothed. Plans are shown on the facing page.

Mohawk Metropolitan Park, Tulsa, Oklahoma

Washington State Park, Missouri

Lake Murray State Park, Oklahoma

TRAILSIDE SEATS, SHELTERS, AND OVERLOOKS

Plate II F-13

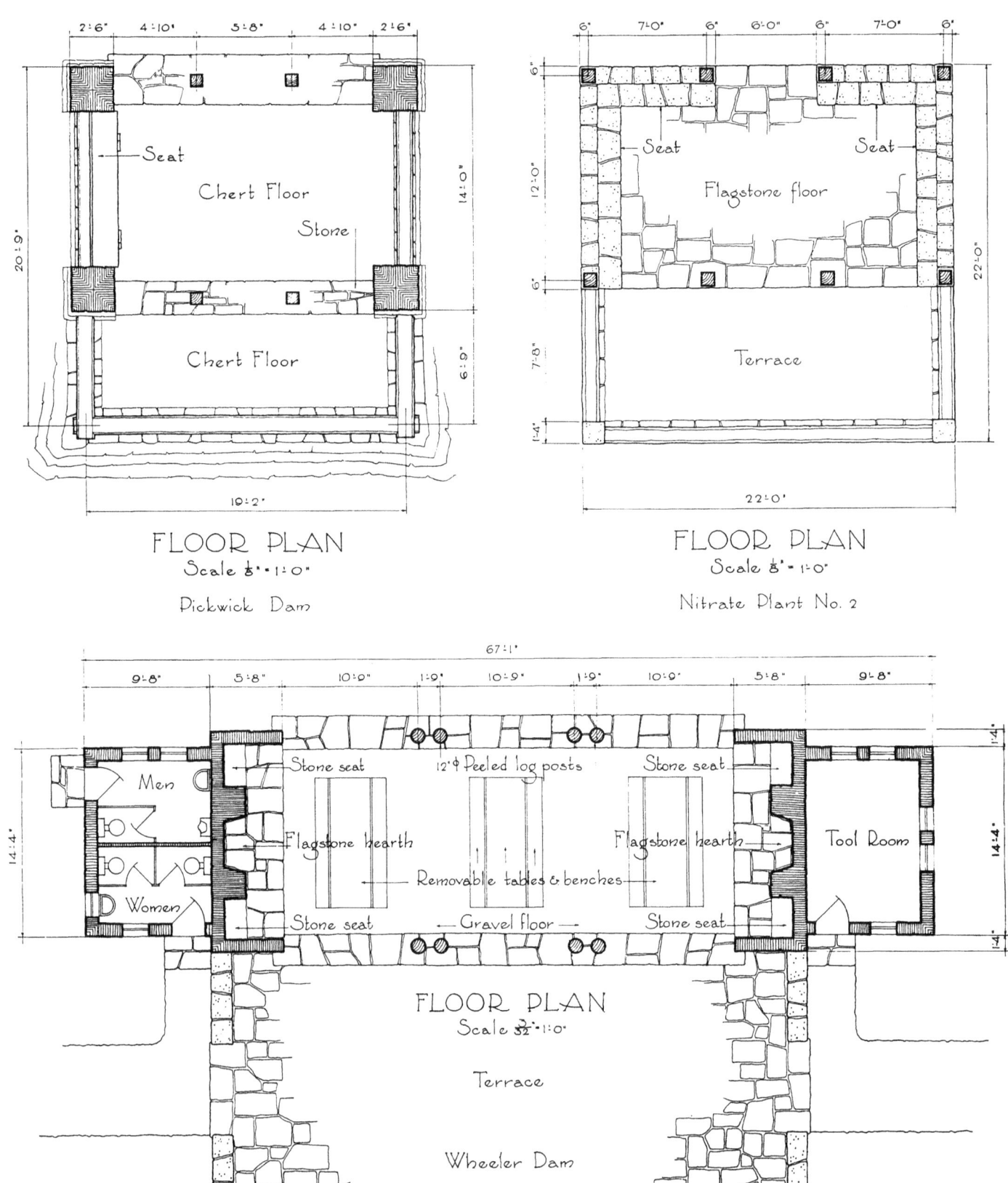

FLOOR PLAN
Scale ⅛" = 1'-0"
Pickwick Dam

FLOOR PLAN
Scale ⅛" = 1'-0"
Nitrate Plant No. 2

FLOOR PLAN
Scale 3/32" = 1'-0"
Wheeler Dam

Plate II F–14　　→→→ TRAILSIDE SEATS, SHELTERS, AND OVERLOOKS

The noticeable batter and moderately rough texture of the stone piers, the sturdiness of squared timbers and railings, and the agreeably "ragged" roof are details that here pyramid the merits of a well-proportioned building. The combination of shelter and overlook terrace is very suitable to this site, which gives a broad view of the Tennessee River. For the attention and confusion of all opponents of the hip roof as somehow unbefitting a park building, this example is pertinently and impertinently offered.

Shelter Overlook, Pickwick Dam, Tennessee Valley Authority

Except for the awkwardly abrupt and seemingly unstudied relationships between the log parapets and the masonry parts, here is a pleasing combination of unroofed overlook and shelter. The square posts are proportioned well to the spans and the roof. If the latter appears too flat in the illustration, this should be chalked up against the camera angle. Undoubtedly it appears to better advantage from the higher side and the level stretch beyond.

Shelter Overlook, Nitrate Plant No. 2, Tennessee Valley Authority

This largest of the shelter-and-terrace-overlook combinations, so typical of the recreational reserves of the Tennessee Valley, adds wings to result in an arrangement that is away from the typical. These house toilet facilities and tool room. The choice of materials and the less free manner of their use somehow sacrifice an indefinable quality, present and very appealing, in the smaller structures shown above. The thinness of the masonry walls is disturbing.

Shelter Overlook, Wheeler Dam, Tennessee Valley Authority

TRAILSIDE SEATS, SHELTERS, AND OVERLOOKS

Plate II F–15

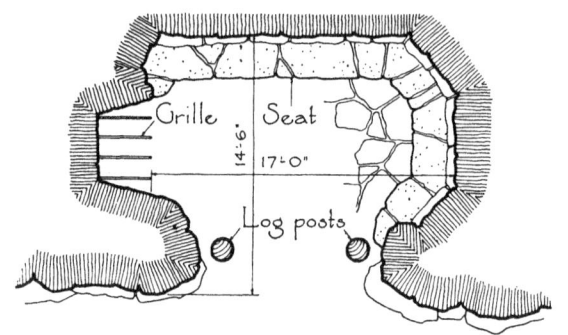

Perry Lake Metropolitan Park — Oklahoma

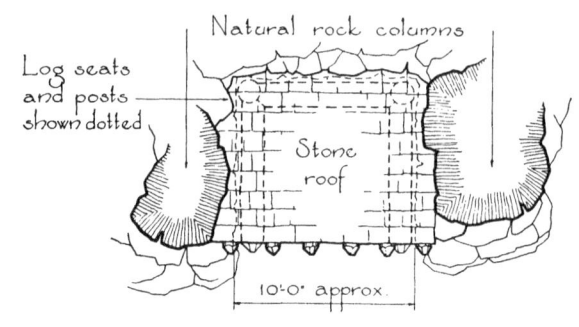

Rib Mountain State Park – Wisconsin

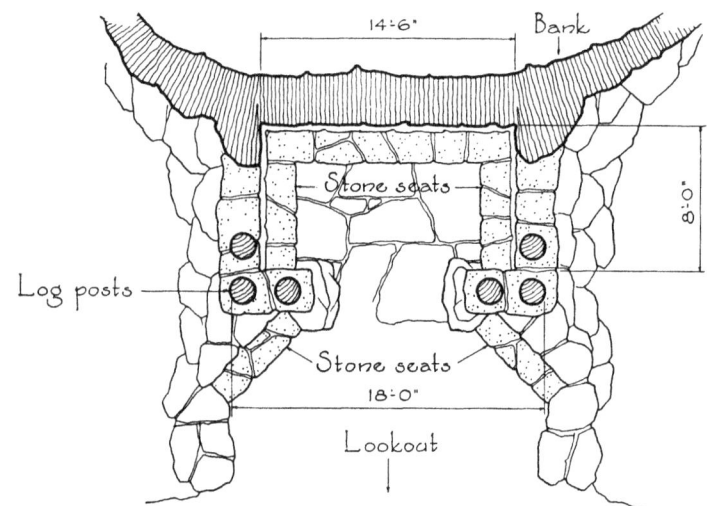

Saratoga Hot Springs State Park – Wyoming

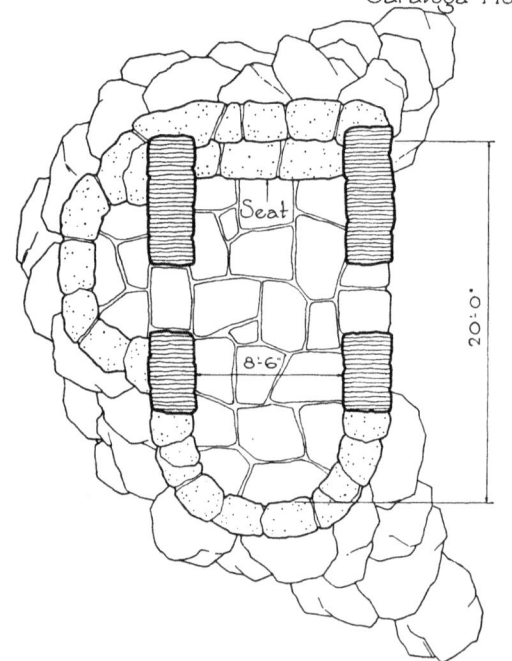

Loveland Mountain Metropolitan Park – Colorado

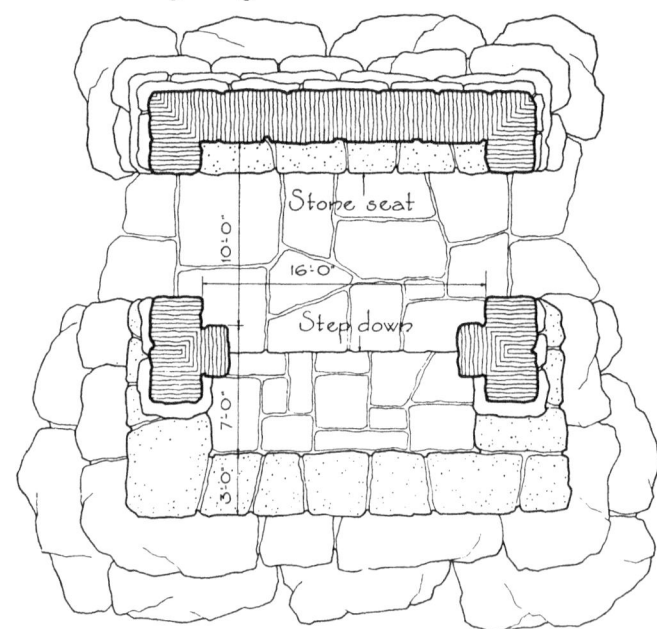

Petit Jean State Park – Arkansas

Scale 3/32" = 1'-0"

Plate II F–16   ⇢⇢⇢ TRAILSIDE SEATS, SHELTERS, AND OVERLOOKS

Perry Lake Metropolitan Park, Oklahoma

Rib Mountain State Park, Wisconsin

TRAILSIDE OVERLOOK SHELTERS

Here are pictures, and on the facing page are plans, of minor shelters erected along foot trails. All occur west of the Mississippi, as their ruggedness of scale tends to disclose. Some make ingenious use of natural site conditions, notably those at Rib Mountain State Park and Perry Lake Metropolitan Park. The latter is a clever "two-decker", having a "sun roof" with protective wall of large rocks naturalistically arranged and cleverly incorporating an open picnic fireplace. The perfection of rugged scale of the Petit Jean overlook delights the eye.

Saratoga Hot Springs State Park, Wyoming

Loveland Mountain Metropolitan Park, Colorado

Petit Jean State Park, Arkansas

105

TRAILSIDE SEATS, SHELTERS, AND OVERLOOKS

Plate II F–17

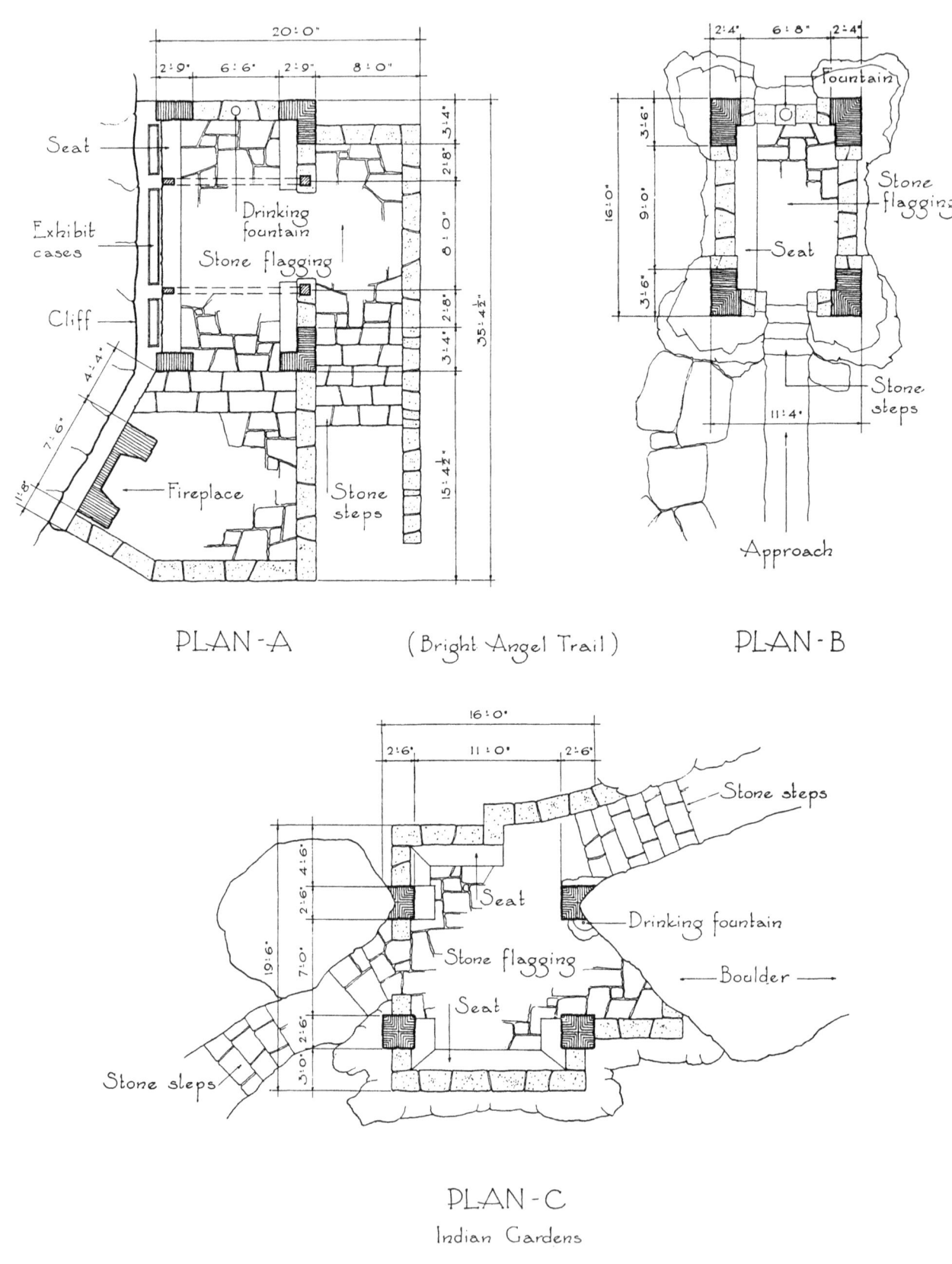

PLAN-A (Bright Angel Trail) PLAN-B

PLAN-C
Indian Gardens
Scale 3/32"=1'-0"

Plate II F–18 →» TRAILSIDE SEATS, SHELTERS, AND OVERLOOKS

Unquestionably useful are shelters along foot and horse trails in the desert country where the going is rough and a shaded place to rest is welcome. Features of this particular shelter (shown in plan at upper left opposite), near the foot of Bright Angel trail are the outdoor chimneyed fireplace and the exhibit cases within the roofed shelter. The exhibits make it something of a trailside nature shrine. The unstructural masonry was probably determined by characteristics of the native rock.

Trail Shelter, Bright Angel Trail, Grand Canyon National Park

This thatch-roofed subject is also along the Bright Angel trail as it winds its way down into the canyon. Its plan is shown opposite at upper right. The considerable batter of the corner piers makes for a silhouette suggesting great stability. Important in all shelters along difficult trails, and especially in hot climates, is a supply of drinking water. It will be noted that this is provided within all three shelters here grouped.

Trail Shelter, Bright Angel Trail, Grand Canyon National Park

This shelter is nestled between huge boulders in the Indian Gardens area of this park. The adjustment of steps and approaches to the surrounding natural obstacles is of interest. In offering drinking water and shaded, sheltered seats like the two foregoing examples, it truly serves as a way station. The low-pitched roofs of these three shelters are in good character with a desert setting and with the rock stratifications which form the canyon wall.

Trail Shelter, Indian Gardens, Grand Canyon National Park

TRAILSIDE SEATS, SHELTERS, AND OVERLOOKS   Plate II F-19

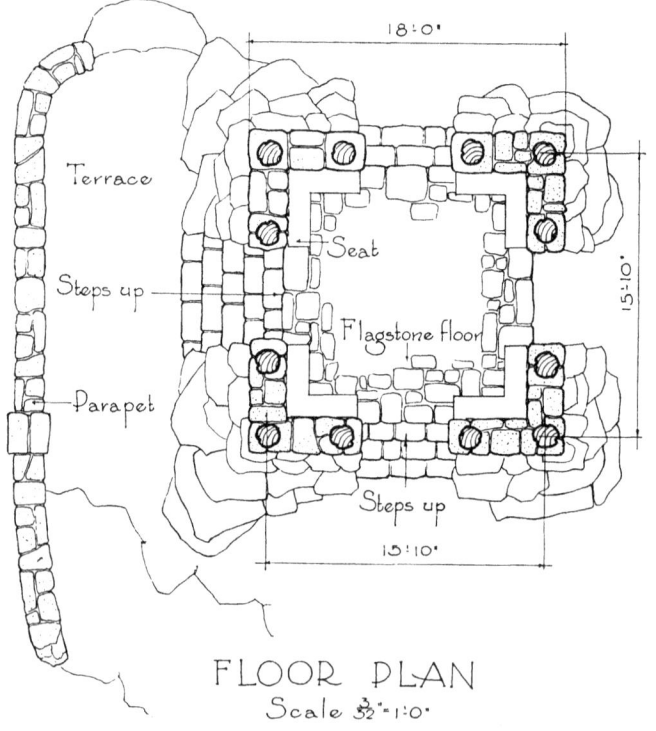

Overlook Shelter, Devil's Den State Park, Arkansas

Nominated from the floor as a candidate for a Pulitzer Award for Park Structures, if and when created. This little structure will cause chagrin and consternation among experts in destructive criticism who will be hard pressed to ferret out its shortcomings. An inventory of all its points of high merit is impossible in a limited space, but would surely lead off with skillful blending to site and vigorous scale and character of rock work and log timbers. The picturesque tree is flattering to the structure, but, it must be admitted, with unquestionable justification.

108

Plate II F-20   ⇒⇒ TRAILSIDE SEATS, SHELTERS, AND OVERLOOKS

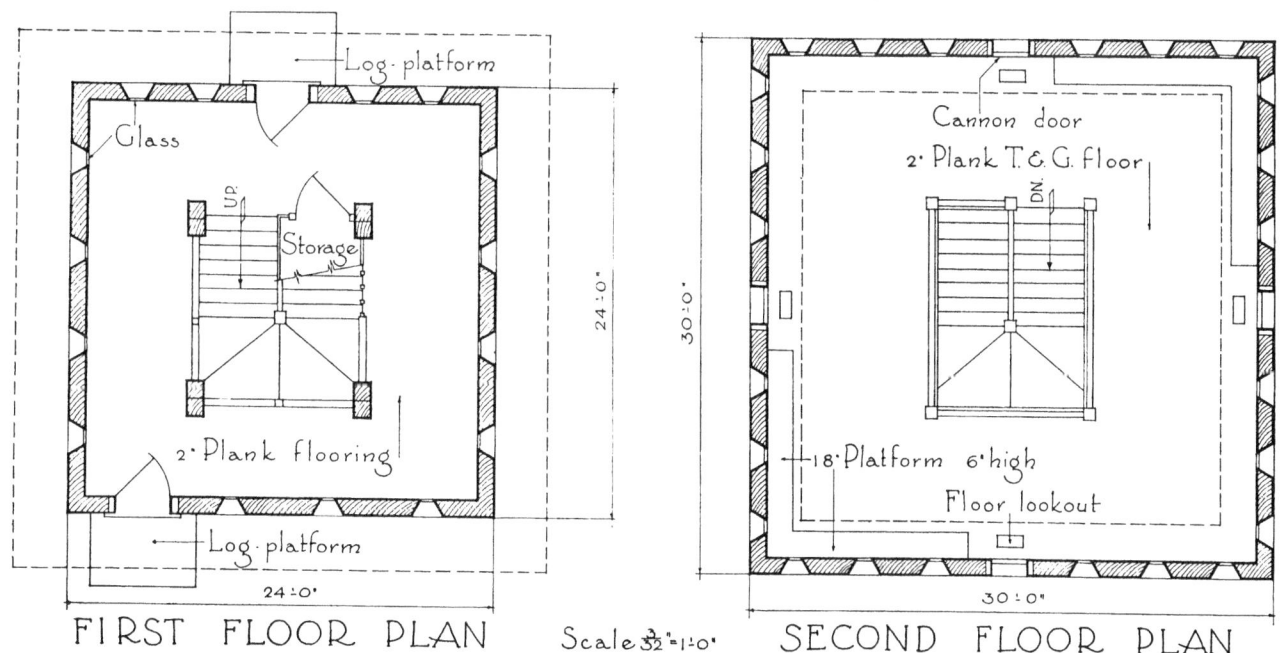

Overlook Shelter, Muskegon State Park, Michigan

A graceful salute to the days of the frontier! For the pleasantly dishonest authenticity of this new-old blockhouse we are indebted to the salvaged timbers of a wrecked lake vessel. This lookout inspires recall of vanished men and vanquished wilderness—a shrine to the Unknown Pioneer.

TRAILSIDE SEATS, SHELTERS, AND OVERLOOKS

Plate II F–21

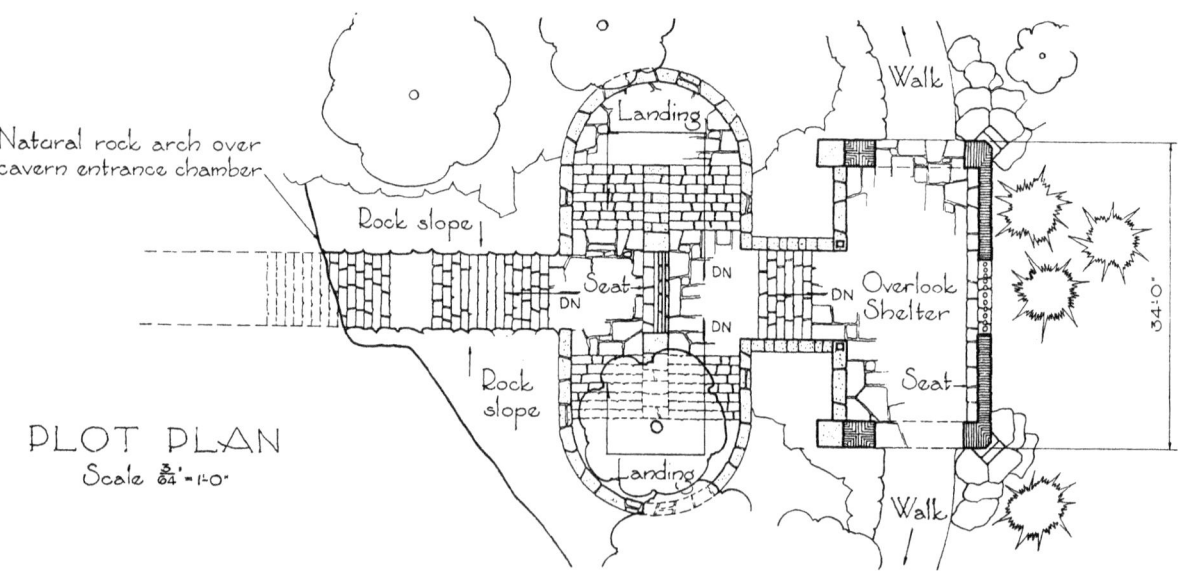

Overlook Shelter, Longhorn Cavern State Park, Texas

Naturally, the feature of this park is its interesting cavern. It is reached from this overlook shelter by the stairway leading down into the rocky depression. At the foot of the stairway is a natural arch giving entrance to the cave. This shelter and the combined overlook and administration building illustrated on the opposite page face each other across this sink on an axis established by the cave entrance.

Plate II F–22 ⇢⇢⇢ TRAILSIDE SEATS, SHELTERS, AND OVERLOOKS

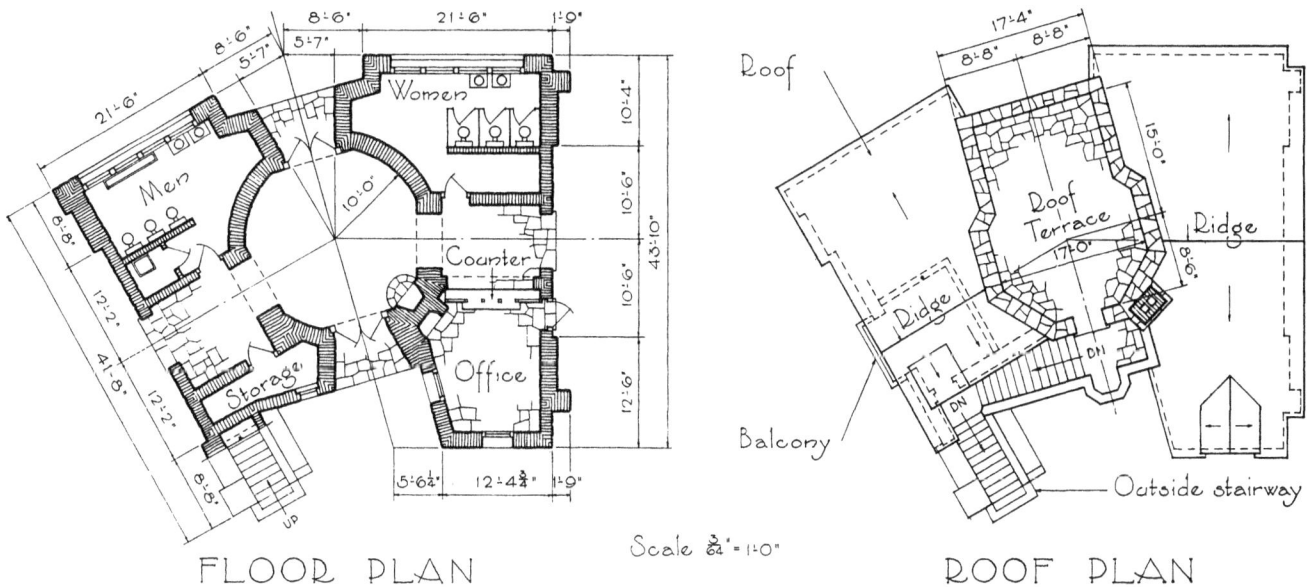

Overlook and Administration Building, Longhorn Cavern State Park, Texas

FLOOR PLAN   ROOF PLAN

Scale ¾"=1'-0"

An extraordinary creation for a park setting, doubtless transported here by the Magic Carpet. It is so cleverly imaginative in mass, variety of materials, and manner of their use as to be very attractive indeed. The outcropping rock ledges contribute in no small way to the pleasing effect. This building and the overlook shelter, shown opposite, are harmonious in architectural treatment.

TRAILSIDE SEATS, SHELTERS, AND OVERLOOKS

Plate II F-23

Lookout Tower — Mt. Nebo State Park — Michigan

More picturesque than most braced timber towers, this example is not thereby any less vulnerable to the deterioration that time brings. The overhanging landings mask but do not entirely eliminate the oil derrick implication of all structures of this general type.

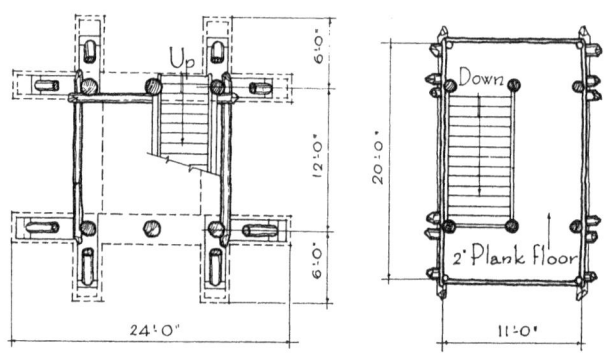

GROUND PLAN — TOP PLAN

Scale 16' : 1'-0"

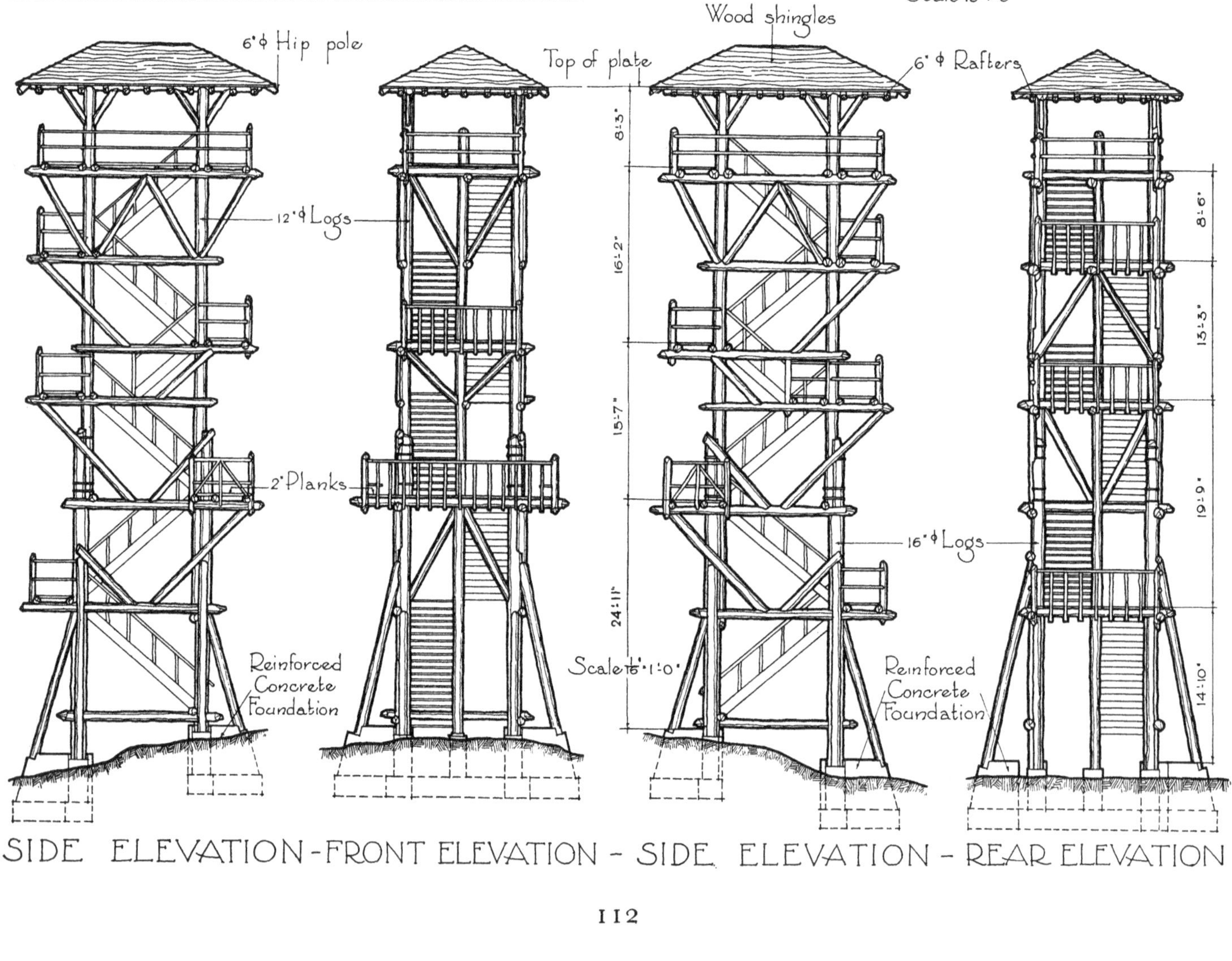

SIDE ELEVATION — FRONT ELEVATION — SIDE ELEVATION — REAR ELEVATION

Plate II F-24   ⟫ TRAILSIDE SEATS, SHELTERS, AND OVERLOOKS

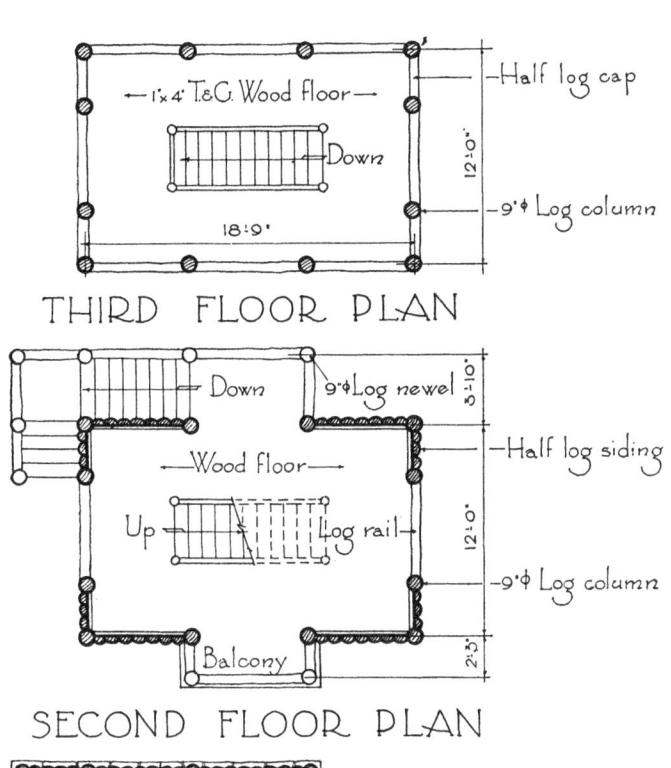

Lookout Tower – Cumberland Falls State Park – Kentucky

The answer to a demand for a wood-framed lookout tower of modest height may lie in the direction of the solution pursued with some degree of success by this example. The structural weaknesses of the typical trussed wood tower are avoided here by limiting the height and by enclosing the framing in large part with vertical logs. The design of future lookouts of logs might well be developed from this pioneering structure rather than from the hazardous latticed type.

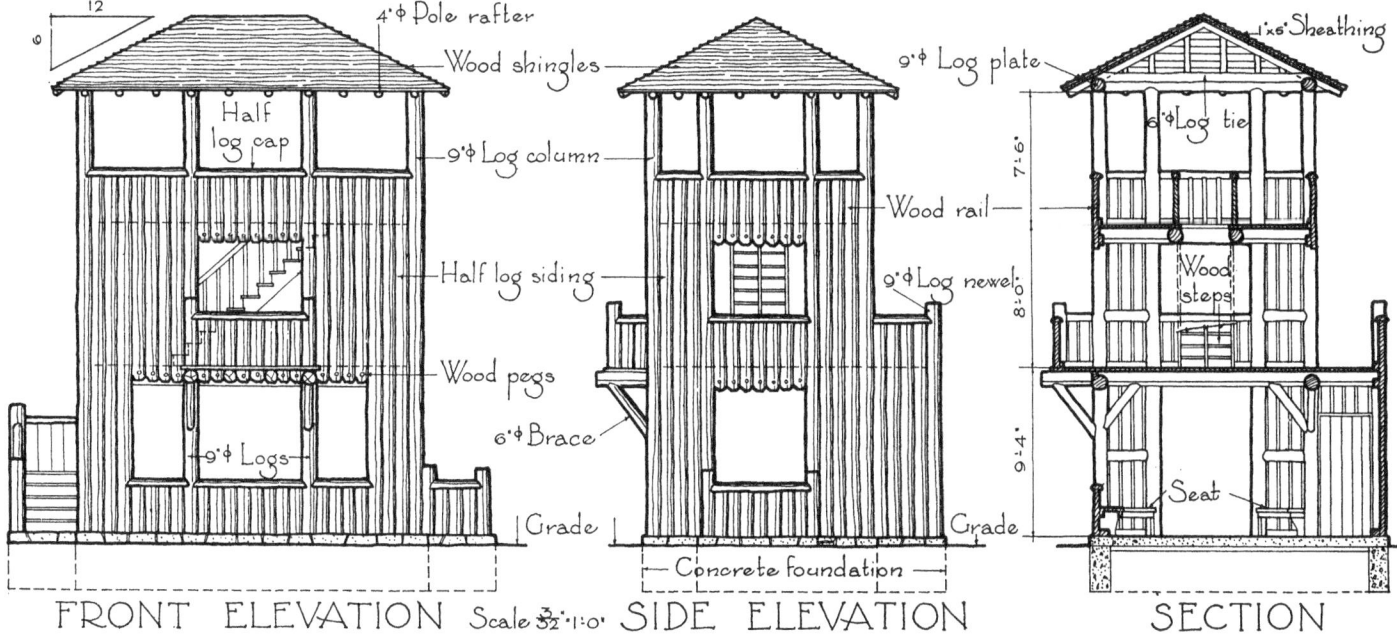

TRAILSIDE SEATS, SHELTERS, AND OVERLOOKS

Plate II F–25

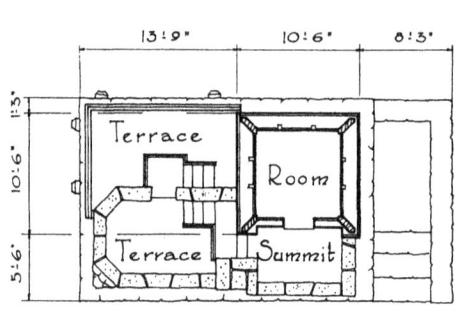

SUMMIT-HOUSE PLAN

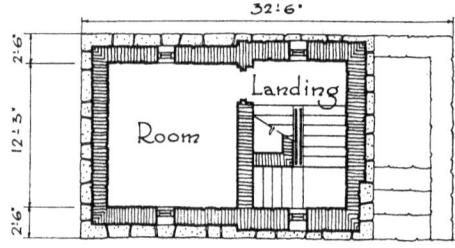

TYPICAL PLAN

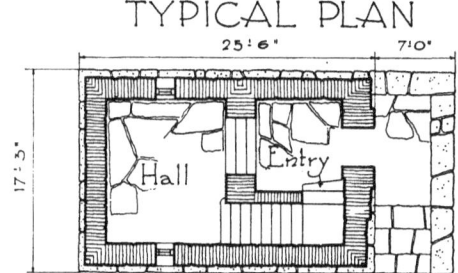

GROUND FLOOR PLAN

Observation Tower – Moran State Park – Washington

Of dual purpose, this tower sensibly isolates the fire lookout's station well above the platform given over to public observation. In consequence there is no conflict of functions

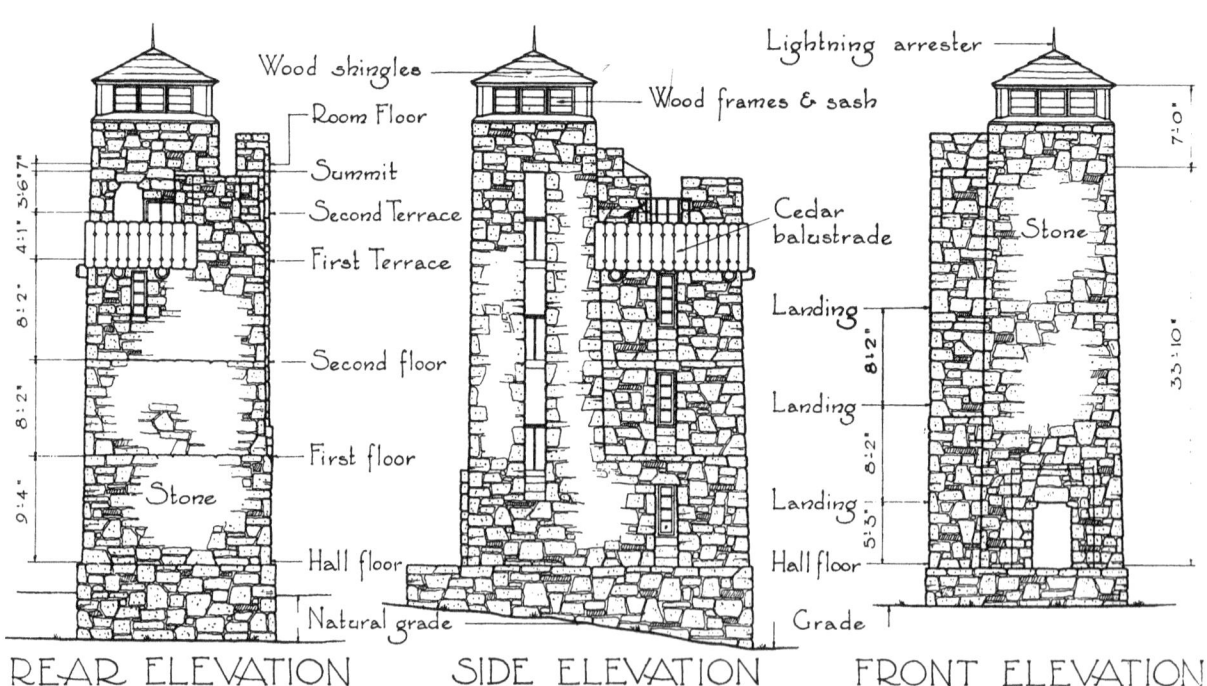

REAR ELEVATION   SIDE ELEVATION   FRONT ELEVATION

Scale $\tfrac{1}{8}" = 1'-0"$

Plate II F–26   ⇝ TRAILSIDE SEATS, SHELTERS, AND OVERLOOKS

Observation Tower – Blue Hills Reservation – Massachusetts

This tower, erected for the single purpose of observation, by magnificently waving aside the opportunity for dual use, spikes the canard of the super-thrifty Yankee. This high accomplishment is dimmed somewhat when we note an unfortunate disregard of the better traditions of Yankee masonry.

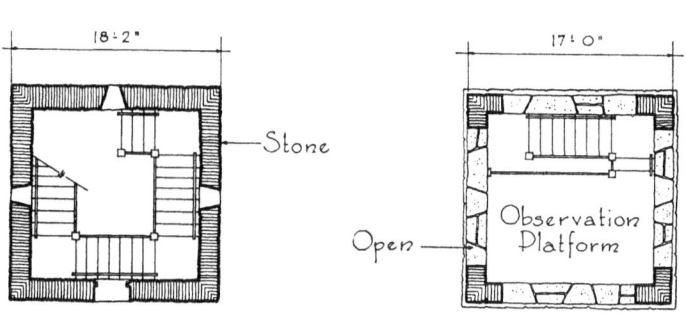

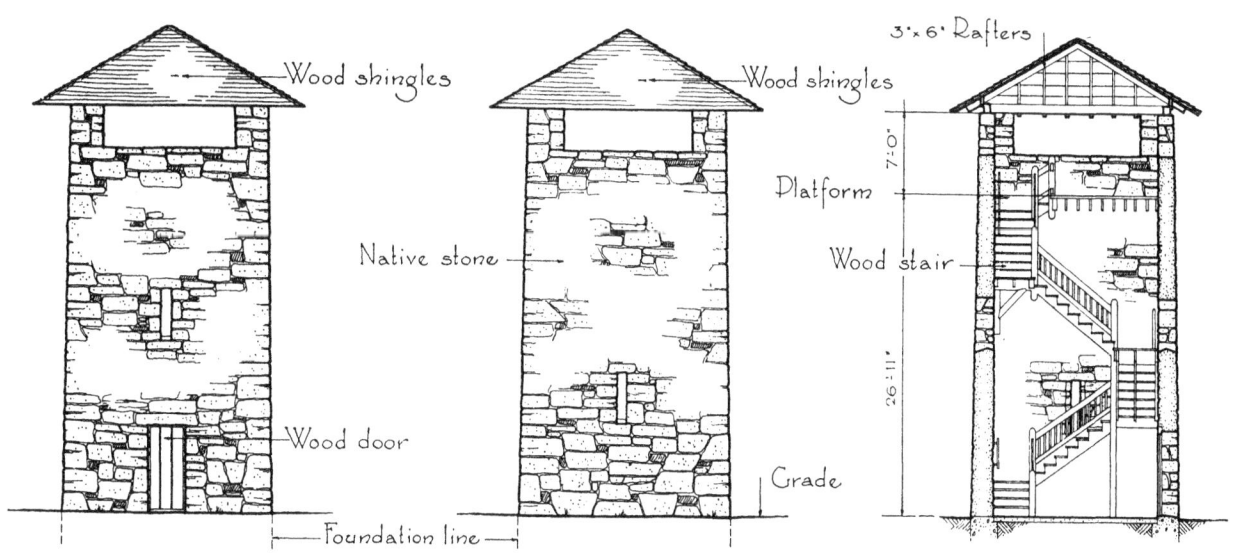

115

TRAILSIDE SEATS, SHELTERS, AND OVERLOOKS *Plate* II F–27

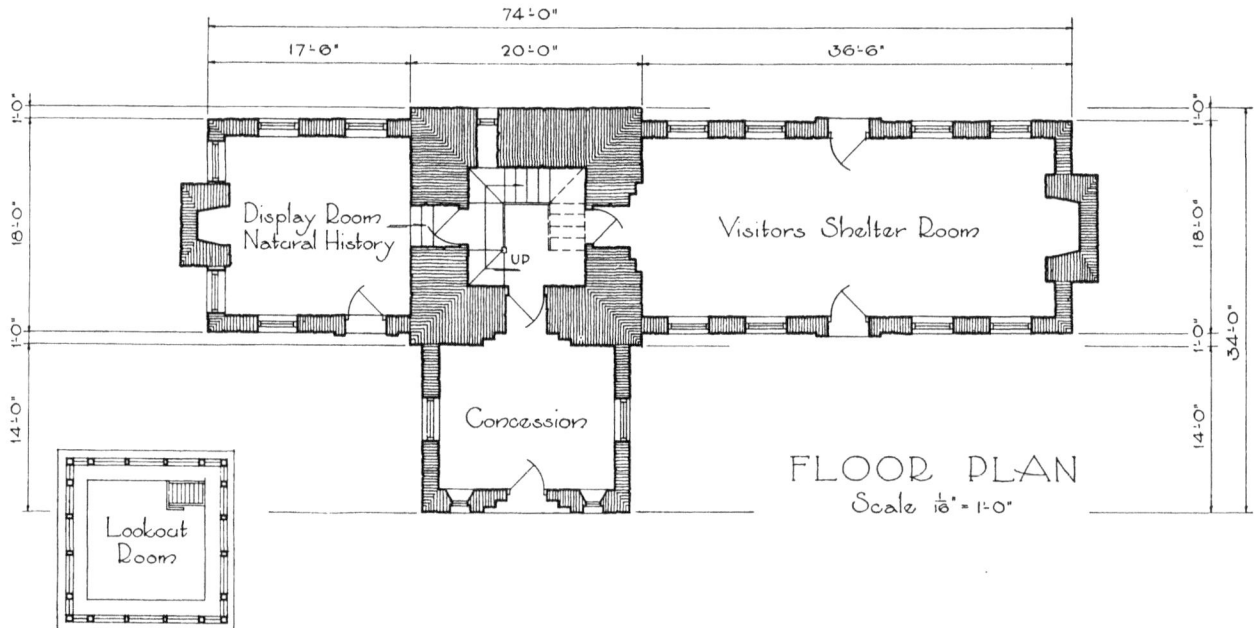

Observation Tower, Cheaha Mountain State Park, Alabama

Erected on the highest point in Alabama, offering a magnificent panoramic view, this lookout tower has its measure of justification. It serves scenic observation and fire detection, and the facilities grouped at its base add to the public's greater use and enjoyment of the lookout area.

Plate II F–28 ››› TRAILSIDE SEATS, SHELTERS, AND OVERLOOKS

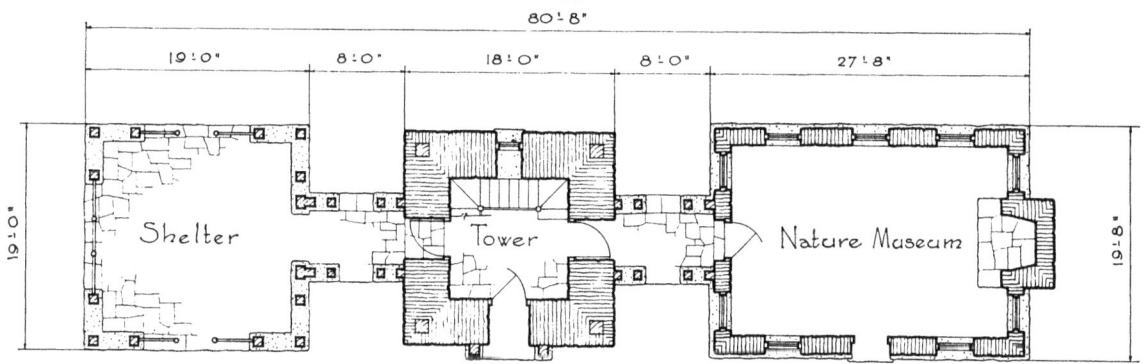

Observation Tower, Weogufka State Park, Alabama

FLOOR PLAN
Scale ⅛"=1'-0"

An observation tower that combines other useful purposes seems somehow to validate itself. Here shelter and nature museum lend their purpose to gain favor for a tower structure. The observation room is such that it is suitable for the operations of a fire lookout. The ensemble is altogether amiable architecturally and novel in its restrained half-timber treatment.

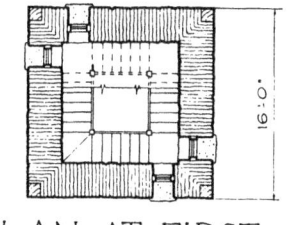

PLAN AT FIRST LANDING

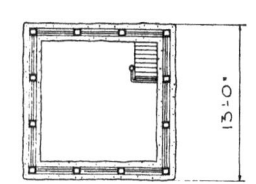

PLAN AT LOOKOUT

117

TRAILSIDE SEATS, SHELTERS, AND OVERLOOKS

Plate II F-29

South Mountain Reservation, New Jersey

Saltwater State Park, Washington

VIEWPOINTS

Above and below are overlooks in their simplest form—merely a natural vantage point of no great elevation, offering a view and railed for the protection of the observer. In one case seats for visitors are included. To the left are two towers of trestle construction, the ultimate in a striving for view. Both are more attractive than it is usually given to such towers to be. Particularly is the tower at upper left proportioned well in its members and stable in appearance by reason of the considerable rake of the corner posts. Sadly enough, regardless of merits of design, the threat of eventual deterioration of structure and insecurity of users haunts all trussed, wooden towers.

Levi Jackson-Wilderness Road State Park, Kentucky

Wheeler Dam Reservation, Tennessee Valley Authority

DAMS AND POOLS

→›› ALTHOUGH IT IS an inviolate principle with respect to national parks and monuments that artificial control of stream flow is to be rigidly avoided, the situation with respect to lesser parks is somewhat different. While it is felt that in some cases such artificial control has been exerted to the detriment of valuable natural conditions without creating adequate compensatory values, there are undoubtedly situations, such as that in which a serious regional shortage of facilities for water recreation exists, which justify this sort of modification of natural conditions. Those who feel that primary emphasis should be placed on preservation of really natural scenery and on historic and scientific values earnestly urge a careful weighing of all prospective losses and gains before any decision is made to create an artificial body of water in a park that is other than primarily for active recreation. Granting then the occasional wisdom of such undertakings, dams are considered with certain reservations to be within the scope of this compilation.

Because the large masonry or concrete dam is a complicated engineering problem, it will not be here discussed. Anything short of the most complete technical information might prove more misinforming than helpful. Furthermore, it has not so far proved very susceptible to coercive attempt to adapt its stubborn functionalism to a harmony with natural environment. It is true that large dams have been faced with stone to some softening of hard, rigid surfaces and lines. But always the failure of the undertaking to register anywhere near a perfect score in straining for harmony with environment has shown that the result has not justified the method. As with certain other facilities in parks, the large dam calls for a philosophical counting of its recreational blessings, and for a blindness to its incorrectible hostility to Nature. The recreational benefits of the made lake alone must be counted on to justify it, without reliance on its feeble efforts to appear a parklike "feature." This, in a development of any considerable size, it can never be.

Only dams that cleverly insinuate themselves into park settings by virtue of appearing to be waterfalls of natural origin, or lake-impounding topographic features having natural aspect in considerable degree, are considered to fall within the scope of this discussion. Herein, even in the case of such dams, concern is with appearance rather than with engineering principles. Readers whose interest goes deeper than the mere naturalizing of a minor impounding instrument will find A Manual for the Design of Low Dams, prepared for the Water Resources Committee of the National Resources Committee, authorative.

The small dam pretending to be a waterfall usually has a structural core wall against and over which the "naturalism" is applied as a veneer. Frequently the rock veneer follows too closely the regularity of the core wall, and betrays the fact that the dam is artificial. This can be avoided if the veneer strives for irregularity both in plan and in vertical section. The latter is accomplished, where ledge rock is native, by building out the lower courses in imitation of natural ledges. The surface treatment of the dam should acknowledge the geology of the area; in a gorge or glen in which rock stratifications are exposed, attempt should be made to bring to the face of the dam all the characteristics of the native ledge rock. The imitation of rocky ledges in a boulder-strewn setting would be sorely out of place—only a dam contrived by a massing of boulders would carry a suggestion of naturalness. Variety in size of the rocks will add much to the natural appearance of the dam. Likewise construction should insure such a distribution of water that all possible rock work of structural purport is screened by the flow. To have portions of the dam exposed during low water may unmask an otherwise well-contrived naturalism.

DAMS AND POOLS

Swimming possibilities in parks and recreational areas can be classified broadly in two groups. Streams, rivers, and lakes comprise the one. The small pond created especially for swimming by the construction of a minor, and usually naturalistic, dam and the formal swimming pool make up the other. The first group is not a present concern; although it may involve the construction of dams, these are generally of such size that the attainment of park character is out of the question.

Only the second group claims our interest here and that largely for its inclusion of the naturalistic pool created by a dam that simulates a waterfall. It might be said that the aspect of the swimming pool and the relationship of the pool to the bathhouse are the points which engage our attention. The plates and illustrations which follow explore these points. There is no intent to treat in detail the construction of the swimming pool, which is an engineering and sanitation problem, so complex as to warrant thorough and detailed treatment if gone into at all. It is assumed that desired information bearing on the construction principles and details of swimming pools, being elsewhere available, will be elsewhere sought. These are ably set forth in Part 1100—Miscellaneous Structures of the Engineering Manual of the National Park Service.

To provide swimming in minor parks where active recreation is a strong demand and overcrowding seems unlikely, a plea is made for the return of the "old swimmin' hole" of fond recollection. The claims of hygiene make a strong case for the thoroughly modern, infection-controlled swimming pool and for the alternative of swimming in a large body of water which well dilutes, may it be said, the contagion risk of mass bathing. But there are areas primarily recreational serving small communities through which an uncontaminated stream may flow. The creation of a large artificial lake may be unwarranted for one or more of a number of reasons—limited area, lack of suitable site or sufficient funds for building a large dam, unreceptive topography, or perhaps only obstinate preference for Nature less modified. Here, if the flow of water is not seasonally stagnant, a swimming hole of "neighborhood" proportions, controlled against overcrowding and periodically checked for pollution, is certainly a logical project. A minor dam is the means by which this communal facility is brought into being, and, if it registers great naturalness, the swimming hole of boyhood's suitless swimming may be convincingly revived.

Pool, Prairie Creek State Park, California

Pursuit of facts regarding the creation of this idyllic pool was deliberately sidestepped owing to a suspicion that man had little to do with. Suffice that it here represents the swimmin' hole of everyman's boyhood—as glorified in retrospect.

Wading Pool, South Park, Pittsburgh, Pennsylvania

This delightful wading pool for youngsters in a metropolitan park is that very rare accomplishment—the spirit of great naturalness created without resort to a single detail truly imitative of Nature. This must be Art.

Plate II G–1   ⇢ DAMS AND POOLS

Palmetto State Park, Texas

Mohawk Metropolitan Park, Tulsa, Oklahoma

MINOR NATURALISTIC WATERFALLS

Here are shown some rock arrangements purposed to simulate small natural waterfalls. In a sense, small dams are structural accessories before the fact, and the visible rock sculpturings are aesthetic accessories after the fact, of a created little pool and flow of water. Nature has been a good teacher in the examples shown, for the fact of artificiality is cleverly hidden. Minor dams, naturalized to look like waterfalls, and trail steps are probably the only elements in the development of a natural area to suffer human use which can make successful pretense at being Nature's handiwork.

Pittsfield State Forest Park, Massachusetts

Platt National Park

Platt National Park

121

DAMS AND POOLS

Plate II G-2

Turner Falls State Park, Oklahoma

October Mountain State Park, Massachusetts

Levi Carter Metropolitan Park, Omaha, Nebraska

NATURALISTIC WATERFALLS

The large illustration above shows outstanding accomplishment in bringing the aspect of naturalness to a large dam. Varying flow, irregular plan, distribution of the rocks—all contribute to the success of this man-made waterfall.

At lower left is proof that the spillway of an earth dam need not invariably be an expanse of inharmonious concrete or stone pavement. At lower right picturesqueness is given to a precipitous rush of water by the skillful suggestion of rock ledges.

Plate II G–3   ⇶ DAMS AND POOLS

Naturalized Dam, Boyle Metropolitan Park, Little Rock, Arkansas

Boyle Metropolitan Park, Little Rock, Arkansas

Boyle Metropolitan Park, Little Rock, Arkansas

Particularly interesting in these three pictures of the same man-made waterfall are the seasonally varying volume of water recorded, and the changing appearance that results. The large illustration must show nearly normal volume and is featured by a pleasing distribution of active flow of water between well-massed rock forms. At lower left low water stage is evidenced, at which time the rocks forming the dam serve as stepping stones for crossing the stream. At lower right is flood stage, the rock forms being almost completely hidden beneath the rush of water.

123

DAMS AND POOLS

Plate II G-4

Dam and Pool, Hot Springs National Park

All subjects on this page represent the swimming pool of modest size created by the construction of a dam which foregoes the imitation of a waterfall but does not altogether sacrifice what we refer to as park character. In this example the pool has a naturalistic outline, and the exposed stone surfaces of the dam have an agreeably rustic texture. The rocks placed below the spillway bring a hint of Nature up to the base of the dam and by association invest the dam itself with natural quality.

Dam and Pool, Enfield Glen State Park, New York

Here is presented not just an attractive swimming pool but photographic evidence in support of the contention that an artificial body of water never adds to, usually detracts from, natural beauty present. The recreational value of a pool for swimming is not to be gainsaid, but the appropriateness of its intruding to the base of a fine natural waterfall to a diminution of scenic beauty may properly be challenged.

Dam and Pool, Cook County Forest Preserve District, Illinois

This pool pays Paul without robbing Peter, by adding recreational value where scenic value hardly constitutes a claim. It has a bottom of concrete and shore line and dam of stone. The stone is employed in a masonry typical of the Chicago metropolitan area. The artificiality of the facility is softened to a considerable extent by the informality of the pleasing sweeping curves of the shore line and bordering steps.

Plate II G–5 →→→ DAMS AND POOLS

Swimming Pool, Grand Canyon National Park

This artificial swimming pool with its naturalistically fabricated rocky banks occurs at Phantom Ranch, deep down in the Grand Canyon. It must present a welcome sight and serve a useful purpose after the difficult descent of the canyon wall by horse trail. The casual appearance of the boulder-strewn banks of this pool is by no means casually arrived at, as those who have tackled any similar problem will be quick to testify.

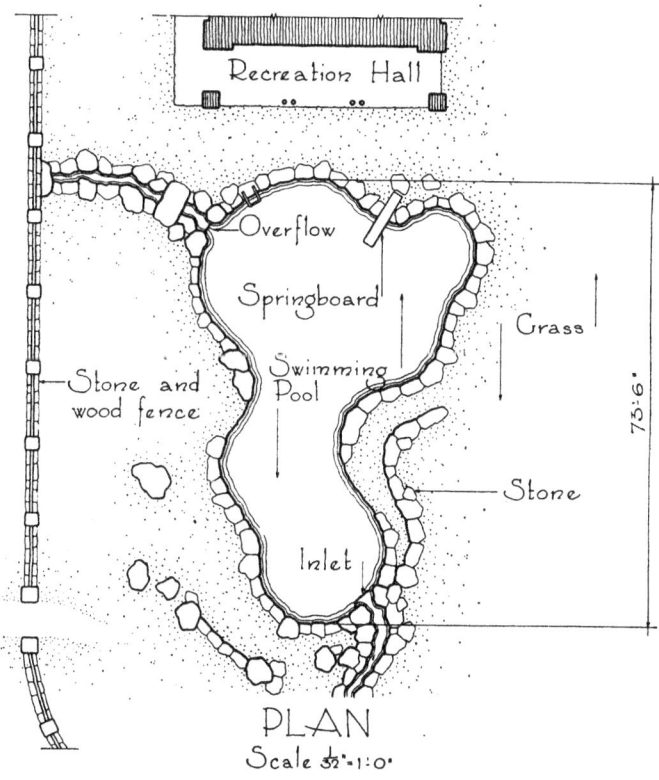

DAMS AND POOLS

Plate II G–6

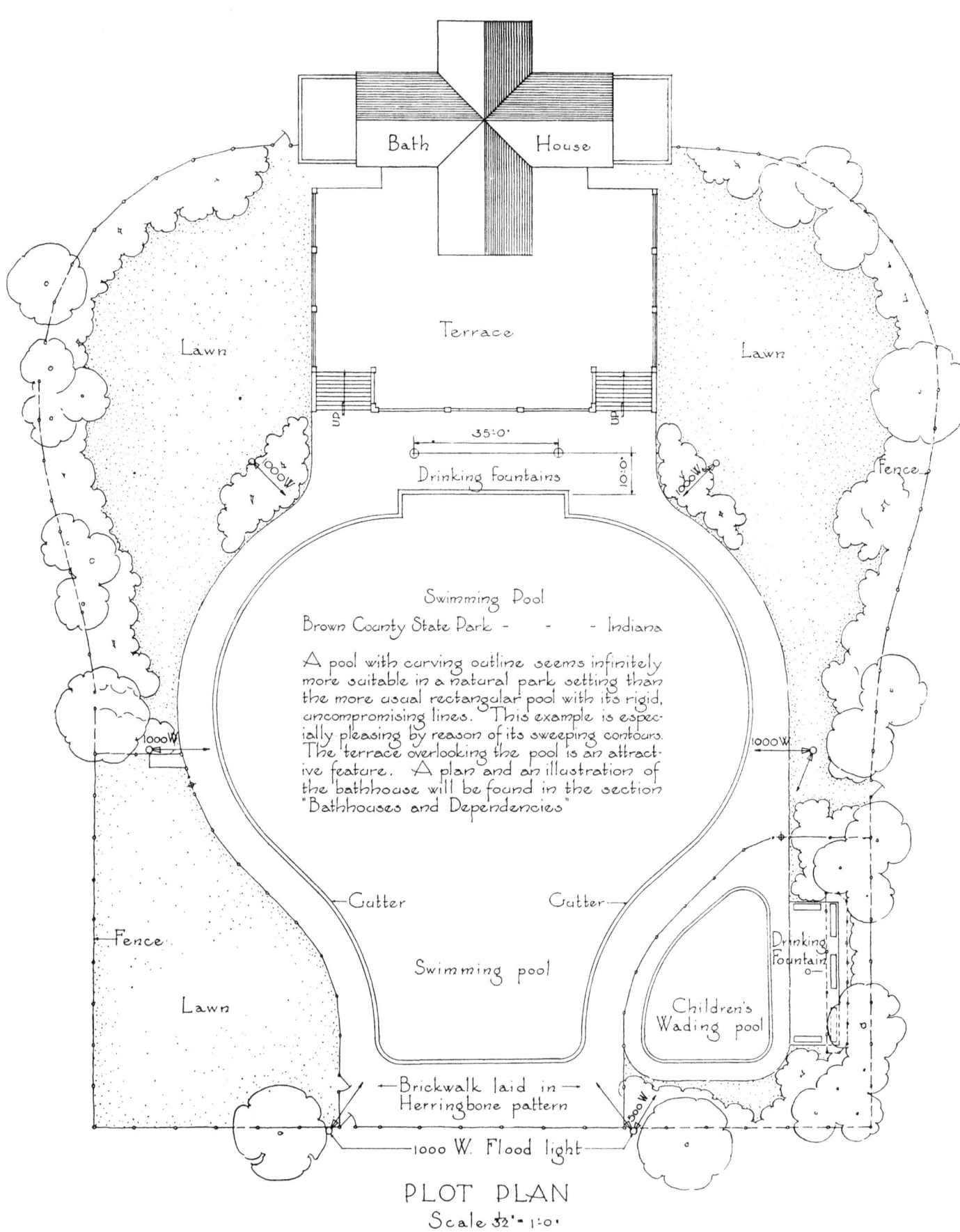

PLOT PLAN
Scale ½" = 1'-0"

BATHHOUSES AND DEPENDENCIES

THE ERA of the casual bathhouse in facilitation of swimming within publicly owned parks is passing. This more or less unsupervised building of the past, now giving place to the controlled bathhouse, is within the memory of all of us. As we dwell fondly on the summer holidays of youth, we perhaps find it difficult to recall clearly that dingy, ill-arranged, ill-maintained, and unhygienic building. It was one of those pioneer structures in recreation that, after worthy apprenticeship cherished in memory, has since moved on to a more orderly and complete fulfilment of function. To cling in nostalgic recall to the bathhouse of horse and carry-all days is as illogical in present day park recreation as to insist upon that means of transportation, or bathing apparel of the same period.

Progress has overtaken the primitive bathhouse, just as it has forced more positive and more complex systems of sanitation within parks grown beyond the safe limits of that lack of sanitation tolerable only in the little-patronized area. Beyond doubt the ever-increasing use of public park facilities by people of widely different social strata is responsible for this trend, and its effects are beneficial and many.

Supervisory control of the bathhouse or bathing pavilion has brought with it higher standards generally in all details of the structure and its accessories. It has been subjected to tests for efficiency and hygiene and emerges very much in step with this year of grace. Whether operated directly or as a concession, a bathhouse in a public area should be so efficiently arranged and constructed that the greatest number of people are suitably accommodated at the lowest possible capital cost. This means, or should mean, the lowest possible charge for use. Here is no place for unnecessary spaciousness, or luxury, or operating system that does not fulfil this requirement, nor is there place for private dressing booths only, claimable under one rental for periods of many hours, and leading to vastness of structure if the use demand is to be met.

Large and spacious buildings can only lead to an exorbitant use-fee if the investment is to be served, or to an inadequate financial return if the public is to be served as it has the right to expect—at a moderate charge. A system that provides for a checking of possessions while a patron is not actually occupying the dressing booth multiplies the capacity and at the same time curbs the size of the building, and should lead to subsequent scaling down, theoretical at least, of the fee. The adoption of such a system is therefore an obligatory demand upon any park authority charged with determining the operating method of a bathhouse on public property, and not unaware of his responsibility.

To meet the need for efficient conservation of space, the old practice of issuing keys for private dressing booths is replaced with open dressing space, or with booths that are only claimable during actual occupancy. Various arrangements for the safe keeping of the bather's possessions while he is on the beach have developed. With the locker system, the bather is issued a key to a small compartment in which his effects may be locked up. With the basket system, he is furnished a basket or tray in which his possessions may be placed and checked with the attendant. The Westchester County Park Commission has given up the use of bathhouse lockers in favor of basket checking, for the reason that baskets can be sterilized more thoroughly and readily than lockers. This Commission prefers aluminum trays to wire baskets, because buttons and clothing are apt to catch and tear in wire mesh.

The number of lockers or baskets provided should be nicely scaled to the capacity of the available dressing space, with due regard for whether the bathing is done in an artificial pool where the time in the water is limited, or in a large body of water where the time element is not a factor. For a given number of people, fewer lockers need be provided in connection with a pool than with a larger swimming beach where many of the bathers hold lockers or baskets for several hours.

Dressing space may be arranged in any one of several ways, or in combinations of these. For men and boys, one general open dressing room with benches and clothes racks is usual. Dressing booths, each equipped with seat and clothes hooks, either open-front, curtained, or with doors, are sometimes provided. There is, however, hardly sufficient reason for providing these exclusively. It seems more reasonable to provide a limited number of dressing booths for the older generation, and a general dressing space for those younger patrons bred in the gymnasium-equipped public schools.

A general dressing space is less acceptable to women. Booths with curtains or doors are probably preferred by them, and if not provided to the exclusion of all open dressing space, should utilize the greater portion of the space available. The younger woman of today, with her increasing participation in sports, probably does not demand the private booth as generally as her elders.

Showers are not only a desirable facility in all bathhouses, but are absolutely essential, and desirable in greater numbers whenever the swimming is done in an artificial pool and bathing with soap before entering the pool is obligatory. Showers for men may be in one general open area. For women they should be individual. It is illogical in bathhouse planning to make provision for women to dress in privacy in booths, and at the same time make necessary their traversing a public aisle to and from the showers. It would seem reasonable, if modesty is to be served, that it be served consistently. In a proper proportion, some few showers might well be provided in direct communication with groups of two or three booths, if available funds permit. Particularly is this true if the swimming is to be done in an artificial pool, with its compulsory preliminary bath.

If the swimming is in an artificial pool, a footbath containing disinfectant to minimize the spread of foot infections should be provided in the passage from the dressing room to the pool so that its use cannot be avoided.

Toilets should be conveniently and conspicuously placed where they must be passed on the way to beach or pool.

An understanding of hygiene has brought other changes to the construction and operation of the bathhouse. Almost always when swimming is in an artificial pool, bathers are required for sanitary reasons to use suits, caps, and towels provided by the management. In connection with some swimming pools in metropolitan park areas, a physical examination is compulsory before entrance to the pool is permitted. This is a sensible precautionary measure in the instance of a heavily used facility.

The value of sunlight and ventilation is lately more fully understood. One bathhouse dressing room arrangement that reflects in maximum this enlightenment is roofed only over the booths and toilets, leaving the aisles and any general dressing space open to the sky. What is more logical than this casting off of the frayed tradition that dressing space must be entirely sheltered? When the weather is too cold for dressing in semishelter, it is likewise too cold for outdoor swimming.

Almost without exception a charge is made for the use of the bathhouse. The income is applied to operation and maintenance. The attendants' station or room, where fees are collected, where suits, towels, baskets, or keys are issued to patrons, and possessions are checked, should be adroitly and compactly laid out in relation to entrance lobby and to passages leading to the men's and women's dressing rooms, so that complete supervision is had with the fewest possible attendants. This is important for the curbing of operating cost.

ALL THE FOREGOING is by way of outlining the basic essentials of the modern bathhouse in a park. There are supplementary appurtenances that are often desirable but not exactly requisite, such as lavatories, drinking fountains, wringers for bathing suits, hair driers, and public telephones. There are dependencies, the incorporation of which will be determined by the operating policy or the funds available, such as office, rest rooms, first aid room, and lifeguards' retiring and locker room. If suits and towels are rented, a laundry and drying room are necessary, unless the laundering is done off the premises.

There are also unrelated features which policy, expediency, and economic and other considerations may make it reasonable to incorporate, and which forthwith transform the bathhouse into a pavilion, community, or combination structure. Police or employes' retiring and locker rooms, employes' living quarters, winter storage space, concessions for the sale of food, drink, candy, tobacco, and toys, and for the rental of beach gear, with all the necessary dependencies of these, may make the bathhouse a large and complex structure.

In connection with a swimming beach, a pier or a float for the bathers' use is a needed accessory. Both these facilities are usually equipped with one or more diving boards, and sometimes include an elevated diving platform and benches for the swimmers.

The float is a level platform built on solid foundations, preferably, or carried on pontoons and anchored where the water is of suitable depth. The latter arrangement is an especially practical feature where the water level is not constant, and where there is real benefit from the offered possibility of mooring at different locations. The pier sometimes takes the form of an enclosure to limit the range of children, nonswimmers, and beginners. So built, it helps greatly to regulate use and promote safety.

Those persons not bathing but wishing admission to the shore are often required to pay a nominal fee for this privilege if the beach area is limited and can be enclosed. This practice regulates crowding, and a turnstile entrance with change booth nearby is the usual and businesslike means of control. Park regulations against taking food onto the beach and against persons in bathing suits leaving the immediate beach area may be most easily enforced at the turnstile. Many parks see fit to prohibit the changing of clothes in automobiles or places other than the bathhouse provided for this purpose.

To back-track from the features that are only auxiliary to bathhouses to a concluding consideration of the bathhouse proper, it cannot be too forcefully urged that in the choosing of materials and equipment entering into such a structure, the readiness with which these can be maintained in whole and clean condition should be carefully weighed. Just as for park toilets, the standard of maintenance is geared to the durability and cleanability of the materials used. Maintenance funds are too often insufficient, yet a wise choice of materials can offset this lack within a reasonable limit. Failure to maintain bathhouse and toilet facilities in sanitary condition is a fair target for complaint by a public that will be apathetic to equivalent lack of maintenance in the case of almost every other park facility.

The diagrams and illustrations of specific successful examples which follow seek to convey typical groupings and relationships of the several component parts, as well as the dependencies, of the bathhouse that has place in public parks.

Diving Platform, Crowley's Ridge State Park, Arkansas

BATHHOUSES AND DEPENDENCIES Plate II H-1

Floating Swimming Pier
Lake Guernsey State Park - - - - Wyoming

Here the characteristics of wilderness construction are brought to a swimming float, a facility seldom given the benefit of any consideration beyond complete practicability. The venture is highly commendable for the effort and the accomplishment. Careful thoughtful design is in evidence and the sturdy proportions of the rustic members are very agreeable to an eye accustomed to the utterly commonplace and merely functional in swimming floats.

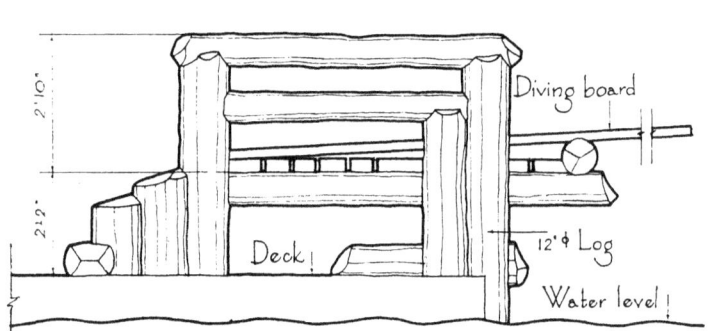

SIDE ELEVATION

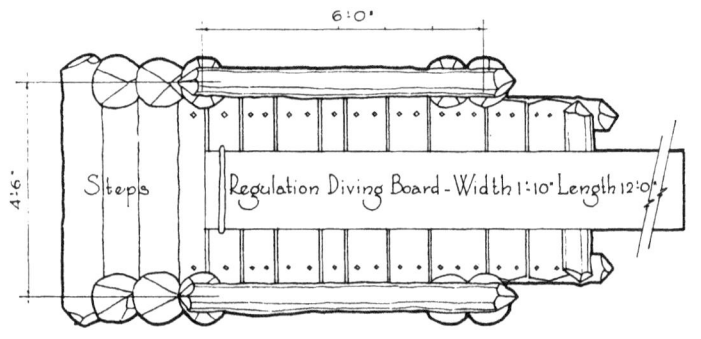

PLAN OF DIVING PLATFORM

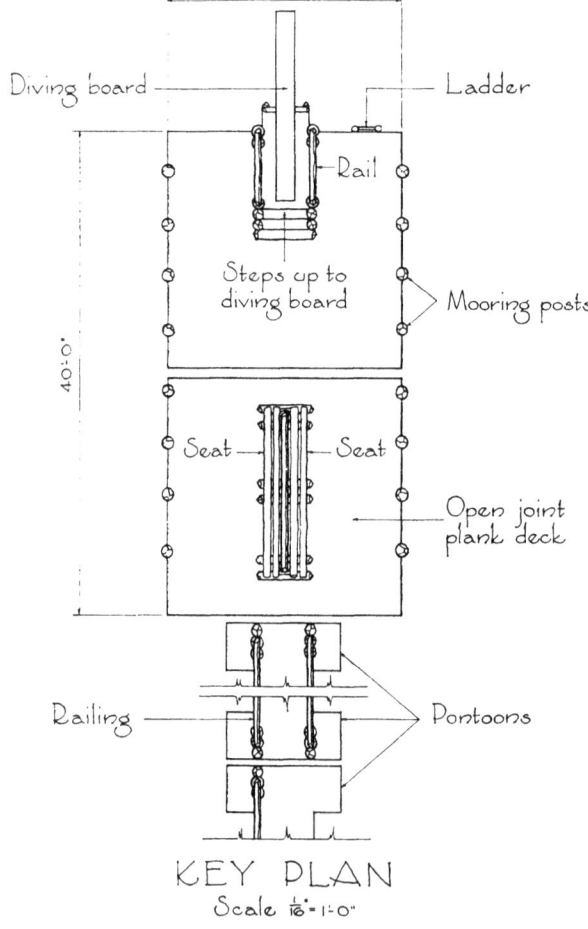

KEY PLAN
Scale 1/16"=1'-0"

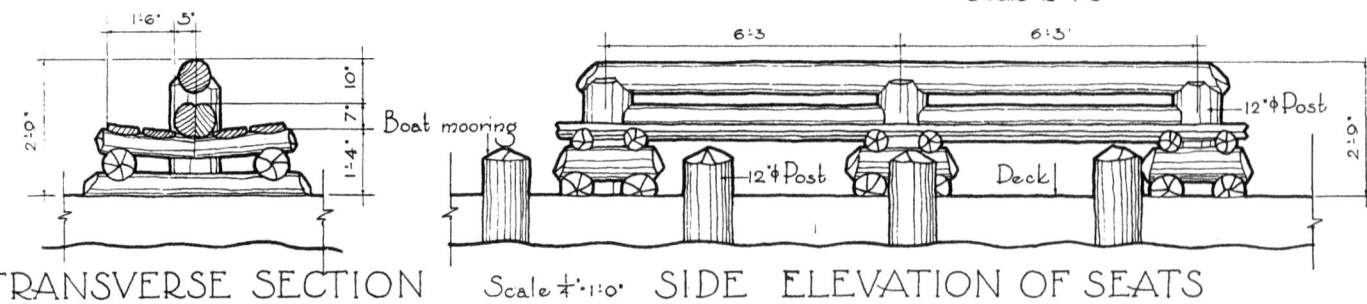

TRANSVERSE SECTION   Scale 1/4"=1'-0"   SIDE ELEVATION OF SEATS

130

Plate II H-2 — BATHHOUSES AND DEPENDENCIES

Pier
Stockade Lake — Custer State Park — South Dakota

This combination of swimming pier and boat landing has in large measure the character of the swimming pier detailed on the facing page and there commended. Both are noteworthy for the rugged scale of the benches and the understructure and railings of the elevated diving boards. In a wooded setting, the use, as far as possible, of timbers in the round, goes far to relate a facility so utilitarian to its surroundings.

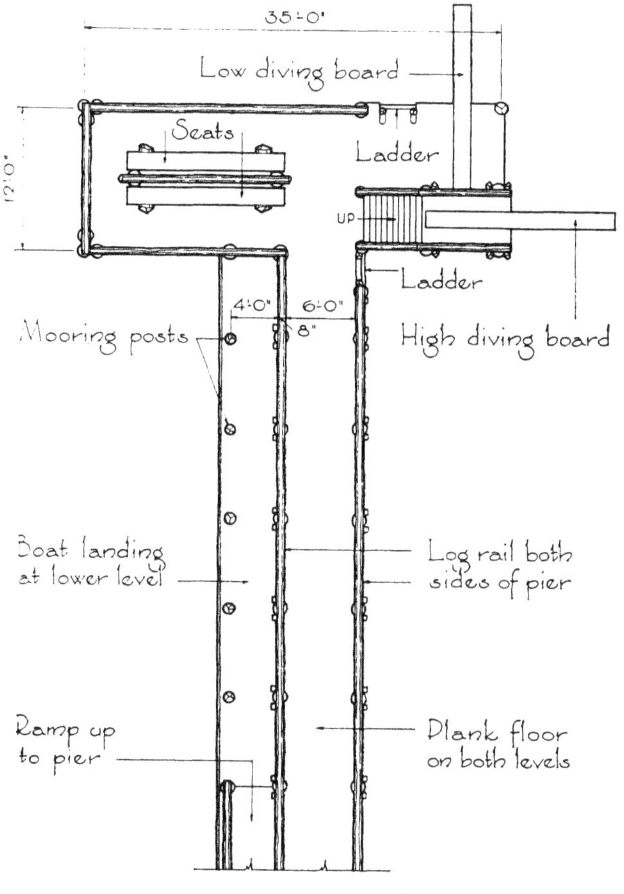

KEY PLAN — Scale 1/16" = 1'-0"

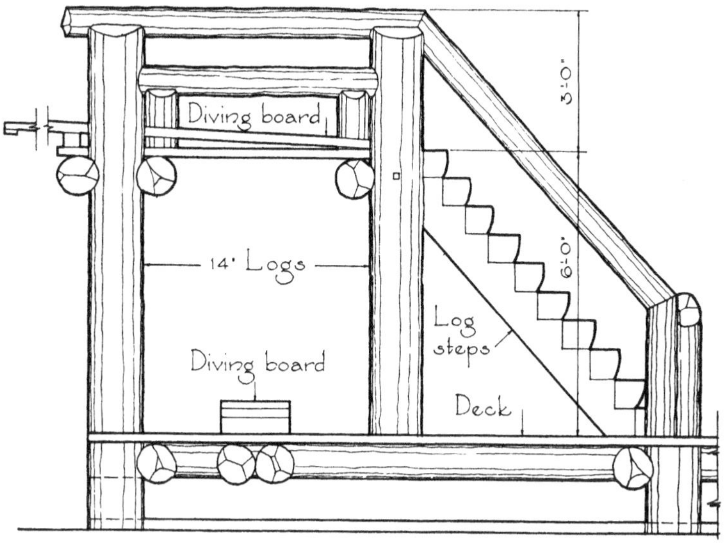

SIDE ELEVATION

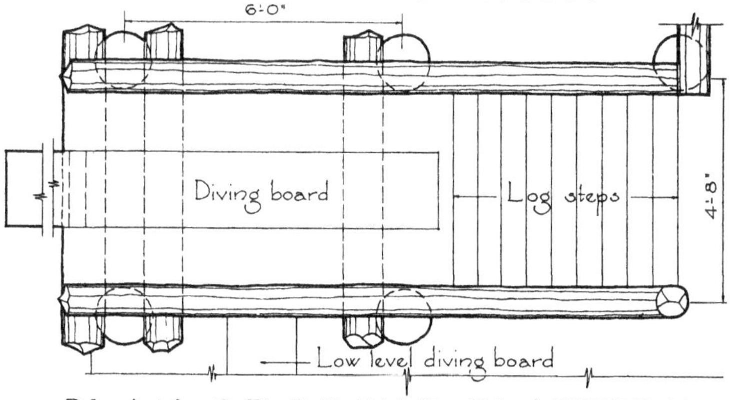

PLAN OF DIVING PLATFORM

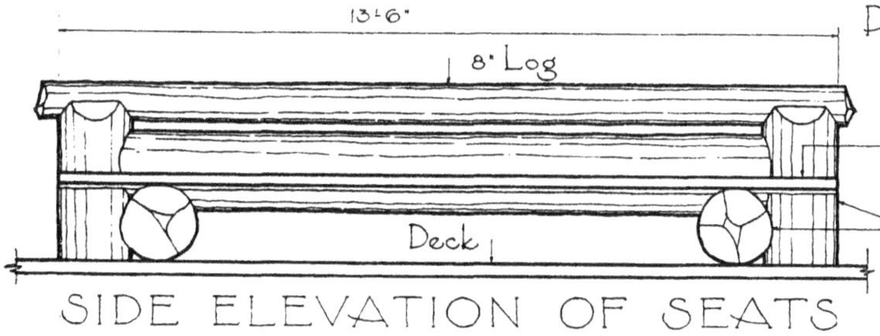

SIDE ELEVATION OF SEATS

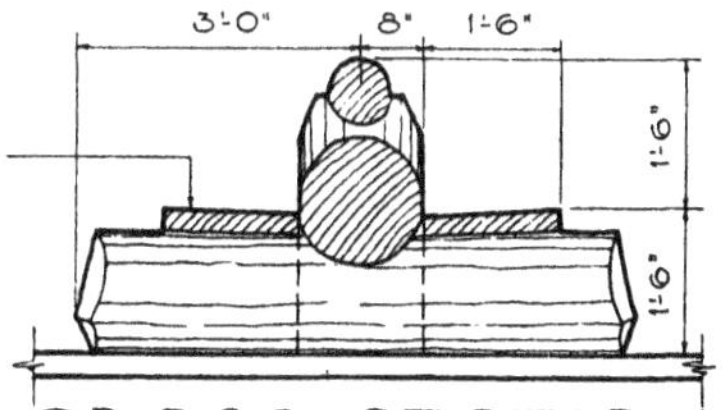

CROSS SECTION — Scale 1/4" = 1'-0"

131

BATHHOUSES AND DEPENDENCIES

Plate II H-3

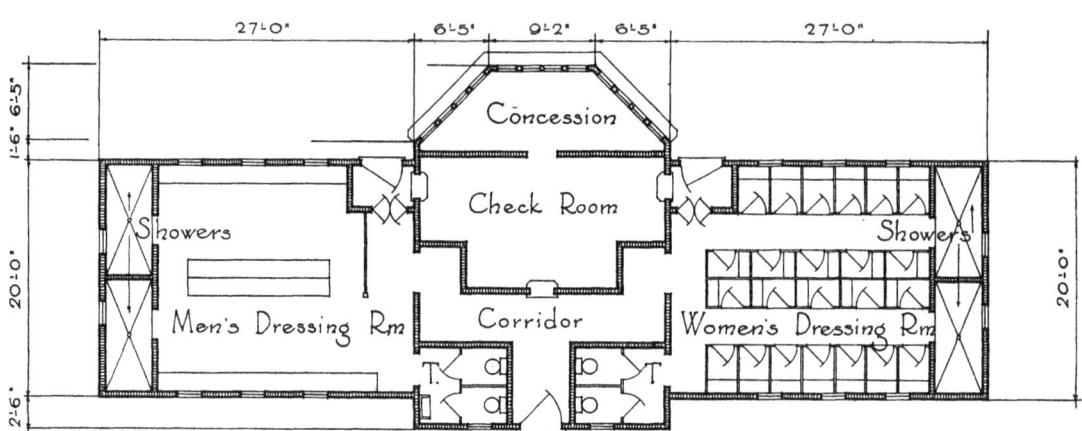

Westmoreland State Park - - Virginia

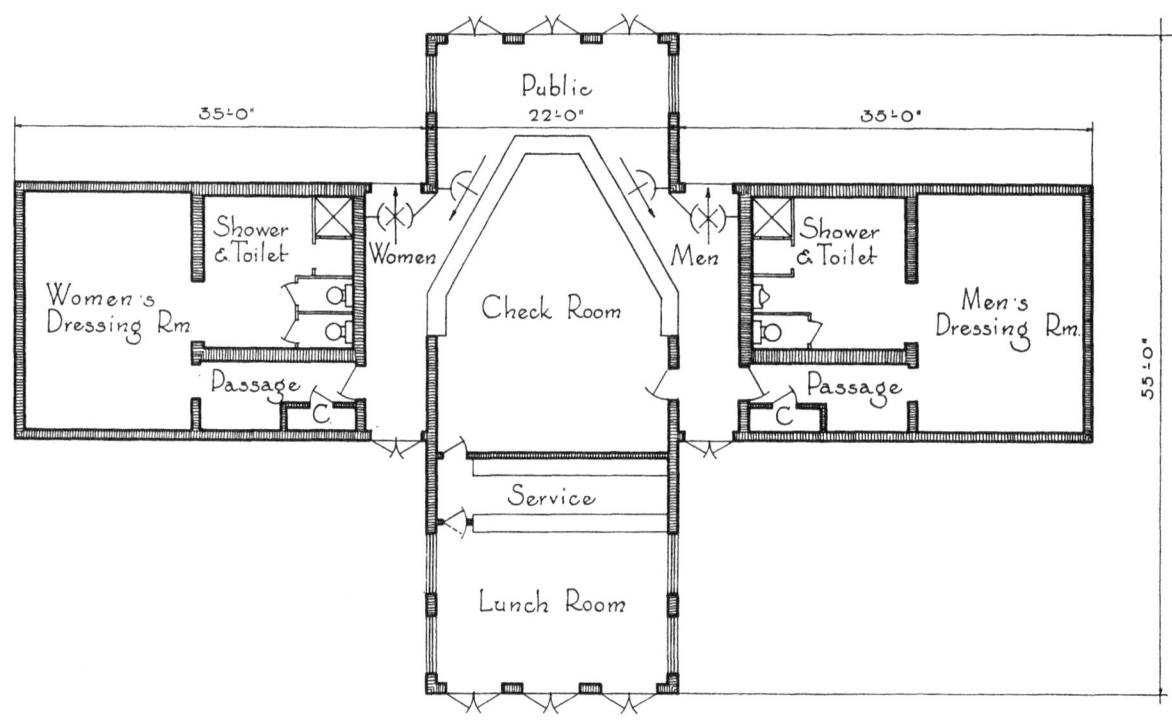

Brown County State Park - - Indiana

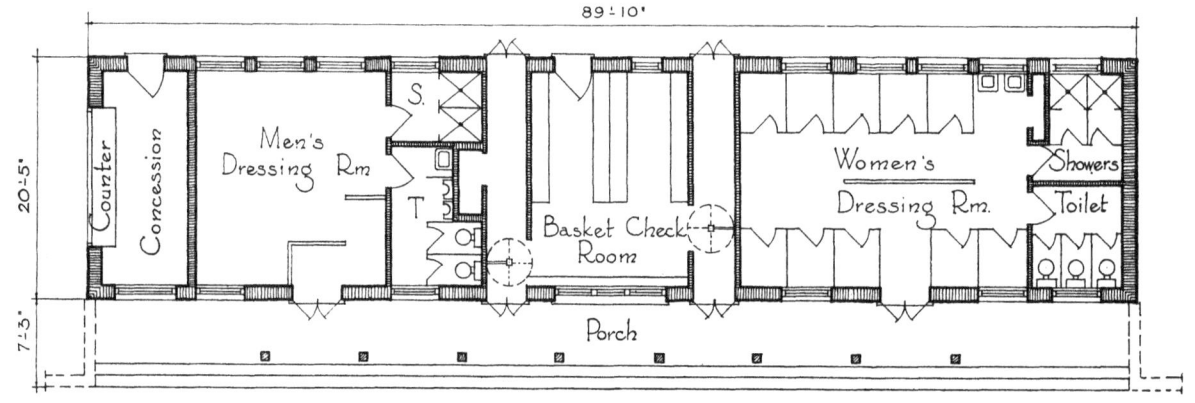

McCormicks Creek State Park - - Indiana

Scale 1/8" = 1'-0"

Modest in size and in materials employed, this bathhouse has many excellent features. The plan permits one-man control of both bathhouse and adjoined concession. The sight lines are well-baffled. The provisions of individual booths in the women's section and open dressing space in the men's section are very reasonable. If it were sought to adapt the building to use with a swimming pool, the plan offers possibility for installing turnstile controls and disinfecting footbaths with only minor revisions.

Bathhouse, Westmoreland State Park, Virginia

This example, like the bathhouse shown above, is an achievement in well-planned and well-proportioned use of inexpensive material. The general arrangement and control features are excellent. Dressing rooms are sensibly without roofs. Because this bathhouse is in connection with a swimming pool, disinfecting footbaths between bathhouse and pool would be very much in order. The terrace overlooking the pool is an attractive feature. A plot plan, showing the relationship of this bathhouse to the pool, is to be found in the section which deals with swimming pools.

Bathhouse, Brown County State Park, Indiana

This bathhouse, which serves a swimming pool, is highly practical in arrangement. One attendant centrally located can wait on both men and women customers, who, upon payment of the fee, enter the fenced-in pool area by one-way turnstiles, then reenter the dressing rooms. Booths are provided for women, open dressing space for men. The absence of footbath between dressing rooms and pool will properly be questioned. Architecturally the building is agreeable, although "finished" in a degree more usual in metropolitan than in natural park areas.

Bathhouse, McCormicks Creek State Park, Indiana

BATHHOUSES AND DEPENDENCIES «« Plate II H–5

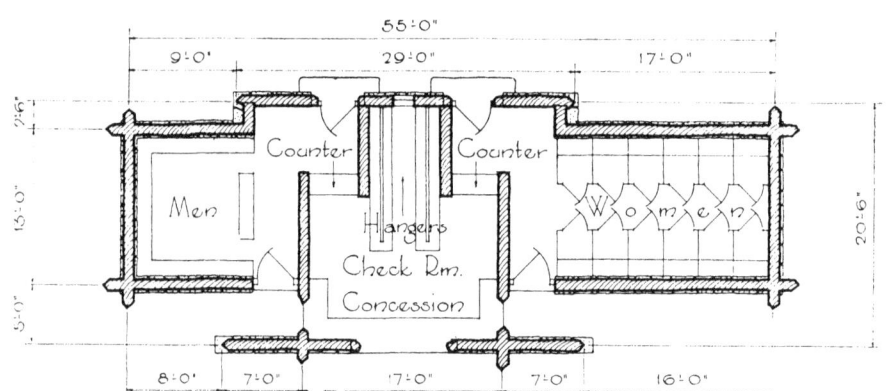

Scenic State Park – – Minnesota

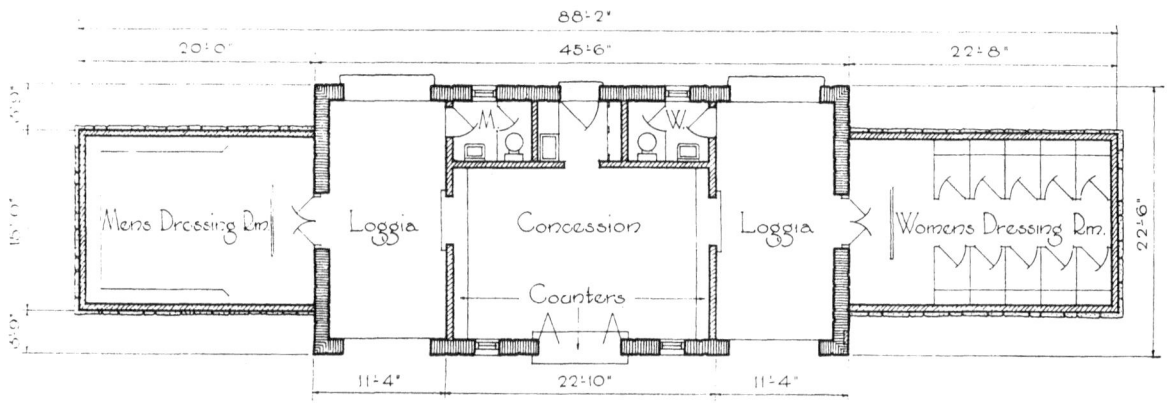

Sibley State Park – – Minnesota

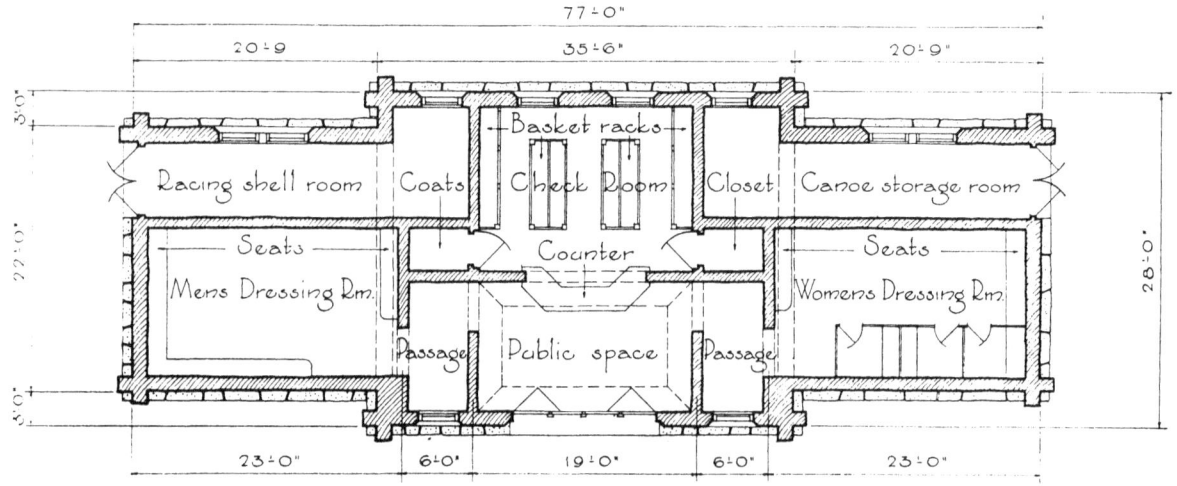

Bewabic State Park – – Michigan

Scale ⅛" = 1'-0"

This minor bathhouse is designed around the conviction that dressing rooms need not be roofed. There is double benefit to derive from this policy—reduced cost and increased light and air. The handling of the masonry leaves something to be desired, but the high quality of the log work and other excellences of plan and treatment go far to make up for this. The compactness of checkroom concession is suitably scaled to the limited dressing room capacity.

Bathhouse, Scenic State Park, Minnesota

This bathhouse and one at Camden State Park, Minnesota, are similar in plan. The view is of the approach side of the building. The refreshment concession faces the bathing beach. The combination of masonry and vertical boards and battens is attractive. Because the loggias allow free circulation through the building, and the attendant can only with difficulty control entrance to the dressing rooms, the plan is most suitable where the operating policy permits free use of the dressing rooms and the concession privilege is limited to renting suits and towels and checking property. Dressing rooms are unroofed.

Bathhouse, Sibley State Park, Minnesota

A fine log bathhouse structure that incorporates storage for boats but with wings so handled that the full benefits of unroofed dressing space are missed while the disadvantages remain. The economy of the practice is lost because the smallness of the well openings has forced the building of what amounts to a full roof. The small and high openings greatly limit the air and sunshine admitted, while the chief nuisance of the open dressing rooms—the litter of dead leaves—persists. Unless the roofless program is embraced in maximum, it would seem better to provide a full roof and rely on sidewall openings for light and air.

Bathhouse, Bewabic State Park, Michigan

BATHHOUSES AND DEPENDENCIES

Plate II H–7

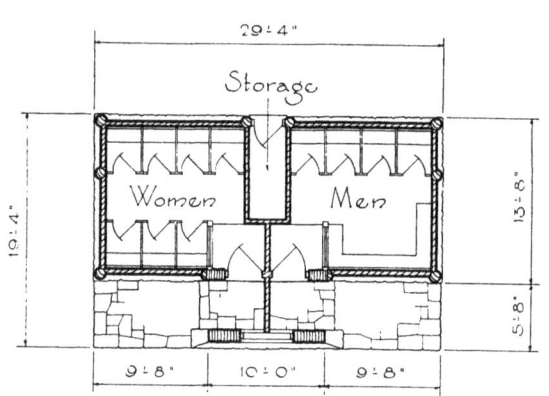

Heyburn State Park – Idaho

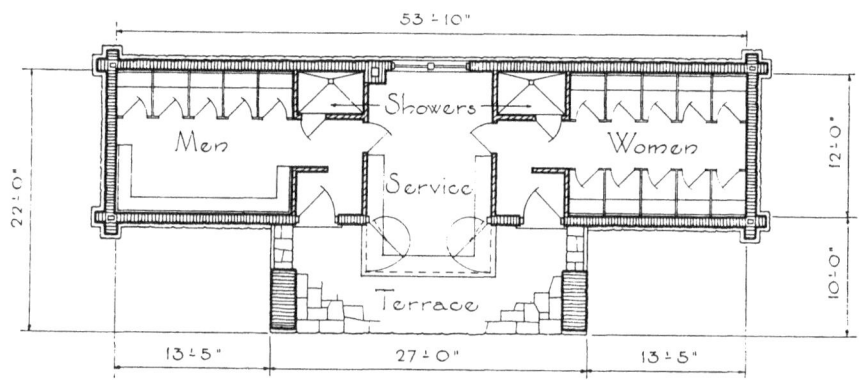

Deception Pass State Park – Washington

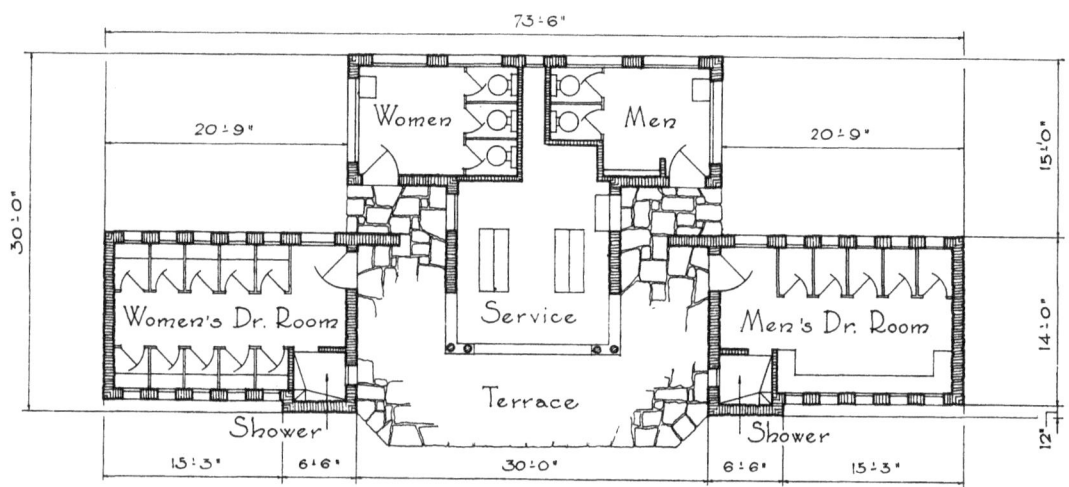

Deception Pass State Park – Washington

Scale 1/16" = 1'-0"

Plate II H–8 →›› BATHHOUSES AND DEPENDENCIES

Here is a bathhouse so miniature that to provide for the rental of bathing suits and towels and an attendant for the task would virtually amount to 100 percent subsidy. In such cases the control feature is very properly omitted. The abbreviated plan arrangement is simple, compact, and altogether reasonable. Dressing rooms are unroofed. The exterior is pleasing notwithstanding the fact that the view indicates that clean-up of the site was not completed.

Bathhouse, Heyburn State Park, Idaho

The small bathhouse has been well studied in the parks of the State of Washington. This one makes use of open-air dressing rooms, roofed only over the compartments. Note the simple, practical plan combining minor food concession without interference with the bathhouse function. The disposition, unfortunately general, to litter concessions with advertising signs is here evidenced. Behind the signs there will be found a very attractive building.

Bathhouse, Deception Pass State Park, Washington

In this example principal variation from the preceding is the addition of comfort stations accessible both to patrons of the bathhouse and to nonpatrons. Thus are what might have been three or four small buildings assembled into one to good advantage. Note that the dressing rooms are roofed, that the men's dressing room provides some private compartments, and that excellent supervisory control of all units is possible from the attendant's station.

Bathhouse, Deception Pass State Park, Washington

BATHHOUSES AND DEPENDENCIES **«** Plate II H-9

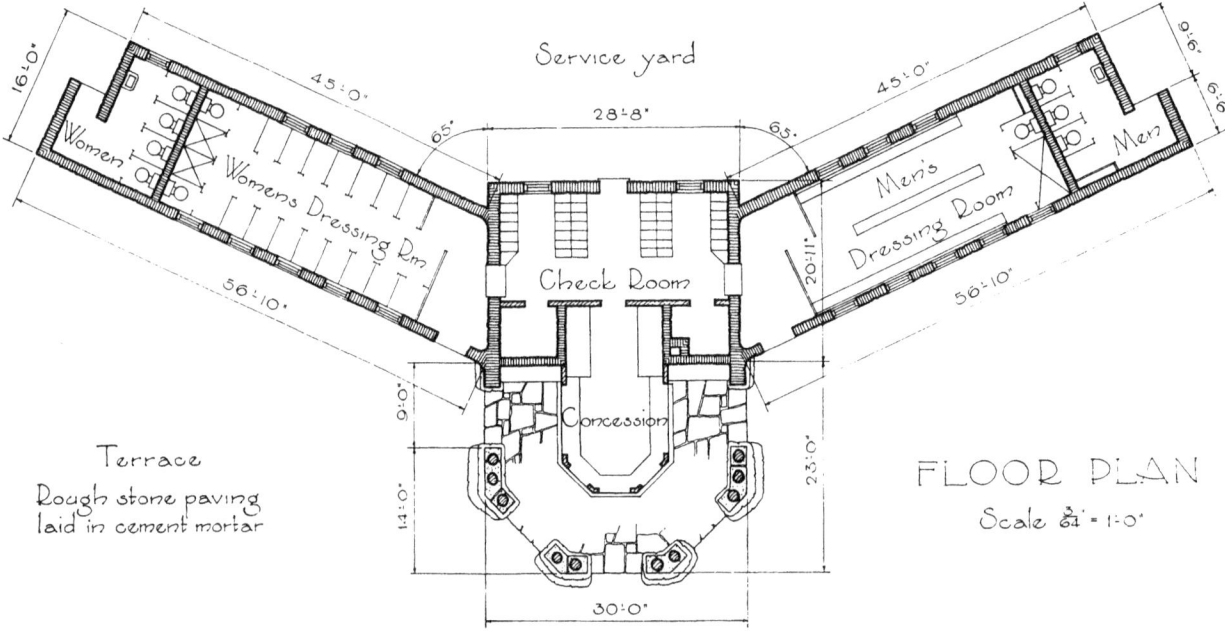

Bathhouse, Boiling Springs State Park, Oklahoma

To the requisite structural elements of a park bathhouse, here are added refreshment concession and comfort stations in an out-of-the-ordinary plan having splayed wings. These house the dressing rooms which are unroofed. There is wise planning for one-man attendance of both checkroom and secondary concession when patronage is light. The sheltered standing room for patrons of the refreshment stand is desirably ample. There is sturdy park character in the architecture of the building.

138

Plate II H-10 →›› BATHHOUSES AND DEPENDENCIES

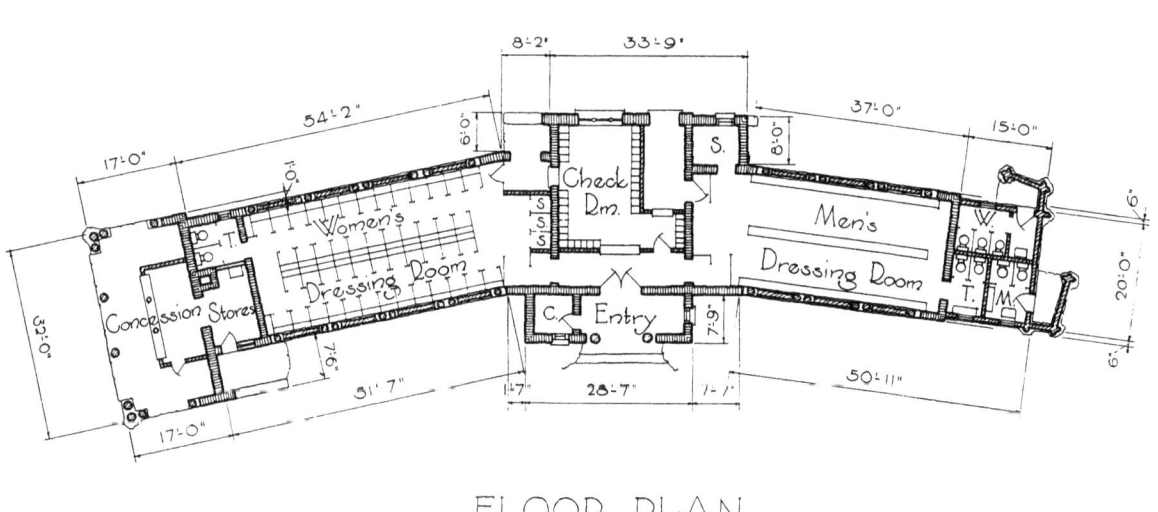

Bathhouse, Robbers Cave State Park, Oklahoma

FLOOR PLAN
Scale 1/32" = 1'-0"

In this multi-purpose building, the principal feature of which is dressing facilities for bathers, stone and log construction are combined to an agreeably vigorous result. Here is proof of the pleasing informality to be obtained in a park building if symmetry and rectangularity are avoided. Entrances and exits and supervisory control over both are organized exceptionally well in a small space. Secondary facilities of this structure are a small food concession and toilets accessible to the general public.

139

BATHHOUSES AND DEPENDENCIES

Plate II H–11

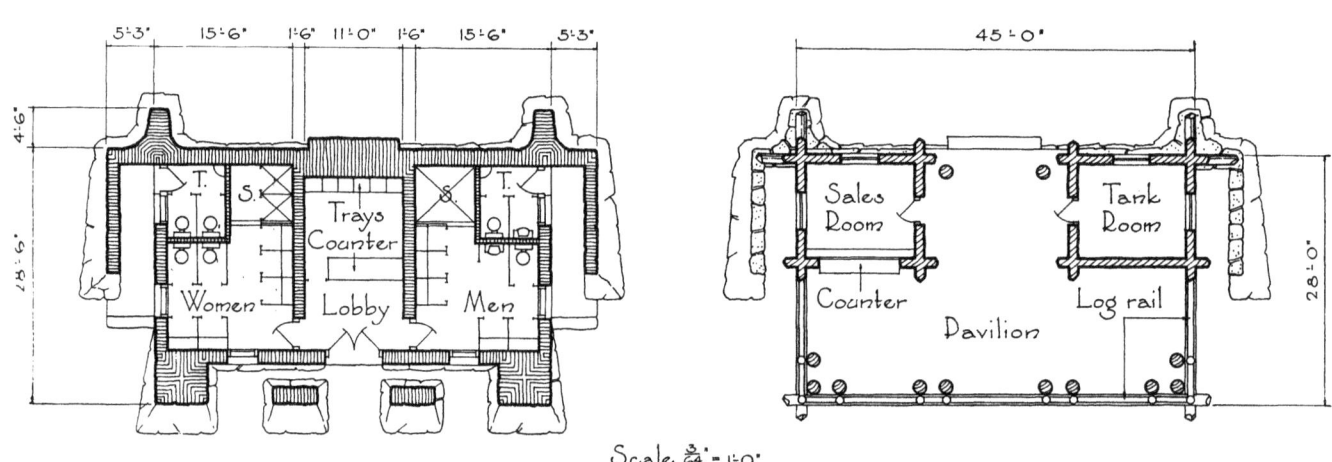

Bathhouse and Shelter, Crowley's Ridge State Park, Arkansas

GROUND FLOOR PLAN

FIRST FLOOR PLAN

Here is no pinchpenny employment of rock and logs. Both materials are happily scaled to the mass and to each other. The plans indicate the lower floor devoted to toilet facilities and dressing rooms for bathers, the upper floor to shelter, concession space, and tank room. In hillside structures there is likely to be insufficient light and ventilation for the rooms of the lower level.

Plate II H–12   BATHHOUSES AND DEPENDENCIES

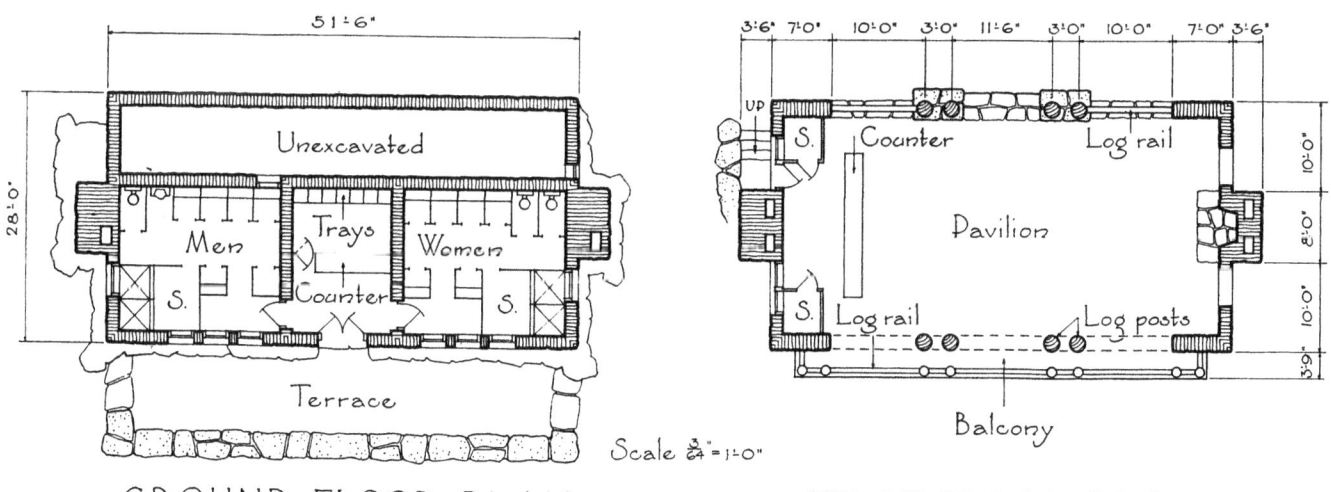

Bathhouse and Shelter, Petit Jean State Park, Arkansas

GROUND FLOOR PLAN   FIRST FLOOR PLAN

Apology for the presence in a natural park of a structure so appealing as this need not be profuse. Possibly the building, as here presented, is a triumph that the designer must share with the photographer. If aesthetic shortcomings exist, the quality of the photograph blinds us to them. Complete harmony with surroundings and a primitive informality are noteworthy. Steep slope makes both shelter above and bathhouse facilities beneath accessible from grade levels.

141

| BATHHOUSES AND DEPENDENCIES | *Plate* II H–13 |

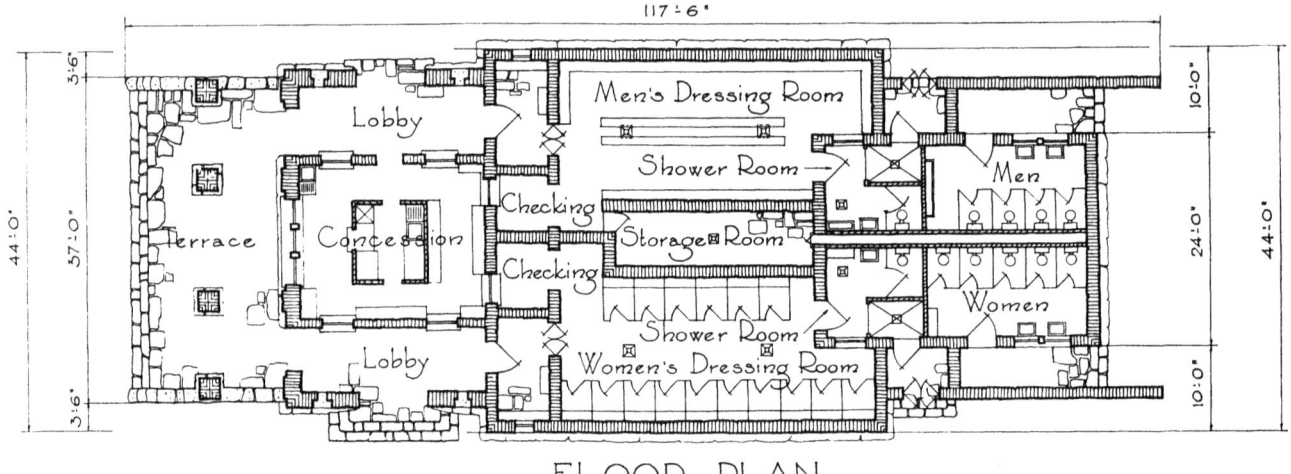

Bathhouse, Bonham State Park, Texas

FLOOR PLAN
Scale 2/64" = 1'0"

A most excellent example of a small park bathhouse that acknowledges the logic, economy, and hygiene of unroofed dressing space. The arrangement of toilet facilities for the use of the general public is such that conflict with the circulation of the bathers is avoided, yet centralization of all plumbing is well accomplished. Working space for the concessionaire's secondary activity—selling soft drinks and the like—is cleverly concentrated and well out of view. In all details of arrangement and architectural treatment this building is deserving of close study.

Plate II H-14 　　　　　　　　　　　　　⇶ BATHHOUSES AND DEPENDENCIES

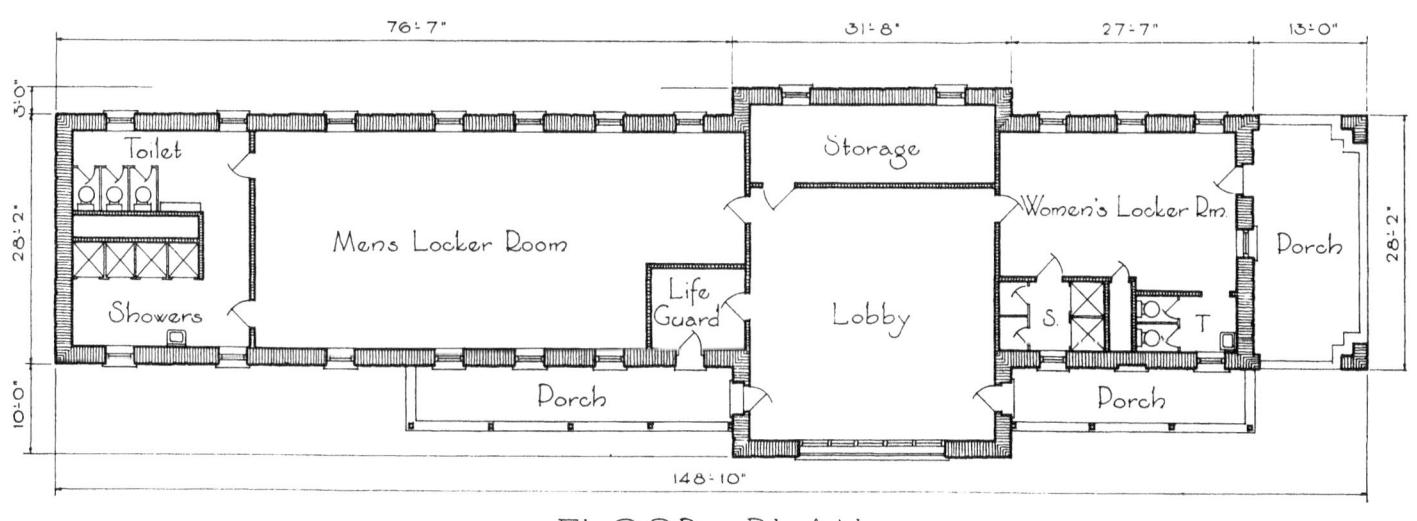

Bathhouse, Delafield Pond, West Point Military Reservation

FLOOR PLAN
Scale ⅛" = 1'-0"

A bathhouse of sophisticated appearance and considerable size interpreted in streamlined colonial which sweepingly eliminates all surplus moldings. A room for a lifeguard, a feature not included in the plans hitherto shown, is provided. The huge window guarantees a well-lighted lounge. Various details contribute to a beach club atmosphere, by no means inappropriate to park bathhouses in some locations.

BATHHOUSES AND DEPENDENCIES

Plate II H-15

Bathhouse - Saltwater State Park - Washington

Here is another of those manifestations of the tremendous character possible in a simple structure by reason of sheer competence in the employment of inexpensive materials. The vigorous scale is more the result of studied effort than it is the actual bulk of the material used. The bold water table and other details of complementary scale are admirable

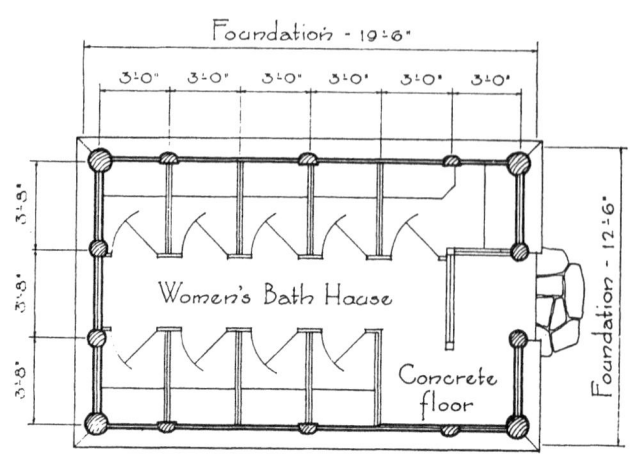

FLOOR PLAN

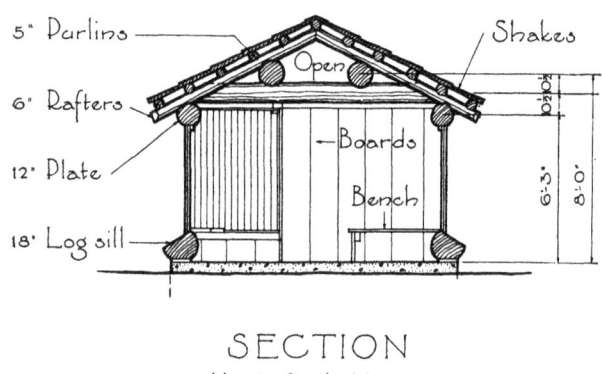

SECTION
Men's Bath House

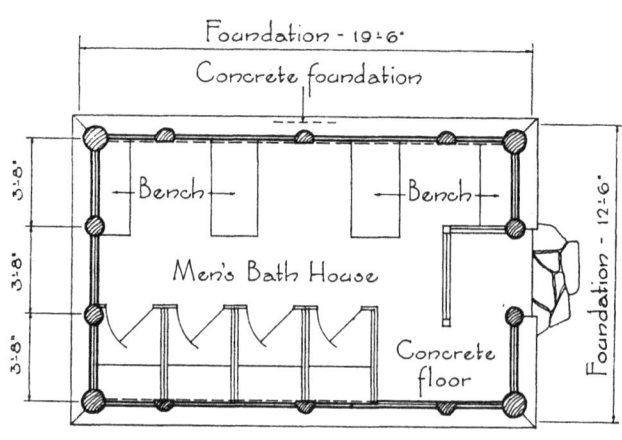

FLOOR PLAN

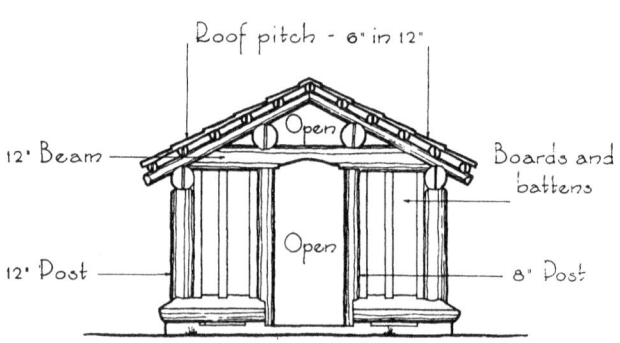

FRONT ELEVATION

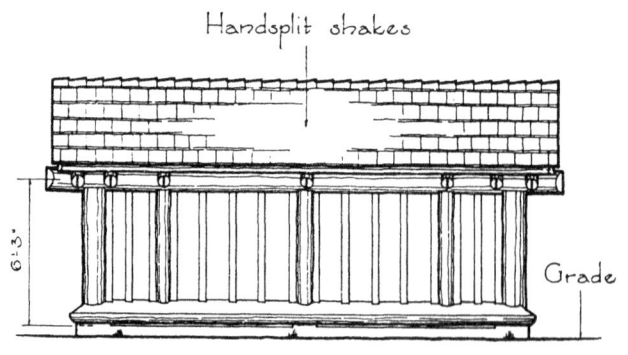

SIDE ELEVATION

Scale ⅛" = 1'-0"

144

BOATHOUSES AND DEPENDENCIES

Boathouses which do not incorporate other park facilities are the exception rather than the rule. Structural facilities providing for boating and bathing are so often housed under one roof, resulting in a combination building designated a water-front building, that two separate classifications here may seem unwarranted.

The boathouse proper implies space allocation for the storage of boats, for their painting and repair, and lockers for motors, oars, paddles, and other boating gear, as well as the effects of the boaters while they are on the water. Inclusion of lounge, office space, and shower and toilet rooms depends upon the elaborateness of conception of the boathouse and its remoteness from such facilities elsewhere provided in the park. Sometimes linked with the boathouse is a shelter, effecting increased usefulness to the boating public.

In no other park building is the foundation of such importance as in the boathouse. It can be only as long-lived as its substructure, and the hazards of high water and swift current and the threat from ice in northerly climates should be appraised and guarded against in construction. In the boathouse there is no virtue in economical construction below the high water level.

On a lake or river of widely fluctuating water level, due to tide or flood conditions, the boathouse is often built out from the shore or bank so that it is usable at low water stage and is reached by a runway from the high water shore line.

Some form of landing or dock is usually auxiliary to the boathouse. This may extend out to deep water to permit the mooring of larger craft, or merely to reach beyond the shore line at low water. Again, the landing may be more useful as a platform paralleling the boathouse on the water-front side. Especially is this desirable where canoes must be pulled out of the water and berthed under cover when not in use. Where the water stage is variable within suitably narrow limitations, such a dock or incline is often hinged to the boathouse structure and its outer edge is permitted to float, so that the inclination changes with the rise and fall of the water. Too wide a variation in water level will naturally preclude the use of such a landing. A smooth, steep incline, when drenched with water, offers uncertain footing to those straining to haul a heavy boat ashore. Rollers for skidding the boats and cleats for a firm foothold are especially useful in connection with such landings. Another provision to meet the exigencies of a changing water level is a stepped landing.

In instances of broad shallow beaches and varying shore line, a floating dock for mooring boats may be the best solution. Such a facility may or may not incorporate slips for small craft. Floated by means of logs, kegs, or other buoyage, it is connected with the shore by a runway. There is the advantage of mobility, for such a pier can be shifted about as conditions may require. Secure anchorage is vital to a landing of this type.

It is highly desirable to remove canoes from the water when not in actual use, and to store them indoors. It is usual to provide racks three tiers high for this purpose. The equivalent of barn doors on the water side of the boathouse gives the fullest possible opening to the platform or incline. The moving of canoes in and out with a minimum of damage to them is made possible by such an arrangement. Rowboats, other than delicate racing shells, are customarily kept in the water during their season of use and are berthed under shelter only out of season. Slips for each rowboat are, of course, the ideal provision.

The floors of the boathouse proper and of docks, runways, and inclines in connection should be of woods that do not deteriorate rapidly when subjected to alternate drenching and drying out in the sun. Ample natural ventilation and floor boards spaced well apart will facilitate drying out and check the tendency to rot out quickly.

BOATHOUSES AND DEPENDENCIES

Plate II I–1

Mooring Float

Moran Lake State Park — — — Washington

Here is a solution of the problem of docking small craft where the water level and shore line are variable. The buoyage for the slips is large logs. The runway from the shore, supported on fixed piers, is in sectional units, of which the one adjoining the float inclines with the changes in water level. Thoroughly practical, this example might well have had the aesthetic benefit of something of the character of the swimming float at Lake Guernsey State Park, Wyoming, elsewhere shown herein.

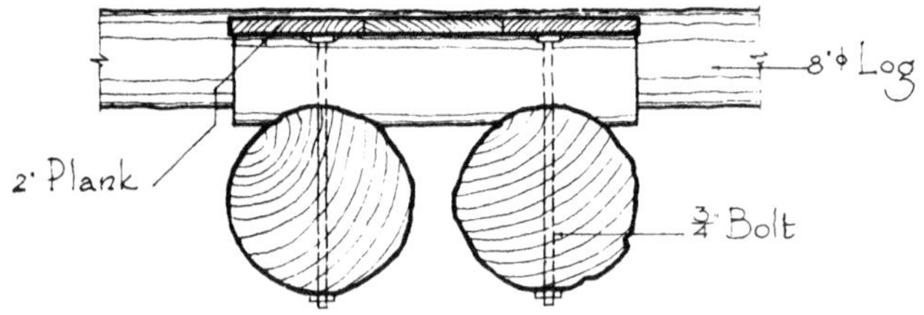

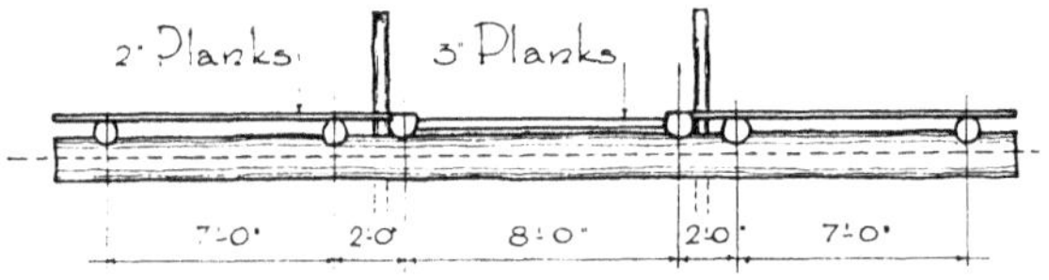

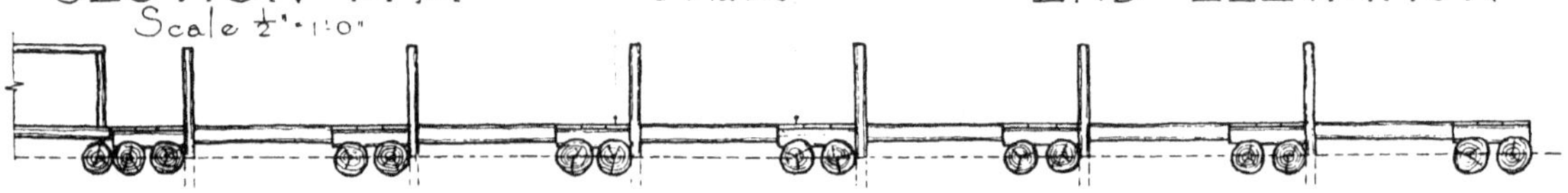

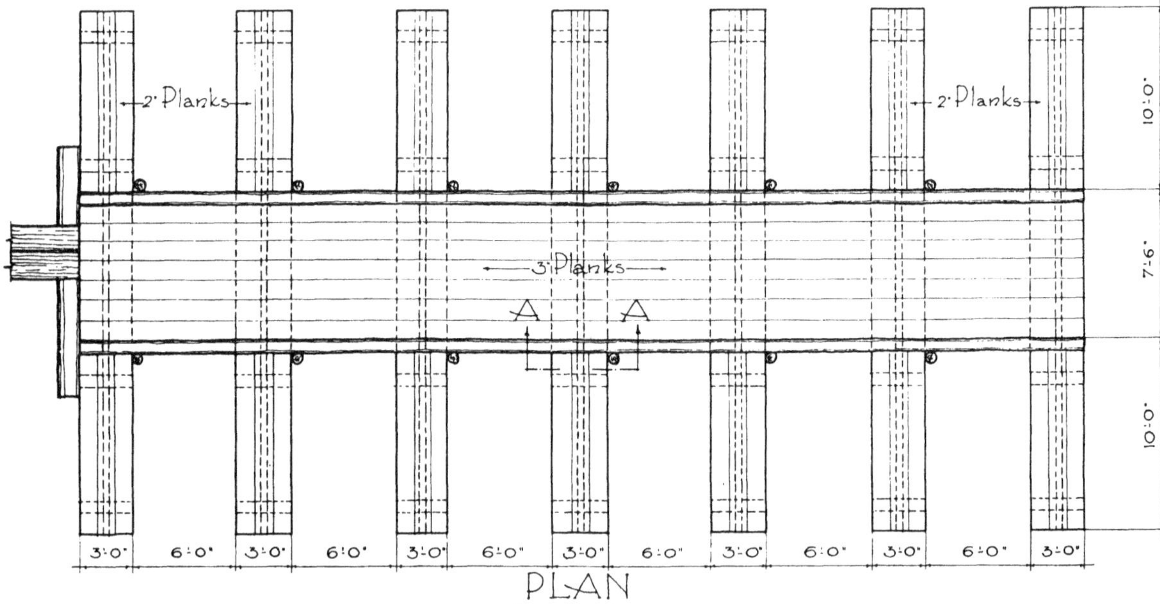

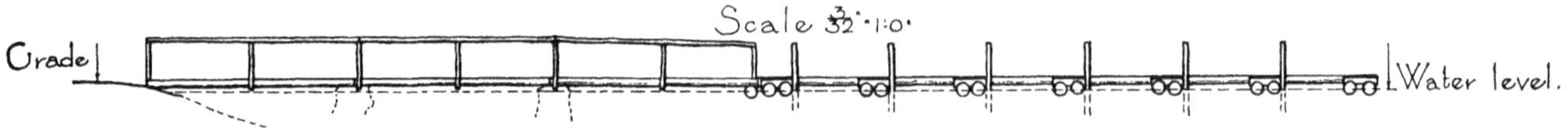

146

Pier - - Gulf State Park - - Alabama

In the deep South a boating and fishing pier with some provision for shelter from a bright sun seems a logical combination. In this example, the solution is simple and pleasing. The hewing of the timbers of the superstructure and the resulting softening of line and surface contribute much to the quality achieved.

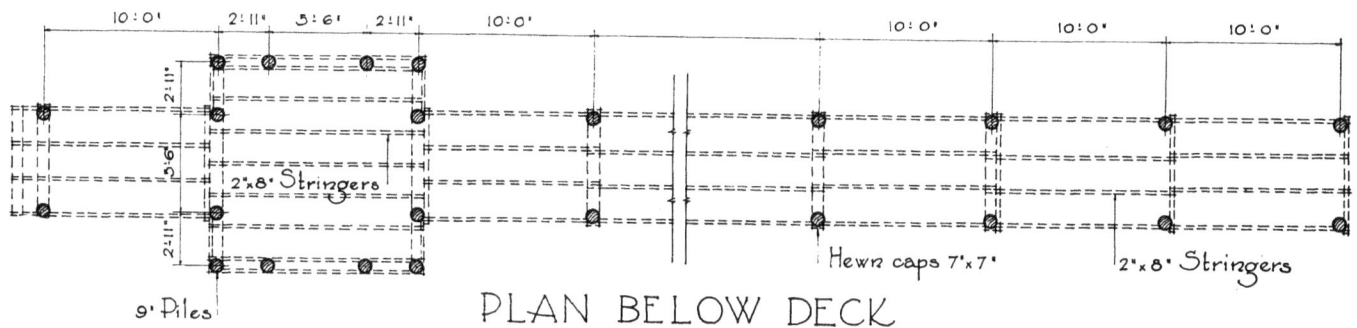

PLAN BELOW DECK

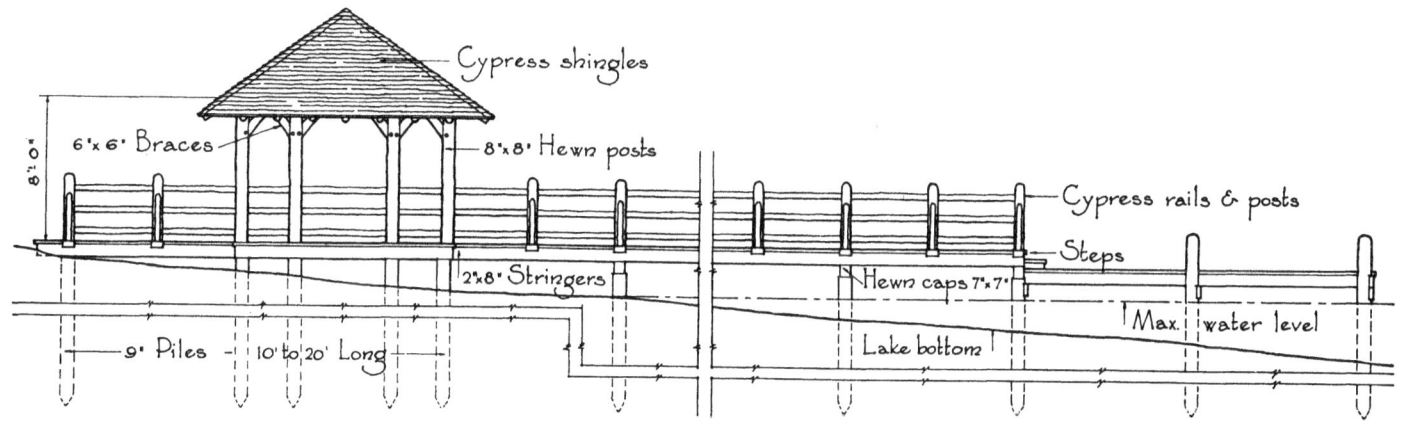

SIDE ELEVATION

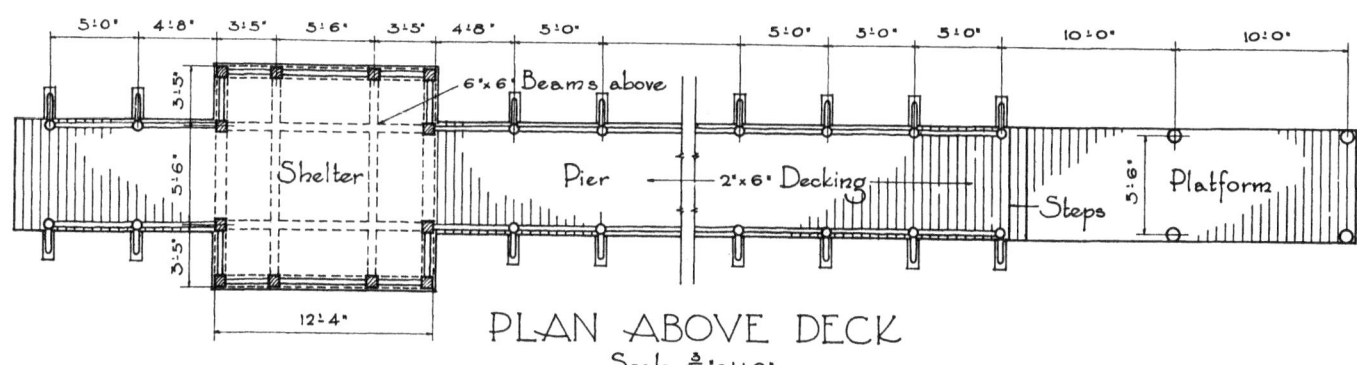

PLAN ABOVE DECK
Scale 3/32" = 1'-0"

BOATHOUSES AND DEPENDENCIES

Plate II I–3

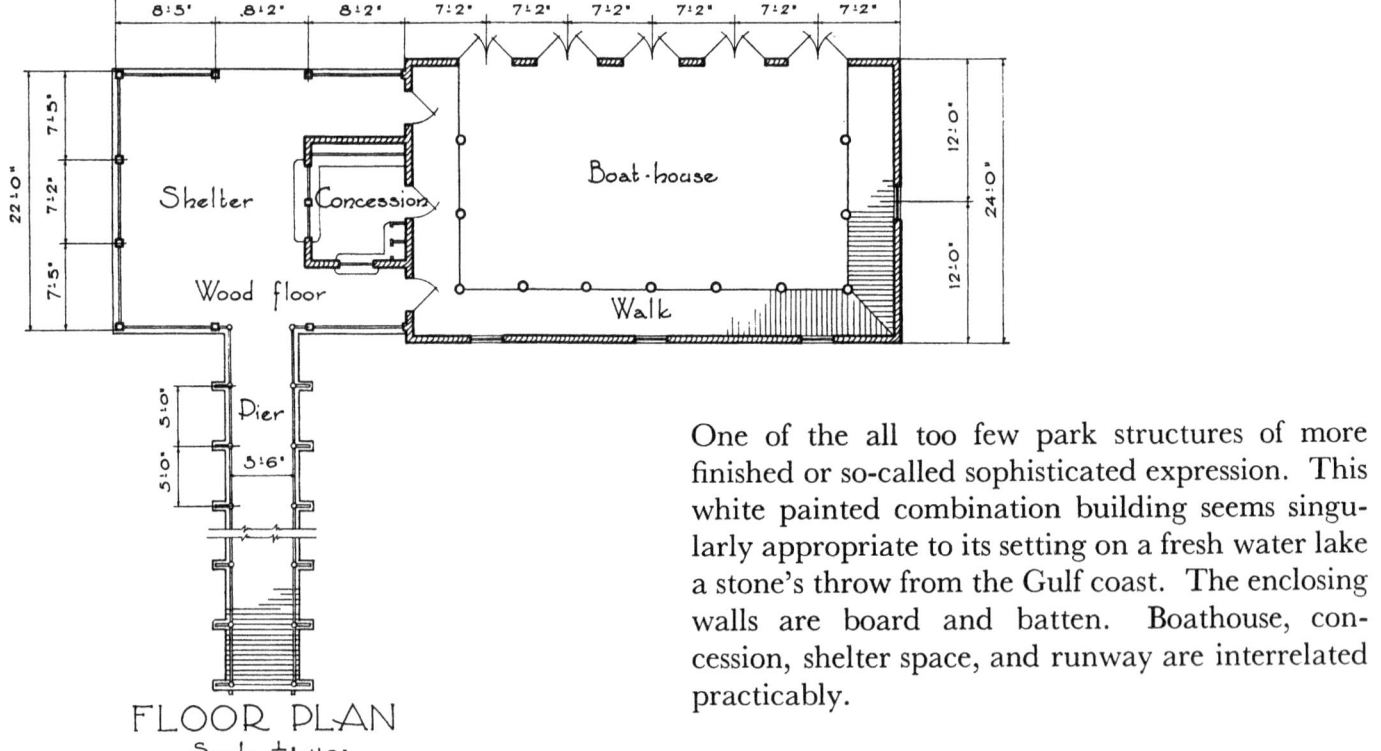

Boathouse, Gulf State Park, Alabama

FLOOR PLAN
Scale 1/16"=1'-0"

One of the all too few park structures of more finished or so-called sophisticated expression. This white painted combination building seems singularly appropriate to its setting on a fresh water lake a stone's throw from the Gulf coast. The enclosing walls are board and batten. Boathouse, concession, shelter space, and runway are interrelated practicably.

Plate II I–4   ⇶ BOATHOUSES AND DEPENDENCIES

Boathouse, Bonham State Park, Texas

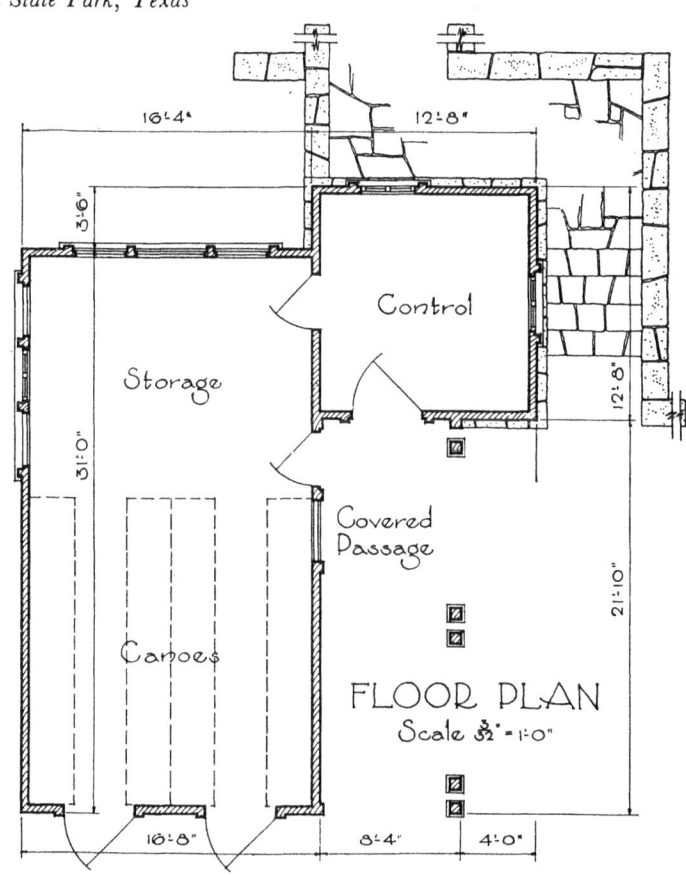

Outstanding and amiable accomplishment in the development of this little park, which cannot pretend to any scenic endowment, is a pervading unity of architectural character in its buildings. The low tower of this boat concession echoes the structure housing the storage tank and pump machinery, the masonry introduced relates it to the stone bathhouse and concession building which can be seen from the boathouse, and the square-hewn posts of the covered passage recall the supports of an open beach shelter pavilion close by. This maintenance of an architectural theme is a monument to the talents and clear vision of the designers.

| BOATHOUSES AND DEPENDENCIES | Plate II I-5 |

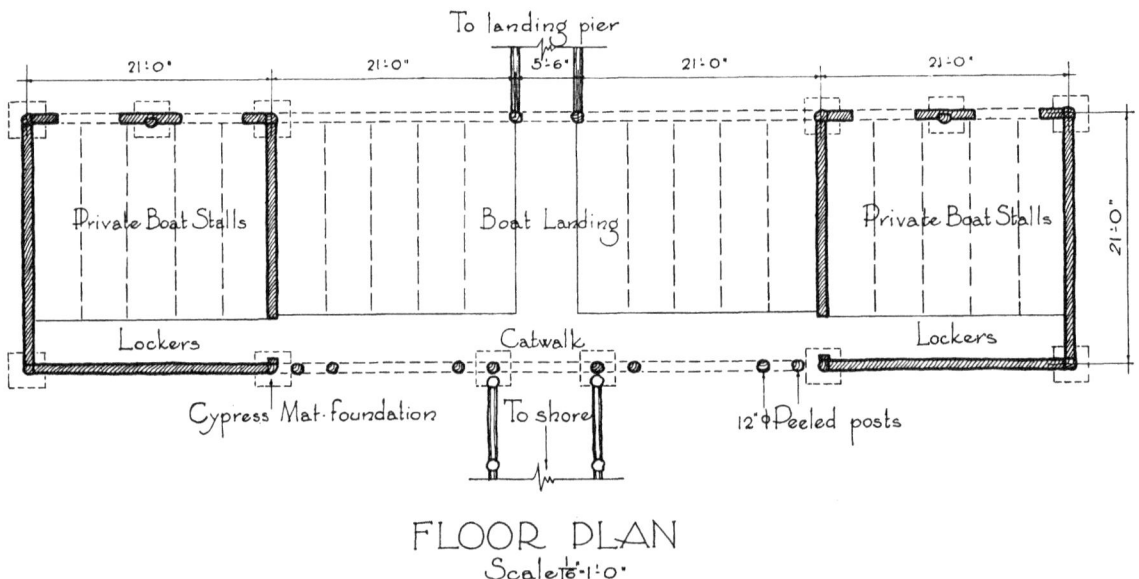

Boathouse, Caddo Lake State Park, Texas

FLOOR PLAN
Scale ⅛"=1'-0"

This boathouse of log construction meets the conditions of a lake subject to flood stages by the provision of a runway to the high water shore line. Opposite this a landing pier is extended to meet the condition of low water. Both enclosed storage and merely roofed shelter for boats are furnished. The building harmonizes with its wooded location. Masking of the piling by a curtain wall of vertical poles or slabs extending well below the water level gives a substantial appearance to the substructure.

150

Plate II I–6 ⇛ BOATHOUSES AND DEPENDENCIES

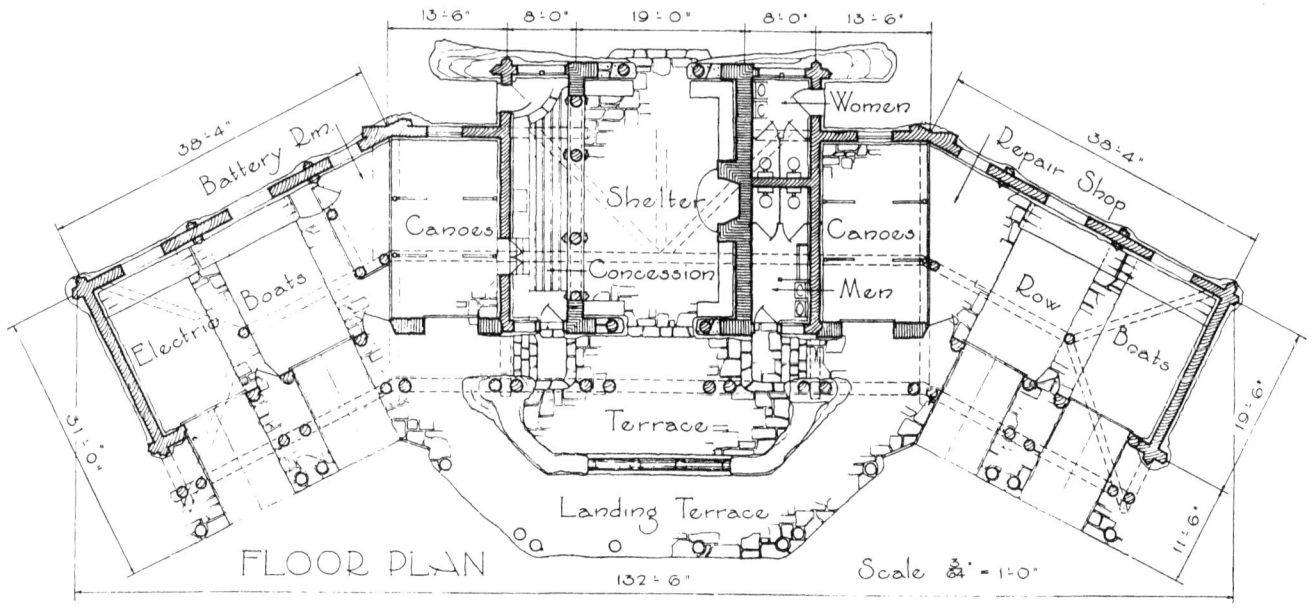

Boathouse, Mohawk Metropolitan Park, Tulsa, Oklahoma

Here a very free and rugged rock masonry and a vigorous log construction, novel in many structural details, are combined to produce a very ambitious and very interesting building. Its location is on a lagoon in a large metropolitan park. It will be noted that shelter, food concession, toilet facilities, and overlook and landing terraces are provided in addition to storage for three kinds of watercraft.

BOATHOUSES AND DEPENDENCIES Plate II I–7

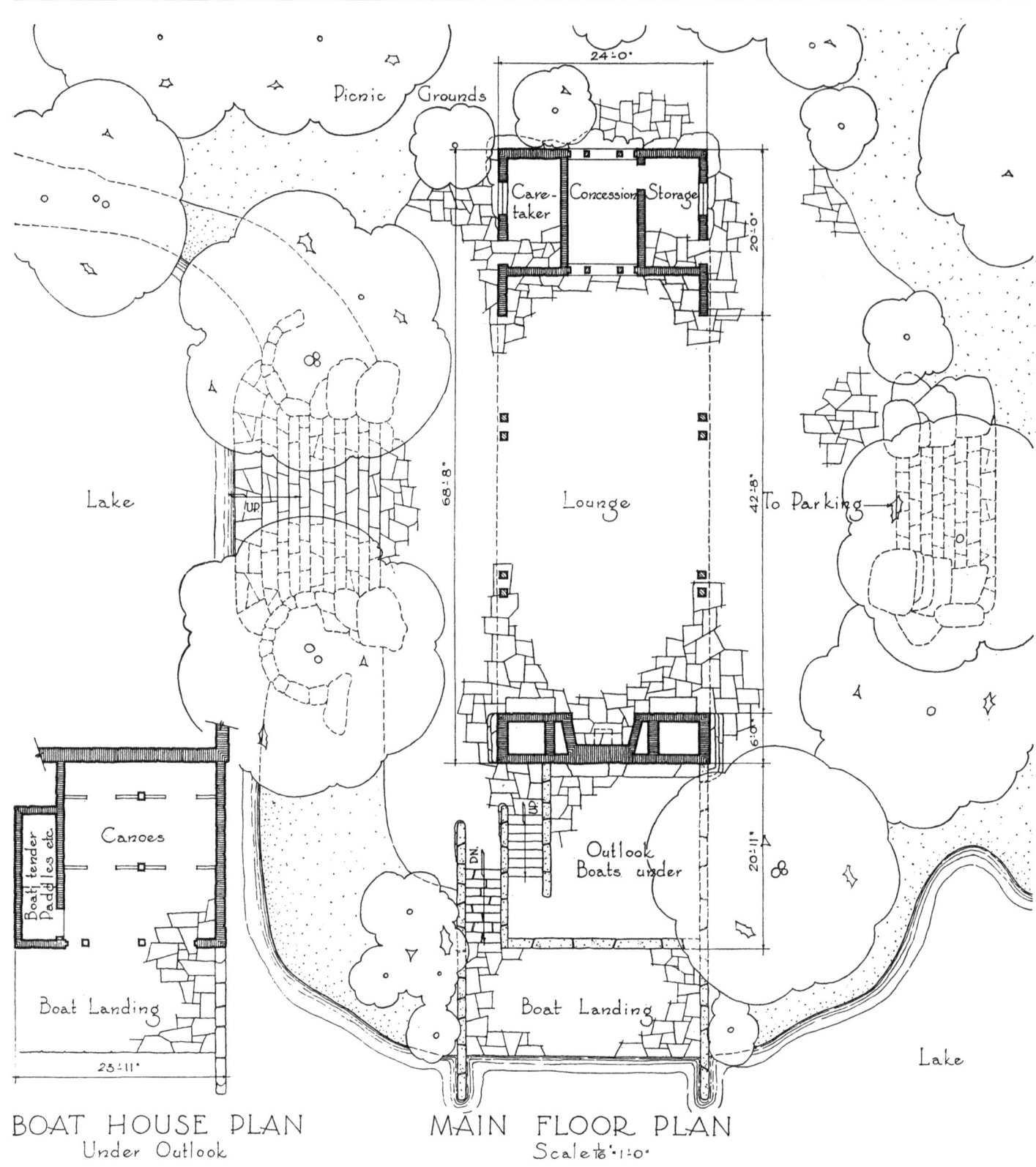

BOAT HOUSE PLAN
Under Outlook

MAIN FLOOR PLAN
Scale ⅛"=1'-0"

Boathouse and Refectory.
Perry Lake — — — — — Oklahoma

An interpretation of sturdy park architecture that turns its back on the tight little patterns of precedent to the attainment of considerable distinction. Its long low lines, massive dominant chimney, the structurally forthright masonry and the broad stone steps that closely link the structure with the environs—all are factors that inspire admiration. The employment of several levels shows a nice attention to the requirements of site.

152

Plate II I-8   ⇶ BOATHOUSES AND DEPENDENCIES

Perry Lake Metropolitan Park, Oklahoma

Perry Lake Metropolitan Park, Oklahoma

BOATHOUSES AND DEPENDENCIES

Plate II I-9

Parvin State Park, New Jersey

Mohawk Metropolitan Park, Tulsa, Oklahoma

Lake Okmulgee State Park, Oklahoma

BOATING—MISCELLANEOUS ACCESSORIES

Here are illustrated several boat landings in character with natural park areas. The stepped levels of the example at Lake Okmulgee indicate a solution of the problem of a landing where the water level fluctuates widely. Below is a view of a facility for hauling boats ashore at Woahink Lake State Park, Oregon, where the bank is somewhat abrupt. One-half the width of the incline is equipped with rollers for skidding the boats, the other half is a ramp furnished with cleats to give a foothold to those hauling in the boats. The end of the dock at Itasca State Park is built of log cribbing, rock-filled to withstand ice pressures.

Itasca State Park, Minnesota

Woahink Lake State Park, Oregon

MISCELLANEOUS SPORTS STRUCTURES

WATER SPORTS AND HIKING, considering the latter as ranging from strolling at snail's pace and tramping to strenuous mountain climbing, undoubtedly include the more widespread types of active recreation in parks and recreational reserves throughout the country. Yet winter sports, horseback riding, archery, and other minor activities are increasingly in favor in many localities and regions.

Trail and mountain clubs have popularized hiking as an active sport along the Appalachian Trail from Maine to Georgia, in the Northeast, Middle West, Rocky Mountains, and along the Pacific Crest Trail from Canada to Mexico. Structures in facilitation of hiking are not various. Open-front lean-to shelters of Adirondack type and closed cabins, where winter use is expected, located easy tramping distances apart on blazed and well-marked trails, and supplemented with campstoves or picnic fireplaces, safe water supply, and simple latrines, make up the full complement. Suitable examples of these structural needs will be found under other sections of this publication.

In the northern and mountainous sections with cold climates, the winter sports of speed and figure skating, ice hockey, curling, and other ice games, ski running and ski jumping, snowshoeing, coasting, tobogganing, bobsledding, and sleighing, among others, are attracting more and more public interest each year. Before undertaking to meet this interest with special facilities, careful studies of snow and temperature conditions in each area of proposed development should be made to determine whether the probable amount of use of such facilities in a short season will warrant the expense of providing them. Except where the expense of importing snow or making artificial outdoor ice rinks can be justified by probable use, it will be feasible to provide these facilities only in areas where snow remains on the ground to a depth of at least six inches, and the temperature stays below freezing through more than 30 days— not necessarily consecutive—during the winter. In fortunate regions such as the West coast where it is possible to enjoy both summer and winter sports throughout the year, there will be other sports competing for interest and attention.

The increasing trek of winter sports enthusiasts by auto, "snow train", and "snow bus" to suitable terrain poses the question of the desirability of winter sports development in those parks, adequate in size and terrain, which are accessible to population centers. It is perhaps needless to say that facilities for winter use, where it is undertaken to provide them, should be coordinated as far as possible with the year-round recreational development of the region, and summer and winter use needs should be combined wherever feasible.

SPECIAL USE STRUCTURES for winter sports activities are necessary or often desirable for the following: tobogganing, coasting, ski jumping, and bobsledding.

Opportunities for coasting may be provided on flat playgrounds by the erection of wooden platforms with short runways of sufficient width to be safe and adequate.

Toboggan slides may be built with snow banks, but they are not completely safe and satisfactory without a specially constructed wooden chute which is slightly wider than a toboggan. This troughlike chute frequently starts from a trestle-built platform and extends down the slope and preferably across most of the level out-run. Toboggan slides may be built singly or in batteries.

Where slides are intensively used, it becomes necessary to time and control the take-off of the sleds and toboggans to avoid accidents. There will always be those who seek to pile thrill upon thrill by stunting—riding backwards or standing up— and the hazards this creates for the orthodox participants and the innocent bystanders, usually grouped

MISCELLANEOUS SPORTS STRUCTURES

at the foot of the slides, can only be checked by having a dispatcher in attendance.

So popular are the toboggan slides of one winter sports area in the Cook County Forest Preserve District that a battery of three slides is now being expanded to six slides, and the proper timing and release of the toboggans is a major consideration of the expansion program. Each slide will have a gate at its take-off. A control tower will be erected above these. Stationed in this tower, an attendant will have a clear view of all slides and toboggans awaiting take-off, and only when the run is clear and all occupants of a waiting toboggan are properly seated, will the gate which will release that toboggan be dropped by operation of a lever. Immediately the toboggan has got away, another shift of the lever will raise the gate to its shut position to hold the next toboggan in check until the way is clear.

A drop gate is preferable to an overhead gate because the latter would obstruct the dispatcher's view of the slide and create one more hazard for the tobogganers in the mishap of a gate dropping to a shut position before the toboggan had completely cleared. It has been pointed out that these gates must be fairly heavy and solid and the start of the runs made otherwise difficult of access to discourage youngsters with bicycles and roller skates from tempting fate by inventing an other-seasonal use for this winter sports facility.

From Germany, Cook County has borrowed the idea of earthen slides. Down a hillside a shallow swale, 12 inches below the natural ground level at the center and 30 inches wide, is excavated. The dirt removed is mounded on either side, and the trough and mounds are then rounded and sodded. The construction is simple, being labor entirely with no materials to be purchased. Moreover, slides so constructed modify but little the natural appearance of an area, and in this consideration are in pointed contrast with wooden runs, especially such as must have trestlelike substructures for desired elevation. The latter can be not only disfiguring but very incongruous out of season, and any possible mental suggestion of January temperatures that these trestlelike structures might invoke in a sun-baked July is hardly compensatory.

The first earthen trough slides built in the Chicago metropolitan area were straight runs. Imagination soon got to work, and simple curves were introduced. These proved so popular that all slides subsequently constructed have banked curves—with variations. The engineer supervising maintenance in this area states that the thrills provided increase as the square of the variations—but has not to date submitted mathematical calculations to prove this interesting formula.

Supervision of the use of these earthen slides is necessary only on occasions of peak load, and accidents are rare. Maintenance is not a big item. If a snowfall is light or the snow melts away in sunny spots, this kind of slide can be quickly conditioned by the application of a few sprinkling cans of water on a cold night.

IN CONCENTRATED USE AREAS for downhill ski running, various means of uphill conveyance for skiers are becoming more and more common. They are called ski tows, upskis, or ski tramways. The common ski tow consists of an endless cable or rope which is operated, with a grooved drive wheel and with a counter weight to take up the slack, by a housed gasoline or electric motor. Hanging ropes, sometimes with detachable handles, are furnished the skiers who are spaced according to the load that can be carried. The return rope, descending the slope, is usually supported on a series of poles by means of pulleys fastened at an angle.

Ski jumping is a specialized form of the sport comparable to high diving. Although small, so-called natural jumps may be used, the safest course is over a specially constructed jump with scientifically accurate proportions between the in-run, take-off, upper transition curve, landing slope, and lower transition curve to the level out-run. A tower and runway, built of steel and wood penetrated with preservative, are usually necessary to provide a steep enough in-run and to give the jumpers a clear view of the take-off from the top.

Unfortunately, ski jump structures of our acquaintance are entirely lacking in park character. Moreover, since the facility must acknowledge factors which cannot bend in compromise with beauty, the prospect of ski jump structures pleasing in appearance beyond the graceful curve they offer for the eye's satisfaction is a remote one. Inasmuch

MISCELLANEOUS SPORTS STRUCTURES

as the design of ski jumps is admittedly a science and not an art, no jump being known which gestures in the direction of the latter, this publication, concerned largely with the consideration of park character, attempts no details of such structures in the plates presented. Doubtless the growth of interest in winter sports will lead eventually to the production of a monograph on facilitating structures, which will be a field for engineering rather than architectural exploration.

Because bobsledding requires a combination of extensive hilly terrain and special structural facilities, a bobsled run should be scientifically laid out according to engineering specifications on a carefully selected terrain. It should have control points at fairly frequent intervals and a telephone line for quick communication.

Areas intensively used for skating, ice games, skiing, and tobogganing should be provided with a heated shelter and refreshment building, sanitary facilities, supply of drinking water, hospital cot, emergency outfit with first aid kit, and either ski stretcher or toboggan. Where all major forms of winter sports may be enjoyed in the same area, a large winter sports lodge may be needed. Such a structure will have lounging room, kitchen, men's and women's toilet rooms, custodian's quarters or office, heated waxing room for skiers, cold room for racks and lockers, and connecting wooden runway to the ice for skaters. Benches, fireplaces, and possibly even picnic facilities may be added. Flood lighting for night use of ski practice slopes, skating rinks, and toboggan slides is usually desirable. Adequate space for the parking of automobiles, accessible over ploughed roads, should be provided near the various use facilities.

For intensive use areas limited to skating and ice games, a commodious warming shelter and refreshment building, located as close to the ice as possible and equipped with sanitary facilities, may be sufficient. Downhill skiing areas may be provided with a small skiers' lodge, having a lounging room, kitchen, and first aid room with sanitary facilities, or an adjacent latrine building, at a trail head easily accessible by automobile. Areas of this kind should at least have closed shelters at the bottom of all trails and also at the top of those over half a mile in length. Each shelter should be accompanied by sanitary facilities, emergency first aid outfits, and, if possible, a supply of drinking water.

The open fronts of Adirondack-type lean-to shelters may be boarded up, with door and window space provided, so that they will give protection from the winter winds for short stop-overs. For those who enjoy winter camping and mountaineering, a series of cabins may be so strategically located in remote areas as to offer convenient overnight shelter on cross country routes for touring skiers and snowshoers. Many foot and horse trails will provide suitable travel ways, except where steep gradients make necessary more winding alternate sections or bypasses for downhill skiing.

Since crowds will always congregate at ski meets, snow fests, winter frolics, and carnivals, adequate provision must be made for handling them on those special occasions. New facilities for winter sports use which are projected for the most suitable locations, based on demand, snow and ice conditions, terrain, exposure, and accessibility, should not be built until provision is made for their proper maintenance and supervision.

HORSEBACK RIDING is another activity which is gaining an enthusiastic following in parks. A stable for the riding horses is the primary structural facility required. It may be limited to suitable shelter for horses and to space for storing feed and equipment. Quarters for an attendant and an enclosure for exercising the mounts are often made part of it. It may even take on some of the aspects of a riding club with lounge, tack room, locker and dressing rooms, and toilet and shower facilities. In parks that offer extended or overnight trips on horseback, supplementing structural facilities may include shelters and corrals for horses and pack animals at objective points and along the trails. Hitching rails and posts, watering troughs, and mounting blocks may be called for in the intensive use areas.

In building structures to further the sport of riding, it is felt there need be no overstriving for park character if increased cost must result from so doing. There are two reasons to justify this viewpoint. First, appealing as the atmosphere of the stable may be to the horse lover, to the majority it is not an ornament, has no just claim to be treated as such, and both theoretically and actually is properly retired in location in much the same manner as other service buildings and facilities. Second, riding is a sport participated in by a small minority of the great field of park patrons and calls for a sober and sound economy in approach, akin to that prescribed for cabins on public areas.

ARCHERY, AS A GAME, has long been more or less in favor in parks, as elsewhere. The recent twist of the sport into hunting with bow and arrow seems to promise an increase in its popularity. Whether limited to competitive marksmanship over a trail course provided with various targets, or actually a sanctioned hunting of certain wildlife over a designated area, during the lawful hunting season, the only structural need in archery is perhaps a trail shelter. There is a hunters' shelter in Brown County State Park, Indiana, furnished with a fireplace and seats, and pegs for hanging up bows and other gear. It is enclosed on three sides. The open side faces an outdoor grill sized to flatter outrageously an archer's pride in marksmanship. Some are sure to believe that its vast expanse is scaled to the archer's lunch basket rather than his bag. If this is not so, then surely the ardent wildlife conservationists of the Hoosier State should view-with-alarm.

The plates which follow in illustration of miscellaneous sports structures appropriate to natural parks and recreation areas are not many. While the currently great popularity of these comparative newcomers to the field of park recreational offerings calls loudly for a comprehensive showing, the brief period of their acceptance in parks has produced few structures of merit. Furthermore, in many parks, particularly where the preservation of scenic values is the primary claim, conspicuous utilitarian structures are properly barred. It is a matter of regret that the showing is thus limited, and must await the completion of additional developments for a truly comprehensive presentation.

Wood Carving, Ski Lodge, Badger Pass, Yosemite National Park

This carved and painted plaque by Robert Boardman Howard represents the almost legendary father of modern skiing technique, Mathias Zdarski, an Austrian, who in the last part of the nineteenth century evolved the use of ski poles and turning. This development brought to skiing the controlled grace of movement of the modern technique.

Plate II J-1 　　　　　　　　　　　　　　»» MISCELLANEOUS SPORTS STRUCTURES

Skaters' Shelter, Blue Hills Reservation, Massachusetts

The essentials of a winter use shelter are incorporated in this building—large warming room, food concession, and toilet facilities. In a shelter projected for skaters' use, a runway or ramp from the shelter level to the ice surface is usually preferred to the steps provided in this instance. Simple form and low cost materials have produced results altogether pleasing. The raw cut in the rear of the structure to be seen in the photograph cries out for remolding and a naturalizing treatment.

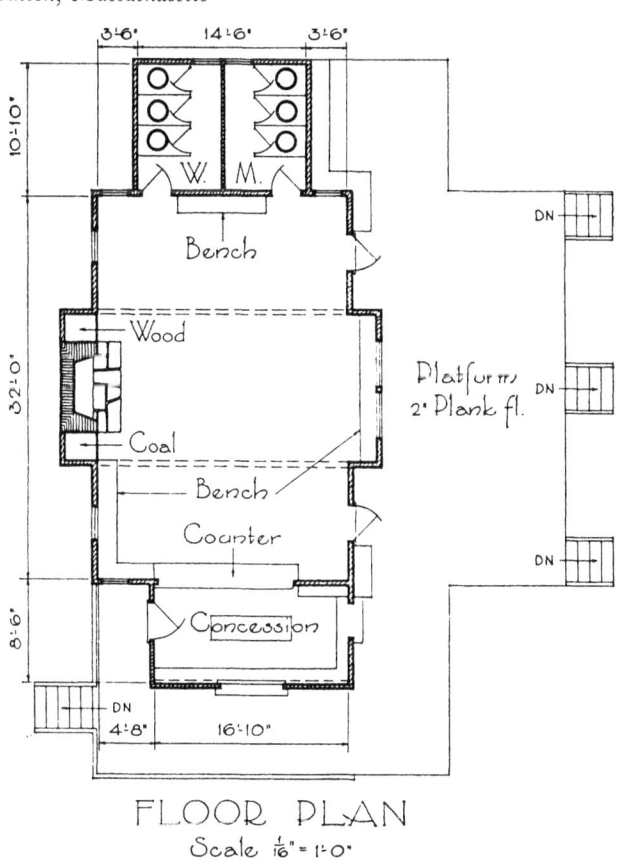

FLOOR PLAN
Scale 1/16" = 1'-0"

MISCELLANEOUS SPORTS STRUCTURES *Plate* II J–2

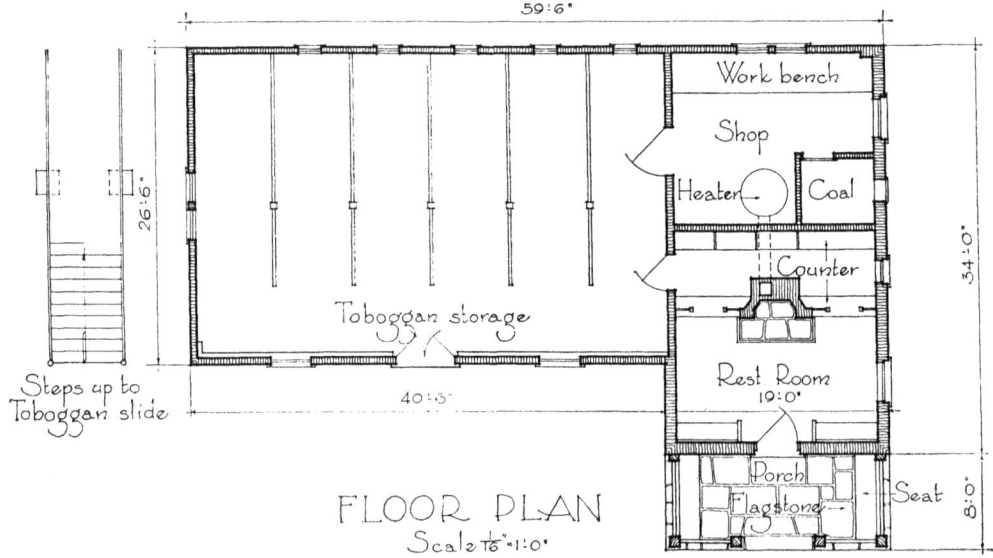

Toboggan House, Beebe Lake, Cornell University, Ithaca, New York

Although actually constructed on a university campus, here is a building both function and character of which are suitable to some of our northern parks. In the main given over to toboggan storage, small lounge space and repair shop are also incorporated. An outside stairway leads up to the slide which can be seen in the rear of the building. The combination of several materials gives interesting informality. J. Lakin Baldridge was the architect.

Plate II J-3   ⇢⇢⇢ MISCELLANEOUS SPORTS STRUCTURES

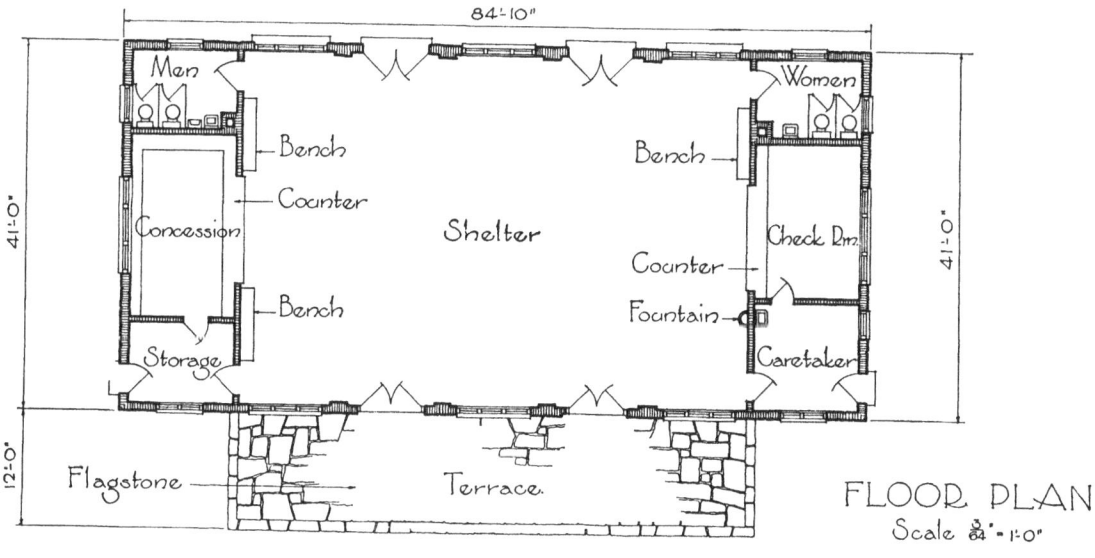

Warming Shelter, Daniel Ryan Woods, Cook County Forest Preserve District, Illinois

A large shelter so located in a metropolitan recreational area that it offers year-round use. On the hill back of it are a low ski-jump structure, a low toboggan-slide structure, and a number of earthen-sled slides. Its terrace overlooks a broad playfield, which in winter serves as runway for the various slides and is flooded in part for skating. In summer the playfield accommodates baseball diamonds. Thus the building serves as warming shelter in winter and picnic shelter in summer.

161

MISCELLANEOUS SPORTS STRUCTURES *Plate* II J-4

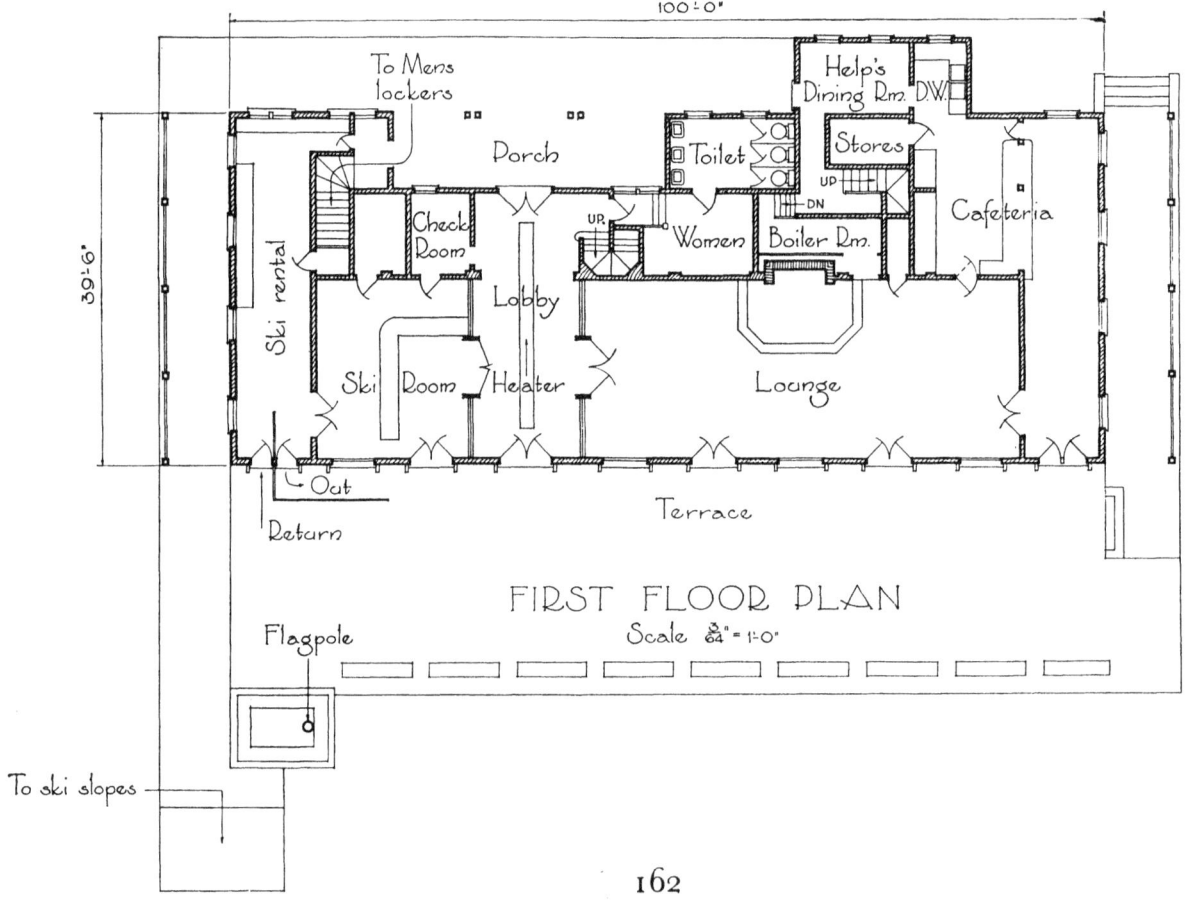

Ski Lodge, Badger Pass, Yosemite National Park

FIRST FLOOR PLAN
Scale 3/64" = 1'-0"

Plate II J–5 →» MISCELLANEOUS SPORTS STRUCTURES

Ski Lodge, Badger Pass, Yosemite National Park

The lay-out shown on the facing page indicates that this lodge specifically serves skiers and onlookers, and that it has no other-seasonal use. Note the lengthy floor heater in the room through which guests arriving and skiers returning from the ski slopes enter to seek the comfort of the lounge and the refreshment of the cafeteria. Note also the ski room with rental and checking space and the broad terrace from which the sports activities may be viewed.

The illustration above shows the facade and terrace facing the sports arena in actual winter use. At the right will be seen a view of the lounge with its highly original fireplace treatment utilizing skier motifs as ornament for the metal hood.

Ski Lodge, Badger Pass, Yosemite National Park

MISCELLANEOUS SPORTS STRUCTURES

Plate II J-6

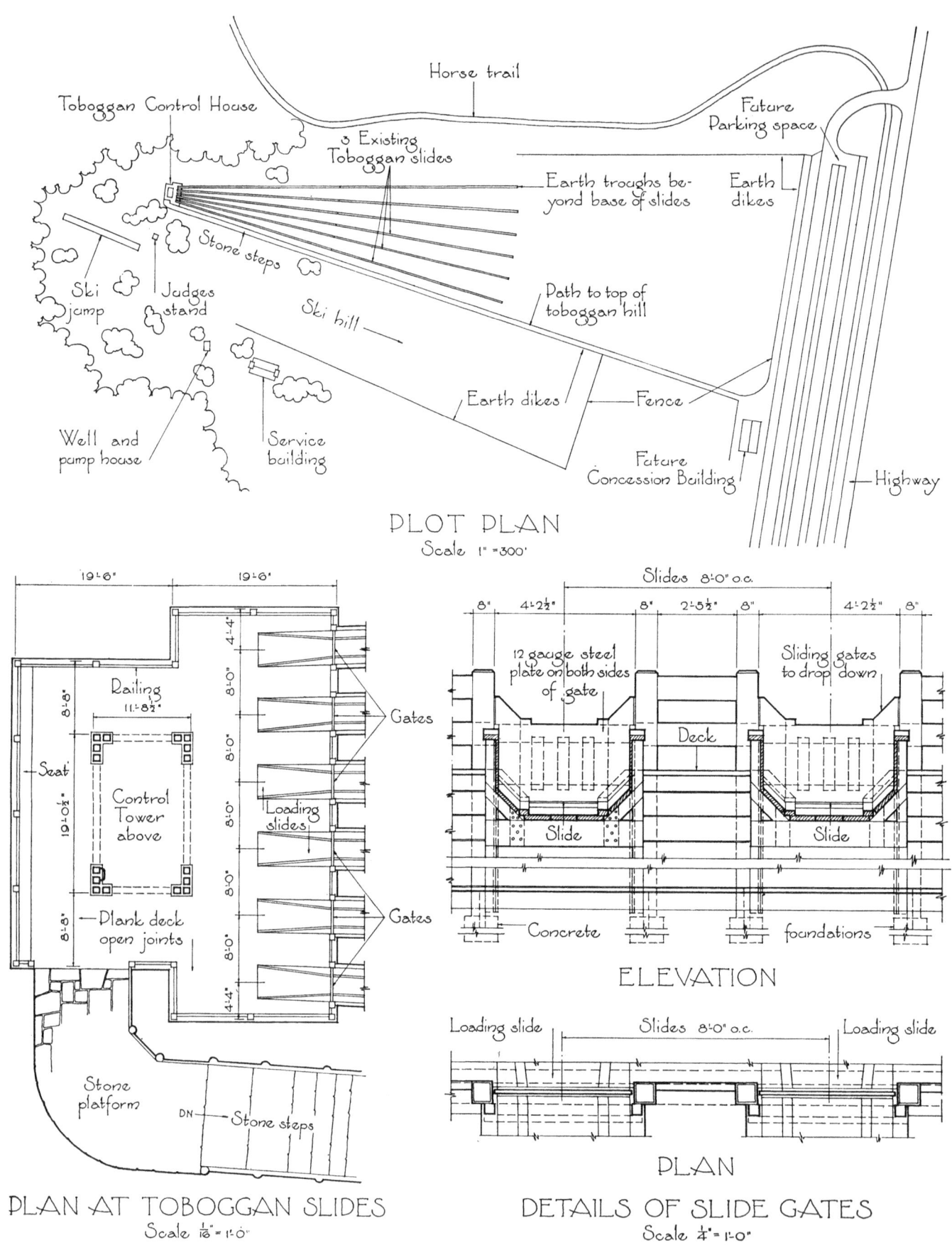

Plate II J–7   ⇉ MISCELLANEOUS SPORTS STRUCTURES

Ski Jumps and Toboggan Slides

Toboggan Slides

WINTER SPORTS FACILITIES, COOK COUNTY FOREST PRESERVE DISTRICT, ILLINOIS

This and the facing page show a winter sports development in the Chicago metropolitan area. The photographs illustrate facilities as these existed until recently. The drawings indicate an enlargement now under way to meet an overtaxing demand for winter sports recreation.

It will be observed that three wooden toboggan slides will be expanded to six, and that an overhead tower for controlling the take-off of toboggans will be added. The drop gates indicated are largely conjectural in detail inasmuch as their final method of operation must be determined by cut-and-fit experimentation on a single gate to assure positive, practical results.

The broad steps leading up to the start of the toboggan slides may be seen in the illustrations. One view shows the relationship of a ski-jump structure to the slides.

Toboggan Slides from above

Steps up to Start of Slides

MISCELLANEOUS SPORTS STRUCTURES

Plate II J-8

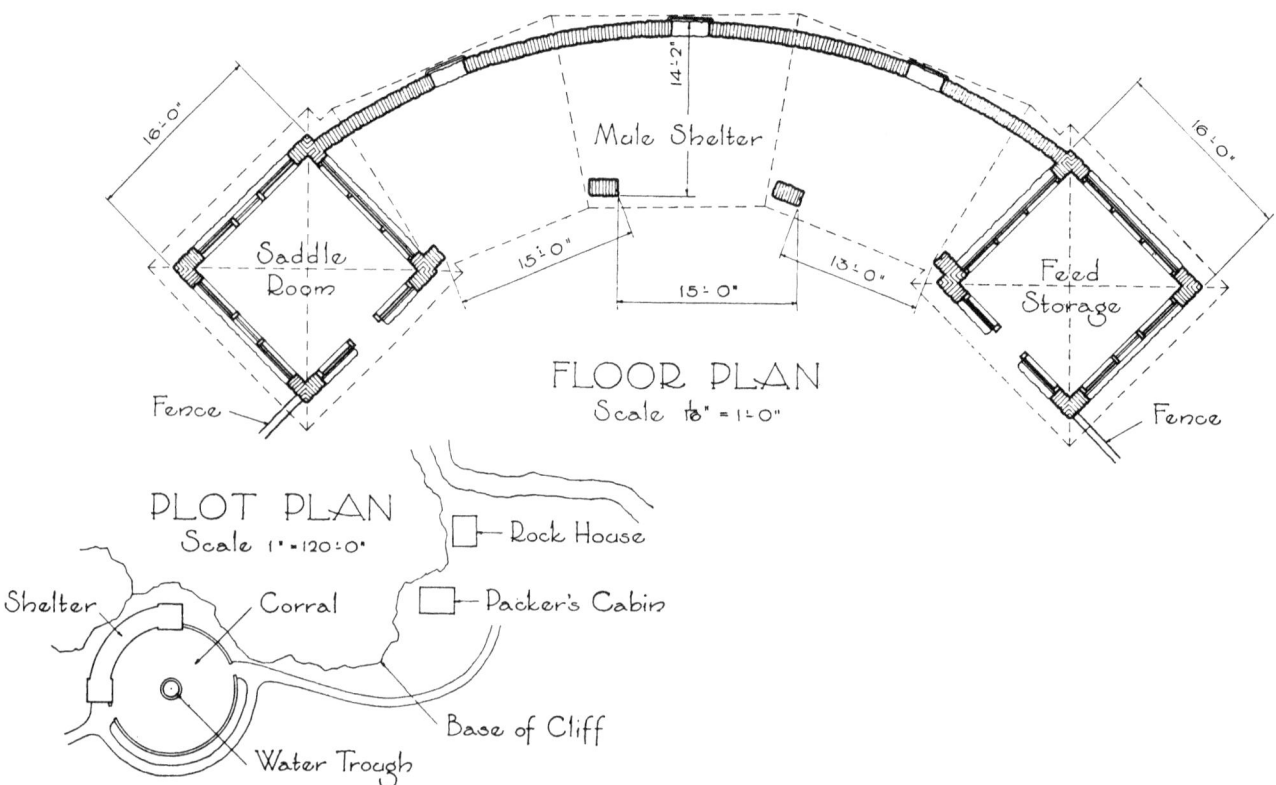

Mule Shelter, Grand Canyon National Park

Shelter, water supply, feed storage, and corral for the pack animals are necessary provisions at the end of the long and difficult trail down into this deep canyon. Boulders are the structural material at hand, which fact, more than the resulting character of the masonry, is justifying of their use.

Plate II J-9   ⋙ MISCELLANEOUS SPORTS STRUCTURES

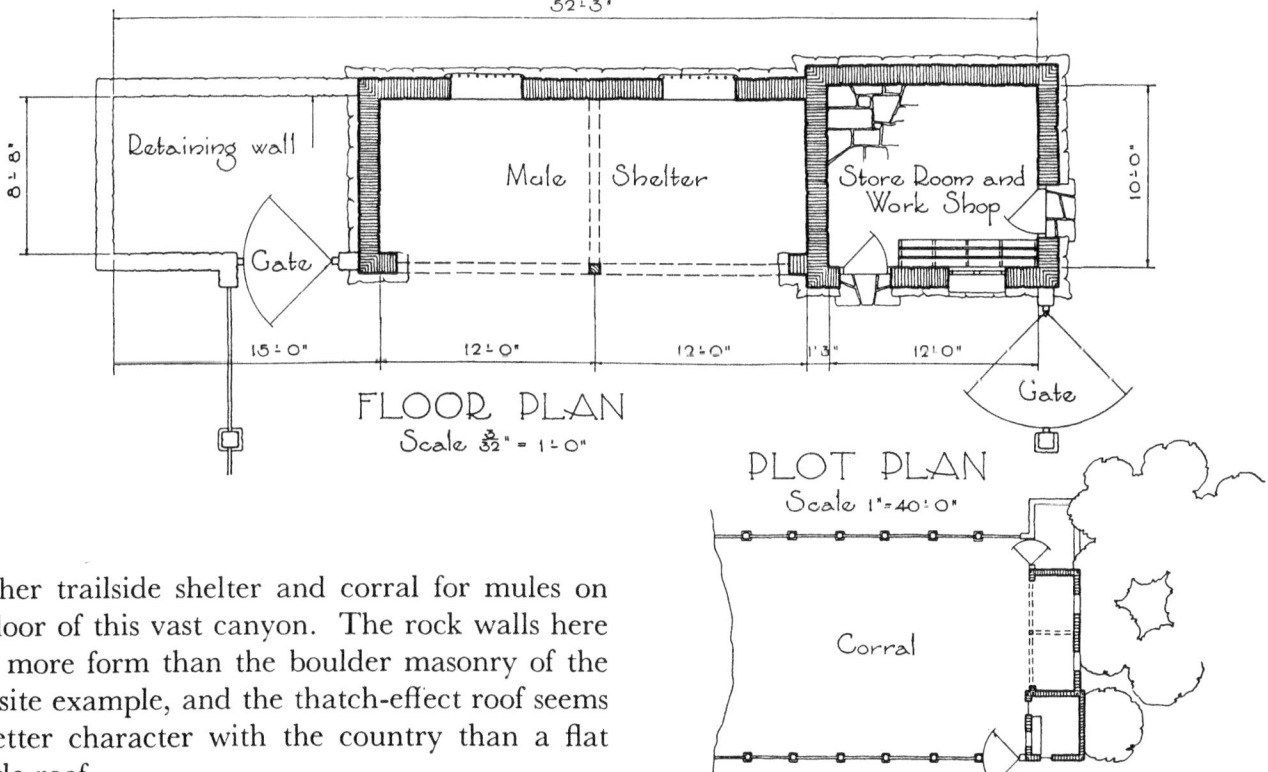

Mule Shelter, Grand Canyon National Park

Another trailside shelter and corral for mules on the floor of this vast canyon. The rock walls here have more form than the boulder masonry of the opposite example, and the thatch-effect roof seems in better character with the country than a flat shingle roof.

MISCELLANEOUS SPORTS STRUCTURES *Plate* II J–10

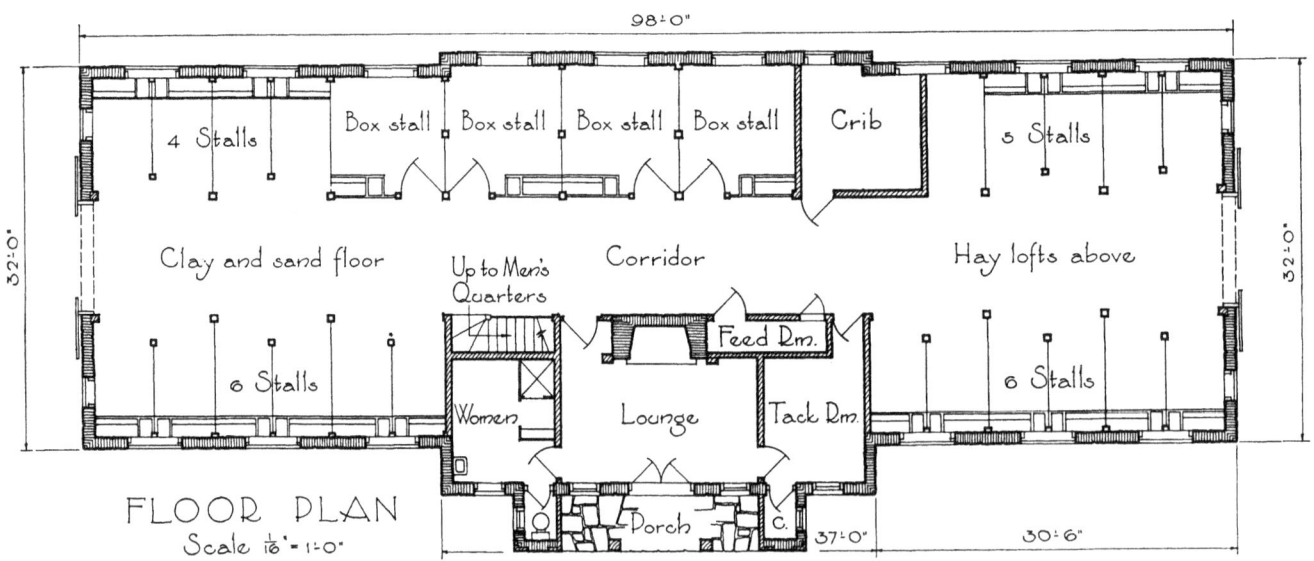

Riding Stable, Brown County State Park, Indiana

Here is a riding stable only to be challenged for being more than a shade on the palatial side. There is no questioning its excellence and completeness of plan and attractiveness of exterior. The stairs lead up to men's locker room, shower and toilet facilities, and stableman's quarters over the lounge, tack room, and women's retiring room equipped with shower and toilet facilities.

MARKERS, SHRINES, AND MUSEUMS

⇢ **B**Y THEIR PURPOSE and intent markers and shrines are differentiated from signs. Signs function to direct, regulate, or caution, whereas the marker and its close cousin, the shrine or graphic guide, serve simply to further the public's understanding and enjoyment of the cultural aspects of a park preserve. These cultural aspects may be in the realms of the natural sciences, history, archeology, and others.

As has been previously stated, it is possible for markers and related devices to capture and convey in greater degree than most other park structures the spirit of a particular area. It is their function, and by no means a minor one, to accent, to "highlight", what might be termed the essential personality of a park.

The markers and shrines of a park the glory of which is some unique or unusual outcome of natural forces can often clearly echo these characteristics to a welcome avoidance of the trite. Witness the nature shrine at Obsidian Cliff in Yellowstone National Park, formed of basaltic columns of hexagonal section in their natural relation to one another, which formation is a phenomenon of this area. There are, as well, other examples herein presented which, through clever and skillful recall of a local feature, are neither banal nor fantastic but succeed in achieving great individuality and distinction.

To the scientific or historical story of a park area, markers are the footnotes and annotations. Judiciously distributed, they are a guide service at the constant command of the park visitor. They can render service quite as fragmentary and irritating, misinformed and obnoxious, as any personal guide service. Effort should be constant to avoid this. A marker, appropriately designed and placed, so as to be neither obscure nor obtrusive, will invite attention. A thoughtfully phrased legend, concise and accurate, will hold attention and stimulate interest without trying the visitor's patience. Its wording and content will meticulously avoid either talking down to the average reader or lifting him to some pedantic level where he is perplexed and annoyed. It will neither be verbose to the point of being tiresome nor so curtly brief that a normal curiosity is left frustrated.

There is an interesting and growing movement to acquaint the using public with the details of a park area through the medium of maps. Informative or educational maps may take the form of simple painted diagrams showing, for instance, the course of a nature trail or historic overland route, the environs of an historic spot, or the reconstruction of remains of military earthworks or Indian mounds. The locations of points of historical, scientific, or scenic interest and the relationships between such notable features and the intensively used areas are graphically told to great advantage.

Lately the educational value of the relief model reproducing at small scale the terrain of an entire park area has come to be more fully appreciated. Created of plaster, such models are already on exhibition in nature and history museums within our parks. Proposed of concrete construction, several have been talked of for outdoor locations. Such models, supplemented with suitable inscriptions, can offer comprehensive visualization of mountain building movements and subsequent erosion of the land by water, wind, and ice or can promote an understanding of a military engagement or vanished civilization that is unapproached by any other medium.

SHRINES OR GRAPHIC GUIDES are devices for bringing exposition to the very scene of an historic event or natural phenomenon, or to the natural abode of a faunal or floral species. Their aim may be to visualize geological cross sections, trace military maneuvers, or chart subterranean caverns. Again it may be their purpose to identify plant or animal species and to present facts pertinent to the habitat and habits of these. They are designed to "answer questions." The interpretative material displayed may be in the nature of specimens, photographs, charts, maps, and such other informative matter, supplemented by legends and detailed explanation.

There is tremendous educational and cultural value in such informative devices. They can supply lucid and at-hand interpretation of the specific features a park was established to commemorate or to preserve. They can offer a wealth of fact, appealing to a variety of interests. They can make possible a broader understanding of an area than endless tramping over the actual ground could give.

A nature shrine usually enframes and shelters one or more weatherproof shallow wall cases with shatterproof glass fronts. It is well to design the cases so that they may be removed and brought into the park headquarters for the winter months.

Since guide and shrine devices are unattended, they are that perfect guide service—the park naturalist or historian par excellence—which, if found dull, may be "walked out on" without reason to feel the pin prick of conscious rudeness. Being thus disadvantaged through their inability to frown at a yawning spectator or physically to force him to remain attentive until the last bitter fact is told, these inanimate guide facilities should be accorded by their devisers all the benefits of interesting presentation and clear, concise exposition. As interpretative media they are in theory and in fact truly transitional between the marker and the museum. They are at once glorified marker and museum in embryo.

ALMOST WITHOUT EXCEPTION, the museum in a natural park or recreational area should confine its presentation to an interpretation of the immediate area. Rarely is there excuse for attempting more. Sometimes a unique, and frequently an unusual, natural phenomenon—be it beauty or science or richness of resource—is the primary reason for the establishment of the park. Wherever such is the case, it seems not unreasonable to hold that interpretative effort should focus intently on that conspicuous feature, unblurred and undistracted by side glances in the direction of the incidental or the commonplace. Few national parks, perhaps no State parks, are outstandingly representative of a vast assortment of natural interests. This might well mean that American park museums committing themselves to a presentation of the universe from Genesis through Revelations could properly be limited to few in number.

When the nature museum interprets one particular phenomenon at hand it may be little more than the nature shrine already discussed. When it exhibits in a permanent arrangement a variety of material found within the park limits, it is more accurately a park museum or what has come to be known as a trailside museum. If the nature museum strays farther afield and accumulates unto itself German helmets, Malay creeses, and the shaving mugs and moustache cups of the hardy pioneers of the neighborhood, we have no word for it. Degenerating into a mere repository for curios and oddities, it has sold out for a mess of pottage. The effectiveness of the park museum is never to be measured in terms of floor area or number of specimens. A bulk of heterogeneous material in a park museum, as in any other, can quickly obscure the very high lights that alone make a museum memorable.

The exhibits may be displayed as in the larger city museums, but there should always be a stressing of the immediate presence of the outdoors. The exhibit rooms should afford an occasional vista into the nearby woodland so that the visitor may have a feeling of being in the midst of the subject matter offered for study. It may be advisable to arrange the plan of the building so that a semi-enclosed courtyard obtains in which exhibits are displayed. Here may be growing flower and forestry specimens, labeled for identification, perhaps a vivarium containing a collection of living reptiles, in seminatural enclosures.

An interpretative policy which attempts to duplicate Nature should be avoided as far as possible. It is better to study living specimens in situ, where that is practical, than to attempt to reproduce them under a roof. A case in point is the advisability of studying wildflower collections actually growing in the field as compared to wax or preserved specimens reproduced in a museum display. As an opposite case, however, it is hardly possible for the visitor briefly visiting a park to make a comprehensive study of the local bird population, whereas a collection of mounted birds of the region will facilitate study materially and therefore is a proper exhibit. It should always be borne in mind that the best museum is that one which functions largely and most efficiently as an interpretative agent.

There is sometimes found in parks another facility for nature study often called a "working museum" or a "camp museum" for the lack of a better designation. It is a structure, usually small and semiopen, in which groups visiting or camping in the area—Boy Scouts, Campfire Girls, and other organized youth groups—arrange their temporary collections of leaves, insects, rock, and other specimens as a part of their nature study work under the guidance of nature counselors.

IN ITS ARCHITECTURE the park museum not only offers great opportunity for capturing the spirit and character of an area or region, but it may be said to exist in no small measure for that purpose. Unless there is the flavor of the locality in the structure as well as in the material it houses, it has failed of its particular assignment and potential accomplishment. There is wide latitude for individuality among museum structures, if each is intent on stressing some particular phase of Nature or of history in its structural expression no less than in its content.

The architecture of our park museums of natural history should above everything else reflect the outdoors. In the design of these buildings it is usually desirable to make use of indigenous materials in a novel way. In the case of one of our national parks the stone corner of the building is the local geological column.

Nearing completion at Lake Guernsey State Park, Wyoming, and Custer State Park, South Dakota, are two small museums that well typify the fitting structural gesture toward rugged untamed settings. The former is scheduled to memorialize the Oregon Trail to the Pacific, highlighting the geological facts that foreordained the trail location and the ensuing civilization so dependent on mining and reclamation. The Custer Museum exhibit will probably closely follow on a small scale the typical pattern for museums of the natural sciences. There are in natural parks examples of museums, too numerous to list, touching on one or more of the natural sciences from the regional or local angle. These may be specialized or mixed, and when the latter, it is sometimes in very shocking degree.

In the case of an historical museum building devoted to a specific era, the structural traditions and methods of that period are a well-justified theme for the design. At Boulder Dam State Park, Nevada, a museum has been built in the traditional adobe of the region, dedicated to preservation of the Lost City archaeological finds salvaged before the site of that ancient culture was inundated by the rising waters of lately created Lake Mead.

There is successful precedent for the restoration of an ancient building to display relics of historic significance or examples of early handcrafts. The old stone mill at Indiana's Spring Mill State Park appropriately houses a collection of farm and craft tools, household utensils, and furnishings of pioneer days. Serving as a nature museum in the Mariposa Grove of Big Trees in Yosemite National Park is the rebuilt log cabin of a pioneer.

The techniques of organization, lighting, case construction, equipment, and storage for a museum are highly specialized—so much so that within present space limitations these can be touched on only to the extent of urging the importance of consulting trained experts before a museum project, even a minor one, is undertaken.

The interpretation of facts and phenomena of Nature can only enjoy vitality in parks as long as there is alert realization that the natural park in a desirably unmodified state is itself the museum, calling only for the creating of secondary and supplemental facilities to furnish reference, interpretation, identification. The wilderness itself is the book, as it were, requiring only marginal notes. With Mohamet philosophically now come to the mountain, there must be no lapse into the old mountain-to-Manhattan techniques of presentation. If natural beauty and phenomena, plant and animal life, are more desirably viewed under glass, then Times Square, by reason of its very convenience of location, must once again become the setting for the embalmed presentations.

MARKERS, SHRINES, AND MUSEUMS

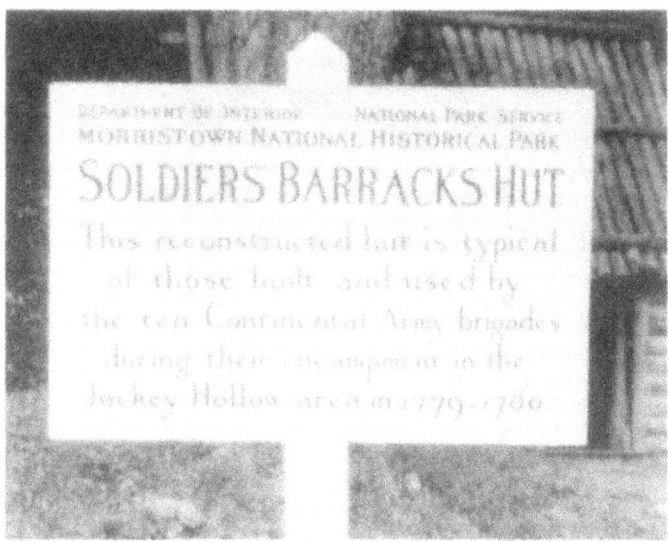

Morristown National Historical Park

Morristown National Historical Park

New Salem State Park, Illinois

MARKERS

Surrounding markers illustrate how this facility may be keyed to an historical period by means of a stylized design of frame and lettering, or to some interesting natural fact or phenomenon by employing native materials appropriately. By their very manner the examples from Morristown and New Salem seem definitely historical, the others, quite as definitely related to some phase of Nature.

Itasca State Park, Minnesota

Crater Lake National Park

Marker — Saltwater State Park — Washington

A truly informative and well located map of the area can prove to be very useful in a park. If the points of interest, and trails and distances to them, are clearly indicated, many queries are automatically answered and time is saved for visitors and park personnel alike. A most durable map may be produced on a wood panel by means of a pyrographic point. It is important that all lines be deeply burned to maintain legibility as normal weathering proceeds. The map here shown might well have been more vigorously traced, and possibly at a larger scale to some advantage. The hood protects the map in some degree from deteriorating exposure to the elements.

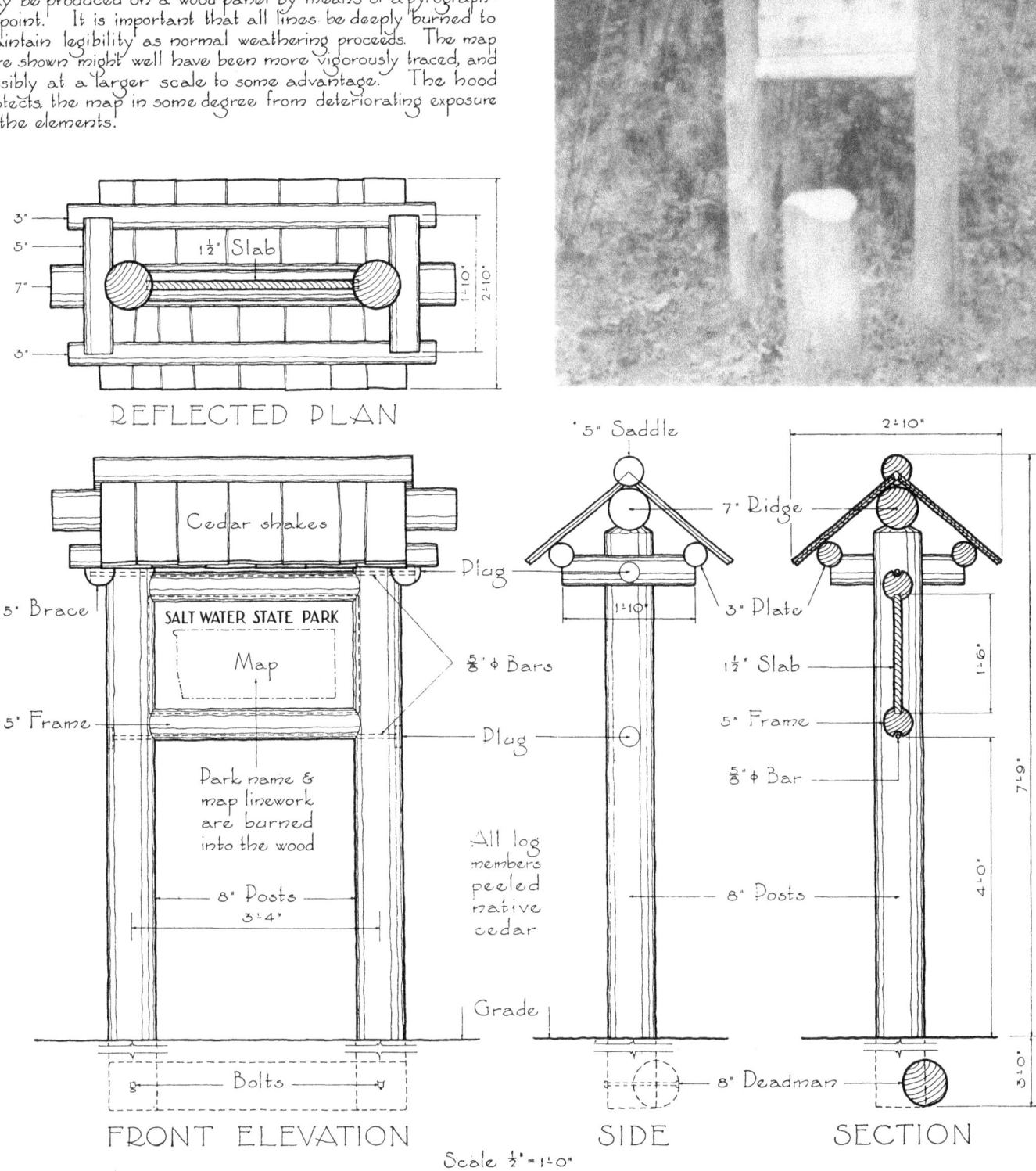

MARKERS, SHRINES, AND MUSEUMS ≪ Plate II K-3

Yaquina Bay State Park, Oregon

Levi Jackson-Wilderness Road State Park, Kentucky

MARKERS INTO MAP AND NATURE EXHIBITS

This two-page spread illustrates the tendency of the out-and-out marker to develop into a more complex facility, which may take the form of a map stand, sometimes elaborate, or a nature exhibit or shrine. Thus, reading left to right from the typical marker at upper left we have a marker and protective enclosure for an historic stump, then an historical marker framed and hooded in a form

Nelson Dewey State Park, Wisconsin

Humboldt-Redwoods State Park, California

174

Plate II K-4   ⇛ MARKERS, SHRINES, AND MUSEUMS

Crowley's Ridge State Park, Arkansas

Highlands Hammock State Park, Florida

almost typical of the nature shrine, and at upper right a glazed map on a standard, furnished with a sun shade. At lower right is a map stand in the manner of a typical shrine, then a well-marked outdoor nature exhibit, and finally two examples of nature shrines in the form become familiar—rustic, hooded frames housing glass-fronted cases to display specimens, illustrations, and printed matter pertaining to a natural phenomenon at hand.

Custer State Park, South Dakota

Yellowstone National Park

MARKERS, SHRINES, AND MUSEUMS

Plate II K–5

Nature Shrine   Yellowstone National Park

This open air museum-in-miniature near Obsidian Cliff is outstandingly representative of individuality achieved by the use of a material which is a phenomenon of the immediate environs. The clustered piers are formed of basaltic columns in their natural relation to one another. The novel motif is altogether amiable largely because it has been employed with logic and restraint.

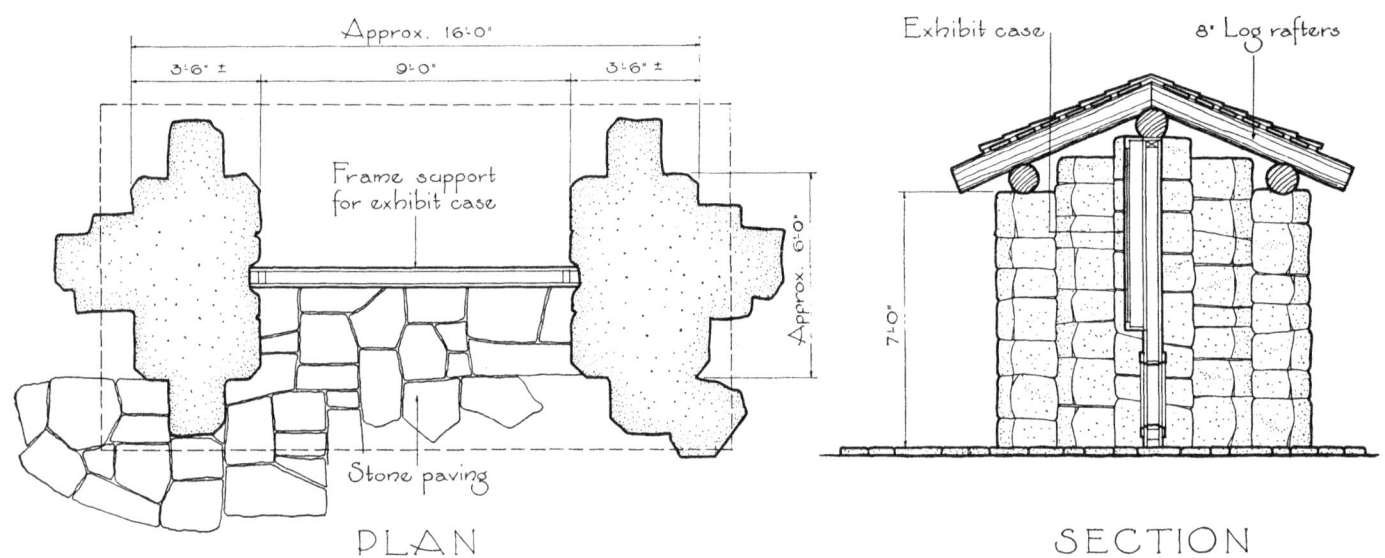

PLAN   SECTION

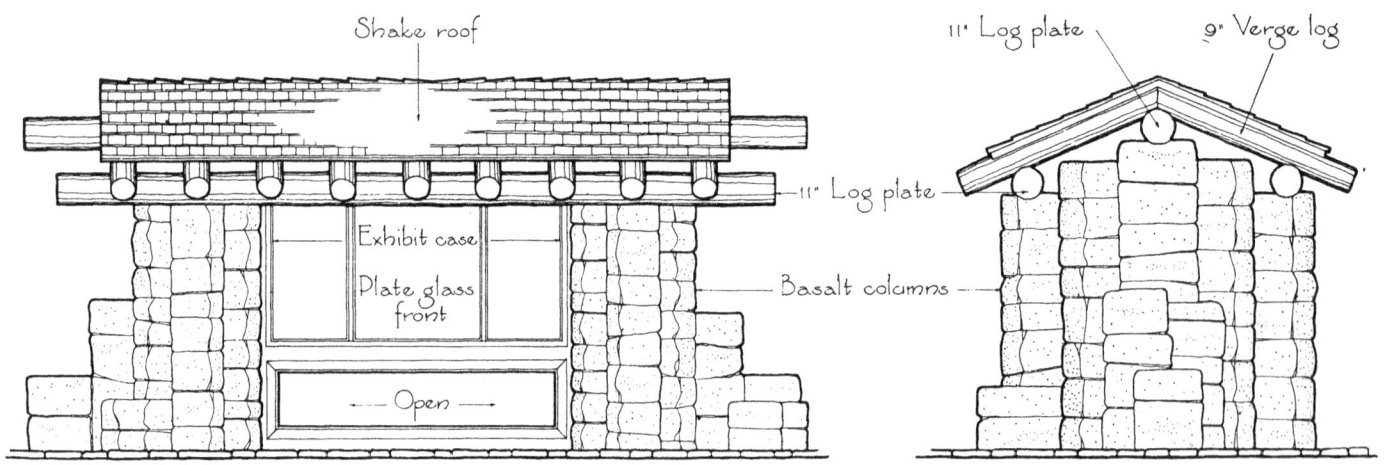

FRONT ELEVATION   END ELEVATION

Scale 3/8" = 1'-0"

Plate II K–6 ⇛ MARKERS, SHRINES, AND MUSEUMS

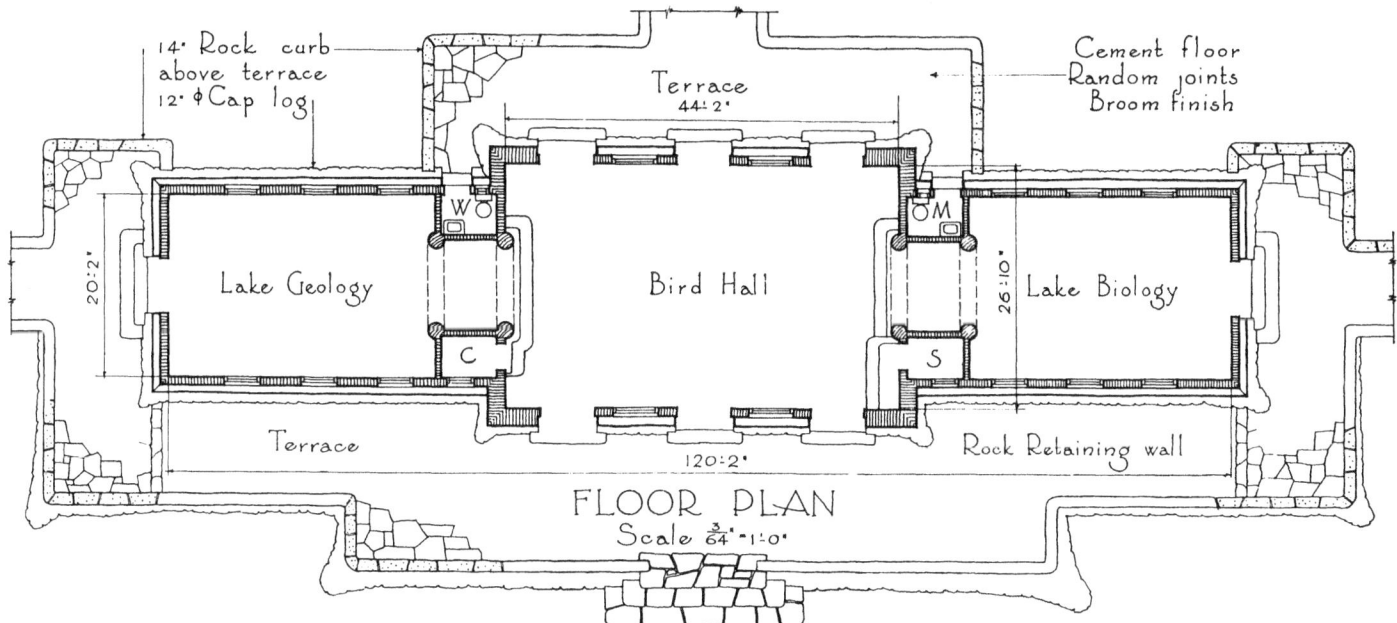

Fishing Bridge Museum, Yellowstone National Park

FLOOR PLAN
Scale 3/64" = 1'-0"

This well-planned and well-lighted nature museum is a successful example of the employment of principles important in the creating of buildings suitable to natural areas—the value of the freehand line, the avoidance of underscale, and the pleasing quality of the furrowed and knotted log.

177

MARKERS, SHRINES, AND MUSEUMS ««« Plate II K-7

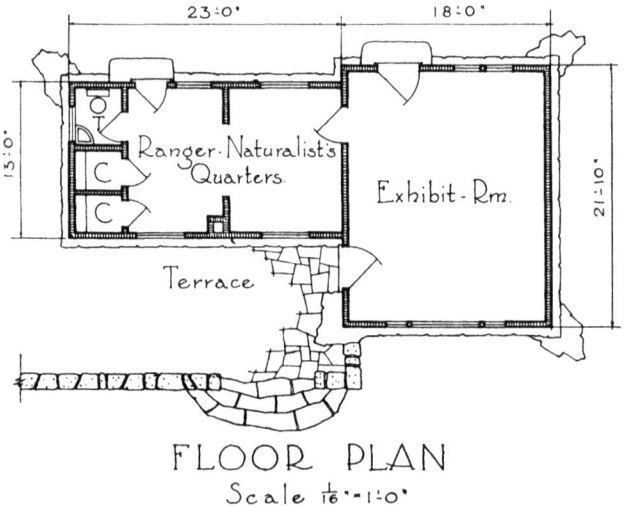

Madison Junction Museum, Yellowstone National Park

Minor in size, but not in its contribution to park architecture. The pitch of the roof and the texture of the selected logs conspire with the rakish buttressing of the well-scaled rock work to deserve unqualified acclaim. The spacious "landscape" window serves to project the outdoors into the museum interior, an illusion to be sought wherever the objective is the interpretation of surrounding Nature.

Plate II K-8   ⇢⇢⇢ MARKERS, SHRINES, AND MUSEUMS

Museum, Grand Canyon National Park

This little museum, perched on the rim of spectacular Grand Canyon forms liaison with its setting by means of its low lines, flat roof, and rugged masonry walls. The foreground is planted with native material as an outdoor exhibit supplementing the function of the museum proper. On the opposite or canyon side of the building is a roofed overlook below which the majestic canyon spreads uninterruptedly. Binoculars which can be trained on distant points of unusual interest are mounted on the guard wall of the overlook.

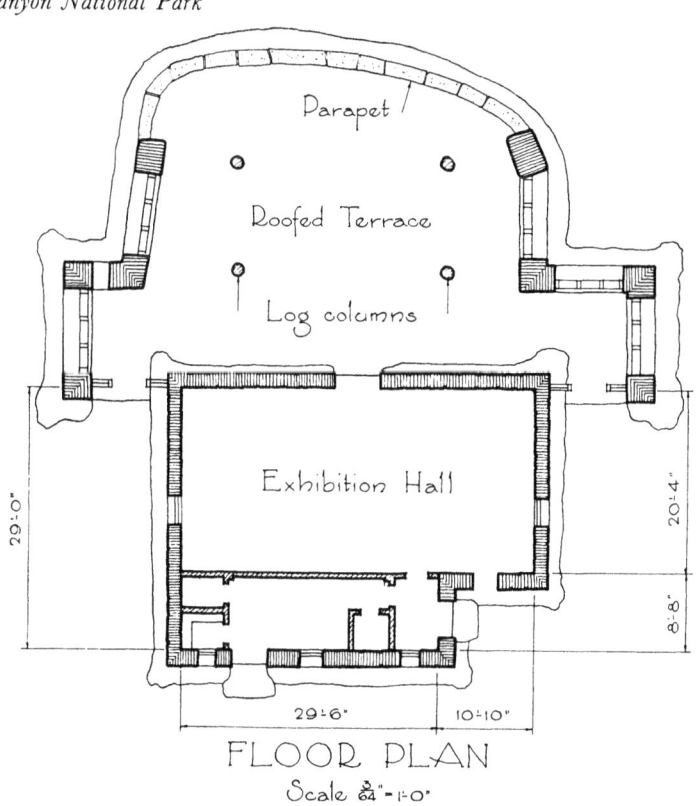

FLOOR PLAN
Scale 3/64"=1'-0"

179

MARKERS, SHRINES, AND MUSEUMS   Plate II K-9

Museum, Custer State Park, South Dakota

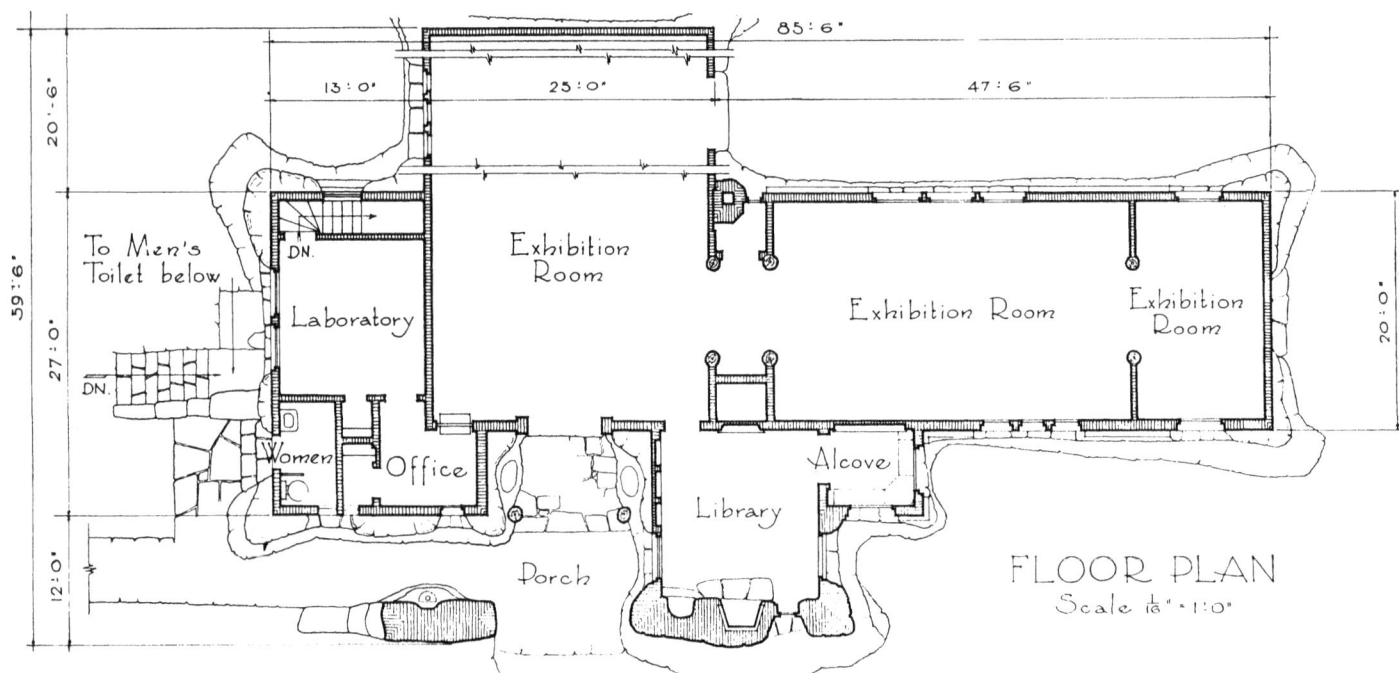

Although uncompleted, this structure, for its rugged, informal character, may not be omitted from a presentation of park museums. It is fittingly related to the Black Hills and their evolution from the unknown—a theme it will strive to interpret. Absence of planting to wed building to site fails to depreciate the merits of this vigorous structure.

Plate II K–10   ⇶ MARKERS, SHRINES, AND MUSEUMS

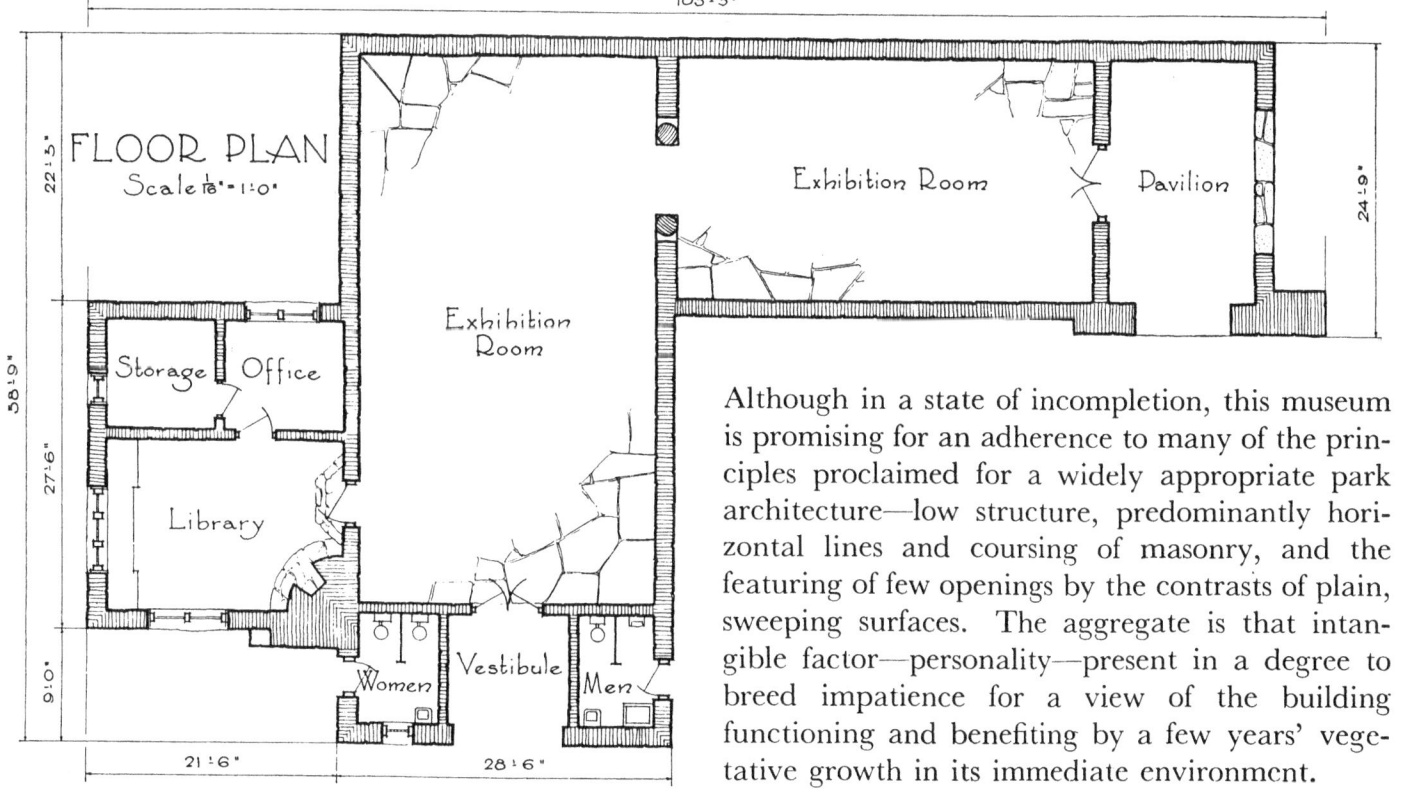

Museum, Lake Guernsey State Park, Wyoming

Although in a state of incompletion, this museum is promising for an adherence to many of the principles proclaimed for a widely appropriate park architecture—low structure, predominantly horizontal lines and coursing of masonry, and the featuring of few openings by the contrasts of plain, sweeping surfaces. The aggregate is that intangible factor—personality—present in a degree to breed impatience for a view of the building functioning and benefiting by a few years' vegetative growth in its immediate environment.

MARKERS, SHRINES, AND MUSEUMS

Plate II K–11

Boulder Dam State Park, Nevada

FLOOR PLAN
Scale 3/64"=1'-0"

Plate II K–12   ⇶ MARKERS, SHRINES, AND MUSEUMS

On the opposite page are a general view and plan of this museum constructed of the traditional adobe of the region. Its remote location is doubtless responsible for the incorporation of living quarters for an attendant. To be noted are the toilet facilities provided for the public, the workroom in its relation to the museum proper, surrounding terraces and low walls, and spaces for native plants and outdoor display of exhibits.

Lost City Archeological Museum, Boulder Dam State Park, Nevada

These Pueblo ruins of Pueblo II culture are reconstructed on an original Indian site near the museum building. In the foreground are remains that give the plan of the plaza walls. All are made of adobe mud and tamarisk branches, a type of construction which provides shelter that is cool in summer and warm in winter. Exhibits such as this bring fuller meaning to the artifacts displayed in the museum cases by comprehensively relating them to the contemporaneous shelter of their creators.

Exhibit-in-place, Boulder Dam State Park, Nevada

This interior view is illustrative of a modern technique of presentation that concentrates on a comprehensive unfolding of prehistoric cultures in series. It illustrates also the adaptation of display equipment to the desirable objective of retaining in the interior of the building something of the structural style established by the exterior. This is here evident in the whitewashed, rough-plastered walls, flag pavement, beamed ceiling, and pole brackets of the shelves above the doorways.

Interior, Museum, Boulder Dam State Park, Nevada

183

MARKERS, SHRINES, AND MUSEUMS

Plate II K–13

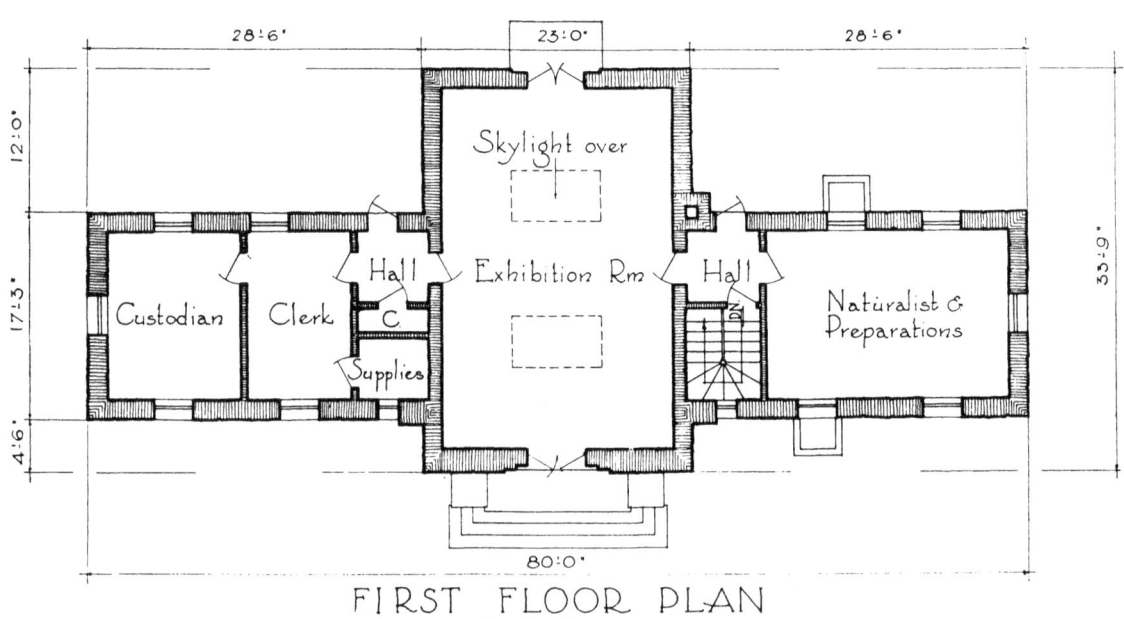

Museum Building, Petrified Forest National Monument

FIRST FLOOR PLAN

With simple dignity, this building happily succeeds both in capturing the flavor of the architecture of the Old Southwest and in gesturing toward contemporary. This is no mean attainment in itself, and with the added score of an orderly workable plan, it is successful beyond cavil.

HISTORICAL PRESERVATIONS AND RECONSTRUCTIONS

PRESERVED or recaptured structural creations by man that have historical, architectural, archeological, or related cultural values are in a sense at once large-scale exhibits-in-place and "living" museums. Museums into which life has been breathed are a comparatively recent development. Chronologically, the American Wing of the Metropolitan Museum may not have been the first exponent of this comprehensive technique in presentation, but most assuredly it has first place as such in the public consciousness.

The "living" museum became even more alive in subsequent developments, wherein the interest-appeal was made to embrace the very housing of the variety of objects that so shortly before had seemed in themselves complete, if dormant, exhibits. It was as though, become aware that both an inside and an outside were part and parcel of its being, the museum became "fourth-dimensional." Restored Williamsburg, Virginia, effectively pictured the apogee of cavalier life in Tidewater Virginia before the Revolution. Dearborn, Michigan, made magnetic by a catholic taste and unlimited funds, attracted to Greenfield Village an anachronistic assortment of uprooted scientific and cultural shrines and their accoutrements for the new presentation.

There are those who will see no tie whatever between these presentations of the past and the wilderness preserve in public ownership. There are those who will challenge the appropriateness in a natural park of any and all structures not absolutely indispensable to human use of the park as a domain of Nature. Wherever the preserve is one of exceptional scenic or scientific interest, their contention is well-grounded. But the wilderness preserve not scenically or otherwise than historically exceptional is a singularly appropriate setting for further "fourth-dimensional" exhibits even more typically American and more widely appealing and understandable to the American public than either Williamsburg or Greenfield Village. This fitting complement of the natural park backdrop is the community of the early American scene—the Frontier Village.

Ohio, Indiana, and Illinois, perhaps other States, have sensed the common touch and ties of that phase of the American past. So, for purposes of recreation and education, traditional pioneer villages have been restored or reconstructed on sites of historical significance in these States. Ohio's Schoenbrunn Memorial re-creates a pre-Revolutionary Moravian mission settlement wiped out by a bloody Indian massacre.

Indiana's Spring Mill brings to life a pioneer outpost that sprang up around the activities of a stone gristmill, built by emigrating Virginia gentry early in the nineteenth century. The mill is so completely rehabilitated that it is again possible to grind corn by primitive methods, an operation which keenly interests park visitors. Its upper floors are given over to the display of early farm implements, household utensils, and handcraft items. The pharmacy is furnished with contemporary equipment and restocked with merchandise of the period.

Illinois' New Salem presents a chapter of the Lincoln legend by bringing back with well-fabricated authenticity the scene of his romance with Ann Rutledge in the village of his railsplitting and storekeeping youth.

Great interest attends upon the survivals of primitive industry as exemplified by the restored mills in Great Smoky Mountains National Park. There is substance to inspire solemn retrospection in the reconstructed hospital and huts that were the soldiers' barracks at Morristown in the War of the Revolution.

Perhaps the time will come when each and every State will be moved similarly to crystallize into actuality some distinctive cultural, empire-building, exploitative, or industrial phase of its beginnings. It may well be that enough Texas longhorn cattle now fast stampeding to extinction can be corralled and managed so that a herd will again exist to bring thrill and meaning to some ranch carefully restored to re-create the heyday of the cowboy. Perhaps a southern cotton plantation—big house and quarters—acquired and put again in operation will lend realism to the romantic tradition of the southern feudalism of ante bellum days. A mining community of midcentury Colorado, a wharf and the paraphernalia of shipping of clipper ship days at Salem or Newburyport, a community actuated by a primitive iron furnace in Pennsylvania, a fur-trading post—these and untold others may some day make the automobile, and not the book, the medium for teaching history and much besides. It is not difficult to imagine a transcontinental motor route of the future linking a succession of phases of the westward march of empire of our past.

All developments of this kind achieve reality and vitality by reason of careful attention to every detail in surroundings and furnishings. In the examples cited relics of historical association contribute to the interest, and minutiae of the period highlight the illusion. The educational and social values potential in such exhibits are incalculable. Surely it is not too much to claim that they stimulate an interest in history and the early arts and crafts and tend to bring about a reevaluation of the pioneering virtues and American ideals that seem progressively remote from us in modern life.

The curse of most historical restorations, reconstructions, or re-creations is an almost irresistible urge to gild the lily. Why persons charged with bringing authenticity to something out of the past feel licensed to indulge their personal tastes and fancies in the direction of improving on known historical or structural fact is not understandable, but it is almost the rule. As an instance, the chimney on a pioneer cabin was typically a strictly practical affair, utilizing no more materials than were needed to encase the flues, and, if it were on the exterior of the cabin, resulted in something probably ungainly and spindling in appearance by today's standards. The currently fashionable silhouette in chimneys is something very much more stocky and ample. The result? Present day reconstructions of the pioneer's cabin generally are garnished with chimneys proportioned to the tastes of today, and the gaunt and gawky utilitarian aspect of the frontier type is completely missed.

Again, it is sought allegedly to recapture the surroundings of an historic personage whose misfortune it was to have made history at a time when architecture and the decorative arts were degraded—so degraded, in fact, that the restorer, with commendable compassion but utter lack of honesty, feels called upon to warp the personage's period by a decade or two in order that his returning ghost may enjoy a décor more glamorous than the revolting black walnut and chromos he had to endure in life. A kindly and artistic impulse, but in violation of the basic obligations of the responsible restoration technician.

Wherever it is proposed to restore or reconstruct anything with pretensions to historical value, there should always be on hand a stubborn horse-sensible codger, skeptical enough to ask "Why?" and too smart-headed to mistake mere enthusiasm and sentiment for a right answer. He should be crowned with laurel forthwith, enthroned as chairman of the project, and charged to ask "Why?" at half-hour intervals until the proposal is tabled or the keys to the finished product are turned over to the Park Authority. This is Recommendation No. 1 for Intelligent Restoration.

This shrewd skeptic is a realist who knows that restorations worthy the designation are not tinkered out of hearsay, three generations removed, and sentiment only. Well and stubbornly may he refuse to become party to a so-called restoration, if he is privy to all that has been done and blithely called by that name. Righteously he croaks his doubt that there can be either evidence or glamour enough in a single excavated hearthstone to validate an entire new building fabricated around it.

Chairman Smart knows that misguided efforts in so-called restoration have forever lost to us much that was authentic, if crumbling. He is aware that the faint shadow of the genuine often makes more intelligent appeal to the imagination than the crass and visionary replica. He recognizes that for a group to materialize largely out of thin air its arbitrary conception of what is fitting and proper is to trespass the right and privilege of the individual to re-create vanished or near-vanished things within his own imagination.

Large or small, restoration and reconstruction projects in parks call for exceptional skill and sympathetic collaboration on the part of the many professions and interests concerned with park planning, if successful accomplishment is to result.

The general restoration policy adopted by the National Park Service, upon recommendation of its Advisory Board on National Parks, Historic Sites, Buildings, and Monuments, reads:

"The motives governing these activities are several, often conflicting: aesthetic, archeological and scientific, and educational. Each has its values and its disadvantages.

"Educational motives often suggest complete reconstitution, as in their heyday, of vanished, ruinous or remodelled buildings and remains. This has often been regarded as requiring removal of subsequent additions, and has involved incidental destruction of much archeological and historical evidence, as well as of aesthetic values arising from age and picturesqueness. The demands of scholarship for the preservation of every vestige of architectural and archeological evidence—desirable in itself—might, if rigidly satisfied, leave the monument in conditions which give the public little idea of its major historical aspect or importance. In aesthetic regards, the claims of unity or original form or intention, of variety of style in successive periods of building and remodelling, and of present beauty of texture and weathering may not always be wholly compatible.

"In attempting to reconcile these claims and motives, the ultimate guide must be the tact and judgment of the men in charge. Certain observations may, however, be of assistance to them:

"(1) No final decision should be taken as to a course of action before reasonable efforts to exhaust the archeological and documentary evidence as to the form and successive transformations of the monument.

"(2) Complete record of such evidence, by drawings, notes and transcripts should be kept, and in no case should evidence offered by the monument itself be destroyed or covered up before it has been fully recorded.

"(3) It is well to bear in mind the saying: 'Better preserve than repair, better repair than restore, better restore than construct.'

"(4) It is ordinarily better to retain genuine old work of several periods, rather than arbitrarily to 'restore' the whole, by new work, to its aspect at a single period.

"(5) This applies even to work of periods later than those now admired, provided their work represents a genuine creative effort.

"(6) In no case should our own artistic preferences or prejudices lead us to modify, on aesthetic grounds, work of a bygone period representing other artistic tastes. Truth is not only stranger than fiction, but more varied and more interesting, as well as more honest.

"(7) Where missing features are to be replaced without sufficient evidence as to their own original form, due regard should be paid to the factors of period and region in other surviving examples of the same time and locality.

"(8) Every reasonable additional care and expense are justified to approximate in new work the materials, methods and quality of old construction, but new work should not be artificially 'antiqued' by theatrical means.

"(9) Work on the preservation and restoration of old buildings requires a slower pace than would be expected in new construction."

Approach Side, Before Restoration

Stream Side, After Restoration

JIM CARR "TUB" MILL, GREAT SMOKY MOUNTAINS NATIONAL PARK

A "tub" mill, or "tubbin" mill, mountaineer for turbine, is typical of the coves of the Great Smokies, and expressive of the determination of the mountain people to exist, independent of the outside world. Craftsmanship cleverly adapts the turbine wheel to local needs. The mill house is a good example of the type, built of squared logs, rib pole and shake roof, and puncheon floor. One view above shows the approach side before, and the other, the stream side after, restoration. The sharply inclined flume is seen in both pictures.

Distinctive feature of the "tubbin" mill is the vertical shaft. One view below shows the grinding mechanism with hopper for shelled corn and tub for ground meal. Ingenious device for regulating the flow of corn to the stones is the cord passing over the housing of the stones. The lower stone is stationary, the upper one revolves, and coarseness of grinding is regulated by raising the upper stone with its heavy shaft and turbine.

The other picture shows the wheel, carved in two halves from a poplar log. These wheels, carved by a local mechanic, using but a few poor tools, are remarkable. The vanes are cut at 45 degrees. The vertical shaft hewn from oak, pinned to the turbine wheel at the bottom, carries a forged gudgeon on its upper end which passes through the lower stone and is keyed to the upper one.

Interior View

Turbine Wheel, Before Replacement

Before Restoration

After Restoration

JIM CABLE GRISTMILL, GREAT SMOKY MOUNTAINS NATIONAL PARK

Near Cades Cove is this primitive gristmill of the southern mountaineers. The need for rescuing this ancient relic is fully proved by the dilapidated condition recorded by the "before" picture, while the "after" picture, from virtually the same viewpoint, attests a sympathetic handling of a preservation problem.

This type of mill is common to all parts of the country, but primitive examples are only to be found in a few places. While the "tubbin" mill shown on the opposite page has a very small output, and is built in the most inaccessible locations, this more common design stands boldly forth alongside large streams to serve whole communities.

The grinding mechanism in one view below is typical, with stones cut from local "gray-backs." The other view shows the gearing, driven by an overshot water wheel mounted on the hand-hewn, eight-sided poplar shaft, which may be as much as 28 inches across. This shaft is fitted with gudgeons, which turn in bearings of hard wood, with no caps, and are lubricated with tallow. The bearing is aligned by driving up the wooden wedges.

The bull gear is built up of layers of plank, with spokes pinned in. Its cast iron rim is one of the few things which must be purchased. All other gears are usually built up of wood, with hickory teeth, although here the large bevel gear is also of iron.

Interior View

Restored Gearing

HISTORICAL PRESERVATIONS AND RECONSTRUCTIONS

Reconstructed Earth Lodge, Fort Lincoln State Park, North Dakota

Interior of Earth Lodge, Fort Lincoln State Park, North Dakota

RECONSTRUCTIONS IN THE MIDWEST

Interesting remains of different periods have occasioned reconstructions in Fort Lincoln State Park, North Dakota, utterly unrelated yet individually identified with the site beyond challenge.

Five earth lodges including one "ceremonial lodge" and the stockade of an ancient Indian village have been constructed over the original foundation posts which were found upon excavation. An exterior and an interior view of a rebuilt lodge of this strange type are shown above. No one knows how long ago the original village was established or abandoned. Modern Indians know nothing of it, and Army records disclose no positive dates of habitation. The many artifacts found in excavating the site are lodged in an historical museum in the capital of the State.

At lower left are Fort McKeen blockhouse and stockade in this same park, reconstructed on the original site from evidence which remained. It memorializes the winning of the West. The original fort was built prior to 1873, when General Custer abandoned it and established Fort Lincoln a short distance away on the plains below.

In Jay Cooke State Park, Minnesota, has been constructed the replica of an early fur-trading post shown at lower right.

Reconstructed Blockhouse, Fort Lincoln State Park, North Dakota

Reconstructed Trading Post, Jay Cooke State Park, Minnesota

Restored Wick House

Restored Wick House Garden

RESTORATION AND RECONSTRUCTION, MORRISTOWN NATIONAL HISTORICAL PARK

Included within the boundaries of Morristown National Historical Park is the restored eighteenth century Wick House, with outbuildings and fenced garden, shown above.

This simple farm house is typical of the more modest dwelling of the Revolutionary period commemorated by the establishment of this historically significant area as a public preserve. The post-and-rail fence and unpretentious garden are details eloquent in proof of the contention that the safe channel to authenticity is charted by restraint.

The structures shown below are strictly reconstructions, purposed to give visitors an impression of the probable type of quarters occupied by the Continentals stationed here during the War for Independence. Exhibits-in-place truly appropriate to a park area are legitimate undertakings, educationally and culturally stimulating, but only as long as the fact of reconstruction and the factor of probability are not obscured.

Reconstructed Barracks Hut

Reconstructed Hospital

Naval Exhibit

Grand French Battery

Fusileers' Redoubt

HISTORICAL EXHIBITS, COLONIAL NATIONAL HISTORICAL PARK

A replica of a portion of the gun deck and of the captain's cabin of a British frigate of the period of the American Revolution displays articles salvaged from British vessels sunk in the York River during the siege of Yorktown in 1781. This setting contributes greatly to a better understanding of the relics and their manner of use. At lower left is the reconstructed Grand French Battery of the first parallel around Yorktown which played an important part in the reduction of the British works and the eventual surrender of Cornwallis. At lower right is the restored Fusileers' Redoubt, the extreme right wing fortification of Cornwallis' defending army.

Plate II L-6　　→» HISTORICAL PRESERVATIONS AND RECONSTRUCTIONS

General View of Mission

Restored Colonnade

Ramada Over Excavated Ruins

MISSION RESTORATION, LA PURISIMA STATE PARK, CALIFORNIA

California has made commendable progress in restoring this old Spanish mission, with painstaking attention to minute details. Already a re-creation of the garden is underway; restoration may ultimately include furnishings and outlying structures. The ramada at lower right, built of adobe piers, eucalyptus posts and beams, and roof thatched with arrow weed, protects excavated remains of tallow vats needed for soap making in a self-contained early mission community of Spanish California. A stone wall prevents the higher ground from eroding into the cleared ruins, and a stout fence discourages the public from climbing onto them.

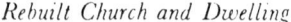

The Reconstructed Village

Rebuilt Church and Dwelling

Rebuilt Dwellings

RECONSTRUCTED PIONEER VILLAGE, SCHOENBRUNN STATE MEMORIAL, OHIO

Schoenbrunn, founded by Moravians and their Indian converts in 1772, grew rapidly into a village of 60 houses of hewn timber, a mission church, and the first schoolhouse built west of the Ohio River. Situated between the English at Detroit and the Americans at Fort Pitt, the position became untenable during the Revolution, and hostile Indians forced its abandonment in 1777. Shortly thereafter the entire town was burned to the ground. Its location lost until 1923, Moravian archives in Bethlehem indicated the site (confirmed by subsequent excavations) and inspired reconstruction.

Plate II L-8   ☛ HISTORICAL PRESERVATIONS AND RECONSTRUCTIONS

Restored Village Street

Reconditioned Mill

Reconditioned Dwellings

PIONEER VILLAGE, SPRING MILL STATE PARK, INDIANA

A modern miracle is this idyllic preservation of early America. Though the Frontier Era of the Middle East is scarcely a century gone, its physical survivals are regrettably few and so isolated and so altered that little of illusion of the past clings to them. Here at Spring Mill Village a little group somehow survived to be intelligently conditioned. Other ancient cabins were gathered in from the nearby countryside to fill the gaps made by Time's adversities. Post-period anachronisms were weeded out. In effect, Time in its flight has here been turned backward.

195

Reconstructed Village Street

Reconstructed "Dogtrot" Cabin

Reconstructed Dwelling

RECONSTRUCTED PIONEER VILLAGE, NEW SALEM STATE PARK, ILLINOIS

The street scene is New Salem, reconstruction of a long-gone frontier community identified with the early life of Abraham Lincoln. The historical value of the site inspired the establishment of the area; findings growing out of careful excavation and search of old documents governed the structural re-creation of the vanished town. The frame-sided building at the end of the street is the village store where Lincoln clerked. The small illustrations show New Salem log houses in the Illinois idiom.

CAMPFIRE CIRCLES AND OUTDOOR THEATERS

THE CAMPFIRE, LECTURE, or council circle or ring, as it is variously called, is merely a foregathering place in the open around the community campfire, where the evening hours may be passed with song and story in the warmth of good comradeship and the friendly fire. Its location is therefore usually close by a development for overnight use, such as tent or cabin colony. It is almost a necessity in connection with an organized camp lay-out, serving as the hub of much of the activities program.

Some form of the lecture circle or its big brother, the outdoor theater, is a desirable adjunct to a park museum, particularly to a nature museum the activities of which include talks by naturalists and related programs. The sole physical essential of the unpretentious example is the campfire itself. Desirable features are a generally level terrain in the immediate vicinity of the fire and surroundings that suggest, if only to the highly imaginative, the glories of a Nature unmodified.

The campfire circle is generally given a fixity of location by arranging a ring of stones to mark and confine the site of the fire. It is often equipped with arcs or rings of seats, especially if conditions of climate or insect life make sitting on the ground unadvisable. Such seating may be merely logs or some more comfortable adaptation of them, or again may be boulders or a more sophisticated masonry construction where stone is the more abundant native material. But there are no fixed principles, no time-revered traditions to be pressed, beyond admonishing attention to the claims of immediate natural environment.

If it would not be construed as flippant, it would here be urged upon park planners who may be contemplating the building of a campfire circle to locate it in a virgin stand of redwoods. Surely nowhere in this world can there be wilderness settings more magnificently impressive and receptive to this particular park facility.

More realistically stated would be the exhortation to consider the campfire circle as it exists in many California State parks along the Redwoods Highway, and to go forth and do as likewise as possible. Attempts in other locations to achieve the glory of a campfire circle ringed by giant redwoods will perforce lack the illusion of a world within a world, the soaring height of these trees, and the lushness of moss and tracery of fern that are their accompaniment in their natural state. Yet in unmodified wilderness of other types there can still be had so many of the impressive attributes of a campfire circle amongst redwoods as to make the efforts to capture some of them well worth while.

All trees with pretentions to age will supply a leafy pattern filtering sunlight or moonlight overhead. Most forests not ravaged by excessive clean-up or human overuse will maintain an undergrowth of greenery to serve as reredos for a chapel out-of-doors. Large trees, other than redwoods, will provide material for benches hewn from a single log. Especially does this type of seating, in reflecting the form and scale of the surrounding large trees, go far to bring to the construction of the campfire circle something of the touch of Nature.

The campfire circle is by no means always of the typical form here described. In fact on occasion it is not a circle at all. A popular variant is something very like an indoors fireplace with a chimney built free-standing out-of-doors, the chimney serving as a kind of votive column for the fire worshipers. The seating may be very like a formal classic exedra flanking both sides of the fireplace, or it may be some modification of natural rock outcropping or naturalized transplanted rocks in an informal approximation of a half-circle. This form of campfire grouping can serve effectively either as a memorial to an individual, or as a symbol of the contribution of some group to a park development. It is one of the few forms somewhat monumental in character yet not altogether ill at ease in a wilderness setting, and lends itself to commemorative tablets or inscriptions within appropriate limits. Being a combination of picnic fireplace and campfire circle, the examples shown will be found under "Picnic Fireplaces."

OUTDOOR THEATERS IN PARKS are points of open-air assembly and seating, ranging from the trivial—hardly more than expanded campfire circles—to the pretentious, having many of the equipment features of the roofed theater. The more extensive developments are apt to be found only in the larger parks where interest is more than local in extent, or in parks within a metropolitan range where large population and civic interest are forceful factors.

Wherever possible the outdoor theater should be located in a natural half-bowl. Unless existing contours truly invite such development, a remolding of them to create a natural effect is likely to require an amount of work out of proportion to the benefits derived. If anything short of accomplishment of complete naturalness results from a remolding of topography in creation of an open-air theater, the park is long, perhaps forever, disfigured by a scar that should be rigidly avoided.

The principles applicable to the creation of amphitheaters or outdoor theaters are numerous. Probably paramount is the consideration of sight lines. Acoustics are here quite as important as for the enclosed auditorium. Many will at first thought regard acoustics as not of the problem, but they should not fail to appreciate that hills and mountains, water surfaces, and forests deflect and echo sound in accordance with their own laws, as do man-made surroundings, and call for just as much advance consideration and study.

It is important that the stage be to the east or north, so that the audience will not face the afternoon sun. A distant view as background for the stage platform is greatly to be desired, or better still a picturesque cliff as at Pine Mountain State Park, Kentucky. A dense stand of forest trees is suitable and impressive. It is well to have the amphitheater encircled by trees. These lend it privacy, provide all possible shade for the audience, and act as barrier against the disturbing noises of other park activities.

The outdoor stage is sometimes merely a platform, the distant view, or cliff, or stand of trees serving as a backdrop. If these are lacking, or some required use of the stage demands it, an artificial background of rustic construction or of planting, or a combination of the two, may be created. When the showing of motion pictures is anticipated, the size of the structural background will be dictated by the size of the picture screen. The screen should be removable in winter, recessed for some measure of protection, and supplemented with dark canvas curtains to be drawn over it when pictures are not being shown. Where dramatic entertainment is to be offered, some provision of dressing room space is necessary. The stage of the amphitheater and any artificial construction in the nature of background, constituting as these do the focal point, must be outstandingly representative of park character. No harshness of line is to be tolerated here, and all the devices of skillful planting and naturalizing of native rock are legitimate in creation of the desired effect.

The seating of the amphitheater in a park setting may be contrived of logs or of stone. It may be said of log seating that it is the more comfortable in use, but the adjusting of the long straight lengths to the segmental arrangement of seats results in angles that are rigid and in a measure inharmonious with the freehand lines of Nature. Although stone seating, on the other hand, offers less physical comfort, it permits flowing and graceful curves in the seating plan that please the eye and complement the surroundings.

The cutting of large trees existent within the limits of the seating of the amphitheater is generally to be avoided. It is usually better to interrupt the seating to accommodate the trees. The trees, if trimmed of the lower branches, will provide shade for the audience with negligible obstruction to view of the stage.

Usually a campfire is built in front of the stage platform, or to one or both sides of it. Sometimes this must serve to illuminate the stage at night in lieu of footlights or other lighting. Whether or not it must serve such purpose, it links the pretentious outdoor theater with the simple campfire ring from which it evolved and provides a temporary home fire for the wanderer.

Plate II M-1   ⇾⇾⇾ CAMPFIRE CIRCLES AND OUTDOOR THEATERS

Campfire Circle
Manzanita Camp Ground - Lassen Volcanic National Park

A campfire circle with budding ambition to become a kind of outdoor theatre. The seating for three-quarters of its circumference is of full round logs, cut out to provide both seats and backs. The rest of the seating is without backs, anticipating the lecture platform, picture screen, and additional front row seats at some future time. Here is all the cleverness of the folding bed brought to park planning.

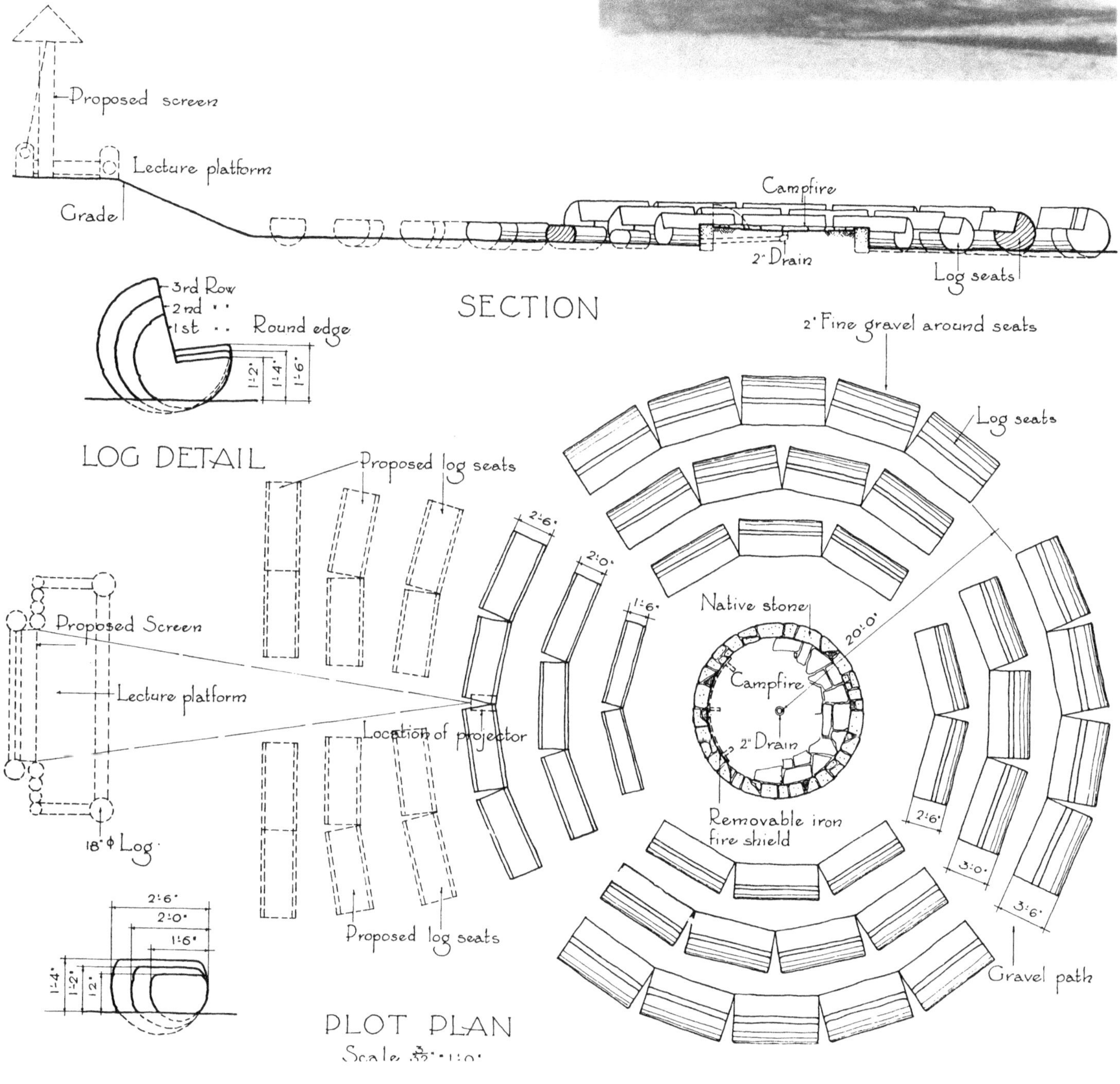

SECTION

LOG DETAIL

PLOT PLAN
Scale ⅛" = 1'0"

199

CAMPFIRE CIRCLES AND OUTDOOR THEATERS

Plate II M–2

Campfire Circle

Summit Lake — — Lassen Volcanic National Park

Here is a simple and well-arranged campfire ring in an ideal wooded setting, offering nearby lake and distant mountain view. The fire is confined to the elevated hearth by a curb of stone masonry. The practical provision of drain for the hearth should be noted, also the increasing sizes of the log seats from front to back row by virtue of which campfire enthusiasts in assorted sizes are catered to.

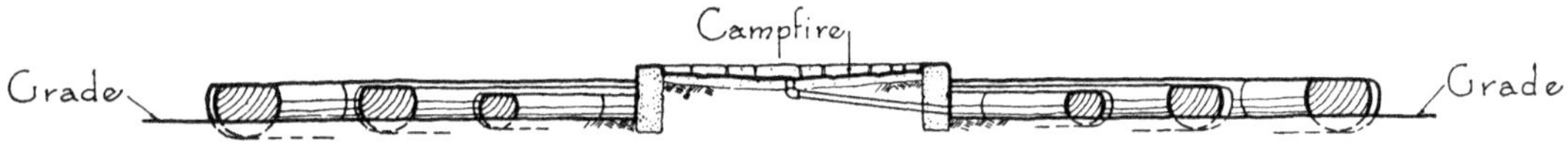

SECTION

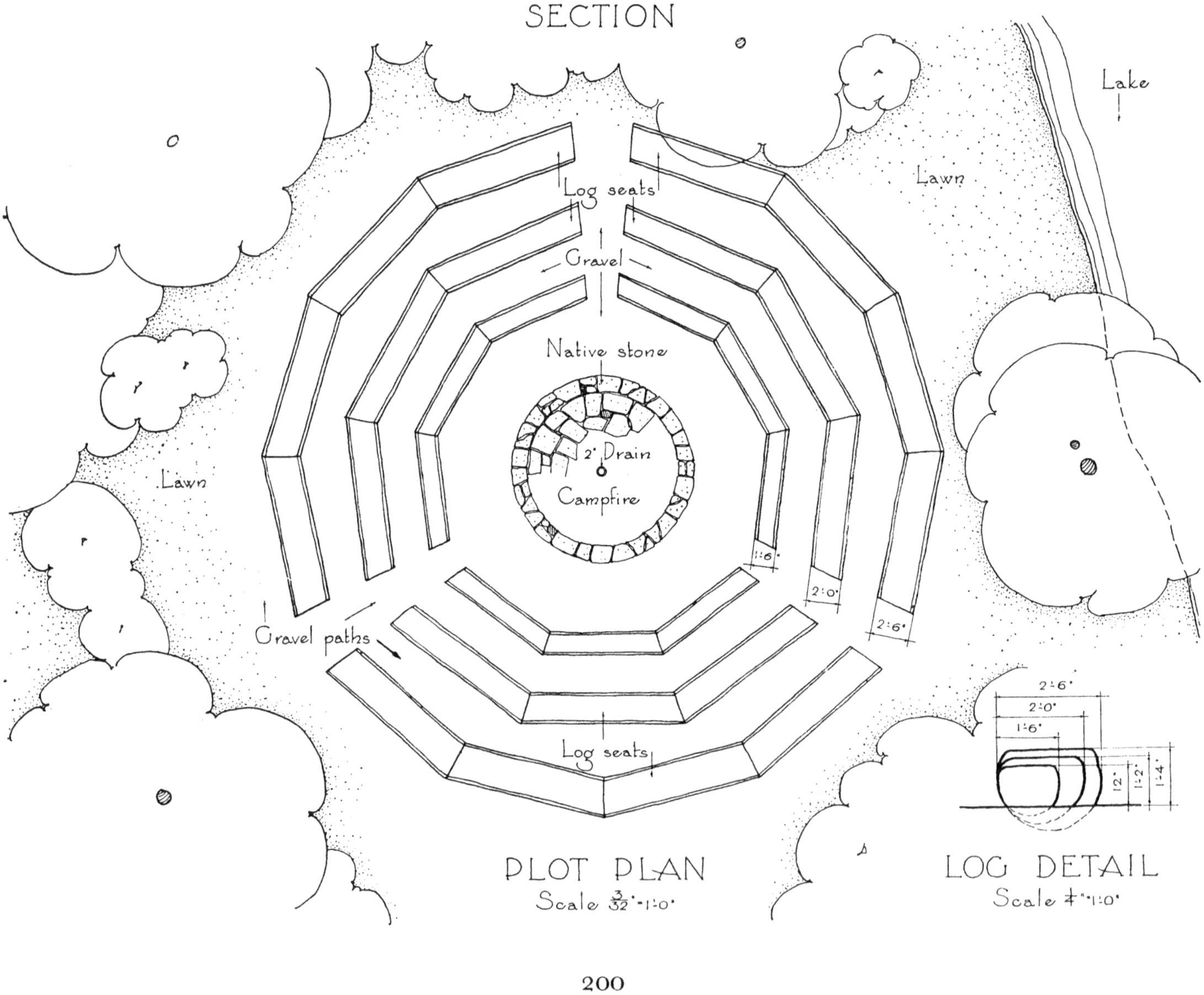

PLOT PLAN
Scale 3/32"=1'-0"

LOG DETAIL
Scale ¾"=1'-0"

Plate II M-3   ⋙ CAMPFIRE CIRCLES AND OUTDOOR THEATERS

Campfire Circle
Stephens Grove State Park   – – –   California

A campfire grouping which, by reason of arrangement, scale and simplicity, avoids being utterly alien in its impressive sylvan setting. The stage is paved with end-grain blocks cut from redwood logs. The two varieties of seating – short lengths of log on end and horizontal logs shaped to provide seats with backs – bring desirably casual informality to the arrangement.

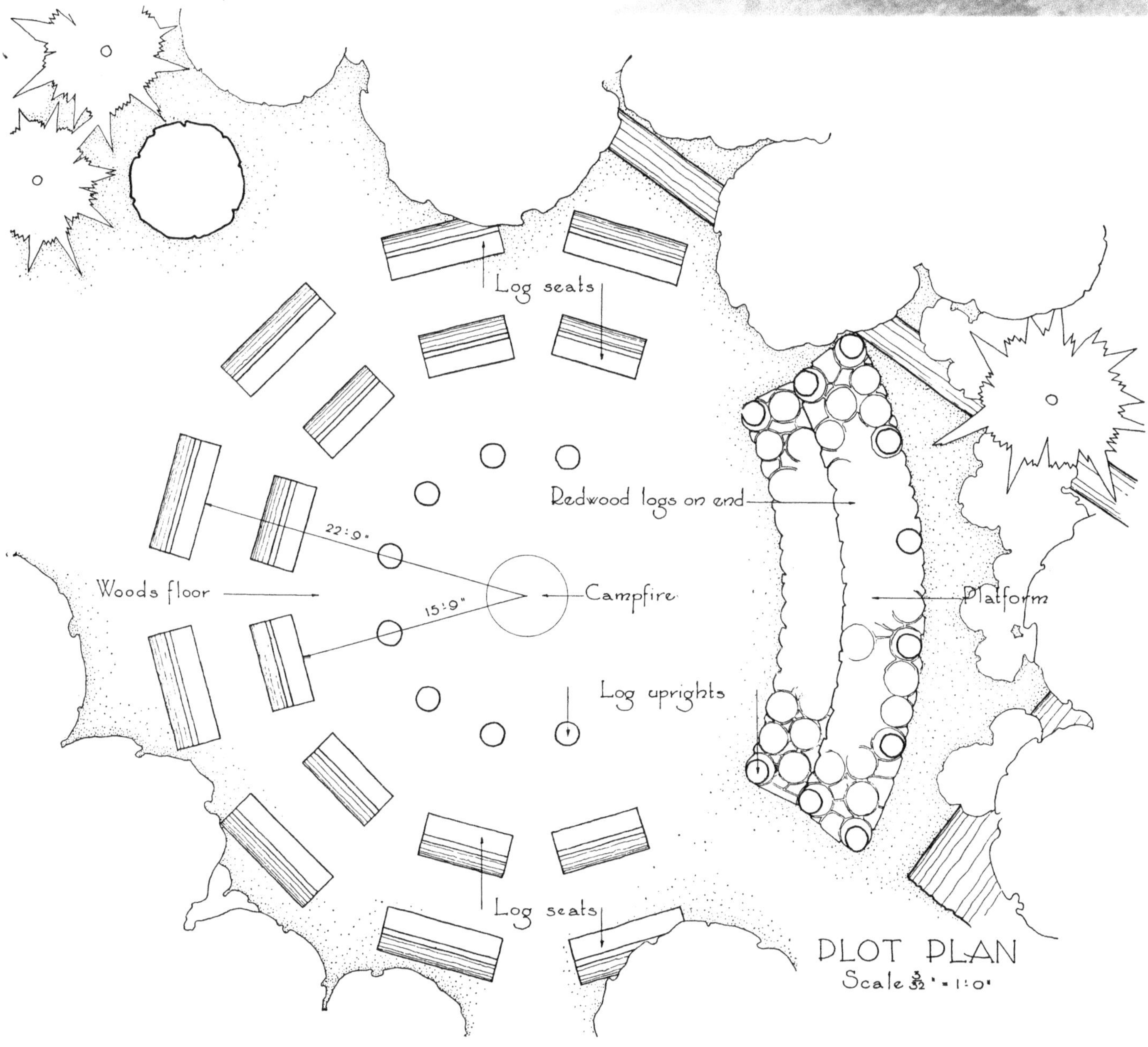

PLOT PLAN
Scale 3/32" = 1'-0"

201

CAMPFIRE CIRCLES AND OUTDOOR THEATERS

Plate II M-4

Campfire Circle

Prairie Creek State Park — — — California

The park planner does well to recognize the paradox which confronts him in a setting so idyllic. It has at once advantaged and handicapped from the very start the facility he hopes to insinuate with a certain grace. Only a simple utilization of material native and in reasonable scale in a fittingly dignified arrangement, and a deep reverence for the surrounding living and fallen trees and lace-like ground cover can save the planner from uttering a sardonic jest.

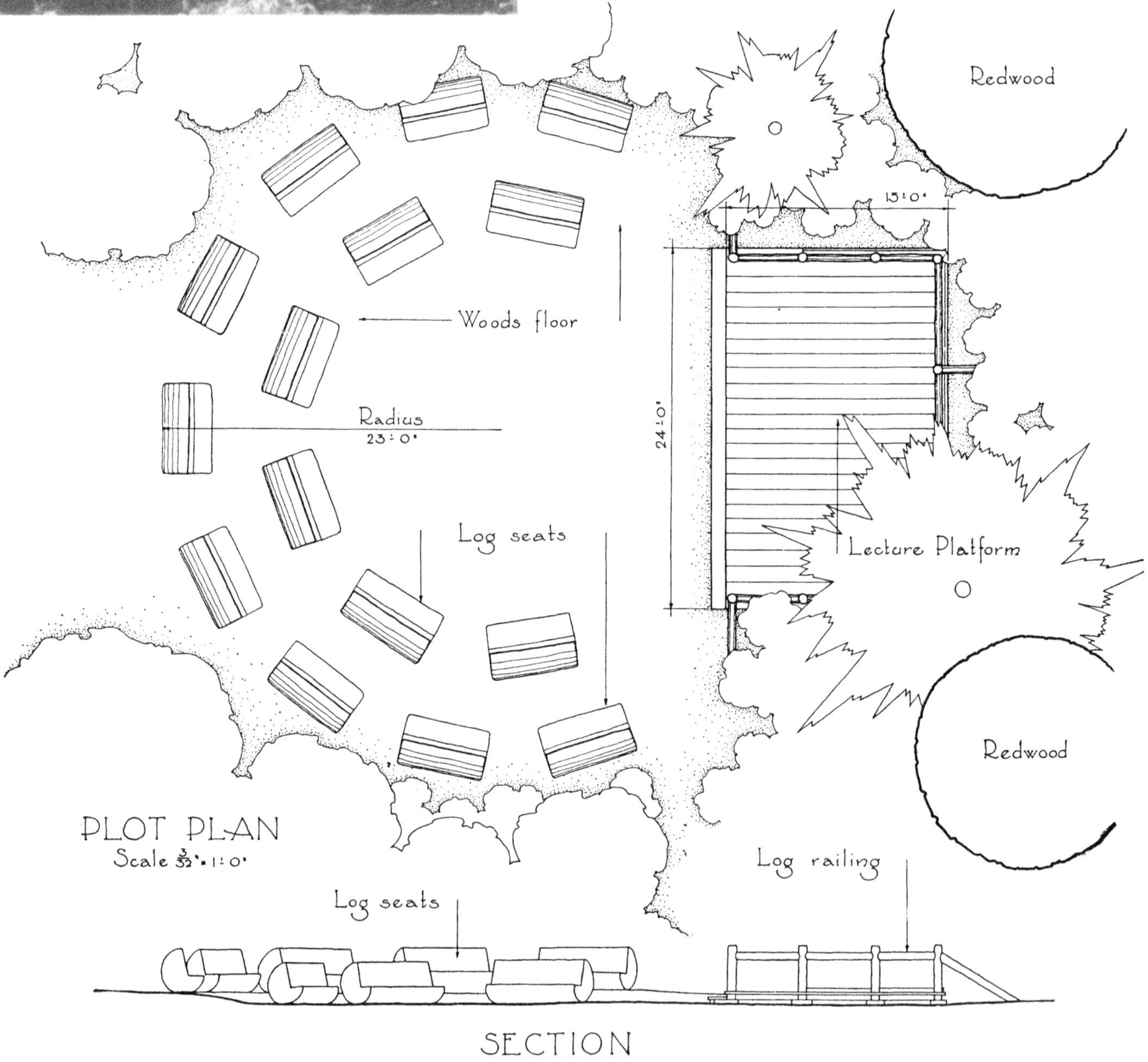

PLOT PLAN
Scale 3/32" = 1'-0"

SECTION

Plate II M–5 — CAMPFIRE CIRCLES AND OUTDOOR THEATERS

Outdoor Theater – Copiague – New York

While this agreeable example is on the grounds of a school, it has conservative and yet definite park character to win it a place here. Its semi-circular plan of seats, surrounding turf stage in front of platform stage, makes it more truly an amphitheater than an outdoor theater. The construction of the seats and the suggestion of foyer achieved by the drinking fountain and two facing log benches should be noted.

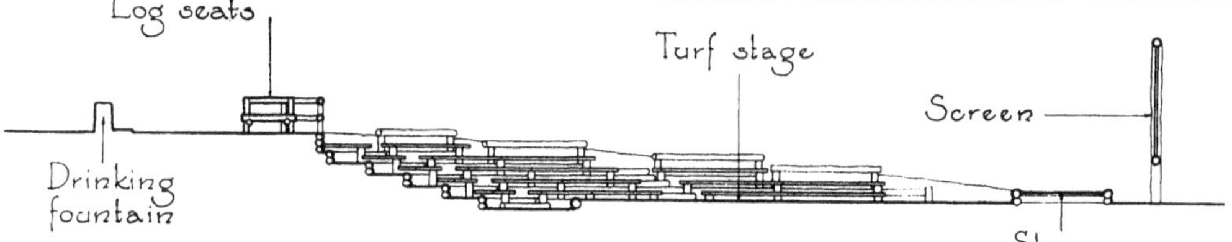

SECTION

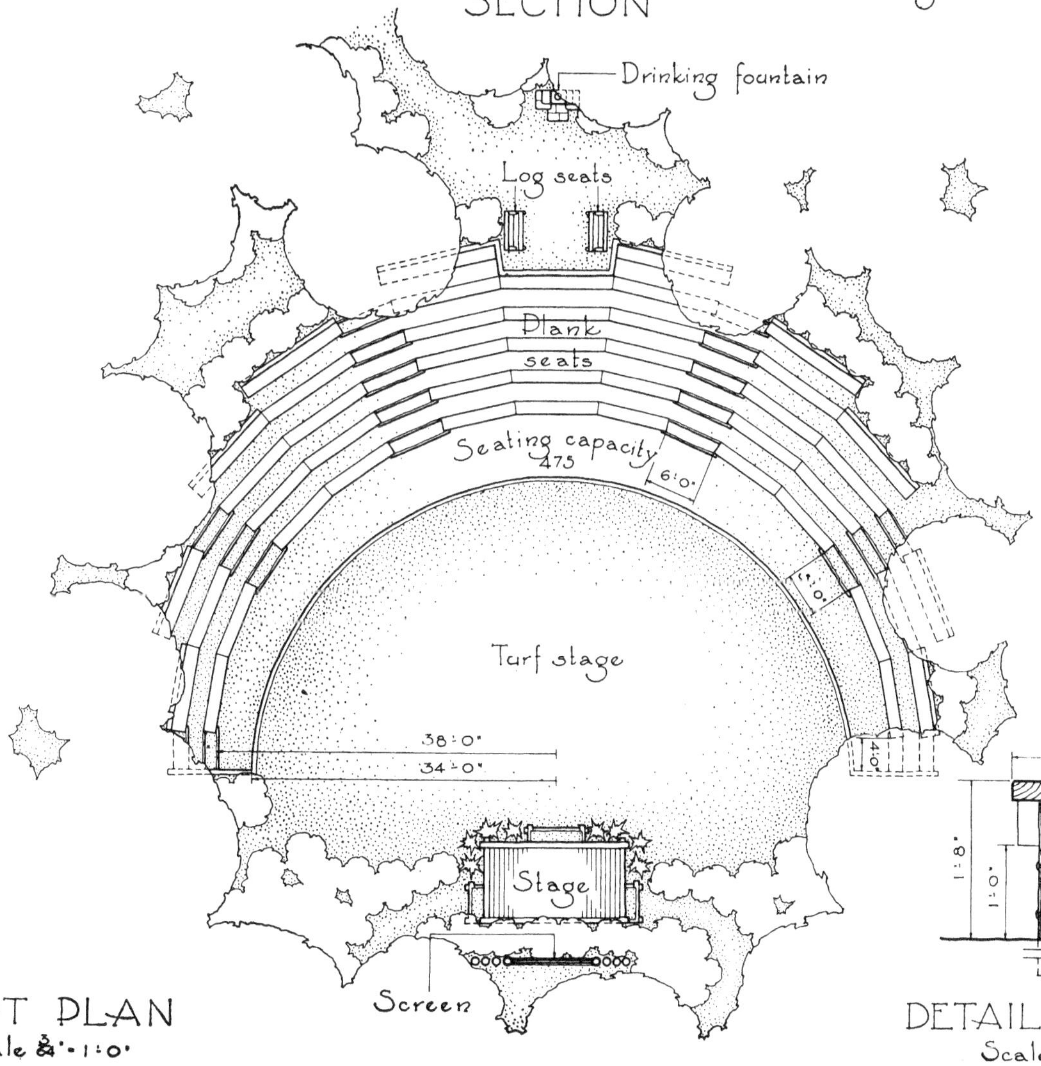

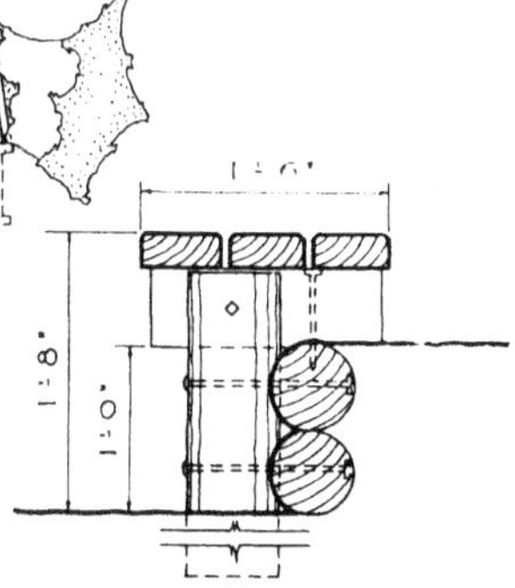

PLOT PLAN
Scale ⅛" = 1'-0"

DETAIL OF SEAT
Scale ½" = 1'-0"

203

CAMPFIRE CIRCLES AND OUTDOOR THEATERS

Plate II M-6

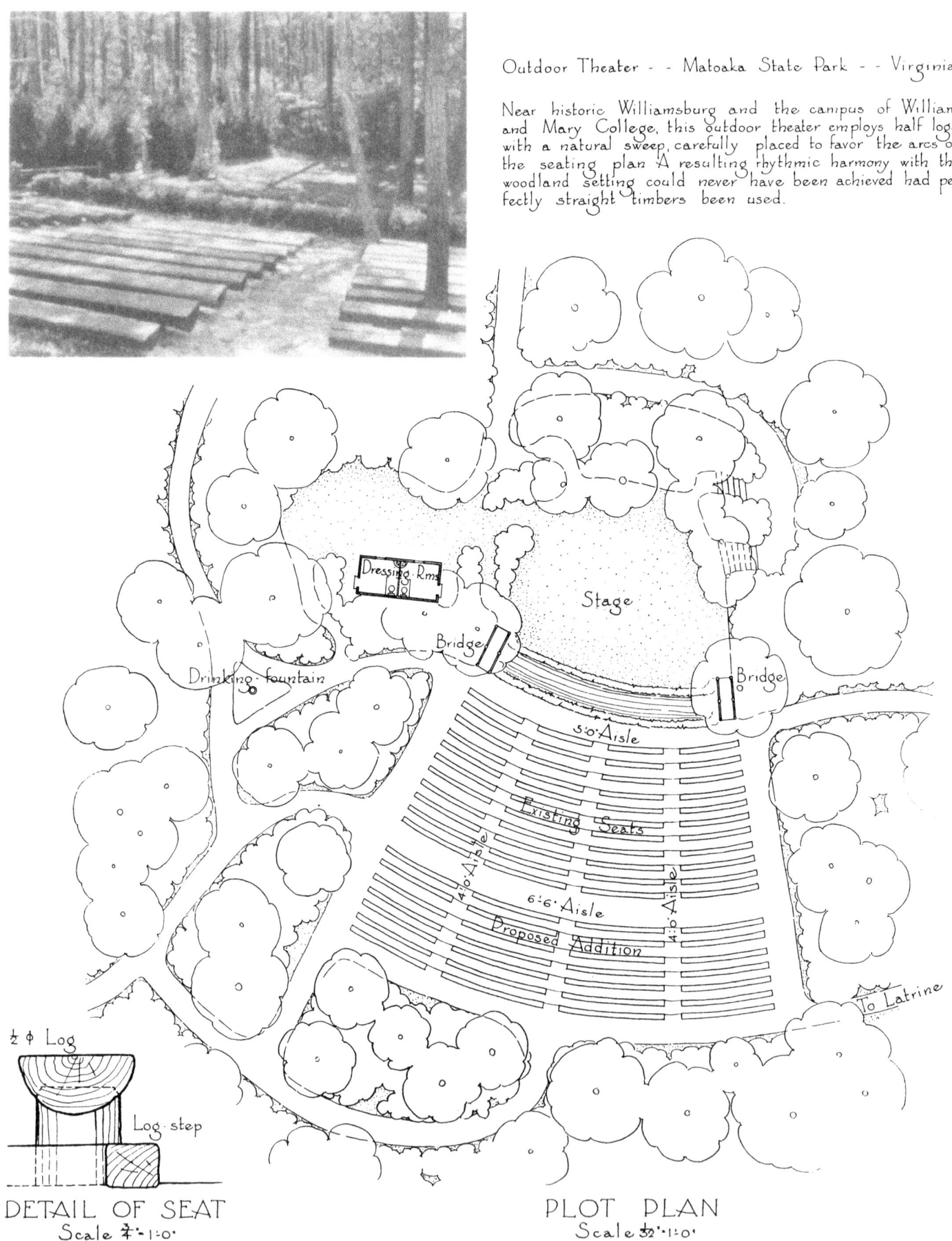

Outdoor Theater - - Matoaka State Park - - Virginia

Near historic Williamsburg and the campus of William and Mary College, this outdoor theater employs half logs with a natural sweep, carefully placed to favor the arcs of the seating plan. A resulting rhythmic harmony with the woodland setting could never have been achieved had perfectly straight timbers been used.

DETAIL OF SEAT
Scale ¾"-1'-0"

PLOT PLAN
Scale 32'-1'-0"

204

Amphitheatre — Forest City State Park — Iowa

The simpler the rendering of an outdoor theater the more fitting in a natural park. Here is an example that does not pretend to outdo its surroundings and as a result justifies its presence. The seats of heavy planks supported on masonry piers do not have the measure of informality attained by the log seating of some of the examples that follow. The state of incompletion and the absence of summer foliage in the illustration obscure the considerable merit, present and potential, of this project.

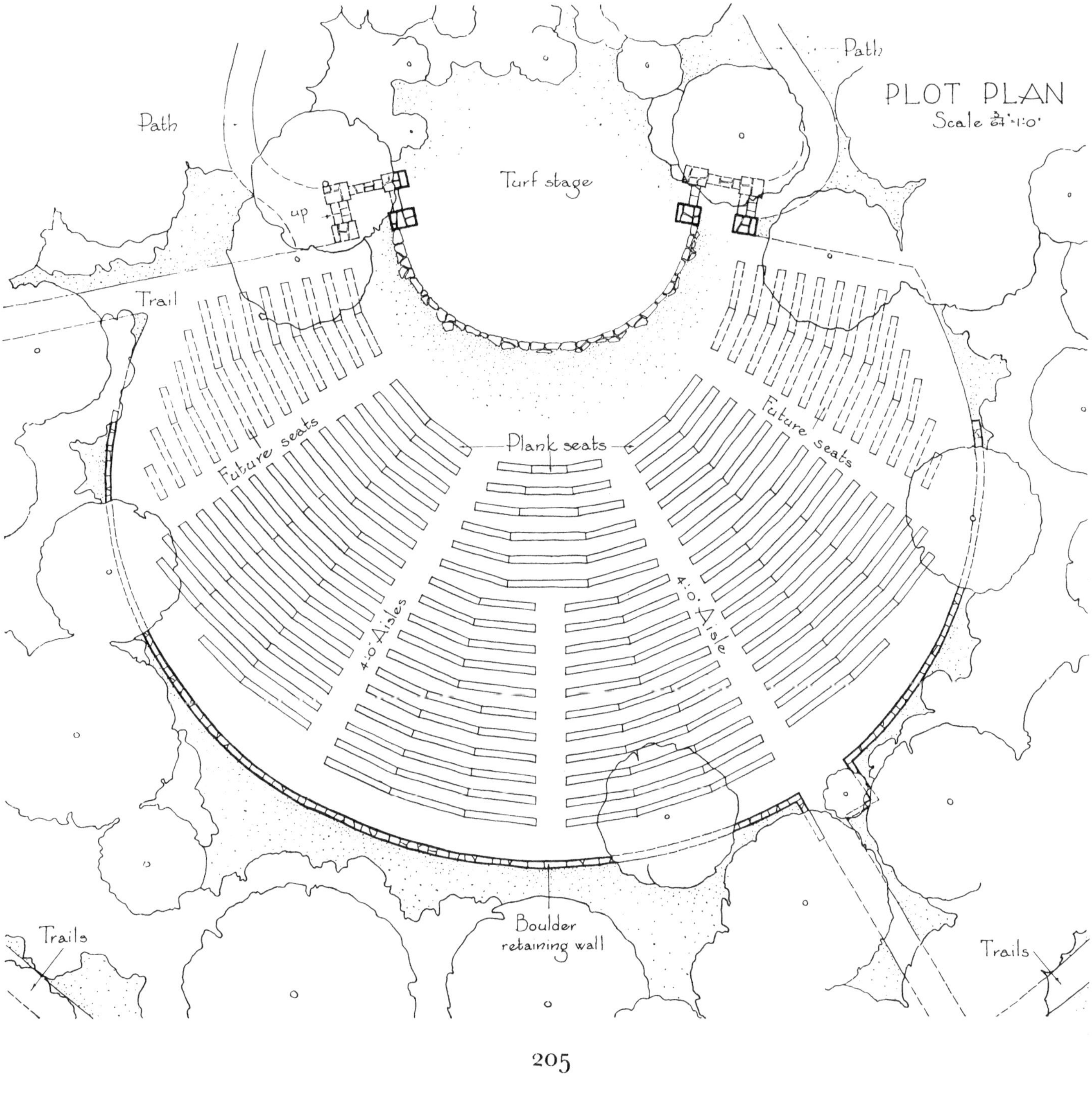

PLOT PLAN
Scale ¾" = 1'-0"

CAMPFIRE CIRCLES AND OUTDOOR THEATERS

Plate II M-8

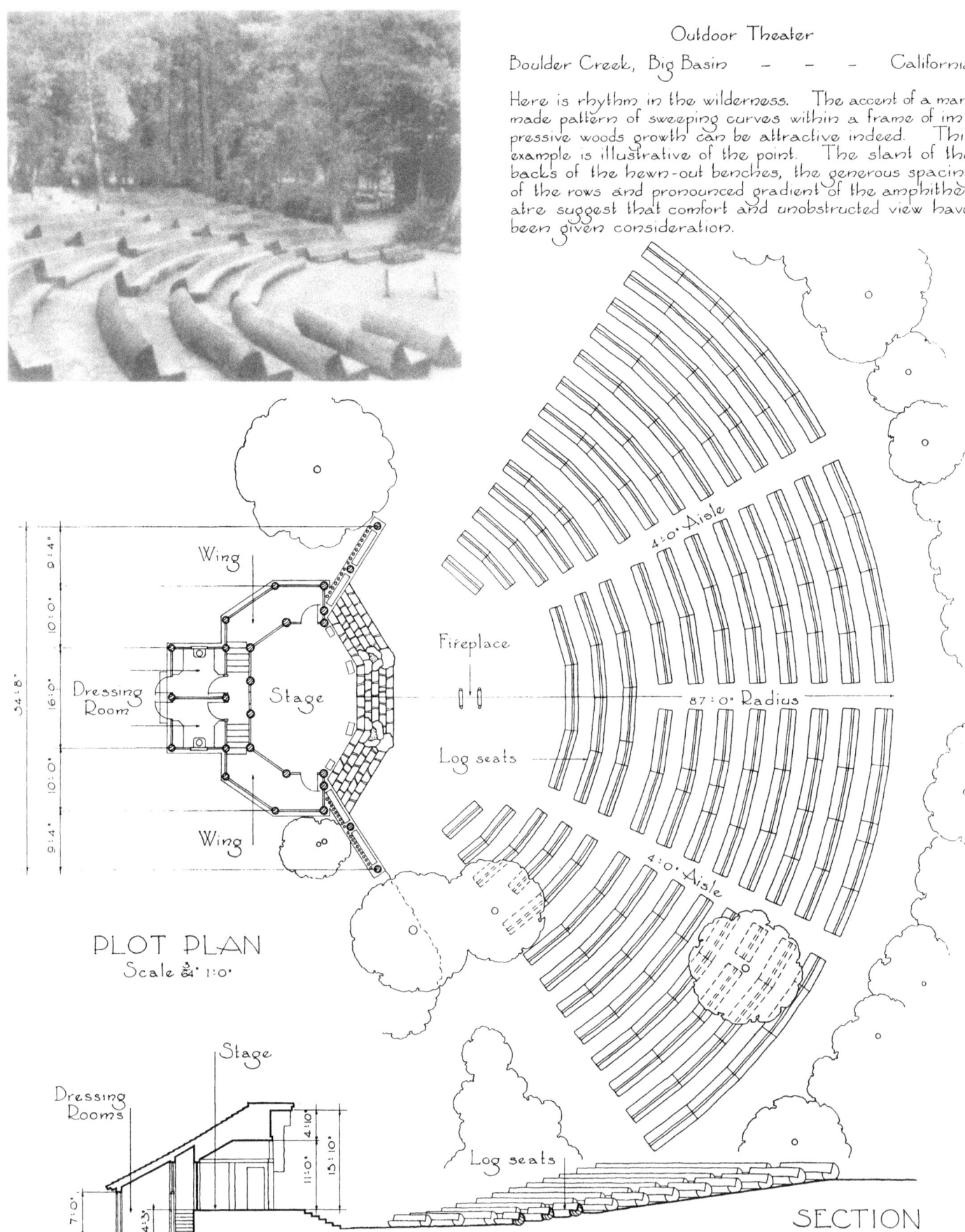

Outdoor Theater

Boulder Creek, Big Basin — — — California

Here is rhythm in the wilderness. The accent of a man-made pattern of sweeping curves within a frame of impressive woods growth can be attractive indeed. This example is illustrative of the point. The slant of the backs of the hewn-out benches, the generous spacing of the rows and pronounced gradient of the amphitheatre suggest that comfort and unobstructed view have been given consideration.

Plate II M-9 — CAMPFIRE CIRCLES AND OUTDOOR THEATERS

Outdoor Theater — — Zion National Park

Most notable feature of this layout, if the magnificent scenic panorama may be excepted, is the disappearing screen and the shelter for screen and equipment. Attention is invited to the projector pedestal, the detail of the seat construction, the asymmetrical location of the campfire and the rock serving as the immediate background of the lecture platform. Future expansion of the seating has been anticipated and well planned.

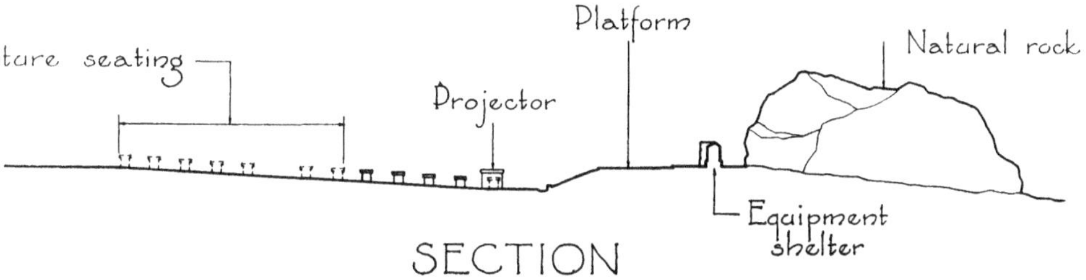

SECTION

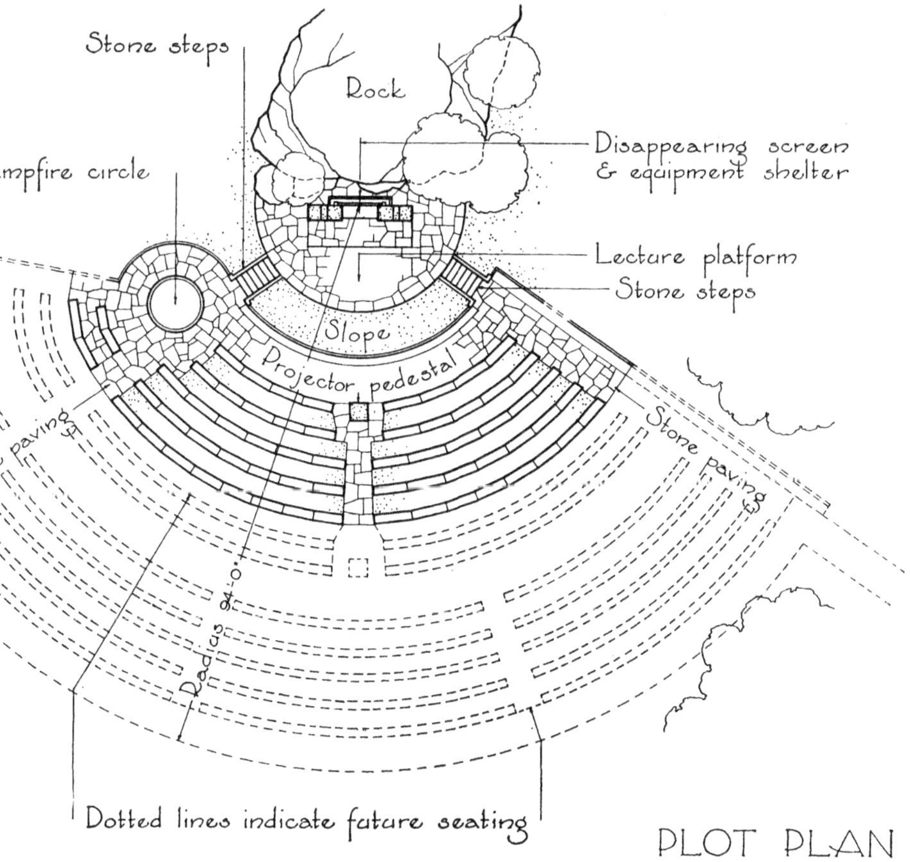

Future seating — Projector — Platform — Natural rock — Equipment shelter

PLOT PLAN Scale 32' = 1'-0"

Stone steps — Rock — Disappearing screen & equipment shelter — Campfire circle — Lecture platform — Stone steps — Slope — Projector pedestal — Stone paving — Stone paving — Dotted lines indicate future seating

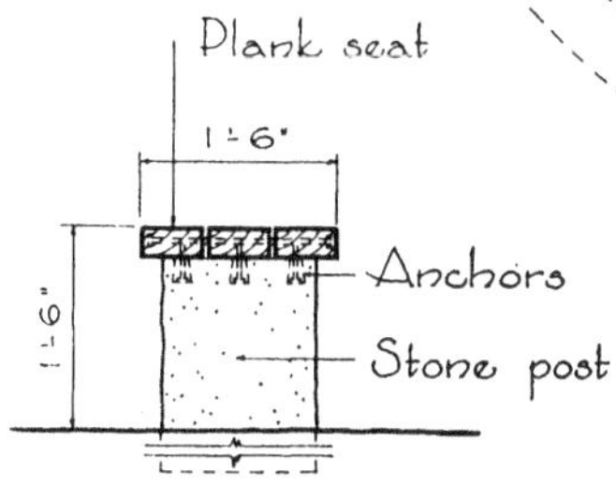

SEAT DETAIL Scale ⅜" = 1'-0"

Plank seat — 1'-6" — Anchors — Stone post — 1'-6"

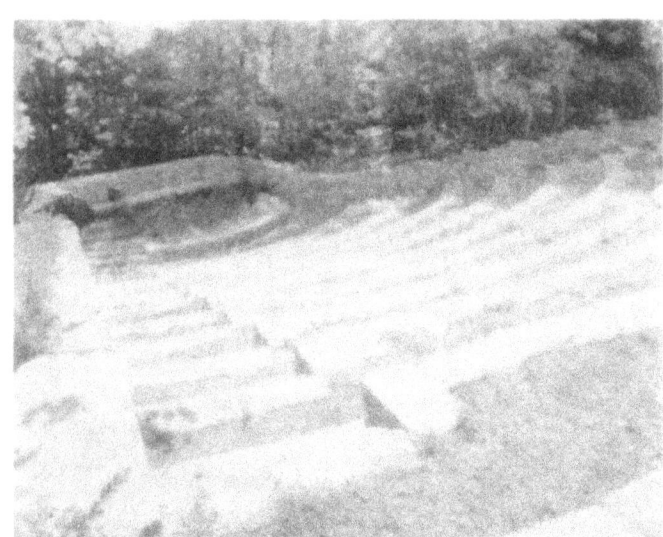

Outdoor Theater

Brown County State Park – – – Indiana

Although uncompleted when the photograph was made this subject promises an altogether happy conclusion. It is desirably framed by trees, which results in an intimate character lacking without them. Its modest size likewise is a factor in this. Patrons will be grateful for the narrow arc plan and sharp slope insuring for all a "head-on" and full view of the stage without need for neck craning and straining for altitude.

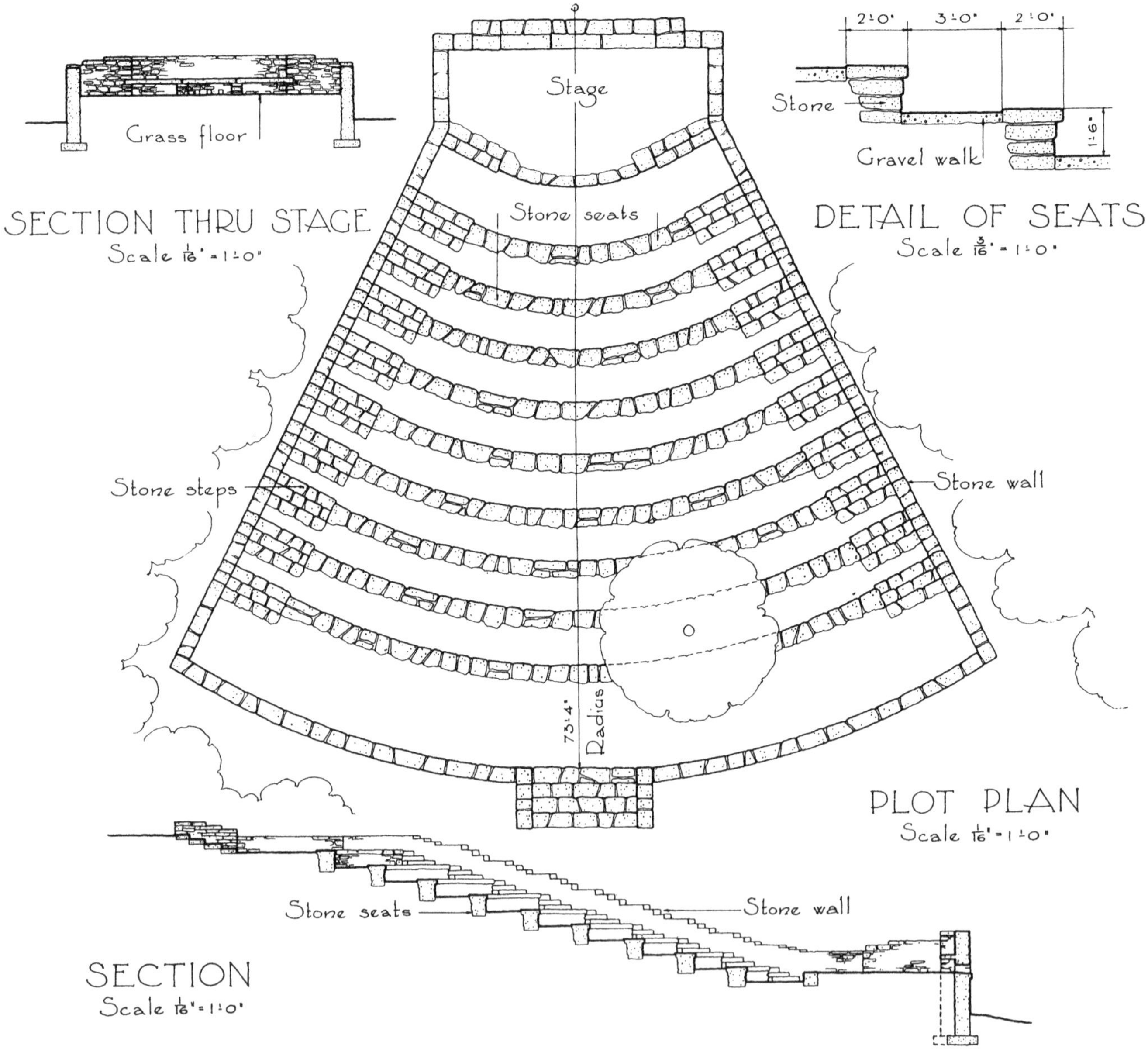
Grass floor
SECTION THRU STAGE
Scale 1/16" = 1'-0"
Stage
Stone seats
Stone steps
Stone wall
73'-4" Radius
PLOT PLAN
Scale 1/16" = 1'-0"
2'-0"
3'-0"
2'-0"
Stone
Gravel walk
1'-6"
DETAIL OF SEATS
Scale 3/16" = 1'-0"
Stone seats
Stone wall
SECTION
Scale 1/16" = 1'-0"

Plate II M-11 — CAMPFIRE CIRCLES AND OUTDOOR THEATERS

Amphitheater — Flagstaff Mountain State Park
Boulder — — — — — — — Colorado

The value of the distant view as backdrop for the stage of an amphitheater is here manifest. The campfire is brought into prominence as the very center of the arcs of stone seats. When time has provided walls of evergreens as a background for the seating, and as a frame for the panoramic backdrop, this example will have come into its own.

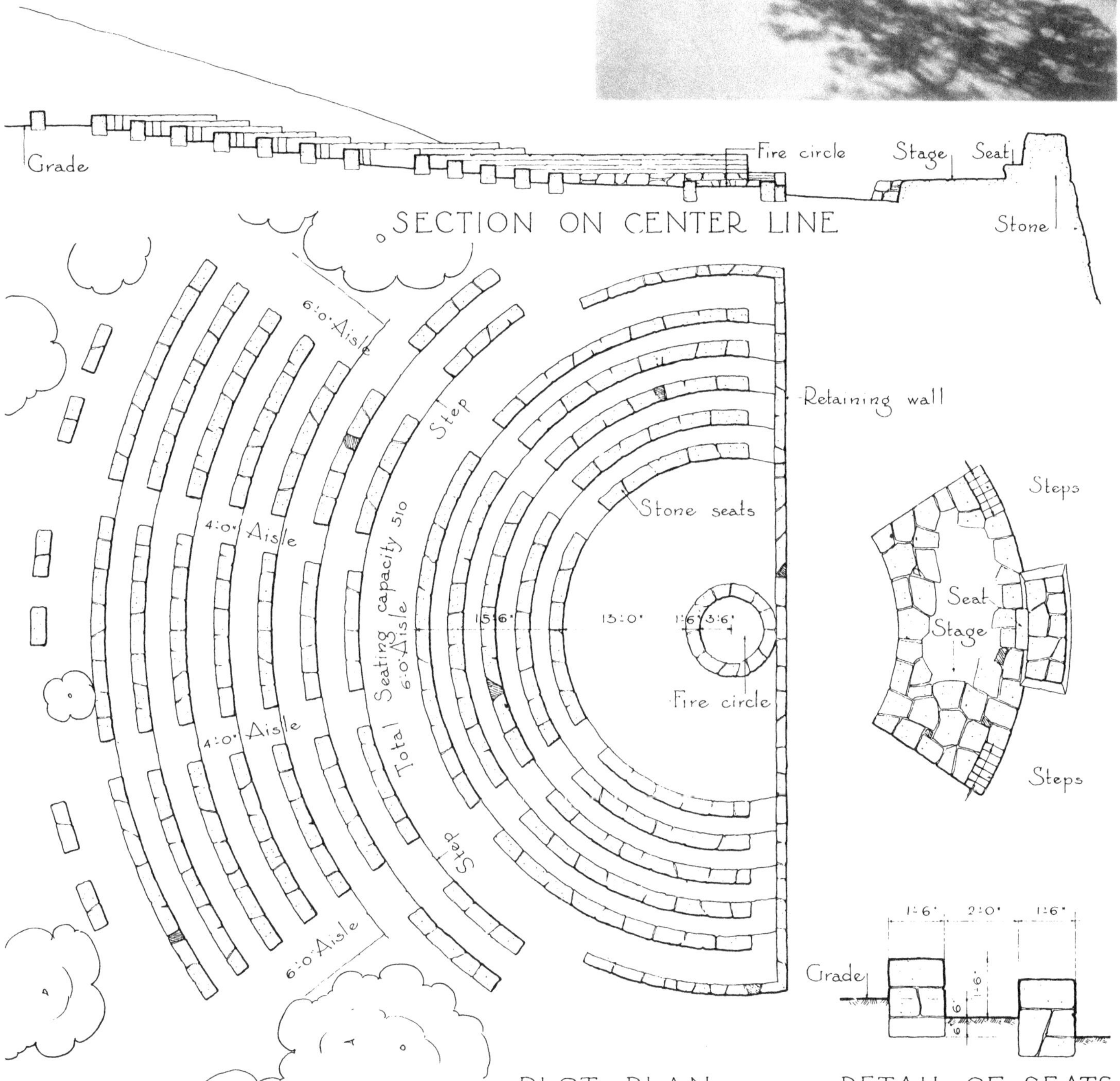

SECTION ON CENTER LINE

PLOT PLAN
Scale 1/16"=1'-0"

DETAIL OF SEATS
Scale 1/4"=1'-0"

CAMPFIRE CIRCLES AND OUTDOOR THEATERS

Plate II M–12

Amphitheater — Yellowstone National Park

In this large national park are two outdoor theaters of nearly identical arrangement. On the facing page both are pictured. The plan shown above is of the Old Faithful amphitheater, which differs from the one at Fishing Bridge, mainly in the greater elaboration of its platform and background. Both platforms are quite shallow front to back.

The campfire pit is axial in both instances. The seating of large, barked logs, resting on log stringers, is boldly scaled to the out-of-doors. The perching of the housing for the projector on log "piles" is of interest. The rocks which outline the paths of one example are so unfortunately placed as to force their eventual removal, unless Nature hastens to supply some ground cover to obliterate them in considerable degree.

Plate II M-13 — CAMPFIRE CIRCLES AND OUTDOOR THEATERS

Old Faithful Amphitheater, Yellowstone National Park

Fishing Bridge Amphitheater, Yellowstone National Park

CAMPFIRE CIRCLES AND OUTDOOR THEATERS

Plate II M-14

Outdoor Theater — General Grant National Park

Typical of an outdoor theater in a Far Western forest, and noteworthy for the seats provided — barked giant logs planted in the earth, leveled on the tops and dressed smooth. The campfire to one side of the vestigial orchestra pit is a usual appurtenance of the amphitheater in a National Park. The dissymetrical seating plan, favoring trees and topography evidences deferential regard for the setting. The restless complexity of the stage background is doubtless necessary to meet the demands of the varied forms of entertainment offered.

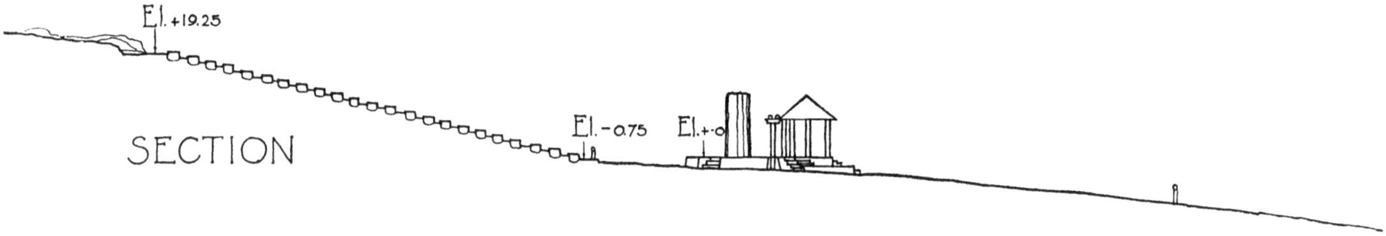

SECTION

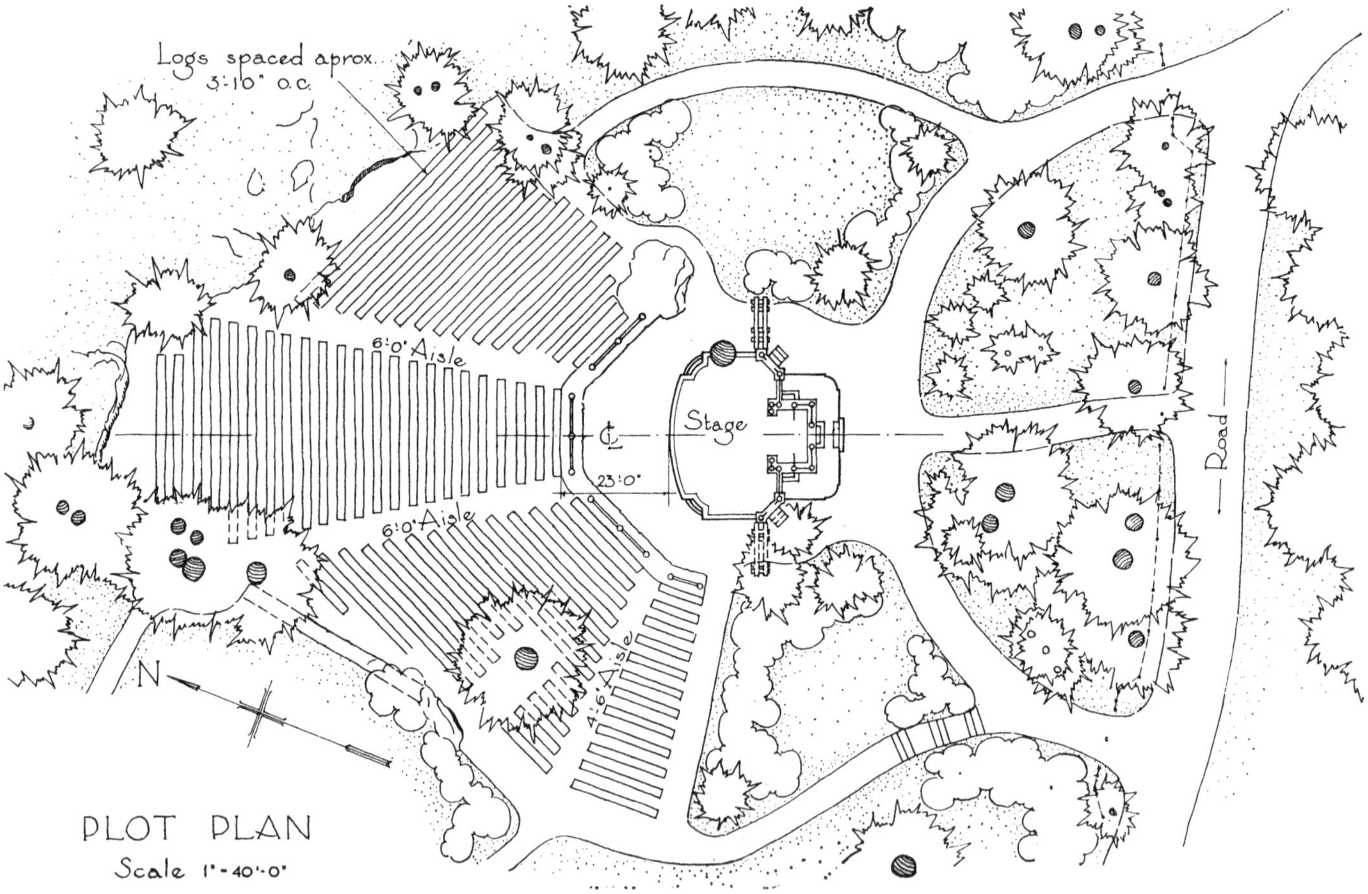

PLOT PLAN
Scale 1" = 40'-0"

Part III

OVERNIGHT AND ORGANIZED CAMP FACILITIES

CONTENTS

	PAGE
OVERNIGHT AND ORGANIZED CAMP FACILITIES	1
TENT AND TRAILER CAMPSITES	5
Plates III A–1 *to* III A–7	
CABINS	17
Plates III B–1 *to* III B–36	
LODGES, INNS, AND HOTELS	57
Plates III C–1 *to* III C–15	
COMMUNITY BUILDINGS	75
Plates III D–1 *to* III D–6	
WASHHOUSES AND LAUNDRIES	83
Plates III E–1 *to* III E–7	
CAMPSTOVES	91
Plates III F–1 *to* III F–6	
FURNITURE AND FURNISHINGS	99
Plates III G–1 *to* III G–8	
CAMP LAY-OUT	109
Plates III H–1 *to* III H–7	
CAMP ADMINISTRATION AND BASIC SERVICE FACILITIES	121
Plates III I–1 *to* III I–18	
CAMP RECREATIONAL AND CULTURAL FACILITIES	143
Plates III J–1 *to* III J–13	
CAMP COOKING AND DINING FACILITIES	161
Plates III K–1 *to* III K–9	
CAMP SLEEPING FACILITIES	173
Plates III L–1 *to* III L–17	

OVERNIGHT AND ORGANIZED CAMP FACILITIES

BEFORE facilitating structures can be discussed with clarity, the nomenclature of overnight accommodation and organized camping in parks calls for examination—indeed organized camping as an institution may even stand in need of exposition. Perhaps an attempt to differentiate between "overnight use" and "organized camping" as the terms are herein applied should first be made.

Overnight facilities in a park are structures ranging from tents to hotels in which an individual or a family, or combinations of either or both, may obtain sleeping accommodations for one or more nights. Facilities for organized camping likewise include tents or cabins in which individuals or families may obtain sleeping accommodations within the park but with the distinction that their group tenancy, generally for a week or longer, is sponsored and supervised by some character-building, educational, welfare, or other organization. This sponsored variety of day and night use of a park constitutes a collective recreational use, so to say, in contrast with the free lance tenancy that characterizes other overnight accommodation. If the distinction is ill-expressed, perhaps it will become more clear as the structural facilities individually are discussed.

Among the variety of means for stopping overnight in a park, the simplest is tent camping, so long practiced that it probably invaded most park areas even before they were officially established as such. Perhaps for this reason tents, clotheslines, and campers in the most outlandish dress and undress, and the propriety of all these in areas of extraordinary natural beauty, have been seldom challenged. The tent camper seems to exercise (and to get away with!) an inversion of the right of eminent domain. He holds any attempt to regulate his tenancy and conduct in the public interest to be ultra vires and inhibiting of his ruggedly individualistic prerogatives.

Then comes trailer camping, comparatively a recent development, more submissive perhaps to regulation, but also more demanding of space and facilities for comfort and convenience. At present the appropriateness of elaborate accommodations for trailers in natural parks of distinction is a subject of lively debate. There is also diverse current prophecy concerning the future of the trailer, ranging from a view that it is a passing fad (as was once said of the automobile), already on the way out, to the statement of a once eminent statistician that within 20 years half the population of the country will be living in trailers. In the latter prediction, considered thought cannot have been given to the schooling of children. Apparently the typical American family of that future time will consist of a man, a wife, and a trailer—probably children, schools, and schooling will then be obsolete. If the birth rate is to drop and the trailer rate to rise, the figure representative of one-half the population in 1956, and so of trailer registration, is highly speculative.

There is everywhere abundant proof that trailer popularity has lately been increasing, and the very present problem of parks is whether to ban them or arrange to make them welcome and as little destructive of park values as need be. In any rush to anticipate the demand of visitors with trailers for parking and camping space in parks, it is recommended as foresighted to keep one trend-conscious ear to the ground to prevent possible overenthusiastic provision of trailer campsites.

In contrast with the aforementioned overnight accommodations of transportable character are those of fixed type. Of this series the cabin is the simplest example. The meaning of the term "cabin" is probably generally well understood. Still, in addition to designating a detached structure accommodating a family or small group vacationing independently, it is applied to a one-room building sleeping campers of an organized camp. In discussions of structures of organized camps, cabin generally means this latter type. It could be termed a "dormitory" if the word did not smack of crowded or substandard sleeping conditions. This taboo and the appearance of no differentiating term in substitution make it incumbent on the reader to interpret the specific intent in each cabin reference herein.

In some parks the need for overnight cabins in great numbers and the difficulties which attend finding a solution satisfactory to the many interests involved have led to centralizations of fixed overnight accommodations, more or less complex. These are variously called inns, lodges, and hotels, and the terms are so interchangeably applied to varying physical set-ups that exact definitions are arrived at with difficulty.

In national parks what is termed a "lodge" is usually a building containing lounge, dining room, and kitchen, together with the dependencies that relate to these. It supplements or serves cabins grouped around it. The hotel in national parks is usually self-contained; instead of supplementing detached cabins, it provides guest rooms under the same roof. But this difference even within the national parks is not always sharply defined. Elsewhere the terms "lodge", "inn", and "hotel" are so generally interchangeable in use that lodge, in these discussions, will be used as the generic term for all combinations, whether the sleeping quarters are integral or detached.

Except for organized camps, the roll of overnight accommodations in parks, from tents to hotels, has been called. Following later textual and graphic exploration of these several facilities, certain necessary supplementing structures will also be discussed and pictured.

ORGANIZED CAMPING is either very old or relatively very new, depending on the perspective in which its background is seen. Only a century ago, when about 75 percent of the population of the United States was rural, primitive conditions made living throughout vast areas not far different from a camping existence except that it was conditioned on the hardest kind of labor. Even when the frontier was pushed westward and rural life in the wake of it became less rigorous, dwellers in rural districts might still enjoy close touch with Nature in its many moods. But the coming of the machine age brought a rapid movement of population from farms to cities and towns. When eventually less than 50 percent of us could experience the satisfying and revivifying contacts with Nature afforded by nonurban existence, these contacts in themselves had lost value. Sprawling, overcrowded cities were expanding on every hand to a far reaching contamination of countryside; natural resources were being squandered to obtain the raw materials for a wasteful, industrial civilization. Lacking only a date line, the obituary of a Nature that had once gloriously spanned a continent and nurtured a nation was on the way to the linotype.

Reaction against the cramped and artificial living conditions imposed by this revolutionary way of life naturally developed. The phrases "the simple life" and "back to Nature", current at the start of the century, evidence an awareness that something highly prized had vanished from the American scene. They indicate, moreover, a will to restore it. When it is remembered that for countless centuries camping was man's normal manner of living and that a settled life in permanent structures is a matter of comparatively few centuries, this nostalgia for the out-of-doors is understandable.

The first excursions in response to the "back to Nature" urge were doubtless made by individuals and small groups geographically scattered. But the idea of camping for camping's sake, not just as a means to some such end as hunting, fishing, migrating, or exploring, carried immediate, far reaching appeal to Americans in great numbers. Small camping groups soon became large groups, and with these had to come organization of a sort. Conflicting interests yielded to a pooling of interests for the greater benefit of all. Individualistic pursuit of recreation gave way to a running with the pack. In this trend was further reversion to man's nomadic past. The tribal organization supplies a centuries-old precedent for the organized camp. Just as the tribal bands, more than the lone wolves among prehistoric hunters, moved the shadowy past into historical focus, so have organized camps, more than the individualistic camping expeditions of limited groups, high-lighted the history of camping and mainly evolved its modern practices.

Most of the first organized camps were private enterprises. Later, educational and character-influencing organizations—church, lodge, and club groups—and political units such as towns and counties were sponsoring, building, and operating camps for the moderately circumstanced and the underprivileged. Today there are organized camps for families, for adults, for boys and for girls of all age groups, for both boys and girls, for mothers and infants, for crippled children and others impaired in health.

In the discussions and illustrations that follow, bearing on the lay-out and construction of organized camps, there is predominant concern with the organized camp evolved to serve generally the somewhat varying needs of many camping groups and coincidently to avoid any serious restriction of the practices particular to any one. There is a stressing of principles and policies relevant to what might be termed a composite organized camp.

Underlying this approach is the realization that many camp lay-outs are used by several very different groups during a single season. Furthermore, vicissitude may lead to a camp built for the exclusive use of a particular group being shared with, or even relinquished to, another organization. Indulging a whim for too individualistic and experimental camp lay-out and construction parallels flying a revolutionary type of airplane without a parachute. It testifies to daring rather than good judgment, and is exceedingly ill-advised if undertaken with public or institutional funds on public lands.

To be sure, where the undertaking is a private venture on a privately held site and sole use by a particular organization appears to be guaranteed, there are some desirable though minor departures from the composite or typical organized camp construction. Especially are the physical set-ups of camps for families, for crippled children, and those occupied simultaneously by children or young people of both sexes improved by variations from the typical. These variations will be later touched on, although none, save the rearrangement of toilet and shower facilities, and perhaps a revision of distances between buildings and between units, is so major as to make the generally typical very much less serviceable by contrast.

Some camp structures that do not adhere to principles promoted herein are included among the plates. Theories of organized camping other than the one here recommended have their proponents, and have led to the creation of camp buildings, imaginative architecturally, and meritorious structurally. Presentation of these here seems completely justified, because of the inspiration to be had from the highly original designs and excellent construction, even though it has sometimes been felt necessary to challenge underlying concepts.

THE IMPORTANCE of structures and facilities of the organized camp may seem to be overstressed, and the contribution of able leadership to the success of such a camp to be neglected, in this publication. This is but natural in a compilation which has for its announced purpose the exploration of structural accessories.

It is admitted at once that a full complement of the buildings and facilities herein rated as essential or desirable will never become a perfect organized camp until competent leadership directs the use of them. On the other hand, experienced and capable camp directors, utilizing structural accessories limited to a very minimum and individually short of ideal, can still achieve something notable in camping. Probably a very able leadership, starting with only a small lodge, sanitary latrines, and tent platforms, will eventually produce a better all around organized camp by the addition of needed structural facilities as opportunity permits than will result where a camp, initially complete structurally, suffers from inept leadership. Even so, it cannot be denied that the greatest potential accomplishment exists for camps when capable leadership is reinforced with structural perfection and completeness.

Naturally in the earliest organized camps there was much freedom for the individual. Programs were impromptu; schedules, rather sketchy; regulations, few. Ensuing development tended to overorganization and overregulation. Camp lay-outs patterned on army camp lines became popular. Tents and buildings more or less formally lined a company street or bordered a virtual parade ground. The camper's day became a succession of periods during each of which everyone in camp was expected to cavort simultaneously at some scheduled activity, devised with good intent for recreation or physical benefit, but often resulting in rebellion and overfatigue. It will probably sometime be recorded that regimentation of camping wrote its own death warrant on a day when a leader of extraordinary inventive genius hit upon the idea of a mass brushing, morning and night, of all the teeth in camp to a kind of dance routine and timing.

Retreat from that kind of camp direction, with its crowded programs, disregard of differing physical capacities, and stifling of individuality, became general and continues a marked trend in camping today. It has greatly influenced the planning of organized camps, and has led to the building of so-called unit camps, a type which will be described later. The formal arrangements on army camp lines have lost favor, and in the most successful and admired campgrounds recently built, the buildings seem to have been plunked down by what has been described as "dice throw" planning. Actually the informal placing of buildings is by no means as casual as might be inferred from this phrase; rather is it a conscious effort to avoid geometric formality and take full advantage of favorable site factors.

Deregimentation of camping has changed the use, design, and number of buildings which comprise a camp group. The one-time acceptable "barracks" housing has given way to smaller units accommodating four campers, preferably, and never more than eight where recommended practices prevail.

In the trend to humor and respect the camper's individuality, there has been very properly no relaxing of standards involving his health and safety. On the contrary, these constantly become more rigid. Safe drinking water, positive disposal of sewage, unpolluted water for swimming, suitable spacing of beds, and the like are increasingly matters of vital concern among camp leaders and jurisdictional agencies.

It is interesting to review the practices in modern camping which derive from the American Indians' way of life and the adaptations from it made by the early pioneers. The influences of these on camp lay-out and construction, in addition to the almost dominating Indian and pioneer influences on activities programs, have been considerable. The council or campfire ring comes immediately to mind. As used, it is an out-and-out revival of Indian custom. The craft shop first came into being for the practice of pioneer and primitive crafts. Organized camps arranged in units are somehow analogous to the villages of certain nomad Indians, wherein the placing of tepees acknowledged groups within a group, and provided fixed positions for related families which were always reassumed in each new encampment.

Log construction is a widely popular style for camp buildings, just as for park buildings, and carries on the structural traditions of the pioneers. Generous fireplaces such as the pioneers built are popular in camps. Among the architecturally most inspired and engaging camp buildings herein shown are those at Dunes State Park, Indiana, where the spirit of the Indian tepee is expressed in wood construction.

The romantic appeal, especially to young children, of camp buildings imaginatively designed is not as widely acknowledged as it might be. Because the primary objective of organized camping is so frequently social welfare—a problem of making an expenditure benefit a maximum number of persons rather than benefit in maximum some lesser number—it is usually, but unfortunately, necessary to forego any overburden of cost that might be solely assessable to "imagination-stimulation" or "romantic appeal." In such situations the dictates of social consciousness must be bowed to, certainly. But there is no possible reason, save the ineptitude and ignorance of camp planners, for the cheapest of camp structures being other than pleasing in proportion, appropriate as to materials, and painless to the eye. If in camps the underprivileged, even the moderately circumstanced, may not eat cake, in an aesthetic sense, it remains an obligation on planners to contrive a substitute that is not less than palatable.

TENT AND TRAILER CAMPSITES

SWEEPING CHANGE in travel and the camping habits of tourists is in process that must shortly force revisions of present day park campground lay-outs if these are to continue functioning to serve campers and preserve parks from misuse. The deus ex machina is the automobile trailer or house car. So popular has this accessory to more abundant travel become that estimates from some parks indicate that one camper out of three has already "gone trailer."

Current production schedules of manufacturers of this equipment evidence that the end is not yet. Although the saturation point is unpredictable, there are indications that taxation and regulation may eventually place limits on the growth of trailer popularity. While the current sharp up-curve of trailer production may level off, as the graph-makers phrase it, at some not distant time, there exists an immediate and pressing need for the suitable accommodation of trailer campers in or near our parks which may not be disregarded. It is a problem to be met squarely and adequately, without lag behind demand and yet certainly without feverish overbuilding based on speculation alone.

It is not unanimously agreed that trailers should be admitted to parks. Some feel that it would be better to ban them entirely and leave their accommodation to private enterprise beyond the park borders. Reasons advanced in support of this opinion are the traffic hazard of trailers on narrow park roads, their destructive effect on light roadways and campsites and, where the camp lay-out must be compact, the likelihood of slum conditions developing and spreading to infect in more or less degree the park area beyond the campground.

It is not here sought to prove that trailer camps belong or do not belong in parks. Probably there are areas where their introduction would be grave error, and others where their presence would not have adverse effect. The intent herein is rather to consider what a trailer campsite in a park can be, once it has been determined that a trailer campground may properly be undertaken on a given area.

In the pamphlet, "Camp Planning and Camp Reconstruction", issued by the United States Forest Service, Dr. E. P. Meinecke analyzes principles of camp planning for automobile-and-tent campers. Until the advent of the trailer, developments based on these principles served to bring order to camping activities in natural parks and to preserve natural aspect without hobbling campers' use and enjoyment of a camping area.

Basic in this campsite concept is a short parking spur, taking off from a one-way road at a readily negotiable angle, and bounded by naturalized barriers defining the parking space and confining the camper's automobile therein. Supplementing principle is a logical grouping of tent site, picnic table, and fireplace in suitable relation to the parked automobile, existing tree growth, and prevailing winds. Finally, a screening of undergrowth around the fringe, to limit and give a desirable privacy to the individual campsite, completes the picture. This arrangement when properly executed met well the needs of the tent camper. He could head into his allotted parking spur, pitch camp, and back his car out with ease whenever he wished to do so.

But when the camper decided to live in a trailer instead of a tent, he discovered that the campsite, ideally arranged for tent camping, was far short of ideal for a trailer. After he had driven his car into the parking spur, dragging his trailer behind him, he found his tow-car stymied by the trailer in the rear and by barriers ahead. In order to "go places" on casual errands he must either back out trailer and all at great inconvenience, or try to hurdle, or worm his way between, barriers in front. The results were certain destruction of the campsite and probable damage to his car.

Vainly seeking a more workable solution, he might then make a fresh start and attempt to back the trailer into the parking spur in order that his automobile might be free for daily comings and goings. If it be recalled that the parking spur for the tent camper's automobile was laid out to be easily swung into head-on from a one-way road, the sharp angle will be appreciated as correspondingly unnegotiable with an unwieldy trailer leading off in a reverse approach. Further, this backing operation creates both obstruction and hazard to traffic that cancel the benefits of a one-way road system.

The more perfectly suited an object, idea, or plan to a given set of conditions, the less readily adaptable it is to different conditions. The very perfection of the ideally executed tent campsite seems to doom it to considerable revision if it is to be made convenient for the trailer.

MOST ADVANTAGEOUS for the head-on parking of the tent camper's automobile was a spur approximating the familiar 45-degree angle parking of some city streets. Best suited to the backing-in of tow-car-and-trailer, if backing is to be tolerated, is this same spur, but only if approached from the opposite direction. It is quite possible that many existing spur campsites, laid out on a one-way loop road, can be made more receptive to tow-car-and-trailer occupancy by the simple expedient of reversing the direction of travel on the camp road and increasing the length of the parking spurs. The results of an intelligent remodeling of certain old campgrounds can be satisfactory in considerable degree, although there will remain the hazards potential in backing a trailer.

Opinion about the difficulty of this operation is divided. There are those who maintain it is no trick at all and that it may be utterly disregarded as a factor in campground lay-out. Others are just as certain that backing a trailer, particularly into a parking spur laid out to minimum requirements, calls for much skill and long practice, and that only camp lay-outs which eliminate all necessity for the backing operation are sufferable. It would seem that the very existence of the latter opinion must demonstrate that backing a trailer is not a trifling task. Those who have observed on the highways the ineptitudes of some citizens for driving a single car forward will sense the havoc that can lurk in their maneuvering a trailer train in reverse. It is felt that the exploration here of alternatives of the spur, which can eliminate in future campground development all necessity for backing trailers, will be tolerated, if not actually welcomed, by serious readers.

There are two alternatives to spur parking. Herein these are dubbed the "bypass" and the "link."

The bypass is any arrangement permitting the trailer camper to drive tow-car-and-trailer off the traveled camp road, park, and drive onto that same road again without backing. In its simplest expression it is merely a defined widening of the camp road to allow tow-car-and-trailer to park out of the traveled lane. In its elaborations an island is created between bypass lane and camp road. This may be compact or extended, formal or informal in plan, screen-planted or not, all as influenced by the distance it is elected to allow between points of take-off from, and return to, the camp road. The bypass may be surfaced like the camp road or merely graded. Where conditions of soil and climate permit, it may be developed as a well-defined grass-grown wagon trail and not as a roadway, particularly where an island provides physical separation. A range of bypass treatments is shown among the plates which follow.

The link is any arrangement allowing the trailer camper's rolling stock to be driven off a traveled camp entrance road to suitable and sufficient parking whence it can be driven onto another roughly parallel camp exit road without any necessity of backing. Variations of the link result mainly from the distance between the entrance and exit camp roads. This may be as little as 50 feet or, owing to affecting topographical conditions or desire for greater privacy, 100 feet or even more. Under favorable conditions the link lane, like the bypass lane, may be in the nature of a well-defined grass-grown wagon trail, rather than a roadway, to a preservation of natural aspect and a saving in development cost. Variations of link campsite lay-outs are presented among the plates.

Included in the diagrams which seek to show the gamut of campsite possibilities more or less receptive to tow-car-and-trailer parking are several spur parking arrangements. None of these requires the extremity of awkward backwards-maneuvering demanded by the tent camper's parking spur when appropriated to trailer use. Wherever there is a disposition to accept a limited backing of trailer, these spur parking arrangements will receive interested consideration for their many points of merit. They make possible a maximum number of campsites per acre. This is an advantage where a more generous space allotment per campsite and the resultant sprawling campground will mean the dissipating of high scenic or wilderness values. The compactness of these spur sites makes for economy where the campground development contemplates the provision of water, electric, and perhaps sewer connections on every campsite, especially where the site is underlaid with rock. But only a generally level terrain, uninterrupted by any natural features which must be preserved and protected, will lend itself to a geometric, space-conserving grouping of minimum campsites.

There are numerous factors acting to sabotage an arbitrary decision to create a campground providing a maximum number of campsites per acre. Very generally, and it is believed fortunately, some of these influences will operate to prevent trailer campgrounds from becoming too formal in lay-out and too conserving of space to be attractive.

First of all, there is not an abundance of terrain over which it is feasible to construct straight, parallel roadways in the pattern of suburban subdivisions. More often than not it will be necessary to build curving roads in adaptation to contours, and the results will be a pleasing informality and a certain welcome "slack" in space use.

Although there may be very grim determination to be ruthless in sacrificing every tree that chances to be within the blueprint confines of the parking spurs and lanes, it is difficult to believe that there will not be a pardonable warping of geometric perfection in order to preserve especially desirable tree and plant growth, with coincident retention of camp-ground assets and some easing up of space limitations.

Then there is that human trait that stubbornly persists in some of us—a desire for privacy in some degree. Ringed in by the most ideal of tree and undergrowth screening, the minimum campsite has at best only the illusion of privacy. If soil or climate is such that effective vegetative screening between campsites is sparse or lacking, greater distances in lieu of foliage barriers may be adopted to real advantage.

In a park wherein primary scenic splendor might be coupled with an extensive, unspectacular buffer area, lacking competing use claims, there will be less reason to compress the areas sacrificed to the modifying effects of camping. If a sizable park is magnificently forested through its entire extent, and camping is determined to be permissible, a camping area will most certainly not be completely cleared for the dubious benefits and close quarters of a treeless gridiron lay-out of minimum campsites.

Among the influences on the other hand tending to compress campground lay-out, most important is the immunity from trespass rightfully established by the presence of outstanding natural values. Another potent factor in this direction is the extent to which it may be determined to provide utilities—water, electricity, and sewerage. Obviously, installation costs of these increase in direct ratio to the distances involved.

THE EXTENT to which campground equivalents of public services and utilities—water, electricity, and sewers—should be made available in trailer camps is much debated. A tent campground has long been felt to be suitably equipped if safe drinking water were provided not more than 200 feet, toilets not more than 400 feet, and washhouse and laundry not more than 1,500 feet distant from any individual campsite. Should not these same facilities provided within similar maximum distances be satisfactory in a trailer camp? Is it really desirable to go further and provide on each individual campsite so many of the refinements of a hotel room that camping fees must climb to virtual competition with hotel rates—to make vacationing out-of-doors so de luxe as to pass beyond the economic range of the majority?

Surely in our parks we should cling tenaciously to a policy of "live and let live" with respect to human beings. This enlightened attitude has inspired our policy with respect to native flora and fauna in parks. Why not accord man the dignity of treating him as a native faunal species and permit him to vacation in a park with some lingering trace of the simple style which he could once enjoy—and could afford?

It is not incumbent upon park authorities to give aid and comfort so abundantly to the nomad that he can only be dislodged from the campground by the first frost. Nor is there any apparent gain to derive from depriving camping of the last semblance of adventure and the primitive.

Where site conditions make for moderate installation costs, it would not be unreasonable to go so far as to provide a drinking water tap adjacent to every campsite, whether laid out for tent or trailer.

It would be a great convenience certainly to the trailer camper if he could plug into an electric connection on the campsite and tap park current during his stay. If lighting only were involved, a flat rate per day could fairly cover the cost. But because some trailers are equipped with electric stove, iceless refrigerator, electric iron, electric heater and electric whatnot, is it good business to furnish electric current except by a coin meter? And the camp management, before electing to become an electric service distributor on such a basis, may well ponder the abuses, short circuits, blown fuses, and general distress potential in the nondescript equipment which will be driven into a park.

A campsite waste connection into a sewerage system might also prove convenient to the owner of a de luxe trailer. But would trailer owners generally be truly grateful for the step-up in camping fees to result from the capital and maintenance costs involved in making this convenience available? Doubtless the campground operator for his part would be recurrently, and more than mildly, annoyed by some of the abuses to which this little utility gadget would be heir.

Park planners should not be stampeded into a wholesale introduction of more and more of the complexities of urban living into vacationing out-of-doors. There is every reason for proceeding cautiously with campsite refinements at least until such time as there comes into being a considerably greater degree of standardization of trailer equipment than prevails today. Sewage disposal for individual campsites certainly, and electric service possibly, are public utility fields where angels might at this writing fear to tread. Shall we then rush in?

WHERE CAMPGROUNDS IN PARKS offer some campsites suitable only for tent camping and others devised for trailer accommodation, and when capacity or near-capacity occupancy is the rule, the troubles of the operating staff can be very complicated indeed. Checking the registering campers' equipment and assigning a campsite receptive to it consumes considerable time. There are occasions, with relatively more in prospect, when the trailer campers knocking at the gate exceed the number of campsites laid out for trailer use. There may be many campsites vacant which, laid out as tent campsites, cannot be negotiated by trailers. It is submitted that a lay-out of campsites each of which is suitable for either tent or trailer occupancy is an ideal solution.

The trailer camper, be it remembered, will usually have no reason to pitch a tent. He will not always resort to cooking on an outdoor campstove or fireplace. Of the several units requisite to the complete tent camp menage, the table and bench combination probably will be used most by the trailer camper. Regardless of these facts, none of these campsite accessories should be omitted from the ideal campsite. Although, in general, the trailer camper cannot use the tent camper's spur site without great inconvenience to himself and eventual disaster to the site, the tent camper on the contrary can make convenient use of any trailer campsite without resulting damage. The adaptability of trailer lay-outs to both tent and trailer use means 100 percent flexibility. It dissolves the camp operator's nightly nightmare of speculation as to how many campers-with-this-kind-of-equipment and how many campers-with-that-kind-of-equipment may register. Where campsites accommodating all comers are provided, the varying ratio of trailers to tents in an area need not be the disturbing concern that it now so often is.

The same obstacles, obstructions, and barriers needed to define the outlines of individual tent campsites and to keep the tent camper's automobile from encroaching upon parts of the campground where its free circulation would tend to injure plant life are likewise needed in connection with trailer campsites. Where there is a disposition to forego a maximum number of campsites per acre in favor of preserving desirable plant and tree growth, the principles of preservation by naturalizing transplanted rocks and large down timbers are especially applicable. Far too many campgrounds look as though a five-ring circus only yesterday had played to a capacity crowd on the site. The only safeguard against such threadbareness lies in providing obstructions and barriers on an effectual scale. Unfortunately, interpreters of the technique of preservation by means of obstructions and barriers have generally failed in the past to achieve a truly effectual scale. Their manipulations of peewee pebbles and saplings to pass for the rock and down timber barriers of the text and their consternation at the inadequacy of these are not without humor.

In the drawings that follow it is attempted to delineate possibilities for campsite lay-out receptive to the tow-car-and-trailer and making for the pleasure and comfort of the camper. Coincidently, protection of natural values and of the sensibilities of the park patron-at-large has been sought by one or the other of two theories of approach. One is to allocate a minimum space for the individual campsite and achieve a compactly geometrical arrangement of campground regardless of the ensuing despoliation of natural values over the limited area appropriated. The other approach acknowledges and preserves all such natural assets as forest cover, screening undergrowth, rock outcrops, and natural contours, and results in a more or less sprawling, informal campground that affects a greater area but modifies it in a lesser degree. Either theory has its points, and only a careful survey of the affecting site factors can determine which of the approaches, or what stage of compromise between them, is most appropriately adopted in a particular instance.

The drawings show one-way camp roads 10 feet wide and two-way camp roads 16 feet wide. In the case of either there should be an additional 3 feet to the center line of the gutter. Parking spurs, bypasses, and links are shown 10 feet wide. The minimum space allotment for an individual campsite is largely governed by the minimum turning radii of tow-car-and-trailer.

It will be seen that, because a majority of trailers have doors on the right hand side, flexibility in the grouping of some of the campsite lay-out types is limited. Some are adaptable only to the left side of a camp road, others only to the right. Unless a type adjustable to both sides of a road is used, left hand and right hand types must be selectively combined where development on both sides of a camp road is projected.

Immediately below is a lay-out illustrative of the lack of receptiveness to tow-car-and-trailer characteristic of the typical tent campsite—a dangerously awkward condition which, in the lay-outs presented by the plates following, it has been sought to avoid.

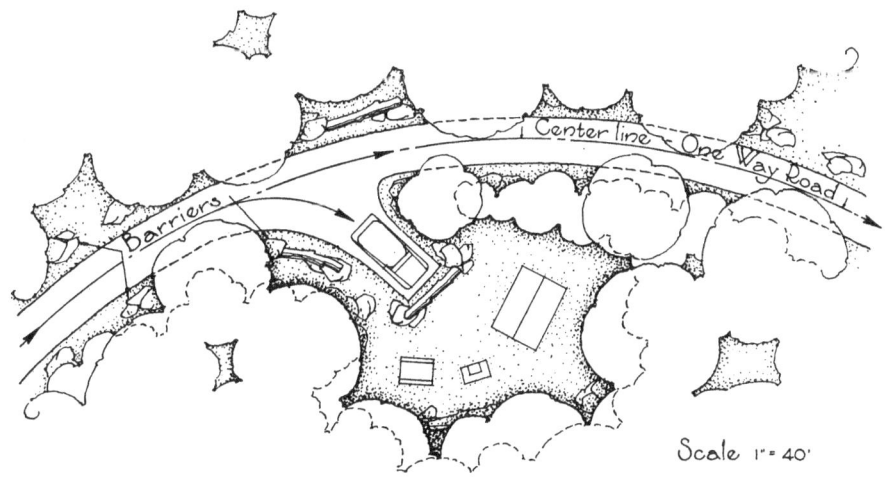

TENT AND TRAILER CAMPSITES

Plate III A-1

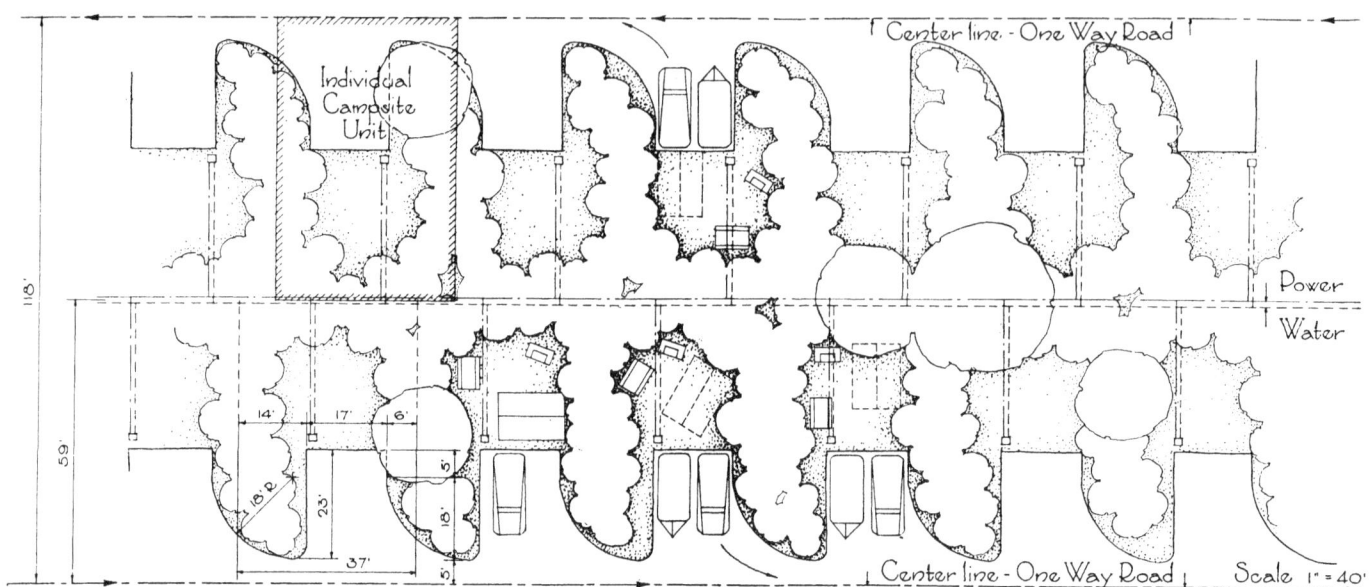

TRAILER CAMPSITE UNIT A (*Area per unit—2,183 square feet including half of roadway. Approximate road surface per unit including spur—80 square yards. Campsites per acre—approximately 20*).

In this compact spur type unit the tow car and the trailer are parked side by side. The type is shown adapted to the left side of a one-way road which permits the right hand side of the trailer (normally the door side) to face the open area. A campground might be laid out to utilize both sides of a one-way road by combining this type on the left and types such as C or D on the right. Unit A might also be adapted to the right side of a road, by interchanging the parking berths of the tow car and the trailer. In that case a less compact spacing will make for easier maneuvering of the vehicles.

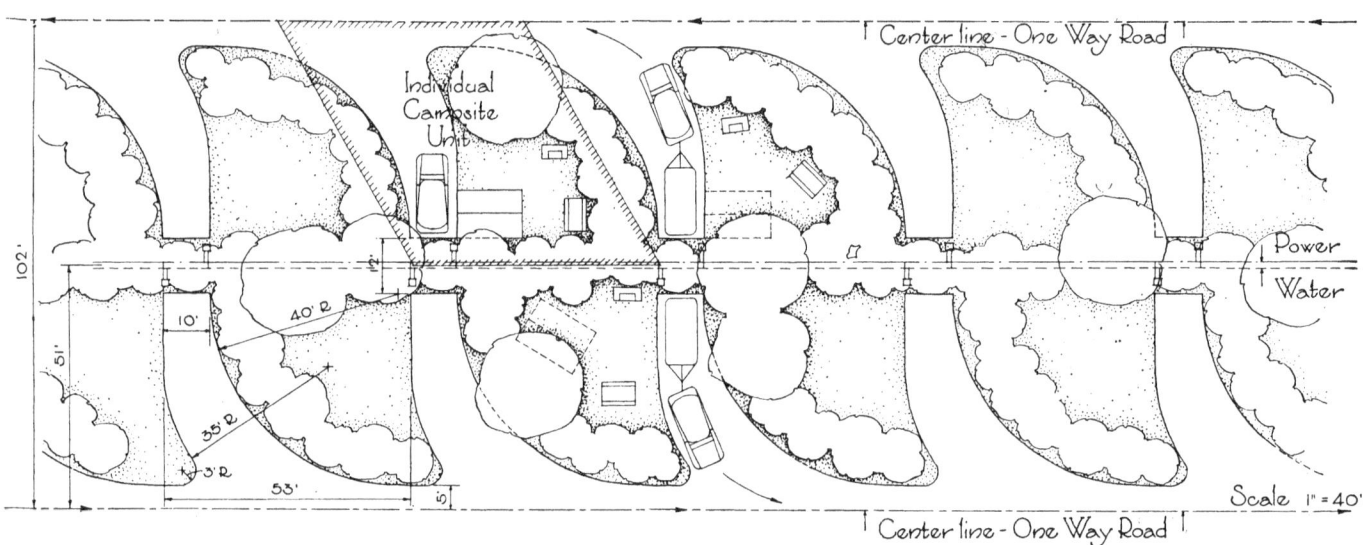

TRAILER CAMPSITE UNIT B (*Area per unit—2,703 square feet including half of roadway. Approximate road surface per unit including spur—106 square yards. Campsites per acre—approximately 16*).

In this spur type of unit the trailer is backed into its parking place and the tow car is parked in front of it. As shown, adapted to the left side of a one-way road, the right hand side of the trailer faces the camp clearing. The unit is convertible to the right side of a one-way road and the door will still front on the open area, if the cleared campsite is rearranged to be on the opposite side of the spur. Combinations with other types of units for variety are, of course, many.

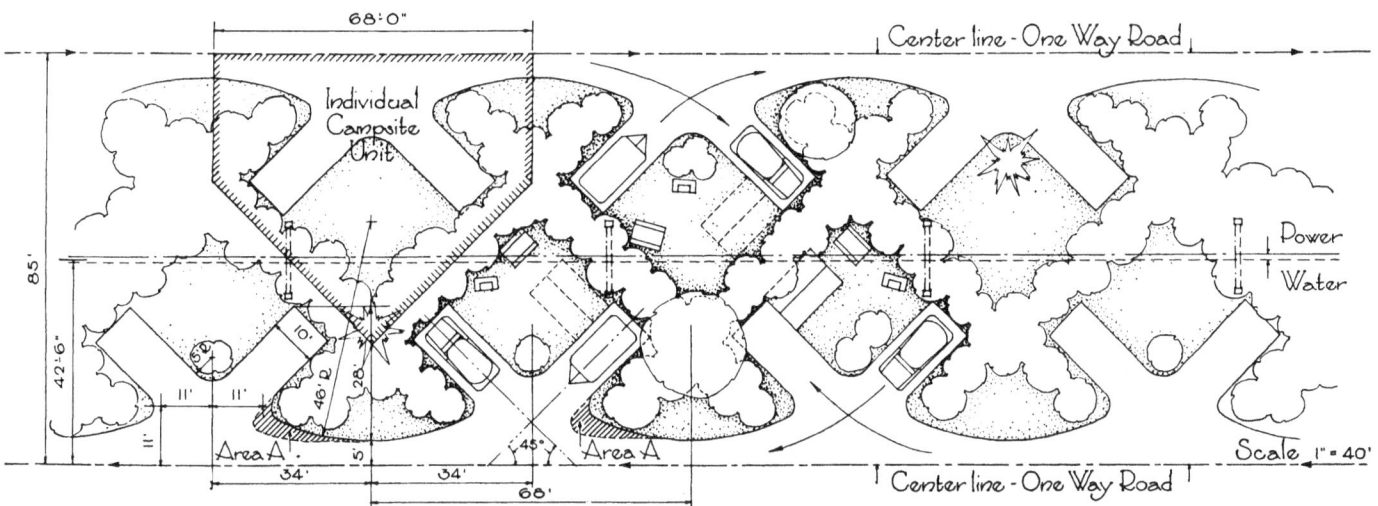

TRAILER CAMPSITE UNIT C (*Area per unit—2,890 square feet including half of roadway. Approximate road surface per unit including spur—130 square yards. Campsites per acre—approximately 15*).

This unit offers separate parking spurs for the tow car and the trailer in an arrangement that makes for a hemmed-in privacy. As shown above, it occurs on the right side of a one-way camp road, yet it might be used on both sides of a two-way road of suitable width and still desirably allow the normal door side of the trailer to face the camp clearing. C units can also be laid out along a one-way road in combination with the strictly left hand types. The adaptability of this unit is considerable. Parking of the tow car can be negotiated without the shaded area "A" being surfaced as a road.

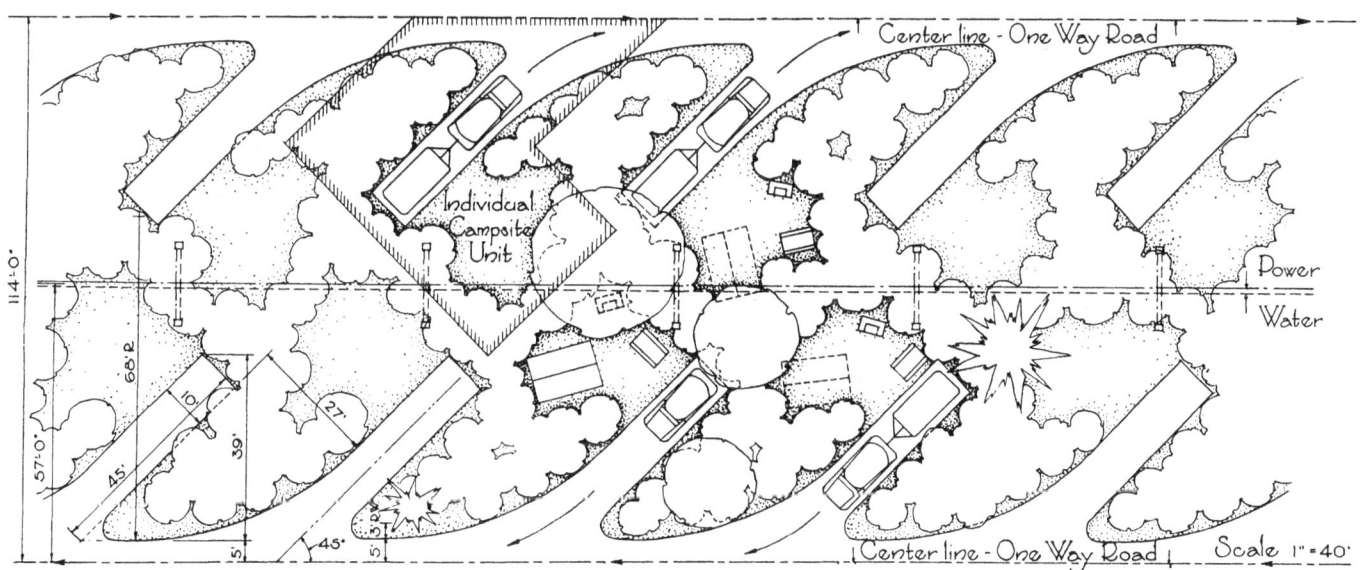

TRAILER CAMPSITE UNIT D (*Area per unit—3,076 square feet including half of roadway. Approximate road surface per unit including spur—118 square yards. Campsites per acre—approximately 14*).

A type of spur parking site, in which the trailer may be readily backed into its fixed parking berth with space between it and the roadway for parking the tow car, as in type B. Although, as shown above, these units are only on the right side of the one-way roads, it will be apparent that they might at the same time be repeated on the left side of these same roads, subject only to an entirely feasible rearrangement of the cleared areas to front on the right hand side (normally the door side) of the trailer in its parked position. Several lay-outs combining this and other unit types are possible.

TENT AND TRAILER CAMPSITES

Plate III A–3

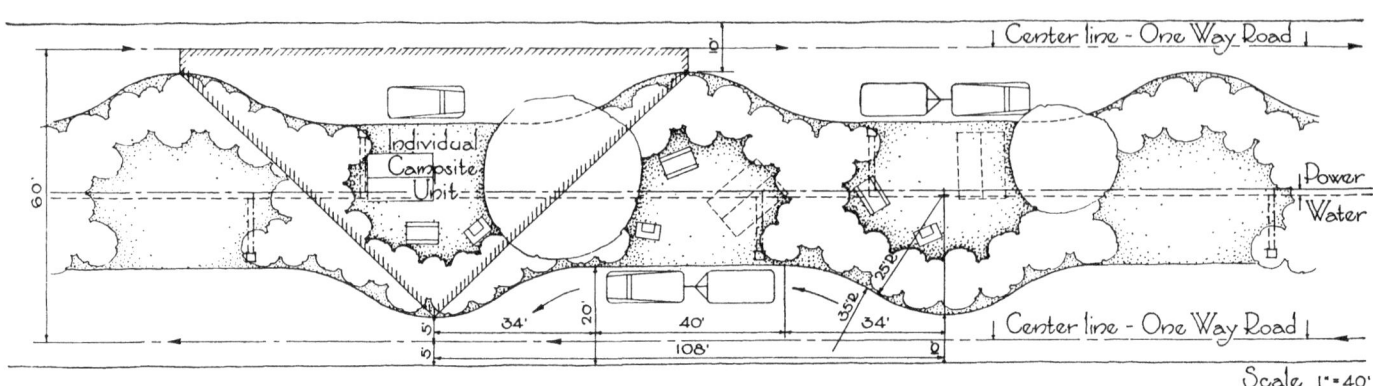

TRAILER CAMPSITE UNIT E (*Area per unit—3,240 square feet including half of roadway. Approximate road surface per unit including bypass—130 square yards. Campsites per acre—approximately 14*).

This simplest and most space-conserving of all campsite units based on bypass parking of the tow-car-and-trailer is merely a defined widening of a camp road so that the two vehicles can be parked off the traveled roadway. Where consideration is properly given to the normal right hand door of trailers, this unit lends itself only to locations on the right side of a one-way road. The drawing above is so arranged. In one-way road systems, combinations with other left hand types are possible. Adjacent to two-way roads, E units are usable on both sides without sacrifice of the desirable feature of the right hand trailer door facing the campsite clearing.

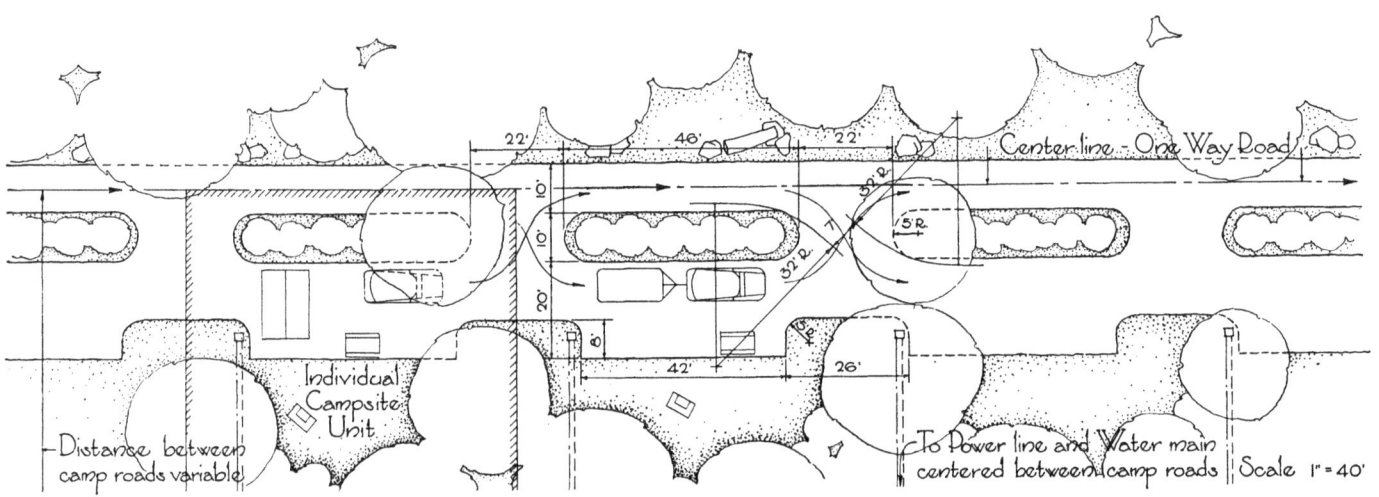

TRAILER CAMPSITE UNIT F (*Area per unit, assuming depth of 60 feet—4,080 square feet including half of roadway. Approximate road surface per unit including bypass—190 square yards. Campsites per acre—approximately 11*).

This bypass unit employs a formal island to separate the bypass parking space from the traveled roadway. As above drawn, the units are laid out along the right side only of a one-way road. There is no apparent reason why these units could not be ranged also along the left side of a one-way road. The surfaced bypass of considerable width allows leeway for parking the trailer so that its right hand door need not be blocked when the bypass is thus entered. Obviously, F units are usable on both sides of a two-way road.

Plate III A-4 →» TENT AND TRAILER CAMPSITES

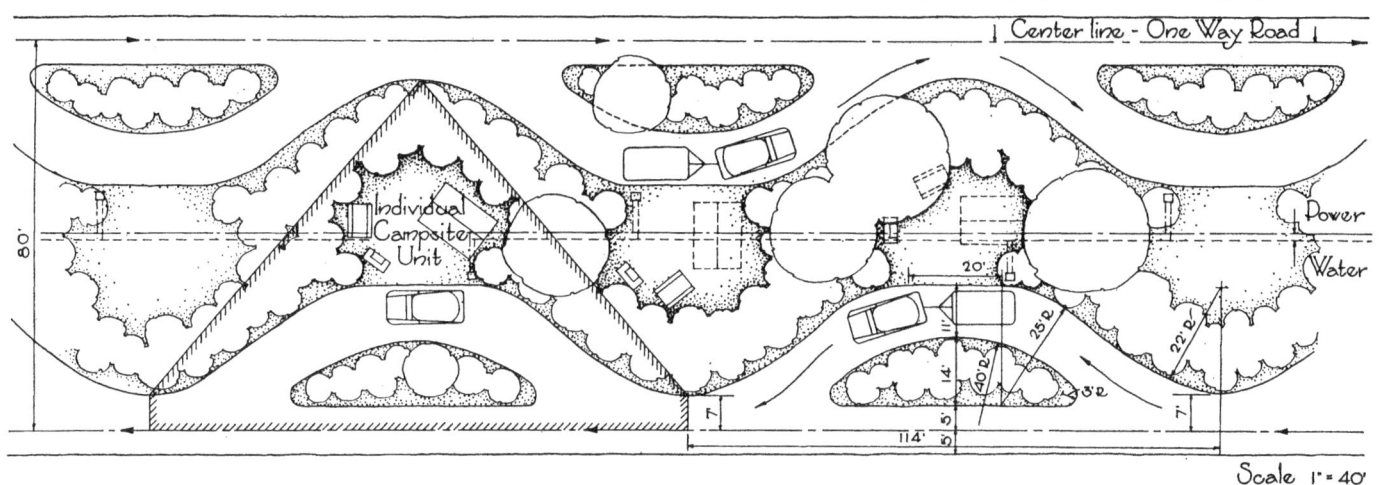

TRAILER CAMPSITE UNIT G (*Area per unit—4,560 feet including half of roadway. Approximate road surface per unit including bypass—183 square yards. Campsites per acre—approximately 10*).

Here again an island separates the bypass parking lane serving the individual campsite from the traveled roadway. These units, if the more customary right hand trailer door is to be served, are only usable on the right side of a one-way road; therefore, if campsites on both sides of a one-way road are projected, some more adaptable unit is better chosen for the left side. Naturally, if a two-way road system is projected, G units are well-suited to both sides of the roads. With all units shown on these facing pages, backing is unnecessary in berthing either tow car or trailer.

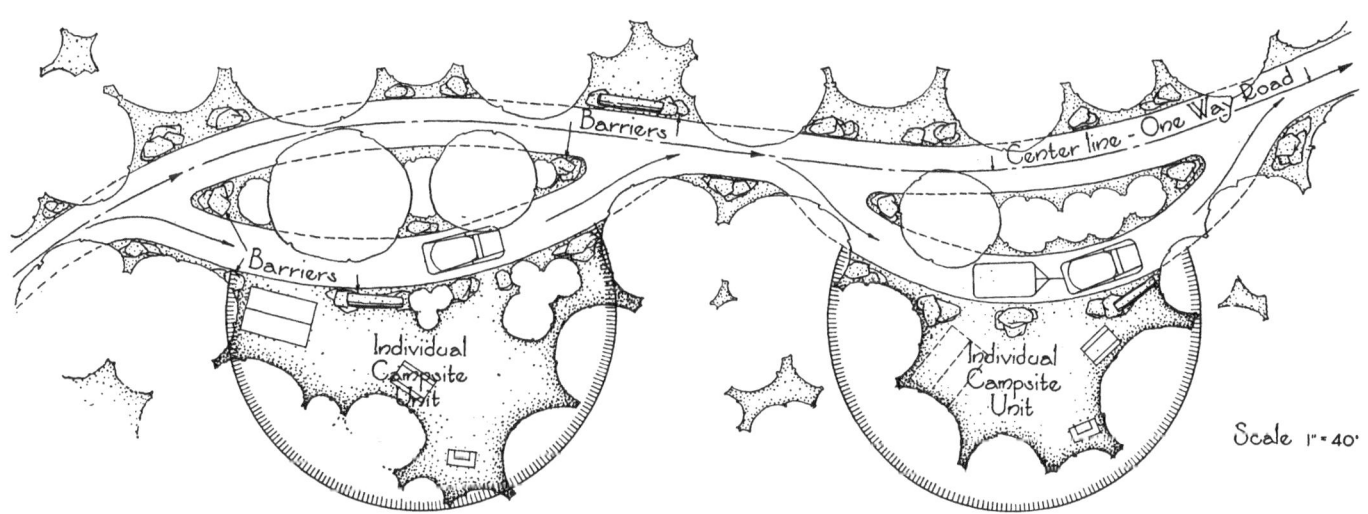

TRAILER CAMPSITE UNIT H (*Statistics of campsite units such as these are indeterminate, because space allocation, road surface area per unit, and the number of campsites per acre are governed entirely by natural factors individual to site*).

This bypass unit is obviously a development of unit G along less formal lines, approached not with a determination to produce the maximum number of campsites per acre, but instead with the triple objective of (1) suiting an irregular topography, (2) sparing existing desirable natural features, and (3) gaining greater privacy for each campsite. The roadway curves to follow natural contours; spacing and naturalized barriers acknowledge, preserve, and protect natural features of site deemed of value; and retained cover and wider, varied spacing of units add to the privacy of individual campsites. Although only well-suited to the right side of a one-way road, and so shown above, these informal units are adaptable to both sides of two-way roads.

TENT AND TRAILER CAMPSITES

Plate III A-5

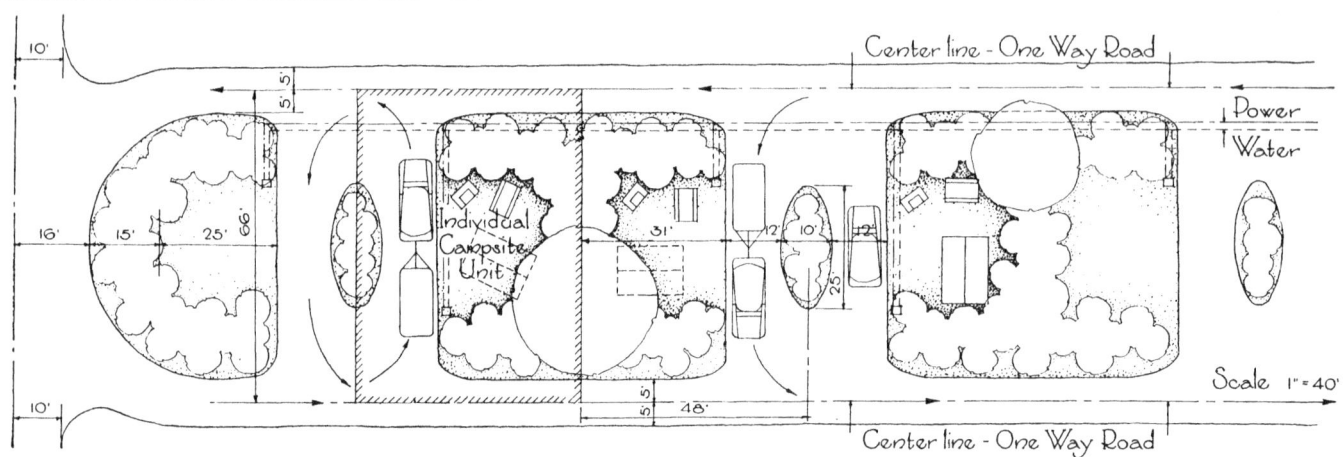

TRAILER CAMPSITE UNIT I (*Area per unit—3,168 square feet including half of roadway. Approximate road surface per unit including link—160 square yards. Campsites per acre—approximately 14*).

As usual, a lay-out along one-way roads is shown in the above delineation of this most compact of the link-lane types of parking here presented. Use of this particular unit in any two-way road system is to be discouraged, for every entrance into and exit from a parking link requires a left turn, crossing an opposing traffic lane. An ingenious and space-conserving unit, but combinations with other types will wisely be limited to the utilization of a right hand unit along a one-way road.

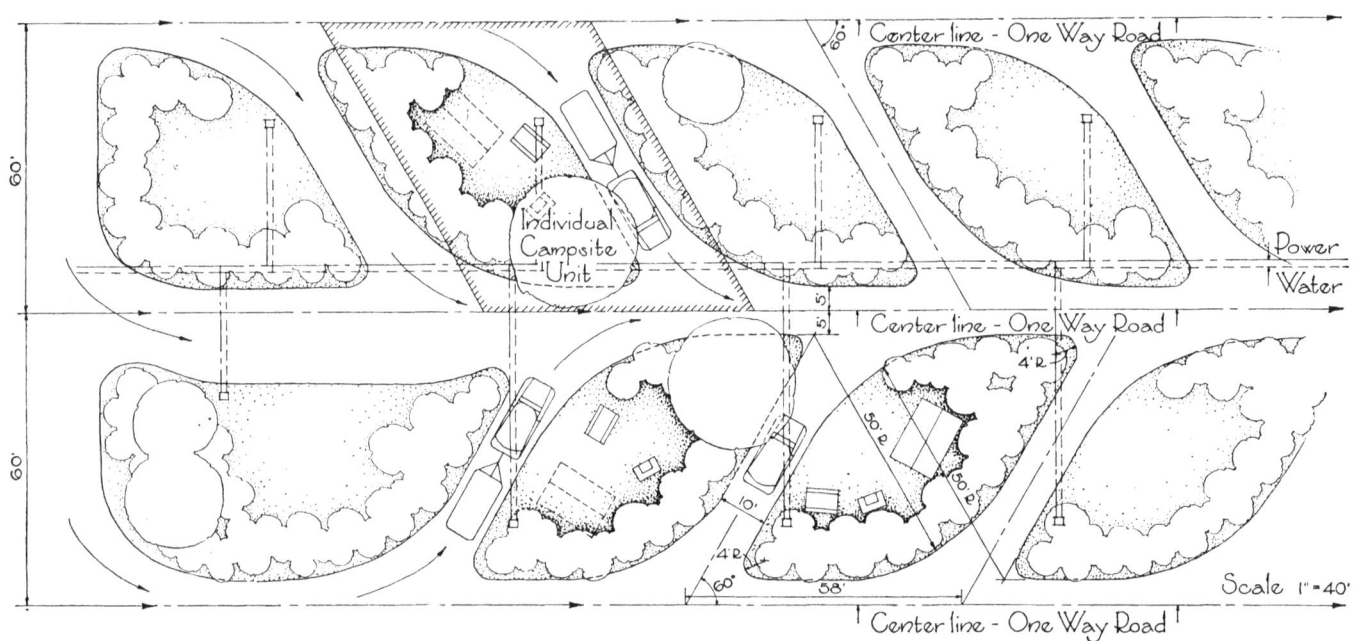

TRAILER CAMPSITE UNIT J (*Area per unit—3,480 square feet including half of roadway. Approximate road surface per unit including link—163 square yards. Campsites per acre—approximately 12*).

That link lanes for parking are desirably confined to campground lay-outs employing one-way roads exclusively is proved again by this example. The fact that traffic of all roads in the arrangement above shown is in one direction suggests that the best possible utilization of this scheme would be a large-scale adaptation in which the one-way roads serve as links between the entrance and exit stretches of a main camp road that loops around the entire campground development. The parking lanes would constitute links between links, so to say, and the result would be one-way traffic throughout the campground and traffic hazards at a minimum.

Plate III A-6 →→→ TENT AND TRAILER CAMPSITES

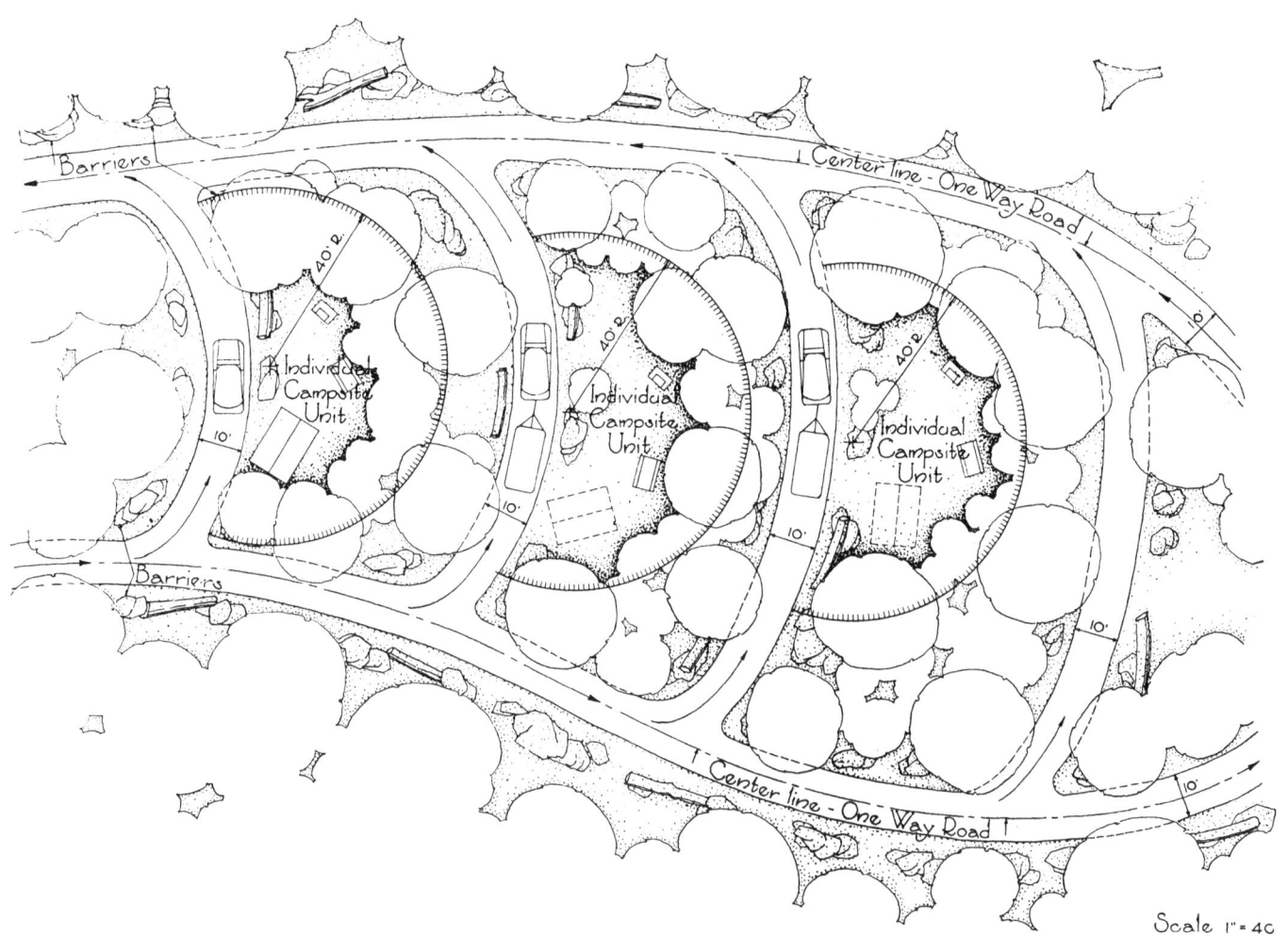

TRAILER CAMPSITE UNIT K (*Because campsite units of this type conform to no prescribed pattern, statistical data cannot be compiled*).

Just as unit H represents a loosely informal and spacious adaptation of bypass parking for tow-car-and-trailer, so this type amounts to an informal and expanded version of the link idea. In connection with both there is the same adjustment of roads to meet existing contours and spacing of parking lanes and cleared areas to spare valuable natural features and afford greater privacy to campers—all as might be motivated by a conviction that, under certain conditions, it is better to modify a larger area only partially than a lesser area completely. In this theory of campsite lay-out, naturalized barriers against damage due to uncontrolled driving of cars play an important part. These must be placed strategically throughout to protect all those natural assets of a campground, in the preservation of which the sprawling campground finds its chief justification.

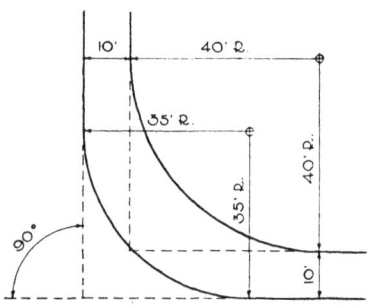
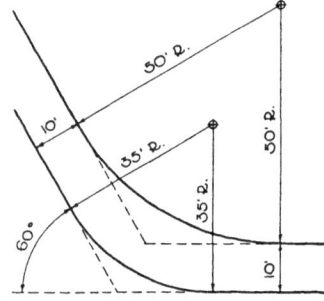
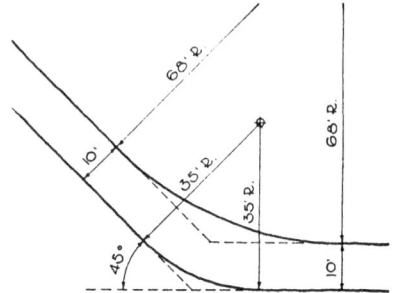

Minimum turning radii for Car and Trailer – One Way Road

Minimum turning radii for Car and Trailer – One Way Road

Minimum turning radii for Car and Trailer – One Way Road

The diagrams above show the development of turning radii for tow-car-and-trailer which have governed a number of the campsite lay-outs of the preceding pages.

The illustrations below indicate the sort of low growth and ground cover which must extend through trailer campgrounds to screen individual campsites if the illusion of privacy is to obtain.

Although both picture the superlative undergrowth found in the redwood forests of the Pacific slope, something approaching the density and varied height of these is possible in many other sections of the country if encouraged by barriers of such effectual size that they will prevent the destructive movement of vehicles and by unremitting replanting and care.

Prairie Creek Campgrounds, California

Patrick's Point Campgrounds, California

CABINS

AMONG BUILDINGS which have come to be regarded as on occasion justified within our present conception of a natural park, the cabin alone has the favorable advantage of long familiarity to us in woodland and meadow. So accustomed are we to survivals of frontier cabins dotting the countryside that we have grown to look upon them as almost indigenous to a natural setting. Of all park structures, those cabins which echo the pioneer theme in their outward appearance, whether constructed of logs, shakes, or native stone, tend to jar us least with any feeling that they are unwelcome. The fact that park cabins are usually erected in colonies or groups (frontier cabins as a rule were not) destroys somewhat the feeling of almost complete fitness that is produced by a single primitive cabin. The further fact that the true cost of such structures is usually much higher than their purpose or the prospective income from them would justify often imposes upon the designer the necessity of availing himself of cheaper and more easily handled materials than those employed by the pioneer, and of using these the best way he can. Hence cabin groups must always be something of a dissonance in parks, acceptable only when their obtrusiveness is minimized insofar as possible.

If the cabin on publicly owned lands is to justify itself, it is essential that it at least pay its own way during its lifetime, and that charges for its use bear a logical relationship to its true cost. Any evaluation of that cost which fails to assign a reasonable value to materials acquired on the site or to all labor involved, however compensated, would be faulty.

Often overlooked, but certainly the primary objective in providing cabins in public parks, should be adjustment in cost and rental of facilities to the income range of the using public. There ought to be just as sincere an effort to furnish habitable vacation shelter to the patron of very limited means as there seems now to exist an enthusiasm to supply the more ample facilities which the higher income brackets can afford and demand.

At the lack of spread in cabin facilities and rentals observable in many parks, just criticism can be leveled. It would seem to be not only better park planning, but better business planning, to offer accommodations in a wide price range bearing some logical ratio to the wide income range represented by park patrons. It might be pointed out as an abuse of democratic principles if the benefits of park areas are withdrawn from availability to the many to the selfish enjoyment of the few. An abundant provision of cabins such as only the few can afford and a blind, or callous, disregard of the budget limits of the vast majority are not social arithmetic.

LET US EXPLORE the range of cabin accommodations that parks might well offer in order to extend availability.

The simplest type of cabin, the "Student" or "Tourist" class (to initiate the figure of the passenger liner), must seek to bring the required minimum of space need in shelter within a most rigid limitation of cost, which must relate definitely and logically to the very limited rent the humble park user can afford to pay. This problem will tax the ingenuity of the ablest designer desirous of producing a nice balance between traditioned charm and reasoned practicability.

Of necessity such a cabin must be a very modest affair, affording merely the most compact sleeping and living space. Required economy will compel the omission of toilet and bathing facilities from this simplest type of cabin. Naturally, concentrating the toilet and bathing facilities will reduce the cost of a cabin group, as compared with that of other cabin groups in which toilet and bathing facilities are integral with every cabin. If provision is made for preparing meals in these cabins, the kitchen must be truly of kitchenette proportions— merely compact cabinet, closet, or small shallow alcove. A possible alternative to the modest kitchenette allowable is an outdoor campstove, preferably with sheltering roof. If strategically treated, the campstove may be a multiple unit, and the kitchen shelter thus made to serve several cabins. Desirable as a fireplace may be, it is scarcely within the economy of the simplest of cabins unless climate makes such a feature an absolute necessity.

Such is the prospectus for recreation or vacation cabins within the budget range of the many and, it should be borne in mind, available to them only for brief periods and by dint of most careful economy on the part of the family unit.

A narrowing field of potential users results when greater spaciousness and added facilities, naturally accompanied by mounting costs and proportionately higher rental charges, are offered in "Second Class" cabins (to continue the figure of the liner). Cabins of this type might contain a kitchenette, a bedroom, and a living room to serve also as a sleeping room at night. The kitchenette will tend to be something more than the simpler cabin type permits. A fireplace is an allowable feature, since the larger cabin will probably have a longer season of use. If a nearby central recreation building is not provided as a gathering place, the cabin is forced to a greater self-sufficiency. Toilet and bath facilities, although naturally desirable features, are not usually possible in this class of cabin because of the cost involved.

Of cabins of the next group, which might be termed "First Class" cabins, distinguishing features are toilet and bath facilities, along with perhaps added spaciousness and more privacy in sleeping quarters. Arbitrary pronouncement of limitations in space and facilities for these cabins is considered beyond the province of this general discussion. When examples of the "First Class" cabin give hint of elaboration to the point of becoming "Cabins de Luxe" or "Royal Suites", their appropriateness within natural parks will be challenged by many and defended by but few. It is certain that pretentious cabins are only justifiable if their vacancy ratio is negligible and if they are rented to produce an income consistent with their initial cost and maintenance expense.

It is not argued that the several "classes" of cabins must rub elbows in the park area as a condition of serving equitably the patrons from different social or financial strata. On the contrary, this is something to be rigidly avoided in lay-out. There is less emphasis on social differences and therefore less dissatisfaction for all concerned if cabins of each type are discreetly grouped somewhat to themselves.

Along with providing a range of rentals, variety in the number of persons to be accommodated in the several cabins of a group should be given consideration. The American family group averages somewhere between four and five persons. It would, therefore, appear reasonable to plan perhaps a majority of cabins to sleep four people. There will be some demand for cabins accommodating two, and a sprinkling of six-cot cabins would not be amiss.

While many cabins built as a single room are large enough to sleep four or six persons, it is very desirable to provide a certain privacy by means of partitions, or curtains on poles, around one or more of the bed locations. Furthermore, potential tenants are not always a family group, and failure to provide some measure of privacy results in a narrowing of the tenant field.

In most localities some form of porch will be a serviceable feature of a cabin. In certain climates a simple terrace may serve, but in a majority of cases a roof will add greatly to usefulness. Rather generally it will be necessary to screen in the porch if its full benefits are to be enjoyed.

When a screened porch is provided, a wide opening between it and the living space is a space-saving possibility to be considered by cabin designers with a praiseworthy urge to provide the utmost for the cabin dollar. Such an opening about eight feet wide, framing sliding doors or three or four folding doors, throws together the limited space allotments of living space and porch and makes for a roominess very useful on occasion.

IT MUST BE ADMITTED that the need in some parks for cabins in considerable numbers presents some very real problems, one of which is the spacing of them. A cabin, when occupied, along with a certain ground area bordering it, is in effect privately leased, for a night, or a week, or longer, as the policy of a park may dictate. It becomes virtually private property serving an infinitesimal portion of the park-using public, and the greater the spacing between the cabins within a group, the greater the area that is withdrawn from the use of the public-at-large. For this reason the spacing of cabins dare not be determined entirely on the basis of a splendid isolation for each cabin.

Frequently observed in connection with cabin groups is a tendency to spread the effects of their presence over a needlessly large area. In groups composed of the simplest cabin types, wide spacing either compels a multiplication of toilet installations or renders the use of central facilities so difficult that the cabin occupant, particularly after dark, will often not go to the required trouble, with consequent development of unpleasant and insanitary conditions. It also compels establishment of additional water outlets—one more item of cost.

Even in the case of cabin groups equipped with toilets and with running water, wide separation means added road construction to make them accessible and longer runs for electric service. After all, it seems fair to assume that, where cabins are erected in parks, their purpose is to facilitate enjoyment of the park itself, and that complete seclusion during the hours when they are occupied is not the supremely important goal it is so frequently assumed to be. To repeat, spacing cabins far enough apart to satisfy fully the desire of the occupants for seclusion tends to encroach on the interests of the public-at-large by reducing its range, so to speak. On the other hand, if the spacing of cabins must so yield to the interests of the public (and perhaps to the influence of economy) that the cabin area becomes row upon row of trifling, and too often identical, cabins—with ground cover and shade traded in for a few inches of seasonally alternative dust or mud underfoot—we have simply infected the outdoors with tenement substandards and made Nature an outcast.

Another problem is the size of the cabins individually and the determining of a proper assortment of cabins of the several possible sizes. If the cabin is small and compact to a minimum, a large family or group finds it cramped. If it is made more spacious, it is in excess of the actual space needs of a family of two. Recently, at Spring Mill State Park, Indiana, some novel cabins have been developed which seem to present the solution to the practical need for accommodating from two to eight persons, without either waste of space or overcrowding. "Multiple cabin" has been suggested as a suitable designation for the type.

Successfully accomplished in these is an ingenious space arrangement of great flexibility. These cabins have four rooms, each of which is served by a separate outside entrance, is equipped with water closet and lavatory, and sleeps two persons. One group of eight, two groups of four, four groups of two, or other combinations are possible by the simple operation of locking or unlocking communicating doors.

Equivalent in flexibility and interest to the Spring Mill multiple cabin is the development adjacent to the Bright Angel Lodge on the South Rim of the Grand Canyon. In this particular setting a large building would have been incongruous. It is avoided, and the problem is solved by linking many small guest houses to the lodge proper by covered pergolas. The guest houses contain from two to sixteen bedrooms and are in effect multiple cabins, permitting the renting of rooms individually or en suite.

SOMETHING ON THE SUBJECT OF CHIMNEYS cries to be heard, but since chimneys have no separate entity in these discussions, their case must be presented and pressed by cabins, as "next friend."

In the discredited "whatnot" or "mission" period of the past, some evangelist of grim determination must have been possessed of an hypnotic ability to implant his debased preference in cabin chimneys through the length and breadth of the land. Apparently it was a lifelong fixation of this crusading apostle. Nothing else will account for the far-flung faith that developed in the supreme appropriateness of boulder masonry for this purpose. The unfortunate circumstance seems to have been further aggravated by a quaint conviction that the less structural in appearance, the less evident the bonding mortar, and the less apparent any reliance on physical laws for stability, the happier and more creditable the accomplishment.

Need it be more than pointed out that from time immemorial good stone work has always been that stone work which appeared incapable of toppling even if all mortar were to be magically removed? It is possible that there has been throughout history recurrent abandonment of this principle as something just trite and old-fashioned in masonry technique. This is mere speculation, of course, because somehow the evidence of such experimentation, other than the execrable "peanut brittle" chimney technique for log cabins, has not survived the ravages of time to our day. It is indeed to be regretted that the most recent sponsor of formless masonry drew no conclusion from this fact. Surely, if he had, his disciples would be spared over the years many chimney replacements, if not necessitated by actual collapse then eventually blasted to ruin by the trumpets of good taste. As from time to time these reconstructions must be made, it is hoped that the reconstructors will appraise the chimney survivals of the American pioneer, and if they are led to offend with globular masonry no more often than did he, a weird ghost will have been laid.

The tailpiece illustration is of a cabin which recalls the handiwork of the pioneer and the splendid timber resources which over wide areas awaited his axe. Only the sworn statement of one who is well-informed, to the effect that this cabin was built from windfalls and not cut timber, permits conservationists to show this cabin here. Almost humorous in its scale, it is far from that as a reminder of magnificent forests all but extinct. As a relic of the days when trees were trees, this cabin can inspire us to firm resolution to permit them to be so again in the long-term future. Somewhere between the scale of this log work and the spindling scale of the majority of present day log structures is the happy and satisfying medium that is too infrequently seen. The random informality of the axe-hewn log ends contributes greatly to the naive charm of this little building.

Cabin, Itasca State Park, Minnesota

Plate III B–1   ⇢⇢⇢ CABINS

Giant City State Park, Illinois

Levi Jackson-Wilderness Road State Park, Kentucky

ONE-ROOM CABINS

The surrounding illustrations evidence the variety of structural treatments possible in a mere one-room cabin. The plans of these, although not shown, are essentially similar to those presented on the following pages. These cabins carry special interest for the fact that each is so characteristic of locality and tradition. The Letchworth cabin is our old friend, the Adirondack shelter, enclosed. The Kentucky cabin at lower right is certainly something of a southern mansion in miniature. The Palo Duro cabin is typed at a glance as of the Southwest. The two structures above approximate the sleeping cabin of an organized camp.

Letchworth State Park, New York

Palo Duro State Park, Texas

Butler Memorial State Park, Kentucky

CABINS

Plate III B-2

One Room Cabin - Letchworth State Park - New York

A wall closes the open side of the typical Adirondack shelter and produces a cabin of the simplest form. Walls sided with so-called "log-siding" are a compromise with traditional primitive log structures and do not entirely sacrifice harmony with a woodland setting. The reduction in the amount of lumber required is not to be scorned lightly nor is the coincident item of lower cost.

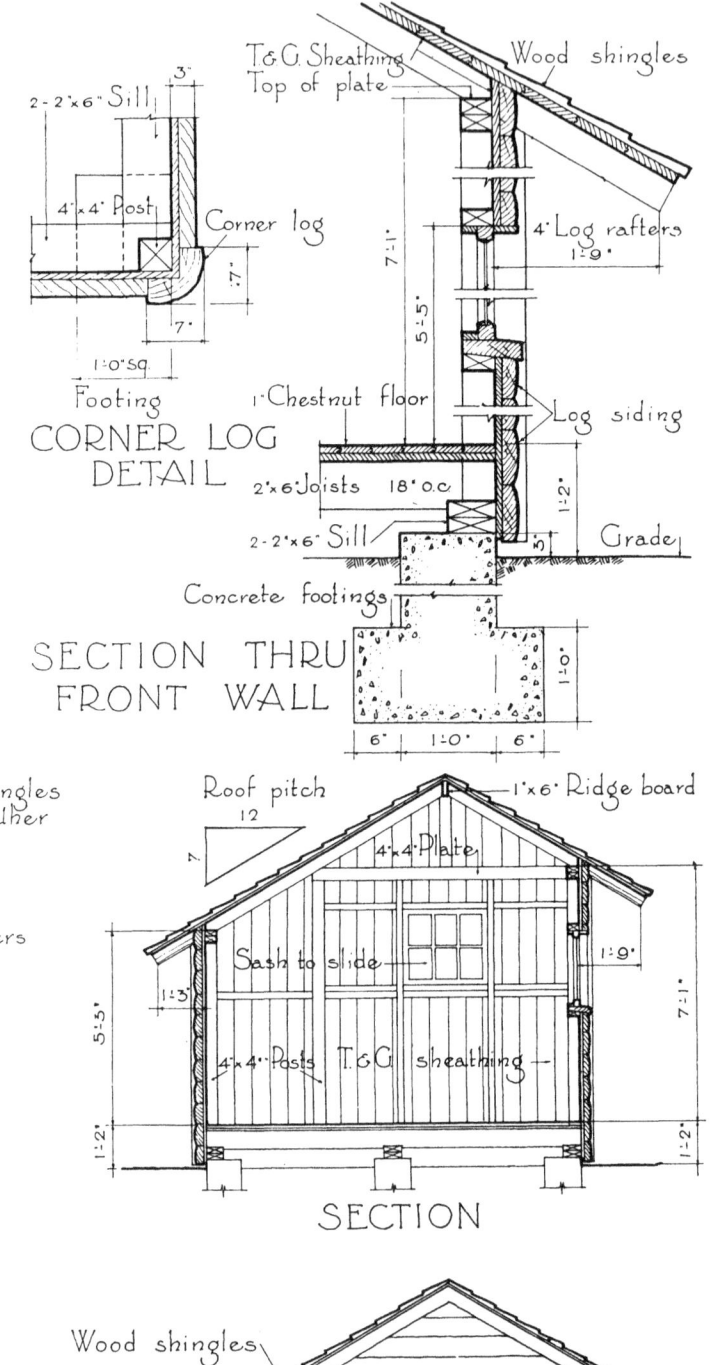

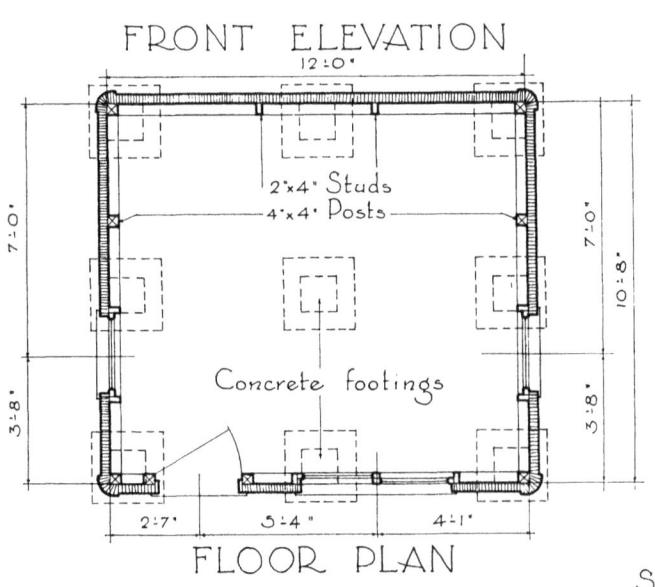

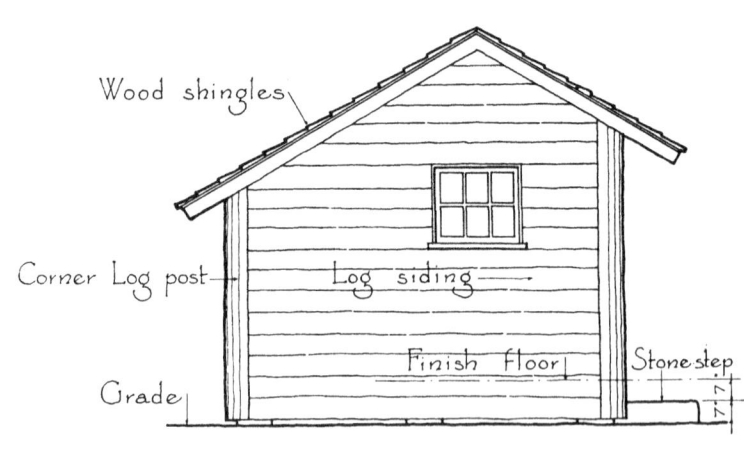

Scale 3/16" = 1'-0"

Plate III B–3 — CABINS

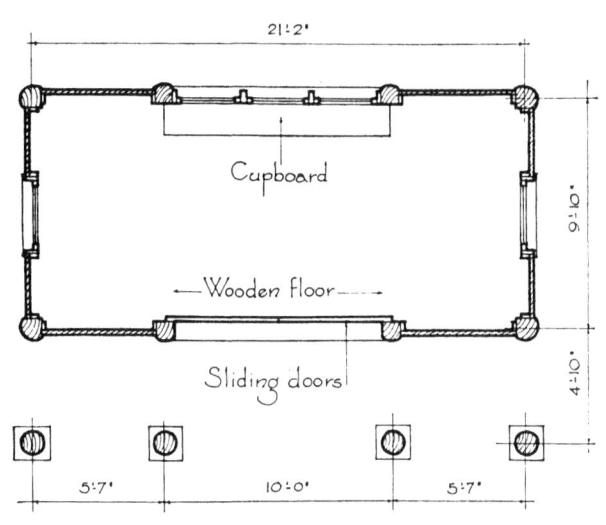

FLOOR PLAN

Cabin

Finger Lakes State Parks Commission — — New York

Deriving from the primitive Adirondack shelter this type of one room cabin with open porch is popular in central New York. The sliding doors are its distinguishing feature. Opened, these relate the cabin intimately to the outdoors.

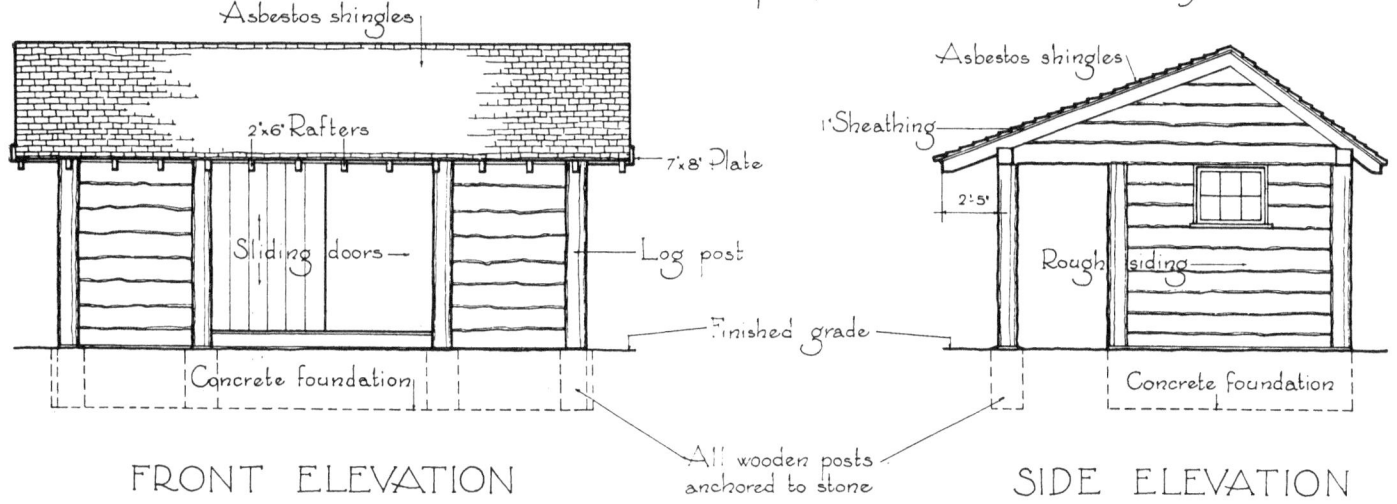

FRONT ELEVATION

SIDE ELEVATION

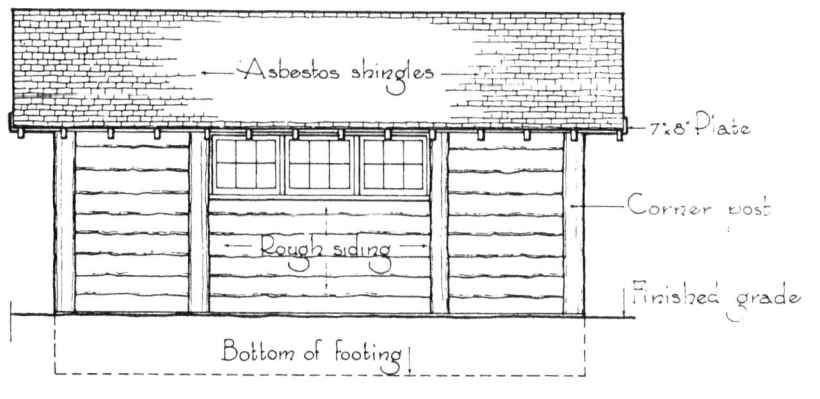

REAR ELEVATION

Scale 8'=1:0'

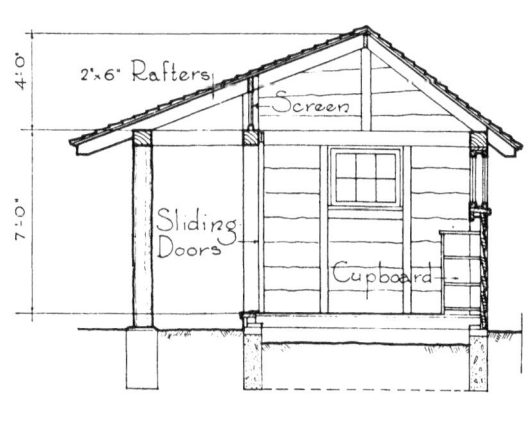

SECTION

CABINS
Plate III B-4

Cabin - Wilderness State Park - Michigan

This example, not content with its achievement of compact plan evidencing careful study and thoughtful design, curries further favor by reason of an exterior that is picturesque, well-proportioned and forthright. The fireplace nook, stone-paved floor and close-fitted log work are elements of interest and merit behind which only the boulder masonry of the chimney conspicuously lags.

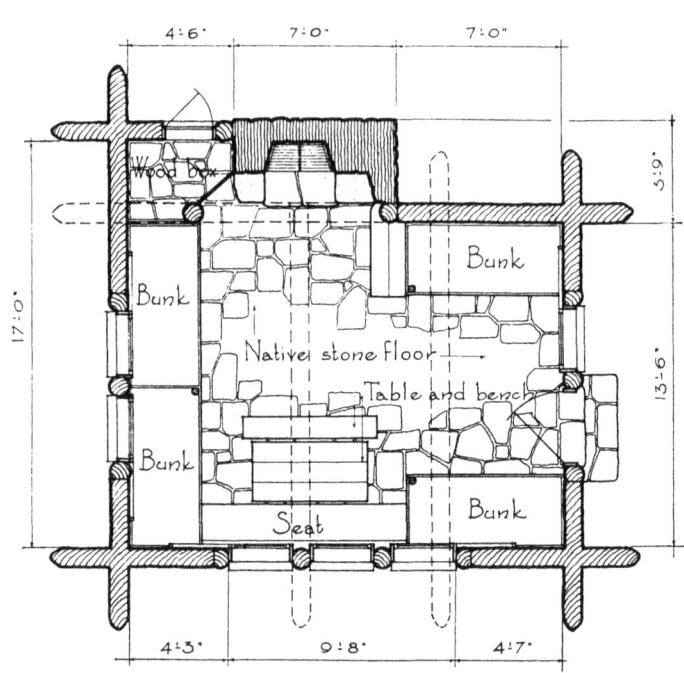

FLOOR PLAN

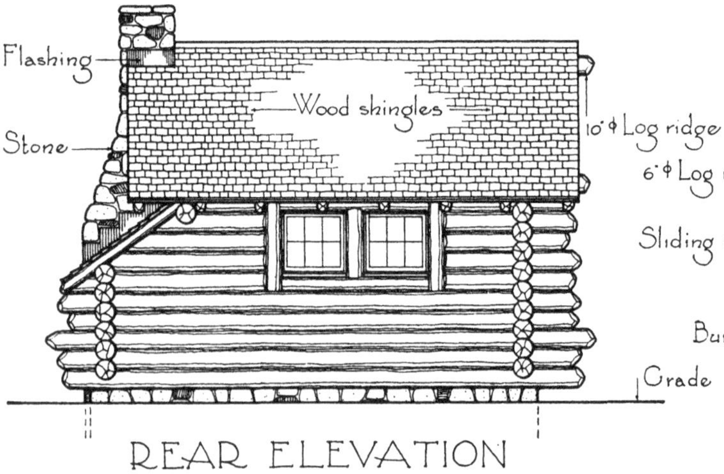

REAR ELEVATION

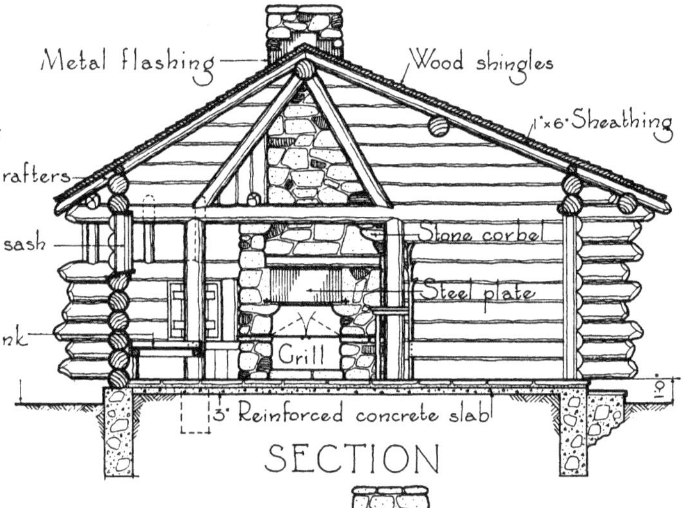

SECTION

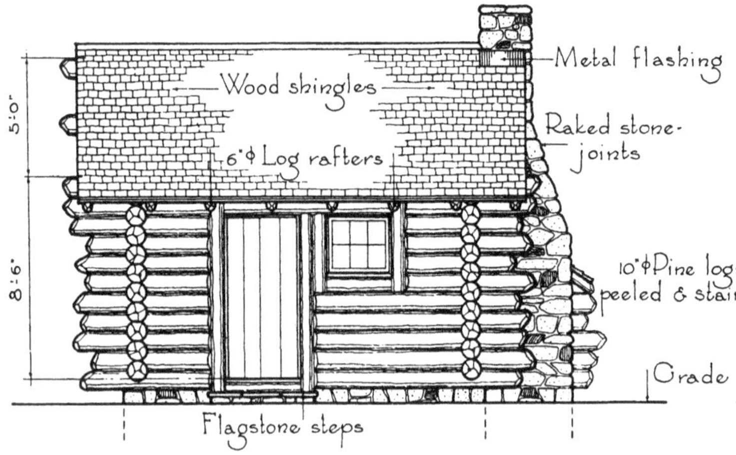

FRONT ELEVATION

Scale ⅜" = 1'-0"

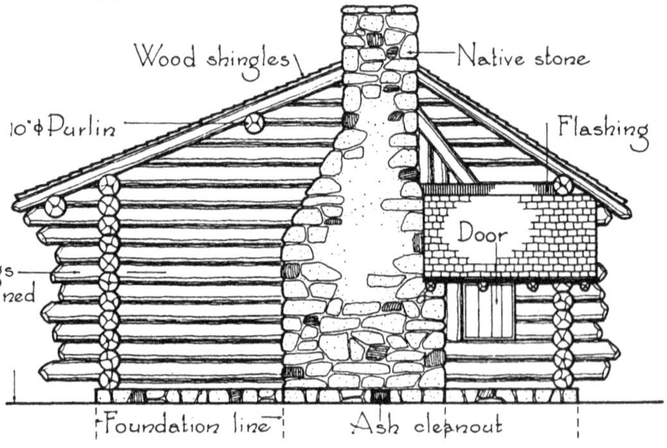

SIDE ELEVATION

Plate III B-5 — CABINS

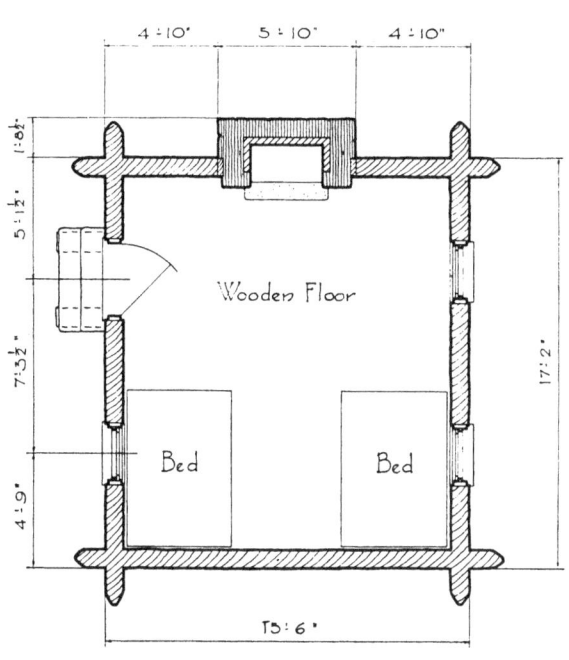

FLOOR PLAN

Cabin - - White Pines State Park - - Illinois

A fine example of the use of true log construction in a present day need for a small cabin of simple lines. The stone foundation and the cupping of the logs to shed moisture promise a long life span for this cabin. Attractive are the scale of the logs, the roof covering and the overwhelming chimney, appealing subtly to the universal weakness for miniature objects.

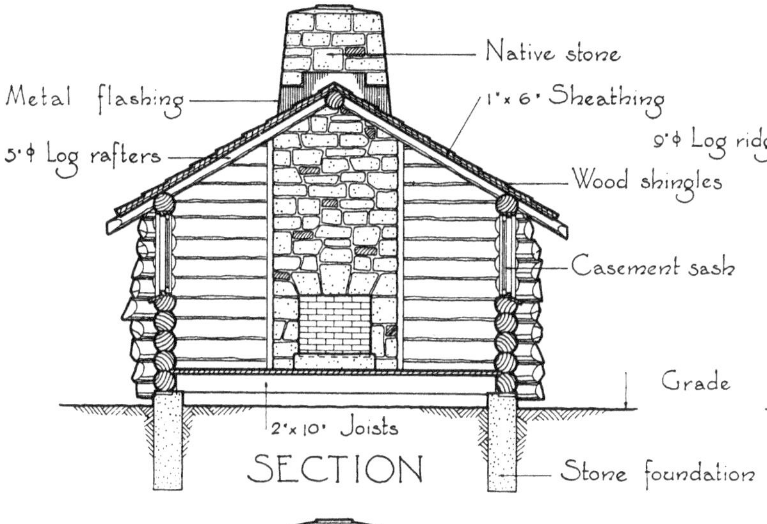

SECTION

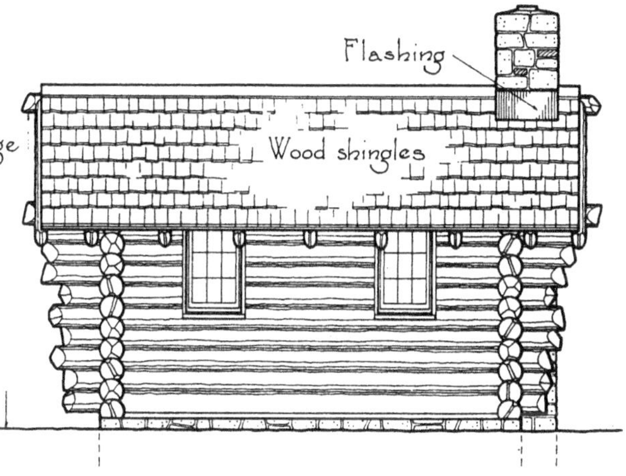

REAR ELEVATION

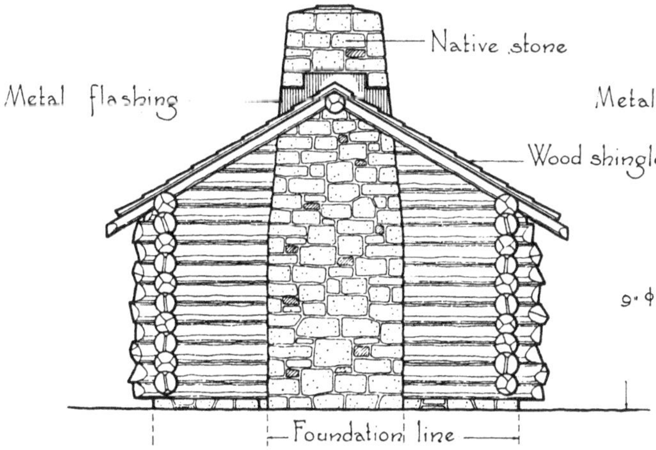

SIDE ELEVATION

Scale ⅛" = 1'-0"

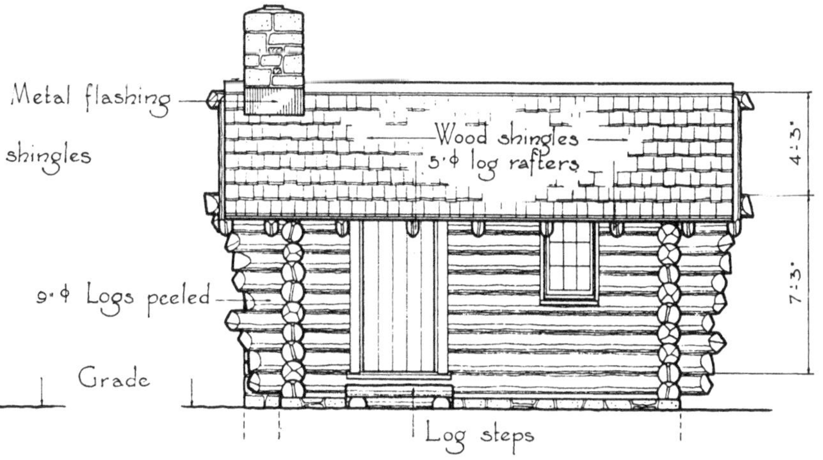

FRONT ELEVATION

25

CABINS

Plate III B-6

Cabin - Mohawk Trail State Forest Park - Massachusetts

This expertly put together log cabin derives of course from the Adirondack shelter. It is disadvantaged by its hillside location to a measurable loss of the pleasing proportions it would have on more level terrain. It offers as compact vacation habitation for two as any cabin here shown.

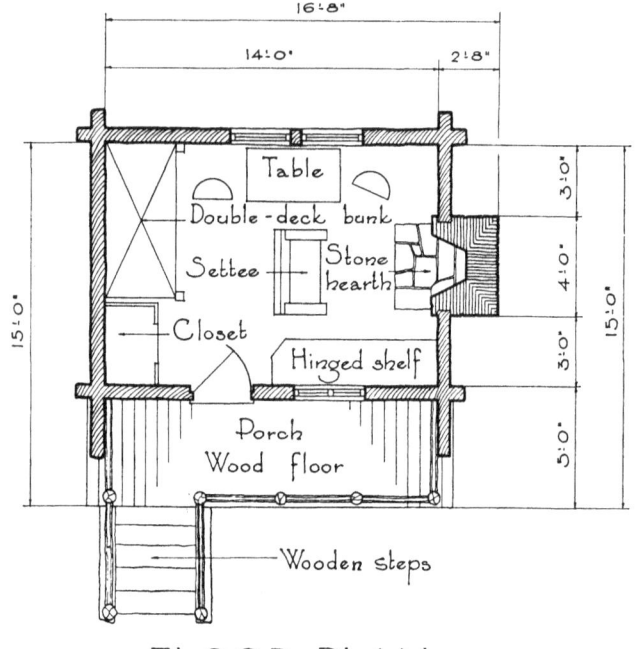

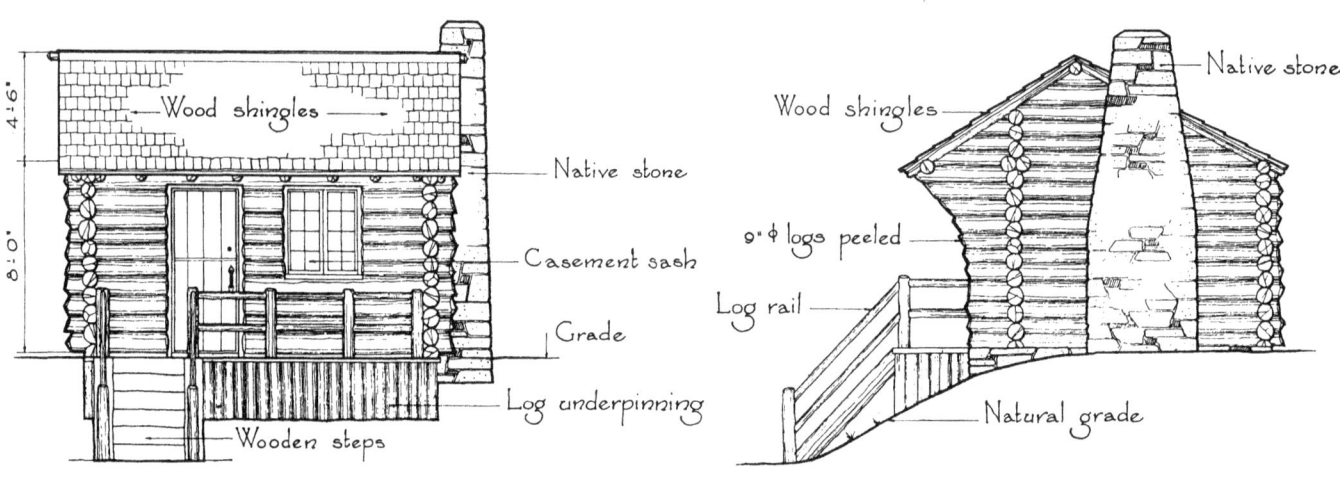

Scale ⅛" = 1'-0"

Plate III B–7 ≫ CABINS

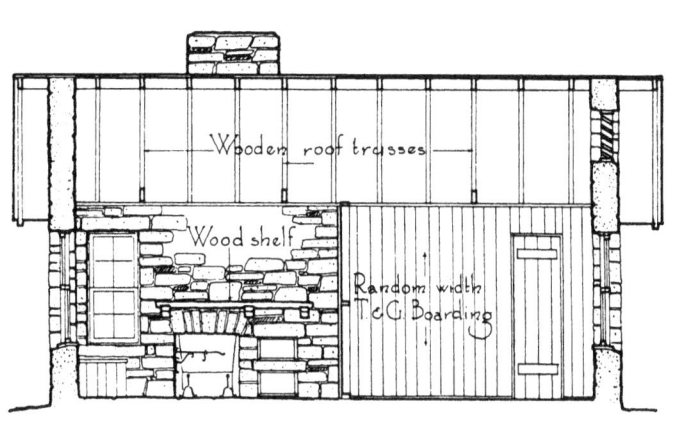

SECTION

Cabin — Cheaha Mountain State Park — Alabama

A plan representative of a compact grouping of all the elements that can be considered essential to a cabin in a state park. Apparently limited in sleeping accomodations to two persons this could well be increased by the addition of a screened porch sized for two or three cots.

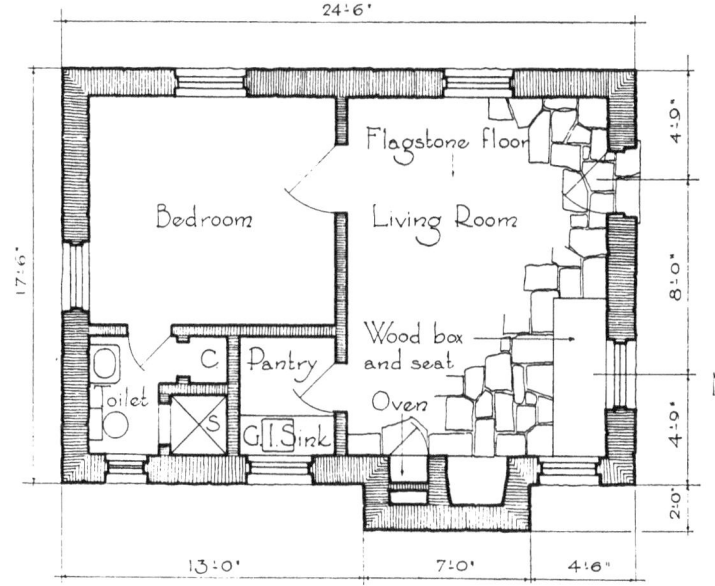

FLOOR PLAN

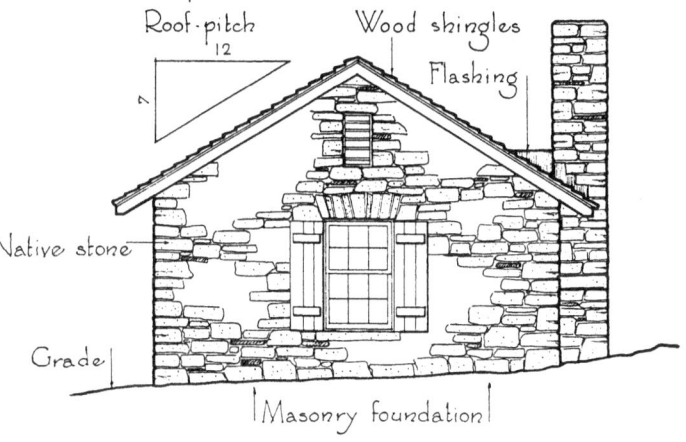

REAR ELEVATION

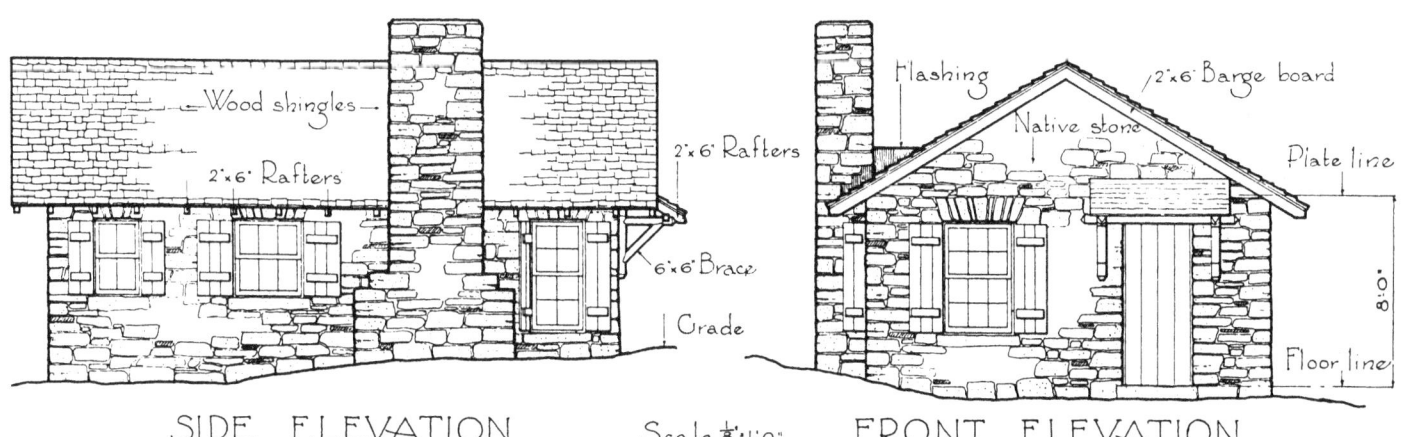

SIDE ELEVATION   Scale ⅛"=1'0"   FRONT ELEVATION

CABINS

Plate III B-8

Cabin - - Scenic State Park - - Minnesota

The space allotments here provide vacation accommodation for a family of four. There are those who will approve of double-deck bunks for family cabins, while frowning on them for being unhealthful and unsafe in a less restricted use, in children's camps, for instance. It should be noted that there is no fireplace in this cabin. Instead an iron stove for both heating and cooking purposes, connects into the small chimney. The saving in cost this alternative effects is often considerable, and so deserves to be weighed well when a cabin policy is being studied.

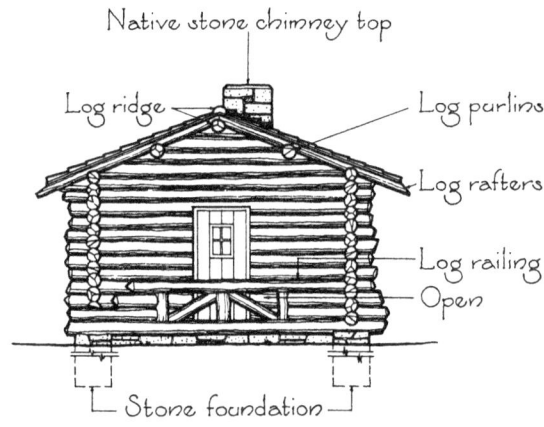

FRONT ELEVATION

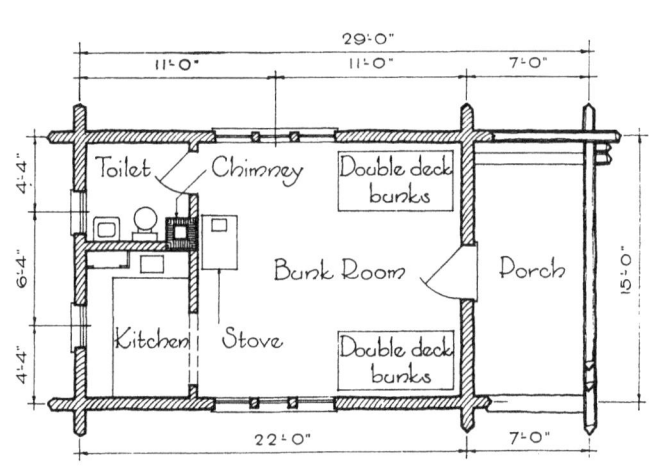

PLAN

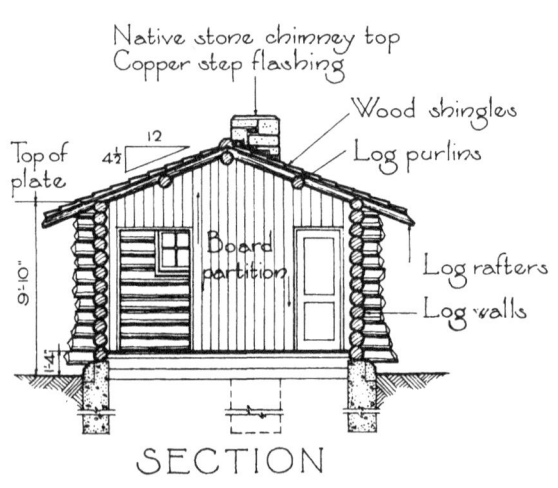

SECTION

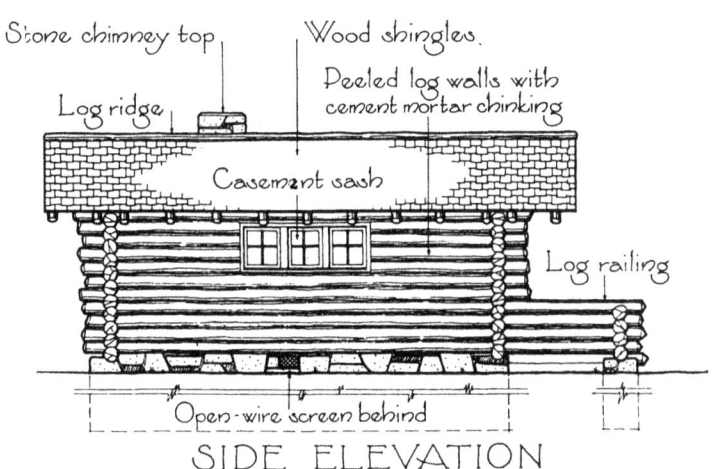

SIDE ELEVATION

Scale 3/32"=1'-0"

Plate III B–9   ⇛ CABINS

Hikers Cabin – – – Shenandoah National Park

Unique in purpose among the cabins here presented is this overnight shelter for a hiking group. Usually the facility is a shelter with one side open facing an outdoor fireplace or campfire. In this case, the fireplace has a chimney, and is integral with the cabin, and roofed over by a porch. A second flue serves a stove in the bunk room. The sleeping capacity of twelve in double-deck bunks is by way of being a master work of compact planning in a room so small. Some will deprecate this clever accomplishment because cubic capacity per sleeper is far below the recommendations of most health authorities.

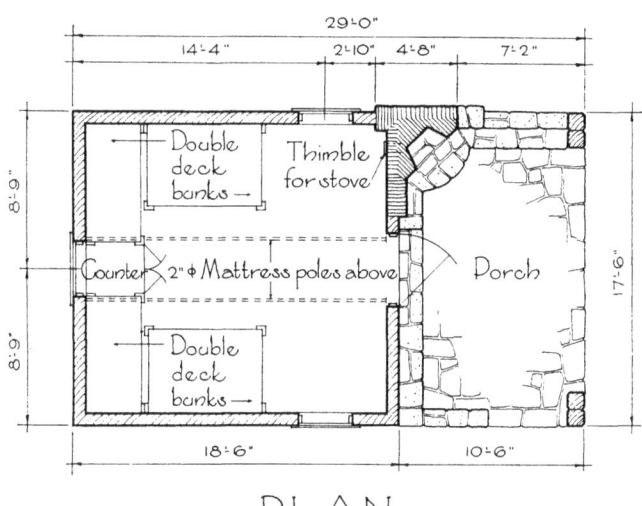

PLAN

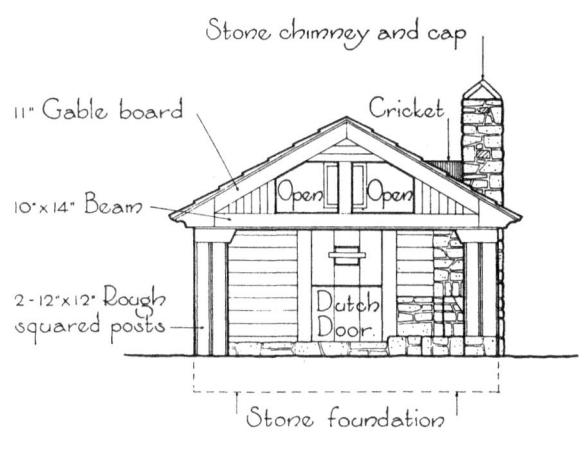

FRONT ELEVATION

SIDE ELEVATION

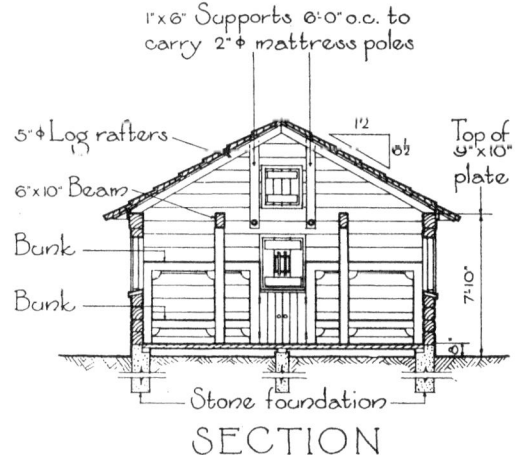

SECTION

Scale 3/32" = 1'-0"

CABINS   Plate III B–10

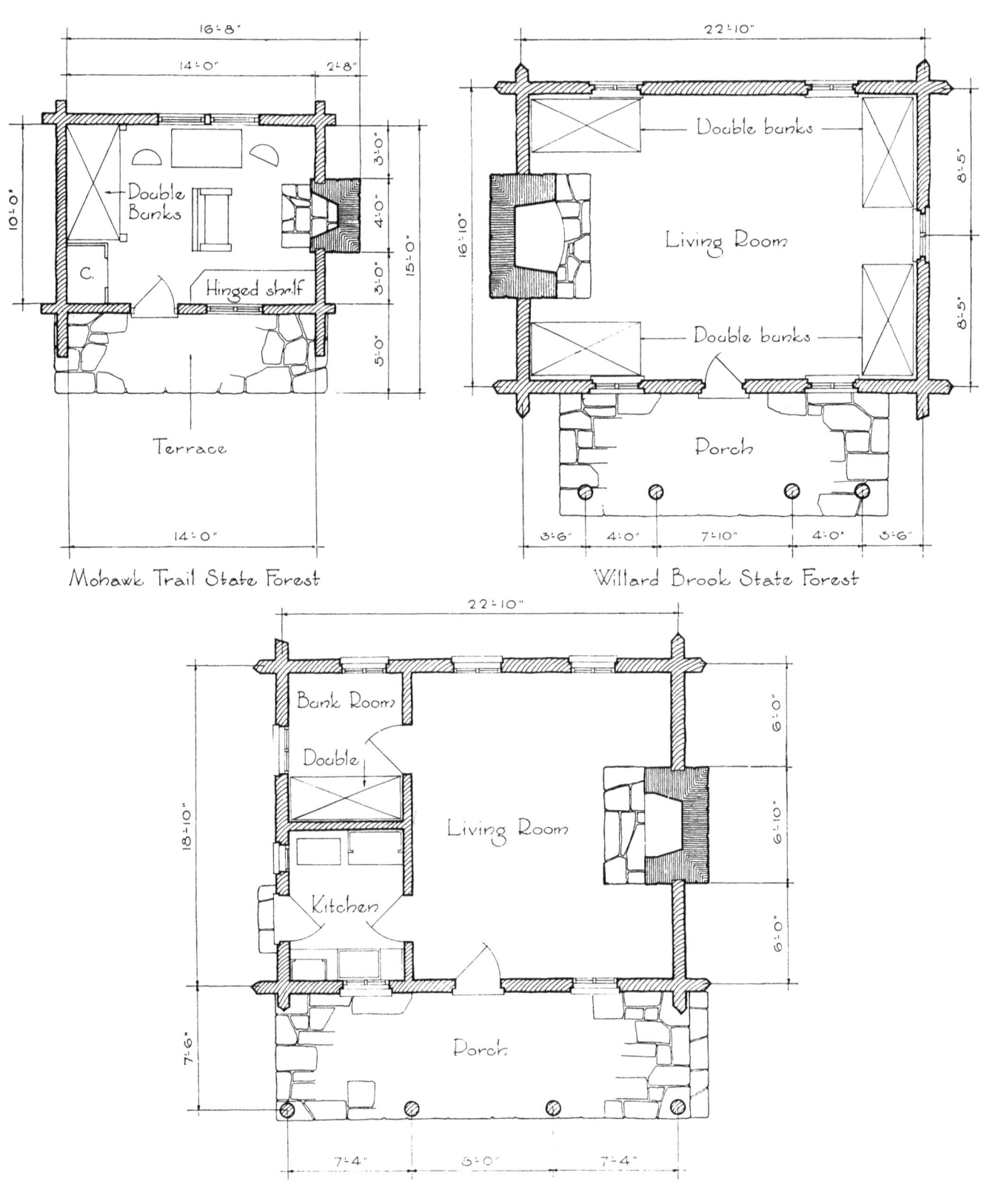

Mohawk Trail State Forest

Willard Brook State Forest

Mohawk Trail State Forest – Massachusetts

Scale ⅛" = 1'-0"

Plate III B–11   →»› CABINS

The plan at upper left opposite proves this little cabin might well represent the minimum in comfortable accommodation of two persons in a cabin colony developed on a basis of community toilet and shower facilities and campstoves provided out-of-doors. The hinged table shelf makes for economy of space. Excellent log joinery is a feature of all cabins on this page.

Mohawk Trail State Forest Park, Massachusetts

Likewise dependent on toilet and shower facilities in a separate nearby building, this larger one-room cabin, shown in plan at upper right opposite, utilizes double-deck bunks to achieve a sleeping capacity of eight. It seems particularly adapted to the use of an age group for week end or other short-term camping, although double-deck bunks are in disfavor with many organized groups.

Willard Brook State Forest, Massachusetts

The plan at the bottom of the facing page reveals a sleeping room separate from the living room and the kitchen. Here the preparation of the occupants' meals is not at the mercy of the weather, as is the case with the two cabins above. Toilet and shower facilities, however, are still a community matter. Cots in the living room can increase the sleeping capacity to four.

Mohawk Trail State Forest Park, Massachusetts

CABINS   Plate III B-12

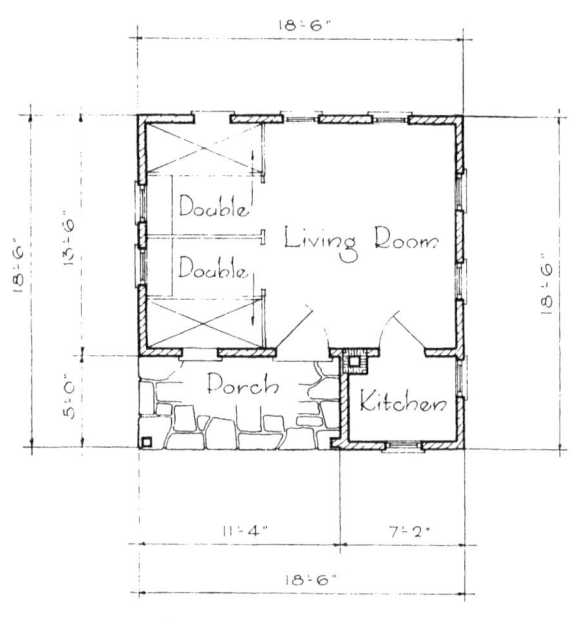

PLAN - A

PLAN - B

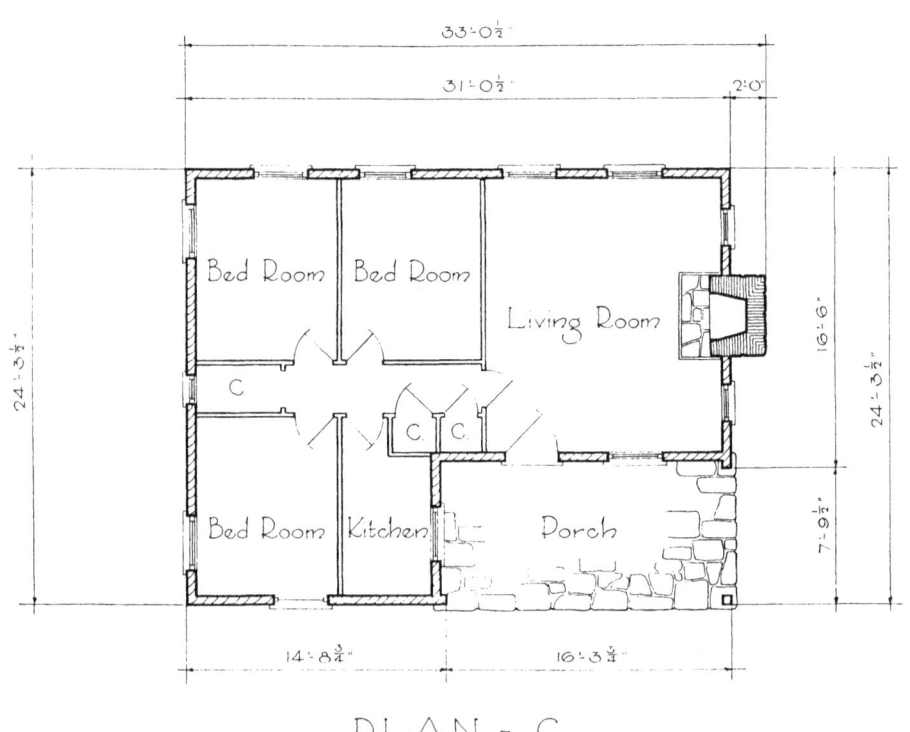

PLAN - C

Lake Taghkanic State Park - New York

Scale 3/32" = 1'-0"

Plate III B–13   →» CABINS

The plan at upper left on the facing page indicates that this cabin is the smallest of this group. Nevertheless, it accommodates four persons, by reason of its built-in double-deck bunks. The waney-edged siding used on all these cabins gives a considerable degree of woods character at a cost that is low in comparison with most other materials that are used to achieve harmony with a wilderness setting.

Cabin A, Lake Taghkanic State Park, New York

The thinness of the stratifications of the native stone used is responsible for the unusual texture of the stone chimney. The plan at upper right promises a capacity of six, and all three bedrooms have the benefit of cross-corner ventilation. Assuming that the living room does double duty in the absence of a dining room, the traffic lane to and from the kitchen seems rather indirect.

Cabin B, Lake Taghkanic State Park, New York

The plan at the bottom of the page opposite suggests that a door between the kitchen and the screened porch would make for convenience in the event it were chosen to use the porch as a dining room. Again the communication between kitchen and living room when the latter serves as a dining room is awkwardly indirect. There are sleeping accommodations for six occupants, and more, with cots provided in the living room.

Cabin C, Lake Taghkanic State Park, New York

CABINS   ««   *Plate* III B–14

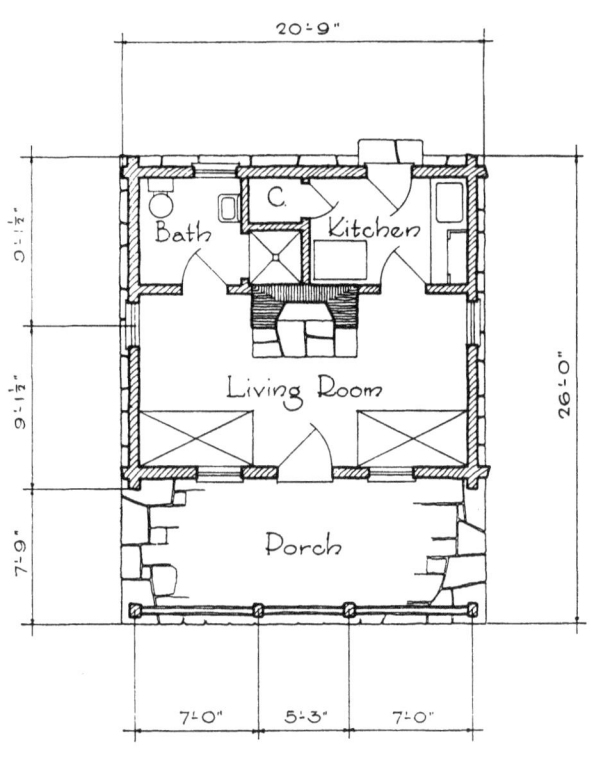

Douthat State Park

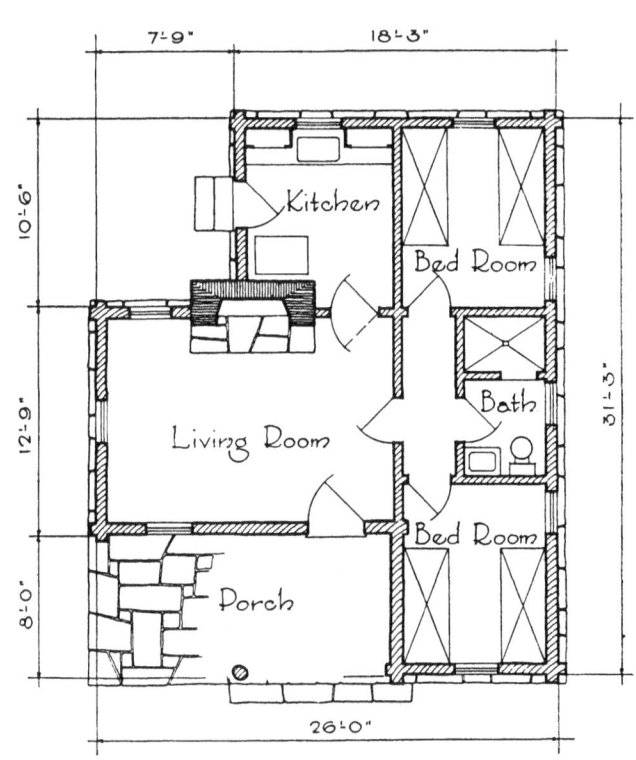

Westmoreland State Park

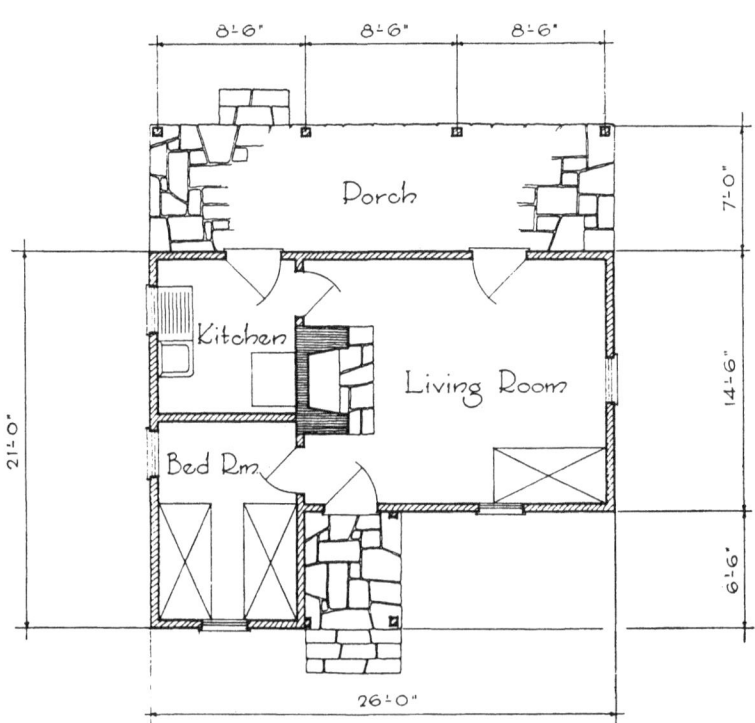

Staunton River State Park – Virginia

Scale 3/32" = 1'-0"

Plate III B–15 ⋙ CABINS

A fine example of vacation cabin, content to follow externally the simple log prototypes of the Frontier Era without apparent aspiration to be bigger and better and gaudier. Inside, it slyly incorporates a modern bathroom just to prove that it is not the venerable relic it appears. The squared logs with hewn surfaces and the simple fenestration contribute greatly to the look of authenticity. There is threat of accelerated deterioration in every log structure in which the spacing of the logs requires such wide chinking.

Douthat State Park, Virginia

Almost idyllic in spirit and setting, this vacation cabin can also claim a plan conveniently arranged with two cross-ventilated bedrooms to accommodate four persons, without either waste or painful economy of space. The quality of the log work, the texture of the shingled roof, are recommended for attention as important factors in the favorable reaction this cabin inspires. The inclusion of kitchen, bathroom, porch, and fireplace produces a cabin that is a self-contained unit.

Westmoreland State Park, Virginia

The exterior treatment of this cabin is typical of a number of park cabin groups in the Old Dominion—walls of wide boards and squared battens, rough-sawn siding in the gables, and steep roof which changes to a very low pitch over the porch. Assuming from the plan that sleeping accommodations in the living room are possible, the "bedding-down" capacity of the cabin is doubtless greater than the one bedroom would indicate. The corners of the porch posts are chamfered.

Staunton River State Park, Virginia

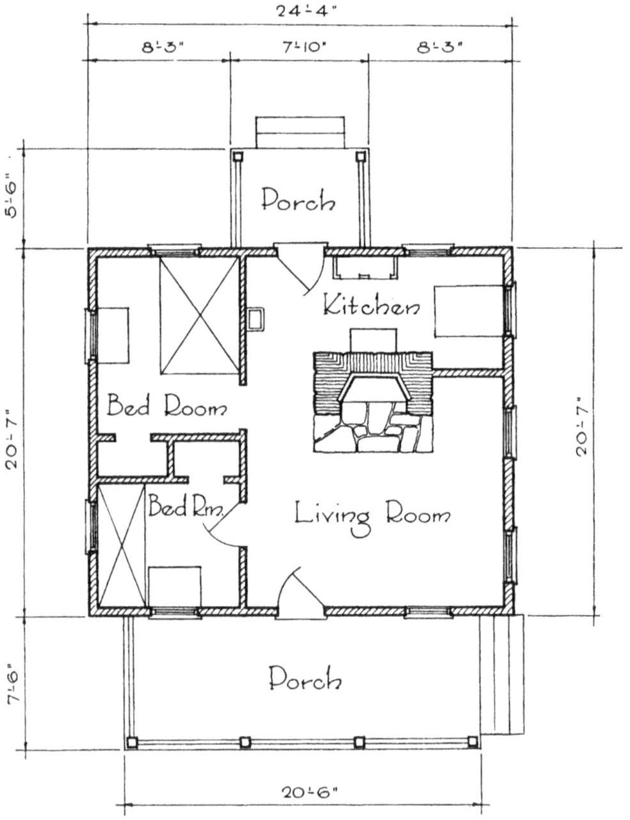

CABINS ⋘   Plate III B–16

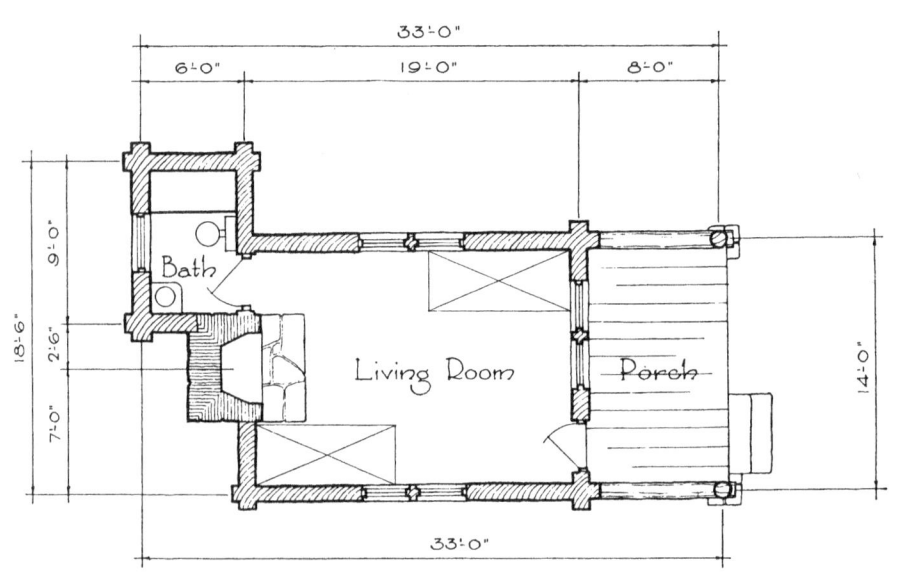

Lost River State Park

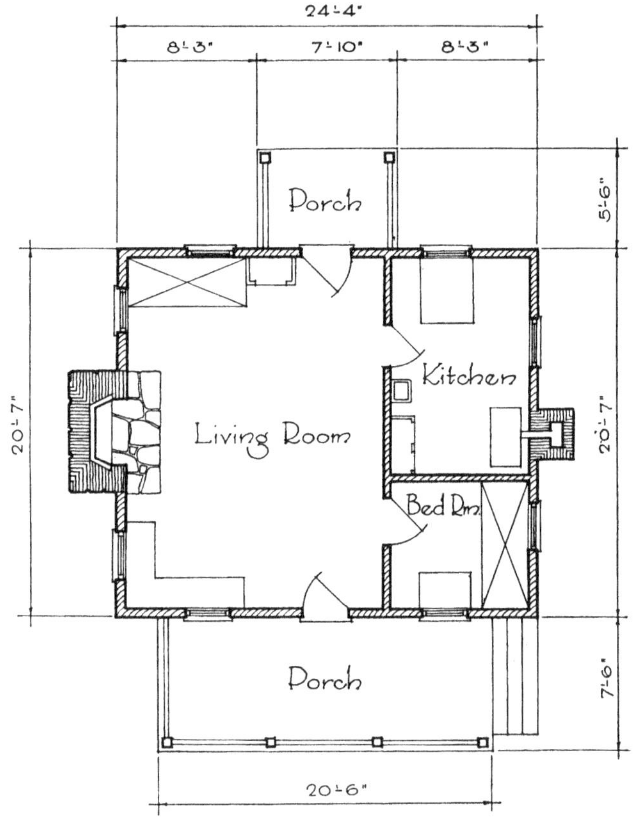

Lost River State Park

Cacapon State Park – West Virginia

Scale 3/32" = 1'-0"

Plate III B-17 　　　　　　　　　　　　　　　　　　　　　　　⇶ CABINS

Squared logs, sided gables, and Georgian symmetry in fenestration and centering of the porches follow the traditions of the earliest cabins of this mountainous region. As a matter of fact, the park includes land once owned by the Revolutionary figure, "Light-horse" Harry Lee. A very early cabin on that tract, said to date from the period of his ownership, may very possibly have inspired these new cabins.

Lost River State Park, West Virginia

Very like the subject above in exterior treatment, this cabin is more extravagant in the two chimneys it requires. The character of the masonry appears excellent until it is observed that some of the stones violate a time-honored principle of good masonry, being set on end instead of the natural bed. The size of the kitchen permits use of it as a dining room also.

Lost River State Park, West Virginia

This one-room cabin with bathroom and porch has modest size, of itself an admirable trait in a park cabin. But it illustrates the inferiority of round log to squared log construction wherever straight logs of uniform size are not available. Squaring eliminates irregularities and results in narrower chinks and better structural appearance generally.

Cacapon State Park, West Virginia

CABINS ≪≪≪ Plate III B-18

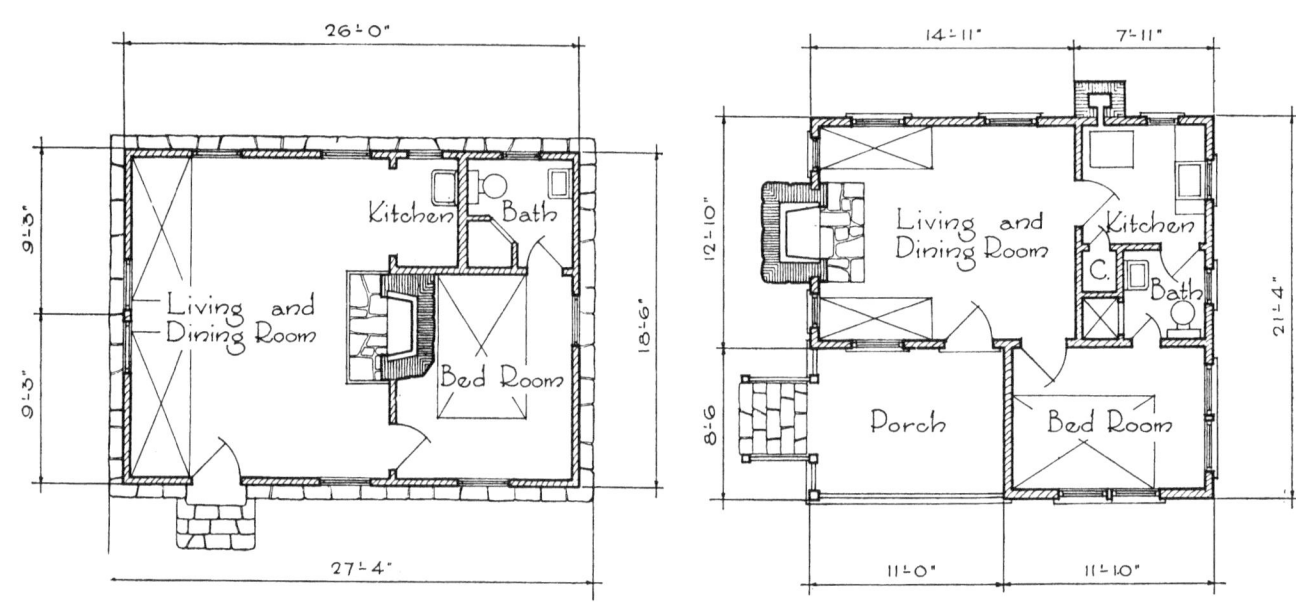

De Soto State Park

De Soto State Park

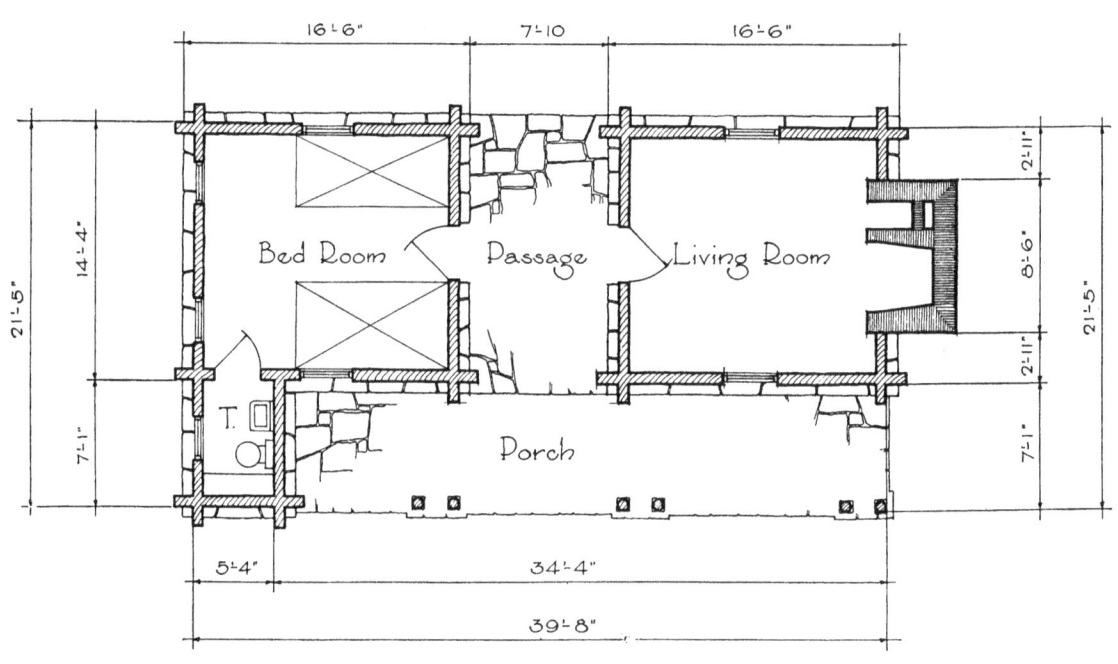

Weogufka State Park

Alabama State Parks
Scale 3/32" = 1'-0"

Squared logs reflect the early cabins of the South. All cabins of this page exhibit well-fitted log joinery promising a lasting weathertightness. The plan at upper left opposite holds to a single chimney with flues for both fireplace and range, an economy that is mandatory in every cabin of modest size. There is further cost saving in an interior chimney because its masonry does not need to be laid with the precision required in an exposed chimney.

De Soto State Park, Alabama

This cabin flaunts two chimneys—an extravagance that is open to criticism in any cabin as small as this. And both chimneys are on the outside and require careful, exposed masonry! Except for its spendthrift airs, there is no quarrel to pick with this cabin. It has both kitchen and bath and is conveniently arranged to sleep four people, which qualifies it to accommodate the average vacationing group.

De Soto State Park, Alabama

The character and workmanship of this cabin are admirable, yet the plan falls short of providing all that its considerable floor area would allow. In relation to the enclosed rooms, too much space is devoted to porch areas. The long porch omitted and the "dogtrot" of southern tradition screened at both ends, would have produced a cabin quite as livable, perhaps more so. The toilet room is inaccessibly located.

Weogufka State Park, Alabama

CABINS

Plate III B–20

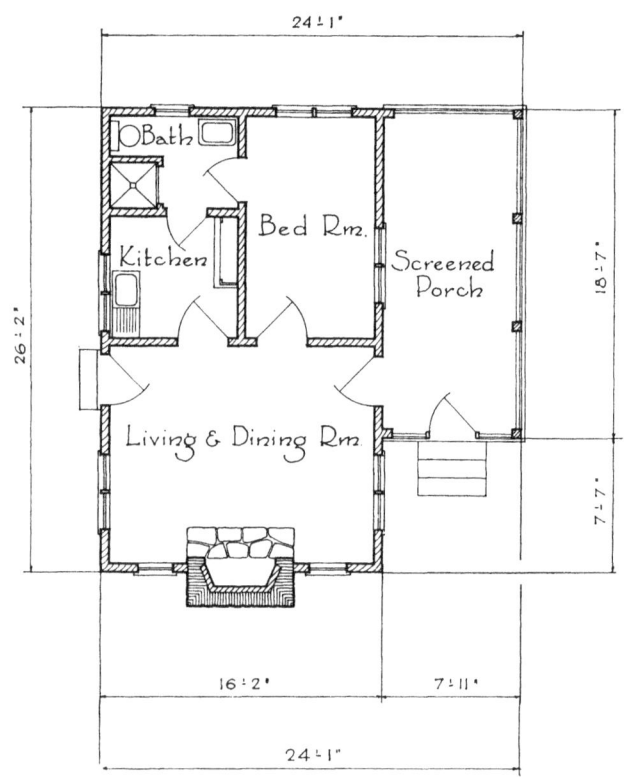

Legion State Park

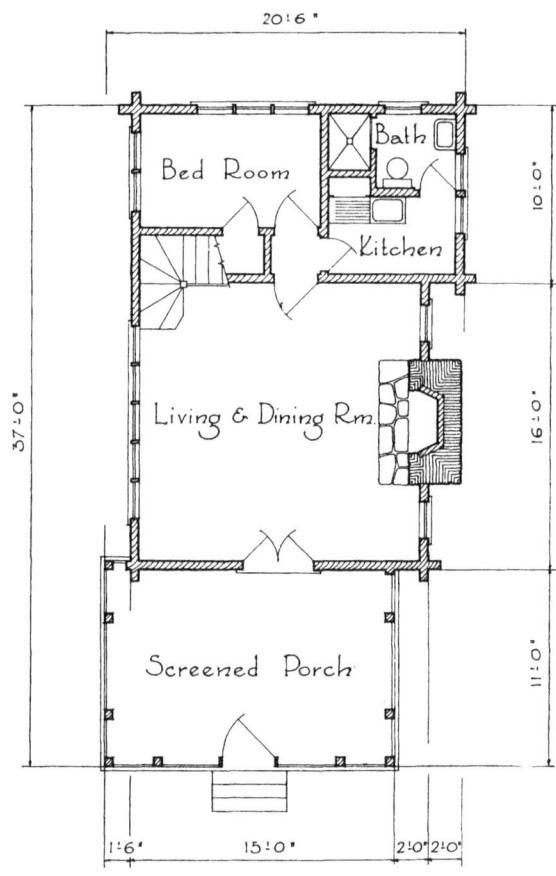

Legion State Park

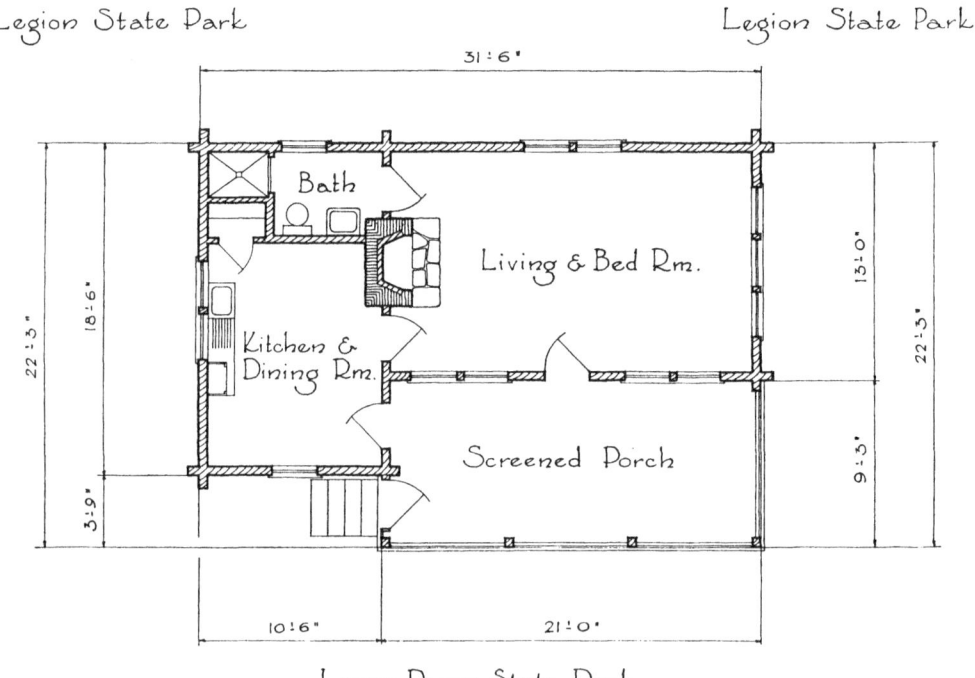

Leroy Percy State Park

Mississippi State Parks
Scale 3/32"=1'-0"

Plate III B–21   ⇒ CABINS

The plan of this cabin of simple lines, economically employing waney-edged siding, is shown at upper left opposite. The porch is an important feature of cabins in the southern parks. Climate dictates a certain spaciousness for it, and insect screening can hardly be omitted. Three open sides as in this example are very desirable, assuring the benefits of air movements.

Legion State Park, Mississippi

This cabin, shown in plan at upper right, rates higher on the score of appearance than convenience. It is awkward to have to cross the small kitchen to reach the bathroom. Perhaps there are sleeping accommodations in the loft indicated by the stairway. Unless such is the case, entrance to the bathroom would surely have been better from the bedroom. A wide opening between living room and porch offers advantages which were here neglected.

Legion State Park, Mississippi

The plan at the bottom of the facing page is economically arranged by reason of the chimney so located that it serves both kitchen stove and living room fireplace. The direct communication between kitchen and screened porch, which permits serving meals on the porch conveniently, is a good feature. An opening seven or eight feet wide between living room and porch was a possibility here. There is always strong feeling of need for foundation planting around every building that lacks an enclosing foundation wall.

Leroy Percy State Park, Mississippi

CABINS — Plate III B-22

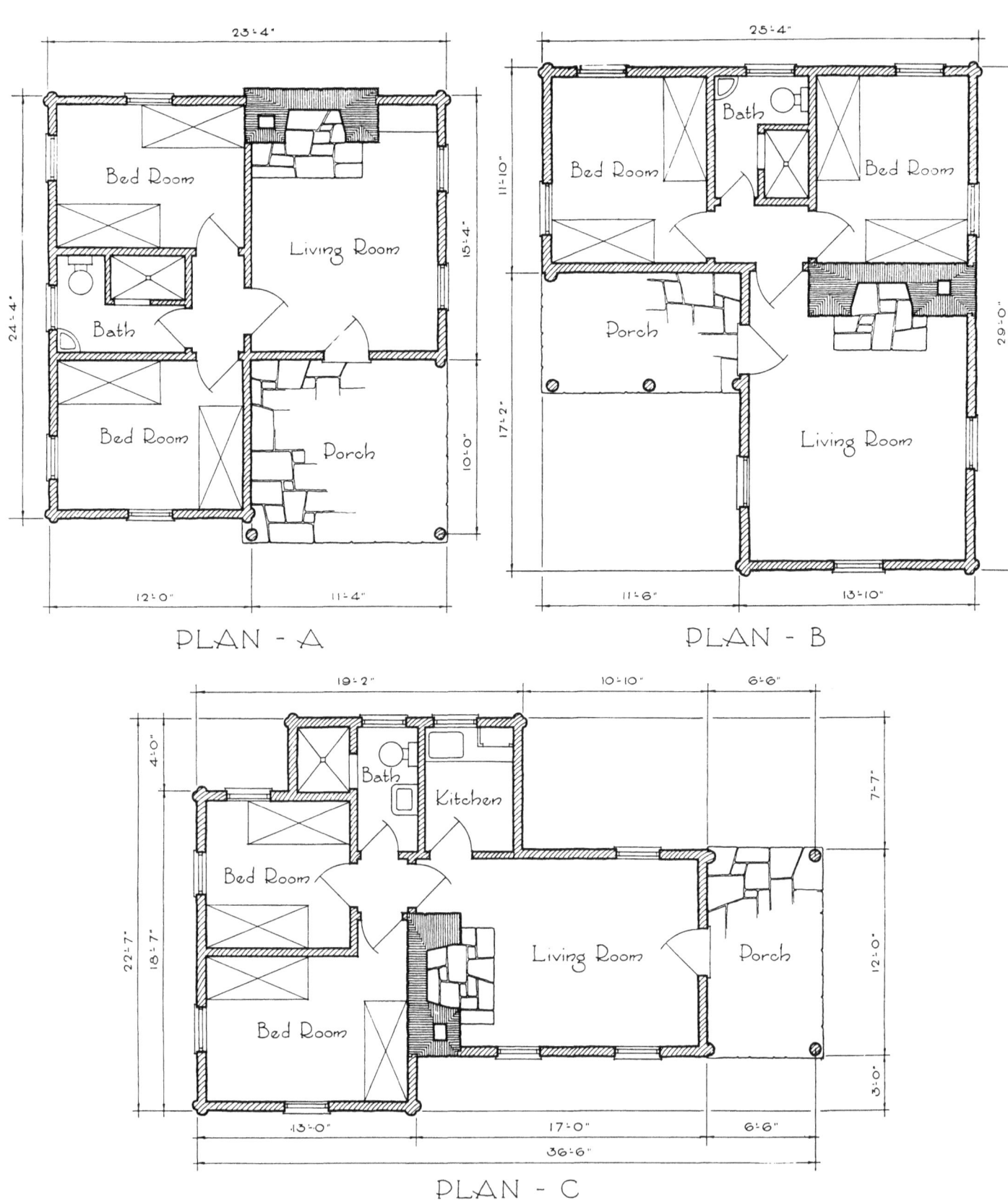

PLAN - A

PLAN - B

PLAN - C

Cumberland Falls State Park - Kentucky
Scale ⅛" = 1'-0"

Plate III B–23 →»› CABINS

The frame wall construction of the cabins in this park is surfaced with horizontally placed slabs. Vertical slabs function as corner boards, and the gables are shingled. The true log cabin is only approximated, yet the effect is one of harmony with a wooded area. The economy of this kind of construction is a factor that goes far to justify the use of it.

Cabin A, Cumberland Falls State Park, Kentucky

The two bedrooms of each of these cabins indicate a sleeping capacity of four persons, which might, when occasion demands, be stretched to six by placing cots in the living rooms. The combination of a normal capacity of four and a potential makeshift capacity of six appeals to the needs of a wide tenant field.

Cabin B, Cumberland Falls State Park, Kentucky

A roll call of the units the plans of these cabins provide includes living room, porch, two bedrooms, and a bath, to which, in the cabin shown at the bottom of these pages, a kitchen is added. Distribution of floor areas is such that well-balanced plans result, and the elements of the plans are so grouped that roofing is uncomplicated.

Cabin C, Cumberland Falls State Park, Kentucky

CABINS ‹‹‹ Plate III B-24

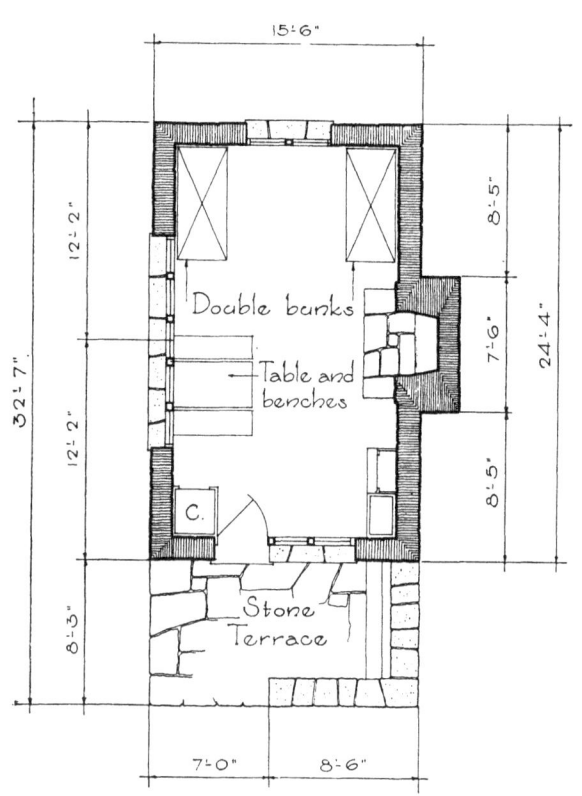

Eldora State Park

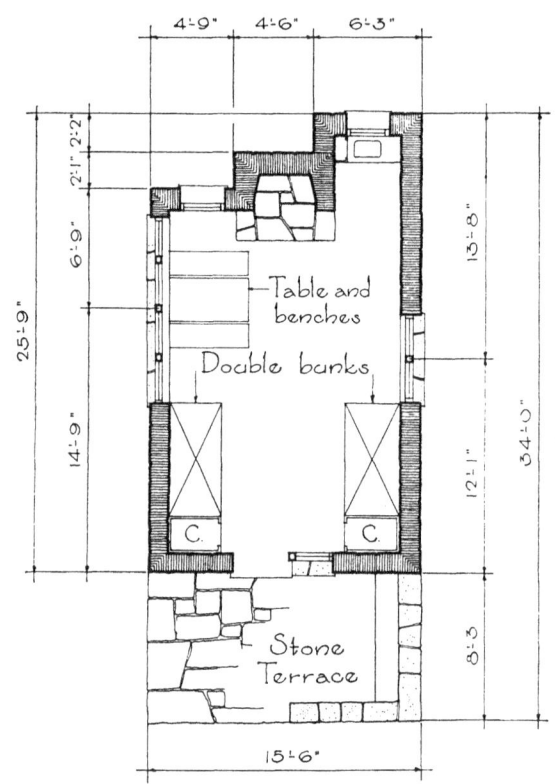

Eldora State Park

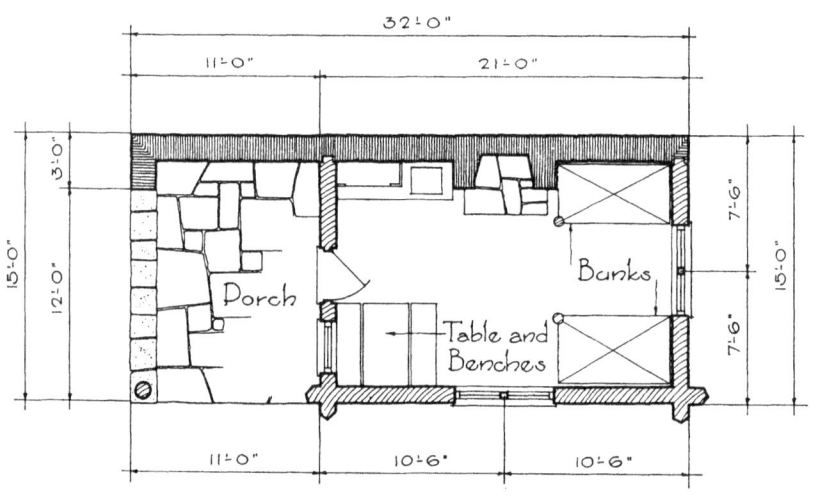

Ledges State Park – Iowa

Scale 3/32" = 1'-0"

Plate III B–25   ⇶ CABINS

These Iowa cabins are contrived for a hillside location and meet well the limitations this situation imposes. The windows are banked on the downhill side where the views are to be had. The stone-paved terraces of the entrance ends are defined by retaining walls at side and rear. These receive the rising grade and form the backs for the seats placed at the rear wall.

Eldora State Park, Iowa

The major items of equipment of the cabins illustrated on this page and shown in plan on the opposite page in the usual order are a fireplace, two "double-deckers", dining table with benches, and sink with running water. Toilet and shower facilities in these parks are a community provision as is usual where the simplest of cabins are the affirmed overnight policy on an area.

Eldora State Park, Iowa

Chief differences between this cabin and those above-presented are the substitution of log construction for masonry walls and the addition of a roof over the stone-paved terrace to provide a porch. In size, equipment, and other details it falls in step with the other two, so that all three may be said to establish an Iowa cabin type having individuality, simplicity, compactness, and well-reasoned limitations in size.

Ledges State Park, Iowa

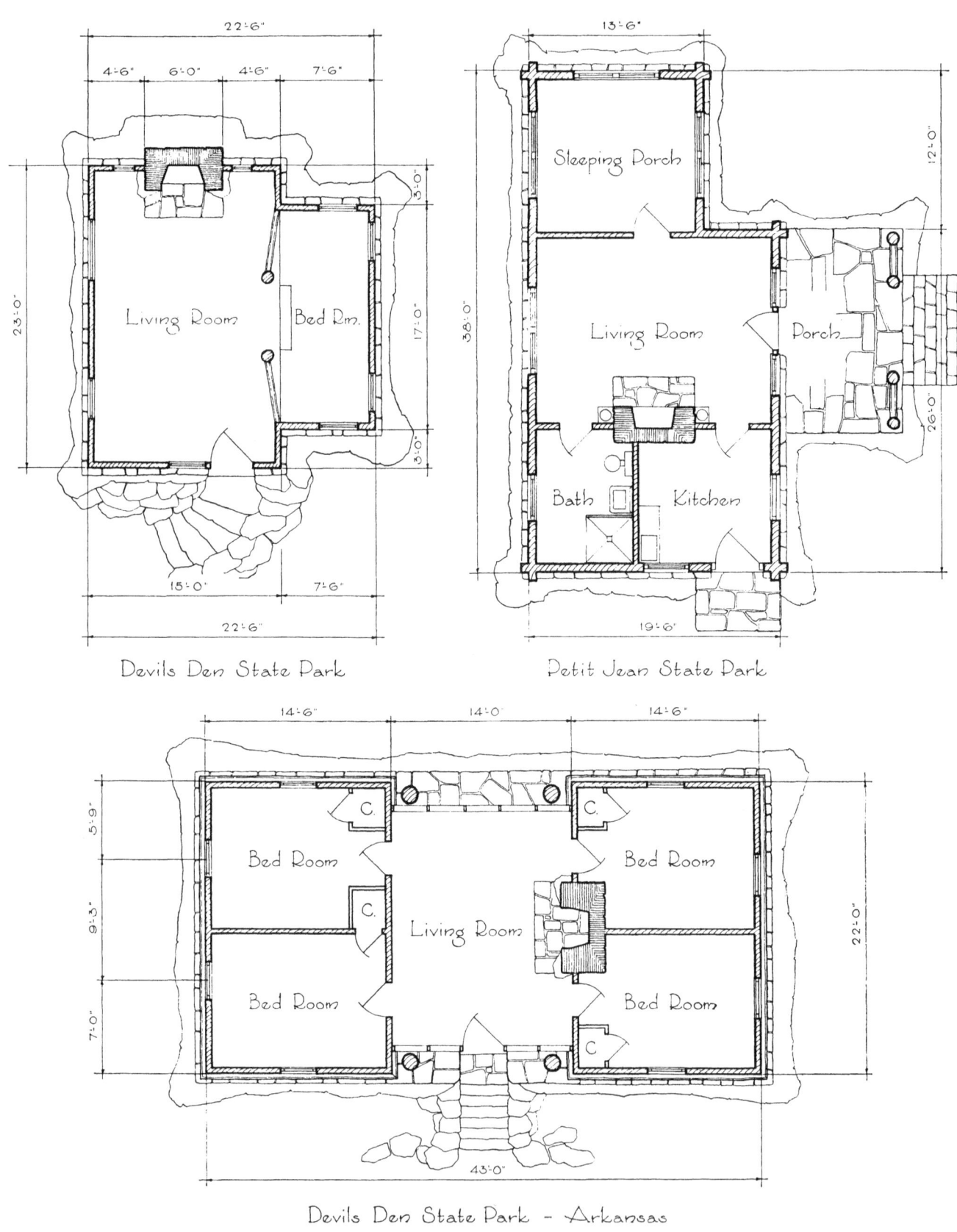

Plate III B–27   ⇾⟫ CABINS

Stone walls up to the sills of the windows of this little cabin—and the one at the bottom of the page—are the practical answer to the demands of a sharp-sloping hillside site. As the grade rises above the floor level, only the masonry is in contact with the earth, and if the masonry is well laid and waterproofed, and if good drainage is provided, the cabin should not be subject to dampness and consequent deterioration.

Devil's Den State Park, Arkansas

There is so much appeal in this cabin that it is difficult to analyze just what characteristics and details are responsible. Pleasing proportions generally, fine log fitting, rugged stone base, good scale of the porch posts, vibrant texture of the roof, all well-visioned and well-executed, and fortified with flattering shadows caught by a photographer of parts, will probably share the merited applause.

Petit Jean State Park, Arkansas

Unusually large for a park cabin is this four-bedroom example with stone and shake-covered walls in combination. All bedrooms enjoy cross-corner ventilation. The centered living room has through ventilation by virtue of the wide windows at the ends. It may be inferred that the typical "dogtrot" cabin long popular in the rural South inspired the very practical plan.

Devil's Den State Park, Arkansas

47

CABINS

Plate III B-28

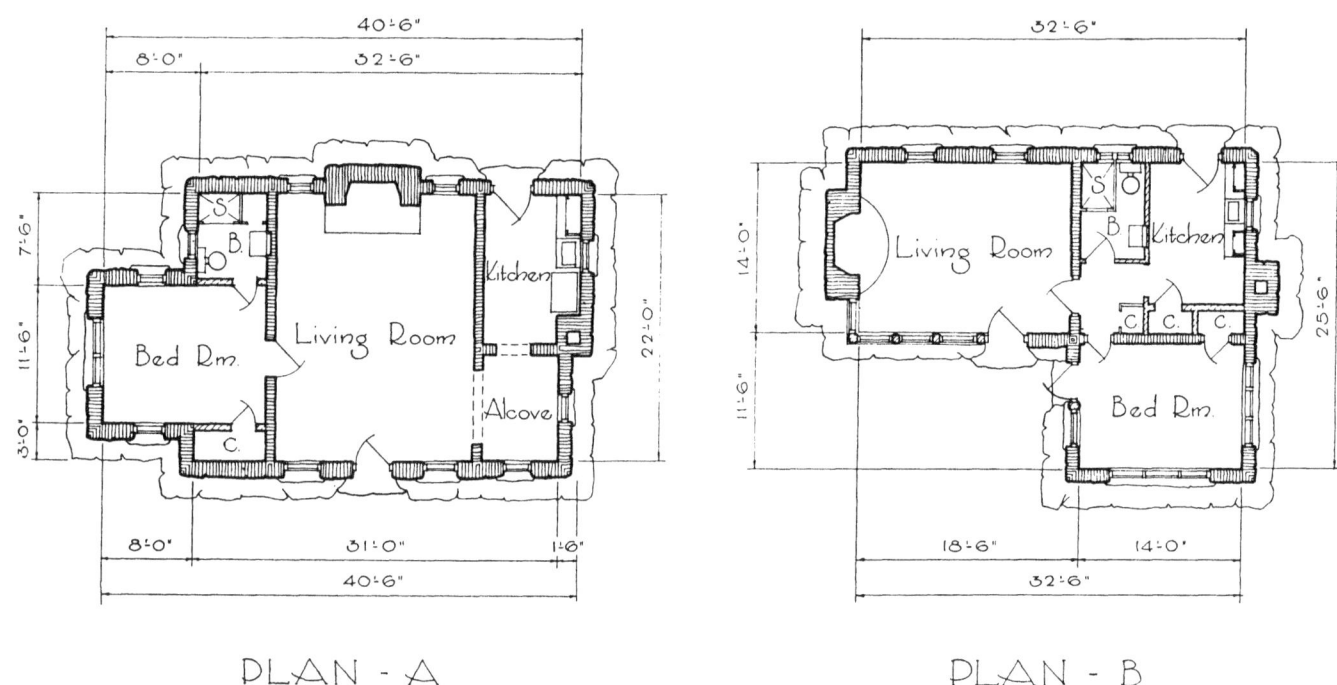

PLAN - A

PLAN - B

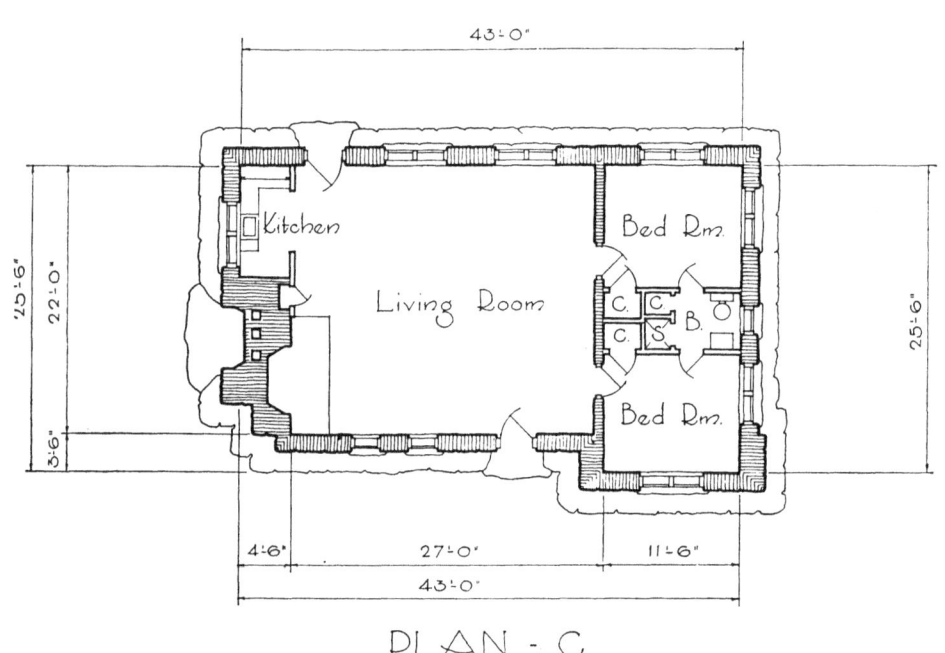

PLAN - C

Lake Murray State Park — Oklahoma
Scale 1/8" = 1'-0"

Plate III B–29 →›› CABINS

These cabins, by reason of the scale and the water-worn edges of the carefully selected, lichen-covered stone units employed, appear very much at home in the boulder-strewn environment. Although barely completed when the pictures were made, the structures betray but little of the rawness natural to new construction except in the scarcity of ground cover in the immediate surroundings.

Cabin A, Lake Murray State Park, Oklahoma

The different plan elements in combination in these cabins may be compared with interest. In the plan of the above-pictured cabin, shown at upper left opposite, a living room is supplemented with kitchen, dining alcove, one bedroom, and a bath; in the example at upper right are the same elements save that a dining alcove is omitted. In the plan at the bottom of the facing page of the cabin illustrated below, there is likewise no dinette; the kitchen is a mere alcove; and a second bedroom is provided.

Cabin B, Lake Murray State Park, Oklahoma

The huge size of some of the stones incorporated in the walls of these cabins is astonishing. The stone sills of the grouped windows and the lintel of the outside fireplace of this example, especially, suggest that Stonehenge may have been sacked for the greater glory of Oklahoma. There is well-defined individuality of style in all the structures completed to date in the Lake Murray area. This is apparent in the concession building, the shelter, and the pumphouse, illustrated in other sections of this publication.

Cabin C, Lake Murray State Park, Oklahoma

CABINS   Plate III B–30

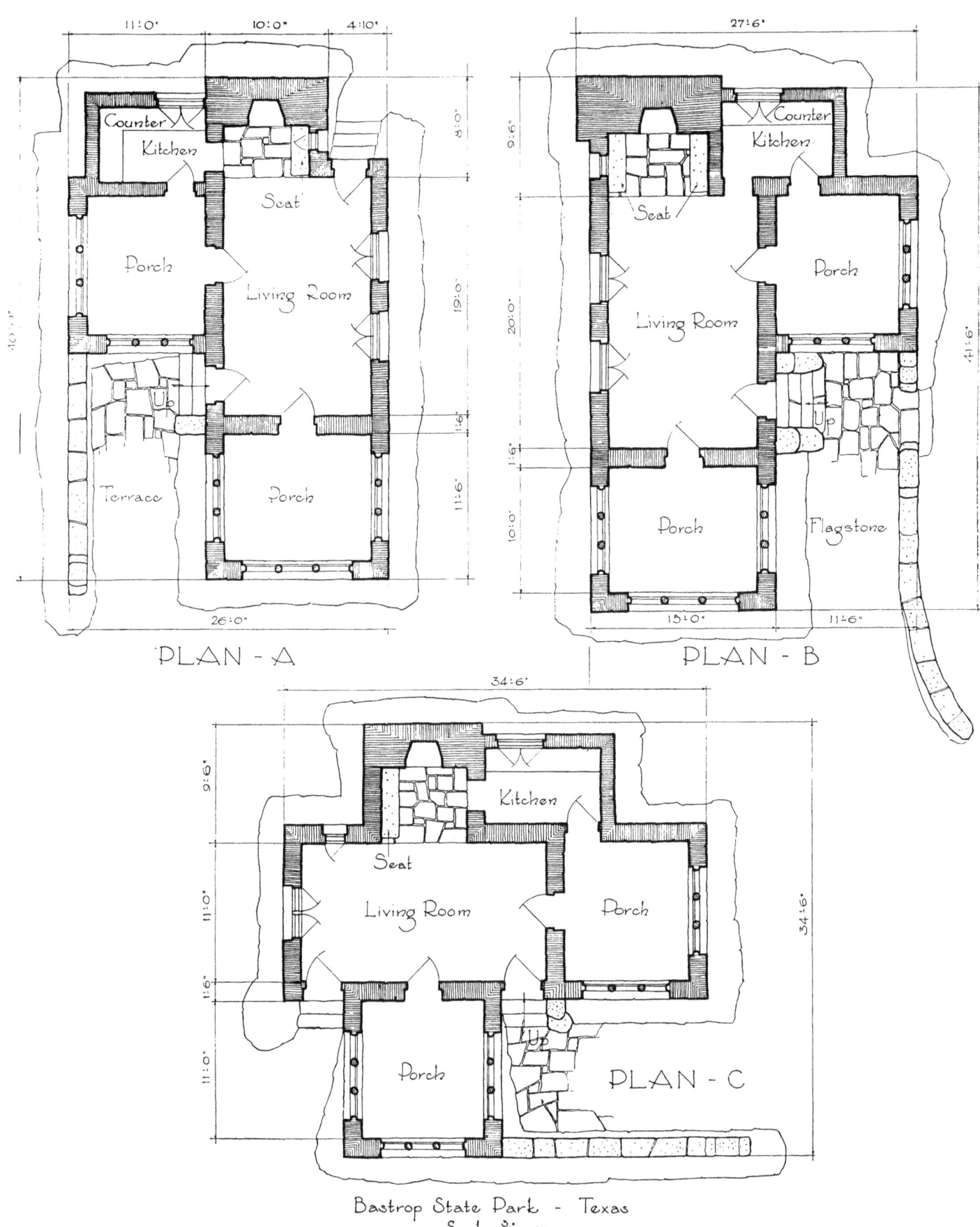

Bastrop State Park - Texas
Scale 3/32"=1'-0"

Plate III B–31 ⇾ CABINS

Low, sprawling, rugged—these cabins seem especially appropriate to the character of the country for which they were designed. The squat, massive chimneys, extreme batter of the walls, roofs of very low pitch, and the low walls which seem to knit the structures to their sites are elements which add up to a total effect that is extraordinarily individual and attractive. This illustration shows the rakish roof lines of the rear elevation of the cabin at upper left of the facing page. Fireplace nooks feature the living rooms of these cabins.

Cabin A, Bastrop State Park, Texas

It is interesting to observe from a study of the three plans shown on the plate opposite that the elements of all are practically identical, and yet so grouped that the cabin exteriors and the outline of the plans are nicely varied. A low wall that follows the natural contours, a feature typical of most of these cabins, is shown in the picture alongside and well demonstrates the picturesqueness such a wall can produce. Plans of this cabin appear at upper right. Obviously, the rooms labeled porches are sleeping porches.

Cabin B, Bastrop State Park, Texas

A basic advantage of stone structures is the opportunity they afford for dropping the floor construction below the natural grade without having to remold the existing contours to a conspicuously artificial appearance. A situation thus happily met can be seen in this illustration. Oftentimes in the determination of the floor level for a frame building on a sloping site a hopeless dilemma confronts the planner; neither warping the grade to accommodate the building nor raising the building to clear the highest natural elevation is an entirely satisfactory solution.

Cabin C, Bastrop State Park, Texas

CABINS   Plate III B-32

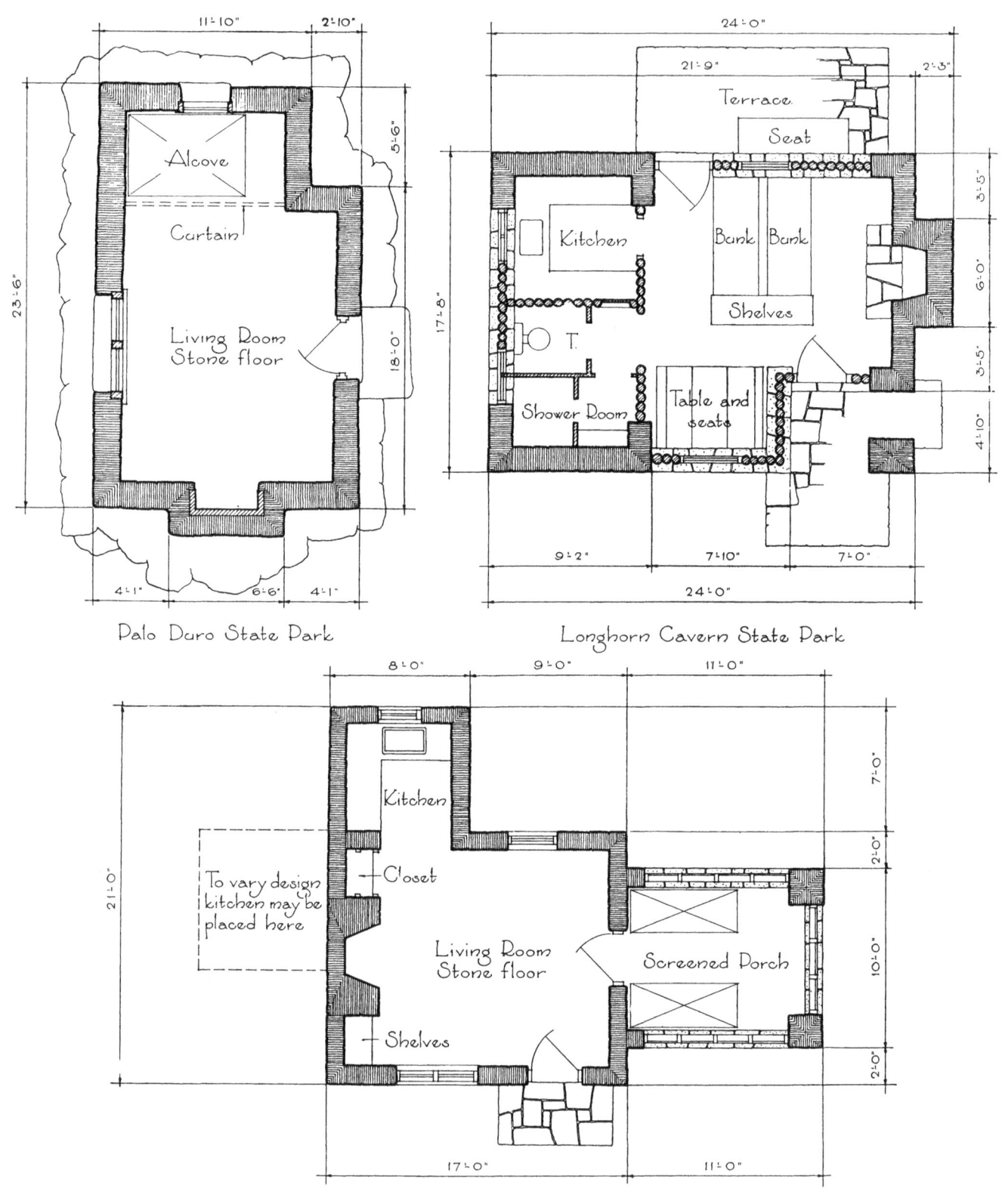

Palo Duro State Park

Longhorn Cavern State Park

Lake Brownwood State Park – Texas

Scale 1/8" = 1'-0"

Plate III B–33 ⇥ CABINS

The infinite variety to be found in Texas State park architecture could not be better illustrated than by the three cabins here grouped. The single room with curtained-off alcove of this Palo Duro cabin, shown in plan at upper left opposite, is overnight accommodation in its simplest terms. Outwardly the cabin evidences a peak accomplishment in the keying of structure to the vast open spaces.

Palo Duro State Park, Texas

The compact plan of this cabin, reproduced opposite at upper right, creates a place for everything, including bathroom fixtures and kitchenette, in a space hardly larger than the little one-room cabin shown above. Externally it has a place for so many of the structural traits of early Texas architecture, and these are so cleverly insinuated, as to reach a high for skillful adaptation in miniature of traditional architecture.

Longhorn Cavern State Park, Texas

In sharp contrast with the tradition-based cabin at Longhorn Cavern State Park is this cabin of contemporary inspiration, the plan of which is shown at the bottom of the facing page. The low lines stressing the horizontal and the fenestration adopted give it a modern cast, yet within limits that keep it from appearing foreign in a natural park preserve. A more pronounced modern treatment would be much less appropriate.

Lake Brownwood State Park, Texas

53

CABINS

Plate III B-34

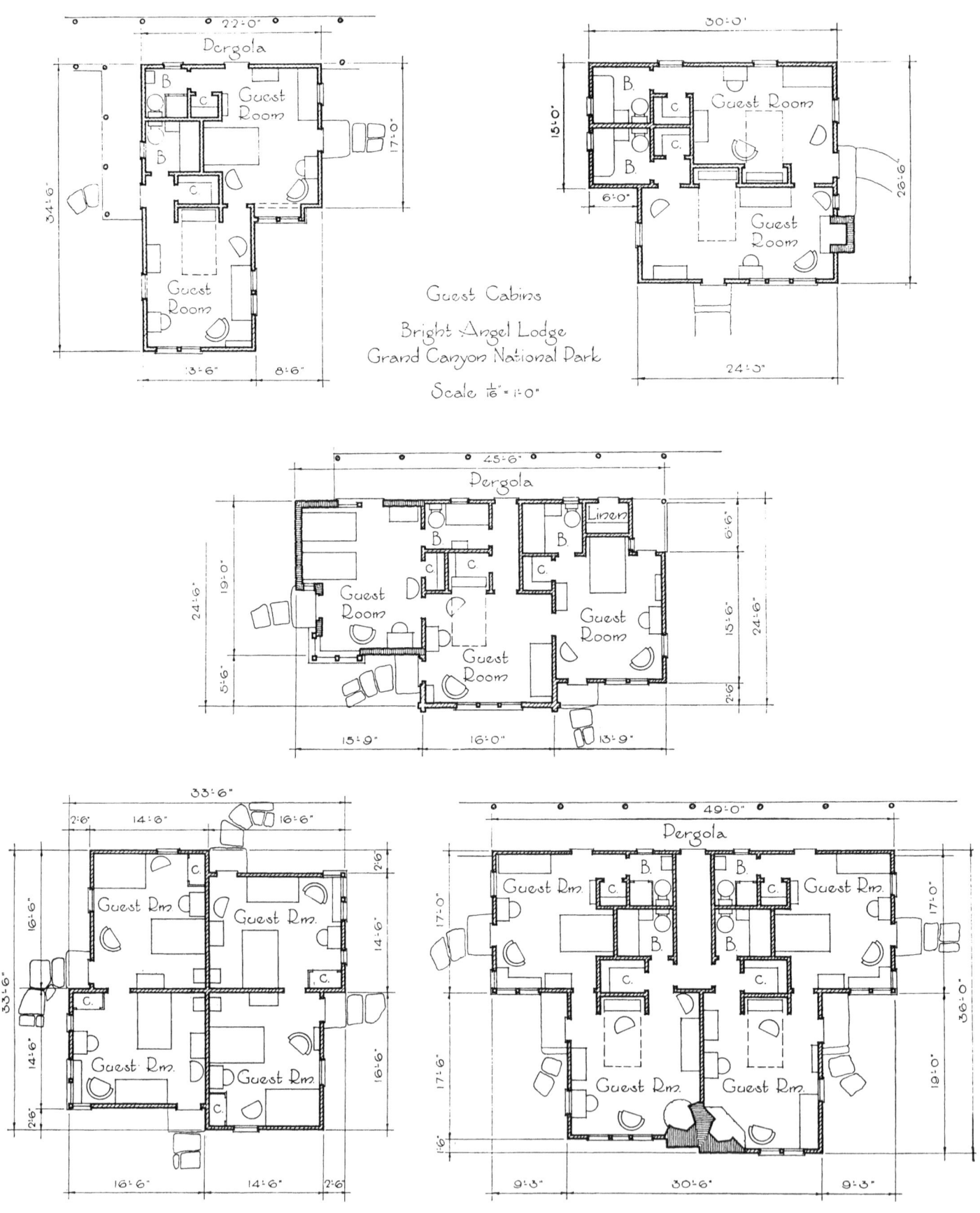

Guest Cabins
Bright Angel Lodge
Grand Canyon National Park
Scale 1/16" = 1'-0"

Plate III B-35 →›› CABINS

Old Post Office

Old Bucky O'Neill Cabin

CABIN DEVELOPMENT, BRIGHT ANGEL LODGE, GRAND CANYON NATIONAL PARK

Above are two historic landmarks which have established the structural theme for the Bright Angel Lodge and all its connecting and outlying cabins. To the left is the old post office building remodeled into a two-room cabin and retaining all its primitive construction. To the right is the Bucky O'Neill cabin which, with its exterior quite unchanged, has become a part of, and given name to, a 17-room guest house. Once occupied by buccaneers of the West's wild days, it later became the lobby of the Bright Angel Hotel, the main hostelry in the stagecoach days of this outstanding scenic area. When the new Bright Angel Lodge and cabins replaced the early hotel, of the old buildings only this cabin and the old post office were preserved.

On the facing page are plans of some of the multiple cabins which derive from the structural traditions of the retained landmarks. Some, it will be noted, have sheltered connection with other buildings of the main group; others are detached. The glimpses of the new construction shown below indicate that harmony with the old construction was achieved in this highly interesting development.

Modern Cabin

Modern Cabin

55

CABINS

Plate III B–36

Spring Mill State Park, Indiana

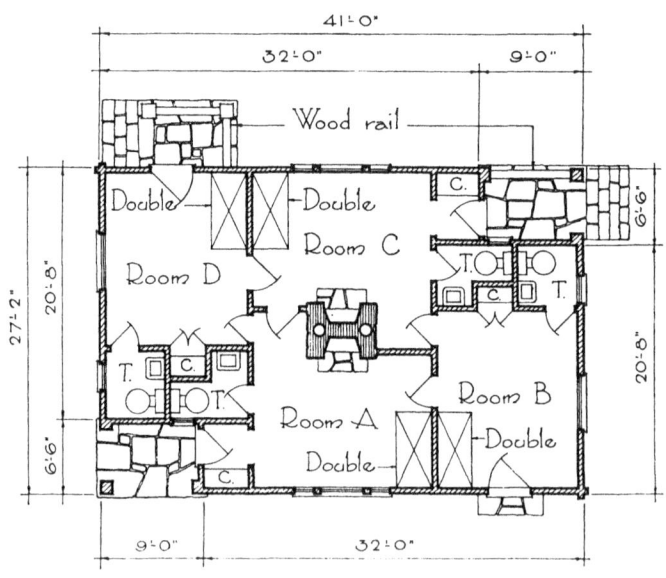

FLOOR PLAN
Scale 1/8" = 1'-0"

MULTIPLE CABIN,
SPRING MILL STATE PARK, INDIANA

Both for its clever, flexible plan and the full flavor of the pioneer generation's log construction it recaptures, this novel overnight unit merits high praise. That it is more acceptable on a public area than four small one-room-and-bath cabins accommodating the same number of visitors seems beyond all reasonable doubt, even though the smaller cabins were built with equivalent fine craftsmanship and feeling for tradition.

LODGES, INNS, AND HOTELS

EVEN IN THE LACK of any current demand for such a building, probably the preliminary development plans for natural parks, with but few exceptions, should designate a suitable location "Future Park Lodge." This is a reasonable sort of advance planning—a kind of hedge or insurance against an unseen future. But just as insurance coverage does not dispose us to seek out fire, shipwreck, or sudden death in order that the full benefits of our policy may be enjoyed, long or eternally deferred use of a potential site for a park lodge, inn, or hotel is nothing to lament.

Much speculation has long centered around the academic question whether the chicken or the egg came first. As between a demand for meals and overnight lodging in a park and the creation of some structure to supply them, there is no debating priority. Demand, not clairvoyantly perceived, but manifest, recurrent, and inescapable, should precede the hatching of any lodge project. Badly confused in his doctrine is the park authority or park planner who thinks he becomes an apostle of advance planning by rushing headlong into the building of a lodge on a public preserve that, in order to promote a semblance of patronage, must depend on ballyhoo by billboard. Not only are the gears of his thinking in reverse, but they give every indication of being badly jammed.

In respect to park buildings generally, it has been many times stated that only urgent need is valid reason for intruding them. In the case of minor structures a breach of this tenet is bad enough. An unrequired shelter, or bench, or picnic unit is a sorry monument to loose planning and miscalculation, but the carrying charges are trivial compared with the staggering losses a park lodge can roll up when it labors under a less-than-capacity patronage. As between accepting an operating deficit and the vain alternative of attempting to reduce or eliminate it by overcharging the less-than-capacity patronage, there is little choice, for both are indefensible.

Since the use of parks is predominantly a daytime one, the only justification for providing overnight accommodations in them is the facilitating of daytime use. There is a distortion of proper objective where overnight accommodations are provided in excess of the actual needs of bona fide park patrons. For those who would arrive at dusk, pass the night, and depart at daybreak, park environment seems hardly an essential. A tourist camp, commercially operated on the highway, can function in supply of their needs. Overnight facilities within a park should essay to serve, not speeding passers-by, but visitors who mean to avail themselves of the typical enjoyments the park can offer. Such accommodation should be incidental to the use of the park, not to the use of the highway.

Any natural park worthy the name will not jeopardize its standards and expose itself to misuse by admitting within its boundaries commercial enterprise that is not dedicated to serving the fundamental purpose and best interests of the park.

The appropriateness of locating a lodge or hotel in a natural park of distinction will be vehemently denied by some who feel that this facility brings a too civilizing influence into any area where retention of primitive aspect is an aim. It will be as stoutly defended by others who plead greater accessibility of natural beauty as the gain. Probably there can never be anything approaching unanimity of opinion on this basic point. Likewise the scale on which lodges may properly be undertaken will be variously argued. Once, however, the construction of such a facility has been authorized and the capacity of it has been determined on the basis of carefully analyzed need, there can perhaps be a certain harmony of viewpoint as regards the theory, form, and details of the structure.

One scheme of development is a central building containing a lounge, dining room, kitchen, and

LODGES, INNS, AND HOTELS

related dependencies, surrounded by individual cabins which provide the sleeping accommodations. In any but a minor development this means many trivial buildings close-crowded in an intensively used area. Such a result is now very generally felt to be subversive of natural park values and therefore bad planning. Moreover, authorities who have made careful studies state that individual cabins are more expensive to operate and maintain than equivalent sleeping accommodations integral with the central structure. Complication of supervision, distances involved in servicing, and, in some climates, the burden of heating a great number of separate units are among the affecting factors.

But the combining of all sleeping accommodations and all functions of the lodge proper under one roof likewise can be criticized when in size the building grows beyond what can be termed a minor development. Somehow or other large buildings in parks appear to be subject to some natural law—increase in volume tends to amplify static interference and cause harmony to fade. The park planner, asked to devise extensive overnight accommodations that are not painfully obtrusive, finds himself in a quandary.

Luckily for parks, there lies between the two extreme courses just described a truly happy mean which, by reducing the appalling number of cabin structures of the one and the offending size of the single building of the other, can avoid the chief disadvantages and retain the points of merit of both. Such a solution is a central lodge limited to lounge, dining room, kitchen, and directly related dependencies, surrounded, not by innumerable individual cabins regimented in a lay-out inspired by the monotony of cross section paper, but by multiple cabins (discussed in the chapter preceding), in some appropriate informal arrangement born of mating imagination, and not geometry, with the site factor. A few low, rambling buildings are more soothing than either a multitude of insignificant voting booth structures in a parking lot congestion, or any rendering in Rustic Renaissance jealously competing with the magnitude of Versailles.

In planning extensive lodge developments in this recommended "middle-of-the-road" approach, it is not necessary to limit the multiple housing units to four rooms, although four-room units make possible two exposures for all rooms. When the units contain more than four rooms, this desirable feature must usually be sacrificed. The more extended the development, the larger should be the housing units in order to maintain a proper scale relationship.

The lodge proper can be connected with the surrounding multiple cabins by covered walkways so that even the most remotely housed guest, by traversing the cabin porches and the covered connecting walks, enjoys overhead protection in travel between his room and the facilities located in the lodge.

These sprawling groups need not be stamped with monotony if there is judicious combining of various materials and varied forms. Nowhere are the potentialities for interest based on a variety of materials and forms more completely realized than in the Bright Angel Lodge and its connected dependencies on the South Rim of the Grand Canyon. The resulting informality of the ensemble is appealing in the extreme, deserving of close study, and should inspire those charged with the design of large-scale overnight housing in parks with a deep desire to create informal individuality of regional flavor in an equivalent degree.

No minor part of the satisfaction experienced on viewing that pleasing development is the contribution made by the long, low, horizontal lines of the buildings. Not less than mandatory in that particular location, the low, horizontal feeling there produced would be the appropriate note in almost any natural park setting one could imagine. The advantage invariably deriving from low height is not restricted to grouped buildings as represented by the Bright Angel Lodge. It has similar importance in the altogether satisfying smaller, single-structure lodge developments at Mariposa Grove in Yosemite National Park and at Petit Jean State Park, Arkansas, both of which are pictured.

There are other characteristics and features, not so major as low horizontality, yet not to be overlooked if, in creating in parks large-scale overnight use structures, something well-differentiated from such facilities as built in cities is to result. It is no light assignment for a designer to be asked to retain the substance of comfort while cutting loose from the evidence of sophistication; nevertheless, that probably analyzes the accomplishment in the illustrated park lodges that readers will most admire.

When the weather turns cold, the guest in the park lodge in the most primitive area will demand well-circulated heat. Even while he is warmed in the comfort of a central heating system, he will be further warmed by the wish-fathered thought that he is miles away from such things as radiators. He will revel in the glow of generously scaled fireplaces, so these must be generously provided in the lodge. He will enjoy originating the thesis that the primitive fireplace was tops in comfort—as long as radiators are at his back, and are not too conspicuous. In a cold climate some auxiliary means of really heating the atmosphere that fireplaces psychologically create cannot be omitted from a lodge that is other than a summer season affair.

The matter of heating is but one item among many. In other details guests will expect the park lodge to be a photograph of all that is primitive—touched up, however, so that all the harsh discomforts that accompany the truly primitive anywhere are somehow obliterated. In the designing of a lodge the stressing of primitive aspect and the disguising of the more major modern comforts combine to produce a problem difficult indeed. The many gadgety conveniences common to urban and pseudo-urban hotels, if incorporated in the wilderness lodge, will only complicate the problem and so have no place in such a development.

In most localities porches and terraces in connection with lodges will be much used. Guests are in the park presumably to enjoy the out-of-doors, and porches and terraces are a means to that end. To function to the best advantage, they should look out on any distant views and points of interest offered.

The two attractive minor structures pictured directly below are accessories of a lodge-with-cabins development. One is a telephone booth, the other a transformer building that includes a telephone booth. The telephones supply communication between the outlying cabins and the lodge proper.

Transformer Building, Grand Canyon National Park

Telephone Booth, Grand Canyon National Park

LODGES, INNS, AND HOTELS

Plate III C-1

Greylock State Reservation, Massachusetts

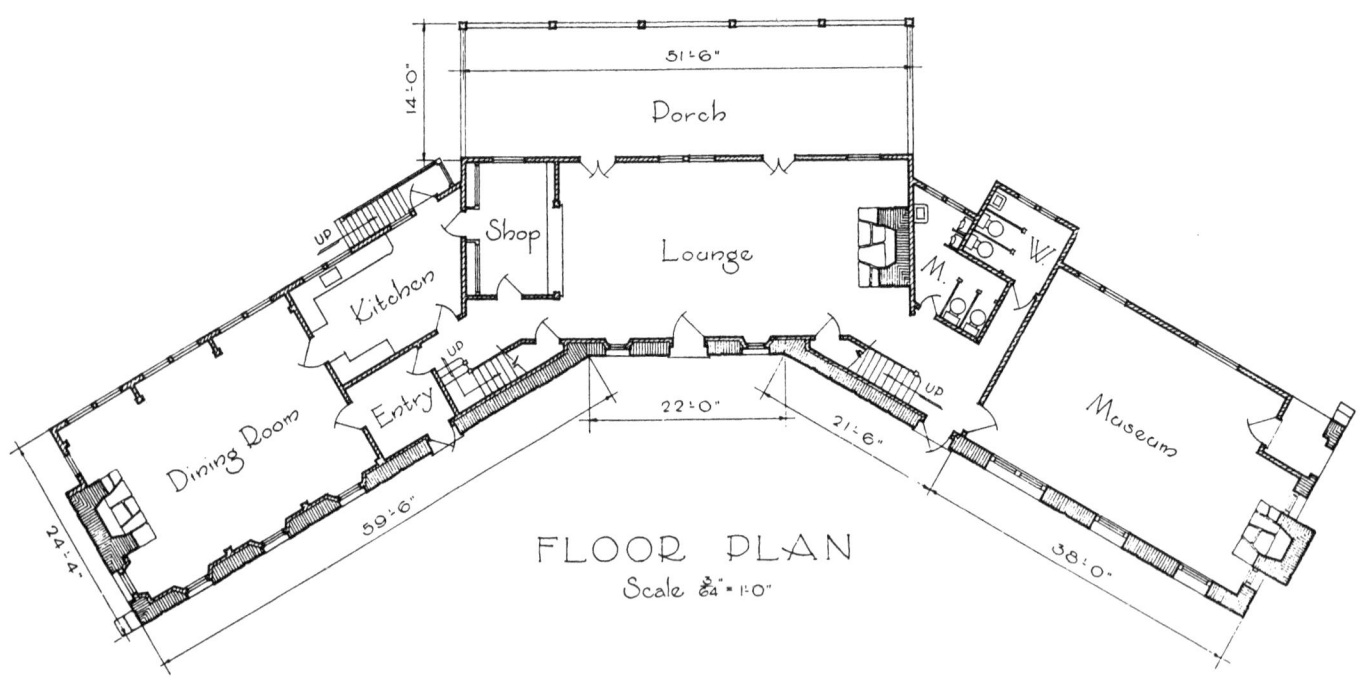

In this lodge structure on the summit of Mount Greylock, stone is utilized for the walls of the approach side and more economical frame construction for the hillside elevation, which cannot be viewed from close range. From the porch may be had views of the Berkshires to the west. A second floor of the central portion houses men's and women's dormitories, reached by separate stairways. The wing which temporarily serves as museum will later be converted into living quarters.

60

Plate III C–2   ⇒ LODGES, INNS, AND HOTELS

Trail Lodge, Blue Mountain County Reservation, New York

The avowed purpose of trail lodges is to supply inexpensive overnight accommodations in parks, particularly for young people on hiking or bicycling tours. The ideal development would be a chain of units located a day's walking distance apart on a scenic trail. Required elements are a common room or lounge, a cooking room in which the hikers prepare their own food, living quarters for a married couple in charge, dormitory, with toilet and shower rooms for girls, and dormitory, with toilet and shower rooms for boys. In the above example, the first such to be built on public areas in this country, there are overflow accommodations in the lofts above the boys' and girls' wings.

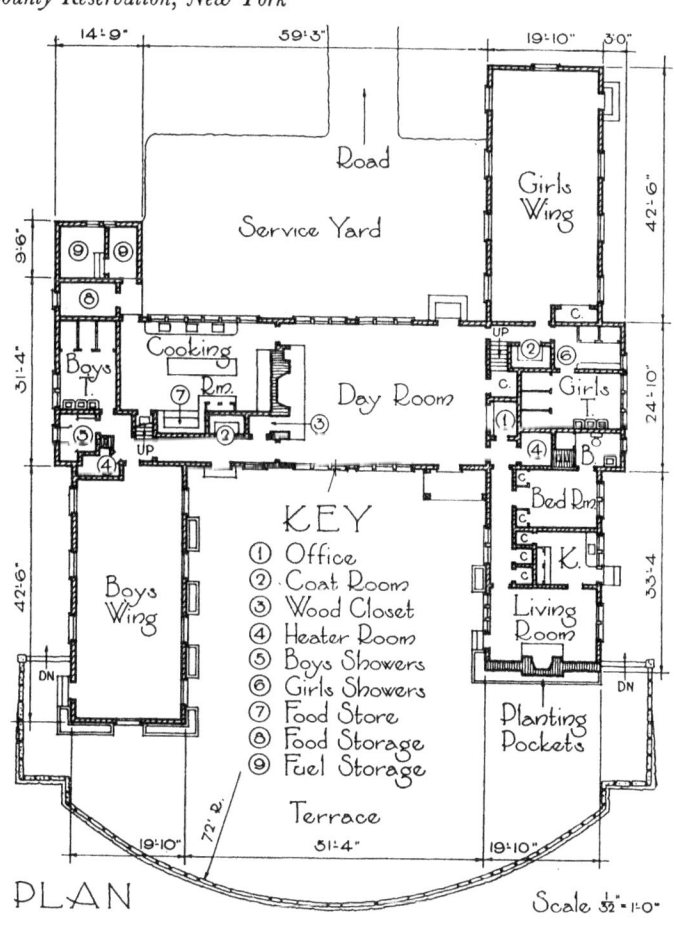

KEY
1. Office
2. Coat Room
3. Wood Closet
4. Heater Room
5. Boys Showers
6. Girls Showers
7. Food Store
8. Food Storage
9. Fuel Storage

PLAN   Scale 1/32"=1'-0"

LODGES, INNS, AND HOTELS

Plate III C–3

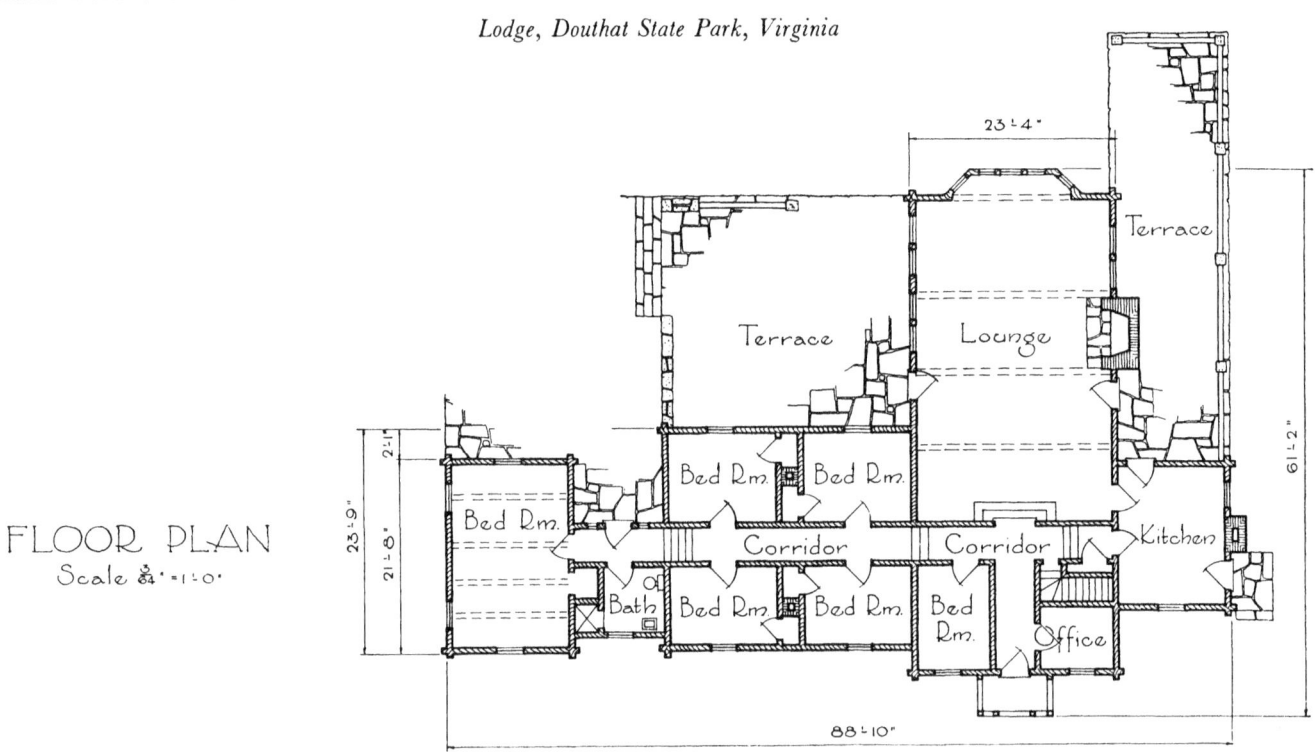

Lodge, Douthat State Park, Virginia

FLOOR PLAN
Scale ⅛" = 1'-0"

This small lodge set high in the mountains of Virginia enjoys commanding views. Above is pictured the approach and entrance side; on the facing page are two views of the opposite or terrace side. Built in the Virginia tradition of squared logs, it establishes, in concert with the custodian's dwelling and many of the cabins in this park, a well-unified structural theme. When patronage warrants, more bedrooms or nearby cabins would create a unit more profitable in operation.

Plate III C-4   →›› LODGES, INNS, AND HOTELS

Terrace Side, Lodge, Douthat State Park, Virginia

Detail, Lodge, Douthat State Park, Virginia

LODGES, INNS, AND HOTELS ««   Plate III C–5

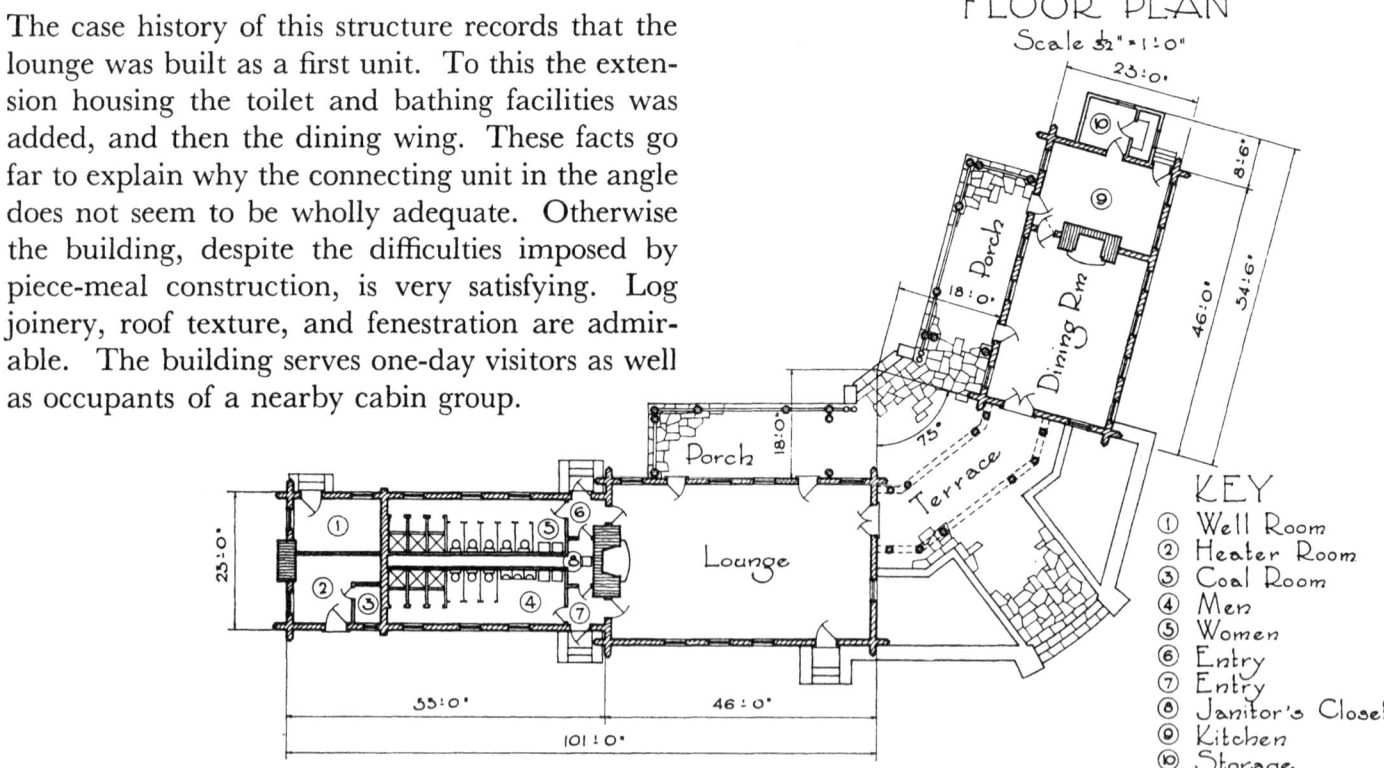

Lodge, White Pines Forest State Park, Illinois

The case history of this structure records that the lounge was built as a first unit. To this the extension housing the toilet and bathing facilities was added, and then the dining wing. These facts go far to explain why the connecting unit in the angle does not seem to be wholly adequate. Otherwise the building, despite the difficulties imposed by piece-meal construction, is very satisfying. Log joinery, roof texture, and fenestration are admirable. The building serves one-day visitors as well as occupants of a nearby cabin group.

KEY
1. Well Room
2. Heater Room
3. Coal Room
4. Men
5. Women
6. Entry
7. Entry
8. Janitor's Closet
9. Kitchen
10. Storage

Plate III C-6 → LODGES, INNS, AND HOTELS

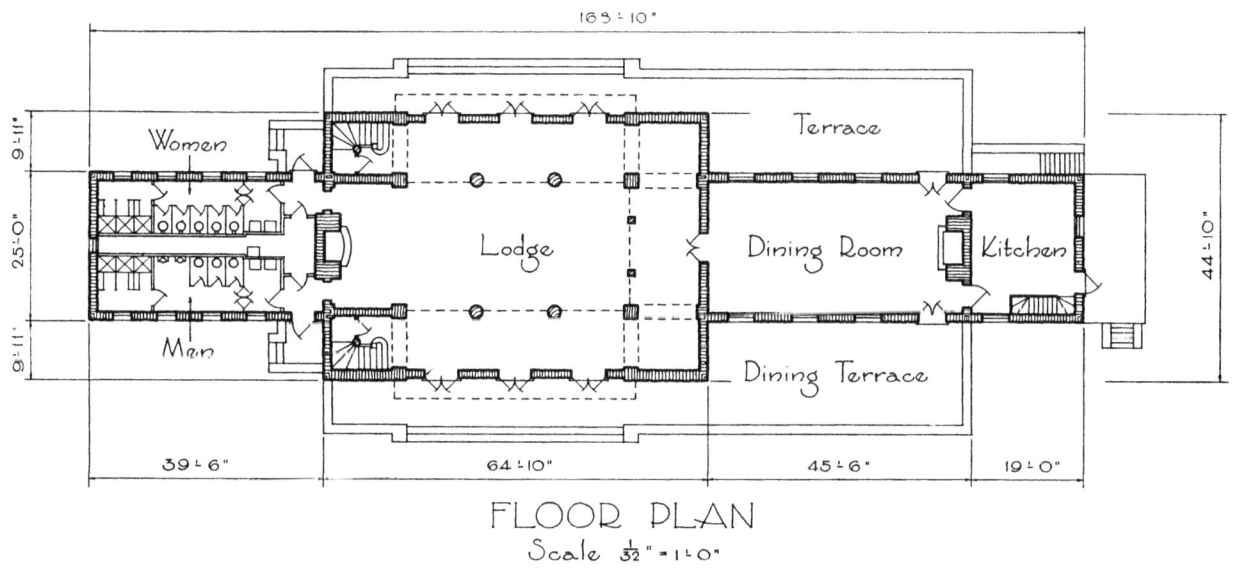

Lodge, Giant City State Park, Illinois

FLOOR PLAN
Scale 1/32" = 1'-0"

This stone building functions both as a refectory for daytime visitors and as a lodge for overnight guests. Sleeping accommodations are in one-room frame cabins situated nearby. The lounge in the central part is impressive. It extends the full height of the building and has balconies on the long sides. The true attractiveness of the building will not be fully realized until the barrenness of surroundings is relieved by the introduction of some tree growth of substantial size.

LODGES, INNS, AND HOTELS

Plate III C–7

Entrance Side, Mather Lodge, Petit Jean State Park, Arkansas

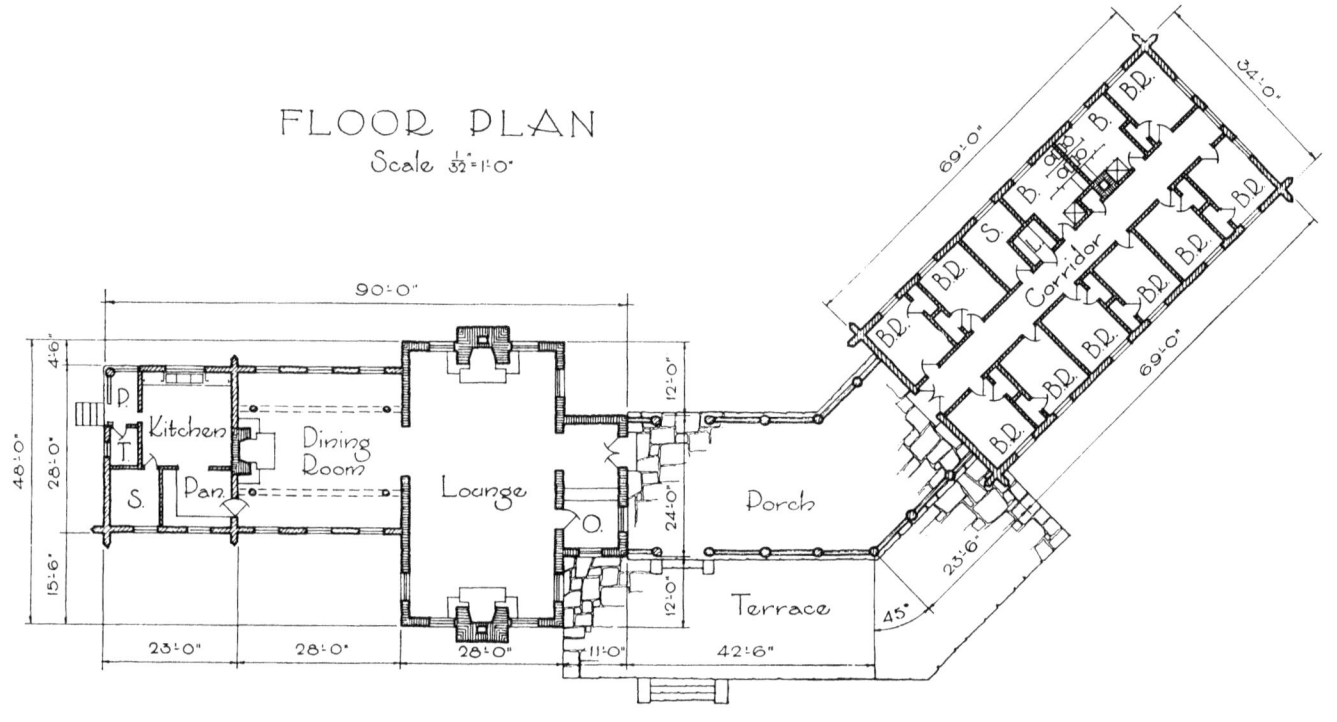

Plate III C–8　　　　　　　　　　　　　　　　　　　↠ LODGES, INNS, AND HOTELS

View Side, Mather Lodge, Petit Jean State Park, Arkansas

Porch, Mather Lodge, Petit Jean State Park, Arkansas

View from Porch, Mather Lodge, Petit Jean State Park, Arkansas

On the facing page are pictured the plan and a part of the entrance side of this most successful lodge, named to honor the first Director of the National Park Service. Above are shown a portion of the opposite side and two views within the porch. Unfortunately, terrain and cover make a complete exterior view unobtainable. For suitably vigorous scale and ingratiating "nativeness" this structure wins a very high rating indeed. Pictures of its interior furnishings are shown elsewhere.

67

LODGES, INNS, AND HOTELS

Plate III C-9

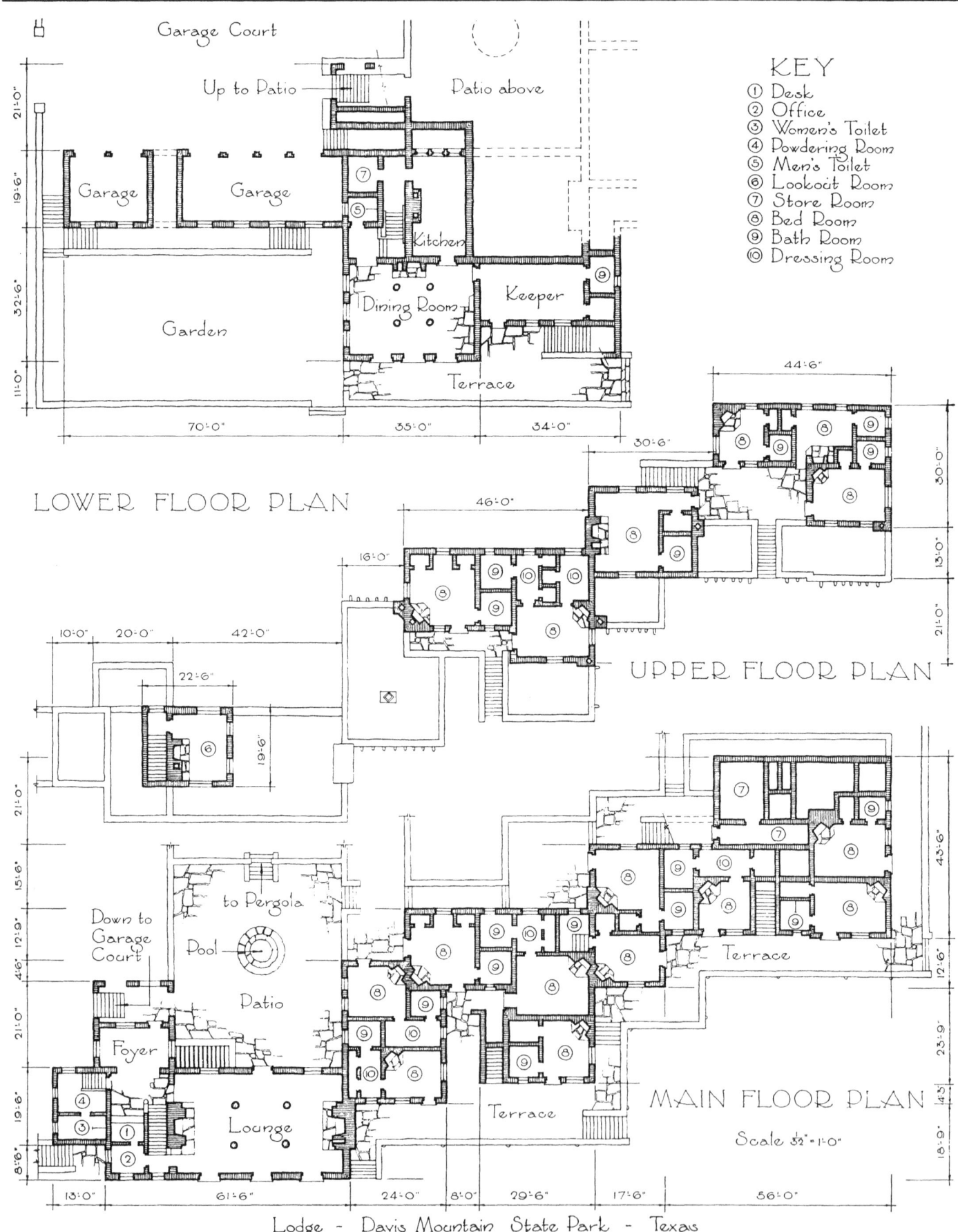

Lodge - Davis Mountain State Park - Texas

Plate III C-10 ⇝ LODGES, INNS, AND HOTELS

Lodge, Davis Mountain State Park, Texas

Detail, Lodge, Davis Mountain State Park, Texas

Detail, Lodge, Davis Mountain State Park, Texas

The plans of this lodge on the facing page, and the illustrations of it above are in rebuttal of any statement that current park architecture is unimaginative, immature, or unaspiring. There is not more imagination, sophistication, and aspiration in Hollywood than is here exhibited. It has size and picturesqueness surpassing its inspirational source—the Indian pueblo—and rivaling the palace of the Grand Lama, as well as many interesting details to hold the attention of the observing.

LODGES, INNS, AND HOTELS   Plate III C-11

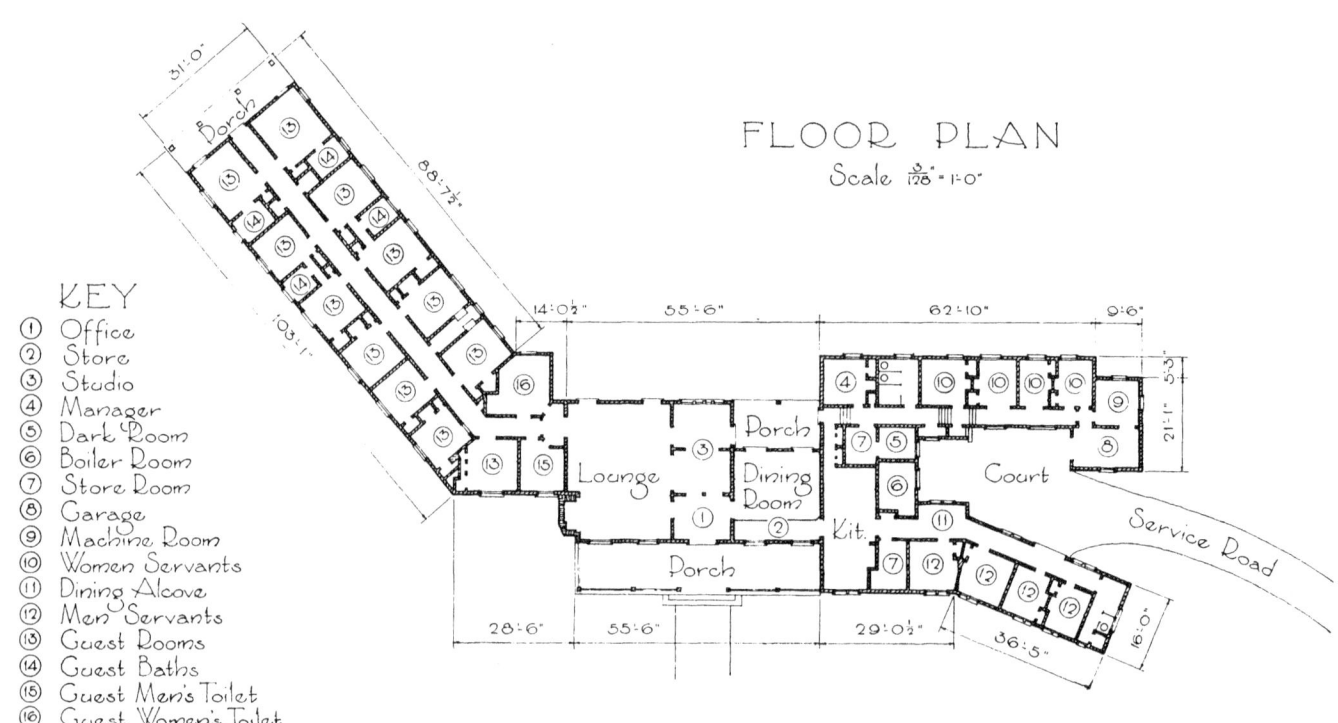

Big Trees Lodge, Mariposa Grove, Yosemite National Park

FLOOR PLAN
Scale 3/128" = 1'-0"

KEY
1. Office
2. Store
3. Studio
4. Manager
5. Dark Room
6. Boiler Room
7. Store Room
8. Garage
9. Machine Room
10. Women Servants
11. Dining Alcove
12. Men Servants
13. Guest Rooms
14. Guest Baths
15. Guest Men's Toilet
16. Guest Women's Toilet

70

Plate III C–12   ⇶ LODGES, INNS, AND HOTELS

Entrance Porch, Big Trees Lodge, Yosemite National Park

Interior, Big Trees Lodge, Yosemite National Park

Interior, Big Trees Lodge, Yosemite National Park

Opposite are pictured the plan and a general view of this small hotel in the awe-inspiring Mariposa Grove of Big Trees. The large cut above shows the entrance porch in closer detail. The surrounding trees prevent the taking of a photograph showing the full expanse of this attractive building. The partial views obtainable evidence a nice simplicity of structure, deferential to the magnificence of the setting. A like simplicity is discovered in the interiors, which have an uncluttered modernity. Eldridge T. Spencer was the architect of this development.

LODGES, INNS, AND HOTELS

Plate III C–13

Aerial View, Bright Angel Lodge, Grand Canyon National Park

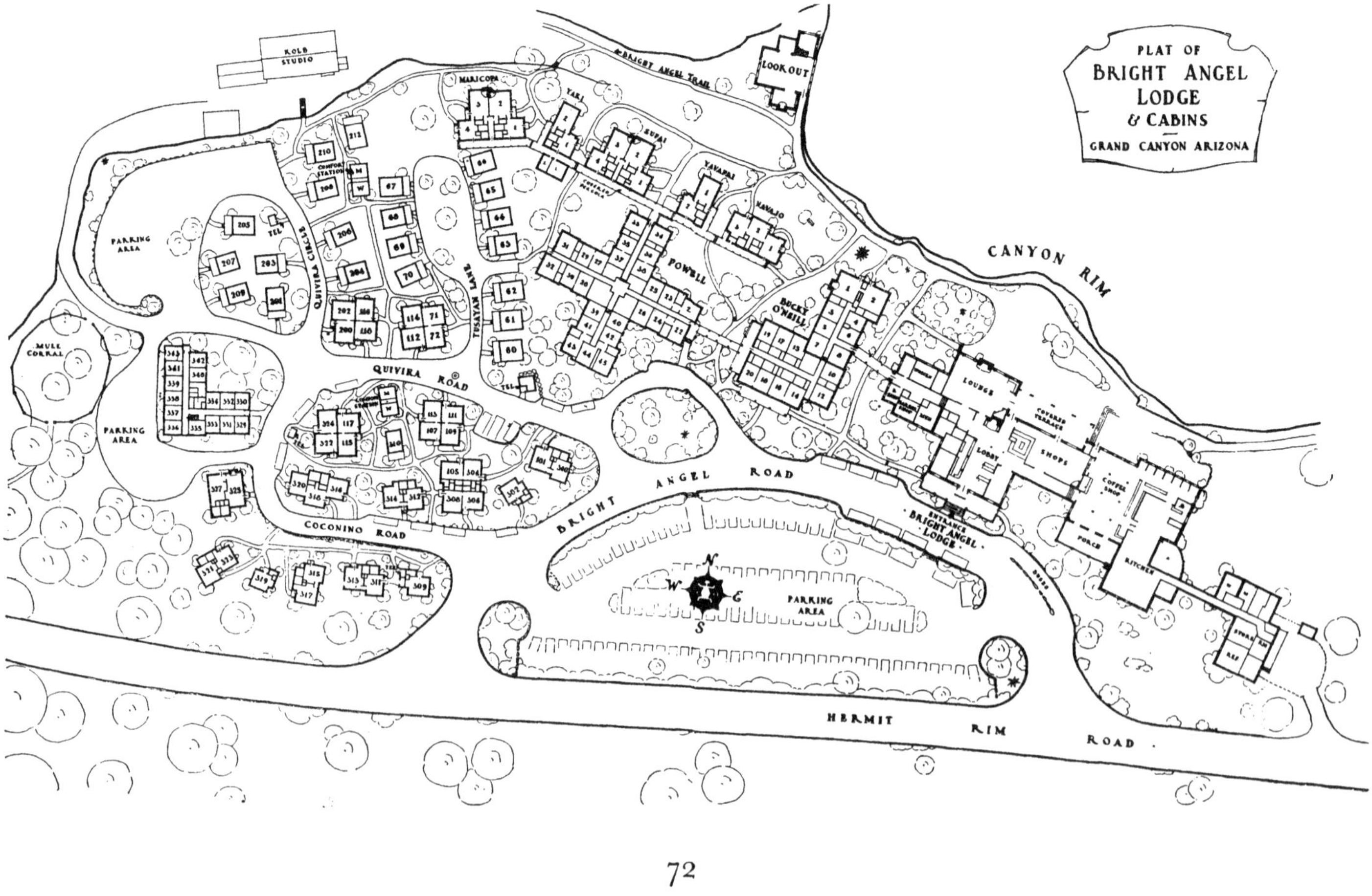

PLAT OF
BRIGHT ANGEL
LODGE
& CABINS
GRAND CANYON ARIZONA

72

Plate III C-14   ⇶ LODGES, INNS, AND HOTELS

Bright Angel Lodge, Grand Canyon National Park

Entrance to Lobby, Bright Angel Lodge

Terrace on Canyon Rim, Bright Angel Lodge

On the facing page are an aerial view and the plan of this imaginative lodge and cabin development on the south rim of the Grand Canyon. Above are pictured the entrance and rim sides of the lodge proper showing portions of the connecting guest houses. On the next following page the structural variety of the guest houses and the roofed pergolas and porches which connect them with the lodge itself will be seen. Inspired architecturally by surviving structures of stagecoach days, and motivated by a conviction that a group of low rambling structures is the only intrusion to be countenanced in a setting of such magnificence, the results are enormously successful.

LODGES, INNS, AND HOTELS

Plate III C–15

Bucky O'Neill Guest House, Bright Angel Lodge

Connecting Pergola, Bright Angel Lodge

Bucky O'Neill Guest House, Bright Angel Lodge

Pergola and Guest House, Bright Angel Lodge

Powell Guest House, Bright Angel Lodge

Lookout through Pergola, Bright Angel Lodge

COMMUNITY BUILDINGS

To TRY TO DESCRIBE what we term community buildings in parks by statements of what they are not is a temptation not to be withstood. It is the easiest way, and by and large perhaps as clarifying as a more affirmative effort, inasmuch as the purposes of the community building seem to be more obscure than those of most other structures having place in parks.

To begin with, this building differs structurally from the open shelter (an essential item of rather similar function) in that it is entirely enclosed. It differs functionally from the concession or refectory building (often a similar item structurally) in that it is seldom identified with the selling or serving of food. Perhaps it need not be so negatively described; it can be more positively defined, after all, as a marriage of something of the function of the shelter and something of the physical aspect of the refectory building.

The community building is almost always located in an intensive use area. It is normally a supplementing facility of an overnight group such as a public campground or a cabin colony. Probably its primary use is as a clubroom or recreation room where tent and trailer campers or cabin occupants can become acquainted and participate in games, music, dancing, and other social diversions. Particularly is this need for it acute when overnight cabins have been pared down in size to a point where they offer only sleeping space and no room at all for indoor activities in bad weather.

However, its use can be more than social and recreational; it can have educational and cultural purpose. Where a park museum is lacking, it often develops that the community building acquires as a side line the offhand display of minor collections of biologic and geologic material and relics or curios of local interest. Sometimes the community building will serve as an indoor "in-case-of-rain" substitute for the campfire circle or amphitheater. The activities of community buildings of considerable size may even embrace platform entertainment.

These varied combinations of purposes encountered in community buildings should result, if structure follows function, in a related variety of structural expressions. Such does not obtain, however, perhaps largely because the combination of functions ultimately housed can so seldom be forecast. And so the community building inclines to be something of a catch-all, functioning for some buildings not yet supplied and for existing others that have proved to be inadequate or overtaxed in use.

If it is to serve advantageously in the many emergenices that can overtake it, the community building must have many windows to supply ample ventilation when it is crowded in warm weather and to light effectively, without need for artificial illumination in daytime, if possible, any collections casually displayed. It should have a fairly high ceiling, since it may have to accommodate large gatherings comfortably in weather when the windows cannot be widely opened. It is no psychologically satisfying substitute for the campfire circle if it is not furnished with at least one large fireplace. Toilet facilities, if not conveniently near in other structures, should be provided in the community building.

If platform entertainment can be foreseen among its ultimate activities, the community building will probably be equipped with something that is more than speaker's platform, yet less than stage. Sometimes this feature is movable. Promoted entertainment will embrace lectures and talks, especially if there is in the vicinity a campfire circle for which the community building will be called on to substitute in bad weather. Since slides and motion pictures are frequently the accompaniment of these outdoor talks and lectures, the community building wisely planned will have, or allow for the future installation of, a screen and a projection booth. In no event should construction of the booth in any detail fall short of fireproofing practices generally recommended for the housing of this equipment item because, along with the usual hazards of film projection and a crowded auditorium, there is likely to be the hazard of a building largely of wood construction.

While platform entertainment in the community building will probably seldom if ever embrace dramatics, it is conceivable that something on the scale of an amateur vaudeville show or a "stunt night", arranged with camper talent, will often threaten. Wherefore the size of the platform might well anticipate the space needs of a song-and-dance act, a quartette, and a dramatic reader with a capacity for sweeping gestures.

It is not intended in the foregoing to impute to the average community building the characteristics of an auditorium. It should stop with being an all-purpose assembly room, nicely scaled to the number of persons likely to make normal use of it in its several uses. Because it may sometimes be overcrowded, there should be no shortage of exit doors, strategically located. If dancing is anticipated as one of its recreational probabilities, a wood floor of good grade is needed.

In common with other park buildings where visitors congregate, community buildings become more useful, and in the summer season actually accommodate more people, if they are provided with wide, roomy porches. Certainly a sheltering entrance porch is almost a necessity.

Since it is an enclosed structure, extra-seasonal use can be made of the community building by appropriating it for week end and other short-term winter camping. Site conditions and climate will sometimes conspire to make it logical to use the building as a shelter house for winter sports participants and onlookers. If this seems probable when the building is being planned, there is justification for providing some means of heating it in winter temperatures, as well as for including a ramp approach, toilet and shower facilities, waxing room, and other refinements which can extend its usefulness.

The well-groomed little structure of the tailpiece illustration is not officially designated a community building and may not even be so utilized. But its plan elements follow so closely those which constitute a serviceable community building in a small park that it is chosen to classify it here as such. It houses a small public room, a tiny office, and toilet rooms for men and women. At one end of the public room are a counter and enclosure that could function as a checkroom, especially if winter sports were an activity, and even as a minor food concession. Besides, it is representative of an appropriate sophisticated park architecture too rarely encountered, compared with which fact, mere accuracy in classification seems unimportant.

Poundridge County Reservation, New York

Plate III D-1   ⇛ COMMUNITY BUILDINGS

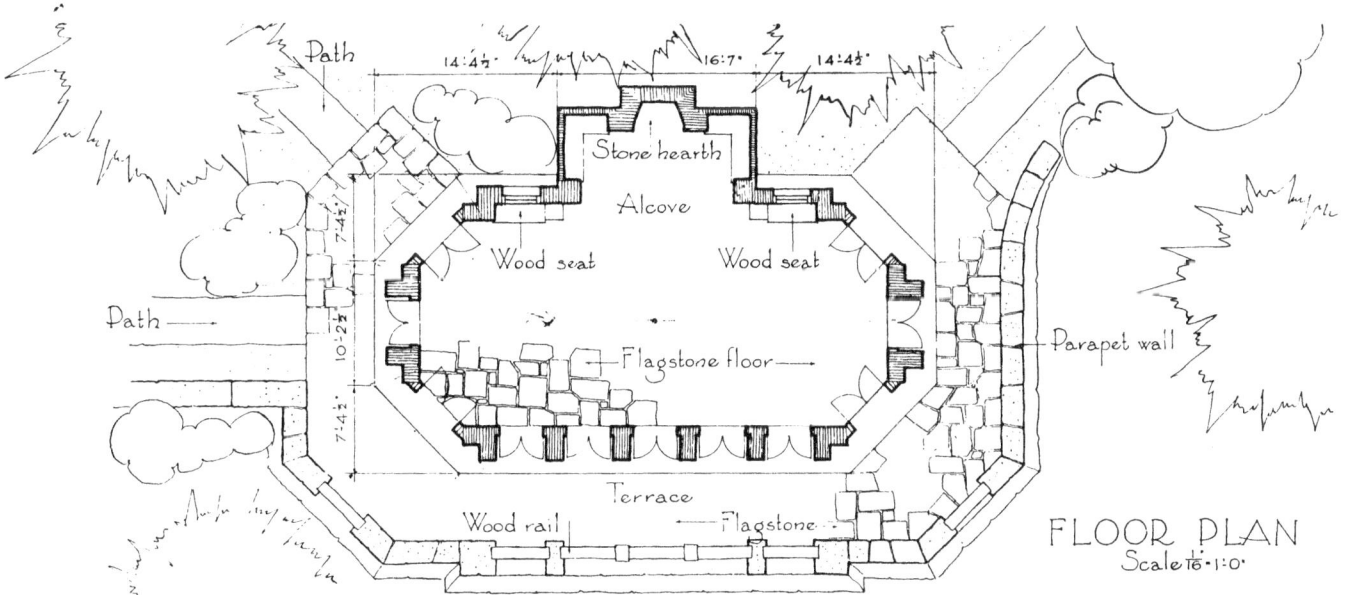

Community Building, Buttermilk Falls State Park, New York

This hillside structure happily escapes the stereotyped, both in plan and exterior treatment. Abundance of doors and windows gives views in all directions. Perhaps the building is not actually used as a community building as the term is applied herein, but being enclosed, it is more than a shelter and closely resembles the community buildings useful in cabin colonies.

COMMUNITY BUILDINGS   *Plate* III D–2

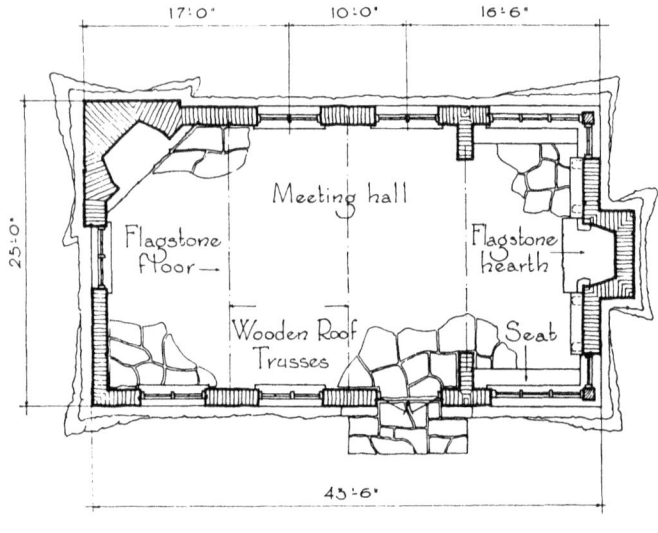

Green Mountain Community Building, Boulder Mountain Park, Colorado

In close harmony with the rock-strewn site, this building seems without false note unless it is the formlessness of the rocks employed to top off the chimney. Even this can claim a measure of exemption from criticism on the plea of relationship to the indigenous rocks. There are many uses for a building of this general type in a park, as a rallying point for Boy Scouts and other organizations visiting or camping in the park as groups, or as a warming shelter where winter sports are indulged in in a small way. The many windows provide good ventilation in summer, yet when these are closed and both fireplaces are lighted, comfort in cold weather is offered.

Plate III D–3   ⋙ COMMUNITY BUILDINGS

Community Building, Scenic State Park, Minnesota

In the fine character of the log construction of this example Minnesota justifies her advantage of superior native timber resources. We are almost blinded to the lesser merit of the chimney masonry, which, for all its sturdy proportions, approaches the "peanut brittle" technique. An imagined ideal park structure might call for a masonry chimney from one of several localities, but it would assuredly specify "logs and log construction by Minnesota." This building accommodates day visitors as well as the residents of a nearby group of cabins.

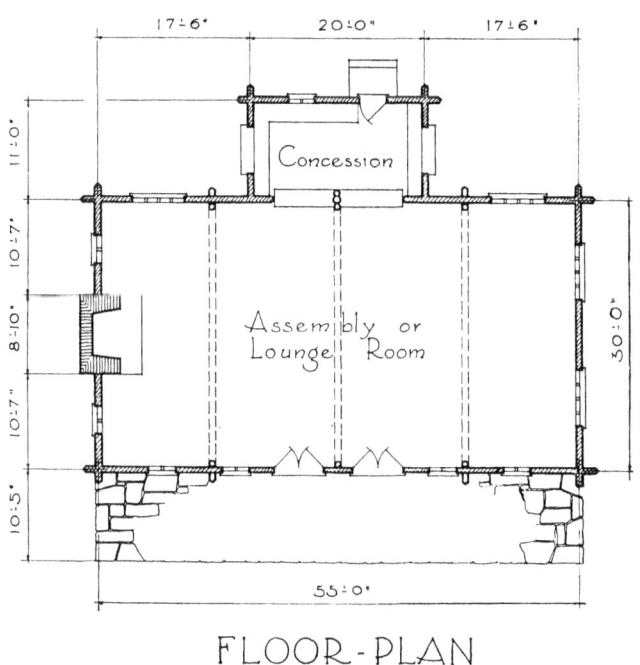

FLOOR-PLAN
Scale 3/64"=1'-0"

COMMUNITY BUILDINGS ««   *Plate* III D-4

Community Building, Longmire, Mount Rainier National Park

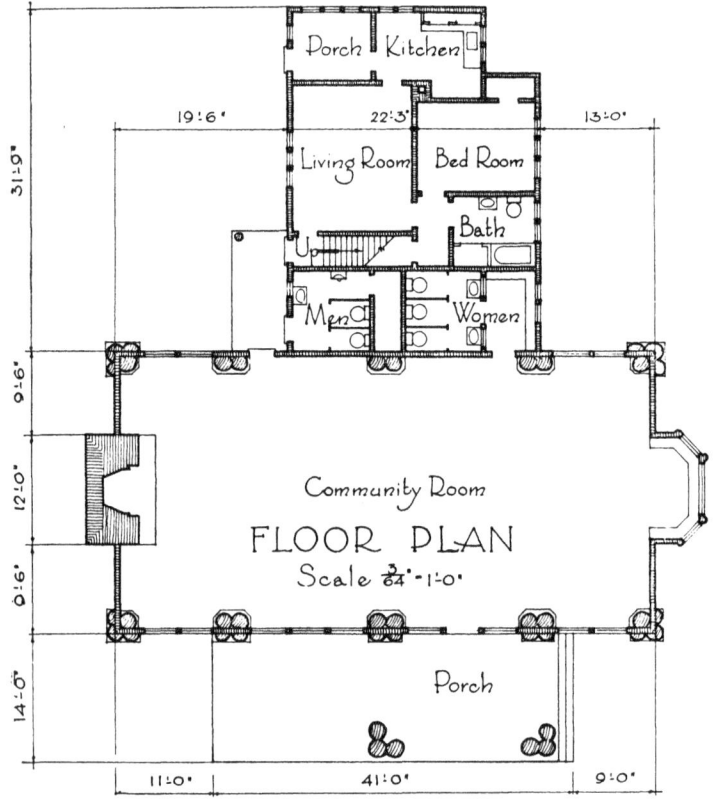

A park structure of importance that, after pointing the way for many later buildings, has been surpassed in achievement of the subtleties of design and execution that make for true park structural character. Comparison of the almost mechanical stiffness of the rafter ends with the handcrafted quality of the "whittled" rafter ends of other subjects more recently built will indicate one such advance in structural technique. The thinness of the roof shingles and the character of the masonry of the chimneys leave something to be desired.

Plate III D–5 　　　　　　　　　　　　　　　　　　　　　　　⇒⇒⇒ COMMUNITY BUILDINGS

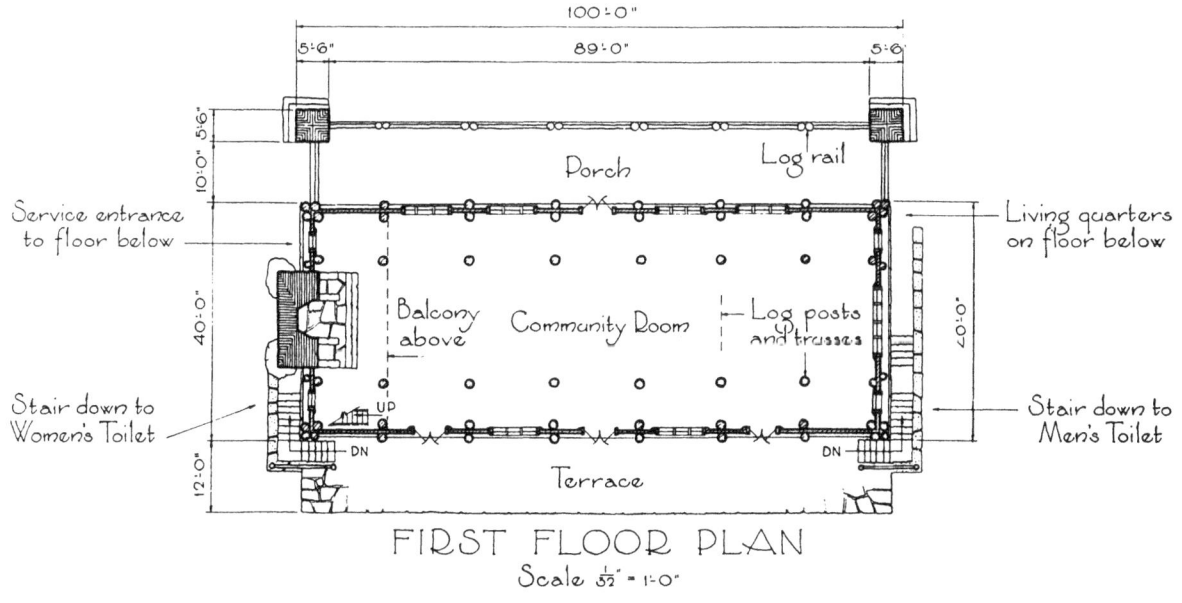

Community Building, Paradise, Mount Rainier National Park

FIRST FLOOR PLAN
Scale 1/32" = 1'-0"

The steepness of the roof of this building, located high up the slope of Mount Rainier, is completely justified by the heavy snowfalls. Features of the plan are the front terrace from which the snow-capped mountain summit can be viewed and the porch with deck roof at the rear from which the lowlands far below can be seen. A balcony is built across the fireplace end of the main room, and public toilets and living quarters are provided in the lower story.

81

COMMUNITY BUILDINGS ⋘   *Plate* III D-6

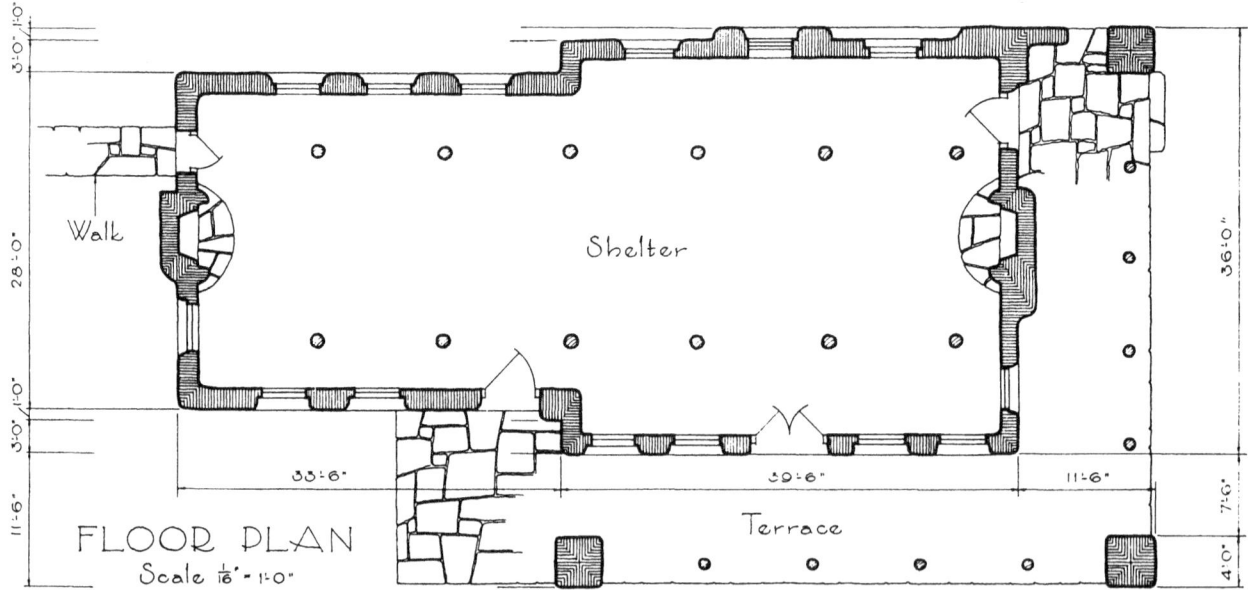

Community Building, Monument Lake Metropolitan Park, Trinidad, Colorado

Lacking any of the dependencies sometimes found in the typical community building of wide purpose, perhaps enclosed shelter is a more exact designation of this stucco-covered adobe structure in the tradition of the Southwest. The floor plan suggests that the building can be readily remodeled in the future to qualify as a refectory building, or, if a cabin colony were developed around it, as a lodge.

WASHHOUSES AND LAUNDRIES

>>> ONLY RARELY are all cabins in a park area individually equipped with toilet, shower, and laundry facilities. More frequently cabins are less pretentious, and groups of such, as well as all public campgrounds, must be furnished with community toilets, showers, and laundries. Wherever, for one or another reason, pit privies rather than flush toilets must serve, shower and laundry facilities should be housed in a separate building. Where flush toilets can be provided, all the needed facilities may be accumulated in one structure scarcely different from the park comfort station save for the addition of shower and laundry rooms.

Because the park comfort station has been already discussed and illustrated, concern here is primarily with shower and laundry facilities for overnight visitors. Although toilet facilities are a part of some of the subjects illustrated, these are considered only incidental to the subject in hand.

Unlike the hot shower and laundry building in organized camps for one sex only, this building in the public campground or cabin colony must have separate shower rooms for men and women. It is not necessary to build the men's showers with individual enclosures and private dressing booths, but it is best, in the women's section, to provide enclosures and dressing rooms with curtained fronts for some of the showers. Although the trend in providing showers for age groups of younger women is probably toward gang showers, such an arrangement for women of all ages, including children, too, does not meet with general approval.

A ratio of one shower to every 12 or 15 persons is reasonable; the same ratio applies to lavatories in the dressing rooms. Windows, giving abundant ventilation and daylight, and electric lighting after dark, wherever electricity is available, are recommended in the shower and dressing rooms, and in the laundry. A careful spotting of the electric outlets, so that all laundry operations are properly lighted, is especially important. In the splash and humidity normal to all the rooms under discussion, smooth and impervious surfaces that are easily kept clean are very desirable. Curbs about six inches high should be built at openings between private dressing rooms and shower stalls and between general dressing rooms and shower rooms. Wood, with its tendency to absorb and retain moisture, swell, and eventually rot out, is to be avoided.

In the laundry, removable mats of wood slats, to keep the campers' feet off the wet floors, will add to comfort. Hot water requirements will mean a large tank and heater, which can be advantageously placed in the laundry room if there are flatirons to be heated. Otherwise, a separate room for heater, tank, and fuel is better, for it will keep much dirt out of the laundry itself.

The average campground laundry will not have all the mechanical equipment the day and age can offer, because of the costs involved and because most campers' laundering is of limited amount. Plentiful hot water, enough two-part laundry trays, ironing boards, and outlets for electric irons or, if electricity is lacking, a stove for heating the old-fashioned kind, will meet the needs of most vacationists. Washing machines, mangles, and driers are not overlooked or here cried down, but these belong to an economy of efficiency rather than the economy of simplicity which largely governs outdoor vacationing.

The vacation season is usually favorable to the drying of clothes out-of-doors. A clearing with clotheslines in orderly alignment should be adjacent to the laundry building. It is fortunate if views of this drying yard can be screened by woods growth. Otherwise, an enclosing fence of vine-covered lattice can be erected to screen sights that might quickly disrupt a housewife's vacation mood.

WASHHOUSES AND LAUNDRIES

Plate III E-1

Washhouse and Laundry
Spring Mill State Park — — — Indiana

Here is a multi-purposed dependency of a cabin group. Toilet, bathing and laundry facilities are grouped in compact arrangement, nicely adapted to a hillside site. The separation of the approaches to Men's and Women's sections is a commendable feature. The successful retention of the "feeling" of Indiana pioneer architecture in the difficulties of topography and to stand comparison with authentic nearby structures in this style is notable.

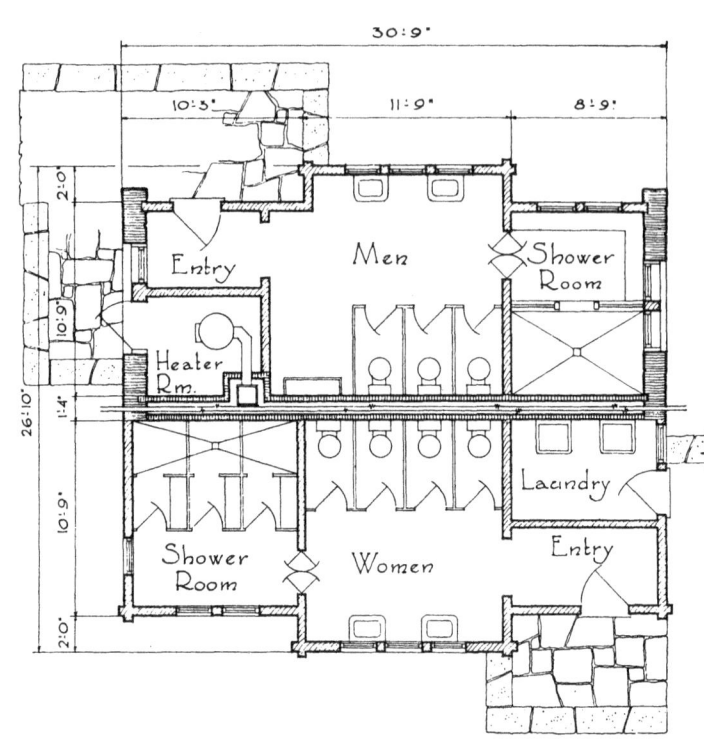

FLOOR PLAN

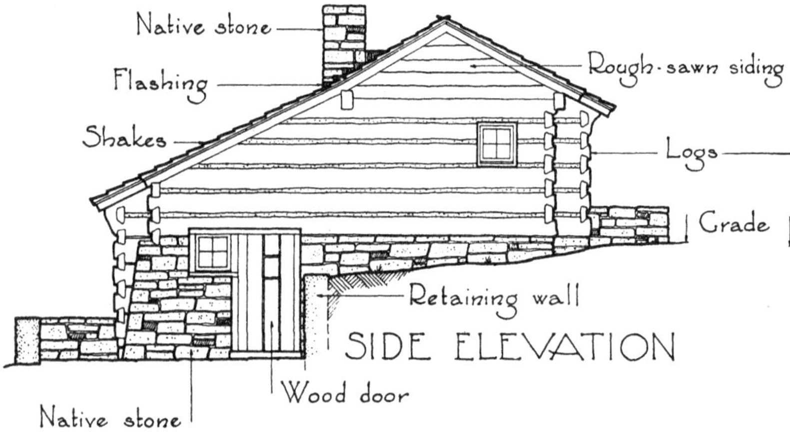

SIDE ELEVATION

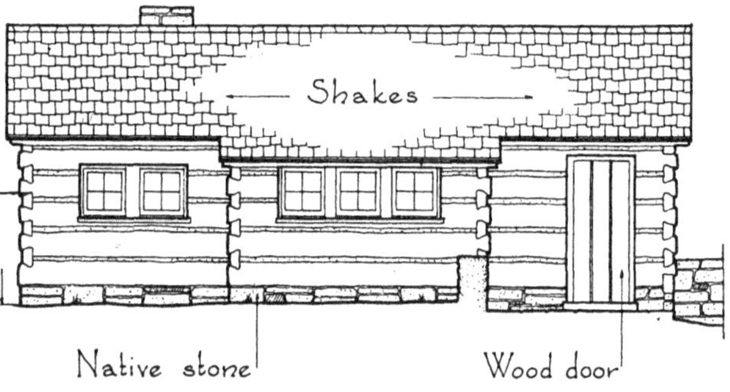

FRONT ELEVATION

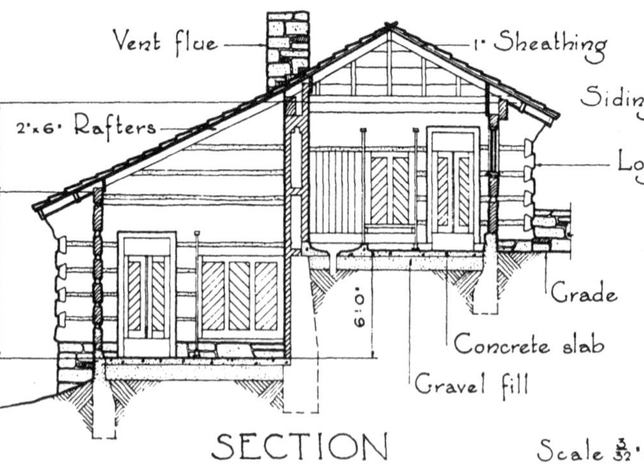

SECTION   Scale 3/32" = 1'-0"

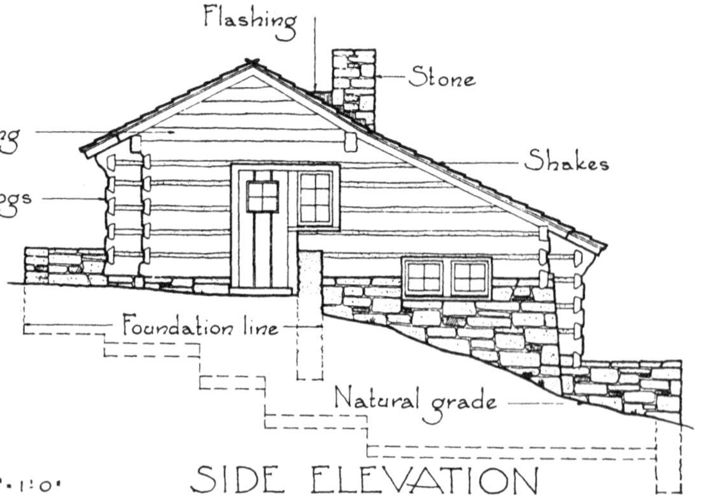

SIDE ELEVATION

84

Plate III E–2 ⋙ WASHHOUSES AND LAUNDRIES

Washhouse, Bastrop State Park, Texas

Architecturally well-related to the stone cabin group it serves, this building houses toilet and shower facilities but contains no laundry. The low-pitched, rough-textured roof, the heavy verge boards, and the character of the masonry please the critical eye. The window guards of stone, not too meticulously laid, give privacy, yet because of the great number of windows, light and ventilation are still provided in proper degree. The entrances to men's and women's sections, screened by the informal rock walls, are suitably distant from one another.

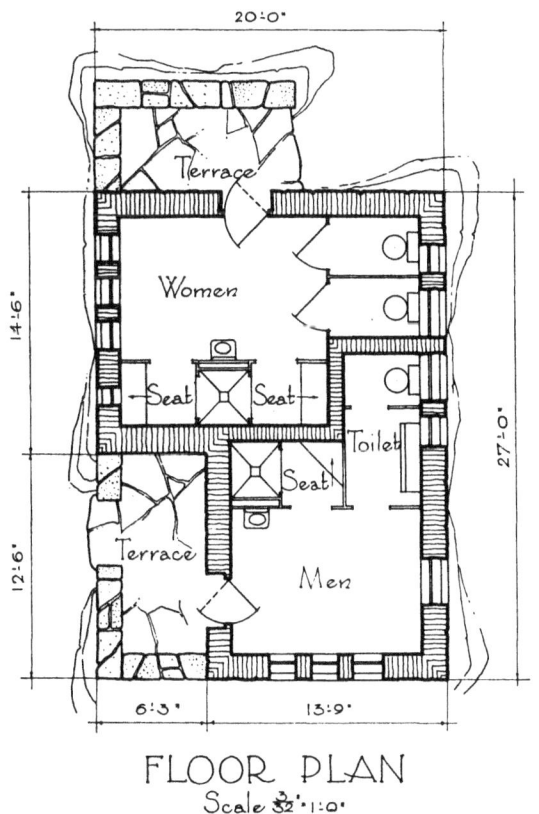

FLOOR PLAN
Scale 32'·1:0'

85

WASHHOUSES AND LAUNDRIES

Plate III E-3

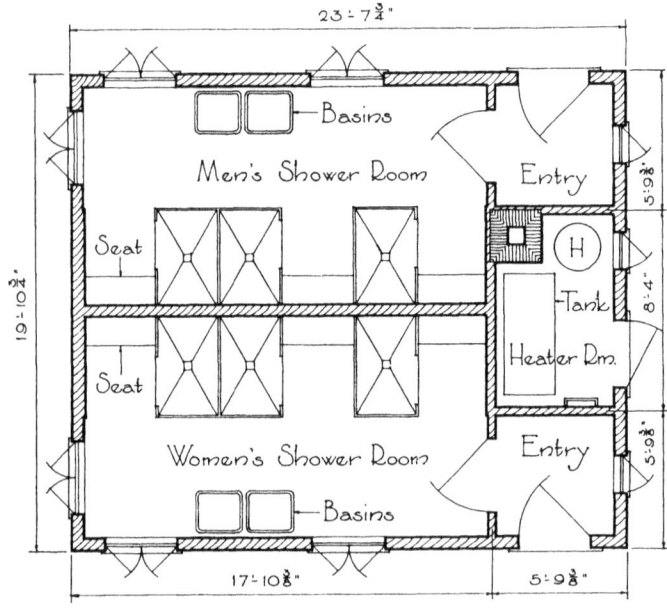

Washhouse, Lake Taghkanic State Park, New York

As built, strictly a washhouse in a cabin colony, this building could add to its function if a laundry room were added at the left end. The plan would lend itself readily to such an addition. The walls of waney-edge siding repeat the material used in the cabins of the group. The large windows of obscure glass suggest that the interiors are well-lighted. Ventilation is provided by ceiling grilles and an exhaust duct.

FLOOR PLAN
Scale ⅛" = 1'-0"

Plate III E–4   ⇛ WASHHOUSES AND LAUNDRIES

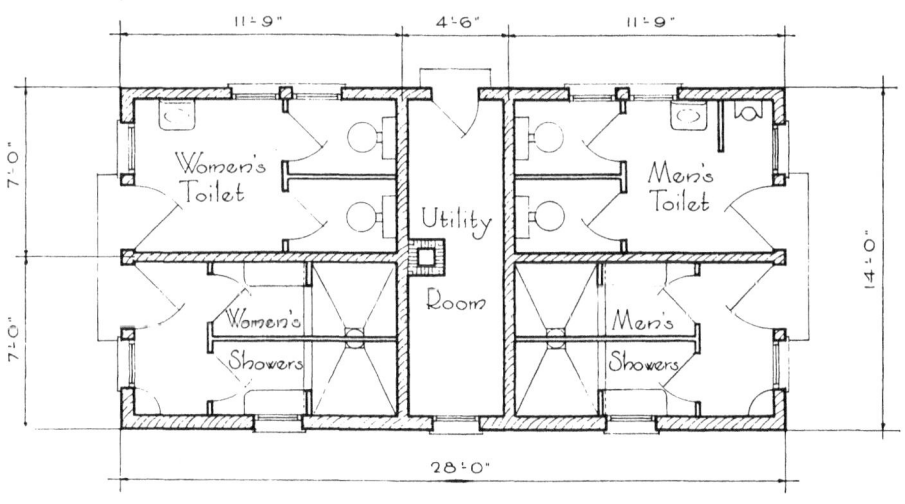

Washhouse, Sequoia National Park

FLOOR PLAN

Scale ⅛" = 1'-0"

This dependency of an overnight area is without pretentions, being content with expressing in plain terms its utilitarian purpose. The separation of the shower bath moisture from the dirt that is tracked into the more often used comfort station makes for more sanitary conditions.

WASHHOUSES AND LAUNDRIES

Plate III E-5

Washhouse, Bandelier National Monument

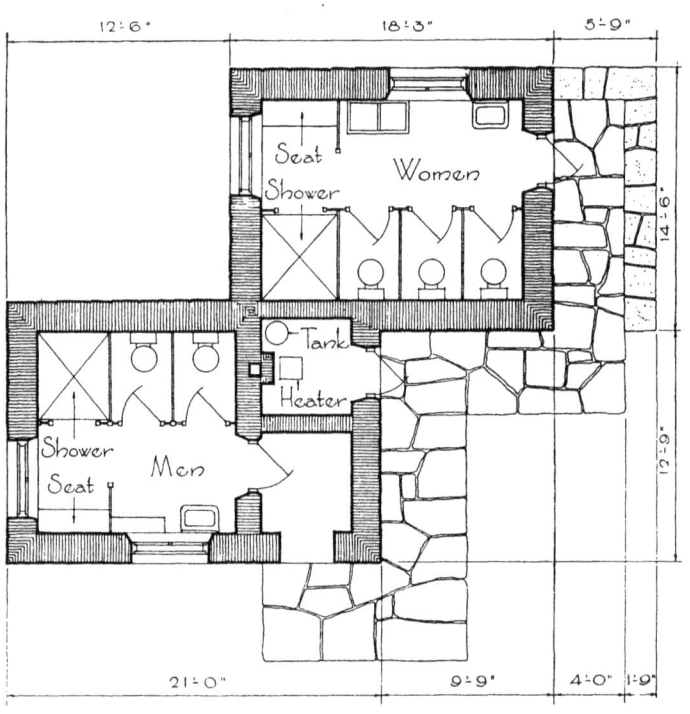

FLOOR PLAN
Scale 3/32" = 1'-0"

This skillful adaptation of the adobe construction of the Southwest to the shower, toilet, and laundry needs of a small campground has architectural excellence in complementary surroundings. Note that laundry trays are an item of equipment in the women's section.

Plate III E–6   ⋙ WASHHOUSES AND LAUNDRIES

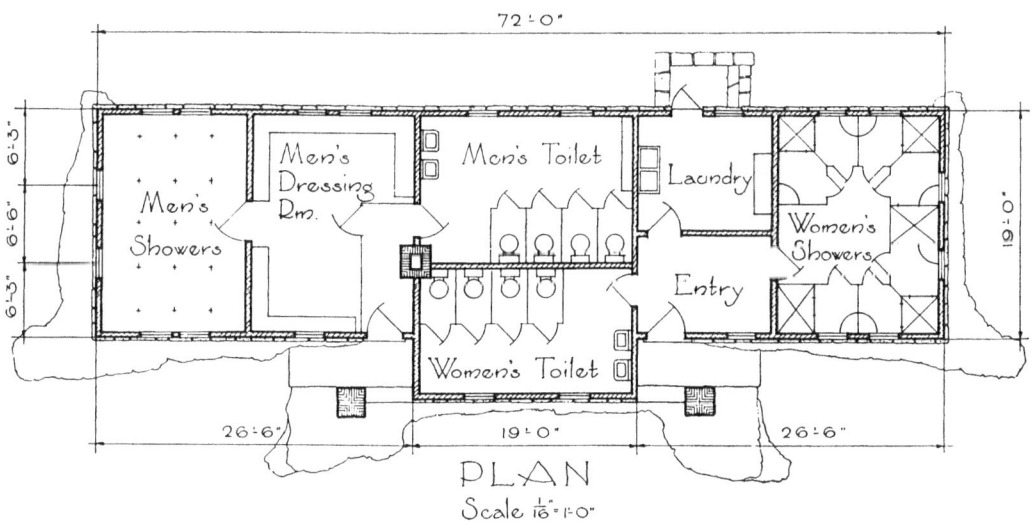

Washhouse and Laundry, Devil's Den State Park, Arkansas

This building is of such extent that it provides showers and dressing rooms for swimmers as well as for occupants of a cabin colony. The usual arrangement of open showers for men and enclosed individual dressing rooms and showers for women has here been adopted. A construction of stone walls to the height of the window sills accommodates the building to the sharp grade. Because of the extreme batter of the walls the building has the look of being well-anchored on the slope.

WASHHOUSES AND LAUNDRIES

Plate III E–7

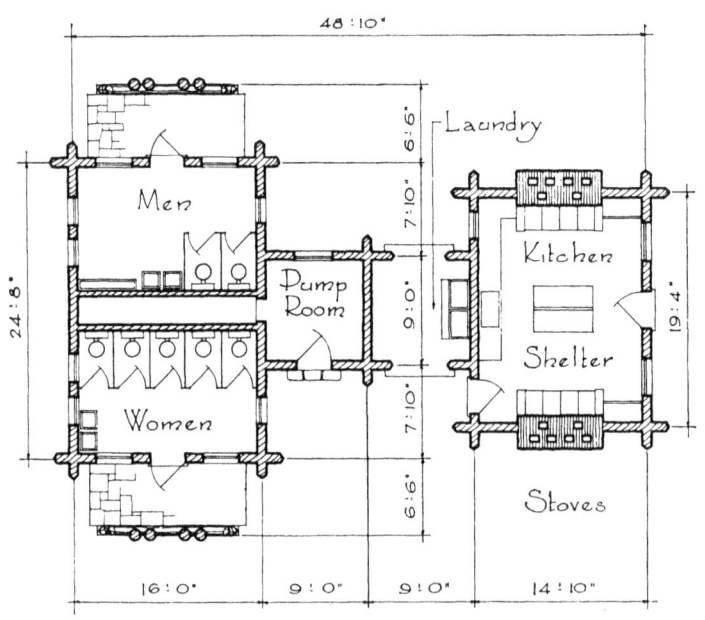

Washhouse and Laundry, Scenic State Park, Minnesota

FLOOR PLAN
Scale 1/8" = 1:0'

While close inspection of this plan will not reveal shower baths along with the pumphouse and toilet, laundry, and kitchen facilities housed, the building is actually a dependency of a cabin group. It could, and perhaps will in the future, as the cabin colony expands, incorporate shower baths, and thus serve to prolong the season of cabin occupancy beyond those months when lake bathing is possible. In plan and in externals the building is excellent.

CAMPSTOVES

>>> TENANTS of campsites, and of those cabins so compact that kitchens or even kitchenettes have been omitted from them, necessarily must be furnished with a means for cooking meals outdoors. The facility is a campstove, and while it has much in common with the picnic fireplace found in parks, there are points of dissimilarity which really differentiate the two.

The chief difference is the height of the cooking surface above the ground. It has long been urged that picnic fireplaces, especially where they are massed in great numbers, be kept low in height so that they are no more obtrusive in the park scene than they need be. The admonition seems fair enough, since a picnic fireplace is used by a picnic group for only one or two meals on a brief outing and any inconvenience caused by the necessity of stooping during cooking operations is offset by the aesthetic benefits to accrue from thus subordinating utilitarian facilities to the natural features of the picnic ground.

Campstoves, on the other hand, are used for a stretch of days or even weeks by camping parties or cabin occupants, and with them cooking becomes a more laborious business than merely warming up picnic fare that has been prepared largely at home. Campstoves are likely to be regarded by their users rather as kitchen stoves set outdoors, and any gestures made toward park environment that result in decreasing their efficiency and convenience will be condemned, and the shortcomings be retailed to all and sundry who will listen. Moreover, campstoves will be on, or hard by, sites that have been rented out for a term of days or weeks, and, in the broad sense, thereby withdrawn from public use. Campers, with some logic, will incline to wonder why any facility they have engaged to themselves by rental should acknowledge any other factor than all possible efficiency and convenience in use. If this attitude is to be met with a conciliatory gesture, the height of cooking surface of campstoves will approximate that of kitchen ranges.

The typical campstove is built of stone and, by reason of its size, cannot be the mortarless piling of rocks that produces the well-naturalized picnic fireplace. All the principles of sound masonry must be acknowledged in constructing it. The surfaces should be true and plumb, the joints solidly filled with mortar, and any top surface on which cooking utensils might be set should be level and reasonably smooth.

The chimney so abhorrent in connection with picnic fireplaces will not be held beyond the pale in devising a campstove 100 percent acceptable to the camper. The cooking surface of campstoves is better a solid iron plate or casting than an open grate of bars or any perforated sheet. The effectiveness of the chimney in drawing off smoke is problematical if the top of the stove is not solid. An arrangement sometimes adopted is a bar grill directly beneath a solid top, the latter hinged so that it can be raised and rested against the chimney, and so that the bar grill can be used when the draft is favorable. In more primitive campstoves the front is left open, but better control of draft results when it is closed and equipped with a fuel door and an ash door having an adjustable damper. An adjustable damper in the chimney flue is a further aid in this purpose.

When rain overtakes a picnic, it can be laughed off as all in a lifetime, and the picnic can be postponed or gone through with as its collective temperament may determine. But if rain intrudes on a vacation of the tenants of a park cabin that is not equipped for indoor cooking, nothing less than a sheltering roof over the open air campstove can stay the vacationists' wrath. After all, if the campstove must have a chimney—and this is very generally conceded—a roof can make the combination a more sightly thing, as several small stove shelters illustrated among the plates which follow prove. Another advantage offered by a sheltering roof is the fact that it makes possible keeping a supply of dry fuel immediately at hand. When the preparation of three meals a day is involved, this is no minor convenience in some climates.

The campstove raised to convenient working height and outfitted with a chimney and a roof, as desirable accessory features, attains a size that invites the challenge that its bulk goes way beyond its function. This may be true if the flue serves and the roof shelters only one campstove. The retort courteous and forehanded defense is to group two or more stoves together and then hope that camping neighbors do not demand the complete isolation that picnicking neighbors are believed to seek, and that the former will share the stove shelter in common and in peace. There are obvious advantages—fewer sources of fire hazard, smoke annoyance, and damage to trees and roots. An operation that, in a frank analysis, is of "nuisance" character is concentrated by this solution.

Where rainfall is heavy, it is sometimes chosen to construct in picnic areas the equivalent of sheltered campstoves instead of low open picnic fireplaces. When built with only one stove under the sheltering roof, what amounts to an individual picnic kitchen is the result. Two or more stoves under one roof produce a structure that is a well-recognized type, several of which are illustrated in the section "Picnic Shelters and Kitchens." These might serve in a campground or colony of cabins that lack kitchens as advantageously as in the picnic area.

The tailpiece illustration pictures the coupling of a practical cooking facility and a masonry hearth and reflector for the evening campfire. The type is built in some of the western national parks. Its chief advantage is that it induces campers to build their campfire in a predetermined location and tends to prevent a wantonness in fire building that quickly destroys the natural values of the campground. Fire hazards are reduced when facilities of this type are supplied. With its metal stove and smokestack, the contraption is not a thing of beauty, but in most campground developments practical, and not artistic, considerations rightly have the call.

Crater Lake National Park

Plate III F-1   ⇛ CAMPSTOVES

Campstove Shelter — Heyburn State Park — Idaho

An individual stove kitchen of this type is suitable in both picnic and cabin areas, particularly in regions where rainfall is heavy. The simple character of this example and the off-centering of the chimney so that the ridge pole is not severed are details of interest.

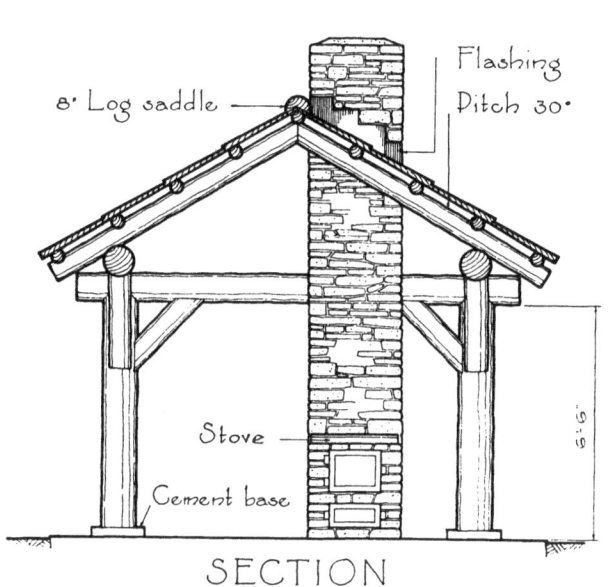

SECTION

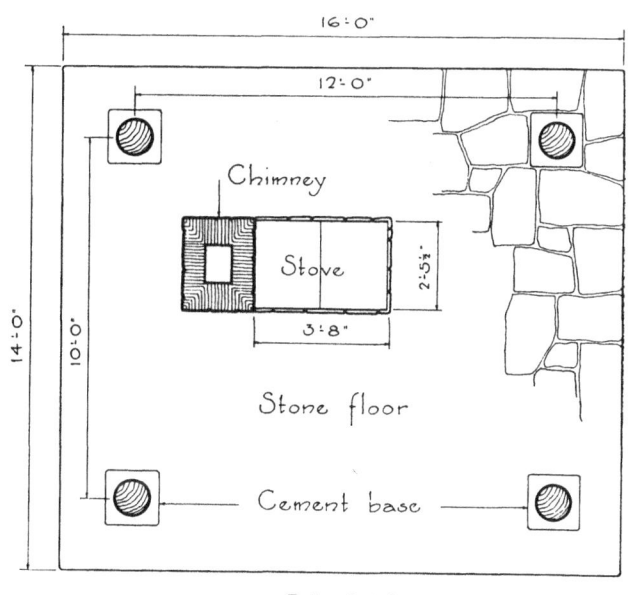

PLAN

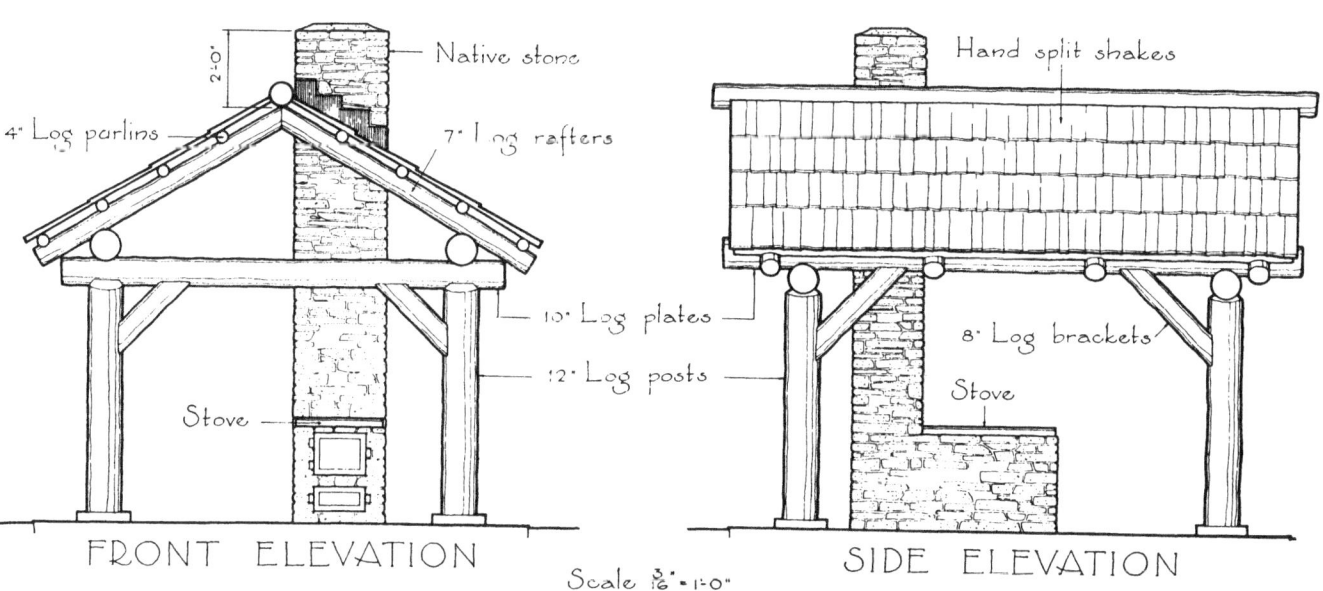

FRONT ELEVATION   Scale ⅜"=1'-0"   SIDE ELEVATION

CAMPSTOVES

Plate III F-2

Campstove Shelter

Deception Pass State Park — — Washington

There is a rakish quality in this individual stove kitchen absent from the little structure of similar purpose in Heyburn State Park. Contributing to this are an informality of masonry and shake roof, wide overhang of cornice and changing level of the eaves. If the facility for cooking out-of-doors must have a chimney, it seems less antagonistic to environment when the sheltering roof is joined to it.

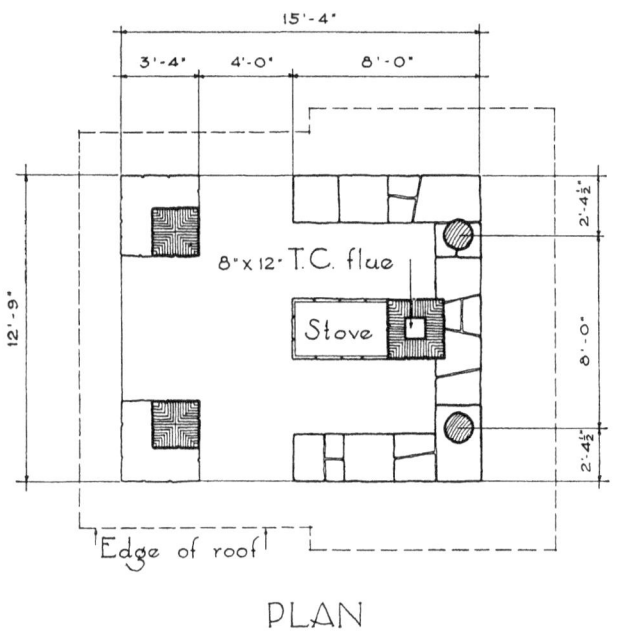

PLAN

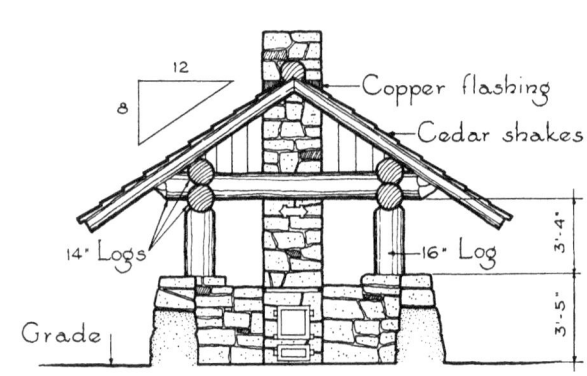

SECTION

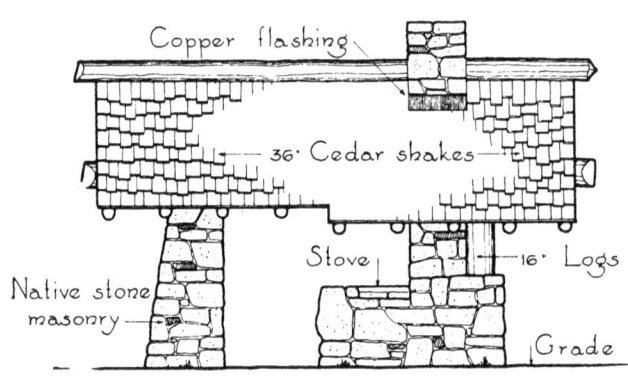

FRONT ELEVATION

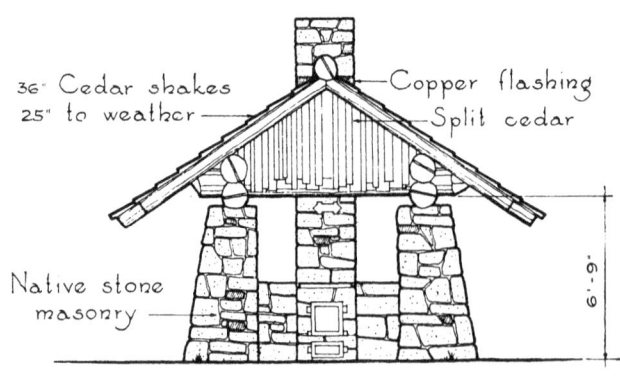

SIDE ELEVATION

Scale ⅜" = 1'-0"

Plate III F-3 — CAMPSTOVES

Campstove Shelter
Deception Pass State Park — Washington

Except that the stove is centered in the shelter and the post braces are omitted this little stove shelter is identical with the Heyburn State Park example already illustrated. Although both structures, it must be admitted, actually exist on picnic areas, they, or multiple phases of them, are in all essentials the campstove shelter urged for campgrounds, where they are really more to be tolerated than in picnic areas.

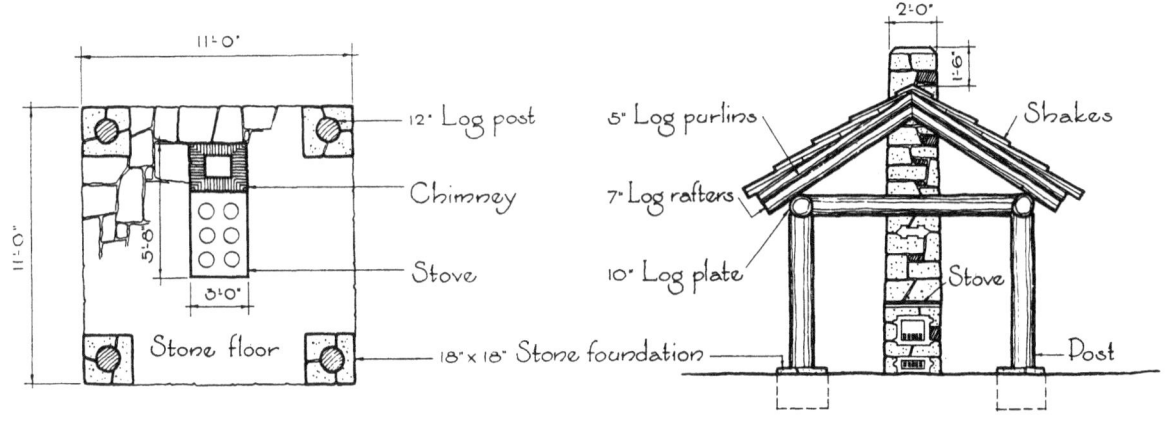

PLAN   FRONT ELEVATION

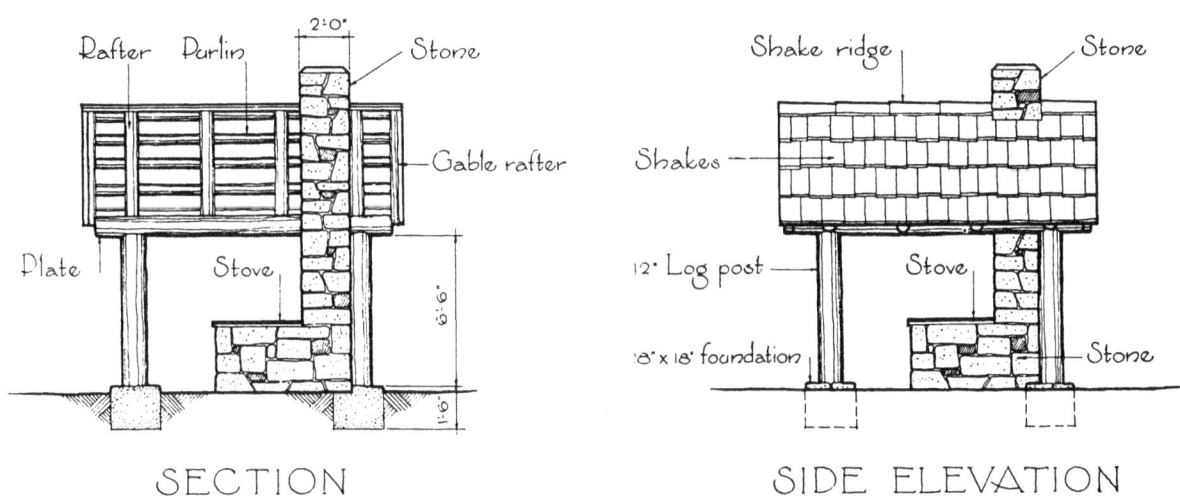

SECTION   SIDE ELEVATION

Scale ¼" = 1'-0"

CAMPSTOVES *Plate* III F–4

Sequoia National Park

This facility for campground cooking is a type widely found in the western national parks. Only its greater height and minor chimney differentiate it from the picnic fireplace. Its side walls are splayed, and its cooking surface is a steel plate. The raised hearth makes for economy of fuel consumption.

Lassen Volcanic National Park

This example, because its cooking surface is lower, is not as convenient in use as the campstove pictured below. If the top could be elevated a few inches without necessitating an increase in the height of the chimney, a more convenient working height and, it is felt, proportions more pleasing to the eye would result.

Bastrop State Park, Texas

Solid tops of cast or heavy sheet metal are best for the diversified cooking done on campstoves. In point of fact a barred or perforated grille top makes the chimney something of a superfluous feature as the blackened masonry seen here proves. The batter of the walls gives the object a pleasing silhouette.

Plate III F-5 ⇶ CAMPSTOVES

In discussing picnic fireplaces, an arbitrary differentiation classified as campstoves those outdoor cooking facilities which have convenient working height and rely on a chimney for draft. On these points, the examples on this page classify more or less as campstoves. This one has a firebrick lining and utilizes a cast top with removable lids.

Pine Lake State Park, Iowa

The cooking surface of this multiple stove is somewhat lacking in height to be altogether convenient in a campground. It might well have been raised to be level with the cheek walls. Apparently the facility offers places for three cooks to operate. If bulk of chimney has anything to do with quickening the draft, smoke does not linger long here.

Mount Penn Metropolitan Reservation, Reading, Pennsylvania

This four-way campstove has many practical features. A solid stove top is hinged and can be rested against the chimney. Directly beneath the solid top is a barred grille which can be used when the fire has been reduced to hot coals. Draft can be controlled by the fuel door. The chimney is topped off just above head height.

Palomar Mountain State Park, California

97

CAMPSTOVES

Plate III F-6

Campstove - Brown County State Park - Indiana

Close-coupled outdoor grilles at convenient working height that could not be accused of being inharmonious in a park setting, despite the considerable size forced by the addition of the attractive and useful, though superfluous, flanking seats. Actually built to face a hunter's shelter of the Adirondack type, it is here written into the record for the consideration of those who would raise the eye appeal of outdoor cooking units in campgrounds and cabin groups.

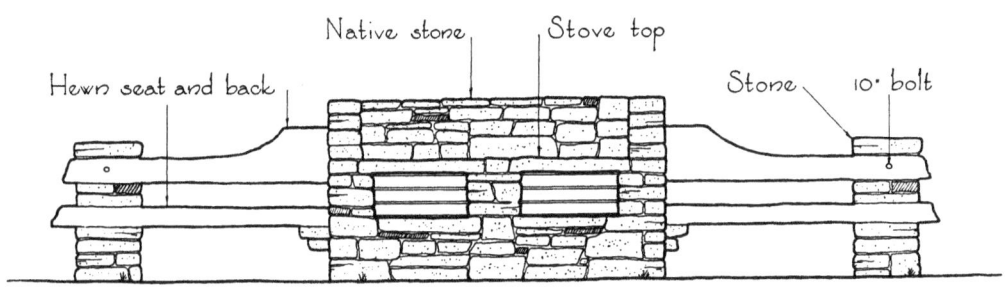

FRONT ELEVATION

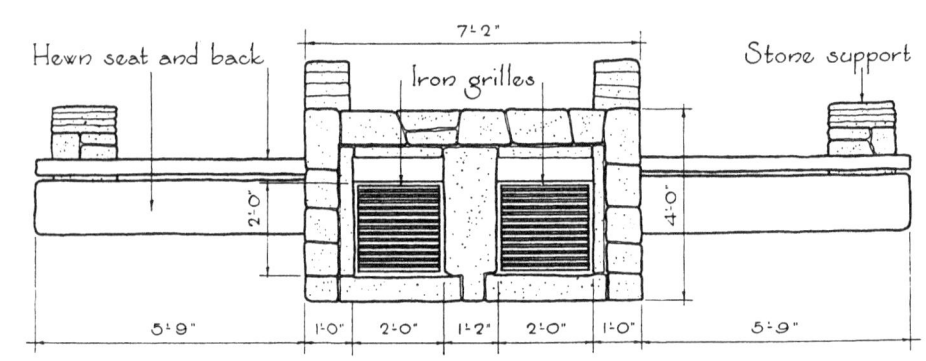

PLAN

SIDE ELEVATION

SECTION

Scale ¼" = 1'-0"

98

FURNITURE AND FURNISHINGS

OPEN SHELTERS in parks do not lend themselves to furniture and furnishings in the sense the terms apply in instances of more enclosed buildings. Mobile equipment of these, whether for picnic or trailside use, is almost exclusively picnic table and bench combinations and trailside seats, a little lighter and more finished perhaps than similar items in the open, but almost as limited in form and variety. The furnishings and decorations of lodges, community buildings, refectories, and cabins, on the contrary, can have great variety and contribute importantly to widen the use and improve the appearance of these buildings. They offer a broad field for the exercise of individuality, taste, and ingenuity.

The well-known principles of all good furniture design—suitability to purpose, appeal to the eye, and adaptation of technique to materials at hand—apply no less to furniture for park buildings than to other types. In the designing of park furniture, however, further considerations, scarcely less important, should be taken into account.

Simplicity must be the keynote if the furnishings are to appear appropriate in structures which themselves must be unpretentious to be successful in natural settings. If the desired simplicity cannot be guaranteed as a matter of course by the good taste of designers, perhaps the usual scarcity of funds for once deserves a cheer for the curb on elaboration it will force.

A certain simplicity of furnishings is reasonably assured when another guiding factor in appropriate design is acknowledged. This is the long tradition of the locality. Primitive and pioneer furnishings were extremely simple; so were the interpretations of transplanted historic styles developed here by the earliest settlers. The same combinations of controlling historical, racial, climatic, and regional influences that produce park structures of varied types should produce furnishings of equivalent variety. Needless to say, the same set of influences that produced a particular building should have play in determining the furnishing of it.

It would be unfitting to transplant Spanish and Pueblo furniture, suited to park buildings of the Southwest evidencing similar influences in their exterior treatment, to other regions, say the Hudson Valley with its early background of Dutch settlement, New England, or the environs of Chicago. The fine, simple furniture styles of the religious sects—the Moravians, Shakers, Amish, Dunkers, and others—are a sound inspiration for the furniture of park buildings in localities in Pennsylvania, Western Massachusetts, Iowa, and Ohio where these groups settled, yet only if the buildings to be furnished testify to the same inspirational sources. Primitive furniture of native handcraft and early origin, still being produced by mountain people in remote parts of the Ozarks, the Great Smokies, and other sections of the Appalachians, offers a pattern for park furniture suitable over a considerable, yet by no means a Nation-wide, area. There is hardly a section of the country but has some historic, racial, or other background for a theme in furnishings and decoration that would be truly individual and appropriate.

The available natural resources of any locality influenced the furniture making, weaving, and other crafts of the pioneers and of the primitive races that preceded them. If the practices of these are to inspire the objects contrived in the present for furnishing park buildings, we too must employ native materials and recognize their peculiar advantages and limitations.

Keeping this in mind, we make use of maple, walnut, and other close-grained hardwoods where tradition calls for turned furniture styles, and avoid sharp edges and turnings when soft woods only are available; we realize the suitability of hickory, ash, maple, and pine to particular uses in Windsor and slat-back chair construction, and of the soft pines to the furniture styles that employ incised ornament.

FURNITURE AND FURNISHINGS

Furniture of rustic type having members in the round with beavered tenons can be made from cedar and hickory. After the outer bark of the former wood is removed, the surface is shaved so that the thin, inner red bark sometimes is not entirely removed, and a striking, mottled surface results. Because its bark stays on better than that of most other woods, hickory made into furniture with the bark intact is quite satisfactory and probably represents the peak in allowable rusticity in furniture.

Happily, furniture items contrived from oddly formed wood growth are no longer popular as they once were. It is hoped that there will be no reaction from the current trend that might result in littering our park buildings with contorted multi-forked logs posing as hat trees, sections of tree trunks hollowed out for barrel chairs, and similar monstrosities.

The seats available for chairs of truly primitive type are in a considerable range—wood slabs, woven rush, woven splint of hickory or elm, many kinds of leather laced on with leather thongs, and even woven fabrics that reproduce early workmanship and patterns.

The need for hangings and upholstering can often be appropriately supplied by reproductions of early fabrics. The weaving of these has lately been revived in different parts of the country, especially among mountain peoples and the Indians. Indian rugs, hooked rugs, and woven rag carpets will quite generally serve for floor coverings, subject, of course, to geographical location and compatibility with the architecture of the structure to be furnished.

Studied effort must be made to introduce color into the furnishings of park buildings if a certain somberness characteristic of interiors built entirely of natural materials is to be offset. Most untreated woods weather to dull grays and browns, and there is only very limited color in most stone masonry. The accent of bright harmonious colors in fabrics and floor coverings is welcome. It is conceivable under certain conditions that the raw wood of certain types of furniture might be stained or painted in relatively brilliant colors to introduce more gaiety into the interiors than it is permissible to express in the exteriors of park structures.

The feeling of the past is accentuated when items of skilled handcrafts associated with the early days are introduced. Products of the loom have already been mentioned. The art of the blacksmith can supply many details important in the creation of "atmosphere." There are types of hand-wrought iron hardware peculiar to the early New England communities, the German counties of Pennsylvania, and the Spanish settlements of the Southwest. In fireplace fittings there are regional characteristics that can be revived in the re-creations of today. There are items of early lighting equipment of wrought iron, other metals, and turned wood unmistakably identified with particular parts of the country and different periods of development. These invite adaptation to present needs.

There is no longer any special novelty about lighting fixtures fashioned from wagon wheels, ox yokes, and parts of spinning wheels and reels. The spirit of pioneer days will only attach to such adaptations as long as they do not become utterly commonplace by reason of being too often used, a fate that is always treading on the heels of innovations popular because of their quaintness.

Plate, III G–1   ❯❯❯ FURNITURE AND FURNISHINGS

Bastrop State Park, Texas

Bastrop State Park, Texas

CEILING FIXTURES

Shown above are the now familiar conversions of wagon wheel and ox yoke to lighting fixture use. In interiors with barnlike proportions having exposed wood trusses and roof framing, these reminders of an earlier day, salvaged to some purpose in the present, seem suitable. At the right is a massive fixture of peeled cedar logs clustered in a pleasing arrangement. It repeats the material of the furniture and relates well to the scale of the room and furniture alike. The fixtures illustrated below exemplify the contribution that the skill of the craftsman in iron can bring to park structures. Crisp wrought iron accents the softer contours of native materials.

Petit Jean State Park, Texas

Bastrop State Park, Texas

Mother Neff State Park, Texas

101

FURNITURE AND FURNISHINGS ««   *Plate* III G–2

INTERIORS, LODGE, PETIT JEAN STATE PARK, ARKANSAS

There is a unified theme in the interior furnishings of this lodge that is very satisfying. Except for the tops of the tables, the sturdy lounge furniture is fabricated entirely of peeled cedar logs. Even the lamp bases and ceiling fixtures are of this material, and yet do not appear bizarre. The bright colors of the lamp shades and of the rough woven fabrics of the cushions on the seating furniture are needed accents against the somber background of stone walls and dark wood ceilings.

Plate III G–3   ⇒ FURNITURE AND FURNISHINGS

FURNITURE, LODGE,
PETIT JEAN STATE PARK, ARKANSAS

Above are pictured some of the furniture items with which the porch, like the lounge illustrated on the facing page, is furnished. The cushions provide comfort without, however, corrupting the basic ruggedness of the furniture itself. To the right are shown the furniture types used in the dining room. The cedar-in-the-round construction is repeated in the understructure of the tables, which are of varying shapes and sizes. The dining chairs are "mountaineer" ladder-backs typical of the locality. Below are bed and divan with which the guest rooms are equipped. The drawer at the foot and the bookshelves at the head of the bed are novel.

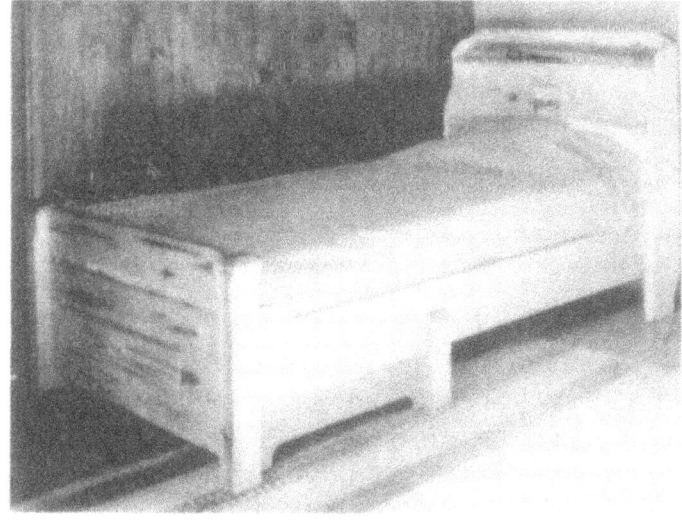

FURNITURE AND FURNISHINGS

Plate III G–4

INTERIOR FURNISHINGS, BASTROP STATE PARK, TEXAS

Illustrated on this and the facing page are typical items of furniture in the lodge and cabins of this Texas park. Here cedar is mill-worked with such decorative features as turnings, shaped shoes and brackets, and other refinements of sophisticated furniture styles, all in striking contrast with the more rustic treatment of the same wood at Petit Jean State Park. The large illustration above pictures a typical cabin interior. The color contrasts typical of cedar are sometimes too striking to appeal to all tastes. Treatment to blend the lighter to the darker wood deserves consideration.

Plate III G–5 ⇛ FURNITURE AND FURNISHINGS

FURNITURE AND FURNISHINGS ««   Plate III G–6

Lodge, Bastrop State Park, Texas

Lodge, Bastrop State Park, Texas

Tavern, New Salem State Park, Illinois

FIREPLACES, FITTINGS, AND ACCESSORIES

Its purpose makes the fireplace the dominant feature—the very center of things—in any park building interior in which it is built. It is therefore deserving of careful design and expert workmanship so that as a focal point it is attractive and as a needed facility it functions perfectly. It should invite the eye to linger—not the smoke to its eventual disfigurement.

The decorative appeal of the fireplace depends first of all on the material selected and its manner

Cabin, Bastrop State Park, Texas

Plate III G–7   →›› FURNITURE AND FURNISHINGS

Caretaker's Dwelling, Riverside State Park, Washington

Kitchawan Tavern, Westchester County, New York

of use. Next in importance are the structural elements integral with it, such as shelf, oven, niches, and many other legitimate interest-giving features. Finally, the fireplace fittings—andirons, cranes, and fire tools—and appropriate decorative accessories of the shelf, chimney breast, and hearth—running from ancient firearms to fabrics and from old-time kitchen utensils to early pottery—can highlight any stylized scheme of furnishings desired.

Caretaker's Dwelling, Cleburne State Park, Texas

Bright Angel Lodge, Grand Canyon National Park

FURNITURE AND FURNISHINGS

Plate III G–8

Bastrop State Park, Texas

Lost River State Park, West Virginia

Mother Neff State Park, Texas

BRACKET FIXTURES

To be sure, not demonstrably interior lighting fixtures, save those pictured directly above. Nonetheless all are illustrative of the appropriateness of wrought iron against a background of native stone, logs, or other rugged materials. The wall brackets at Mother Neff and Bastrop State Parks have a delicacy that suggests that they would not be unsuitable in an interior use. The two lantern brackets shown below have definitely outdoor weight and scale. They might appear fitting in an open shelter but hardly in an enclosed building.

Hereford State Park, Texas

Lake Brownwood State Park, Texas

CAMP LAY-OUT

A DISCUSSION of the lay-out of organized camps is only ventured in a compilation devoted to structures and facilities because lay-out plays such a vital part in determining just what structures and facilities are requisite in a camp and what the details of these shall be. Very definitely the number and size of the camp buildings and the relationship between them *are* the camp lay-out in fact, and any discussion of the buildings individually is difficult without some preliminary consideration of them as a whole.

There is no intention here to examine the structural needs of all kinds of camps, or even of organized camps of every size. It is chosen to limit detailed consideration to the structural requisites of organized camps in that capacity range which embraces the overwhelming majority of organized camps—those accommodating not less than 25 and not more than 100 campers.

There are organized camps of lesser and greater capacity, justified, it is admitted, under special conditions. Week end or other short-term accommodation of groups of less than 25 persons will be briefly touched on later. Larger camps accommodating several hundred campers exist and are deemed by some to be successful. There is a growing realization, however, that camps of more than 125 persons, ranging say to capacities of 200, 300, or 500, in a sense cease to be true camps and become mere cantonments or concentrations where the things that are of the essence of camping somehow cannot be done.

There is now almost general acceptance of the principle that any camp for more than 32 persons should be broken down into groups of 16, 24, or at a maximum, 32 campers. Camps so planned have come to be known as unit camps. A central area provides facilities for general administration; dining; medical examination, care, and isolation; and for the mass recreational and cultural activities of all the campers on the area. Outlying a short walking distance from this central area are the units, each of which is a colony of sleeping cabins or tents for campers and their leaders, centering around a unit lodge which is the recreational and social rallying point of the group. A unit washhouse and latrine completes the unit lay-out.

One figure of speech has the central area the "hub" and the units the radiating "spokes" of a wheel. Another has the units as outlying "hamlets" suburban to a "village" in which the mutual interests of all the units in orderly government, food supply, medical care, and recreational and cultural pursuits center.

Camps laid out in units allow for the variations that exist in all human beings. In children's and young people's camps, a break-down into small units permits a logical grouping of campers of the same age and physical ability, similar interests and experience. In these small groups children and adolescents are given opportunity to find themselves, while in "mass camping" they experience a hardly avoidable regimentation and a sensation of being lost in a crowd. Small groups permit a high degree of personal attention on the part of the counselors, while large groups mean a less personal leadership or exhaustion of the counselors who attempt too much.

From a health point of view, there are also sound arguments in favor of small groups in camp. Children in large groups easily become overstimulated, and the possibilities for fatigue are greatly increased when a large number of children eat, sleep, and generally live in close quarters. Should a communicable disease develop in a camp laid out in units, it is less likely to spread through the whole camp.

THE BREAK-DOWN OF A CAMP into units or groups does not mean that each is wholly independent of the others. Many recreational and cultural activities are participated in simultaneously by all groups. But the deadly institutionalism toward which mass camping can tend is avoided through the individualism fostered by the recreational activities and intimacies of the small unit, "on its own" much of the time.

Because many youth groups which go in for camping are organized into squads or patrols of eight, or troops of 16, 24, or 32, there is good reason for laying out camp units in multiples of eight. Units of 24 campers are considered both practical and desirable. There can be an efficient supervision of groups of 24, which escapes being either repressive or insufficient. Units of 16 are perhaps more desirable than practical, for in order to accommodate a given number of campers there must, of course, be a greater number of units, resulting in a more extended camp and increased costs of construction and operation. Units of 32, on the contrary, are probably more practical than desirable, for while such concentrations mean some reduction in the costs of construction, maintenance, and operation, the supervision will tend to be inadequate and the groups to be unwieldy for a properly unified leadership. All things considered, units of 24 seem to be the happy mean. It is assumed that the logic back of units which accommodate 16, 24, or at the most, 32 persons will lead to most camps being laid out in units of one or another of these sizes.

Camps, ranging roughly from 25- to 100-camper capacity, laid out in multiple-of-eight units, seem to group into three sizes. There is the small camp accommodating 24 to 32 persons. Although generally a single unit, it may be broken down into two units of 16 where rigid economy is not a weighing factor.

There is next the medium-sized camp of 48- to 64-capacity which embraces camps of two units of 24 or 32 campers. We may also include in this category camps composed of three and four units of 16, if these more ideal standards are economically supportable.

The large camp accommodates from 72 to 96 campers and may be made up of three groups of 24 or 32, or four groups of 24, campers. It, too, may be broken down into units of 16, but the resulting increase in construction and supervisory costs and the probable unavailability of five or six suitable unit campsites, properly central to the administration area, will be deterrent influences. It is sometimes felt necessary to stretch the capacity of a large camp to accommodate more than 100 campers, but 125 is a recommended maximum, and capacity in excess of that is almost invariably to be discouraged.

The distances desirable between the several units composing a camp and between these units and the administration or central area cannot be arbitrarily stated. In selecting the location for any camp, privacy is a consideration as primary as the availability of safe drinking water and the suitability of the soil for sewage disposal. Likewise, a proper degree of privacy is of first importance for the component units of the camp. Studies of a group of camps have revealed an average distance of 600 feet between units. It does not follow, however, that 600 feet or any other given distance may be fixed for spacing units from each other and from the administrative group. The distance necessary for a suitable privacy depends in each case on existing site conditions, among which topography and cover are controlling elements.

In the cabin unit the spotting of campers' cabins in relation to one another, to sun and shade, and to dependencies of the group deserves a word. It is desirable that they be exposed to sunlight a part of the day, preferably in the forenoon, so that clothes and bedding may be sunned and aired. Shade in the late afternoon is equally desirable in warm climates so that the cabins will be comfortable for sleeping at the early hour campers usually go to bed. The distances between cabins are naturally subject to site conditions, but 50 feet is the recommended maximum for age group camps where supervision is an important consideration. Family cabins can string out with greater space between them, for, in groups of these, supervision is limited or even unnecessary. No sleeping cabin in a children's camp should be more than 150 feet distant from the latrine. Cabins for a youth group or a family may exceed this distance somewhat, but more than 200 feet is not good practice.

THE LAY-OUT OF A CAMP, before stated to be synonymous with the number of buildings, their size, and the relationships between them, is governed by a variety of considerations.

Probably foremost is capacity as dictated by the needs of the community to be served. Whether to undertake a small, medium-sized, or large camp, or a camp which falls outside the 25- to 100-range, hangs in any case on carefully analyzed need.

Second and inevitable influence is the availability of funds. Consideration of this may not stop with capital investment in site, buildings, and equipment. It must anticipate all details of supervision, and foresee the extent of the supervisory staff and the full complement of lesser employes required for a proper functioning of the camp in operation. There is opportunity for grievous error in miscalculating the scale on which camp operation may be economically carried on. Overestimate of an economically supportable personnel results in a waste of capital funds to construct some buildings which are not long used. On the other hand, if an essential staffing is underestimated, unfortunate overcrowding of facilities is certain to follow. Operating and maintenance costs must therefore be taken into account when funds for construction, and the physical plant such will provide, are undergoing preliminary examination.

Another set of conditions which has all-important bearing on the camp plan includes site factors such as topography, natural features, and climate. A rugged topography may force a sprawling lay-out or a very concentrated one, both of which are non-typical and short of ideal. Sparseness of cover will suggest a wide separation of units. Because most camps are so largely centered around swimming, the natural feature or man-made facility which will serve for this activity will directly govern the lay-out. A steep lakeshore or river bank may make it necessary to string out the camp in a plan that departs from the typical. If the site is a small peninsula, the lay-out will recognize the peculiar advantages this offers. If the site is along a stream, dammed to create a small pondlike "swimming hole", the camp development along both banks will find a different expression. If the hub of activity is a formal swimming pool, the camp and its component units will be arranged in still another pattern. A mild, dry climate may permit a minimum number of buildings and a light, inexpensive construction. A rainy climate will call for considerable space under roof for enforced indoor recreation. In northern areas a better grade of construction will probably be employed, aimed to lengthen a short camping season or even to make winter camping possible.

If a projected camp is to be built on public lands as a public or semipublic undertaking, the sponsorship indicated for it is an important consideration in the planning. When it seems definitely assured that a single organization can be relied on to assume continuous responsibility, there might be some minor warping of typical lay-out to meet particular needs of the single using agency. Naturally, a camp planned exclusively for families could differ in some of its details from one planned for occupancy at one and the same time by boys and girls, or young men and young women. Similarly such co-recreational camps would not with logic duplicate camps planned to be continuously occupied by very small children, mothers with infants, or crippled children. But if, as is often the case, the use of the publicly or semipublicly owned camp is to be divided among several using agencies, it follows that any departures from a typical lay-out in the interest of one of them will be likely to handicap the program of the others. A generally typical arrangement represents a nice balance between extremes that should prove practical and satisfactory to the great majority of all potential users. Obviously, the restrictive factor of multiple sponsorship and use does not involve the designing of private camps on privately owned lands. Neither will the lay-out of private camps be forced to acknowledge the claims of other competing recreational interests which very often affect the planning of camps built on publicly owned lands.

Whether the public or private camp under single sponsorship will be occupied by one group of campers for its entire season of use or by successive groups for short-term periods will also influence the lay-out. There are items, almost essential for full-season occupancy, which for short camping periods may be foregone.

THE STRUCTURES AND FACILITIES which make up an organized group camp may be classified on the basis of function in categories which broadly parallel the groupings of park structures and facilities as these have been hereinbefore presented.

One group embraces structural facilities identified with administration and the basic services, among which the administration building, infirmary, unit washhouse and latrine, and central hot shower and laundry building are the principal items. Another includes facilities which further recreational and cultural activity—the unit lodge, recreation building, accessories to water sports, museum, craft shop, and campfire ring. A third deals with construction that provides for the preparation and serving of meals—dining lodge and kitchen with related dependencies, as well as the outdoor kitchen occasionally favored. Finally, there is the group which embraces sleeping quarters for the campers, the staff, and the employes.

There is also purpose in classifying organized camp structures and facilities on the basis of need. There are those deemed essential, or essential under certain conditions. Others rate as desirable though not essential, and there are varying degrees of desirability determined by a host of influences such as availability of funds, competence of leadership, the age and sex of the campers, co-recreational occupancy, and many another.

The plates which follow show ideal unit camp lay-outs on hypothetical sites, conjectured to illustrate the variety of topographic conditions likely to be encountered in problems of camp planning. It has also been sought to show the differences in relationships between buildings and between units which logically come about in camps of different sizes. There is furthermore an attempt to differentiate between essential construction and items, sometimes desirable but nonessential.

It will be observed that the ideal location for the administrative center is one easily reached by automobile from the outside and by foot from the rest of the camp. It should not be assumed, however, that the administration center is of necessity the exact geographical center of the camp. The entrance road to the camp should penetrate a minimum distance, to a small parking area for automobiles near the administration building. It is well to supplement this with an overflow parking area on the approach road further removed from the camp. From the termination of the entrance road a strictly service drive should lead to the service area, which, in most cases, is the kitchen wing of the dining lodge. The garage is the only other building necessarily served by a road, and, if properly located, is in the immediate vicinity of this terminal point. There is no purpose in an actual roadway to the other camp buildings. Should there be occasional need to reach other buildings to collect rubbish, for instance, or to distribute any heavy equipment at the opening and closing of a camp, a cleared truck or wagon trail, treated merely as a widened foot trail, under all but the most unusual conditions, will suffice. In laying out and clearing a roadway for use during the construction of the camp, it is farsighted to anticipate any service trail travel needs in the finished camp, so that the two purposes can be served by the one operation.

To build the service road between the parking area and the kitchen wing so that it invites travel other than by delivery trucks is a tactical error. It is undramatic in the extreme to lead campers and visitors, on the occasion of their first entry into the camp, right up to the kitchen door, after perhaps passing the incinerator and help's quarters en route. First impressions still remain important, and it is an obligation in camp lay-out to arrange the stage so that the setting for the first act of a camping experience will disclose something more romantically thrilling than its back yard operations. A more effective approach will be a well-laid-out foot trail from the parking area to the administration building and on beyond to views that reveal more favorably the campsite and its buildings and activities.

The distance between the campsite and the place of water-front activity is important in the planning of the organized camp. The temptation to indulge in unsupervised swimming, despite the fact that it is outlawed in every well-conducted camp, is great. Particularly are employes, busy during the day, inclined to disregard this first of camp commandments and go swimming at night. The desirable thing, of course, is by moral suasion to make unsupervised swimming unthinkable to everyone in camp. Where it is felt that this attitude can be attained 100 percent, the camp buildings can be on the water-front. The cynical planner may see fit to reinforce moral restraint with physical distance and spot the structures from 1,000 to 2,000 feet from the swimming beach.

When the swimming facility is a constructed pool, there is need for close relationship with the shower house, which will mean locating the pool centrally in the camp. Likewise, in a large camp a naturalized swimming hole, contrived by damming a small stream, must be in the heart of the camp if the recommended relationships between the several units are to obtain. Formal pools and shallow millponds, however, are without some of the hazards to swimmers that exist in large lakes and in river currents.

There are other desirable, if less important, relationships in lay-out. These will be mentioned as the different structures of the organized camp are discussed in detail.

Not for any bearing on plan, but because they are of very general nature, some further details should not go unremarked. Important and commendable as is a determination to limit modification of the site and surroundings of camp buildings to a minimum, it sometimes occurs that vegetation, particularly low growth, in the immediate vicinity of the buildings is retained to the detriment of other, not less important, considerations. Too dense cover up to the very walls of the buildings tends to produce damp and unhealthful conditions by obstructing sunlight and movements of air. To insure against such conditions, the less desirable cover near the buildings should be judiciously thinned out, but in such a manner that there is a smooth transition to the unmodified cover beyond.

The menace of fire should be recognized and guarded against in the planning and construction of camp buildings in such reasonable degree as available funds allow. To this end it is desirable to provide continuous enclosing masonry foundations under the building. If this is not possible by reason of its cost, the alternative of setting the floor construction high enough off the ground that dead leaves and other combustibles can be raked out from under the buildings should be adopted. There should be no slighting of well-recognized fireproofing measures in the building of chimneys and the installation of stoves. Electric wiring should conform with approved standards. The construction of the camp buildings can contribute only to the prevention of fires; once fire appears, fighting it is a matter of equipment and action.

There are some recommendations general to camp buildings that, however trite, still bear repetition. For health and comfort in the majority of locations, most of the structures should be completely screened against insects. If wall construction is not insect-tight, as is likely to occur when waney-edged siding or green lumber has been used, it becomes necessary to line the interior with some type of building board or other material to make the cabin insectproof. Types of floor construction which do not allow for a circulation of air between the cabin floor and grade, such as concrete or masonry laid on the ground, are unsatisfactory, and in a long spell of damp weather become a health hazard.

CAMP LAY-OUT

Plate III H–1

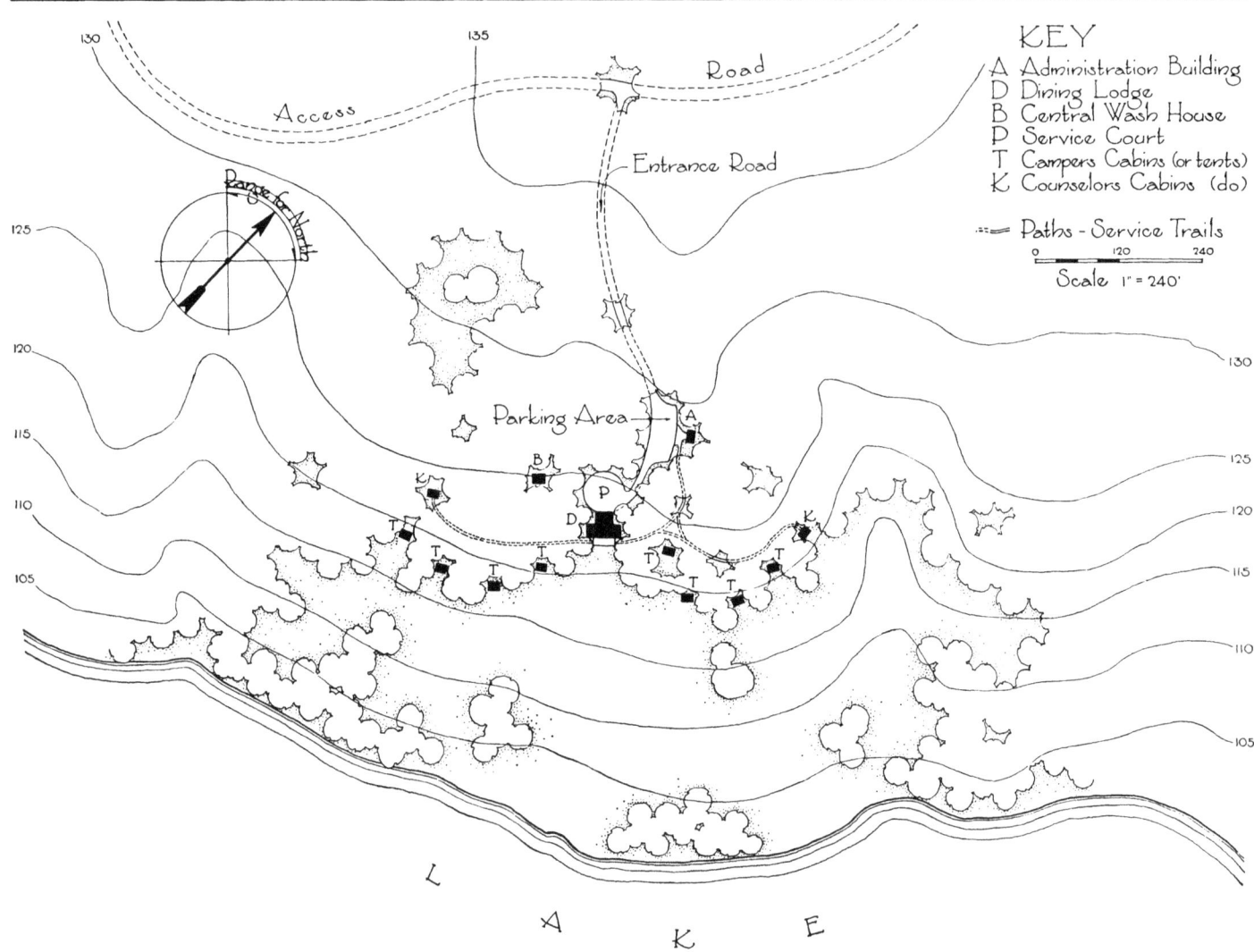

A SMALL ORGANIZED CAMP ON A LAKE-FRONT SITE

The conditions which inspire the camp lay-out shown above are a hypothetical lake-front site and the accommodation of 32 campers, the maximum capacity somewhat arbitrarily established for what herein is termed a small camp.

Eight four-cot tents or cabins in two separate groups or units provide sleeping quarters for the campers. A tent or cabin for two or more counselors is a part of each unit. The only other structures deemed essential in this small camp are the dining lodge and the central washhouse, which latter is assumed to include flush toilets as well as shower facilities. If conditions do not permit the use of flush toilets and if pit privies must serve, two privy structures, one close to each cabin unit, are recommended.

The administration building shown is not considered an essential building, although the operating practices of some camps might make it a desirable one. It is possible to perform the limited administrative duties of a small camp in the lodge or one of the counselors' cabins or tents.

This imagined lay-out assumes that meals are prepared by the campers themselves. If a camp cook is employed, he may be lodged in a duplicate of the campers' quarters. This is best located so that it controls the service drive to the kitchen wing of the lodge and yet is not too remote from the central washhouse.

114

Plate III H-2 ⇛ CAMP LAY-OUT

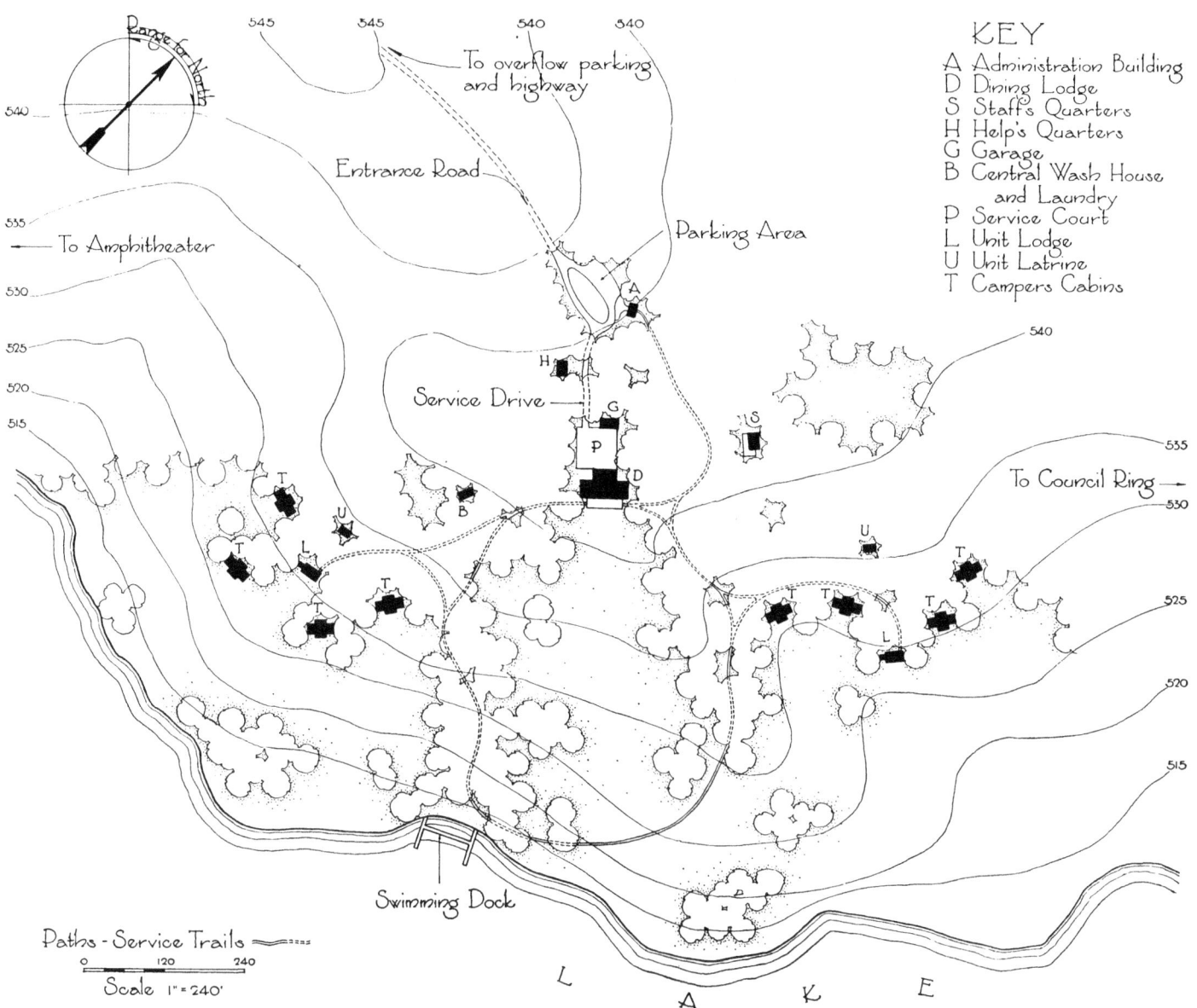

A MEDIUM-SIZED ORGANIZED CAMP ON A LAKE-FRONT SITE

The camp lay-out pictured above assumes a lake-front site and a capacity range of from 48 to 64 campers, which are the extremes hereinbefore specified for a medium-sized camp. The plan divides the campers into two units, each unit supplied with a lodge and a latrine. The sleeping cabins indicated are of the "saddlebag" type recommended in camps for very small children—a counselor's room and entrance porch flanked by two four-cot campers' rooms. Thus each unit accommodates 32 campers and from four to eight counselors.

For older children or adults eight four-bed tents or cabins in each unit are a preferable arrangement. Better still than two such units are three units of four or five four-cot tents or cabins, with a leader's cabin, lodge, and latrine to serve each unit.

In camps of this capacity, dining lodge, central washhouse, and separate quarters for the director and central staff and for help are probably essential; administration building and garage are less important. In the absence of a building that is specifically an infirmary, a cabin can serve when illness descends on the camp. Nature study and craft work in a camp of this size can be outdoor pursuits mainly. In inclement weather the unit lodges can harbor these activities.

CAMP LAY-OUT

Plate III H-3

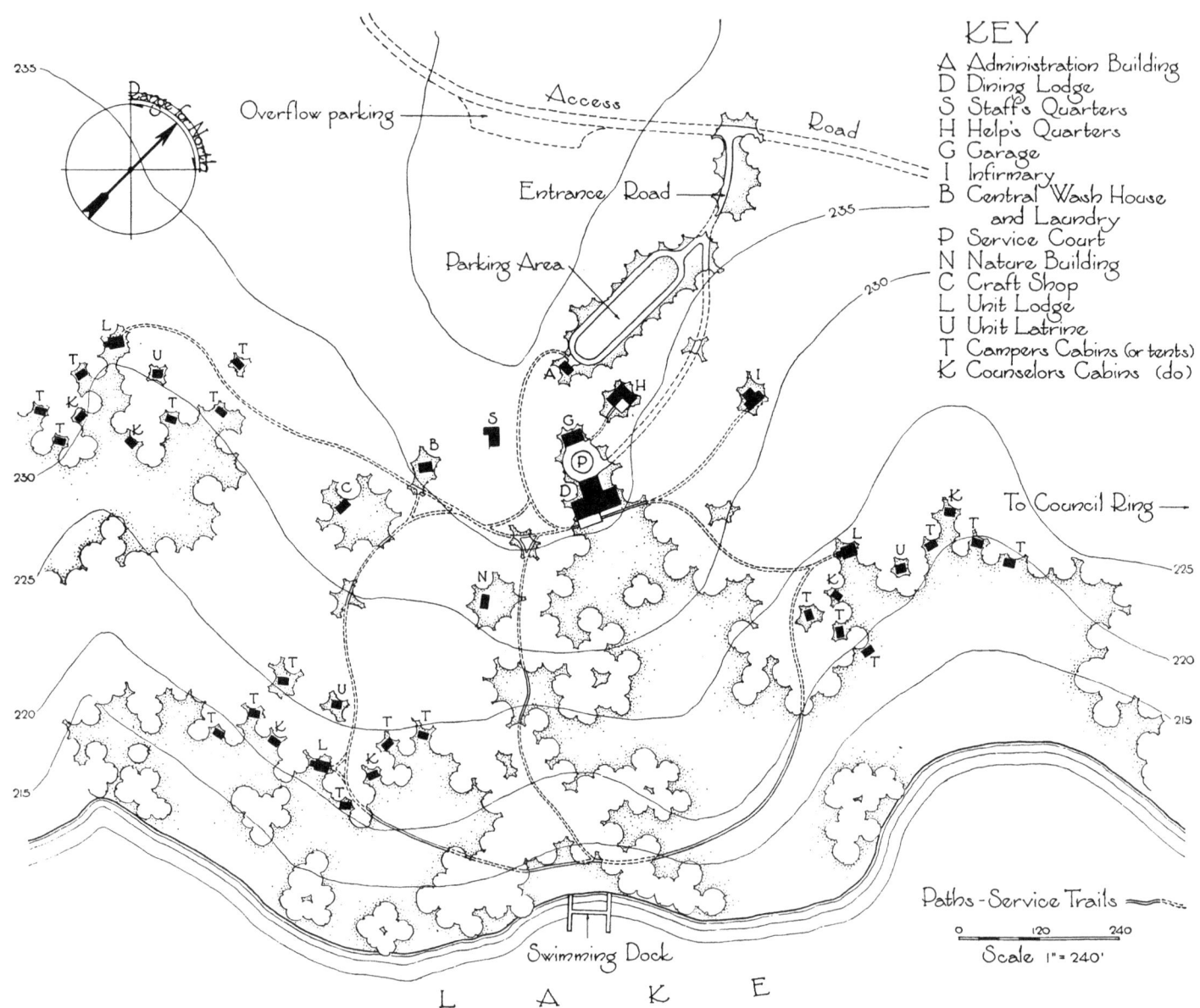

A LARGE ORGANIZED CAMP ON A LAKE-FRONT SITE

A lake-front location like those of the two preceding lay-outs is shown above, developed for an organized camp of from 72 to 96 campers, which is a large camp in the terminology of these discussions.

In addition to essential structures, other buildings of varying desirability are indicated in this lay-out. Some camp directors might contend that the nature building and craft shop could be dispensed with; others might as positively insist that the lay-out is incomplete because a general recreation building, or a water-front building, is not included. But these are "borderline" items to be rated as essential plus, essential minus, desirable plus, or desirable minus, entirely on the basis of the individual case, on which a multitude of factors bear.

As shown, this 72-capacity camp embraces three units, each made up of six four-cot sleeping units, which might be either tents or cabins. Each unit contains two two-cot counselor's tents or cabins, a lodge, and a latrine. Naturally, if this were used as a family camp, two latrines would be necessary in each unit. Variations of this lay-out within the 72- to 96-capacity range might be based on three units of 32, four units of 24, or five or six units of 16 campers. Topography will sometimes be found to place limits on the number of suitable unit sites within convenient range of the central buildings which constitute the hub of the camp lay-out.

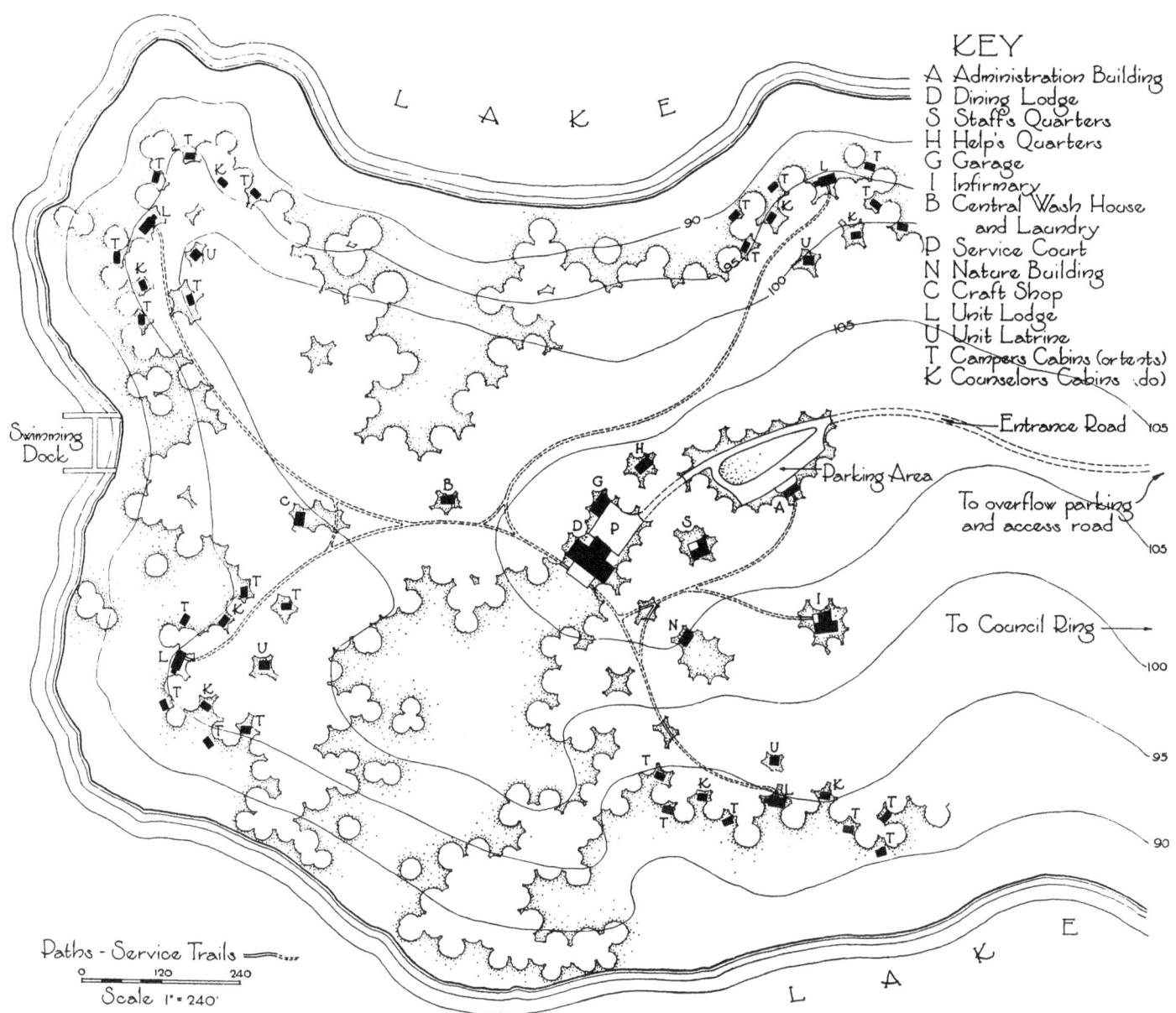

A LARGE ORGANIZED CAMP ON A PENINSULAR SITE

It has been sought in this conjectural lay-out of an organized camp of 72- to 96-capacity to show an advantageous utilization of a peninsula as a campsite. Such topography is perhaps not typical of sites widely available, yet it is not too rare to deserve consideration for the advantages it offers. Important among these are the privacy and scenic outlooks afforded each unit and the likelihood that breezes and tempered climate will result from water area in so many directions.

In the specific detail shown, four cabin colonies or units are ranged around the central buildings. Each includes six four-cot tents or cabins, supplemented with lodge, latrine, and counselors' quarters. The capacity of each unit might be either more or less than the 24 campers this lay-out indicates.

In this lay-out distance between the nature building and the craftshop and failure to include a general recreation building and a water-front building are probably invitations to controversy. It is reiterated that these details are scarcely of first importance though they be meat or poison to equally experienced camping experts. There is no intent to press recommendations concerning these minor, if moot, points. Unanimous agreement is not sought, much less expected.

CAMP LAY-OUT   Plate III H-5

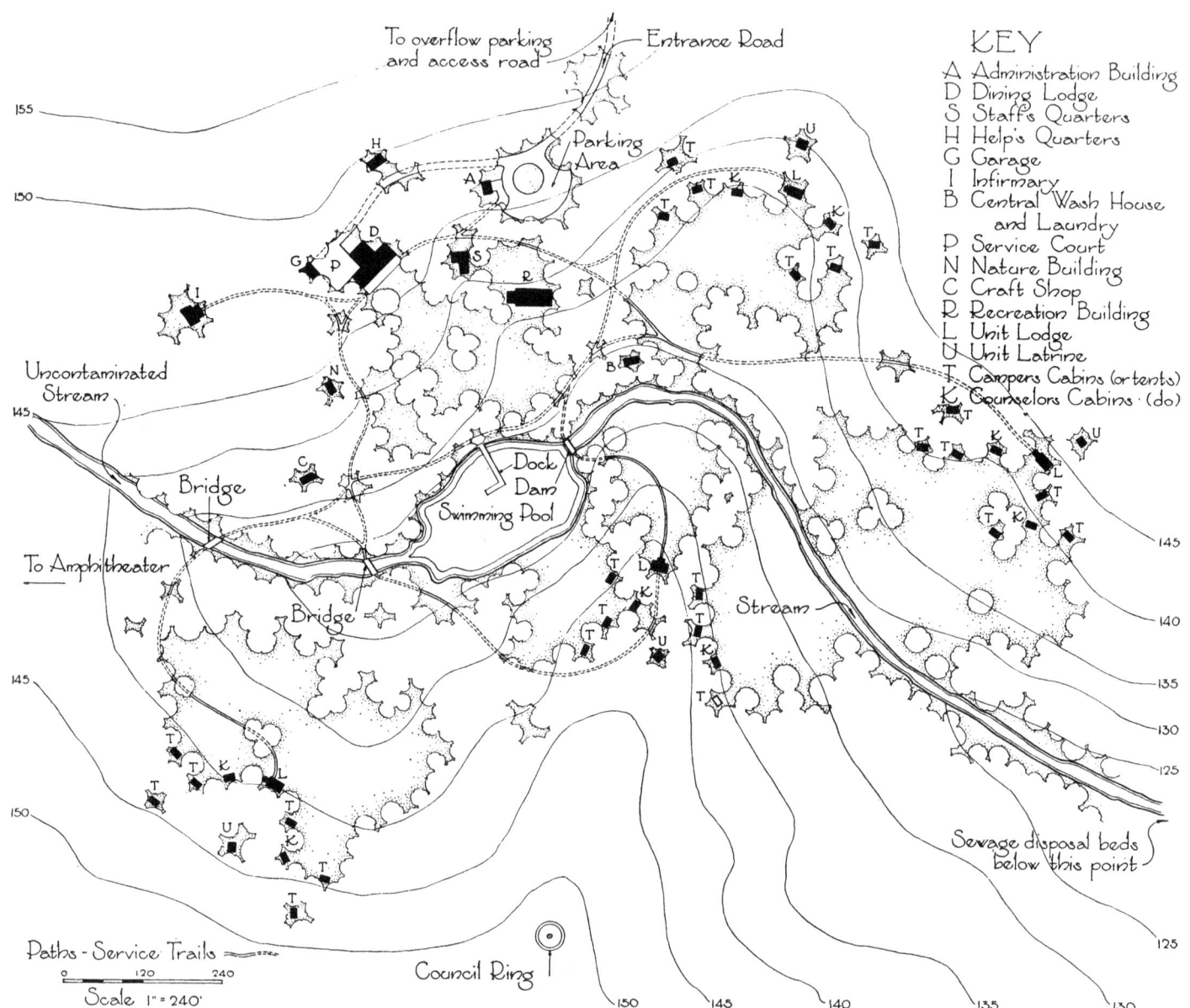

A LARGE ORGANIZED CAMP ALONG A DAMMED STREAM

Up to this point the camp plans shown have been premised on lake frontage—always conducive to an outward-looking plotting of buildings. When lake frontage is lacking, a camp plan that faces in upon itself naturally evolves. By damming an uncontaminated stream, something in the nature of a millpond or miniature lake can be created. A naturalized swimming pool, the modern version of the "swimmin' hole" can be scenically very attractive in a quiet way. The distribution of camp buildings so that they face the pool is logical. The structures may be located on one side of the stream only, but, if the pond is small, utilizing both sides of the stream makes for a more intimate lay-out.

As arbitrarily detailed above, this 72- to 96-capacity camp is formed of four 24-camper units, each comprising six four-cot campers' cabins. The lay-out might be varied to range from three to six units of other capacities if recommended maximum camp population were not exceeded. Probably the central recreation building among all the structures here shown is least important to the successful operation of most camps.

The primary requirements for a camp on terrain of this character are an unpolluted stream and a carefully installed system of sanitation that insures discharge from the sewage disposal beds serving the camp well downstream from the site.

Plate III H-6 →›› CAMP LAY-OUT

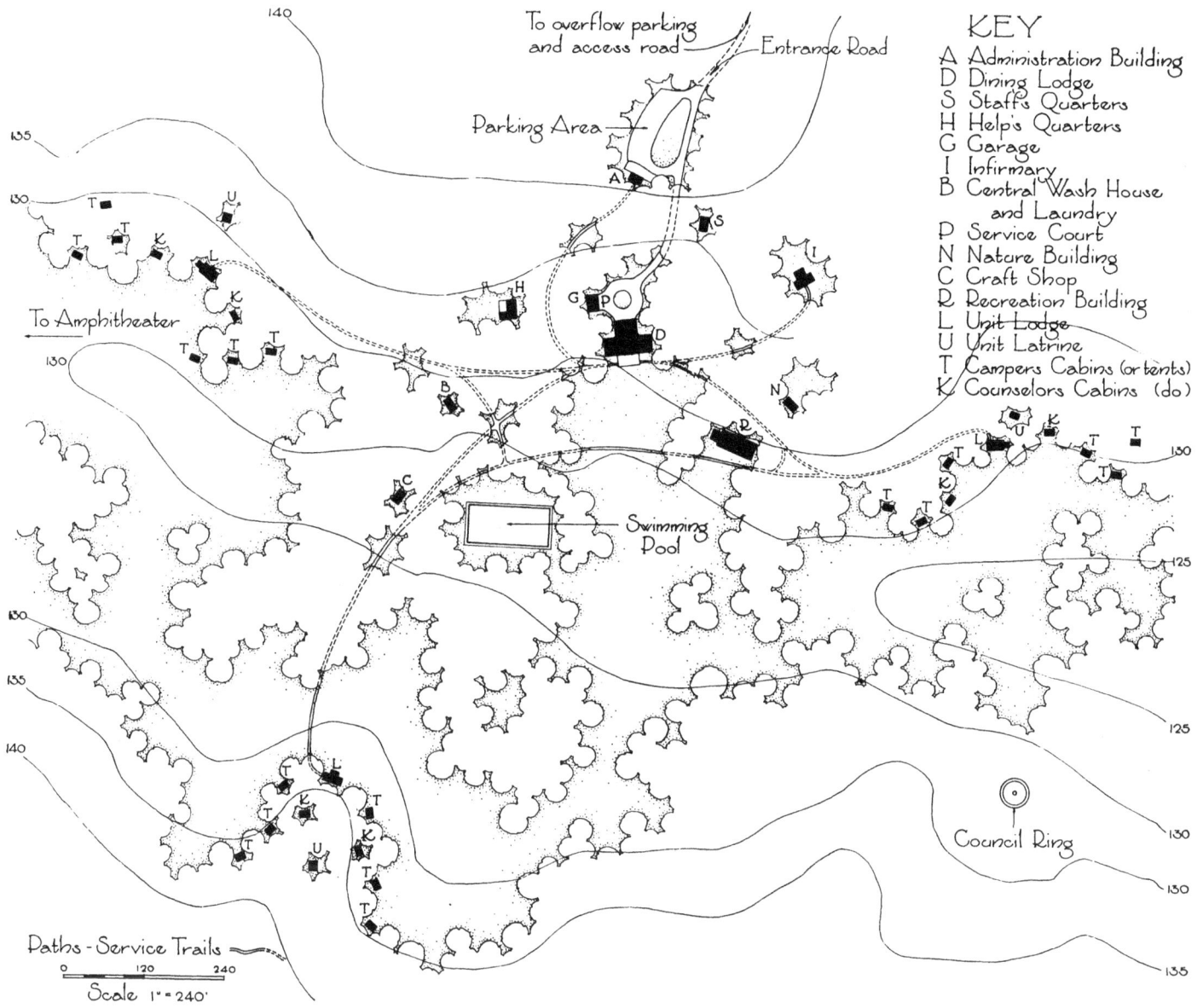

A LARGE ORGANIZED CAMP WITH FORMAL SWIMMING POOL

When lake frontage is lacking, the formal swimming pool is the alternative of the naturalized lake of the preceding lay-out. In fact, with no uncontaminated stream nearby, the formal pool supplied with water pumped from a well or piped from a distance is the forced substitute. It induces a lay-out that looks inward, with the swimming pool often located centrally in the campsite.

The lay-out above shows three units outlying from the administrative group. Each includes six four-cot cabins, two counselors' cabins, a lodge, and a latrine. This makes a 72-capacity camp, but within the 72- to 96-population range of the large camp, other combinations of units of several capacities are naturally many.

A central recreation building has more purpose in a camp without lake frontage than in one which benefits from the many activities offered by a recreational lake. A restricted field of outdoor activities justifies, indeed forces, the substitution of other recreational pursuits for those that are denied.

In a well-conducted camp dependent on a constructed pool for swimming, the swimmers will be required to take shower baths before entering the pool. Therefore, the central washhouse to be most convenient will be located near the pool.

CAMP LAY-OUT

Plate III H-7

CHART ILLUSTRATING THE FACTORS INVOLVED IN
LOCATING, DEVELOPING, AND OPERATING AN ORGANIZED CAMP

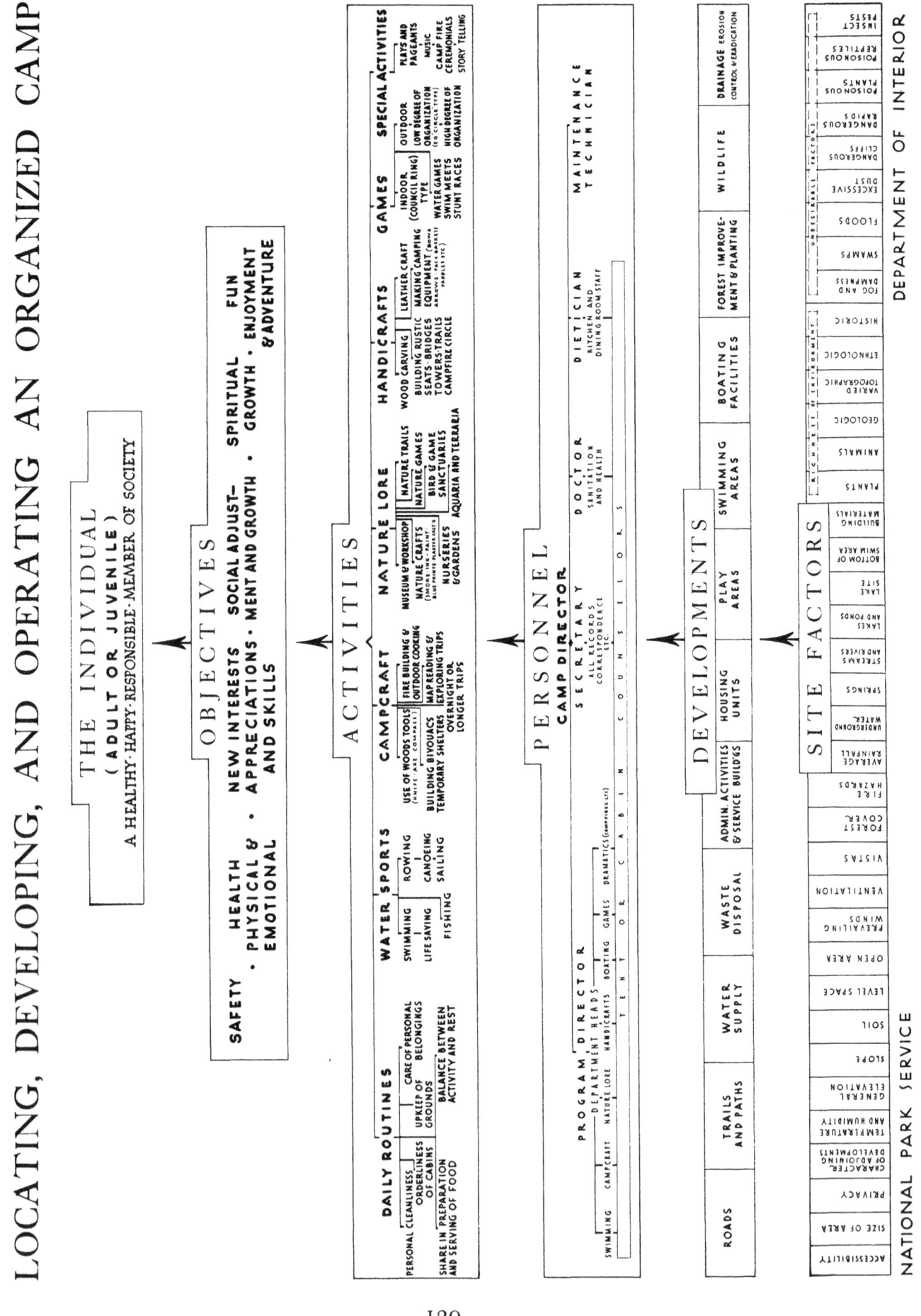

NATIONAL PARK SERVICE — DEPARTMENT OF INTERIOR

CAMP ADMINISTRATION AND BASIC SERVICE FACILITIES

→» Basic SERVICE FACILITIES of a camp are those necessary structural items without which other construction, more apparently identified with the feeding, housing, and recreational pursuits of the campers, could not function properly and ought not to be undertaken. In large part these are the camp counterparts of the public utilities and services of any community. The camp office or administration building is in a sense the "town hall" of the camp village—the point of control. The fact that it is the first building reached on entering a properly planned camp will serve as the logic for discussing it before other structures.

Office space requirements in the typical camp are not great. The administration building should provide a private office for the camp director and an ante room with space for files and desk for a secretary or clerk. In very large and very completely staffed camps there may be need for office space for an assistant director, program director, and additional clerical help. Bookshelves, a storage closet for office supplies, and a public telephone booth might well be included. If not otherwise available within a short distance, a toilet and a drinking fountain should be provided. It is not good practice to combine living quarters and administrative space under one roof.

In a small camp the administrative function may be made a part of the dining lodge or the recreation building, but the kitchen noises of the one and the hub-bub of rainy day recreational activities of the other are likely to prove distracting.

It is logical to incorporate in the administration building the canteen, trading post, or camp store as it is variously called. The combination may be said to be usual. Since the camp store is customarily open only for scheduled short periods, its association with the administrative function makes it possible for one individual to assume the duties of storekeeper along with those of administrative clerk or secretary. Equipment of the camp store should include shelves, counters, and a storage closet lined with one-quarter-inch galvanized wire mesh or otherwise rodentproofed. The store will require only a small space unless the camp is of the family type, and food is sold to the campers. Even in such an instance the stock will not be extensive except in some unorthodox operation of a family camp in which, no point of central feeding being provided, every family might be expected to prepare all its own meals.

A VERY BASIC NEED in the organized camp is the combined hot shower house and laundry. It is necessary in all camps to provide facilities for hot showers with soap. A soap scrub while swimming is not a substitute. As one health authority has put it, "The swimming place is not a proper place for soap baths unless it is a fast running stream, and a fast running stream is not a proper place for swimming." Because of the great cost of installing and maintaining a supply of hot water at many widely scattered points, it is not considered necessary to provide these facilities in every group of cabins. It involves no great hardship for the camper to go to the administration unit daily to launder his clothing and his person. It is important, however, to locate the central shower house and laundry so that its distance from any cabin group does not belie the designation "central."

It is economically practical wherever possible to include separate showers and toilet rooms for the staff, for employes, and for visitors in the same building which houses the campers' showers and laundry facilities. This multiple functioning will further incline the camp planner to locate the hot shower and laundry building so that it will be readily convenient to the living and working quarters of staff members and employes. Since all these points are centrally, if properly, located with respect to the entire camp, the desirable central location for the shower and laundry building seems almost to be guaranteed.

Naturally, in very large camps or where conditions force distances between units greatly in excess of the ideal, it will be expedient to build more than one shower house. In family and co-recreational camps it will be necessary to have either two such buildings or one in which the required duplicating facilities are properly separated. The question whether to provide showers in private stalls or a battery of open showers for women and girls remains an open discussion, with the trend probably toward gang showers. Where it is concluded to provide open showers generally, it is suggested that one be enclosed with its private dressing room.

Showers should be provided in the ratio of one to eight or fewer campers. In figuring the number of showers, the largest number of campers in any one unit may be taken as a base, for it is possible to schedule the use of the showers so that but one unit uses them at a time. The floors of the shower room and dressing room should be of cement, compacted and troweled to a smooth, polished surface that can be kept spotlessly clean. A cement base six inches or eight inches high around these rooms will do much to retard the deterioration of walls of wood.

A disinfecting footbath, depressed in the cement floor within the doorway through which the bathers must pass in leaving the shower room, has a useful purpose. It does not function automatically, however, and where evidence of a fixed determination to keep the device clean and conditioned is lacking, it is perhaps as well to omit it entirely.

The shower and laundry building should have a hot water storage tank and heater of ample size, and should provide space for fuel storage. Tank, heater, and fuel supply are best housed in a separate room, in which supplies might also be kept; an alternative location is the laundry room.

A double laundry tub is probably sufficient equipment in the laundry of a camp occupied by restricted age groups. In a family camp, however, more laundering will be done by the campers, and two or three double trays will be required. If the men's and women's showers for a family camp are in separate buildings, the laundry equipment will be mainly useful in the women's shower building, although there will be purpose in installing one set of trays in the men's building, placed in a corner of the dressing room.

It is important to have shower and laundry buildings completely screened against insects.

A WASHHOUSE AND LATRINE building is an essential basic service facility for each group of sleeping cabins. Just as the hot shower house and laundry building should be central to the several cabin groups, so should the location of the unit washhouse and latrine avoid favoring some cabins to the disadvantage of other cabins of the unit. In children's camps no sleeping cabin should be more than 150 feet distant from the latrine. Even in camps serving adults a greater distance is objectionable, although sometimes unavoidable owing to site conditions and spacing for privacy.

By all means should a system of sanitation that provides flush toilets and a positive disposal of sewage by natural processes be adopted wherever possible. There is strong prejudice against sewage treatment by chemical processes alone due to the uncertainty of accurate control. The National Park Service Engineering Manual, Part 700—Sewage Disposal, will be found a valuable reference for its detailed consideration of sanitation with respect to parks and campsites.

In cases, and it is hoped these will be few, where flush toilets and a proper system of sewage disposal are out of the question for reasons of economy or other considerations, the alternative pit privies should be the best it is possible to devise, and be unremittingly maintained. When pit privies must be resorted to, these and the washhouse must be separate structures. Although flush toilets and facilities for washing, on the contrary, may be housed under one roof, it becomes necessary to have pit latrines of temporary character auxiliary to the flush toilet equipment of camps scheduled for winter use.

The combined washhouse and latrine serving a cabin group is desirably made a partially enclosed structure. One end is merely roofed over to shelter the wash basins or troughs, the other end is enclosed to house the toilets in stalls. It is well to devise a line of least resistance for the campers by adopting a plan arrangement that leads the campers past the wash basins or troughs as they leave the toilet stalls. A theory that campers will walk around the end of a building to clean up is not borne out by experience.

A concrete floor, or one of stone on concrete base, is important both for the washing "porch" and for the toilet stalls. A mere earth or gravel-filled floor surrounding the basins can become a most insanitary wallow when the sloshings and spurtings of exuberant youth on the loose are added to a normal splash and wastage of water. Ordinarily showers are not needed in the unit washhouse, if the central shower house equipment is of proper capacity. Cold showers only will be supplied in the unit washhouse, if showers are provided there at all.

An arrangement for washing in running water is the more desirable, because it is the more sanitary. Lavatories, or faucets in connection with a trough lavatory, should be in the ratio of one to eight campers. But this is a wasteful system, and if the water supply is limited or must be pumped at great cost, hand basins must sometimes be used for reasons of economy. A hand basin used in common can carry and spread infections and belongs in the same class with common drinking cup or common towel. In camps where water must be conserved, individual hand basins for every camper are the only tolerable substitute for running water.

Toilets should be provided in the ratio of one to ten campers. The privacy of toilet enclosure stalls equipped with doors is recommended. Urinals, if installed at all, should be a type that extends to the floor, because of the difficulty of keeping other types and their surroundings in a sanitary condition.

For camp units which house both sexes, it is of course obvious that the facilities here under discussion must be arranged differently than in the unit washhouse and latrine just described. Where flush toilets are possible, a single building will serve if the men's latrine and women's latrine sections are placed back-to-back and provided with entrances through wash "porches" placed at opposite ends of the building. With such an arrangement it is recommended that the wash basins or troughs be largely screened from view by lattice to afford more privacy. If toilets are of the pit privy type, two separate latrine structures are recommended, each with its detached, lattice-screened washhouse.

On the "must" list for all unit latrines or combined washhouse and latrine buildings is the complete insect screening of all toilet stalls. Particularly is it mandatory to screen effectively pit privy structures, to see to their maintenance in a clean and sanitary condition, and to resort to self-closing seat covers and any other devices which may be in the direction of preventing contamination being carried by flies, other insects, and animals.

THE INFIRMARY fills the need in every camp for a building in which to care for campers who become ill or injured or who may need isolation and rest. Its location should be removed far enough from the sleeping units and from points of noisy recreational activity to afford quiet, and near enough to the kitchen of the dining lodge to permit serving hot food from the kitchen to the infirmary conveniently. The structure should have a room which can be used as a dispensary where examinations may be made and minor injuries may be cared for. This dispensary or first aid room should be equipped with a sink, a closet, and shelves and cabinets for supplies and equipment.

There is seldom, if ever, need for a separate waiting room, for large groups of campers are practically never waiting for treatment. On the rare occasions when it may be necessary to have them come to the dispensary en masse for examination, they can await their turns out-of-doors. A bench or two on a porch outside the dispensary door will be useful in such situations.

Other space needs in the infirmary are a ward, an isolation room, a bathroom, and sleeping quarters for the doctor or nurse in charge. Recommended capacities are two beds for what has been termed the small camp, three for the medium-sized, and four for the large camp. In each case, the isolation room will accommodate one of these. It should be possible to place all beds, whether in a ward or in the isolation room, so that access may be had from both sides. Wards should be large enough to allow the spacing of beds with a distance of six feet between side rails and four feet between end rails. A plan arrangement that provides fairly direct entrance to the isolation room from the outside without the need to pass through any other rooms is always best.

The equipment of the bathroom will be the usual three fixtures—lavatory, toilet, and tub, a shower preferably over the tub. As it will be used by the doctor or nurse, and the patients as well, it is best to locate it centrally so that it is entered from a hall or passage.

The doctor's or nurse's sleeping room should contain not less than 100 square feet of floor area and should be supplied with a closet of ample size.

Important in the infirmary building are provisions for abundant sunlight and ventilation, a plentiful supply of hot water, some means for heating the rooms if conditions demand, and a positive screening throughout against insects.

Ideal arrangements for heating are a fireplace in the dispensary and a heater for the hot water tank so oversize that, when temperatures demand, this one source can also heat small hot water radiators in the ward and the isolation room. The hot water tank, heater, and fuel bin should be in a separate room, lined to be fire resistant and non-conductive of heat. A small door can be rigged in one wall of the heater room. This will permit taking advantage, in chilly weather, of the heat generated in the heater room. Preferably this would open into the hall or the bathroom.

VERY PATENTLY in the category of basic services or transplantations of urban utilities to the camp community are water supply, electric wiring, and incinerators. Drinking water should be brought to each of the units as well as to the administrative center. Bubblers should be installed at the unit washhouses and outdoor kitchens, and in the unit lodges if these and the outdoor kitchens are not joined. Bubblers are hardly short of essential, certainly very desirable, in the administration building, infirmary, recreation building, craft club, nature club, and the living quarters of staff members and employes. Water must, of course, be brought to the dining lodge, and will be a great convenience in the garage and for the washing out of garbage cans at the incinerator. Assuming flush toilets as equipment and one shower bath per camper per day as inescapable, a minimum of 50 gallons of water per camper per day is needed.

When electricity is within reach, the extent to which wiring should be provided in the organized camp is controversial. Few would argue to withhold its benefits from the administration unit, wherein it will lighten the kitchen tasks and constitute important equipment in the infirmary. Opinions differ as to whether it should be carried to the outlying units. While some would wire every building in camp as a matter of practical convenience, others would ban electricity from the units for the training and experience that campers acquire through contact with elemental processes. Overhead wiring is destructive of the illusion of wilderness; underground wiring, properly done, is expensive. It is the practice of young campers to retire early; this does not prevail among those camping as families. To generalize in arbitrary recommendation of flashlights or floodlights in the units would be foolhardy indeed. In each individual case the considerations cited, and others, deserve to be thoughtfully weighed.

The complete disposal of garbage and rubbish is mandatory in every camp, as in every other recreational area. The effective medium is an incinerator. Because the facilities serving camp and picnic ground are identical, the discussion and illustrations previously presented in the section "Incinerators" will not here be repeated. The proper location for the camp incinerator is one far enough distant from the campsite that the smoke and odors of combustion do not reach the camp. The direction of prevailing winds will be taken into account even though it results in the incinerator being less accessible. A small trash burner near the camp kitchen will be a convenience, and need not be an annoyance if used with discretion.

Another service structure desirable in a camp is a garage to shelter one or two cars and provide space for a workshop. Since this building does not differ from the garage built as a part of the service group on other recreational areas, it is unnecessary to repeat here verbal or graphic exposition of it. The camp garage can rate a classification as essential if it is made to serve a double purpose. It can be utilized for winter storage of equipment to include mattresses and bedding, if it is made rodent-proof; and if tightly built, it is a logical place for the fumigation of such equipment.

Plate III I–1   ⇶ CAMP ADMINISTRATION AND BASIC SERVICE FACILITIES

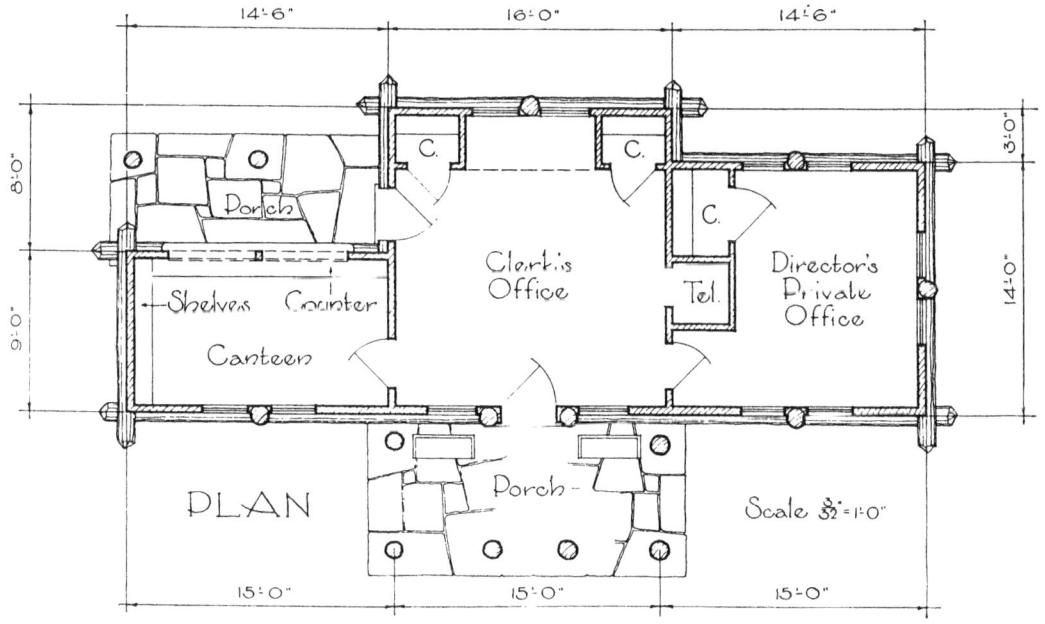

Administration Building, Raccoon Creek Recreational Demonstration Area, Pennsylvania

Among administration buildings serving organized camps, here is one that is planned particularly well, not only in the primary elements of the plan, but also in the ample closet space provided and the separate porch for the patrons of the canteen. The log construction combined with waney-edged siding, typical of the buildings at Raccoon Creek, is an unusual combination of materials.

125

CAMP ADMINISTRATION AND BASIC SERVICE FACILITIES   *Plate* III I–2

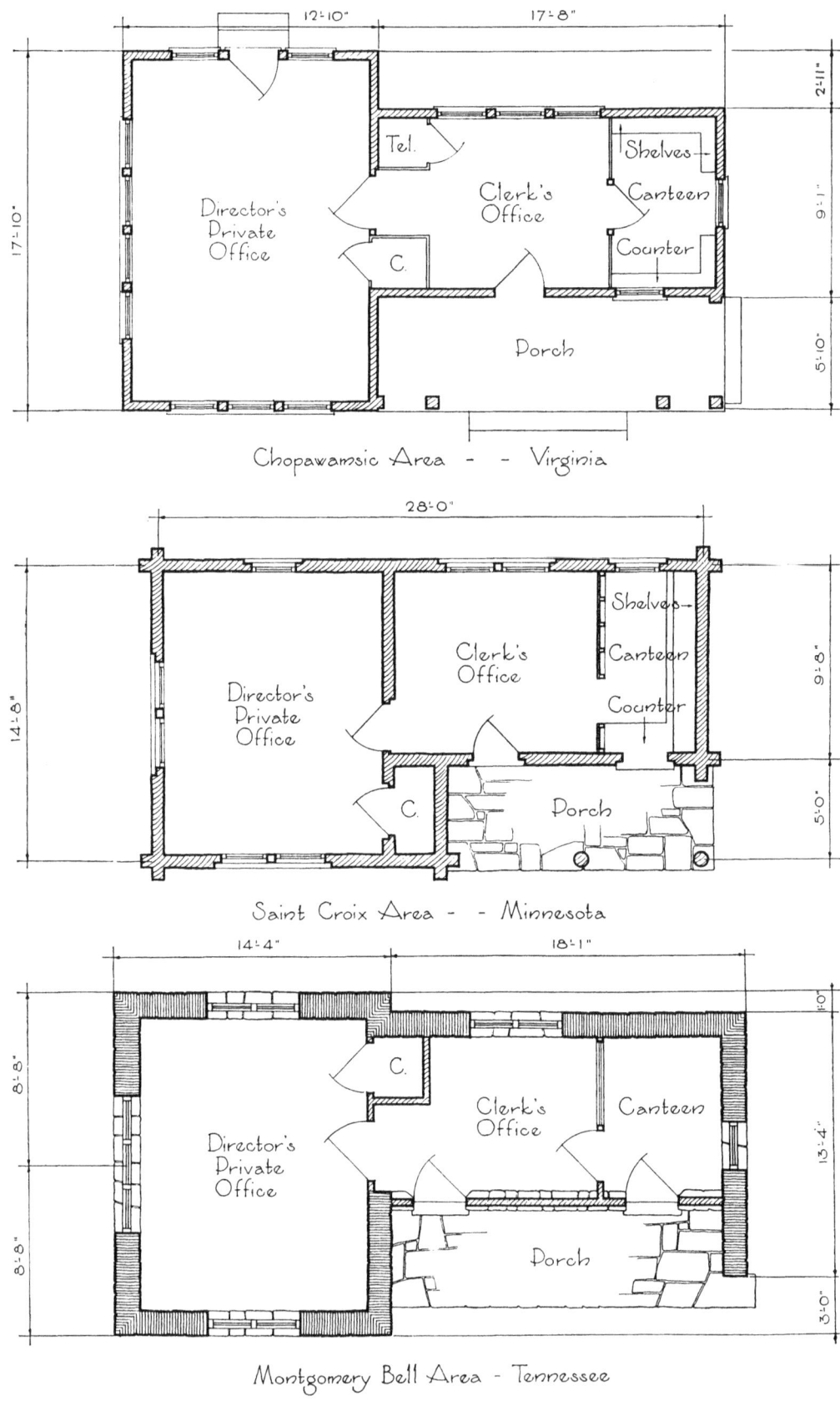

Chopawamsic Area – – Virginia

Saint Croix Area – – Minnesota

Montgomery Bell Area – Tennessee
Camp Administration Buildings
Scale ⅛"=1'-0"

Plate III I–3 ⋙ CAMP ADMINISTRATION AND BASIC SERVICE FACILITIES

All three administration buildings here grouped are of a modest size, adequate for organized camps up to a capacity of 100. All have uninspired similarity of plan because the interrelationship of the primary elements of the plan was made a condition of the problem. The combination of waney-edged siding cut in between clustered vertical boards at the corners of the building is typical of the Chopawamsic Area and gives its buildings a certain individuality.

Chopawamsic Recreational Demonstration Area, Virginia

In this little administration building fabricated of logs in the round, the central waiting room or clerk's office is flanked by the director's office at the one end and the trading post at the other, just as in the administration building above. There is added to some advantage, between the porch and canteen, an arrangement of shutters and counter over which the customers can make purchases during the hours the canteen is open for business.

St. Croix Recreational Demonstration Area, Minnesota

On this area the plan utilized in the two foregoing administration buildings is rendered in masonry, to a result that has a pleasing look of permanence. Like the building immediately above, this one offers canteen service directly to the porch over a counter that is reminiscent of a Dutch door. This makes it unnecessary for the canteen customers to enter the building to make their purchases.

Montgomery Bell Recreational Demonstration Area, Tennessee

CAMP ADMINISTRATION AND BASIC SERVICE FACILITIES

Plate III I-4

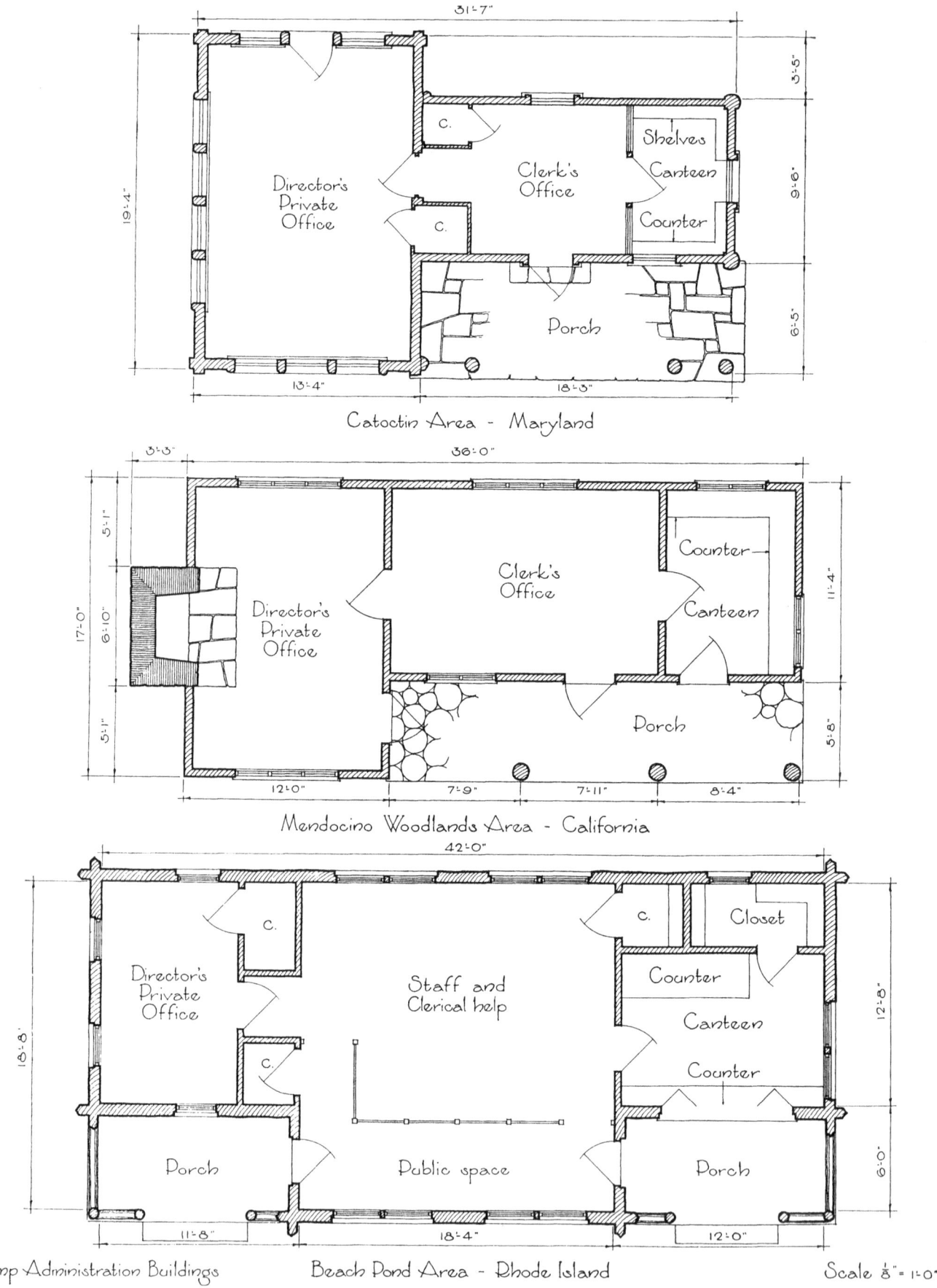

Catoctin Area - Maryland

Mendocino Woodlands Area - California

Camp Administration Buildings   Beach Pond Area - Rhode Island   Scale ⅛" = 1'-0"

Plate III I-5   →» CAMP ADMINISTRATION AND BASIC SERVICE FACILITIES

In plan, this building and the one directly below follow closely the typical arrangement represented by the administration buildings on the preceding page. For a minimum staffing it is almost the rule to incorporate the trading post in the administration building. Inasmuch as the store is open only for a limited time each day, tending it can be a secondary duty of the camp clerk.

Catoctin Recreational Demonstration Area, Maryland

A fireplace, generally felt to be unnecessary in an administration building, makes an appearance in this example, doubtless a mere gesture toward the remote possibility of unusual weather. Closets unfortunately have been omitted, and there is always real need for these for storing records and supplies. In pursuance of a local custom, the porch is paved with wood blocks, roughly circular and cross sectionally cut from logs.

Mendocino Woodlands Recreational Demonstration Area, California

This administration building is ambitious beyond the ordinary and indicates an unusually complete administrative staffing. The several roomy closets and the porch solely for the use of canteen customers are good features. The disfiguring smokestack emerging from a window in the illustration is only temporary, being necessitated by winter use of the building as a construction office while the camp was being built.

Beach Pond Recreational Demonstration Area, Rhode Island

129

CAMP ADMINISTRATION AND BASIC SERVICE FACILITIES   Plate III I-6

Infirmary, Raccoon Creek Recreational Demonstration Area, Pennsylvania

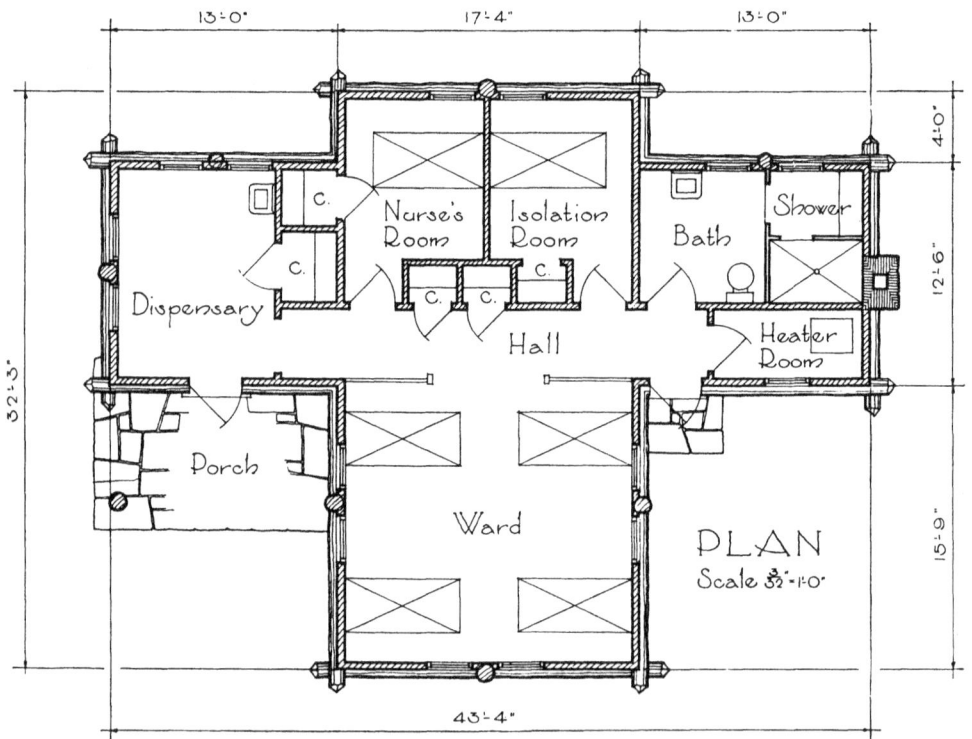

The typical construction at Raccoon Creek—salvaged telephone poles at the base and waney-edged siding above—has striking individuality. The hallway is too much a part of the ward, separated only by a low screen, and as a result the isolation room is not truly isolated. The condition would be much improved if the screen were made a full partition, perhaps largely of glass to give an adequately lighted hall. The windows of the nurse's room and the isolation room seem insufficient.

130

Plate III I-7   ⋙ CAMP ADMINISTRATION AND BASIC SERVICE FACILITIES

Infirmary, Chopawamsic Recreational Demonstration Area, Virginia

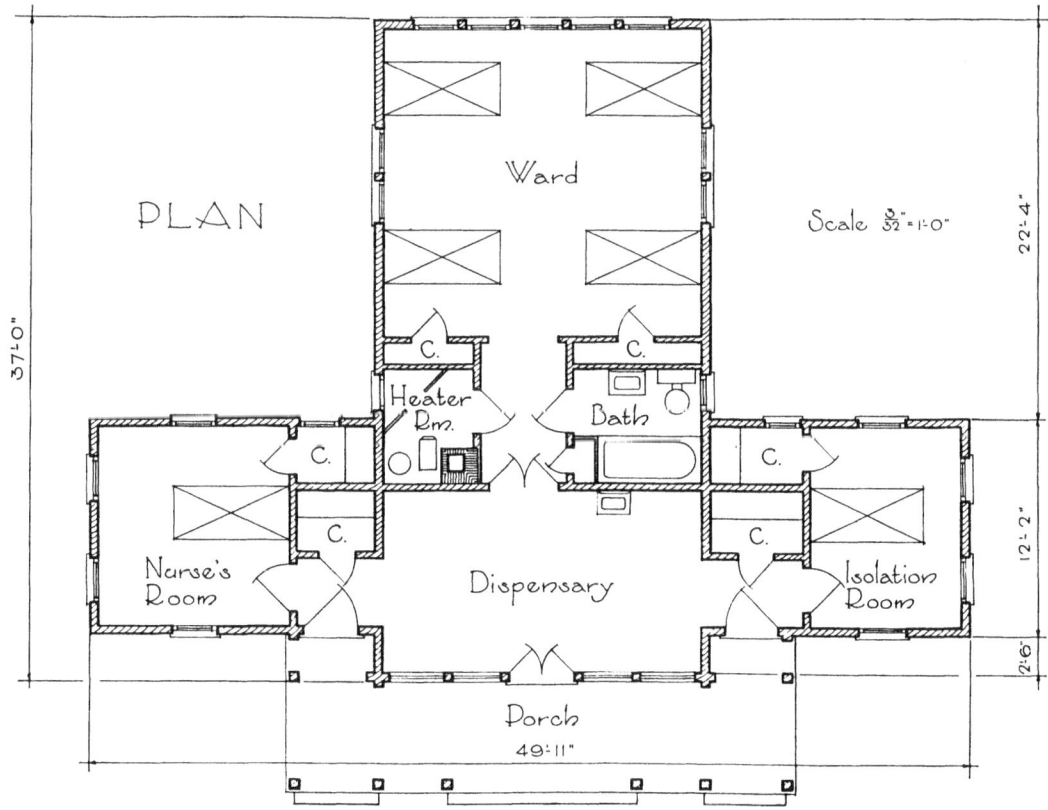

Once again the combination of vertical boards and waney-edged siding that distinguishes the buildings at Chopawamsic gives pleasing results. There is generous provision of closets. The ward, isolation room, and nurse's room are well supplied with windows, promising good light and ventilation.

131

CAMP ADMINISTRATION AND BASIC SERVICE FACILITIES Plate III I-8

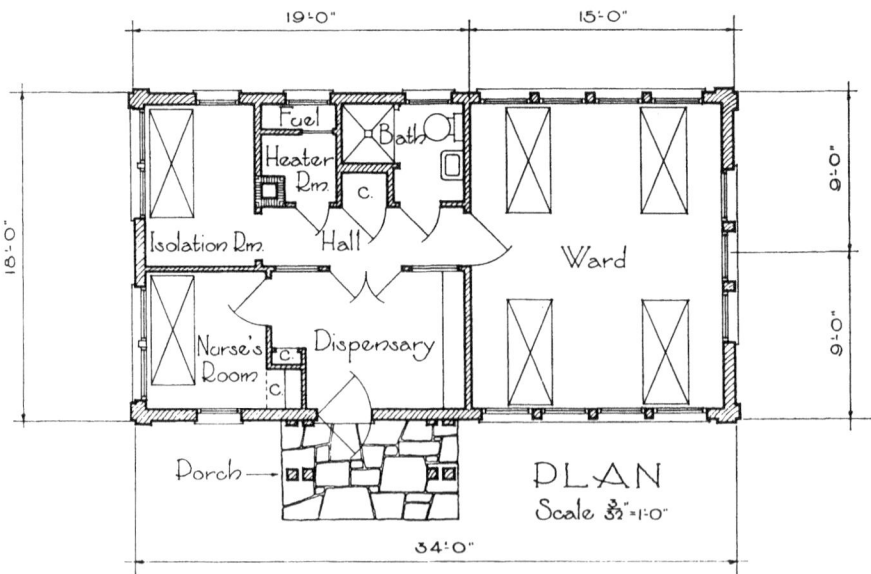

Infirmary, Yankee Springs Recreational Demonstration Area, Michigan

The single roof ridge made possible by the rectangular plan in turn produces a building less complicated and so less expensive to build than the infirmaries already pictured. All the rooms equipped with beds seem to have good natural light and ventilation, and the latter is augmented with a roof ridge ventilator. The interrelationship of the elements of plan is practical and compact.

Plate III I-9   ⋙ CAMP ADMINISTRATION AND BASIC SERVICE FACILITIES

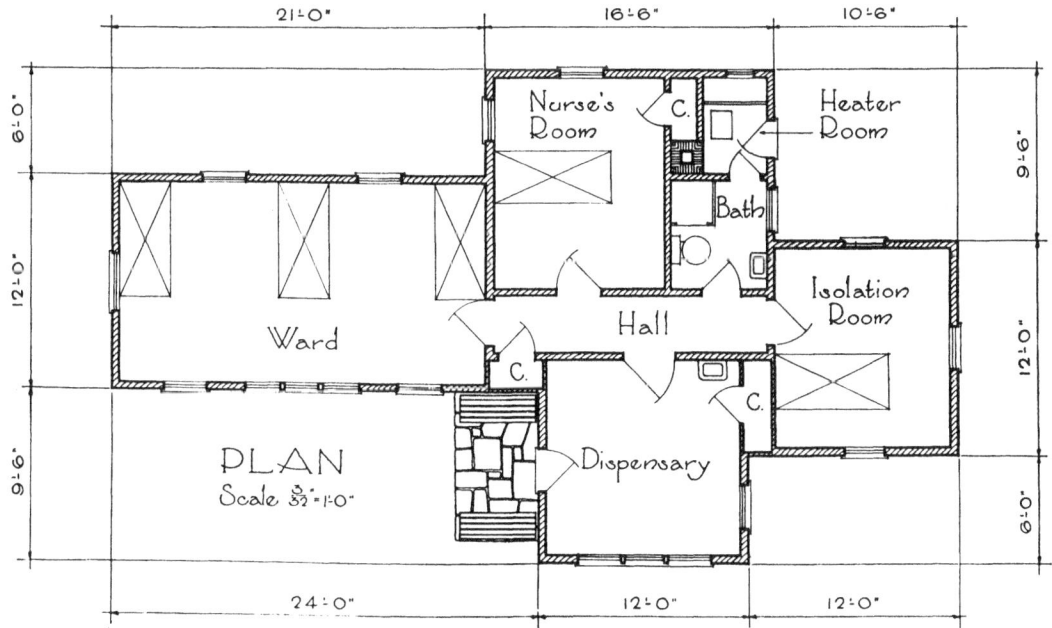

Infirmary, Hickory Run Recreational Demonstration Area, Pennsylvania

Ease of operation and plenty of light and ventilation are indicated by the plan here shown. The bed capacity of the ward in relation to the floor area of that room is somewhat extravagant. Furthermore, hospital beds placed in corners are inconvenient and short of ideal.

133

CAMP ADMINISTRATION AND BASIC SERVICE FACILITIES

Plate III I-10

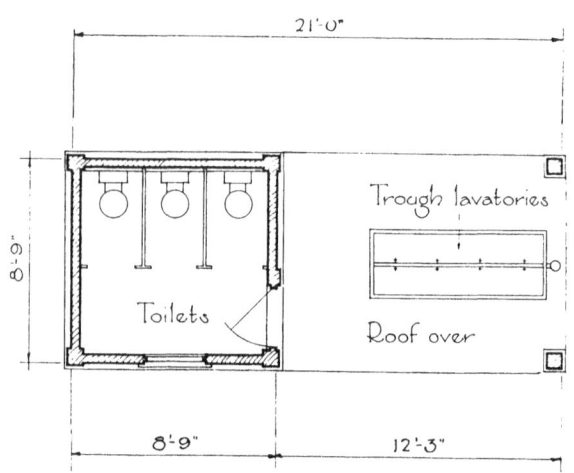

St. Croix River Area - Minnesota

Swift Creek Area - Virginia

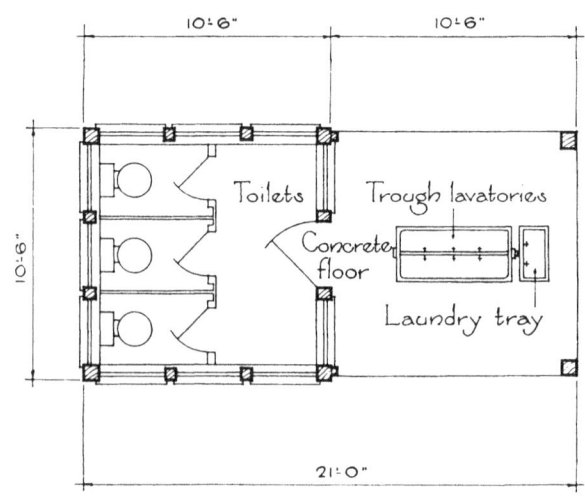 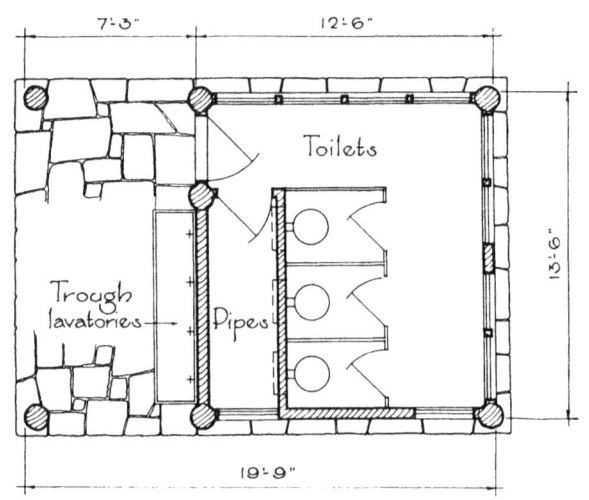

Kings Mountain Area - South Carolina

Lake Murray Area - Oklahoma

Camp Unit Latrines
Scale ⅛" = 1'-0"

Plate III I-11 ⇶ CAMP ADMINISTRATION AND BASIC SERVICE FACILITIES

St. Croix Recreational Demonstration Area, Minnesota

Swift Creek Recreational Demonstration Area, Virginia

UNIT LATRINES

Three of the four plans shown on the opposite page reveal a combination of enclosed toilet stalls and open wash porch which is almost typical of the unit latrine built in the cabin units of recreational demonstration camps. In the plan at upper right, the porch feature is omitted and the trough lavatories are housed in the enclosed structure along with the toilet fixtures. The latter arrangement makes for congestion that is avoided when the lavatories are in the open. Moreover "washing up" in camp has so long been an open-air operation that forcing it indoors amounts almost to violation of time-honored tradition. The dampness that naturally accumulates under foot around wash basins or lavatories used by groups dries up more quickly in the open, resulting in more sanitary surroundings than could prevail indoors unless mopping-up were frequent.

Kings Mountain Recreational Demonstration Area, South Carolina

Lake Murray Recreational Demonstration Area, Oklahoma

CAMP ADMINISTRATION AND BASIC SERVICE FACILITIES Plate III I-12

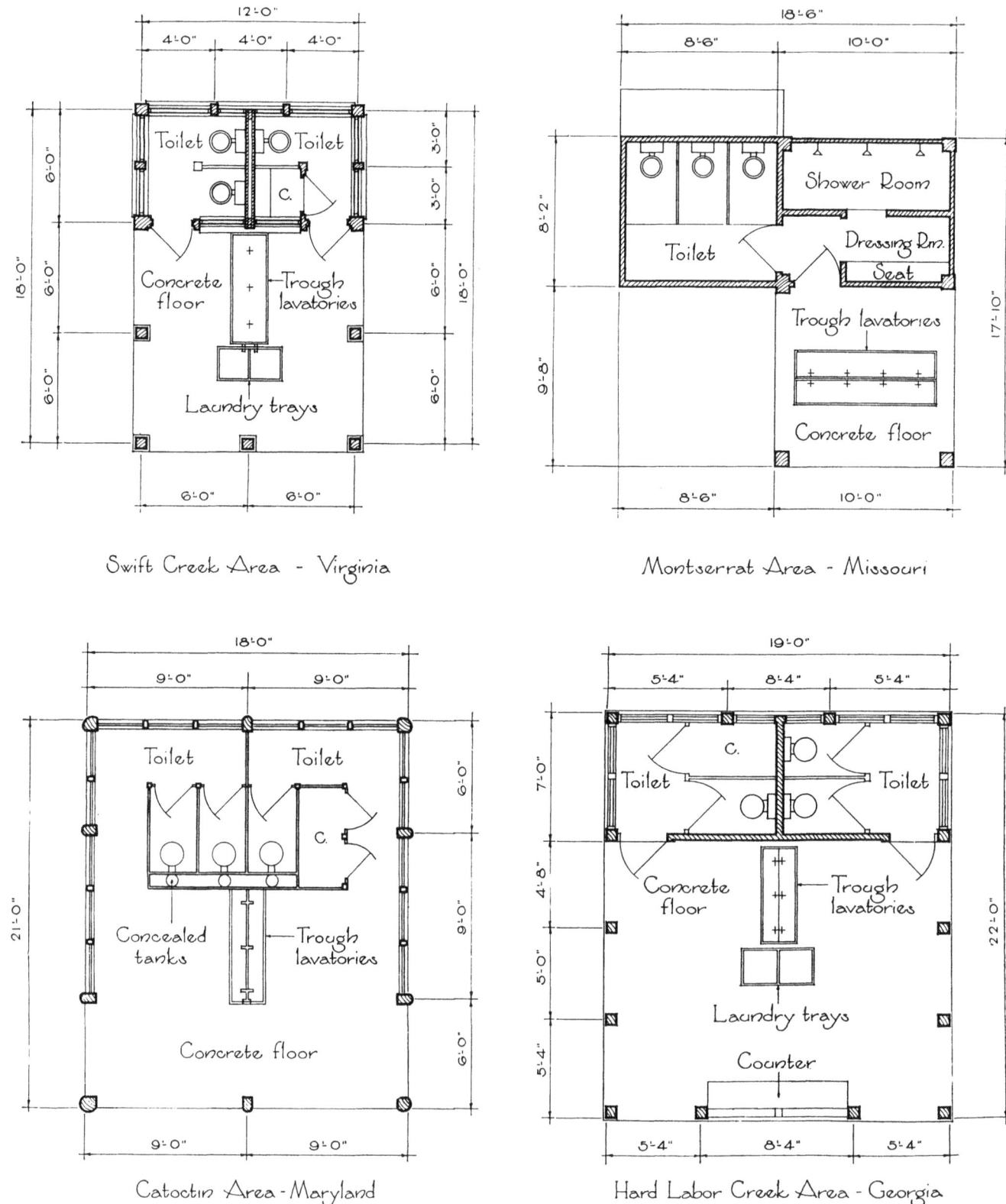

Camp Unit Latrines
Scale ⅛" = 1'-0"

Plate III I-15　　↠ CAMP ADMINISTRATION AND BASIC SERVICE FACILITIES

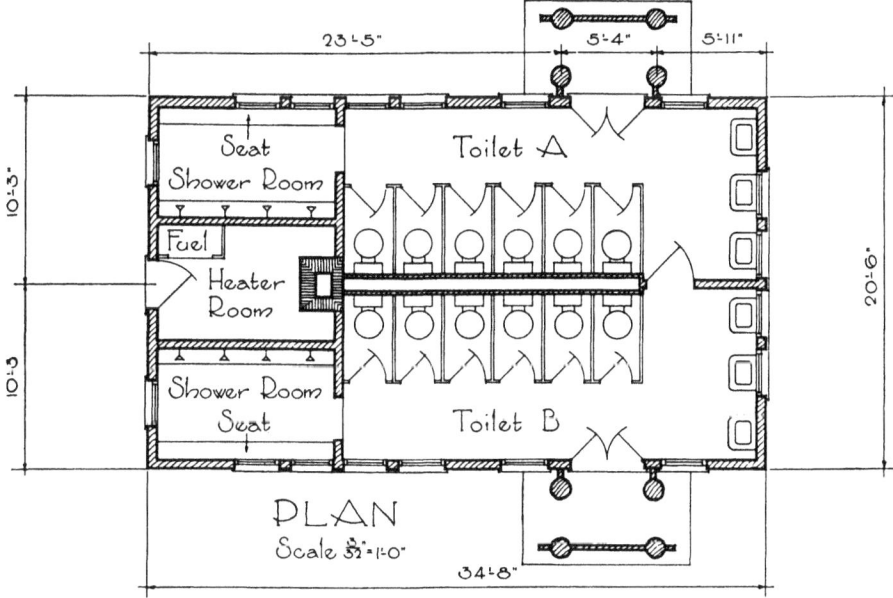

Central Washhouse and Toilet, Dunes State Park, Indiana

The use of this camp is much the same as the one at Pokagon—by youngsters for short camping periods, which call for little or no personal laundry work in camp. If a laundry were added at the shower end of the building, a very complete washhouse, shower, and laundry combination building, useful in a public campground or an organized family camp, would be created. Naturally the camping theory which produces concentrated toilet facilities is at variance with the theory of the unit camp which recommends unit latrines. The recall of the Indian tepee in the architecture is very clever.

139

CAMP ADMINISTRATION AND BASIC SERVICE FACILITIES

Plate III I-16

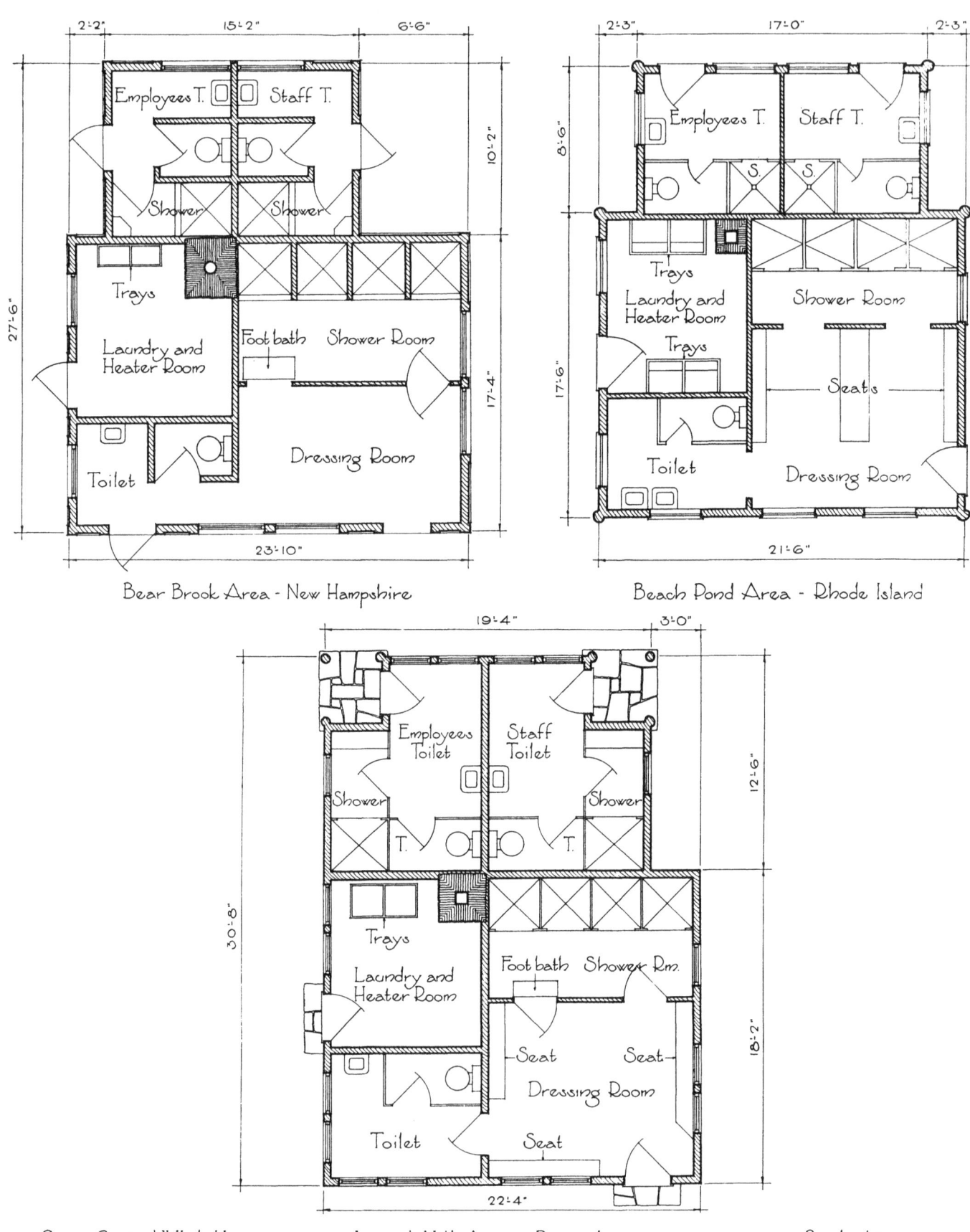

Camp Central Wash Houses

Plate III I-17   ⇶ CAMP ADMINISTRATION AND BASIC SERVICE FACILITIES

The plans of central washhouses on the facing page are alike in all but the more minor details. All are independent developments of one sketch plan issued to insure economy and logical relationships among the several separate uses linked in this somewhat complex dependency of a central unit of an organized camp.

Bear Brook Recreational Demonstration Area, New Hampshire

Assuming a boys' camp, the typical central shower and laundry building provides, first of all, a dressing room, shower room, and toilets for the campers and the male staff members and visitors. Other elements are a separate shower and toilet room for women staff members and visitors, a separate shower and toilet room for the help, and a laundry room. If the camp is occupied by girls, one of the separate shower and toilet rooms is then for male staff members and visitors.

Beach Pond Recreational Demonstration Area, Rhode Island

The minor variations in plan and the different exterior treatments presented by buildings which have evolved within identical, prescribed limits are always interesting. Predetermined floor areas and fixture arrangement, closely followed, permit little leeway. The variety produced in these three structures is surprising in the circumstances.

Laurel Hill Recreational Demonstration Area, Pennsylvania

CAMP ADMINISTRATION AND BASIC SERVICE FACILITIES ‹‹‹ *Plate* III I-18

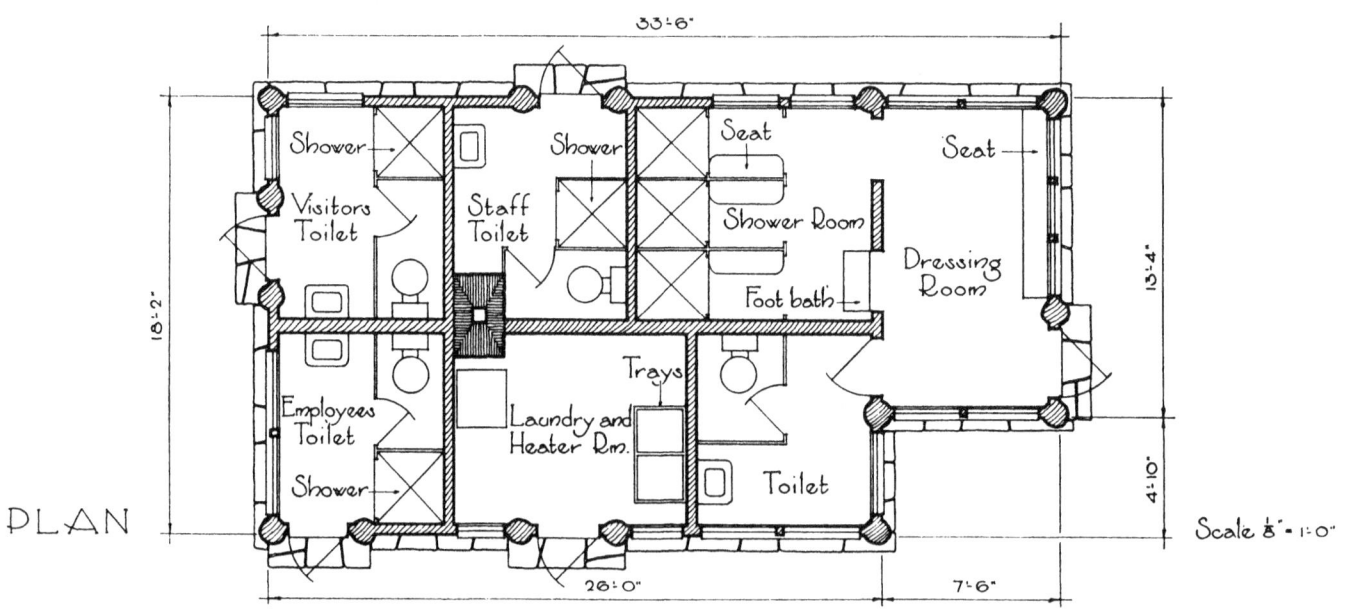

Central Washhouse and Laundry, Lake Murray Recreational Demonstration Area, Oklahoma

This example of a central shower and laundry building in the administration unit of an organized camp differs from similar structures grouped on the preceding page in that it adds a shower and toilet room for staff members and visitors of the same sex as the campers, separate from the facilities used by the campers themselves. The ridge ventilator has great practical purpose for a summer use structure housing a heating unit scaled to provide hot showers for an entire camp.

CAMP RECREATIONAL AND CULTURAL FACILITIES

CHIEF, and perhaps only, structures truly essential to the recreational and cultural program of camping are the accessories which contribute to safe swimming and indoor space for rainy day activities. Purposeful as are a campfire ring, craft shop or craft club, nature lore building or nature club, and water-front building, in the event of the omission of any or all of these, the unit lodge can take over many of their functions without the sacrifice of the major objectives of a worth while camp program.

As has been said, the unit lodge is the rallying point of a camp unit. It has recreational, social, educational, and cultural purpose. It is the common living room or clubroom of the campers who make up the unit, and if joined with an outdoor kitchen—a recommended practice—it can serve as their dining room as well.

In size the unit lodge should allow about 20 square feet for each camper of the group. A room 20 feet wide and 30 feet long has convenient proportions. As with most structures for campers' use, the fireplace is its most important feature and should be of generous size. Closet and cupboard space will be useful for the storage of equipment at all seasons.

For the bearing it has on construction details, thoughtful consideration should be given to the likelihood of winter use of a unit lodge. In that prospect, for instance, it is well to provide in the chimney an extra flue and thimble for connecting a stove for both cooking and auxiliary heating purposes. Projected winter use will also suggest a lower and flatter roof so that the lodge can be more easily heated. It will also lead to the substitution of glazed sash of limited extent in place of the more generous screened openings and batten winter closures recommended for unit lodges planned for summer use exclusively. For comfort in winter occupancy, the higher insulating value of a grade of construction better than required for strictly summer use is advisable.

If the full potentialities of the unit lodge are to be realized, a simple outdoor kitchen shelter, where meals can be prepared, must be erected nearby or, better still, attached to it. The latter arrangement permits one chimney to do double duty and will prove its superior convenience on rainy days. Experienced camping groups may essay to cook all their meals in the outdoor kitchen. Others may use it on occasion for practice cooking or the novelty of preparing a meal or two, on their own. When the camp is not entirely occupied, the outdoor kitchen combined with the unit lodge functioning as a dining room makes possible and practical the operating of units as independent camps accommodating small groups.

It is recommended that the kitchen, if joined to the unit lodge, be open on three sides; if entirely detached, then open on all four sides. The stove should be of masonry of the campstove pattern, built integrally with the masonry chimney. Its iron top, preferably a casting, should be solid, from front to its intersection with the face of the chimney, and should be at a convenient working height. Grills and any perforations or openings in the stove top which would allow smoke to collect within the shelter are to be avoided, likewise removable lids like those of a coal range, which are too easily mislaid or otherwise lost. Control of draft either by a damper in the flue or by a readily adjustable fueling door should be provided.

Needed structural equipment for the outdoor kitchen further includes cupboards for storing utensils and dishes, an ice box, and storage place for food protected against animals and insects. Drinking water should be available at a bubbler and also at a tap where pails and other vessels may be filled.

Generally speaking, the small recreational building of each cabin colony in the form of the unit lodge, as described, will eliminate the need for a large recreation building in the administrative

CAMP RECREATIONAL AND CULTURAL FACILITIES

group. Particularly is this true if the dining lodge is readily convertible and roomy enough for mass recreational activity, and if not too many such demands are made on it. Without the network of unit lodges to take the brunt of enforced indoor activity in bad weather, the taking over of the dining lodge for every minor indoor recreational need would indeed be a disruptive practice, and a central recreation building would become a necessity. While in a choice between a chain of unit lodges and a central recreation building, the former is thought to be better camping practice, some camp planners, for good and sufficient reasons (lack of funds probably a potent first), will elect to build the central facility instead. It should not be assumed that a camp having both a central recreation building and a chain of supplementing unit recreation buildings is necessarily ideally equipped—too many facilities for indoor events may interfere with the realization of a desirably complete outdoor program.

The ideal, if seldom economically supportable, central recreation building will allow from 15 to 20 square feet per camper. It will feature a generous fireplace, perhaps more than one. The main recreation room will have a portable or permanent stage for amateur entertainments and will be arranged so that dressing rooms, if not actually a part of the building, can be supplied by tents temporarily erected outside advantageously located stage exits and entrances. A wide veranda will contribute greatly to the general usefulness of the structure, and an alcove or separate room for reading and writing, equipped with bookshelves and writing tables, will be another important element. The main recreation room will have tables for ping-pong and other games, and benches and other seating furniture suitable to its varied uses. Ample storage space for equipment items that need to be stowed away when the building is appropriated for special events will not be overlooked.

IT CANNOT BE DENIED, with swimming almost the reason for being of most camps, that insuring safety in the water-front area, insofar as lay-out and structural appurtenances can effect this, is the first and foremost demand upon planners of camp recreational facilities. Stating objectives broadly, water-front development should create a confined, safe operating range for beginners and nonswimmers, facilitate their instruction, and provide for the more varied, less restricted, but still safeguarded, activities of experienced swimmers.

Probably the ideal development of a swimming beach is an H-shaped dock, the upright strokes of the letter at right angles to the shore line. Within the shoreward hollow of the H, beginners' flounderings and founderings are confined, and instruction is given. Herein the water should not exceed a depth of four feet. The outer hollow is the sports arena of the true swimmers, and within this area the water is desirably not over seven feet deep. At the ends of the piers the diving boards are installed, where, for high diving, water nine feet deep is necessary.

The many advantages in the H-dock will be quickly sensed. Not the least of these are definitely prescribed limits of water-front for swimming activities which tend to restrain the rash and unwary from venturing beyond the bounds of rescue. Another very real advantage is that boats, where boating is also a camp activity, may be moored outside the piers and kept completely away from the swimmers. The operation of boats within swimming areas, irrespective of the skill and cautiousness of the operators, is a hazard which will not be tolerated in a well-supervised camp.

There are other forms for the swimming dock—T-shaped, L-shaped, and others, but none scores with so many telling advantages as does the H-plan. Regardless of the form adopted, the construction of the dock should be such that there is no chance for campers, diving or swimming under water, to be trapped beneath it. This may be accomplished, where the water level is not widely fluctuating, by building the dock level high enough above the water level to insure "breathing space" between them at all times. Elsewhere barriers of wood piling, heavy wire fencing, or something equally effective, to keep swimmers from getting under the dock, become a necessary part of the substructure and should extend to the bottom. The substructure should be of substantial construction which anticipates and gives promise of surviving ice conditions of the locality. The timbers under water should be heavily creosoted.

CAMP RECREATIONAL AND CULTURAL FACILITIES

There are water-front situations in which a sharply sloping beach, mucky bottom, swift current, or other unfavorable condition will dictate the building of a swimming crib—a floating swimming pool—for the instruction of beginners. The crib is of cross-planked cratelike construction, the spaces between the planks permitting active circulation of water yet narrow enough that there is no chance of a foot getting between the planks and being wedged there. Pockets built in the ends of the crib, weighted with rocks, make it possible to float the crib at the desired level. By building it in sections, bolted together, a crib 80 feet long and 35 feet wide is practicable. Structural members, of course, must be scaled to its over-all size and to affecting conditions such as current and ice conditions. Damage by the latter can only be effectively circumvented where winters are so truly mild that ice normally occurring qualifies as a film rather than anything more formidable. Projected for cold climates, the crib should be so contrived that its superstructure can be readily removed in sections and hauled ashore for the winter months, and the substructure prayerfully weighted down in deep water in the hope it may escape damage by ice. Crib construction should have the preservative benefits of thorough creosoting for submerged parts and painting for the parts above water.

The provision of diving boards is nothing to be undertaken in an offhand manner. There are definite and easily obtained standards for this equipment item governing the pitch and overhang of the board, its dimensions, distance above the water, the clamping device, and other equally important details. Experimental and makeshift departures from generally accepted diving board standards are unwarranted, even dangerous. It is decidedly unfair to campers bent on learning to do something well, to start them off disadvantaged by nonconforming equipment.

The only satisfactory location for diving boards is a fixed structure. Diving boards on floats are hazardous. The behavior of a float in rough weather is unpredictable, and painful accidents to divers can result. It is also possible for a swimmer to come up under a float and be trapped there. In consequence, even though it becomes necessary to resort to a rock crib construction, diving boards should be on fixed structures.

There are a number of water-front accessories, minor as structures, but important to the safety of the swimming area. One is an elevated seat from which a guard can observe all swimmers and quickly speed to the rescue of any who get into difficulties. Other items are rescue and safety equipment—always life rings hanging on racks ready for instant use, life lines, and resting floats, and, if the site conditions warrant, life boats. There should be no shortage of ladders up which to climb from the water to the dock. Trivial structurally as ladders are, the scarce provision of them in many outdoor swimming set-ups is shocking. Wherever swimmers must tread water awaiting their turns to clamor up a ladder, the planning of facilities is under the cloud of criminal negligence.

Where there is neither lake nor dammed stream to afford swimming for the organized camp, the man-made formal swimming pool is the alternative to be undertaken. It will differ not at all from the swimming pool in any outdoor location, thorough information on which is available from so many sources that there is no obligation to discuss it here. Let it suffice here to urge upon camp planners that, where the swimming pool is a required structure, the most authoritative recommendations be not slighted.

CONSIDERATION of camp recreational and cultural structures and facilities now tapers off to embrace those generally held desirable but less than essential. The recreation building in the administrative group has been mentioned as thus classifiable except when, by reason of the omission of recreational facilities from the units, it becomes a truly essential structure.

In the typical organized camp, dressing for swimming can be done in the sleeping cabins, and no water-front construction in provision of dressing rooms is considered to be necessary. There will only be purpose in a water-front building if boating is a camp activity. Then it will be a boat storage building divorced from the bathing area. It will be sized to berth the boats belonging to the camp and will have storage space for paddles, oars, and such accessory boating gear. Perhaps it will have an incline to the water, with cleats for a foothold in hauling in boats. In some instances a landing pier adjoining the boathouse may be desirable. The water-front building may advantageously include winter storage space for some of the bathing beach equipment such as life rings and resting floats. It is a structure that cannot be reduced to a typical lay-out, being affected more than any other camp building by special considerations of site and program. Foundations that will withstand severe ice conditions are important.

Naturally, if the facility for swimming is a treated pool, preparatory shower baths will be required of all who enter it. In that situation the central shower house will logically be located near the swimming pool, its size increased to provide a roomier dressing space and more shower heads.

WORK IN THE CRAFTS is an activity in organized camps of all kinds. With some campers craft interest is merely a rainy day matter; with those of creative bent it is a thrilling pursuit that cannot be made to wait on unfavorable weather. The structure which houses these activities is termed a craft shop, or craft club, and among the interests possible are carpentry, leather work, the graphic arts, metal work, weaving, printing, and photography. The building is normally a simple structure with plenty of light a first requirement. Its equipment will include work benches and tables, shelves, cupboards, even individual lockers for tools, materials, and work in progress. A sink with running water is necessary; a fireplace is desirable. The variety of the craft program will dictate the extent of the other equipment, but a loom, a small forge, a photographic dark room, a potter's wheel, and a small printing press are among the many possibilities. It is recommended that the craft and nature buildings be located in the same general vicinity but not joined under one roof. The often noisy and untidy creative activities will be likely to disturb the more contemplative research of the nature groups.

It has been found to be good practice to place the craft and nature buildings so that they will be passed by the campers in the day's routine travel. Young people, particularly, will not be inclined to seek out these facilities when located off the beaten track, yet their indifference can be broken down, and an enthusiasm can be created, if they are given opportunities for frequent and casual observation of the interest of fellow campers in craft and nature hobbies.

WHAT IT IS CHOSEN herein to christen the nature club is a facility long-provided and variously designated in camps. The terms "museum" and "nature museum" somehow suggest eternally suspended animation, whereas the place, functioning as it should, is one of lively activity. "Nature lore building" seems to carry threat of an innocuous bedtime story approach to the facts of Nature from which sophisticated modern youth will instinctively back away, and more power to him! "Nature hall" has scholastic and World's Fair connotations which make this term not exactly fitting. These names and less used others for one or another reason seeming less than apt, it is here elected to send up a trial balloon for "nature club" as suitably descriptive.

It is the rendezvous of the nature-minded, present and potential, among the campers. It may contain permanent collections of natural objects identified with the locality, but its more important purpose is to serve as a working museum—a combination laboratory-classroom-library for the campers of an inquiring turn of mind in the realm of Nature. Structurally, it will probably consist of a large exhibition-workroom and a small office-laboratory for the nature counselor in charge. It will be well-lighted and equipped with shelves and cases for display, work tables, bookshelves, cupboards for storage, and a sink with running water. Very desirably a wild flower garden, perhaps a vivarium or aquarium, will adjoin it, and it will be the starting point of a nature trail. The building will be expressive of its purpose if it is linked with the out-of-doors by large openings that give vistas into the surroundings and by the use of materials patently native to the locality.

THE COUNCIL CIRCLE, or council ring, only fails of classification as essential in organized camps, for the reason that, in the initial absence of any such facility, persistent need will eventually bring into being a makeshift substitute. The makeshift may serve very well, or not, depending on terrain and other considerations of locale.

The ideal camp council circle will be remote from the camp, at least 1,000 feet from the nearest building. It will be in a secluded spot, wooded if possible, without distracting vistas, and free of disturbing influences. The location must be such that a cleared circular plot, smooth and practically level, of 24- to 30-foot diameter, can be ringed in by the front row of seats. Seating will be benches with low backs. When there is need for a second and third row of seats, each should be elevated slightly above the row immediately in front. The leader's seat, as the focal point, may well be differentiated from the general seating by a higher back. It is fine if a large tree or rock can furnish a background. Entrances through the ring of seats should be few, preferably not more than two or three. The council circle of the organized camp differs from what is termed in some campgrounds a campfire circle, in that it lacks a pit or a fixed hearth ring of stones for the campfire. The enclosed space accommodates a campfire, of course, but is free of any construction which might interfere with the games, stunts, and rituals of the organized campers.

Success has not rewarded a search for a photograph of a council ring on the structural lines just described. Perhaps, after all, the council ring is what one camping expert, to whom appeal for a photograph was made, described it to be: "a group of people bound together by bonds of interest and appreciation around a fire"—something of the spirit rather than of structure. And if this is true, the tailpiece illustration, as the sole example here pictured, ably represents this facility.

CAMP RECREATIONAL AND CULTURAL FACILITIES

Plate III J–1

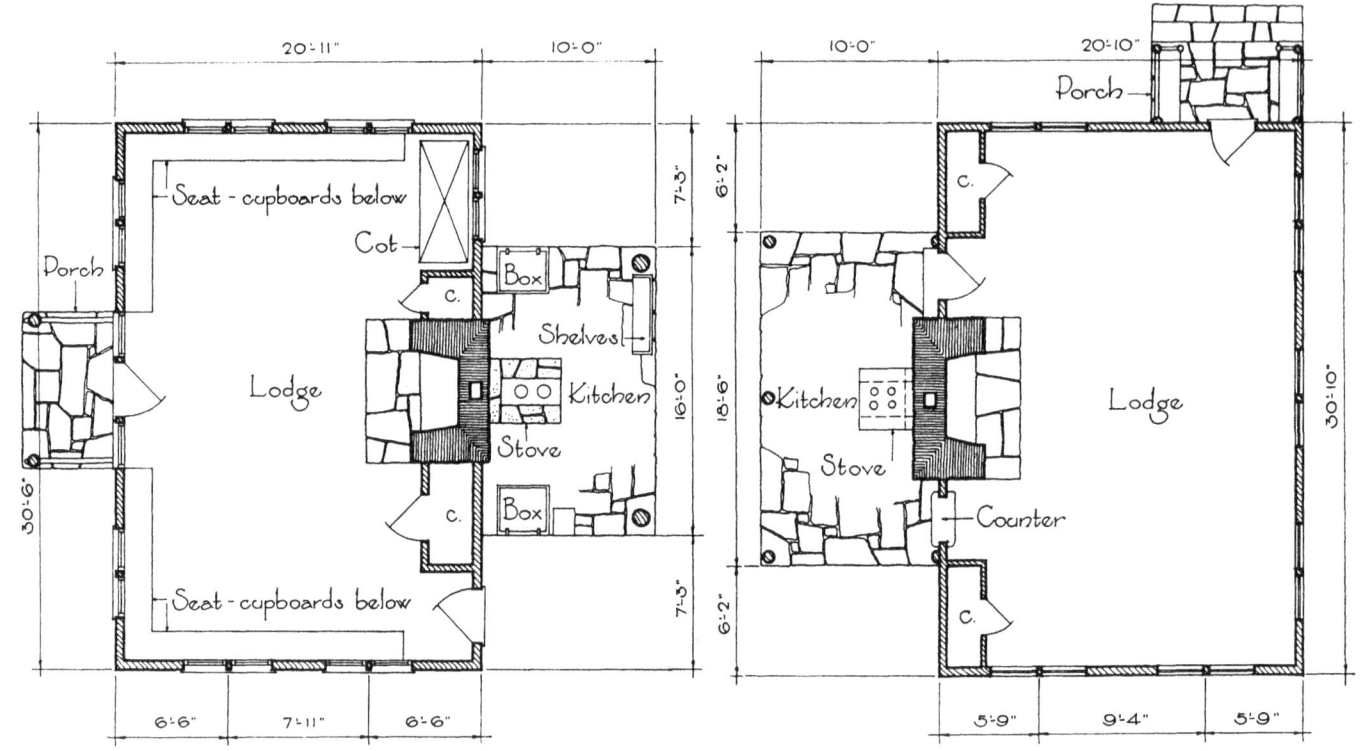

Otter Creek Area – Kentucky

Laurel Hill Area – Pennsylvania

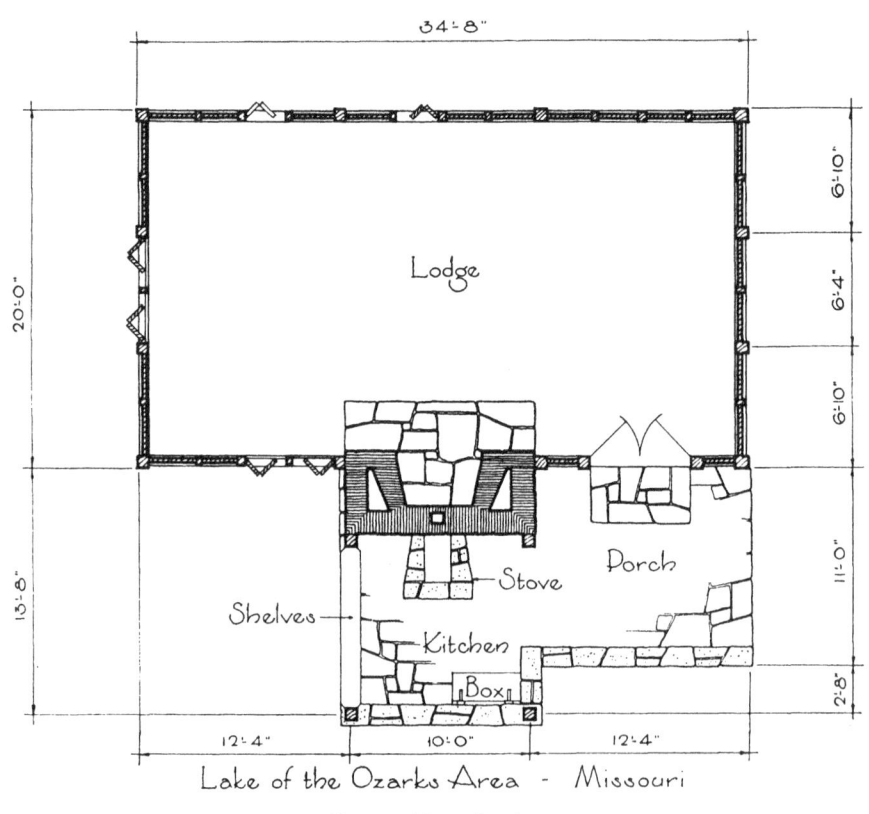

Lake of the Ozarks Area – Missouri

Camp Unit Lodges
Scale 3/32" = 1'-0"

Plate III J–2 →>> CAMP RECREATIONAL AND CULTURAL FACILITIES

The recommended unit lodge, which amounts to the community building of a unit of an organized camp, is produced by coupling an outdoor kitchen and an enclosed shelter. The unit, as a result, is made more self-contained, for in addition to furthering the recreational and educational activities of the small group, the unit lodge provides a place where the group can prepare and serve its own meals.

Otter Creek Recreational Demonstration Area, Kentucky

Linking an enclosed shelter and an outdoor kitchen to produce a unit lodge offers no great variety in plan arrangement. The kitchen porch may be either on the end or on the long side of the shelter. The latter arrangement prevails in the examples illustrated on this page and shown in plan opposite. Ordinarily there is another entrance to the lodge proper than the one which communicates with the kitchen.

Laurel Hill Recreational Demonstration Area, Pennsylvania

This subject differs from the two shown above in that its only entrance is by way of the kitchen. It is lacking in closet space much needed for the storage of equipment and supplies. Unfortunately, photographs made either before the buildings were occupied or out of the camping season fail to show such necessary equipment of the outdoor kitchen as an ice box and cupboards for provisions and utensils.

Lake of the Ozarks Recreational Demonstration Area, Missouri

CAMP RECREATIONAL AND CULTURAL FACILITIES   Plate III J-3

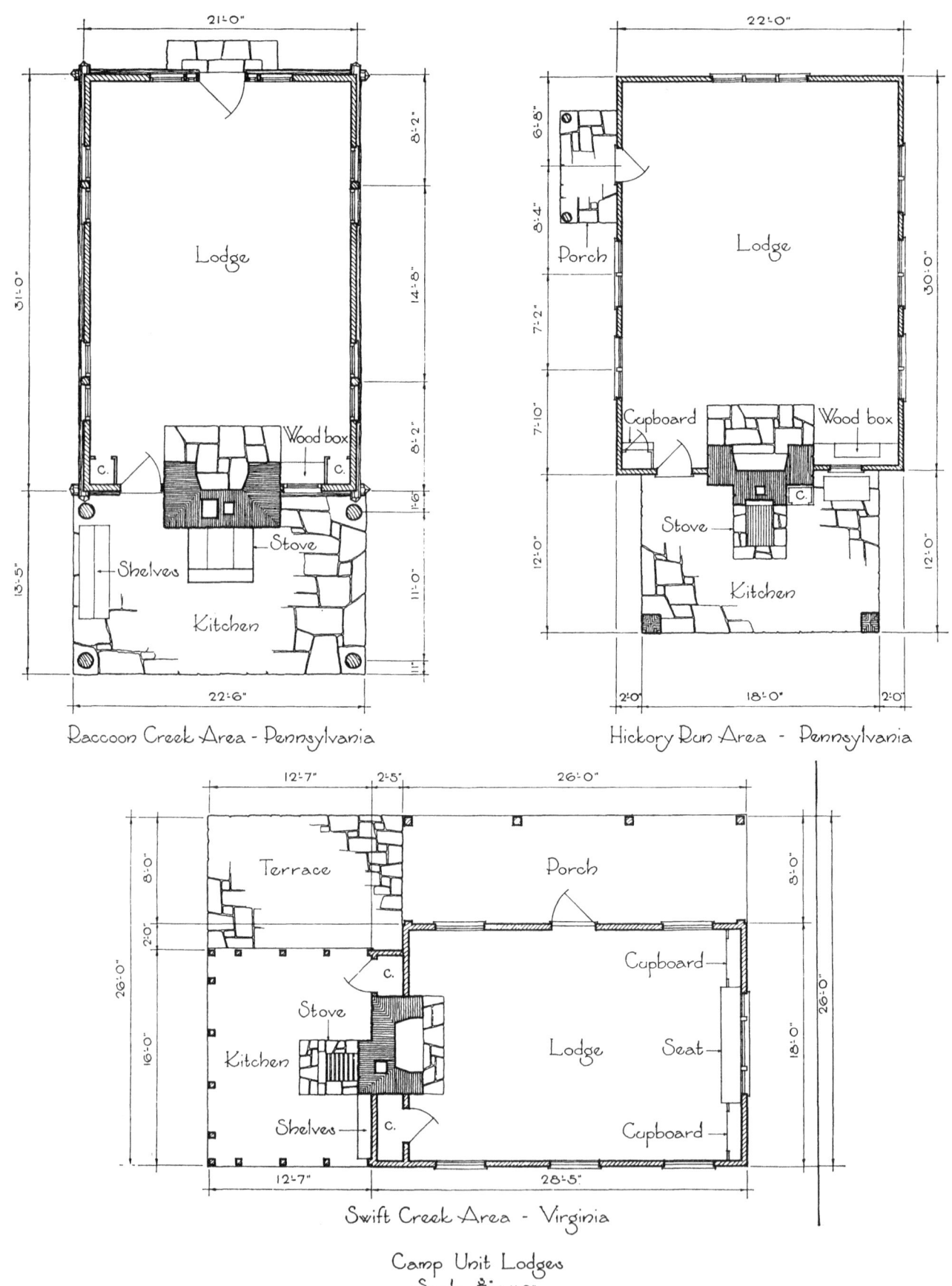

Raccoon Creek Area - Pennsylvania

Hickory Run Area - Pennsylvania

Swift Creek Area - Virginia

Camp Unit Lodges
Scale ⅛" = 1'-0"

Similarity of the unit lodges here grouped is the placing of the kitchens at the ends of the enclosed rooms. In this particular example, shown in plan at upper left opposite, there appears to be insufficient closet space for storage. The quality produced by combining logs and freehand-edged siding, the latter used even on the roof surfaces, is appropriately picturesque.

Raccoon Creek Recreational Demonstration Area, Pennsylvania

The materials used in this subject make for much more precise character than is found in the unit lodge at Raccoon Creek, illustrated above. The roof of the porch that shelters the outdoor kitchen is supported on stone piers and has an open truss of square timbers in the gable end. Again, more closet space would undoubtedly prove useful.

Hickory Run Recreational Demonstration Area, Pennsylvania

Besides the porch that is the outdoor kitchen of the unit lodge in organized camps on recreational demonstration areas, another porch or terrace is sometimes added in southern climates. Here at Swift Creek both are included. The absence of a door between the lodge proper and the kitchen is non-typical and amounts to a fault in this plan.

Swift Creek Recreational Demonstration Area, Virginia

CAMP RECREATIONAL AND CULTURAL FACILITIES

Plate III J-5

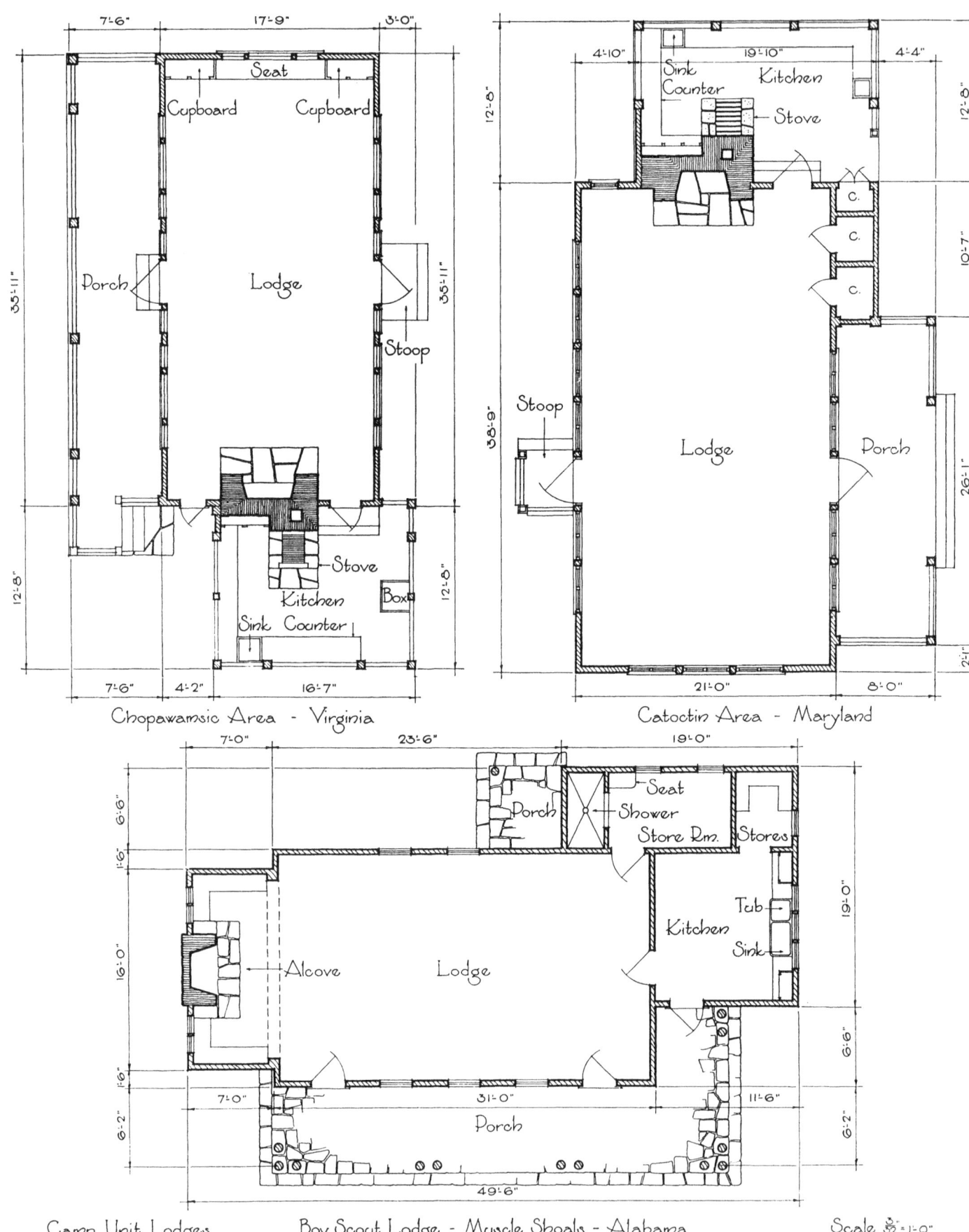

Camp Unit Lodges — Boy Scout Lodge - Muscle Shoals - Alabama — Scale ⅜"=1'-0"

Plate III J–6 →» CAMP RECREATIONAL AND CULTURAL FACILITIES

For the unit lodge, a second porch of the extent of the one shown at upper left of the facing page cannot be termed undesirable, although it is certainly unrequired. There is a tendency to add this superfluity in a hillside location that offers a view. It is one item which may be omitted without hampering use of the building. The native materials and methods here employed bring a pleasing wilderness character to the structure. In size it is scaled to a unit of 32 campers and in a winter camping use would accommodate eight or ten cots in a recommended spacing.

Unit Lodge, Chopawamsic Recreational Demonstration Area, Virginia

The appeal to the eye made by this squared log structure, shown in plan at upper right opposite, is unsurpassed by that of any unit lodge that has been pictured. It is not often economically logical to employ such expertly fashioned log construction in a building program having social objectives primarily. This is a great pity in view of the romance that a revival of pioneer methods can conjure up for youth. The plan is good, although ambitious beyond absolute essentials in the added porch. Louvres in the gable end are an aid in ventilation.

Unit Lodge, Catoctin Recreational Demonstration Area, Maryland

Actually, this troop lodge for the use of Boy Scouts in one of the recreational areas of the Tennessee Valley exemplifies the unit lodge in its most complete form. The plan is at the bottom of the facing page. The kitchen, which was an open porch in all the examples previously reviewed, is here enclosed, and a facility for a convenient year-round use is the result. The advantages are obvious, but funds are seldom available for such winter construction. If winter week end camping is only occasional, it is hard to justify the increased cost. Perhaps the answer is one or two such unit lodges in organized unit camps where more than casual winter use seems guaranteed.

Troop Lodge, Muscle Shoals, Alabama, Tennessee Valley Authority

CAMP RECREATIONAL AND CULTURAL FACILITIES

Plate **III** J-7

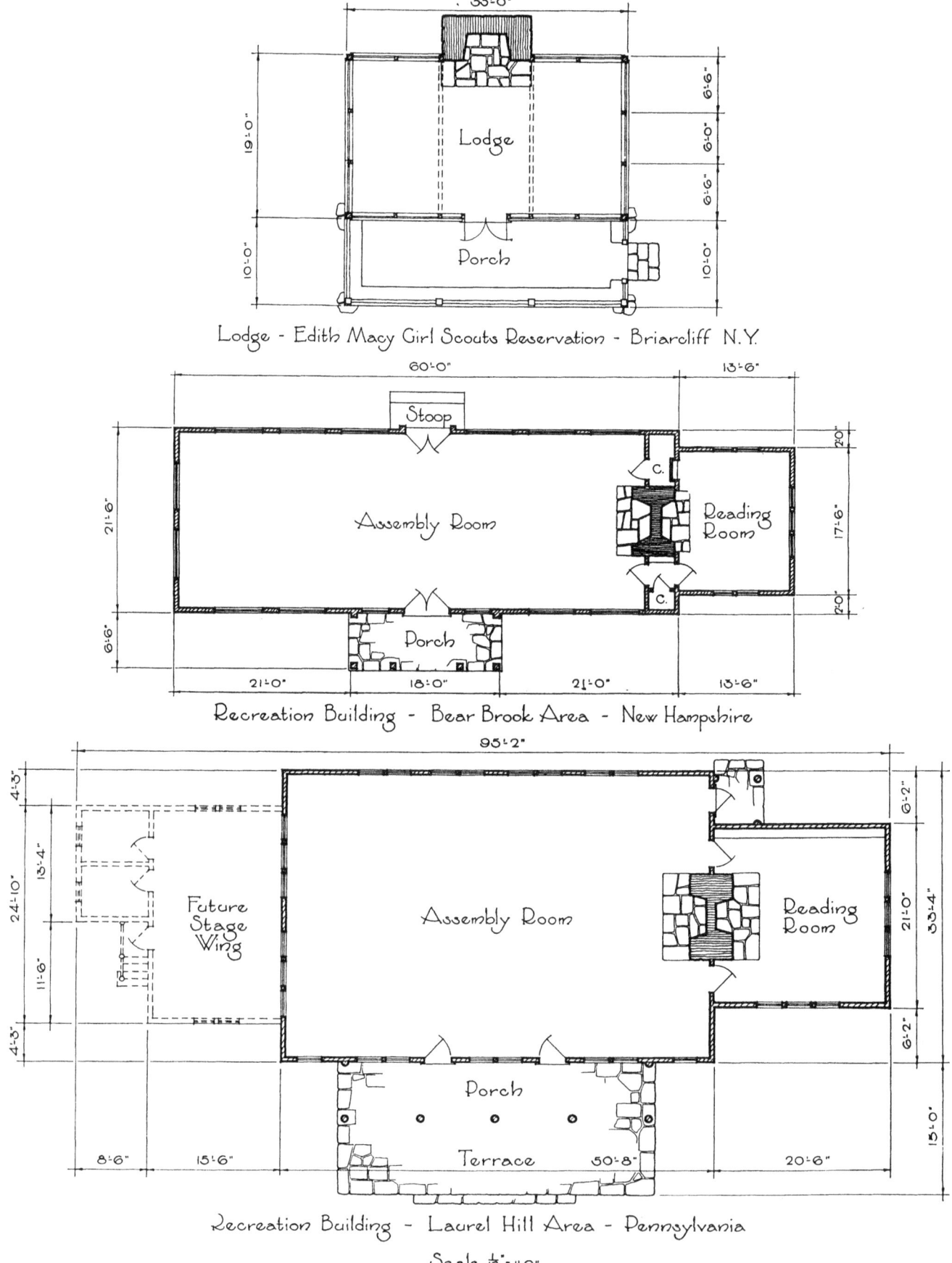

Lodge - Edith Macy Girl Scouts Reservation - Briarcliff N.Y.

Recreation Building - Bear Brook Area - New Hampshire

Recreation Building - Laurel Hill Area - Pennsylvania

Scale ⅛" = 1'-0"

Plate III J–8 ⇶ CAMP RECREATIONAL AND CULTURAL FACILITIES

This attractive building is illustrative of a unit lodge or recreation building in its least terms. Supplemented with an outdoor and detached kitchen, it has much the same function as have the unit lodges with attached kitchens shown on preceding pages. The advantage of the attached kitchen in inclement weather is obvious—and then probably truly appreciated. Architect for this lodge and its complementing outdoor cooking facility, shown elsewhere, was J. Y. Rippin.

Lodge, Edith Macy Girl Scouts Reservation, Briarcliff, New York

If available funds are insufficient to provide a small recreation building in each cabin colony of a unit camp, a central recreation building such as this, placed in the administrative unit, is sometimes a substitute. Occasionally funds will allow such a building in addition to a full complement of unit lodges, in which case it serves when the entire camp gathers en masse for indoor recreation and obviates need of converting the dining lodge to that use.

Recreation Building, Bear Brook Area, New Hampshire

When the wing housing the stage and its dependencies is built in the future, this building will have all the recommended major elements of the central recreation building—assembly room, which will function also as an auditorium when the stage is added, reading room, and porch. Use as an auditorium justifies a height of building that is usually avoided in other structures of organized camps. All doors of a recreation building should open outward, and there should be plenty of them—more than here shown.

Recreation Building, Laurel Hill Area, Pennsylvania

CAMP RECREATIONAL AND CULTURAL FACILITIES

Plate III J-9

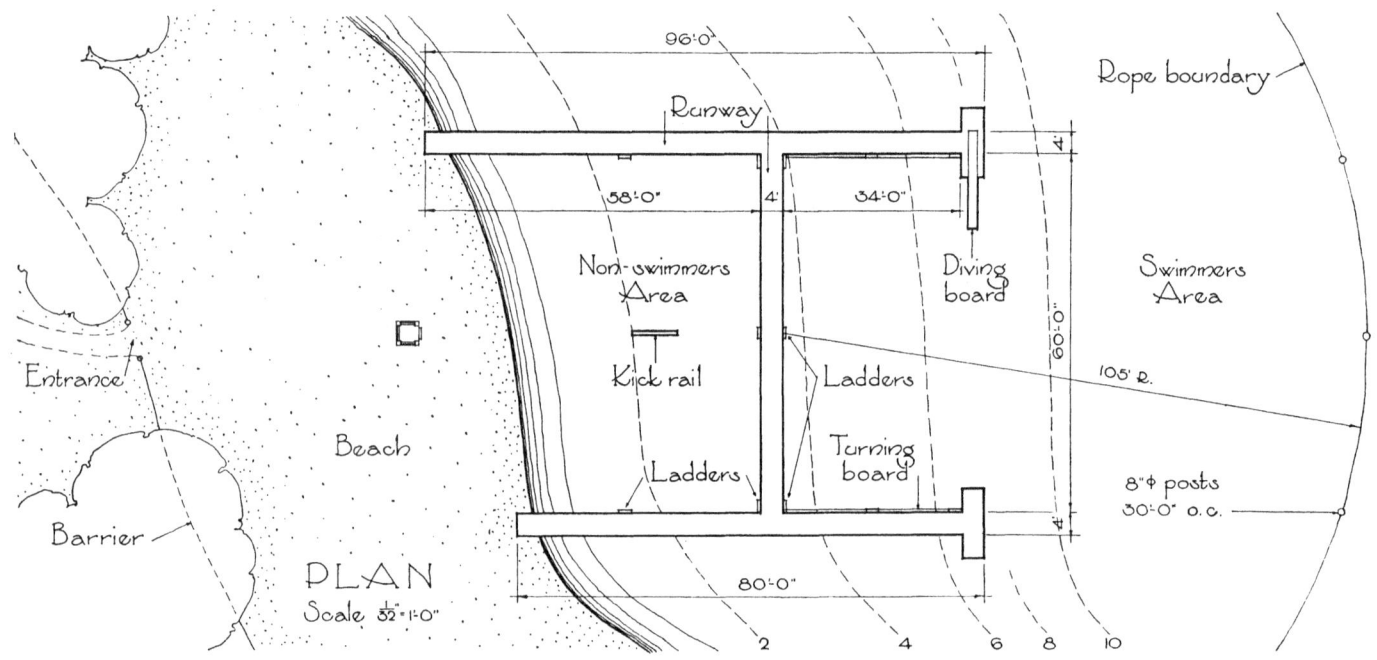

Swimming Dock, Hard Labor Creek Recreational Demonstration Area, Georgia

The H-shaped swimming dock has advantages that those of other forms do not possess. The zone for nonswimmers is completely enclosed so that there is no hazard of boats. This example has an elevated station on the shore from which the lifeguard can survey the swimming area. The many ladders up the sides of the dock deserve notice. The contour lines on the plan, indicating approximate levels over the bottom of the lake, generally accord with recommended depths.

Plate III J–10 →›› CAMP RECREATIONAL AND CULTURAL FACILITIES

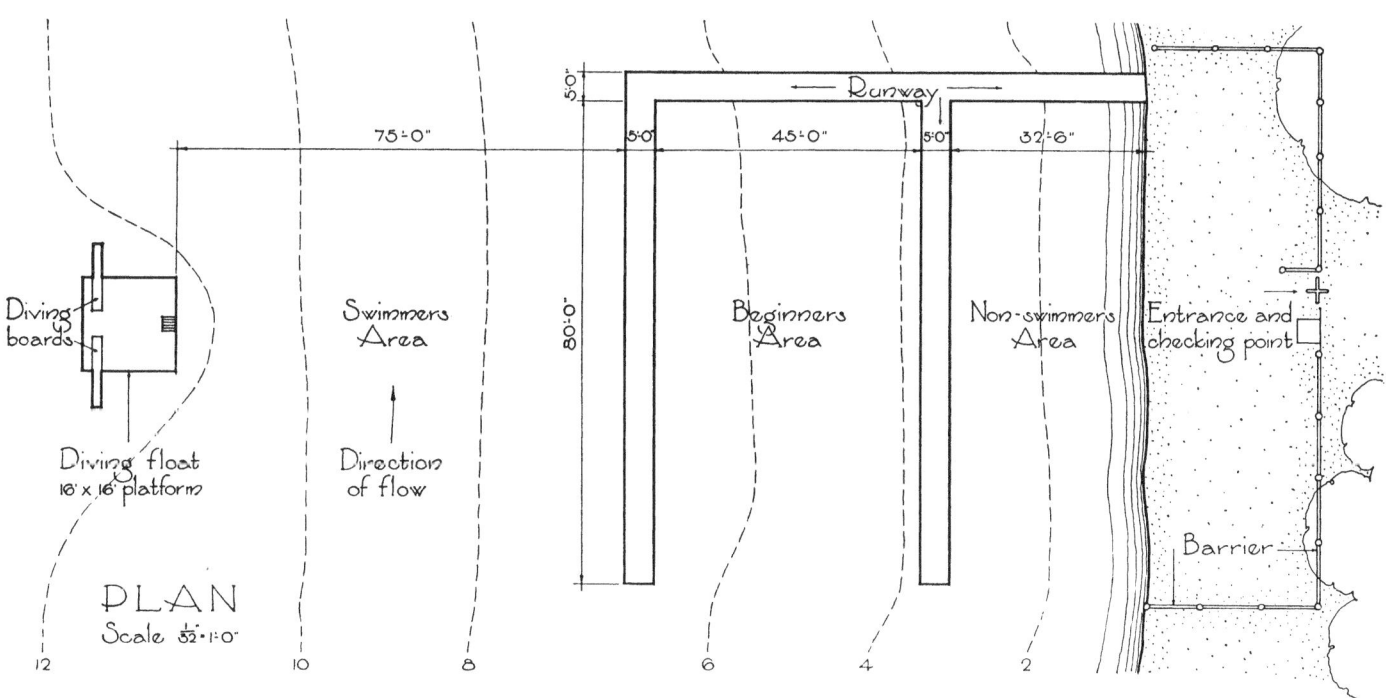

Swimming Dock, Mortimer L. Schiff Scout Reservation, Mendahm, New Jersey

This swimming dock is a good example of the F-type. The open ends of the nonswimmers' and the beginners' areas are marked by ropes supported by buoys. The lateral limits for swimming off the end of the dock and out to the diving platform are indicated by flag buoys. Survey of the swimmers is apparently conducted from the elevated station on the diving platform. The depths of the swimming area conform generally with the recommendations of authorities.

157

CAMP RECREATIONAL AND CULTURAL FACILITIES   Plate III J–11

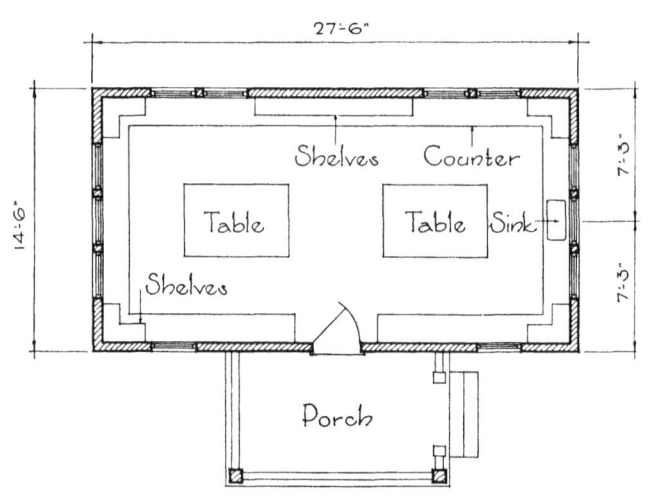

Museum – Bear Brook Area – New Hampshire

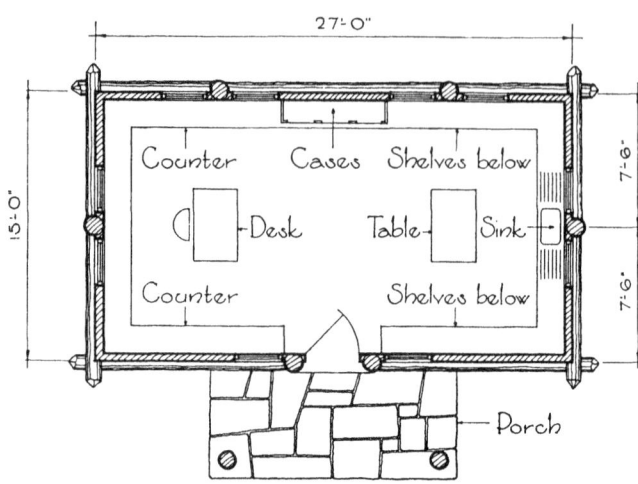

Museum – Raccoon Creek Area – Pennsylvania

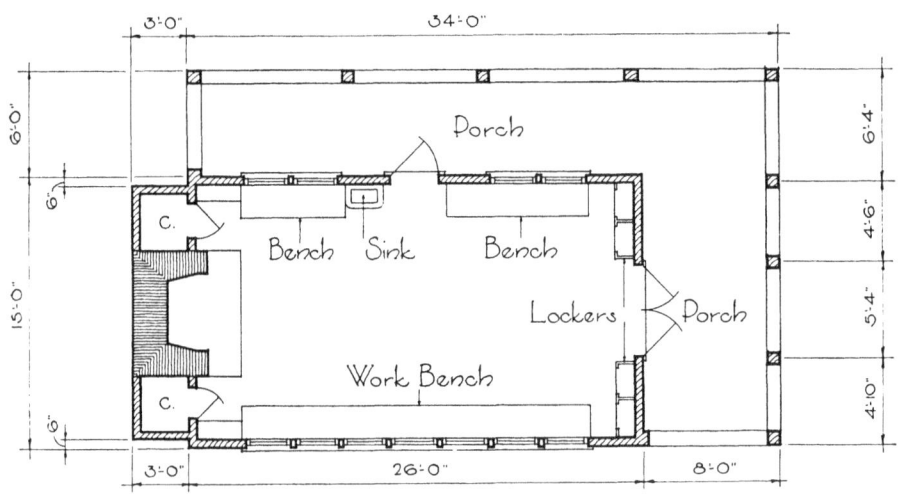

Craft Shop – Swift Creek Area – Virginia

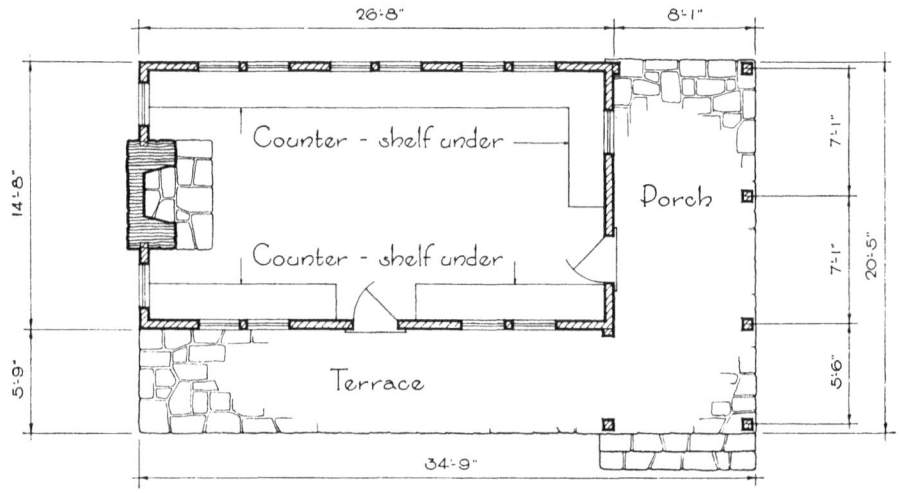

Craft Shop – Laurel Hill Area – Pennsylvania

Scale ⅛" = 1'-0"

Plate III J–12 →›› CAMP RECREATIONAL AND CULTURAL FACILITIES

Bear Brook Recreational Demonstration Area, New Hampshire

Raccoon Creek Recreational Demonstration Area, Pennsylvania

NATURE BUILDINGS AND CRAFT SHOPS

Above are illustrated two nature lore buildings, or camp museums as they are sometimes inaccurately called. Plans of them are shown at the top of the facing page. Both stand for the bare minimum in a facility of this sort for an organized camp, being equipped with sink, work tables, counters, and cupboards. A small office space for a nature counselor would improve both plans. The primary requirement of good natural light is met well in both. The Raccoon Creek example has a rusticity, relating it to the subjects with which its activities are concerned, that is lacking in the other.

Below are pictured two craft shops on recreational demonstration areas. Plans of these are shown at the bottom of the opposing page. In the Swift Creek example length of porch and massiveness of chimney flanked by shed-roofed closets add interest and relieve that "boxiness" which so often results when small buildings must be built economically. Both buildings are equipped with counters, sinks, and lockers, and appear to have ample natural light. Porches and terraces in connection with craft shops are not without purpose, for many camp crafts can be practiced in the open.

Swift Creek Recreational Demonstration Area, Virginia

Laurel Hill Recreational Demonstration Area, Pennsylvania

CAMP RECREATIONAL AND CULTURAL FACILITIES

Plate III J-13

Exterior

Exterior

Interior

GIRL SCOUTS LODGE, DAYTON, OHIO

Although it is impossible to classify this building of many functions in the categorical divisions of this presentation of camp structures, its great architectural interest and excellence dictate that it may not be omitted. The first floor is a common room—almost the kitchen-living room of the pioneer home. The loft, reached by a ladder stair, is a dormitory. The spacing of cots will not have the approval of authorities who urge that distances between sleepers, not cubical contents, govern cot spacing. Chimney, fireplace, and "rose" window developed from a wagon wheel are notably attractive features. Smith-Chamberlain, Architects.

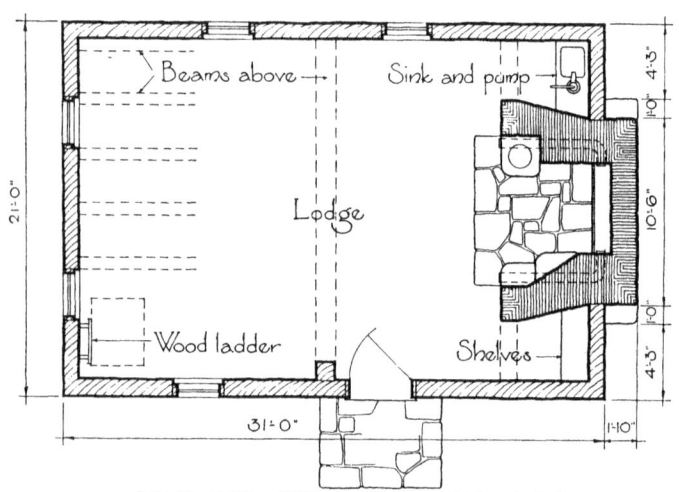
FIRST FLOOR PLAN

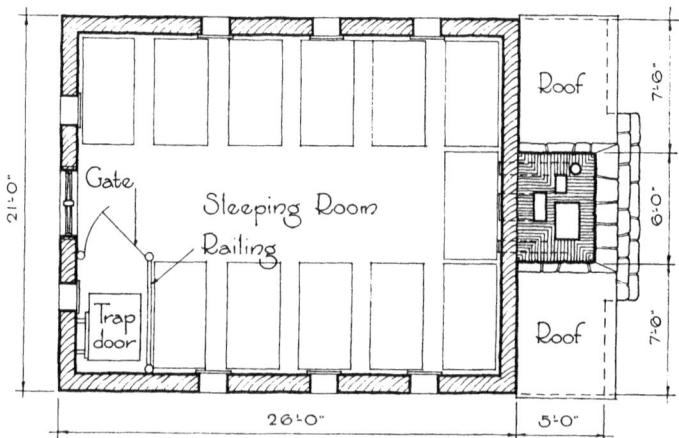
SECOND FLOOR PLAN

Scale 3/32"=1'-0"

CAMP COOKING AND DINING FACILITIES

EXACTLY three times a day facilities for cooking and serving meals become the most important structures in every camp, wherefore too much care in planning them is hardly possible. The primary structure is a dining lodge housing dining room and kitchen with necessary dependencies. While separate structures for cooking and dining purposes are imaginable in some situations, the arrangement promises too little of logic and efficiency to occur very often.

The outdoor kitchen as a joined or detached dependency of the unit lodge has already been touched on. This facility in which the cooking done is normally recreational and occasional, and not an efficient "three-square-a-day" business routine, is not a present concern. After a preliminary reference to campstoves, the discussion here will treat only of the dining lodge, combining dining room and kitchen, and the several minor accessories which may be housed either in it or in small independent buildings clustered around the kitchen wing or service court.

Campstoves have previously been discussed and illustrated as needed facilities in the public campground of a park. They likewise have useful purpose in the organized camp planned for the use of families, where it is likely a family will sometimes wish to prepare a meal on its own. They will differ not at all from the types of park campstove illustrated in the section "Campstoves", for they will properly be built to greater height than picnic fireplaces; they may, or may not, have a sheltering roof; and they may be either single or multiple. When an organized family camp can be built with its full complement of desirable structural accessories, one or more campstoves will be provided in each cabin group.

DESIRABLE OBJECTIVES in devising a plan for a dining lodge are wide and pleasing views from the dining room, ample light and cross ventilation for both dining room and kitchen, and a relationship between these two units which will result in a service of maximum efficiency with a minimum of steps. The T-shaped plan accomplishes these objectives, and is recommended above all other plan possibilities, with a full realization that the recommendation, if widely accepted, will lead to a degree of standardization, and that standardization is frowned on by designers of ability. Nevertheless, the T-shaped plan has too many advantages to justify rejection of it solely on the score of its being too commonly used.

The dining lodge is generally built for summer use only. It can therefore be of very light construction and can have many large screened openings with low sill height for the full benefits of view and ventilation. All openings should be equipped with shutters or closures of a type to give protection in stormy weather while the camp is occupied and to make possible closing the building out of season.

Completely effective insect screening of the dining lodge is essential. This should include all roof and floor ventilators and every other minor opening, for only the most positive precautions against the entrance of flies, where food is prepared and served, comply with recommended camp practice.

A fireplace is a welcome feature in the dining room not too widely open to retain the cheer and warmth a fireplace can spread on chilly mornings and evenings and in wet weather. Its flue and, let it be remarked in passing, the flues of all camp buildings, regardless of purpose, should be topped off with an effective spark-arresting device.

A dining room of suitable size will be had by allowing from 10 to 15 square feet of floor area per camper, depending on the size and shape of the dining tables. Table and bench combinations, that is, tables with seats attached, such as are appropriate in the picnic area, are not recommended in the camp dining room. Chairs or benches independent of the tables will be useful on those occa-

CAMP COOKING AND DINING FACILITIES

sions when the tables must be stored away to clear the room for recreational use. Tables seating four, six, or eight persons have been found practicable. They may be square, round, or rectangular. In camps where the lack of a separate central recreation hall means that the dining room must sometimes be converted to recreational use, light dining tables of folding type, which can be easily handled and stored in a small space, are a possibility.

In most well-ordered camps, a current trend in the serving of meals is to duplicate as far as possible practices that would prevail in a not underprivileged home. Meals are served as at a family table with campers taking turns as waiters and a counselor serving at each table or delegating the serving to one of the campers. Stacking the dishes and skidding them to the end of the table nearest the kitchen may be timesaving, but there is nothing else to recommend it and, as a permissible practice, it is out. There are those who condemn cafeteria service in a camp dining room for being institutional in flavor. There are localities, however, notably along the Pacific coast, where this type of service has been perferred. Regional preferences should be the weighing factor when a choice between the two types of service is to be made.

To prevent kitchen heat, noises, and odors from penetrating to the dining room, the openings between these rooms should be limited to two doors, whichever type of service is adopted. The camper-waiters of the one plan will pass in one door, pick up food from a serving counter extending across the kitchen, and reenter the dining room by the other door. If cafeteria service is used, the counter, of course, will be on the dining room side of the partition separating dining room and kitchen, and the two doors will serve the in-and-out traffic of the kitchen help. In either case the counters should be continuous, with gates or hinged tops at any required openings to bar the campers from the kitchen help's field of operations.

The most vexing problems of camp operation invariably center around these employes. A first and far step in forestalling some of the difficulties which can arise is to keep the campers out of the kitchen proper and away from behind the serving counter. It is appreciated that in many camps the campers will be detailed to set the tables, to assist in the preparation of vegetables, and to perform other tasks, but it is only rational so to plan the dining lodge that this amateur help will not recurrently short circuit the professional and blow the fuse of morale. Very effective insulation against such disasters is to provide a screened porch directly off the kitchen where the campers doing K. P. can work at their set tasks out from under foot of the cook and his assistants.

IN THE CAMP KITCHEN, as in every other kitchen, the lay-out of equipment should adhere to the tried principles of efficient arrangement. In short, it should be zoned for three basic functions—preparation of food, serving of food, and dishwashing—arranged in this proper sequence. In the well-planned kitchen the dishwashing zone will be definitely isolated from the two others, which will be as disentangled one from the other as their inherently close relationship will permit. Range, work tables, counters, dish closets, pan racks, sinks, and all the items which make up the complete kitchen will only find their proper location if the importance and use of each in relation to the others has been carefully analyzed, and if such factors as light, ventilation, and circulation, have been weighed.

Size is a matter of first importance in the kitchen. There is no glib formula for calculating the exact desirable size, yet for every particular case there is a right answer within very narrow limits, about as one might say the answer to 7 times 7 is between 48 and 50. The kitchen a little large is much too large; the kitchen a little small is much too small. And sadly enough, the kitchen that is just the right size is very rare indeed.

Concrete floors under the range and the hot water heater serve as a safeguard against fire. If extended throughout the kitchen, concrete provides a floor surface that is more easily cleaned than wood, though harder on the feet of those who must stand on it all day, and usually costlier. Wall and ceiling surfaces adjacent to the range and to the hot water heater should be adequately fireproofed.

The temper of the kitchen staff and the temperature of the kitchen would appear as parallel movements if shown by graphs. No simple ventilating device which will aid in keeping down temperature and tempers in the kitchen should be omitted from the construction. A long, low ridge ventilator, screened and fitted with movable louvres, will serve as an outlet for the warm air and cooking odors which accumulate under the roof. Louvred screened openings at the floor line will supply fresh air and, in conjunction with the ridge ventilator, effect a helpful natural circulation of air. An abundance of windows for cross ventilation and light is strongly urged. An overventilated summer camp kitchen south of the arctic circle is yet to be heard of. Whereas the sills of the dining room windows should be low enough to afford persons seated views of the outdoors, the sills of the kitchen windows should be high enough to clear all counters and sinks at a suitable working height.

Dependencies of the kitchen desirably joined with it include a cool room; a refrigerator having two compartments, one for meats, the other for vegetables and dairy products; a rodentproof storage closet; and a service porch. The cool room is a storage place for vegetables and need not be large if it is supplemental to an underground vegetable cellar. A secondary function of the cool room, if proper planning has the refrigerator entered from the cool room and not directly from the kitchen, is to insulate the ice box against kitchen heat. In such a plan arrangement, ice is conserved, and some of the cold lost by the refrigerator serves to lower the temperature of the cool room.

To serve a summer camp adequately, the ice box of necessity will be large. Whether it may be a carpenter-built affair that pretends to no exceptional rating for efficiency or should be a commercially built box of guaranteed, proved insulation value depends on the source of ice. Obviously, in northern locations where natural ice has been cut and stored near at hand in abundance, there will not be the same economic reason for efficiency in the ice box as exists where artificial ice must be brought from a distance. An outside icing door placed suitably high in the wall will prove convenient.

In the rodentproof closet are kept the staples and foodstuffs which do not require storage in a cool place. Quarter-inch wire mesh over walls and ceilings and between subfloor and finish floor will prevent animals from entering the closet.

The service entrance steps and porch should be built of masonry or concrete. Not only must these endure much wear and tear due to deliveries and removals, but there will be frequent need for hosing down the platform and steps to keep them in a sanitary condition. Nearby, though preferably not directly joined with the steps, should be a concrete platform for garbage cans. It is convenient to have this at truck platform height.

If toilet and wash basin are not available in another building close by, there will be the economy of saved time if these are provided along with other dependencies in the kitchen wing.

It is conceivable that there might be need in a large camp for a dietitian's or steward's office where accounts and deliveries might be checked and other duties performed away from the kitchen proper. It can be a very small room, and its proper location is near the service entrance door.

DEPENDENCIES OF THE DINING LODGE which are better housed separately than incorporated within the kitchen wing are few. Most necessary is space for fuel storage. If the fuel for the range and the water heater is the usual coal or wood, a small separate structure in which to store it convenient to the service entrance will keep much dirt and dust out of the kitchen. To bring in fuel from the outside may seem less convenient than to dip into an abundant supply stored alongside the range, but the annalist should ponder the more frequent scrubbings of the kitchen floor made necessary when the kitchen doubles as the coal bin.

If gasoline or oil must be used as fuel for the kitchen range and heater in the camp, it becomes mandatory to provide a separate shed a safe distance from all other structures, marked to announce the hazardous contents, and otherwise in compliance with any governing regulations in force.

In some localities an underground storage place for vegetables, convenient to the kitchen wing, will be useful. When ice must be brought from such distances that buying for only a few days' need is uneconomical, or when winter ice is cut on the camp property and a season's supply must be stored on the premises, generous storage space is needed. As for other minor structural needs associable with camp cooking and dining facilities, it is pointless to explore the nontypical further to a possible confounding of typical construction.

CAMP COOKING AND DINING FACILITIES

Plate III K-1

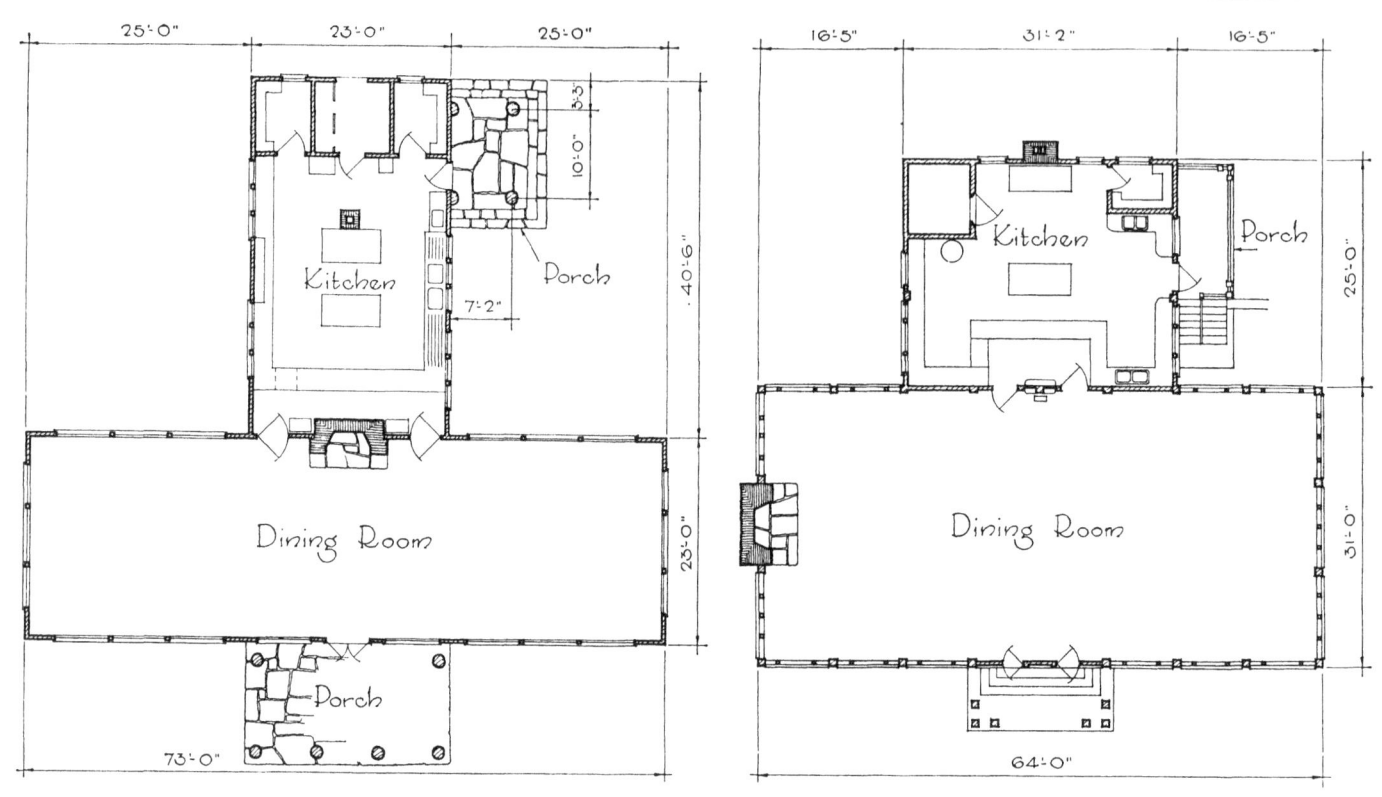

Raccoon Creek Area - Pennsylvania

Oak Mountain Area - Alabama

Chopawamsic Area - Virginia
Camp Dining Lodges
Scale 3/64" = 1'-0"

Plate III K–2   ⇛ CAMP COOKING AND DINING FACILITIES

Common to the dining lodges grouped in plan on the facing page are geographic location east of the Mississippi River and development from the same basic T-shaped plan. The plan of this example, shown at upper left opposite, differs from the other two of the group principally in having a fireplace featured between the serving doors from the kitchen wing. The building is apparently well-lighted and well-ventilated throughout. The type of construction is characteristic of all the Raccoon Creek camp buildings.

Raccoon Creek Recreational Demonstration Area, Pennsylvania

In the plan at upper right opposite will be seen a dining room shorter and wider than average. Similarly the kitchen wing has greater width and less length than those of the other buildings. This may offer the advantage of some saved steps, though obviously at some sacrifice of light and ventilation. The exterior in itself is attractive but any dining lodge is conspicuously at odds with the natural grade when a full flight of steps up to the kitchen door is necessary, as here.

Oak Mountain Recreational Demonstration Area, Alabama

Something more than minimum requirements is in evidence in this dining lodge. Features such as the bay windows flanking the fireplace and the large porch, if quite nonessential, are important factors in the attractiveness of the building. The breezeway between the kitchen and the dependencies behind it has purpose in warm climates. Unfortunately, because of the density of cover, a photograph of the building in its entirety could not be obtained.

Chopawamsic Recreational Demonstration Area, Virginia

165

CAMP COOKING AND DINING FACILITIES Plate III K-3

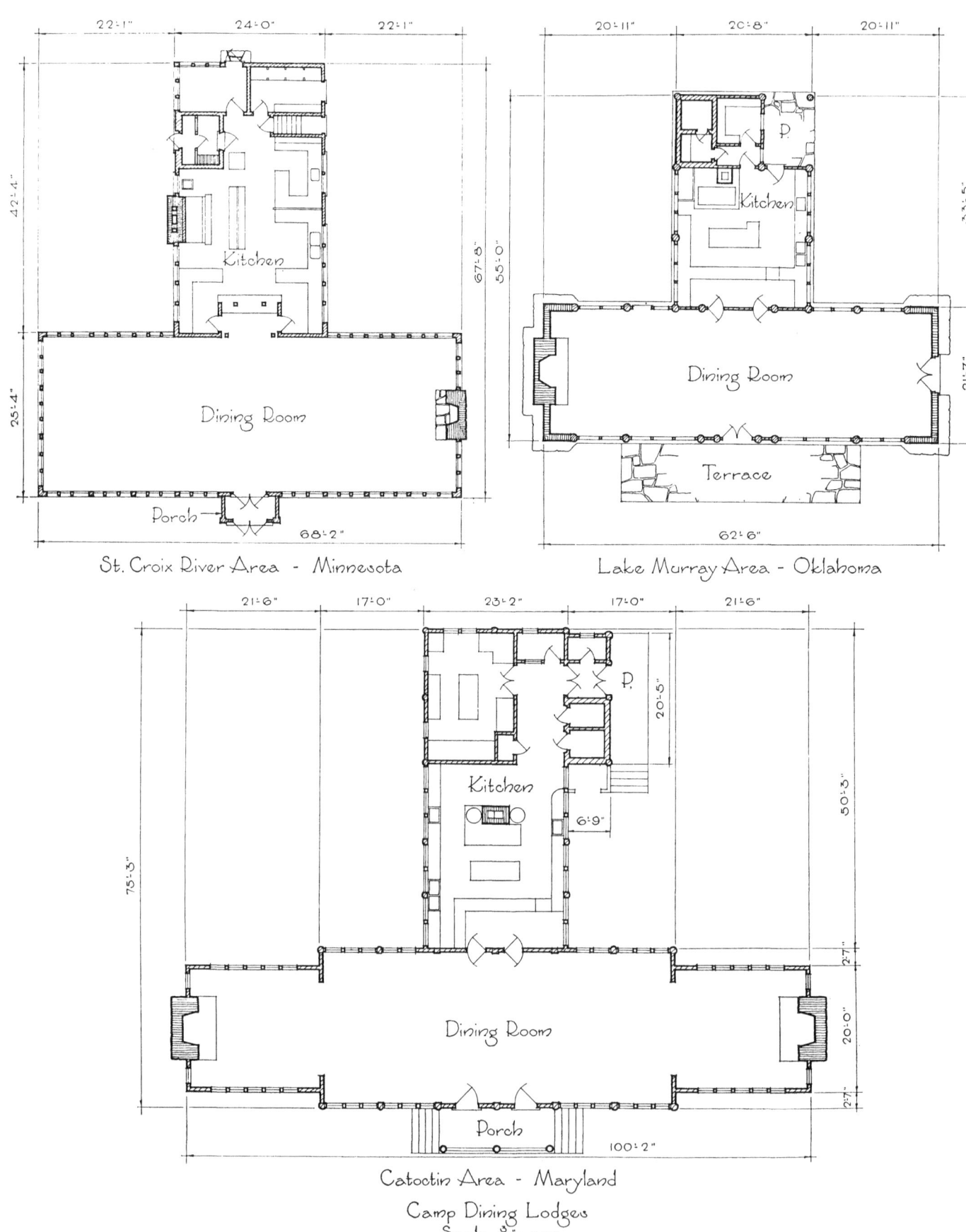

St. Croix River Area - Minnesota

Lake Murray Area - Oklahoma

Catoctin Area - Maryland
Camp Dining Lodges
Scale 3/64" = 1'-0"

Plate III K-4   →» CAMP COOKING AND DINING FACILITIES

Grouped on the opposite page are plans of dining lodges on recreational demonstration areas in widely scattered locations. The plan of this one, reproduced at upper left, shows a kitchen of generous size, well-zoned by the distribution of equipment items for the several operations of a large kitchen. There is adequate provision for light and ventilation in both the dining room and the kitchen wing.

St. Croix Recreational Demonstration Area, Minnesota

This example, smaller than most dining lodges on recreational demonstration areas, is unusual in the masonry end walls of the dining room. These create for a building which is mainly of frame construction an appearance of being built largely of masonry. The simplicity and long, low lines of the building, the texture of the roof, and the character of the masonry are noteworthy. A monitor roof over the service wing helps to ventilate the kitchen.

Lake Murray Recreational Demonstration Area, Oklahoma

The illustration does not do full justice to this building, which harmoniously combines masonry, logs, and slabs in a structure of great interest. The wings which flank the center room to result in a kind of combined dining lodge and recreation building are an unusual plan feature. Ordinarily recreational alcoves, these expand the dining capacity if occasion warrants. If closed off from the main building by doors, two unit lodges for winter use would be created.

Catoctin Recreational Demonstration Area, Maryland

| CAMP COOKING AND DINING FACILITIES | Plate III K–5 |

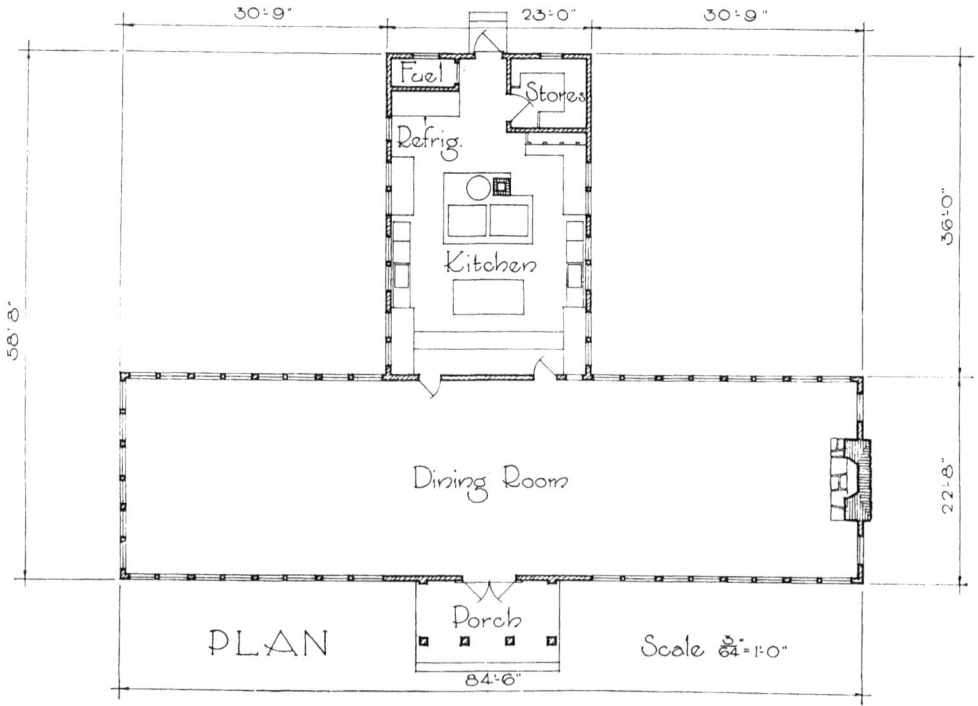

Dining Lodge, Montserrat Recreational Demonstration Area, Missouri

There is considerable regional similarity between this dining lodge and the one at St. Croix Recreational Demonstration Area. Except in surface character, there can be no striking variations in facilities all of which have sprung from certain prescribed basic instructions, calling for a T-shaped plan and establishing floor areas. The roof ridge ventilator should be noted.

Plate III K-6 ⇛ CAMP COOKING AND DINING FACILITIES

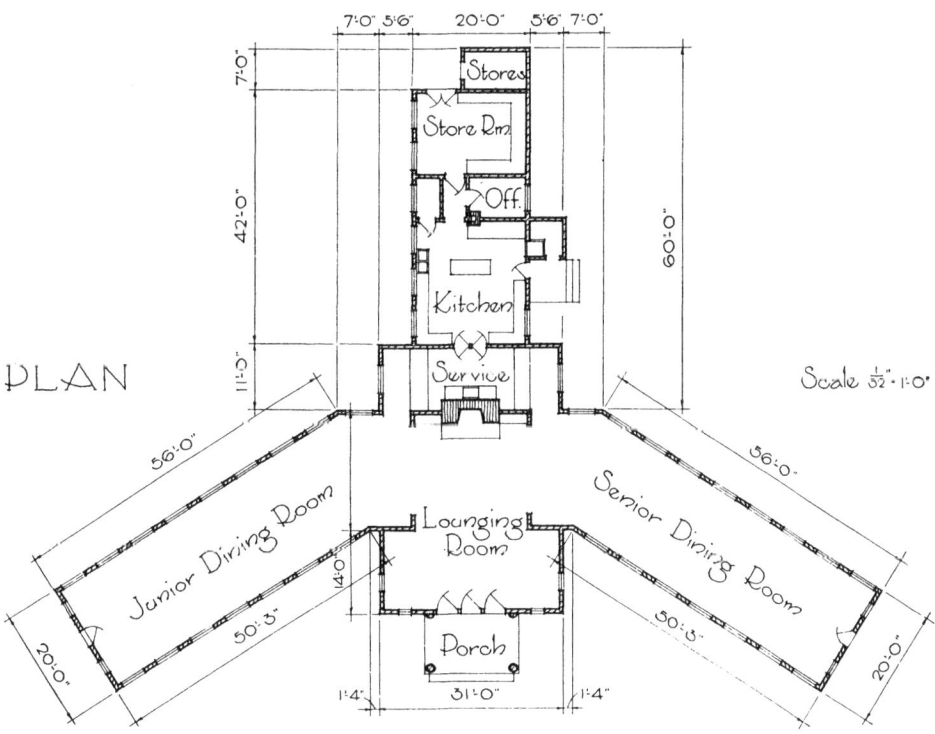

Dining Lodge, Washington, D. C., Girl Scouts Camp, Harrisonburg, Virginia

Except for the angle at which the dining room wings are placed and greater size, this example is generally similar to the dining lodges of the recreational demonstration camps already illustrated. It is scaled to a camp of more than 100-capacity, as against a maximum of that number for the others.

169

CAMP COOKING AND DINING FACILITIES

Plate III K–7

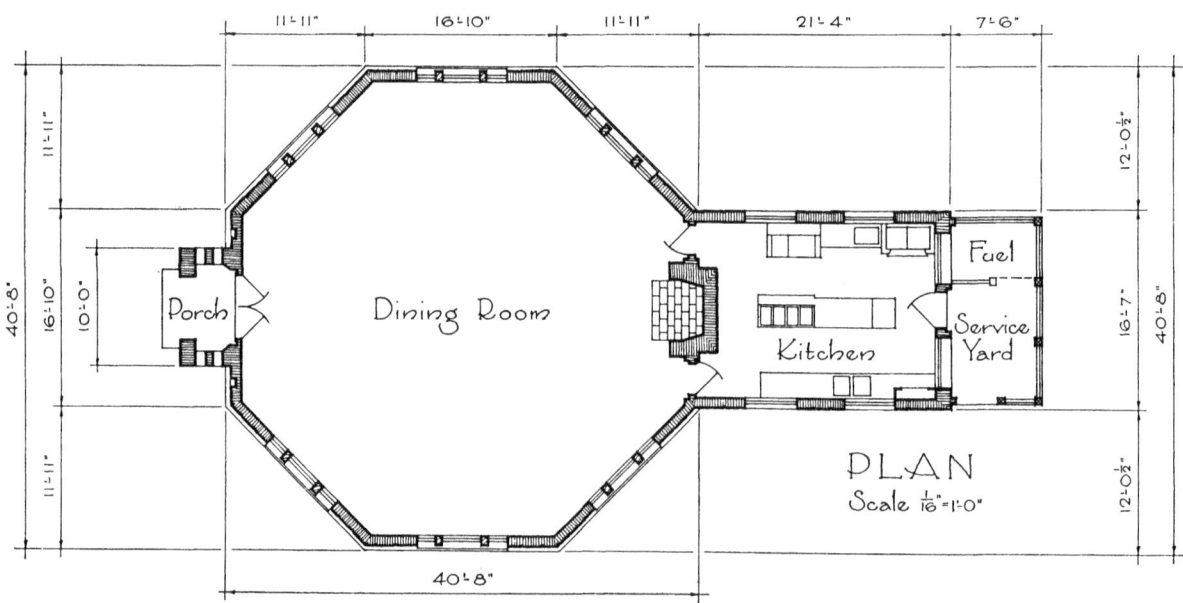

Dining Lodge, Pokagon State Park, Indiana

Here is a novel departure from the stereotyped T-shaped dining lodge plan. Substituting an octagon for the crossing of the T produces a structure of refreshing individuality without forfeiting the merits of the more standard arrangement, save perhaps that the tables cannot be as advantageously placed as in a rectangular room. Dormers serve to ventilate the space under the high roof and to light the central part of the room. The screened service yard should be noted.

Plate III K–8   ⇢⇢ CAMP COOKING AND DINING FACILITIES

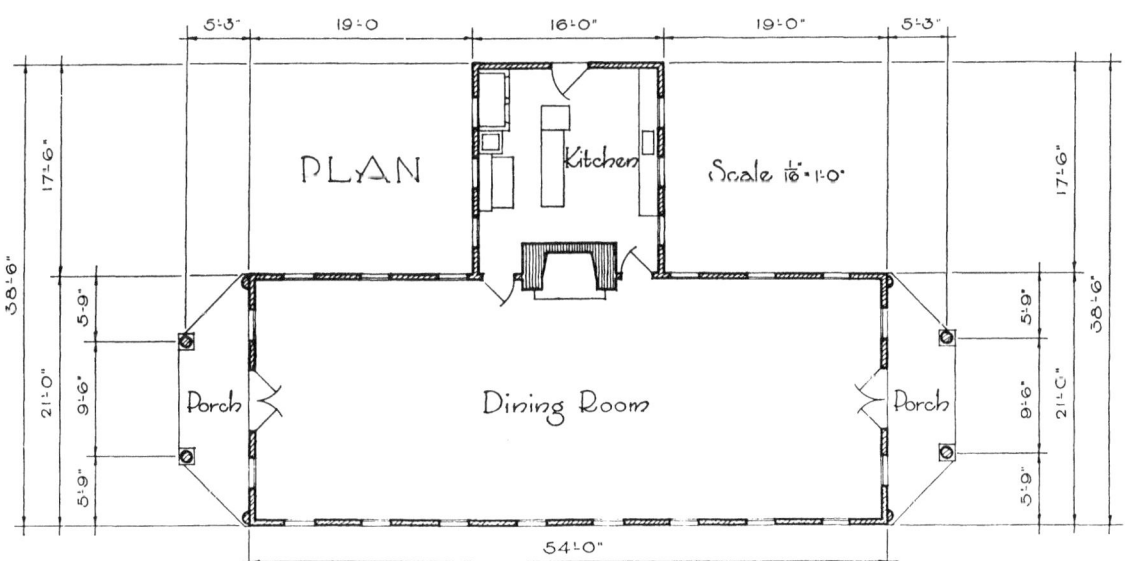

Dining Lodge, Dunes State Park, Indiana

Interpretation of the Indian tepee in wooden architecture is the theme of all camp buildings in this park. Steep roof pitch, poles atop the hips, and Indian symbols painted on the shingled roofs proclaim the inspirational source. By the ultra-practical among camp planners, the windows will be held to be of insufficient size. To these, architects will willingly stand up in debate; larger windows would obscure the provenance of this interesting adaptation. The roof ventilator for exhausting air that might become pocketed under the steep roof is decorative as well as purposeful.

CAMP COOKING AND DINING FACILITIES

Plate III K-9

Outdoor Kitchen
Edith Macy Girl Scouts Reservation — New York

The outdoor kitchen, which is an integral part of all the unit lodges previously shown, is in this instance detached from the enclosed shelter, a less convenient arrangement in inclement weather. The structure is practically equipped with stove, shelves, worktable, and benches and is of attractive appearance.

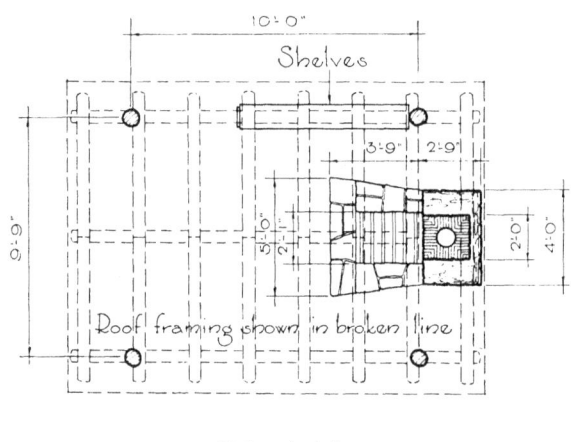

PLAN

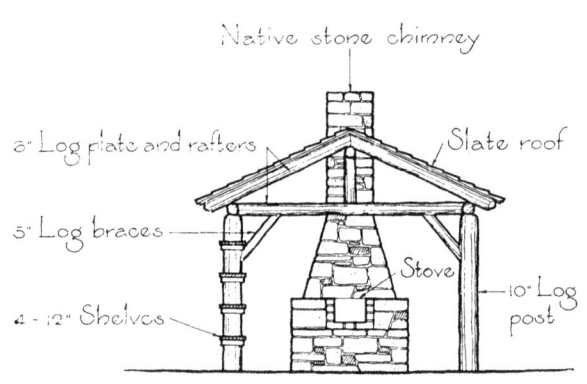

SECTION

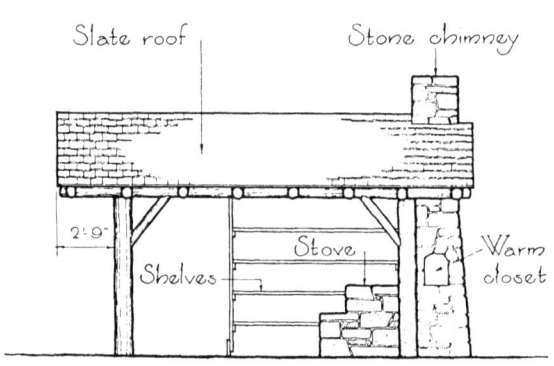

SIDE ELEVATION

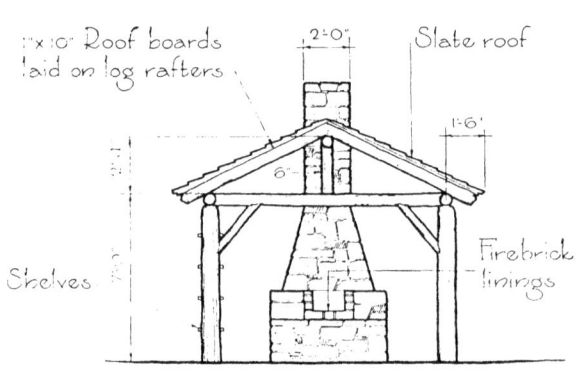

FRONT ELEVATION

Scale ⅛" = 1'-0"

CAMP SLEEPING FACILITIES

TIME WAS, and not long past, when the very word "camping" carried presupposition of sleeping in a tent. Since prehistoric darkness, some form of tent has served man as shelter during his migrations and farings forth to hunt and to fight. In consequence the tent stands as an inherited symbol of high adventure, especially to youth. Naturally then, when on his first camping expedition, a youthful reincarnation of Daniel Boone or Marco Polo finds to his horror that he is expected to sleep in other than a tent, cynicism rears its ugly head, and today's generation is forever convinced that it was born too late.

Probably organized camping must take the lion's share of responsibility for having undermined tentage as the supreme facility for sheltering campers. This institution has had opportunity to observe the high cost of tents (maintenance and replacement considered) and the difficulties of screening them against insects. Conclusion is very generally reached that the "wooden tent" has enough advantages in economy and health to outweigh the thrill of sleeping under canvas.

Some camping leaders will not lightly sacrifice the psychological advantage of the tent and will favor using it for sleeping purposes in spite of its overburden of cost. A tent so used should have a raised platform with flooring tightly fitted. It is pointed out that the actual dimensions of tents often vary by several inches from their nominal size. Hence it is unwise to build tent platforms until the tents are on hand, in order that the platforms may be custom-tailored to a snug fit. Well-braced side rails will contribute to fixity of form and will help in anchoring the canvas.

There is always inclination to try to eliminate the shortcomings of the tent by this change or that addition. This leads to an anomalous fabrication, half-tent and half-cabin, which usually succeeds in rolling into one all the disadvantages, rather than the advantages, of both kinds of shelter and in appearing to be a cross between a corncrib and a cricket box of heroic proportions. Unless the tent is accepted for exactly what it is, the alternative of an out-and-out wood structure is urged.

As a usual thing, sleeping units in camps must accommodate the following different groups: campers, staff members, and those termed collectively the help, but more accurately defined as employes who are not members of the leadership staff. The help will be housed somewhat to themselves within convenient reach of the dining lodge. Quarters for the staff will be at a location so central that general supervision of the camp can be maintained at all hours. The living quarters of the doctor or nurse in charge of the infirmary are necessarily within that building, as has been said. If the camp is planned for young children or youth groups, living quarters for one or more counselors or leaders will be provided in each group of campers' cabins. This practice may or may not prevail in the camp planned for family use.

As to sleeping cabins for the campers themselves, there are material differences between those designed for families and those designed for age groups. Let us consider the two types and their basic structural differences before sleeping accommodations for staff and help are explored in detail.

THE HISTORY of group camping reveals a continual reduction in the recommended number of campers housed in one sleeping unit. Actual experience with age groups in camp, particularly younger children, shows that as "dormitory" groups were made smaller, many behavior problems disappeared and the campers were happier. There are many children and older persons too who find it difficult to adjust themselves to many roommates. It was found that eight campers in a cabin was better than twelve, that six was a still better-sized group, and that four seemed best of all. Because adjustments to camp mates and camp life are more easily made in the small group and because noises, disturbances, and problems of discipline all decrease proportionately as the size of the group, and therefore less supervision is required, it is urged, when campers are over 12 years of age, that not more than four be housed in a sleeping cabin. For children under 12 it is recommended that the cabins be planned with two rooms accommodating four campers each and with a separate room for the counselor between.

Wherever groups of small children are brought together in camp, the sleeping cabins, for reasons of health, safety, and comfort, should comply with United States Public Health Service recommendations. These call for six feet between side rails and four feet between end rails of beds, and ban double-deck bunks. In cabins or dormitories that accommodate more than four young persons, the six-foot spacing can be reduced if well-fitted canvas or light wood barriers are placed between the beds, and if in so doing the cubic content requirements of local health agencies having jurisdiction are met. If the campers are adult or housed as families, it is considered allowable to substitute the space and content regulations of directly jurisdictional agencies for those of the Public Health Service.

In sleeping cabins planned for summer use only, as is generally the case, window openings may be large. The solid walls need not extend more than three feet above the floor, from which level to the plate line screened openings should be provided. Some method must be contrived for closing them in stormy weather. It may be done by means of canvas curtains, wire glass-cloth on frames neither too light nor too heavy, or by solid wood shutters. Canvas curtains flap in the wind, become mildewed if rolled when wet, and will be found to entail high maintenance costs even though mildewproof canvas is used. If not subjected to abusive treatment, wire glass-cloth mounted on sufficiently rigid frames should last for several years. Because this material admits light, it is superior to the canvas curtain and the solid wood shutter, both of which leave the cabin entirely in darkness when they are closed. Everything considered, the most desirable solution would seem to be glass-cloth storm closures interchangeable with wood batten winter closures.

The initial cost of glazed sash in camp buildings is high. And when the buildings are remotely situated and deserted out of season, glass breakage is often considerable with consequent high maintenance costs. It is recommended that the use of glazed windows in camp structures be limited to those buildings planned for year-round use.

As to equipment, sleeping cabins should provide individual clothes closets for the personal belongings of each camper to insure a neat and orderly cabin at all times. These closets may be simple three-sided affairs with canvas curtains across the front. One or two shelves at the bottom or the top will serve to store the camper's small belongings; a rod or coat hooks will accommodate coat hangers. Building these closets in the center of the ends or sides of the cabins will help to insure the cots being placed in conformity with the United States Public Health Service space regulations.

It seems hardly necessary to recommend that all doors of sleeping cabins should open outward as a safety measure in case of fire or other emergency when young children, especially, would be panic-stricken. A small porch at the cabin entrance will protect the doorway in wet weather and offer a place where campers before entering can clean their shoes of mud. If large enough, the porch is a pleasant place for the cabin occupants to sit outdoors, weather and insects permitting.

When it is expected that an organized camp will be occupied part-time by families and part-time by age groups, the cabin just described as desirable for the latter will meet fairly acceptably the needs of a family. If, on the other hand, a full-season family use of the camp is projected, a cabin more favorable to family occupancy can be devised. First of all, this would be less open. A group of family cabins will be inhabited by persons of both sexes and all ages, and more privacy for the family than would be accorded an age group of either sex is very much in order. To this end the amount of screened wall can be reduced by half. Furthermore, it is desirable to divide the family cabin into two rooms, for conceivably a family camp will not operate on so fixed a schedule as other camps, and the children and adults of a family will retire at different hours. It is also proposed that cabins be of several sizes, sleeping four, five, and six persons, when strictly family use is anticipated.

The economy basic in organized camping, founded on the principle of making its benefits accessible to the greatest number, will oppose anything more elaborate in family cabins than has just been described. True enough a fireplace, a living room, and a screened porch would be desirable additions. But these, accompanied by that inevitable other addition—an increased camping fee, resulting in reduction in the broad field it is hoped to serve by organized camps—are unjustified.

SLEEPING QUARTERS FOR STAFF MEMBERS in camps operated for age groups must be widely scattered to effect a proper supervision. In family camps this need is less imperative or may be lacking altogether. There are staff members in age group camps—the counselors or leaders—who are on duty 24 hours a day, being expected to sleep with one eye and one ear open.

The tendency in camp staffing is toward more counselors to a given number of campers than formerly. This has resulted in more varied programs as well as more personal attention. In present practice the camper-to-counselor ratio probably averages around eight to one. Doubtless fewer campers per counselor is the situation where the campers are very young or physically handicapped and more, where the campers are more mature.

The younger the campers, the closer at hand should be the counselors' sleeping quarters. Hence, when the group is made up of very young children, the type of cabin previously described, having the leaders' room flanked on either side by rooms accommodating four campers so that all are under one roof, is desirable. When older children constitute the group, a detached cabin will serve as living quarters for the counselors. It may house three, but two is better. Its proper location is central among the campers supervised by the counselors. Its construction will be similar to that of the campers' cabins, and it will be of a size that permits spacing beds at least as far apart as recommended for campers' cabins. It will be equipped with a closet for each occupant and will be arranged to receive two or three chairs and a table for use as a desk.

In the typical camp there will be need for a cabin with sleeping quarters for the director and other members of the central staff who may be off duty after taps. It is sometimes advantageous to include sleeping accommodations in this cabin for one or two guests, and perhaps a living room or lounge with a fireplace which can be used by other staff members during their leisure hours. Often there will be purpose in building it so that short-term winter use is possible by an arrangement that permits one bedroom to be converted to use as a kitchen. Otherwise, a summer construction, a little less exposed and somewhat more spacious than recommended for counselors' and campers' cabins, is in order. The camp staff, in camp all summer long and composed usually of older people, is entitled to a little more room, privacy, and comfort than the campers will require.

Employes' living quarters should be apart from those of the campers and staff members, yet should be located convenient to the central washhouse, which incorporates their toilet and bathing facilities, and to the dining lodge, in which their work centers. There is advantage too in locating the building that houses help where it will control the service road to the kitchen wing of the dining lodge, as some supplies may be delivered at hours when none of the kitchen crew is on duty.

Size of the help's quarters will be determined by the policies and type of service adopted in the kitchen and dining room, the extent of camper participation in the operation of the dining lodge, and the possibility of employment of some day help in the neighborhood who will return home at night. It is wise to plan one room for a couple. The building will usually be of summer construction, perhaps less open than the campers' cabins.

Anticipated short-term winter use may warrant a better construction in either this building or the staff's cabin, or even in both. When it is a case of one or the other and not both, then such construction and use seem the more logical in connection with the staff's quarters. In some camp lay-outs it will be chosen to duplicate counselors' cabins to house the help. Toilet and bath incorporated in staff's quarters and help's quarters are, of course, convenient, but scarcity of funds usually dictates omission of them.

CAMP SLEEPING FACILITIES

Plate III L-1

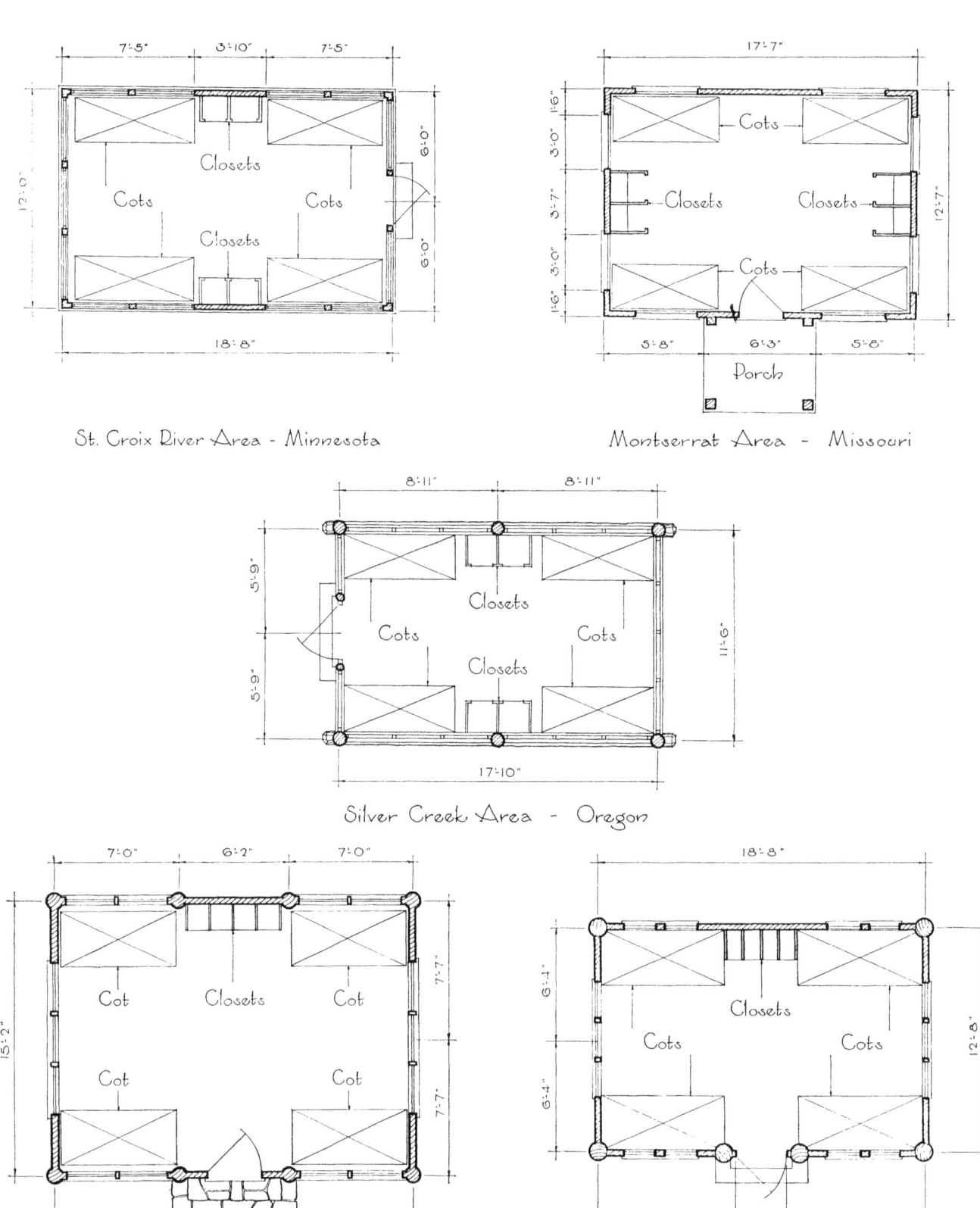

Plate III L-2   ⇶ CAMP SLEEPING FACILITIES

St. Croix Recreational Demonstration Area, Minnesota

Montserrat Recreational Demonstration Area, Missouri

CAMPERS' CABINS WITHOUT PORCHES

All the essentials of organized camp cabins sleeping four campers are present in the cabins here grouped and shown in plan on the facing page. Structural economies, recommended distances between cots, large openings for light and air, and individual closets for the occupants fix size and arrangement. Any individuality possible is largely a matter of surface treatment and the option of whether to have a porch and if so the form it will take. Common to the cabins of this group is the lack of a porch, save the rudimentary one of the Montserrat subject.

Silver Creek Recreational Demonstration Area, Oregon

Otter Creek Recreational Demonstration Area, Kentucky

Lake Murray Recreational Demonstration Area, Oklahoma

CAMP SLEEPING FACILITIES

Plate III L-3

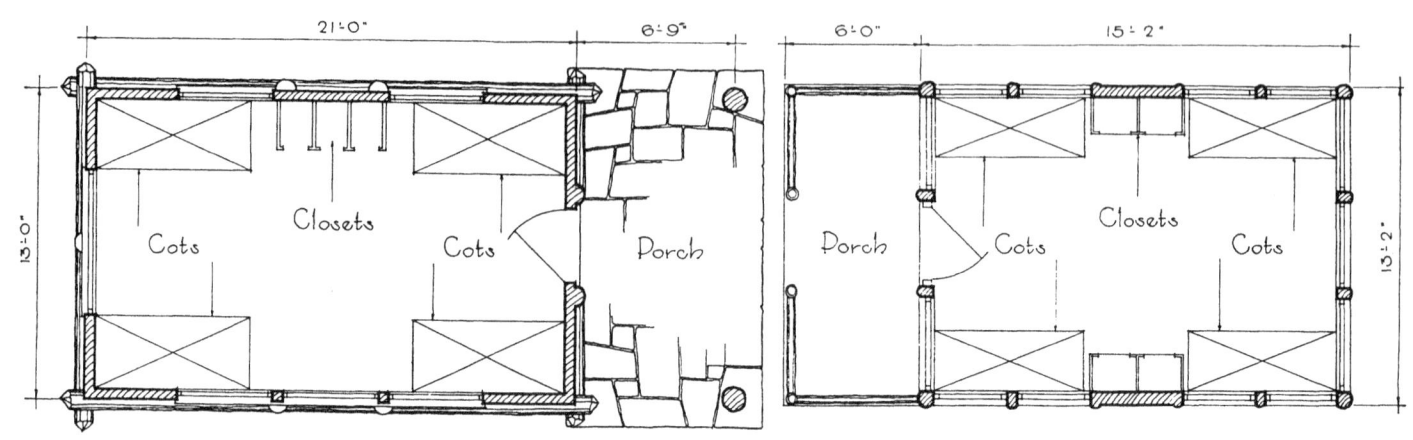

Raccoon Creek Area - Pennsylvania

Catoctin Area - Maryland

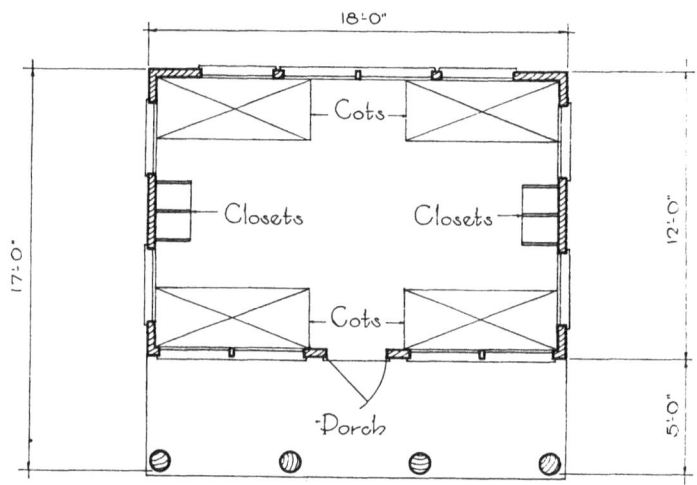

Hickory Run Area - Pennsylvania

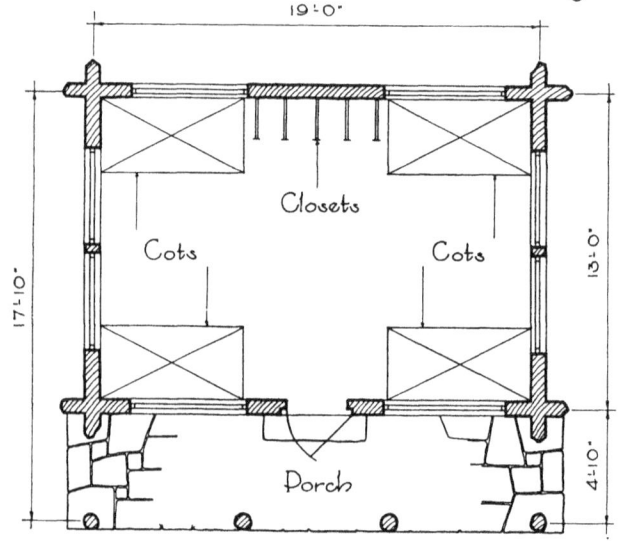

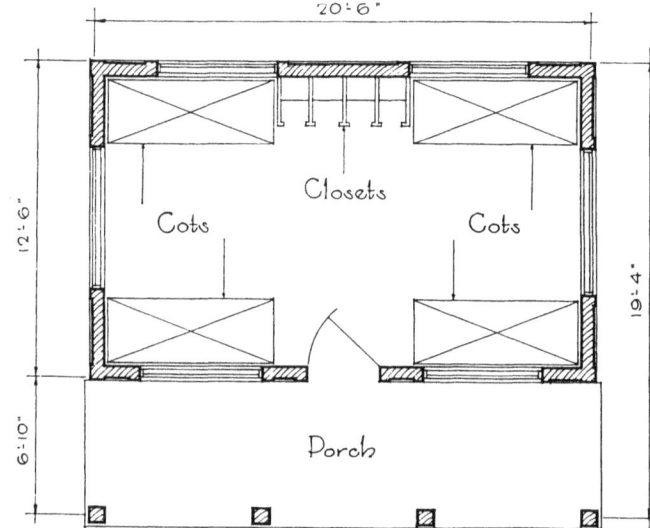

Beach Pond Area - Rhode Island

Campers Cabins
Scale ⅛" = 1'-0"

Bear Brook Area - New Hampshire

Plate III L-4　　　　　　　　　　　　　　　　　　　　⇶ CAMP SLEEPING FACILITIES

Raccoon Creek Recreational Demonstration Area, Pennsylvania

Catoctin Recreational Demonstration Area, Maryland

CAMPERS' CABINS IN THE NORTHEAST

Grouping these cabins together is entirely on the basis of geography. They exhibit no special features unknown in other parts of the country. Two have entrances and porches at the end; three are entered on the long side and so have longer side porches. Noteworthy in the group is the Catoctin cabin, outstanding for its simple excellence and true craftsmanship. If built-in benches are not a part of the cabin porches, the steps should be wide enough to offer a place for the occupants to sit out-of-doors.

Hickory Run Recreational Demonstration Area, Pennsylvania

Beach Pond Recreational Demonstration Area, Rhode Island

Bear Brook Recreational Demonstration Area, New Hampshire

CAMP SLEEPING FACILITIES

Plate III L–5

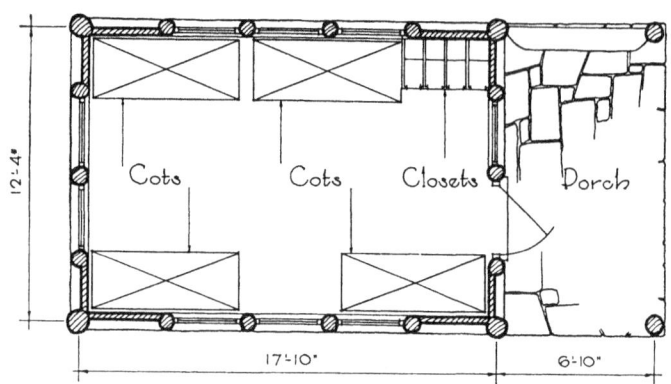

Falls Creek Falls Area - Tennessee

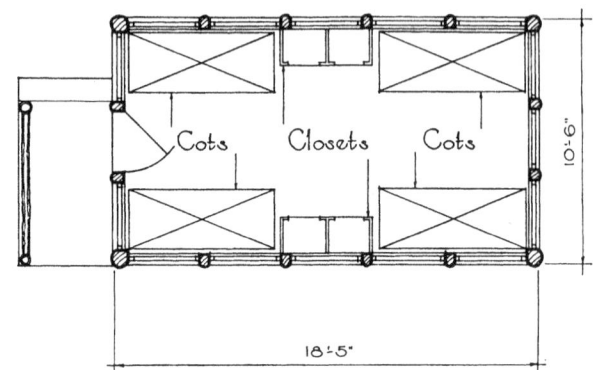

Chopawamsic Area - Virginia

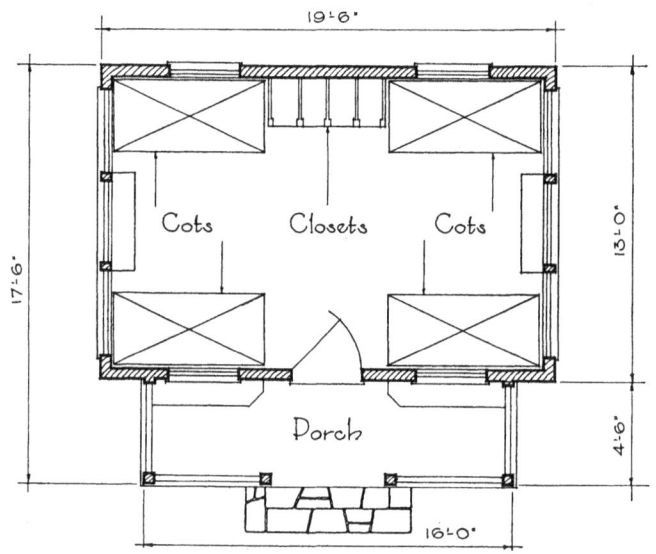

Alexander H. Stephens Memorial Park - Georgia

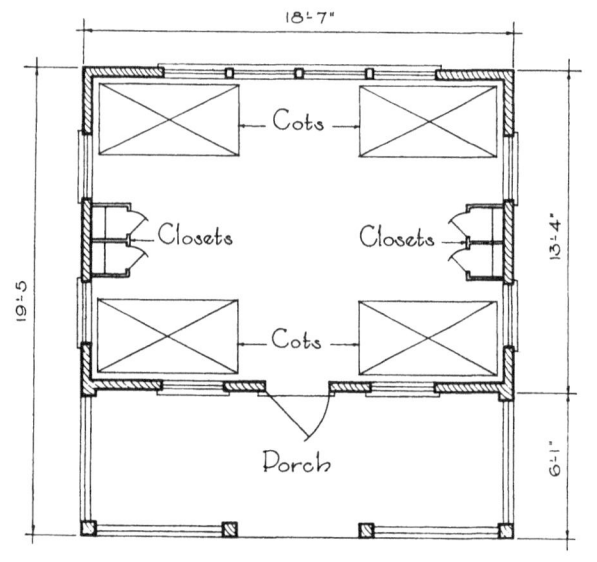

Cheraw Area - South Carolina

Campers Cabins
Scale ⅛" = 1'-0"

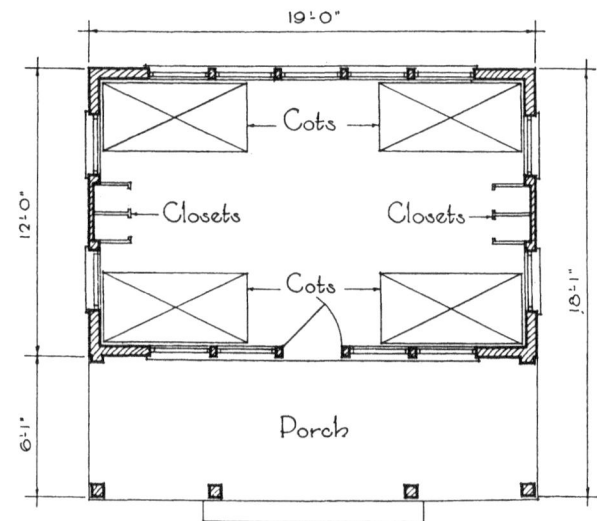

Swift Creek Area - Virginia

Plate III L-6 — CAMP SLEEPING FACILITIES

Falls Creek Falls Recreational Demonstration Area, Tennessee

Chopawamsic Recreational Demonstration Area, Virginia

CAMPERS' CABINS IN THE SOUTHEAST

Another group of camp cabins assembled on a geographic basis and not because of any structural or other close kinship. The plans opposite show the cabins at the top of the page to have end porches and entrance doors and the others to have side porches and entrances. The timbers of the upper cabins are logs in the round; those of the lower three are square. Alternative locations for the closets will be noticed; all four may be banked opposite the entrance door, or two may be spotted on each side between the cots.

Alexander H. Stephens Memorial Park, Georgia

Cheraw Recreational Demonstration Area, South Carolina

Swift Creek Recreational Demonstration Area, Virginia

CAMP SLEEPING FACILITIES

Plate III L-7

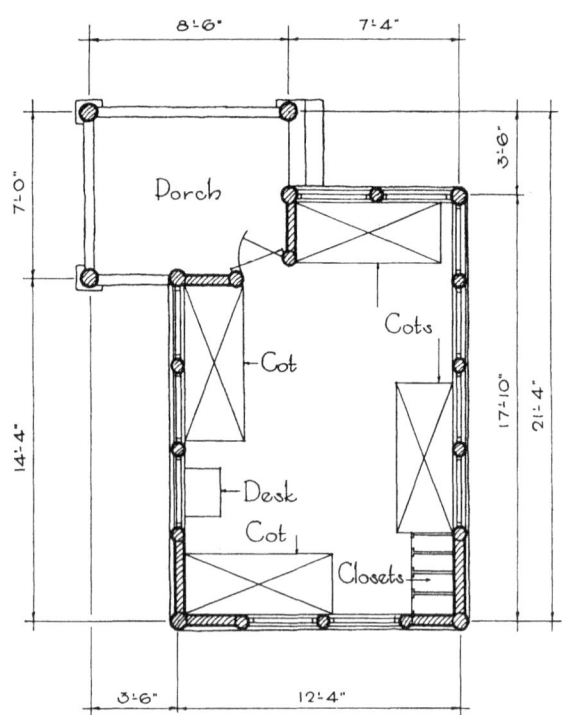

Falls Creek Falls Area – Tennessee

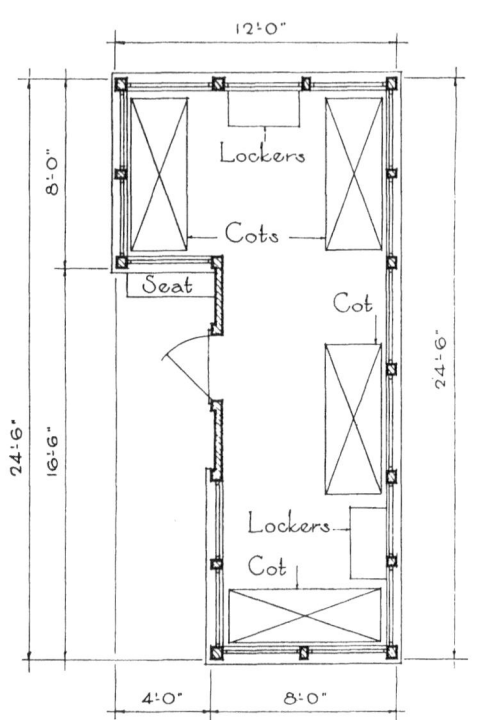

Hard Labor Creek Area – Georgia

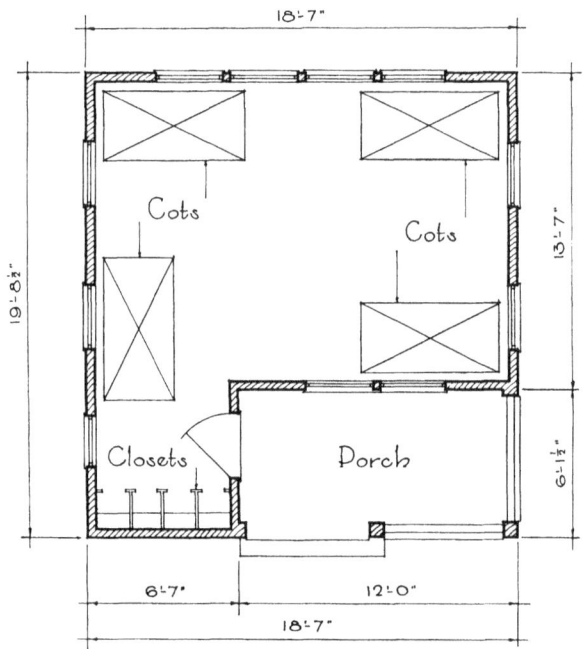

Kings Mountain Area – South Carolina

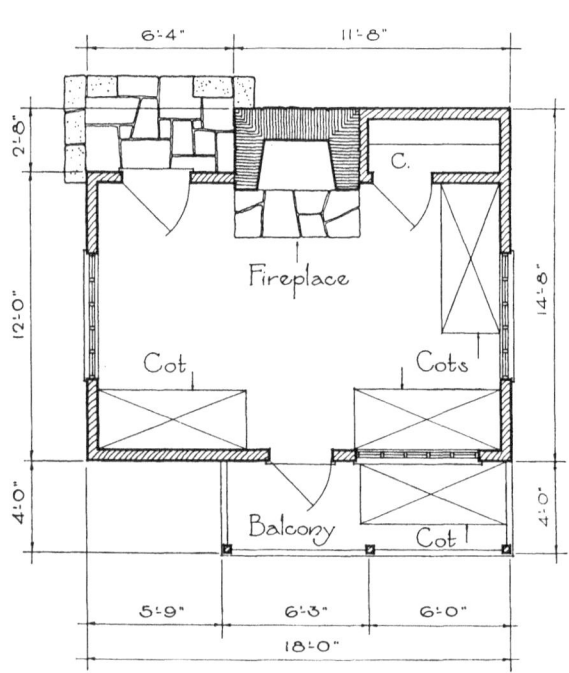

Mendocino Woodlands Area – California

Campers Cabins
Scale 1/8" = 1'-0"

Plate III L-8   ⇶ CAMP SLEEPING FACILITIES

Falls Creek Falls Recreational Demonstration Area, Tennessee

Hard Labor Creek Recreational Demonstration Area, Georgia

NONTYPICAL FOUR-BED CAMPERS' CABINS

The plans on the facing page prove that departures from the typical rectangular sleeping cabin are possible without compromising basic requirements. The variety thus introduced into crowded cabin groups should be welcomed widely. We have now reviewed camp cabins from the Atlantic to the Pacific and only in sunny California has a fireplace been incorporated. This is something to ponder, along with the unique distribution of cots—three indoors near the fireplace and one outside in the fog. This may have something to do with the ratio of native sons to newcomers. Probably that is three to one, and the stranger is quarantined out on the balcony to toughen.

Kings Mountain Recreational Demonstration Area, South Carolina

Mendocino Woodlands Recreational Demonstration Area, California

183

CAMP SLEEPING FACILITIES

Plate III L-9

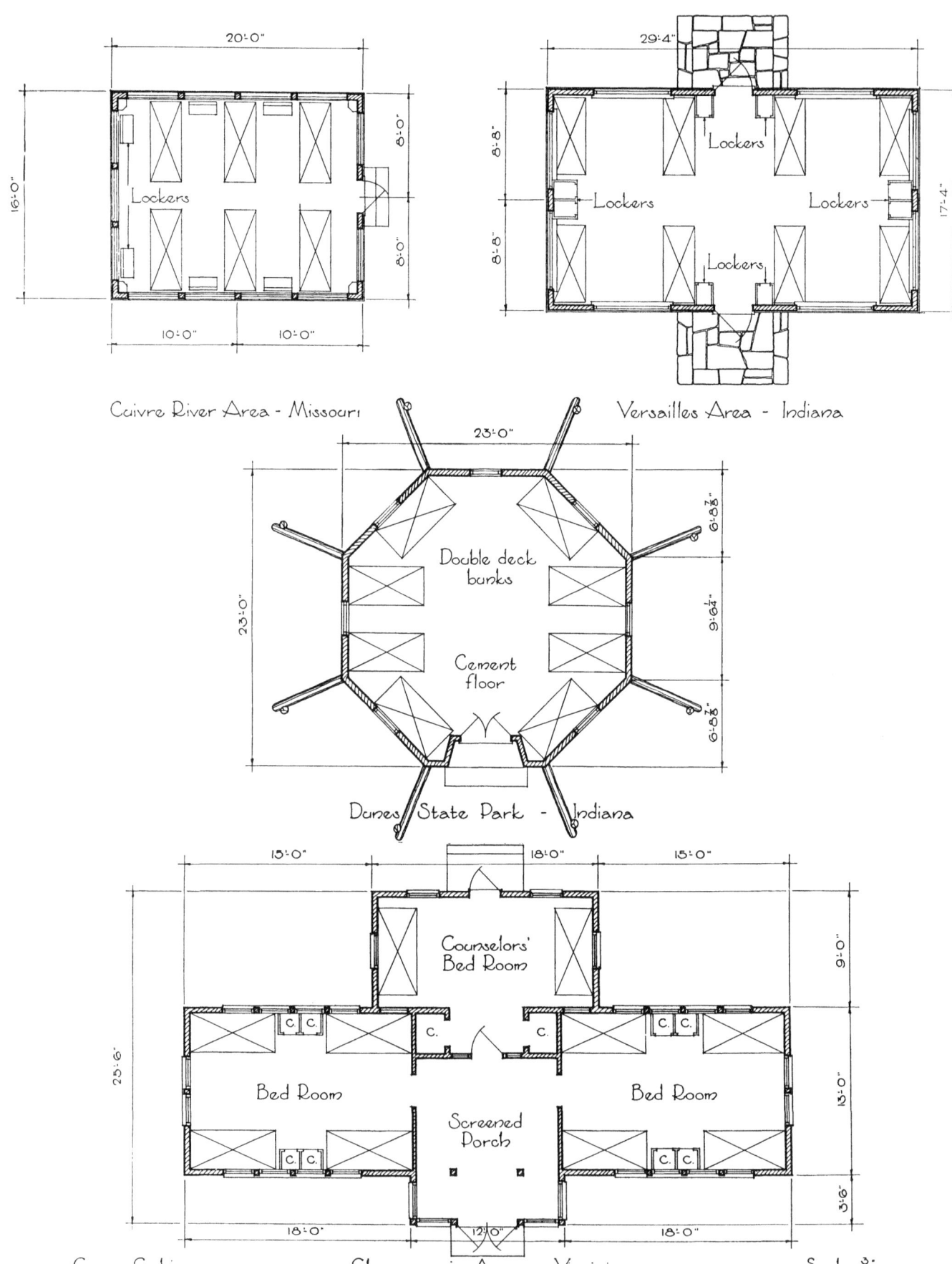

Cuivre River Area - Missouri

Versailles Area - Indiana

Dunes State Park - Indiana

Camp Cabins — Chopawamsic Area - Virginia — Scale 3/32"=1'-0"

Plate III L-10   →» CAMP SLEEPING FACILITIES

Cuivre River Recreational Demonstration Area, Missouri

Versailles Recreational Demonstration Area, Indiana

CAMPERS' CABINS ACCOMMODATING MORE THAN FOUR

Although a sleeping capacity of four in a camp cabin is widely held to be the desirable ideal, some viewpoints consider a capacity of six or eight allowable, as the plans on the facing page indicate.

The six-bed cabin at Cuivre River, shown at upper left, would be more acceptably arranged if four of the beds were moved into the corners to give a bed spacing equivalent to that of the eight-bed cabin on the Versailles Recreational Demonstration Area, shown at upper right.

The chief accomplishment of the striking tepee-like structure of octagonal plan is the thrill it holds for youth. But this is not arrived at without sacrifice. In a housing that is more picturesque than well-ventilated, the eight double-deck bunks crowd sixteen sleepers in serious violation of space recommendations. Even though the eight double-deckers were single cots, the spacing would still be substandard.

The "saddlebag" cabin at Chopawamsic is the arrangement recommended in camps for very small children. It brings eight children together under one roof in two four-room dormitories, separated by an entry and a sleeping room for two leaders. This permits one leader to be off duty at certain hours with no relaxing of supervision.

Dunes State Park, Indiana

Chopawamsic Recreational Demonstration Area, Virginia

185

CAMP SLEEPING FACILITIES

Plate III L–11

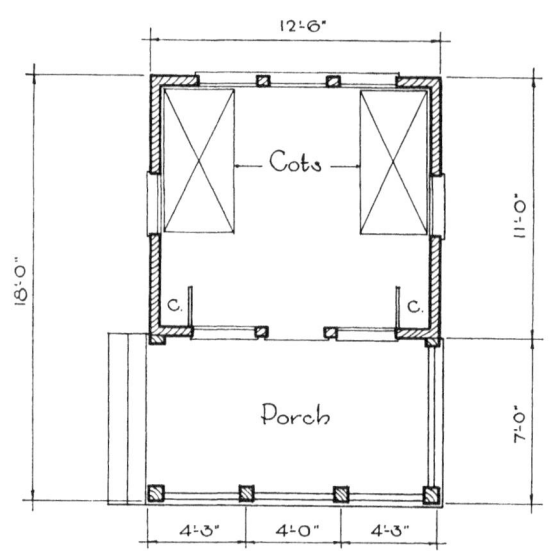

Kings Mountain Area – South Carolina

Hickory Run Area – Pennsylvania

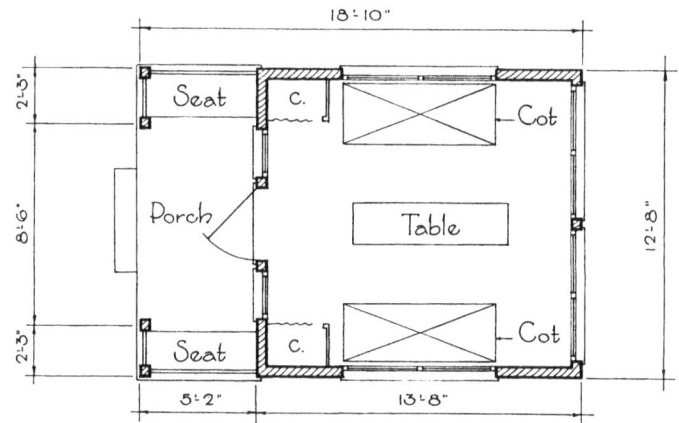

French Creek Area – Pennsylvania

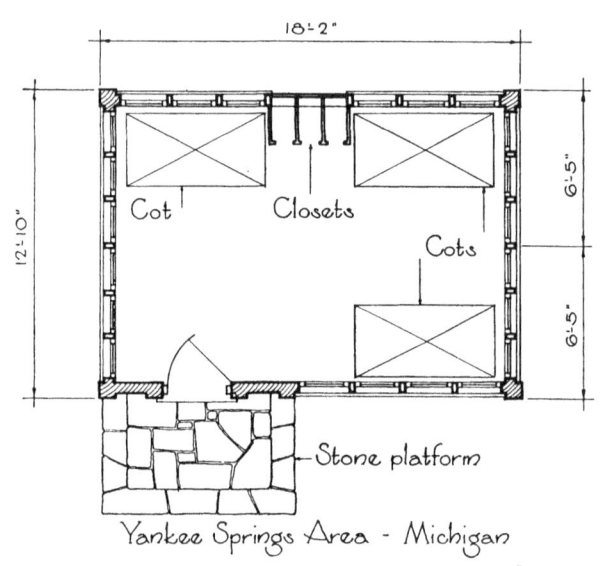

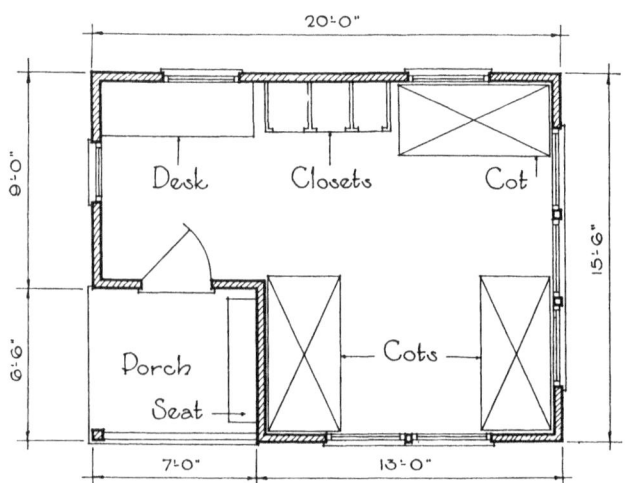

Yankee Springs Area – Michigan

Alexander H. Stephens Memorial Park – Georgia

Camp Counselors' Cabins
Scale ⅛" = 1'-0"

Plate III L-12   ⋙ CAMP SLEEPING FACILITIES

Kings Mountain Recreational Demonstration Area, South Carolina

Hickory Run Recreational Demonstration Area, Pennsylvania

COUNSELORS' CABINS

Sleeping quarters for counselors in the units of recreational demonstration camps are usually very like the campers' cabins of the area, in a reduced size that accommodates two, or at most three, leaders. Both capacities are shown in the plans opposite. The same openness of construction, spacing of cots, and provision of closets that determine the campers' cabins, plus space for a small table, and some chairs, fix the size and arrangement of the leaders' cabins.

French Creek Recreational Demonstration Area, Pennsylvania

Yankee Springs Recreational Demonstration Area, Michigan

Alexander H. Stephens Memorial Park, Georgia

CAMP SLEEPING FACILITIES

Plate III L-13

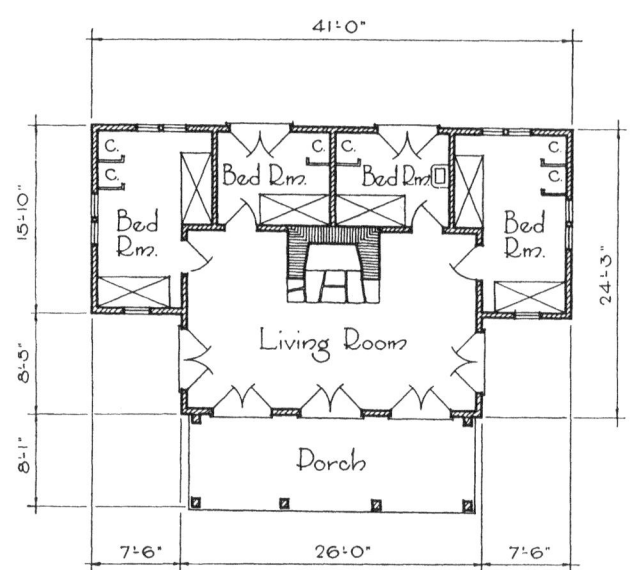

Montserrat Area - Missouri

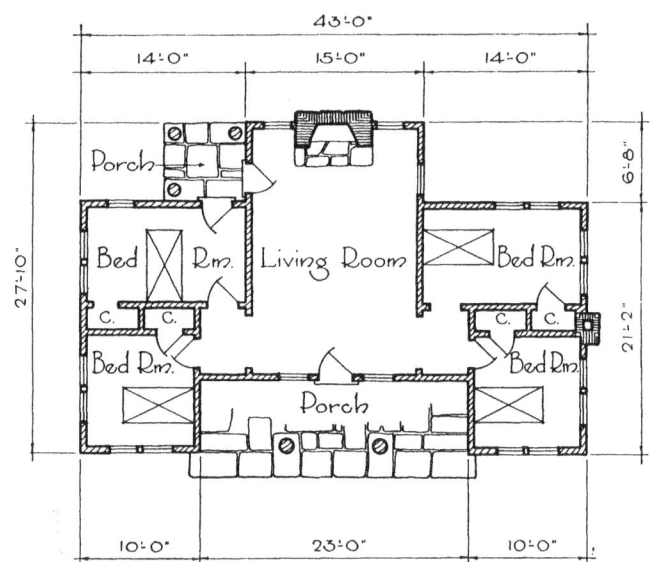

Raccoon Creek Area - Pennsylvania

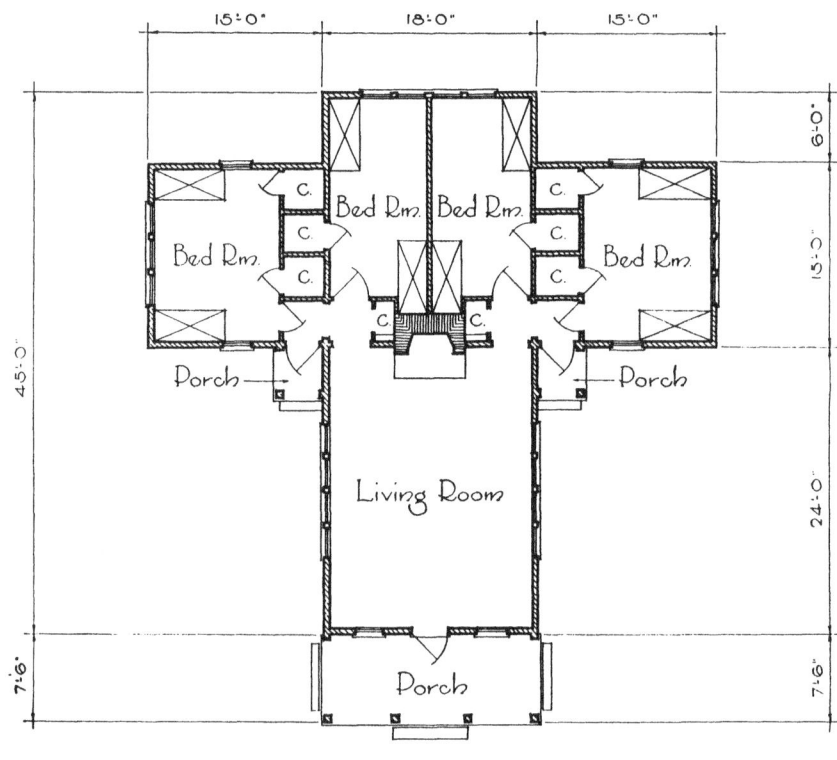

Chopawamsic Area - Virginia

Staff Quarters
Scale 1/8" = 1'-0"

Plate III L–14   ⇛ CAMP SLEEPING FACILITIES

Typical provision of living quarters for staff members who may not be required to sleep in the units of an organized camp is this arrangement of living room, porch, and four bedrooms accommodating six cots. Sometimes a camping program includes winter use of the staff building for short-term camping by small groups. When this eventuates, one of the bedrooms is appropriated for a kitchen, and a thimble in a chimney to receive the smokestack of a small cook stove has useful purpose.

Montserrat Recreational Demonstration Area, Missouri

Almost identical with the staff quarters above in its space allocation and sleeping capacity, this building adds the benefits of cross-corner ventilation for all bedrooms. On the other hand, it does not equal the economy of the other in the matter of chimney location, for, in anticipation of a stove being set up in a bedroom for cooking purposes in any winter use, it has been necessary to include a second chimney.

Raccoon Creek Recreational Demonstration Area, Pennsylvania

Here the same plan elements are to be found as in the two plans above, but less compactly grouped and on a little more spacious scale. Its chimney is located to provide the extra flue for a cook stove set up in a bedroom in the event of winter camping. The three exposures of the living room are a good feature, but two of the bedrooms are ill-favored for light and ventilation.

Chopawamsic Recreational Demonstration Area, Virginia

CAMP SLEEPING FACILITIES

Plate III L-15

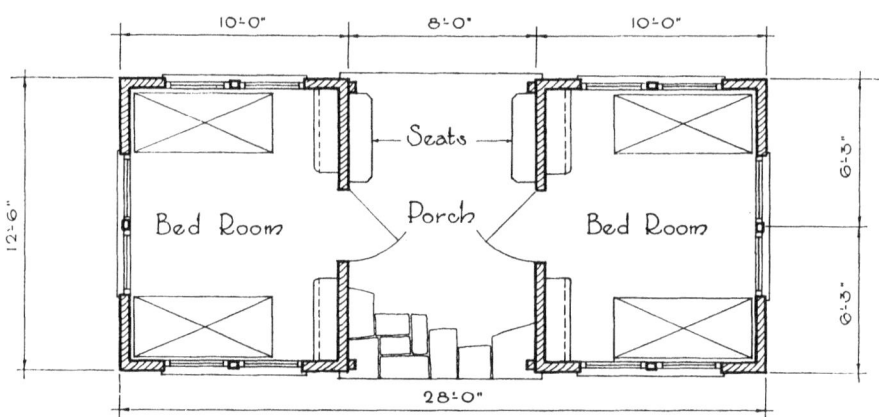

Cuivre River Area - Missouri

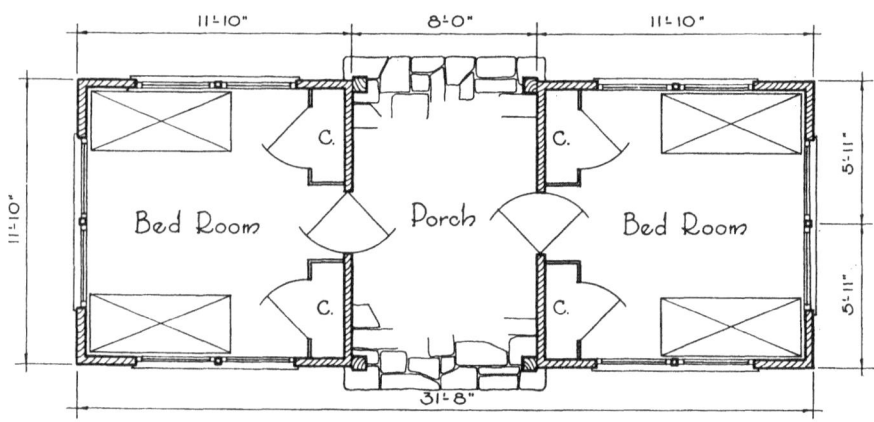

Montserrat Area - Missouri

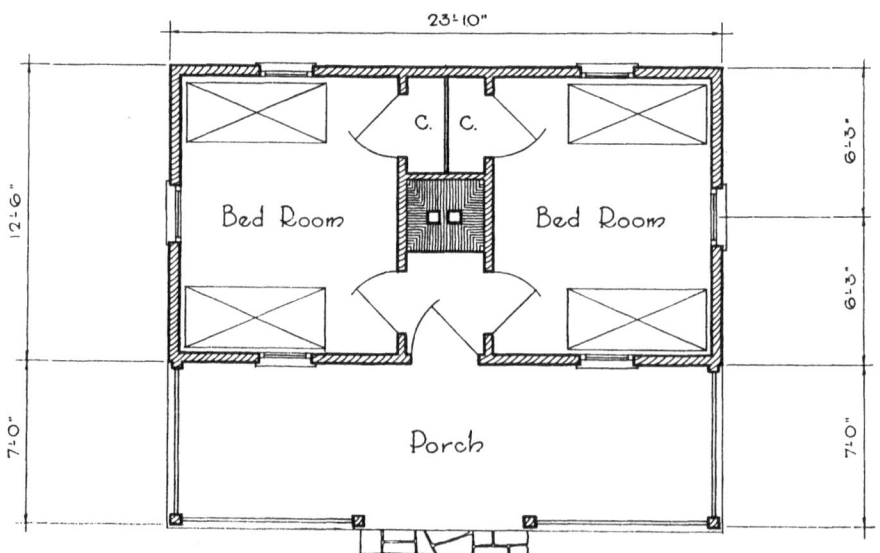

Kings Mountain Area - South Carolina

Camp Help's Quarters
Scale ⅛" = 1'-0"

HELP'S QUARTERS

The breezeway cabin plan is suited well to the housing of camp employes for the greater privacy it gives to the two bedrooms. Because the help may be something of an assortment, there is an advantage in this plan. Whether the porch is placed between the two rooms, as here, or in equivalent area in some other arrangement, has no considerable effect on cost.

Cuivre River Recreational Demonstration Area, Missouri

This help's sleeping cabin of breezeway type is almost the counterpart in plan of the one shown above it. The fenestration is the same. It is a trifle larger. It substitutes closets for the open shelves and hanging rods of the other. Screening the open ends of the breezeway would add to the comfort of these quarters, and this could be done at small cost in relation to size of the area screened.

Montserrat Recreational Demonstration Area, Missouri

If a unified structural theme is to carry through an entire camp, and this is desirable, even the somewhat detached help's quarters should have the same outward characteristics as other buildings. Such is the case at Kings Mountain Recreational Demonstration Area where the help's cabins, save for the added chimney, closely duplicate the campers' cabins.

Kings Mountain Recreational Demonstration Area, South Carolina

CAMP SLEEPING FACILITIES ‹‹‹ Plate III L–17

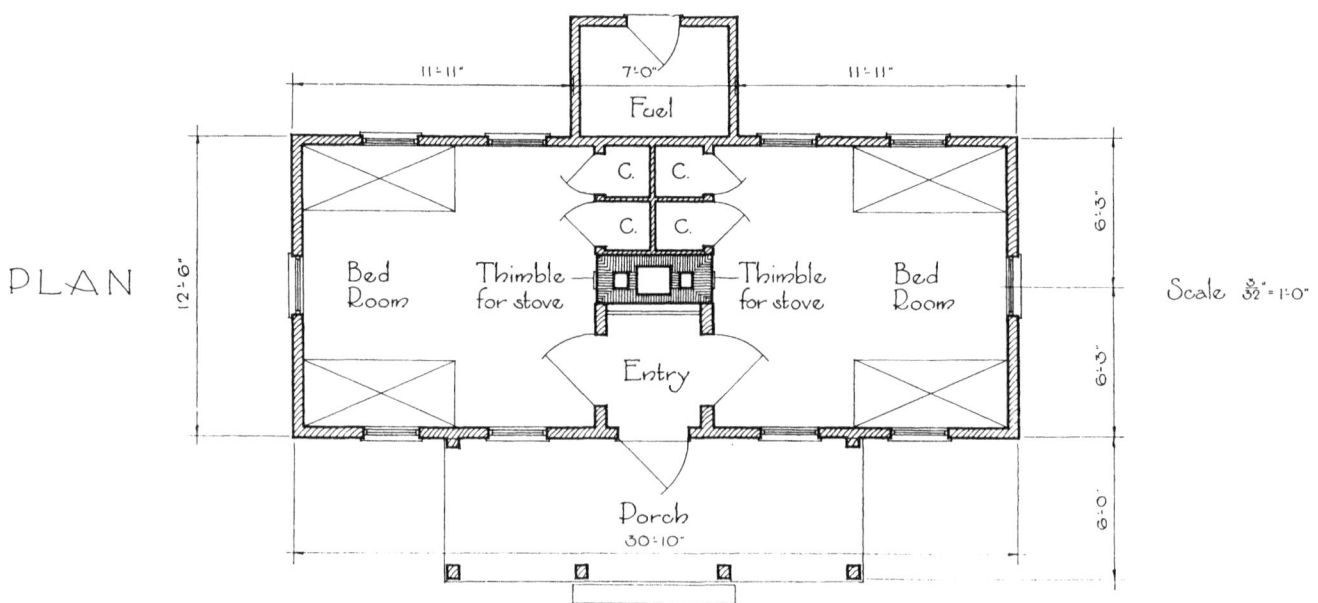

Help's Quarters, Swift Creek Recreational Demonstration Area, Virginia

PLAN Scale 3/32"=1'-0"

The employes' housing here illustrated is more commodious than the examples previously reviewed, and probably larger than absolutely necessary. Where funds are limited, something more compact is recommended. Doubtless space for a stove in each bedroom, in anticipation of short-term winter camping, induced the greater size. The shed at the rear provides fuel storage space.

www.ingramcontent.com/pod-product-compliance
Lightning Source LLC
LaVergne TN
LVHW081549060526
838200LV00048B/2261